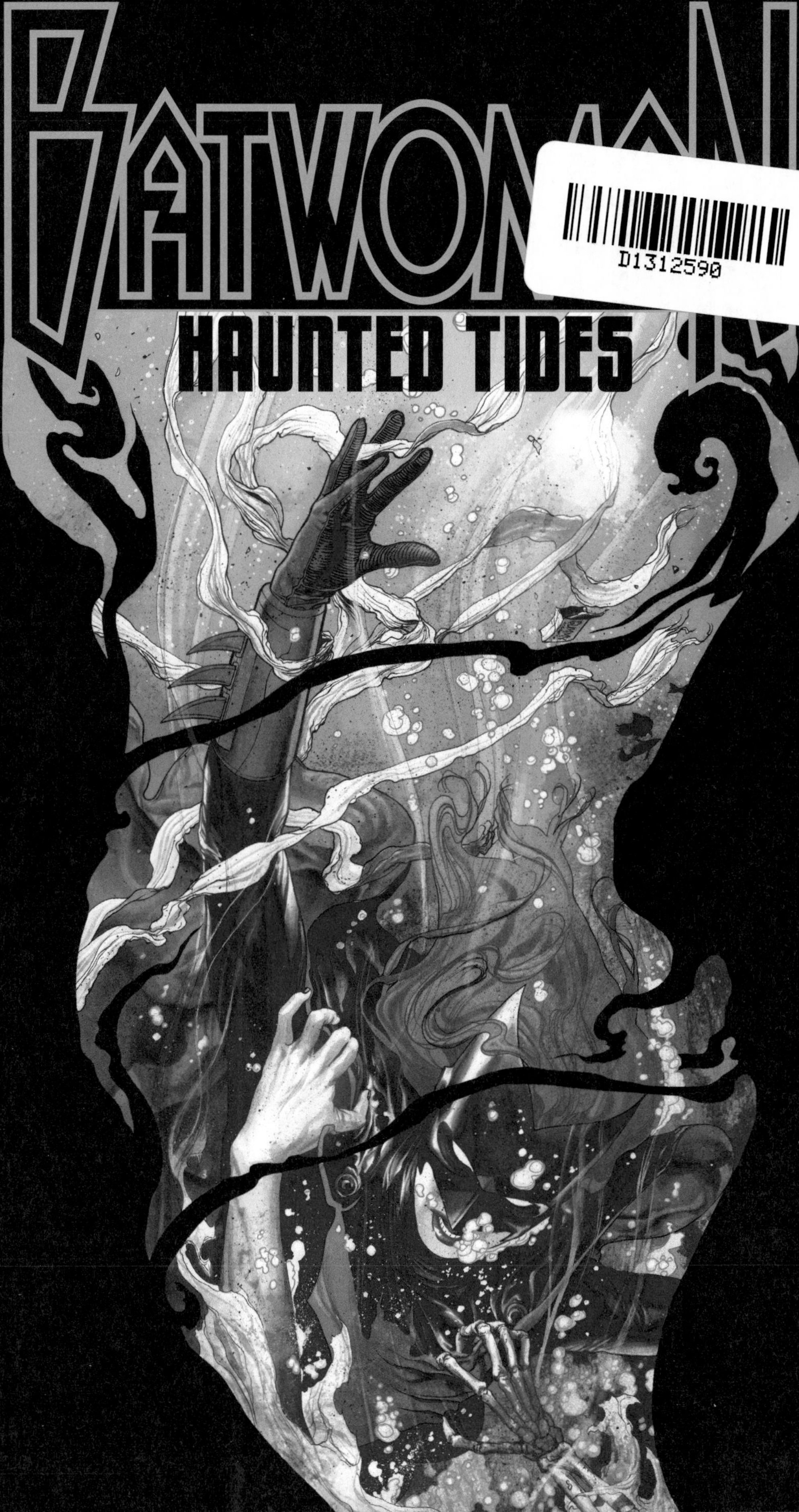
BATWOMAN
HAUNTED TIDES

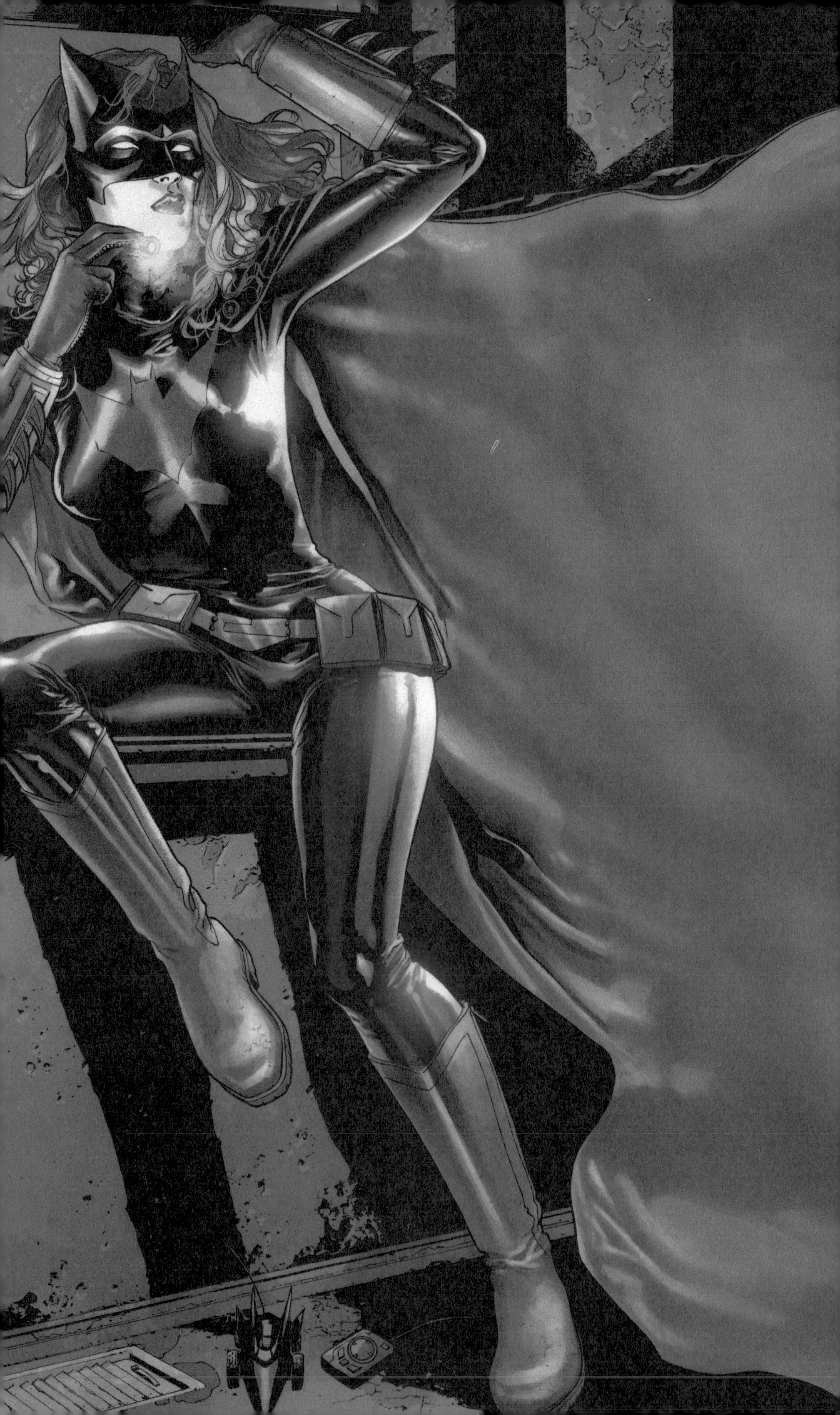

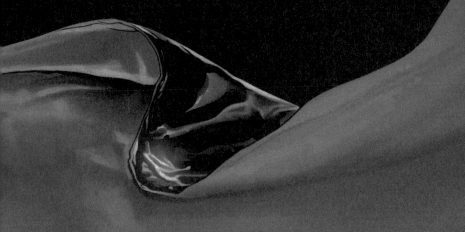

J.H. WILLIAMS III
W. HADEN BLACKMAN
writers

J.H. WILLIAMS III
AMY REEDER | TREVOR McCARTHY
ROB HUNTER | RICHARD FRIEND | PERE PÉREZ
artists

DAVE STEWART | GUY MAJOR
colorists

TODD KLEIN
letterer

BEN OLIVER
collection cover artist

BATWOMAN
HAUNTED TIDES

MIKE MARTS Editor – Original Series
HARVEY RICHARDS, JANELLE ASSELIN Associate Editors – Original Series
RICKEY PURDIN, KATIE KUBERT Assistant Editors – Original Series
JEB WOODARD Group Editor – Collected Editions
ERIKA ROTHBERG Editor – Collected Edition
STEVE COOK Design Director – Books
MEGEN BELLERSEN Publication Design
ADAM RADO Publication Production

BOB HARRAS Senior VP – Editor-in-Chief, DC Comics
PAT McCALLUM Executive Editor, DC Comics

DAN DiDIO Publisher
JIM LEE Publisher & Chief Creative Officer
BOBBIE CHASE VP – New Publishing Initiatives & Talent Development
DON FALLETTI VP – Manufacturing Operations & Workflow Management
LAWRENCE GANEM VP – Talent Services
ALISON GILL Senior VP – Manufacturing & Operations
HANK KANALZ Senior VP – Publishing Strategy & Support Services
DAN MIRON VP – Publishing Operations
NICK J. NAPOLITANO VP – Manufacturing Administration & Design
NANCY SPEARS VP – Sales
MICHELE R. WELLS VP & Executive Editor, Young Reader

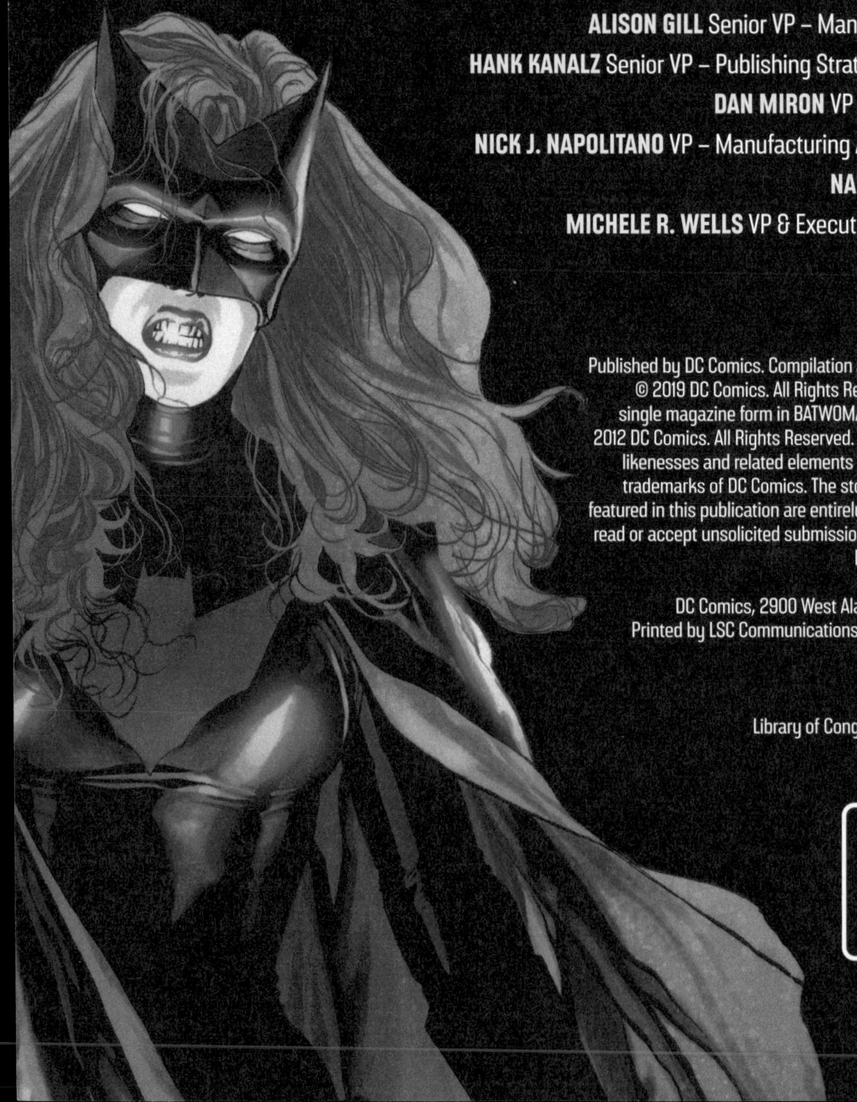

BATWOMAN: HAUNTED TIDES

DC Comics, 2900 West Alameda Ave., Burbank, CA 91505
Printed by LSC Communications, Owensville, MO, USA. 8/30/19.
First Printing.
ISBN: 978-1-4012-9814-2

Library of Congress Cataloging-in-Publication
Data is available.

PEFC Certified
This product is from sustainably managed forests and controlled sources
PEFC/29-31-337
www.pefc.org

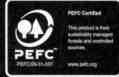

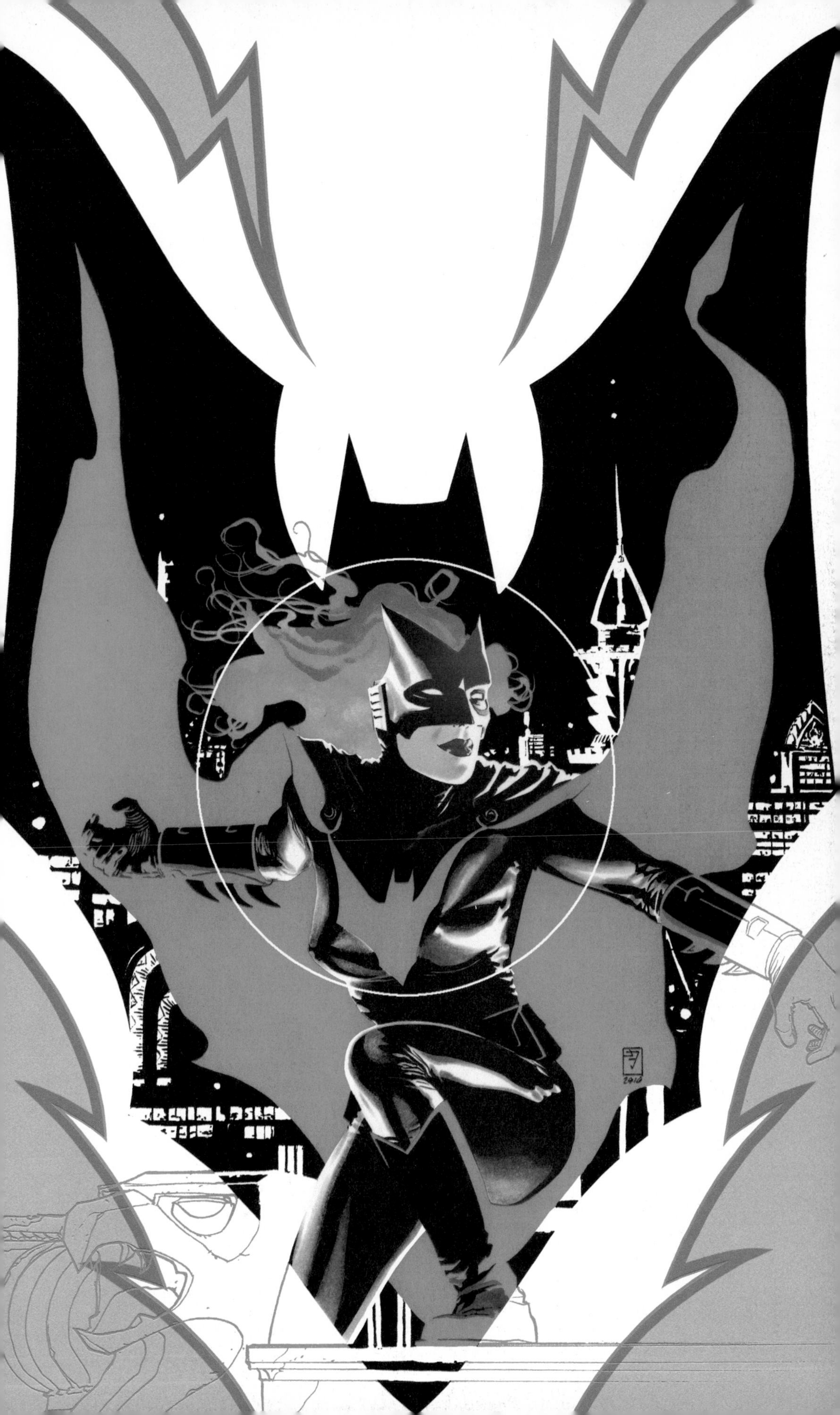

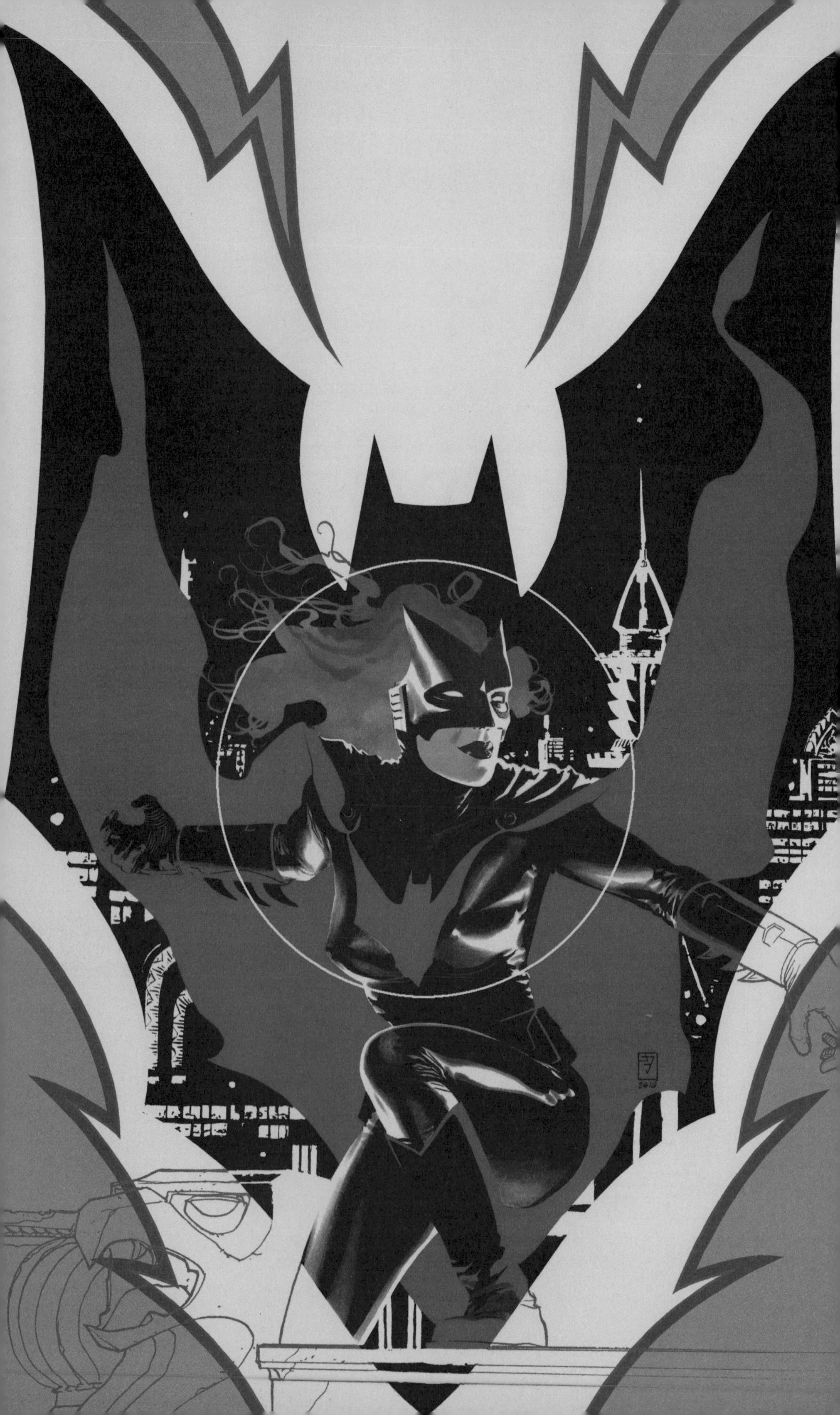

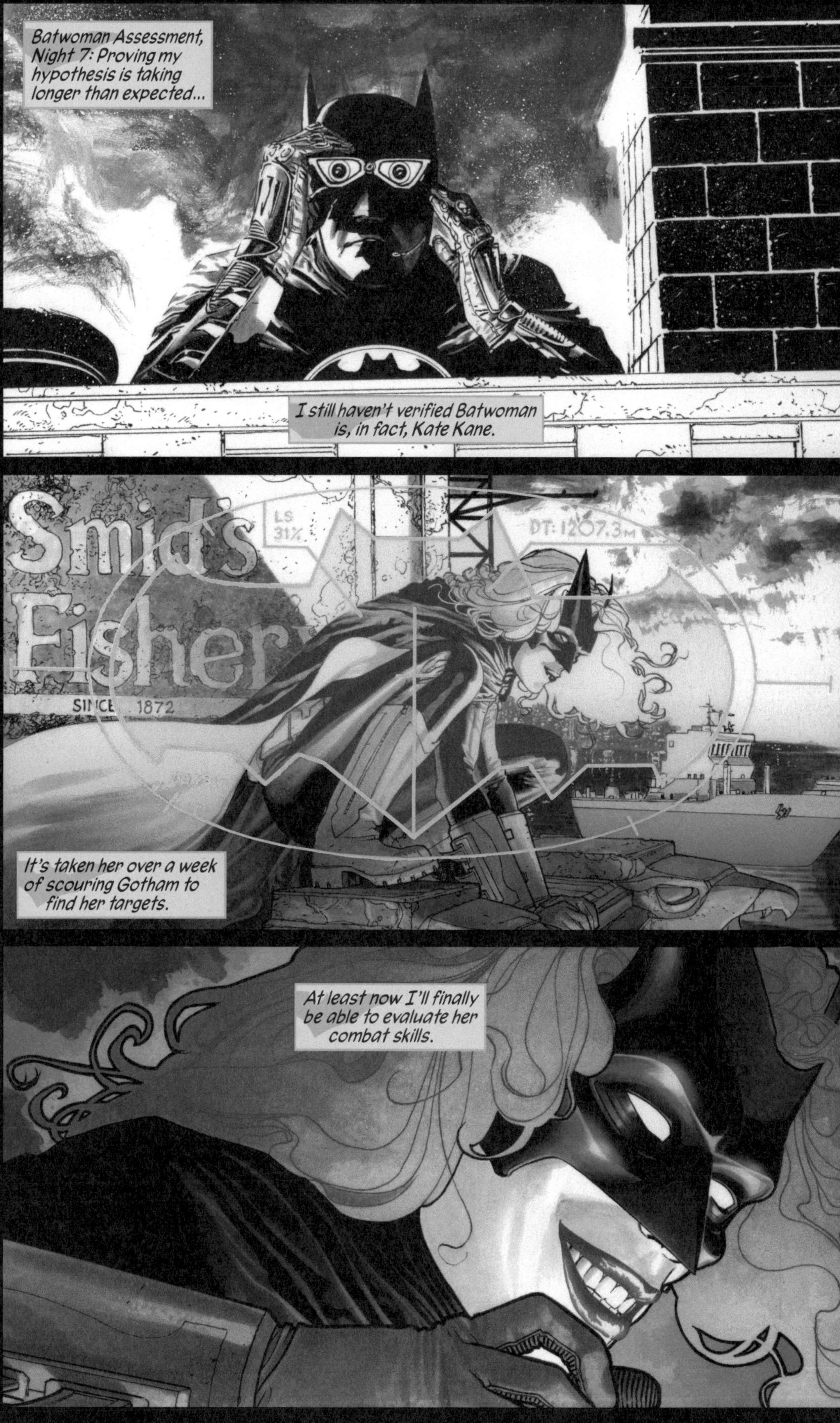
Batwoman Assessment, Night 7: Proving my hypothesis is taking longer than expected...
I still haven't verified Batwoman is, in fact, Kate Kane.
Smid's Fisher
SINCE 1872
LS 31%
DT: 1207.3M
It's taken her over a week of scouring Gotham to find her targets.
At least now I'll finally be able to evaluate her combat skills.

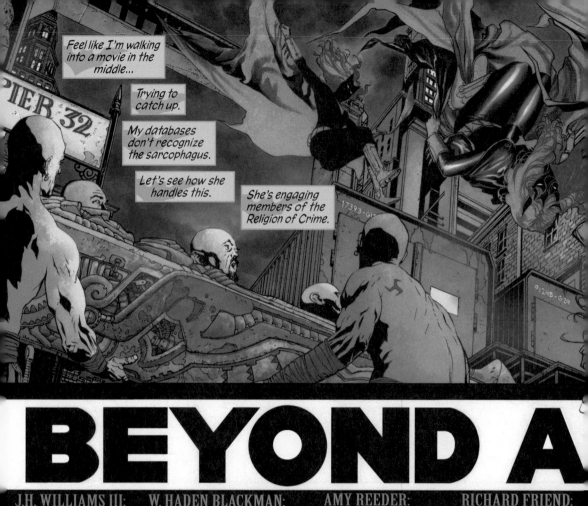

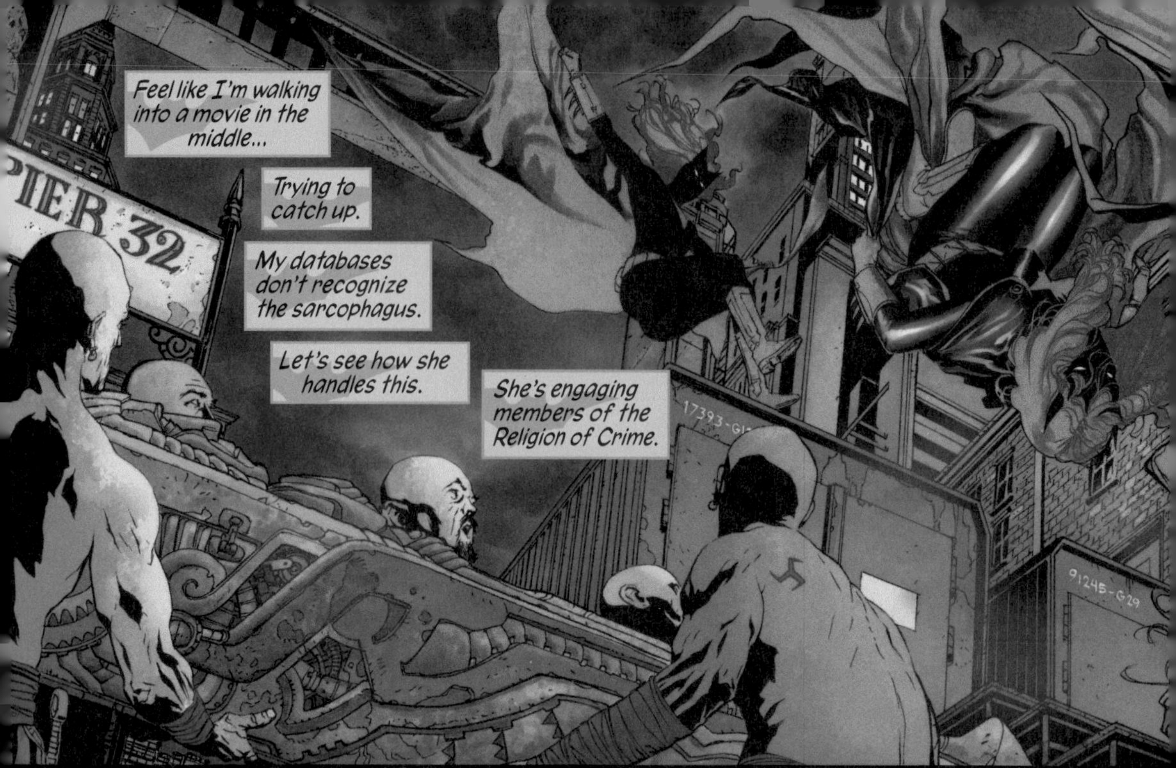
Feel like I'm walking into a movie in the middle...
Trying to catch up.
My databases don't recognize the sarcophagus.
Let's see how she handles this.
She's engaging members of the Religion of Crime.
PIER 32
91245-G29

BEYOND A

J.H. WILLIAMS III: writer - artist
W. HADEN BLACKMAN: co-writer
AMY REEDER: artist - Kate sequence
RICHARD FRIEND: inker - Kate sequence

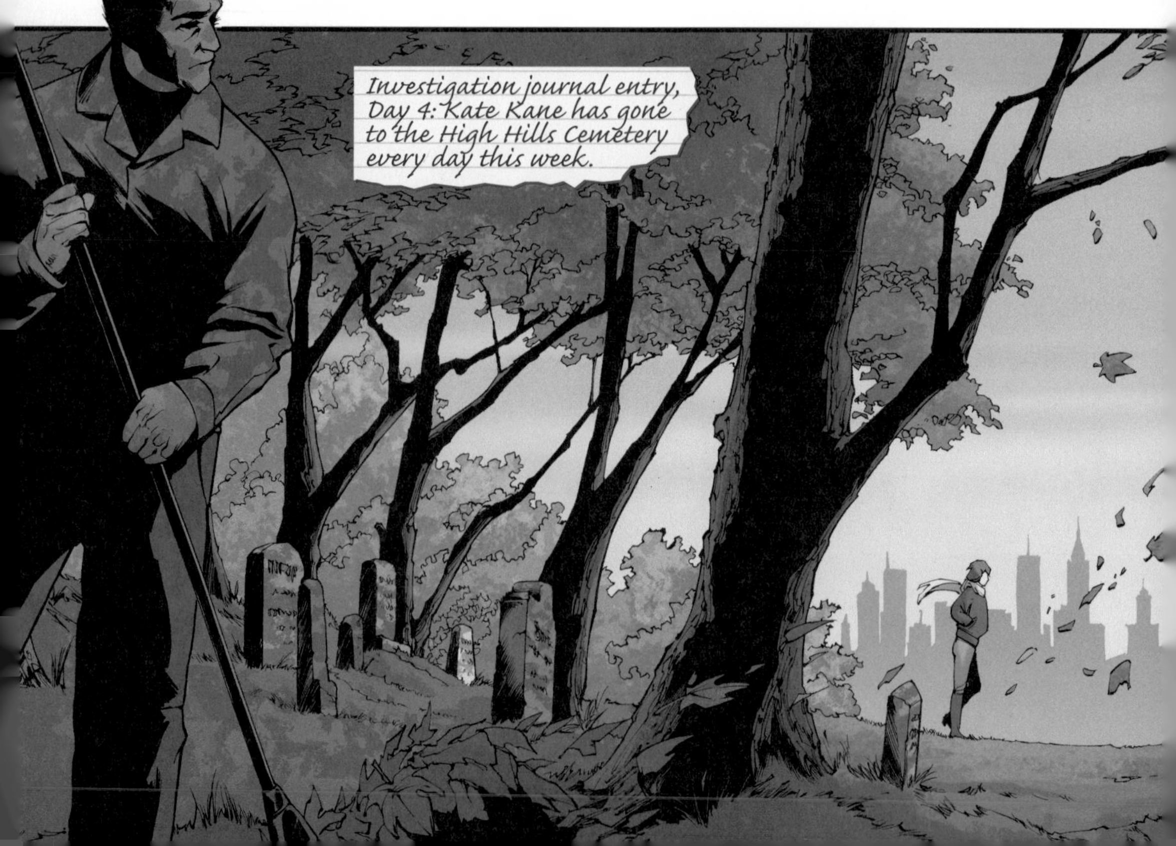
Investigation journal entry, Day 4: Kate Kane has gone to the High Hills Cemetery every day this week.

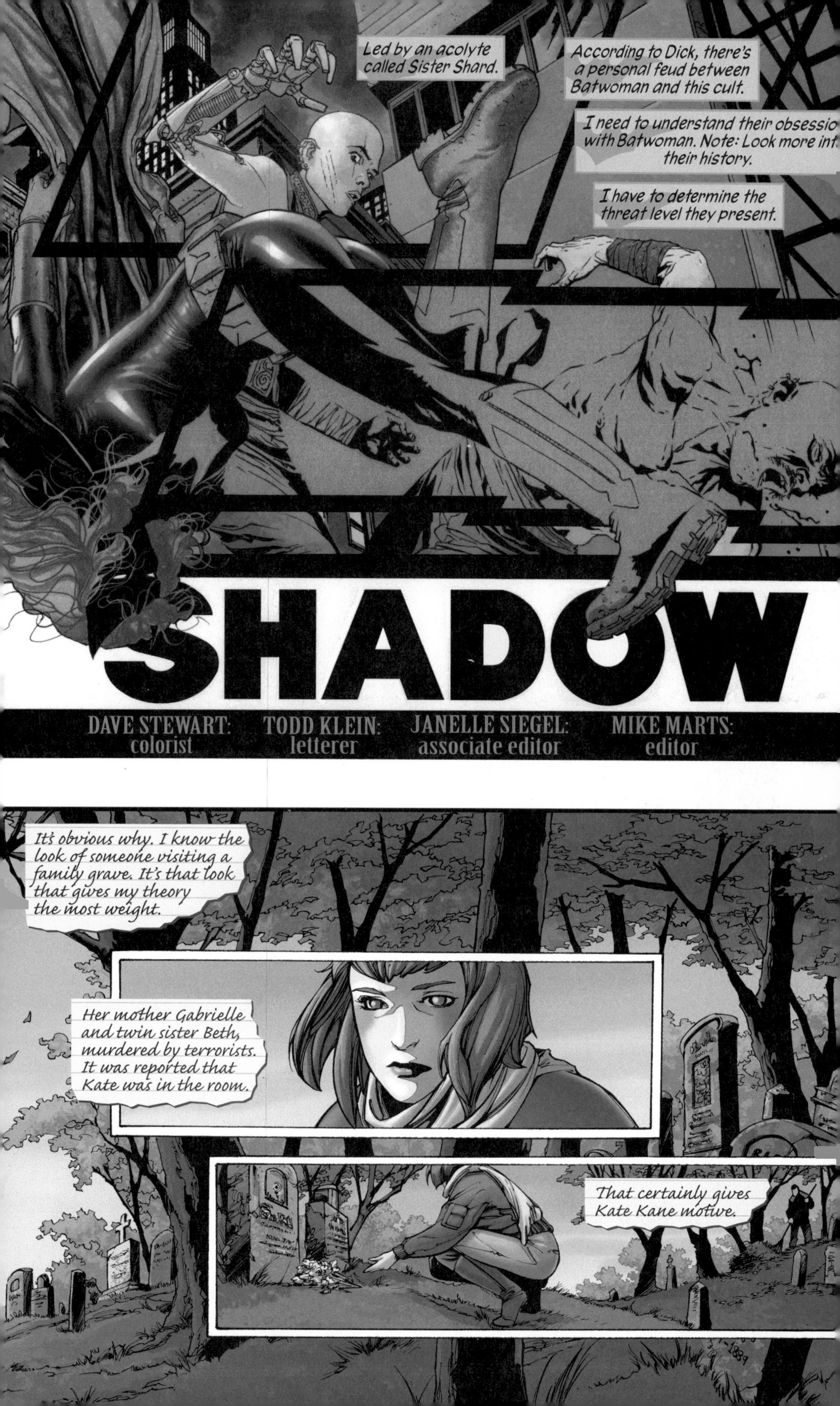

Led by an acolyte called Sister Shard.
According to Dick, there's a personal feud between Batwoman and this cult.
I need to understand their obsessio with Batwoman. Note: Look more int their history.
I have to determine the threat level they present.
SHADOW
DAVE STEWART: colorist
TODD KLEIN: letterer
JANELLE SIEGEL: associate editor
MIKE MARTS: editor
It's obvious why. I know the look of someone visiting a family grave. It's that look that gives my theory the most weight.
Her mother Gabrielle and twin sister Beth, murdered by terrorists. It was reported that Kate was in the room.
That certainly gives Kate Kane motive.

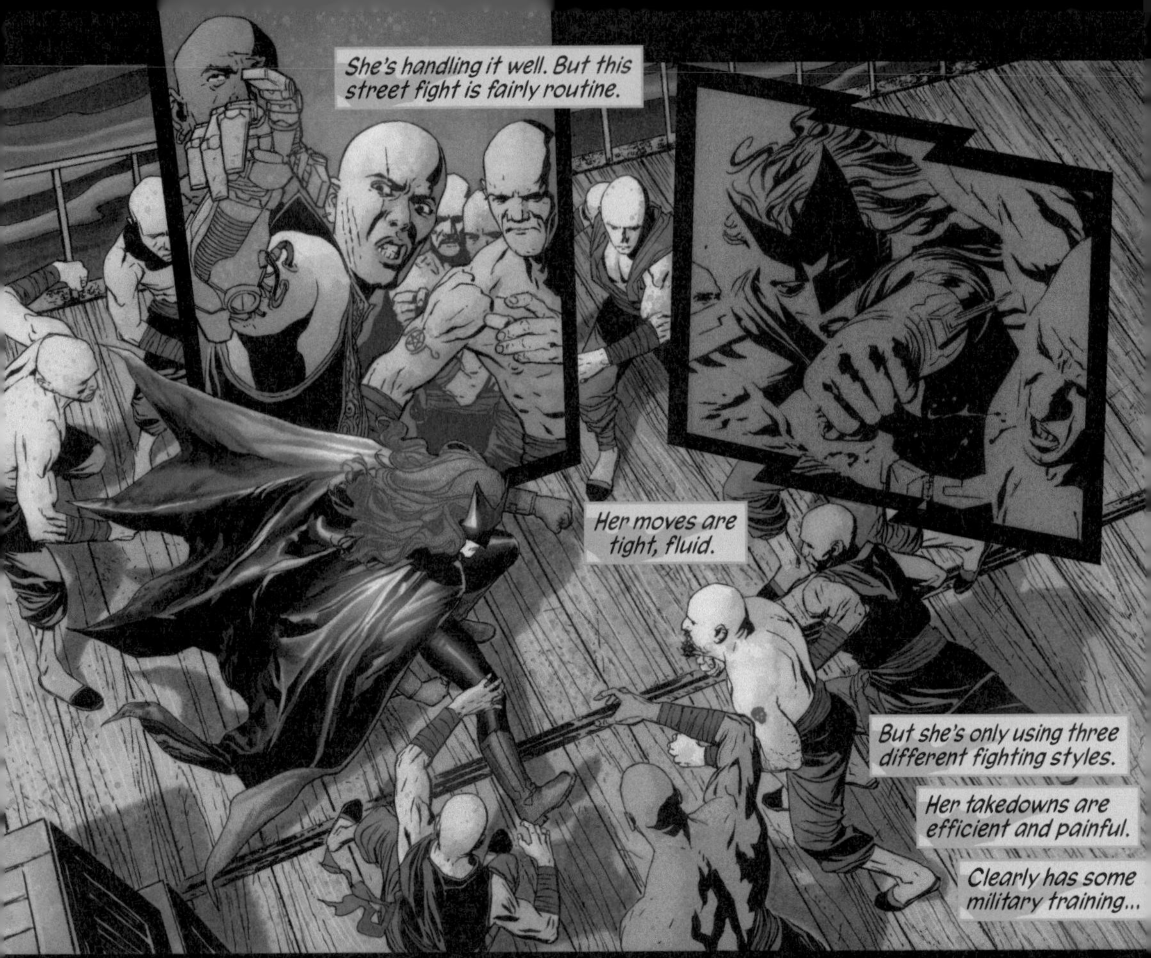
She's handling it well. But this street fight is fairly routine.
Her moves are tight, fluid.
But she's only using three different fighting styles.
Her takedowns are efficient and painful.
Clearly has some military training...

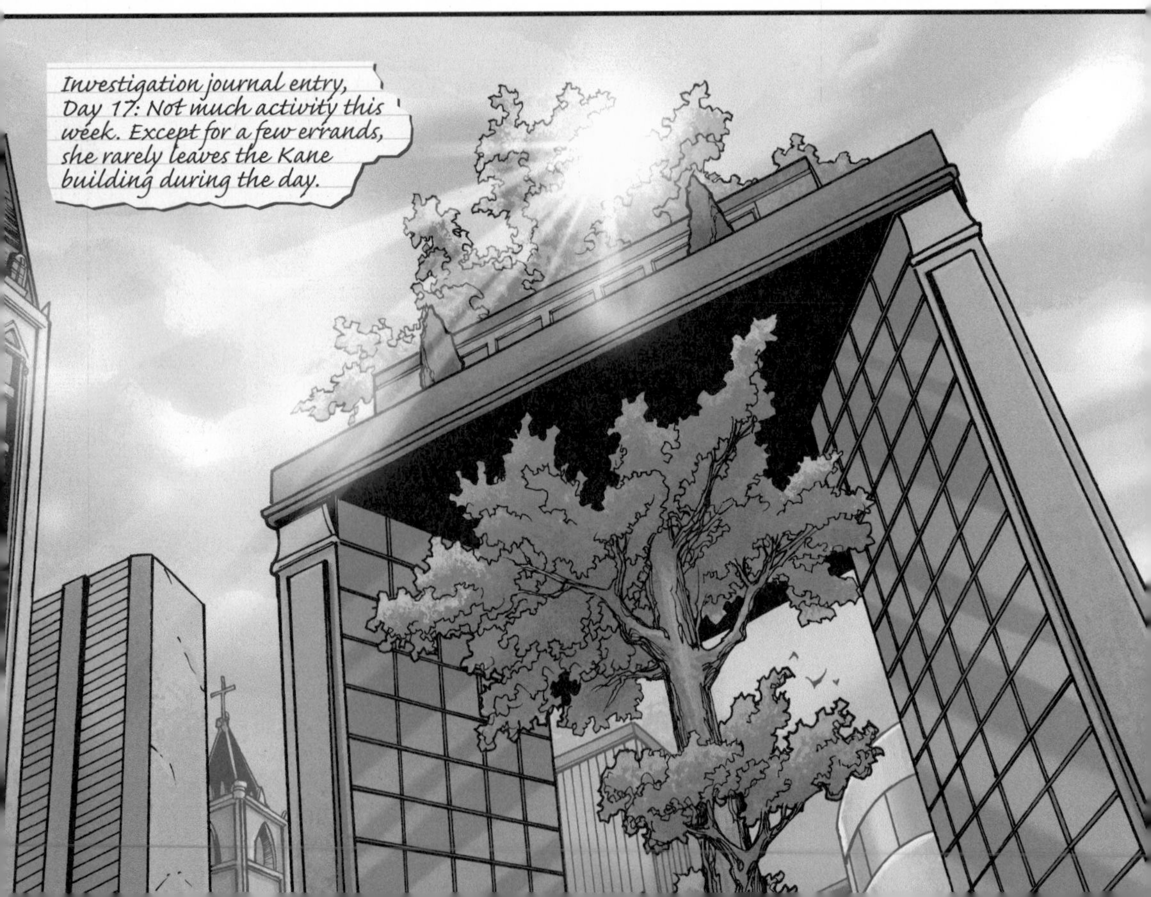
Investigation journal entry, Day 17: Not much activity this week. Except for a few errands, she rarely leaves the Kane building during the day.

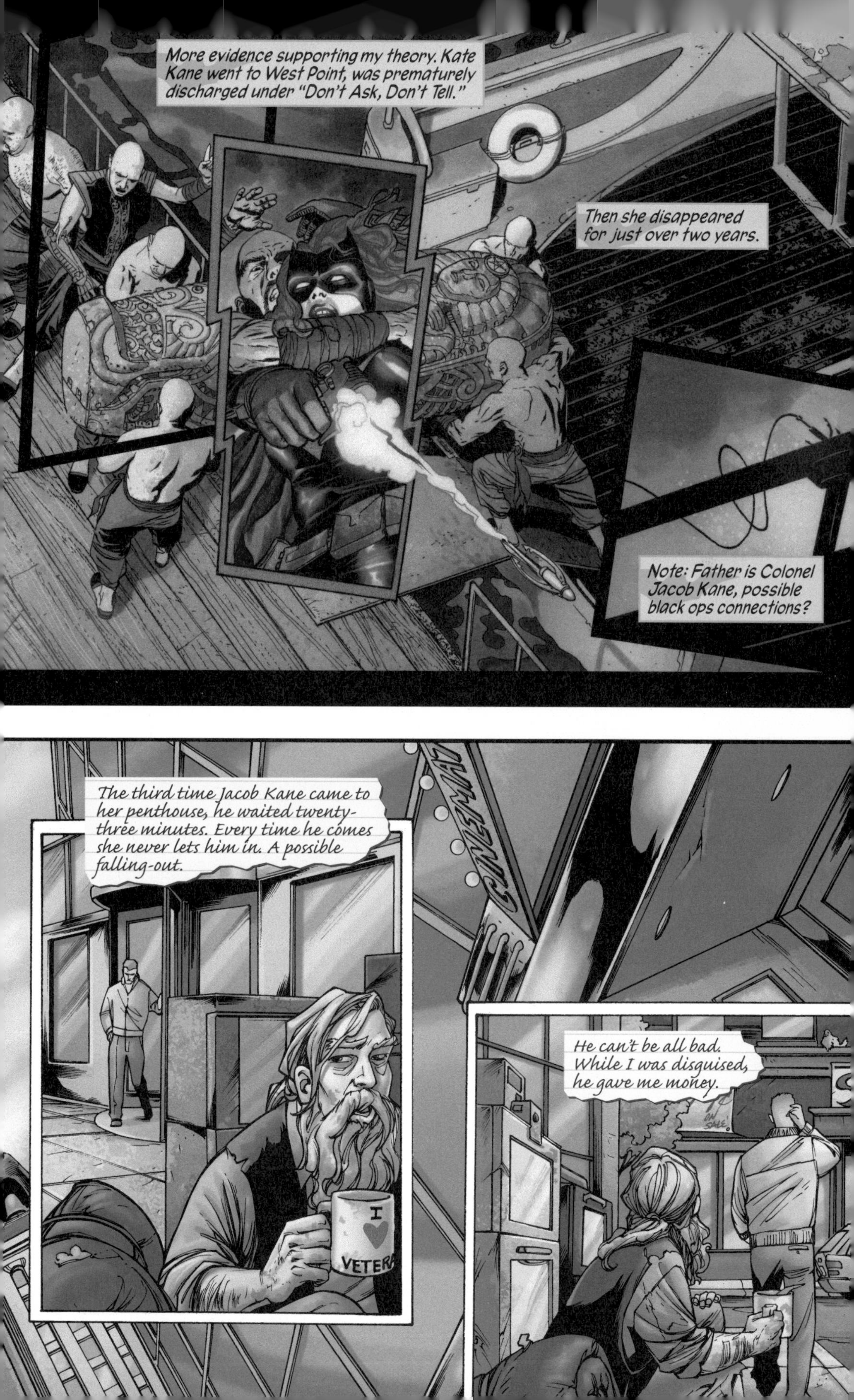
More evidence supporting my theory. Kate Kane went to West Point, was prematurely discharged under "Don't Ask, Don't Tell."
Then she disappeared for just over two years.
Note: Father is Colonel Jacob Kane, possible black ops connections?
The third time Jacob Kane came to her penthouse, he waited twenty-three minutes. Every time he comes she never lets him in. A possible falling-out.
He can't be all bad. While I was disguised, he gave me money.

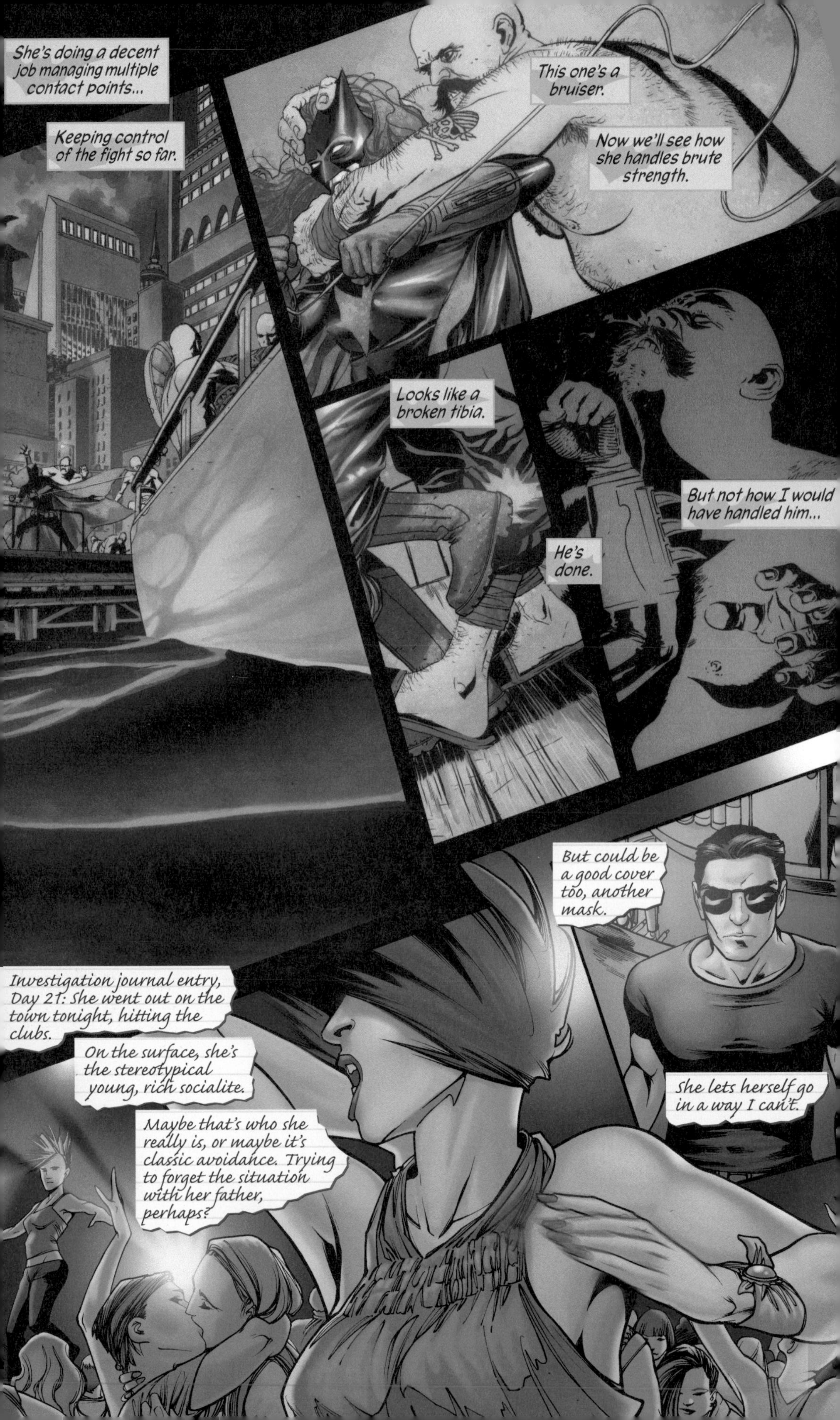

She's doing a decent job managing multiple contact points...
Keeping control of the fight so far.
This one's a bruiser.
Now we'll see how she handles brute strength.
Looks like a broken tibia.
He's done.
But not how I would have handled him...
Investigation journal entry, Day 21: She went out on the town tonight, hitting the clubs.
On the surface, she's the stereotypical young, rich socialite.
Maybe that's who she really is, or maybe it's classic avoidance. Trying to forget the situation with her father, perhaps?
But could be a good cover too, another mask.
She lets herself go in a way I can't.

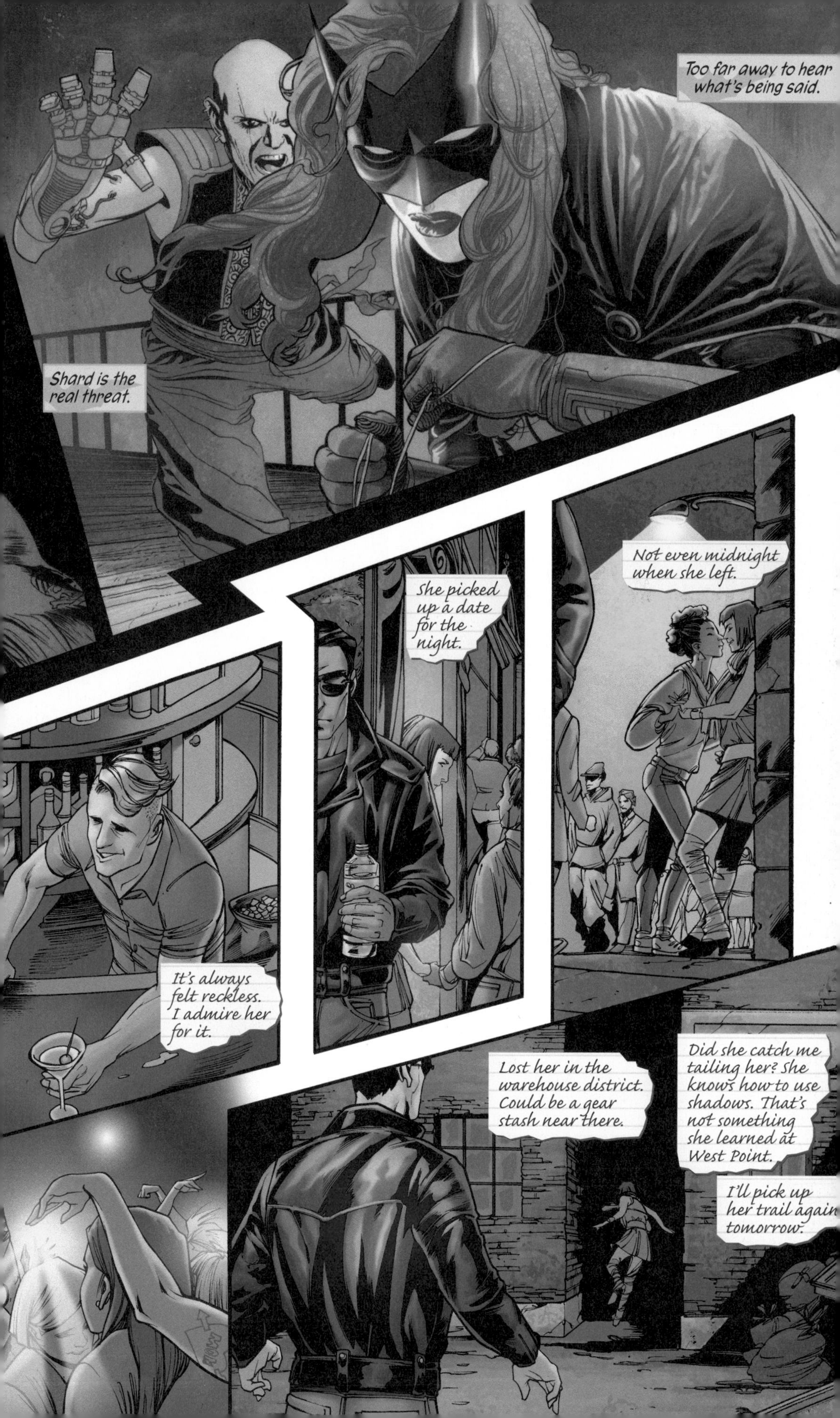
Too far away to hear what's being said.
Shard is the real threat.
She picked up a date for the night.
Not even midnight when she left.
It's always felt reckless. I admire her for it.
Lost her in the warehouse district. Could be a gear stash near there.
Did she catch me tailing her? She knows how to use shadows. That's not something she learned at West Point.
I'll pick up her trail again tomorrow.

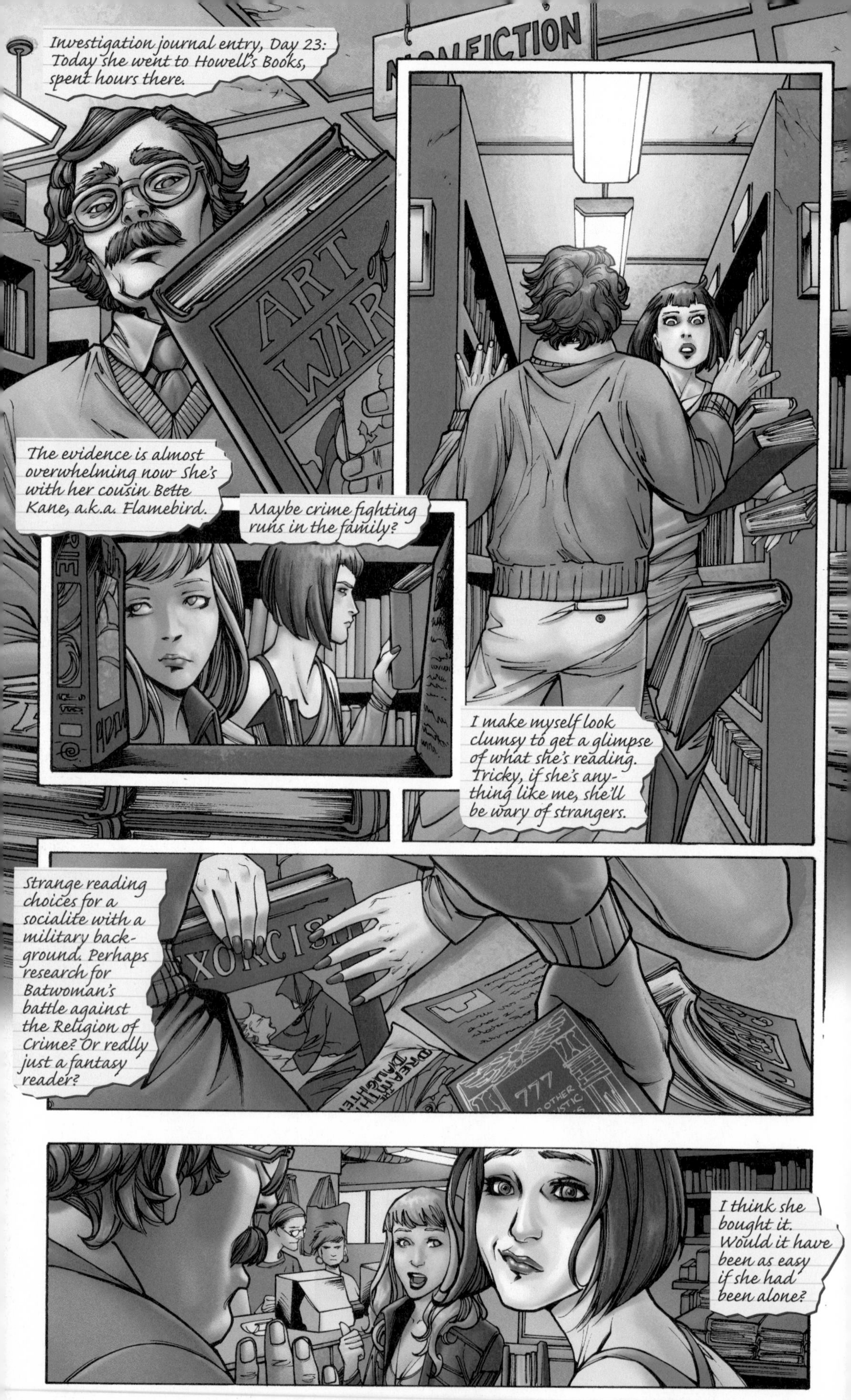
NONFICTION
Investigation journal entry, Day 23: Today she went to Howell's Books, spent hours there.
ART WAR
The evidence is almost overwhelming now She's with her cousin Bette Kane, a.k.a. Flamebird.
Maybe crime fighting runs in the family?
I make myself look clumsy to get a glimpse of what she's reading. Tricky, if she's anything like me, she'll be wary of strangers.
Strange reading choices for a socialite with a military background. Perhaps research for Batwoman's battle against the Religion of Crime? Or really just a fantasy reader?
XORCISM
777
I think she bought it. Would it have been as easy if she had been alone?

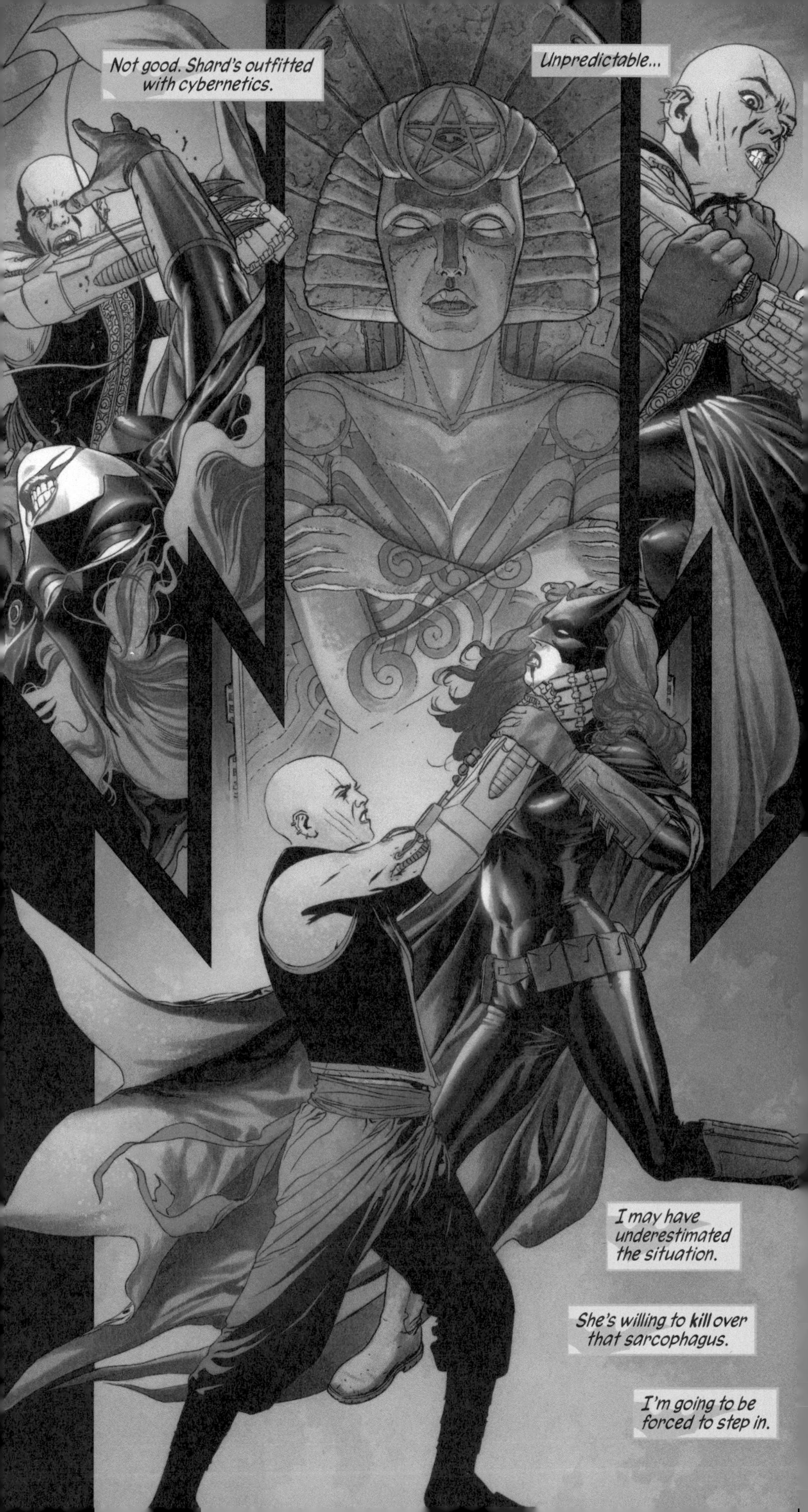
Not good. Shard's outfitted with cybernetics.
Unpredictable...
I may have underestimated the situation.
She's willing to **kill** over that sarcophagus.
I'm going to be forced to step in.

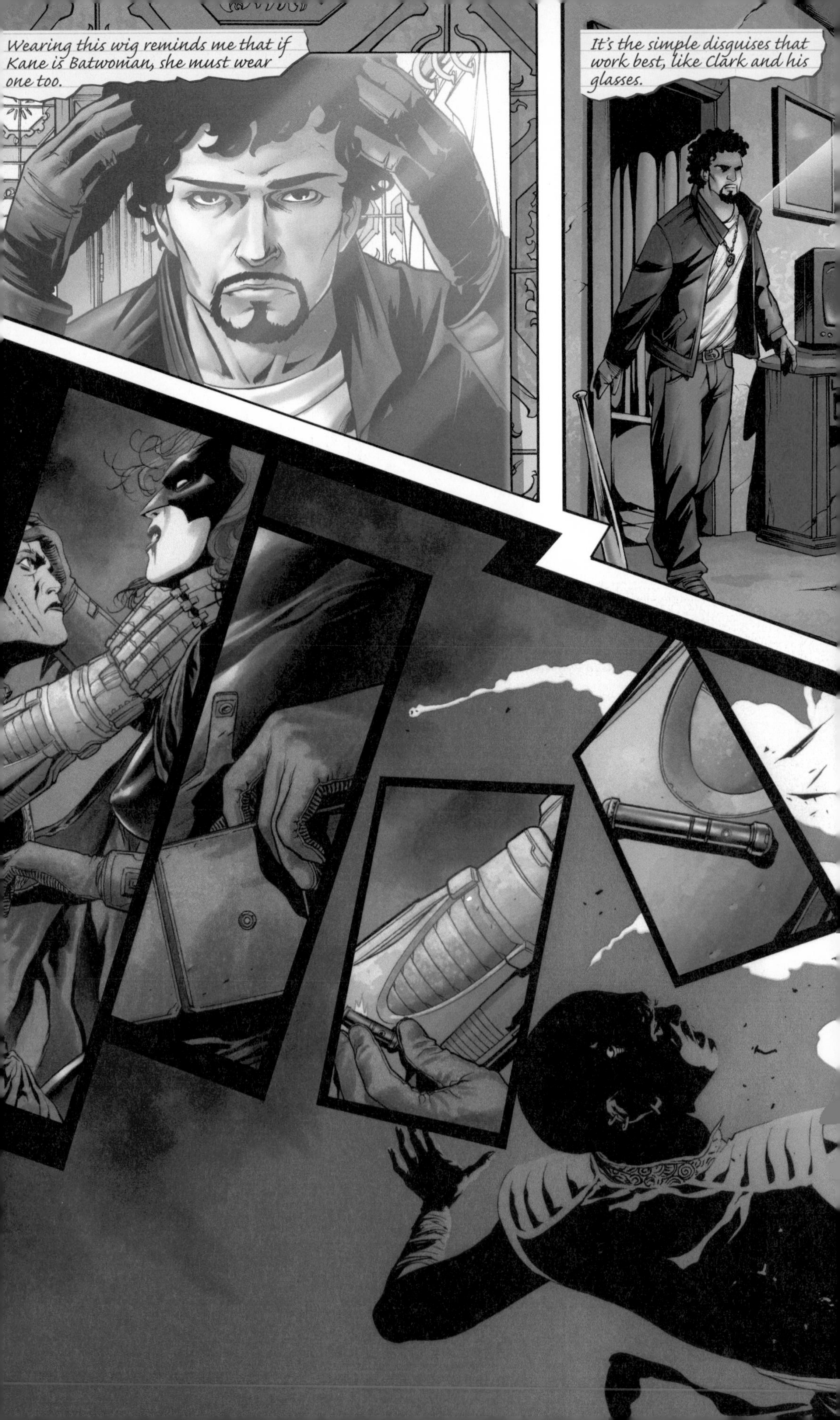
Wearing this wig reminds me that if Kane is Batwoman, she must wear one too.
It's the simple disguises that work best, like Clark and his glasses.

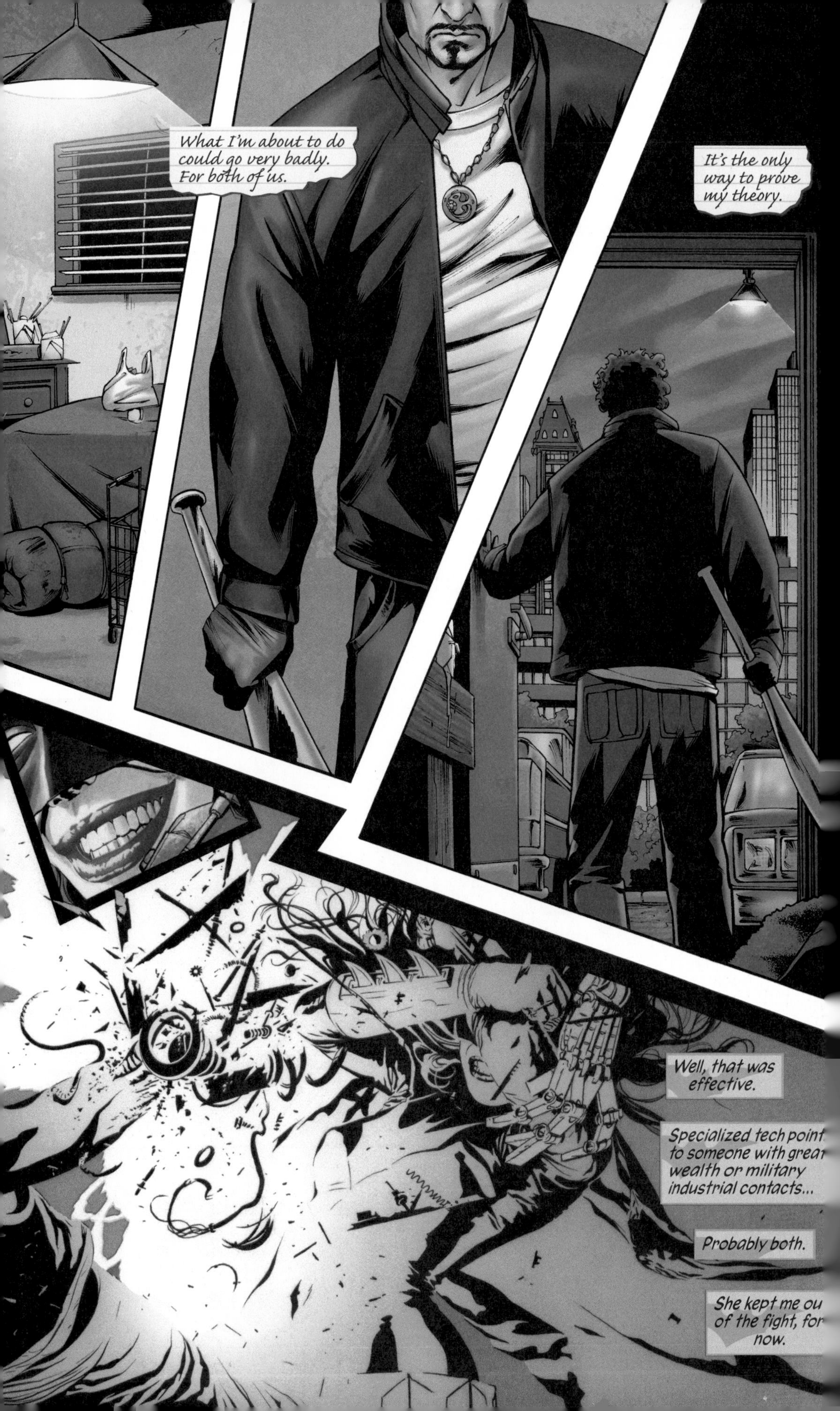
What I'm about to do could go very badly. For both of us.
It's the only way to prove my theory.
Well, that was effective.
Specialized tech point to someone with grea wealth or military industrial contacts...
Probably both.
She kept me ou of the fight, for now.

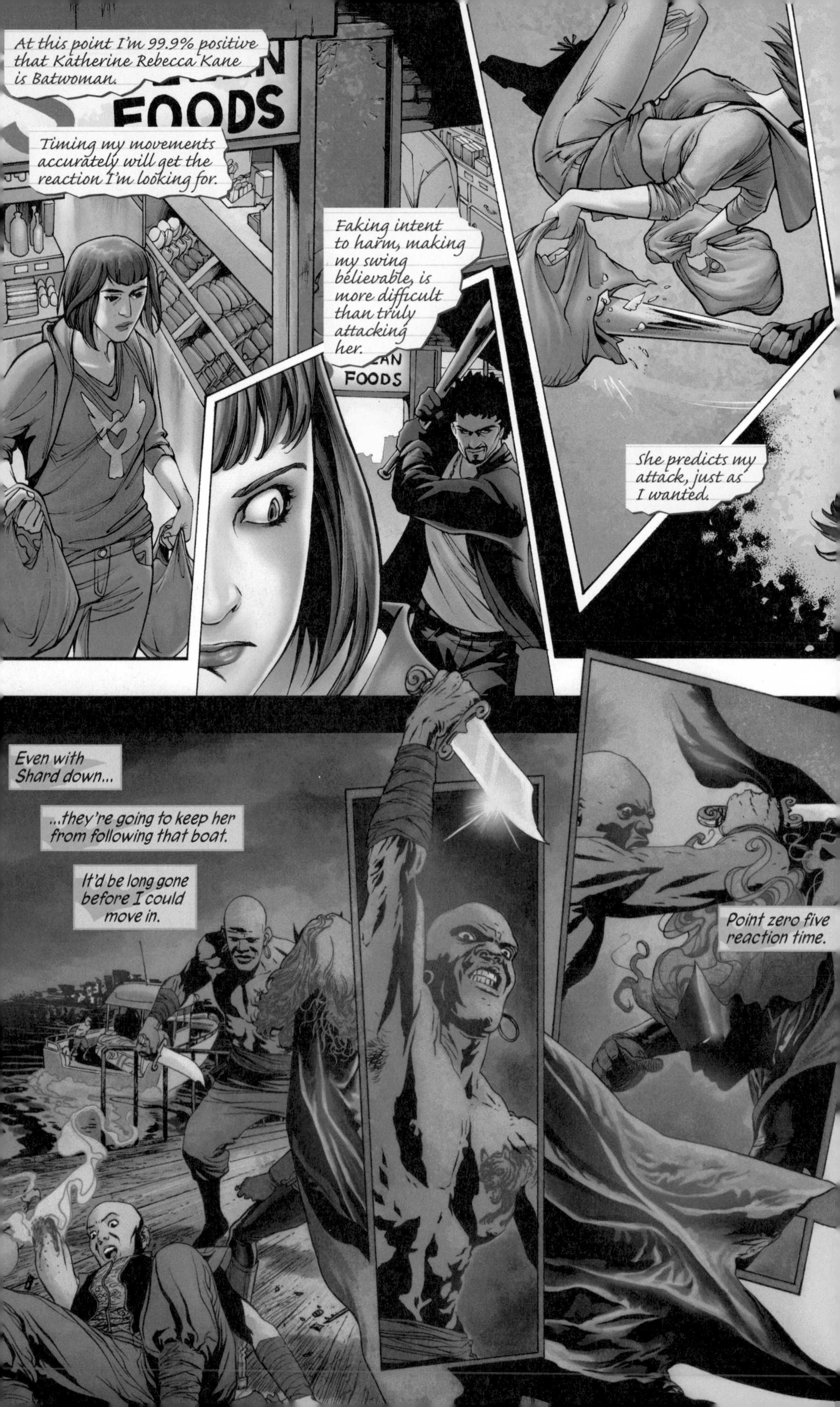

At this point I'm 99.9% positive that Katherine Rebecca Kane is Batwoman.
FOODS
Timing my movements accurately will get the reaction I'm looking for.
Faking intent to harm, making my swing believable, is more difficult than truly attacking her.
FOODS
She predicts my attack, just as I wanted.
Even with Shard down...
...they're going to keep her from following that boat.
It'd be long gone before I could move in.
Point zero five reaction time.

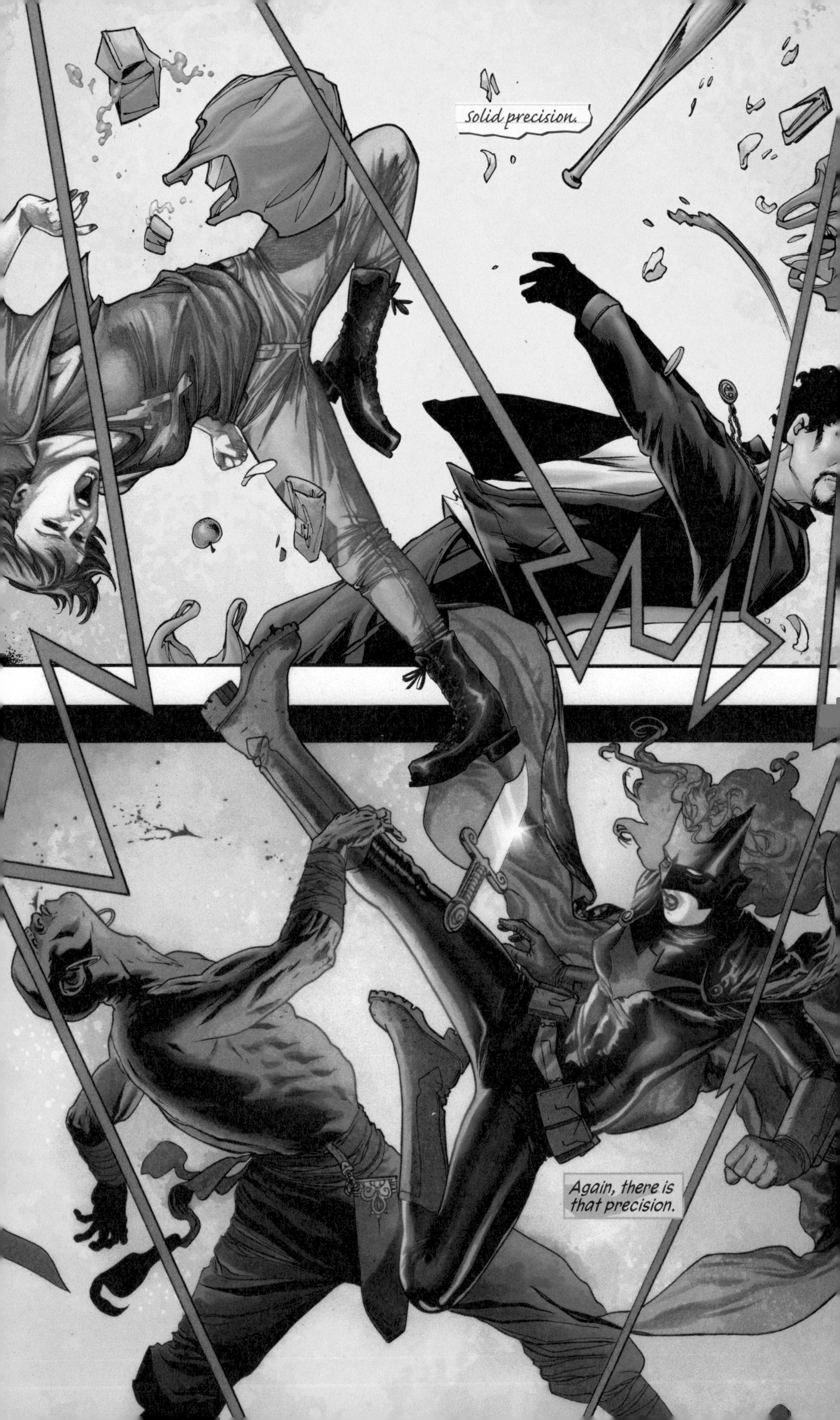
solid precision.
Again, there is that precision.

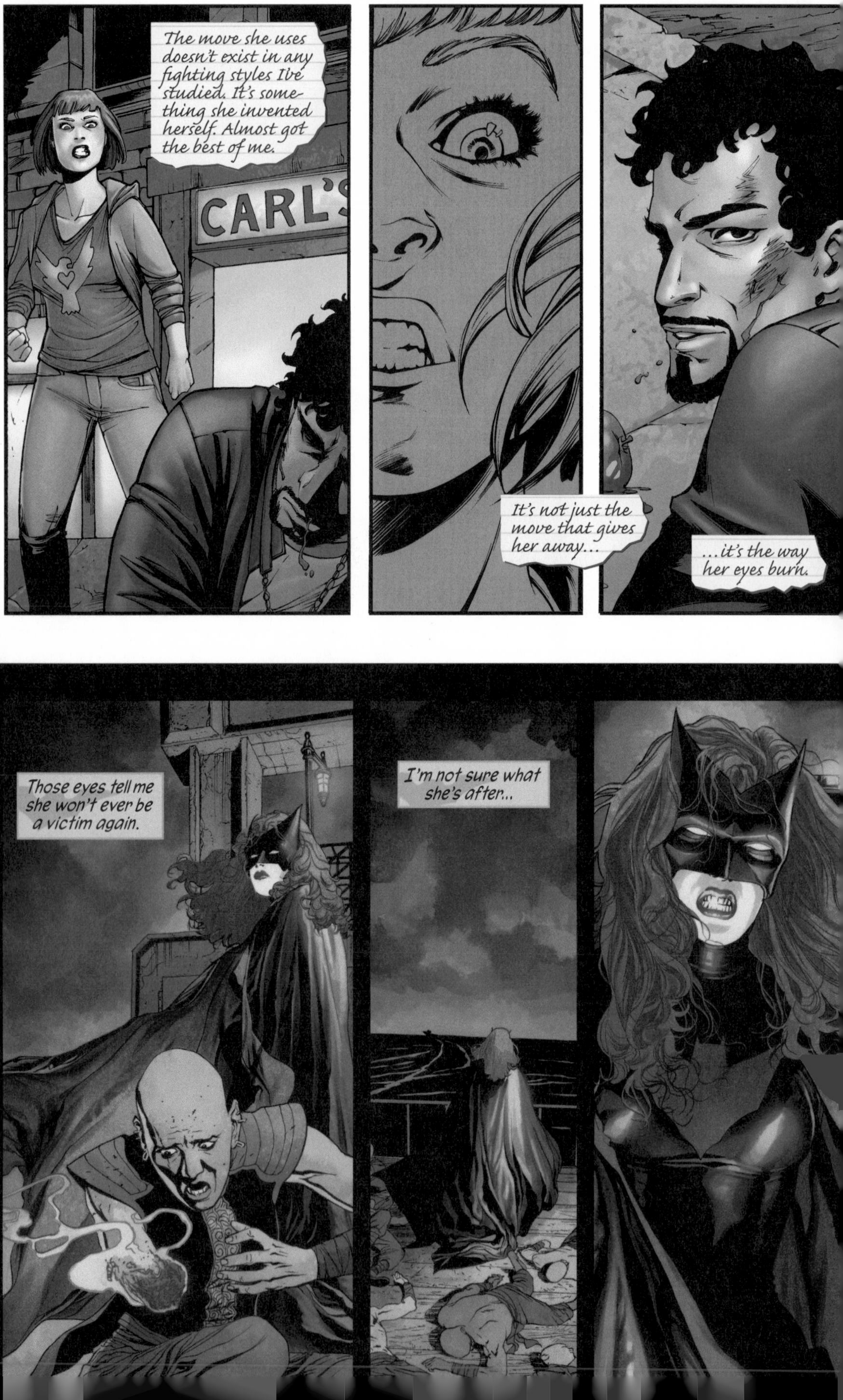
The move she uses doesn't exist in any fighting styles I've studied. It's something she invented herself. Almost got the best of me.
CARL'S
It's not just the move that gives her away...
...it's the way her eyes burn.
Those eyes tell me she won't ever be a victim again.
I'm not sure what she's after...

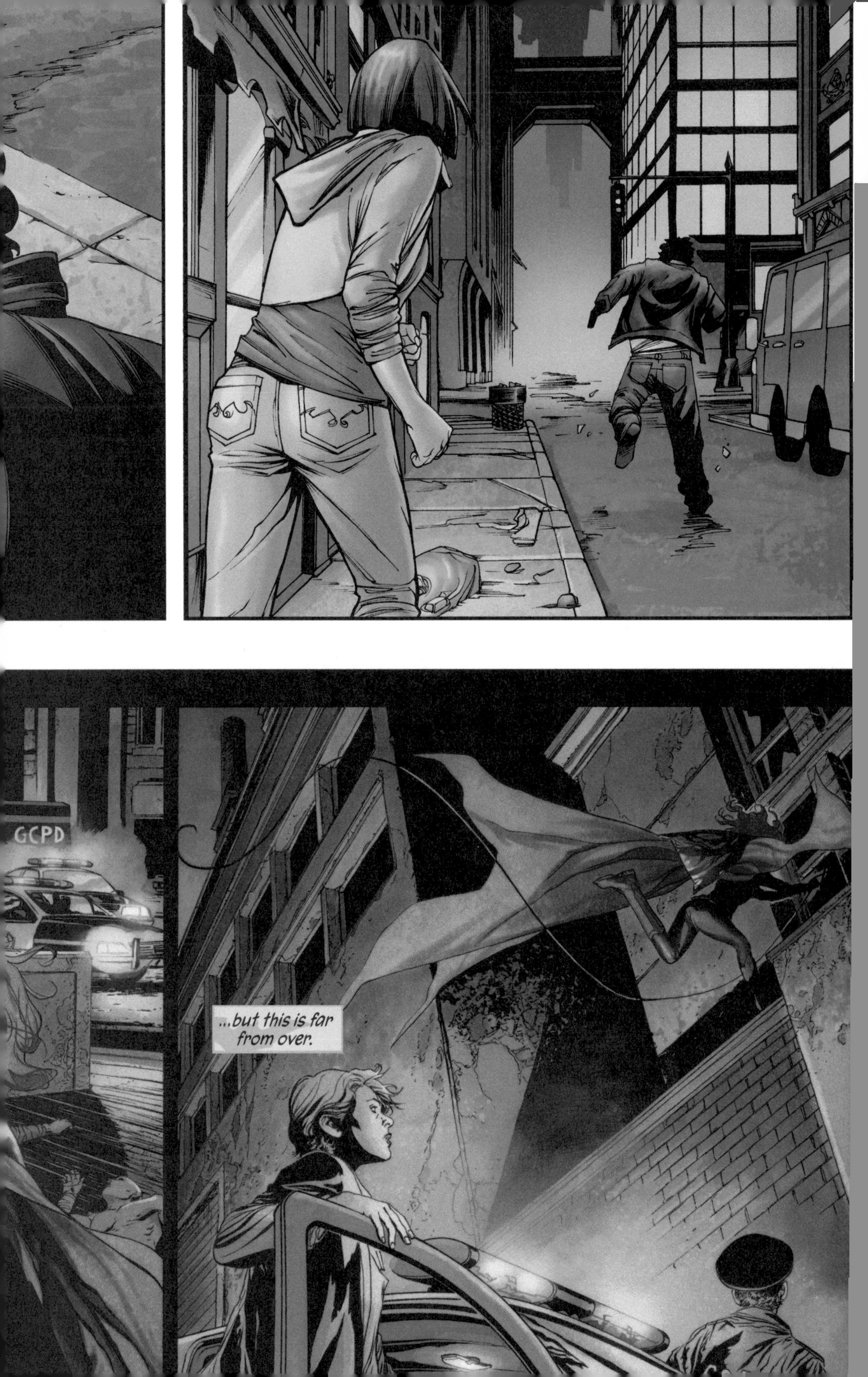
GCPD
...but this is far from over.

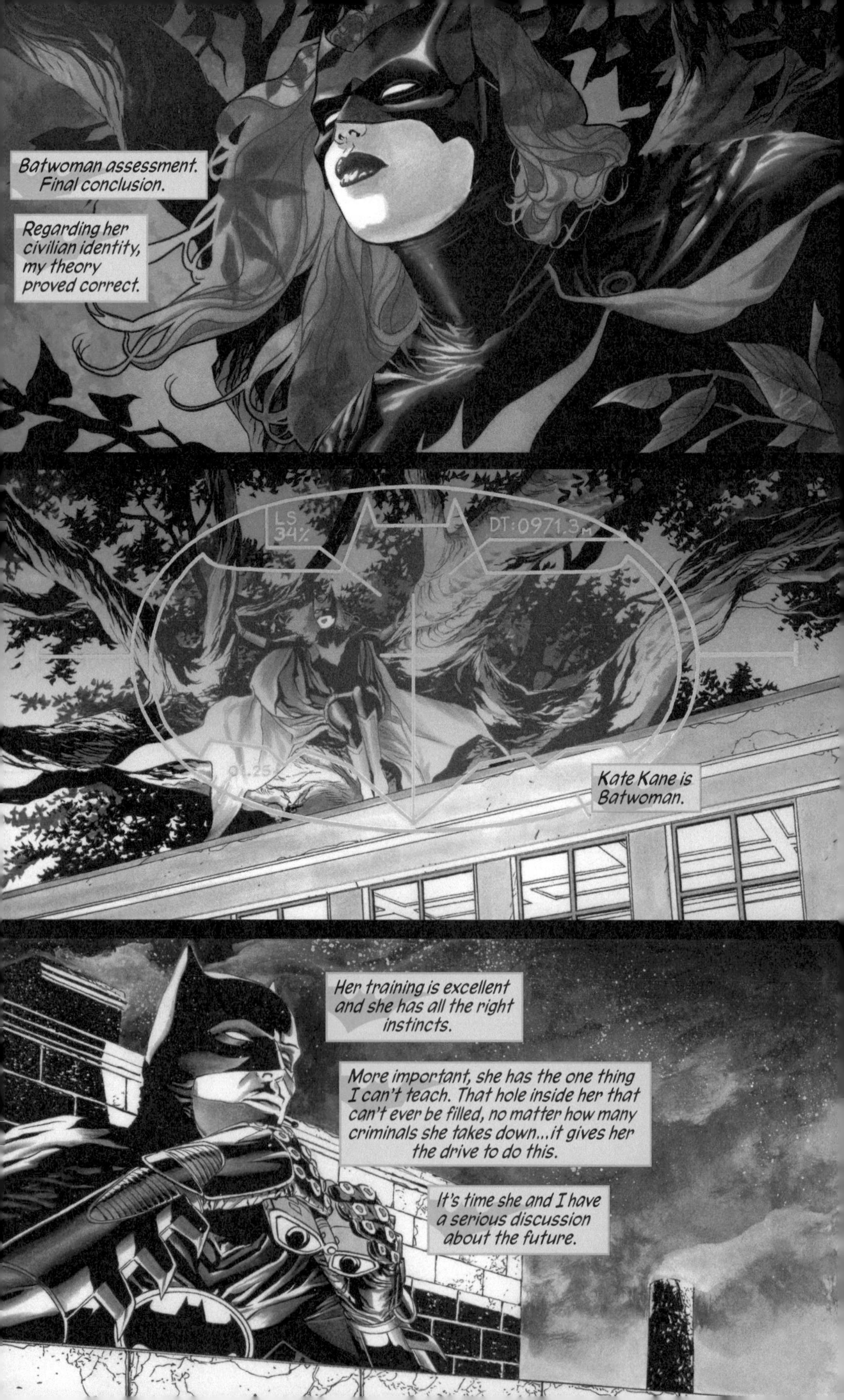
Batwoman assessment. Final conclusion.
Regarding her civilian identity, my theory proved correct.
LS 34%
DT:0971.3M
Kate Kane is Batwoman.
Her training is excellent and she has all the right instincts.
More important, she has the one thing I can't teach. That hole inside her that can't ever be filled, no matter how many criminals she takes down...it gives her the drive to do this.
It's time she and I have a serious discussion about the future.

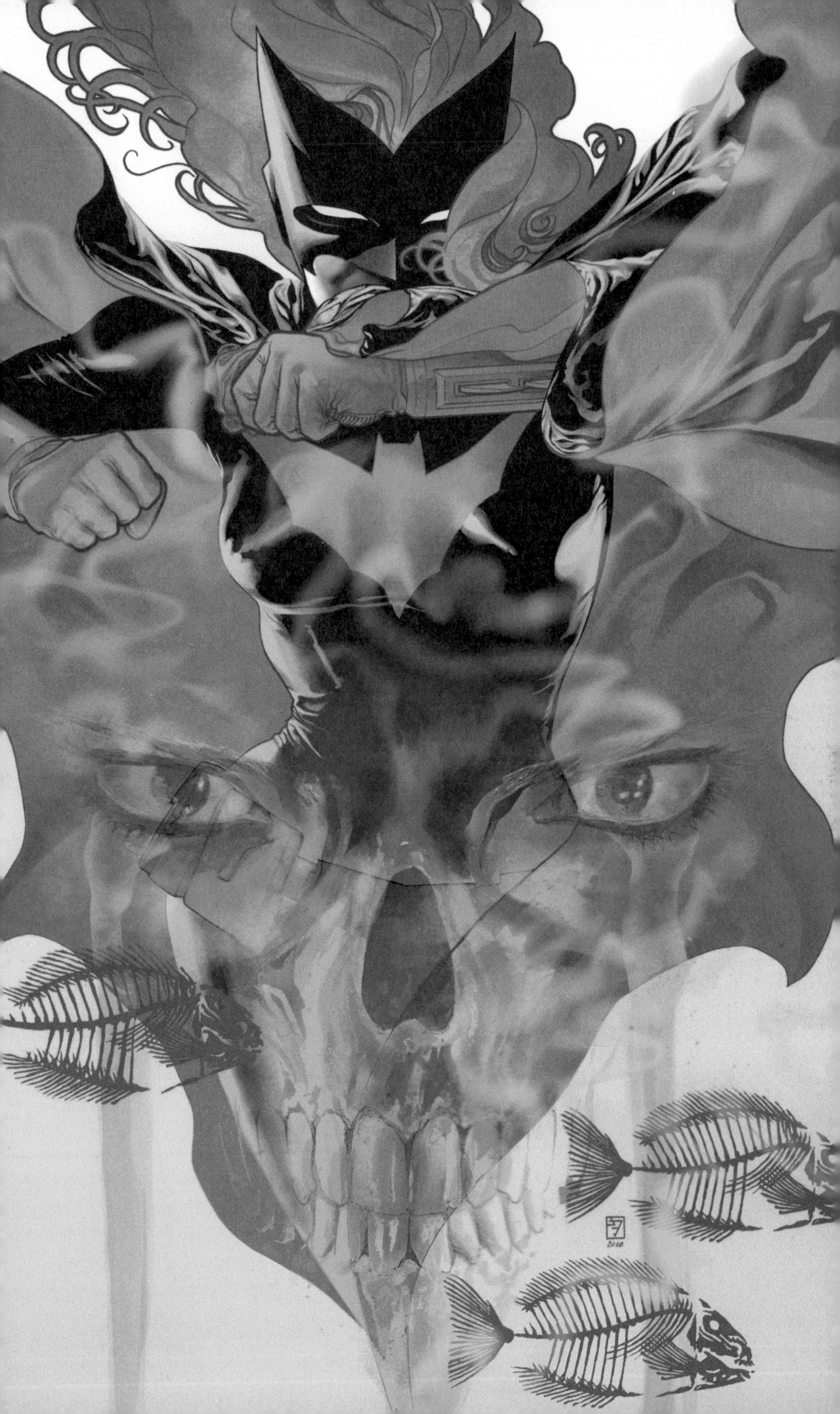

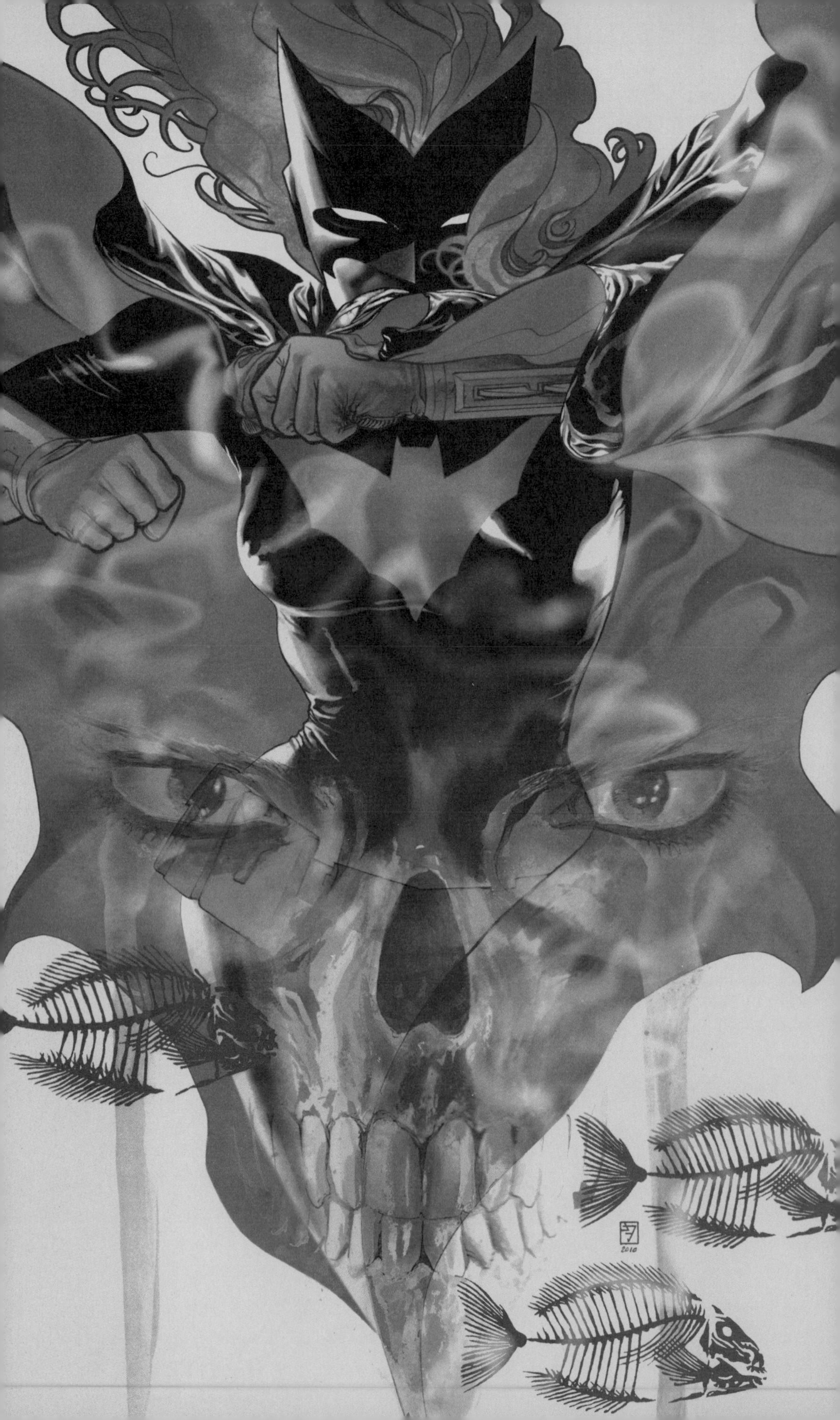
2010

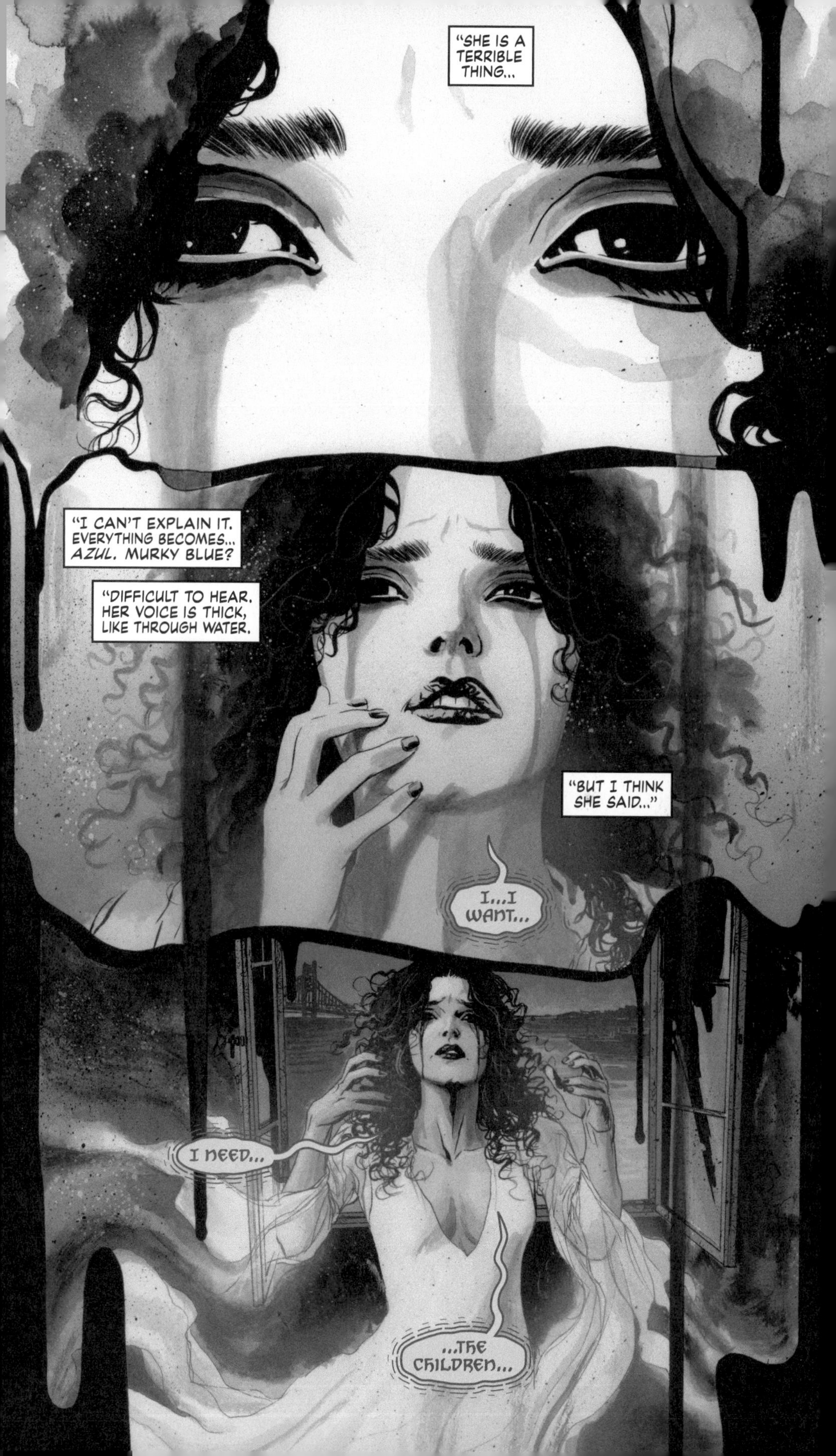
"SHE IS A TERRIBLE THING...
"I CAN'T EXPLAIN IT. EVERYTHING BECOMES... AZUL. MURKY BLUE?
"DIFFICULT TO HEAR. HER VOICE IS THICK, LIKE THROUGH WATER.
"BUT I THINK SHE SAID..."
I...I WANT...
I NEED...
...THE CHILDREN...

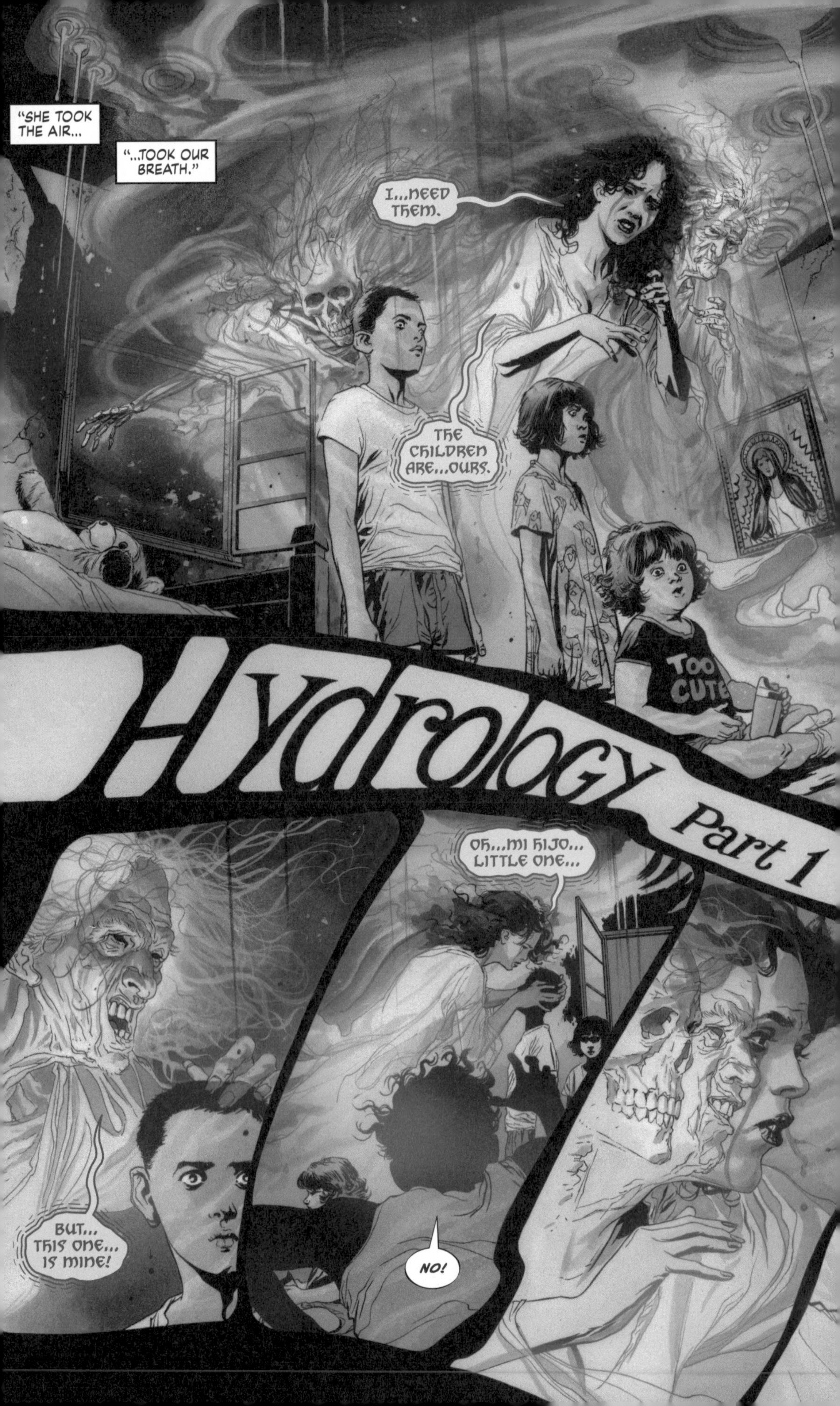
"SHE TOOK THE AIR...
"...TOOK OUR BREATH."
I...NEED THEM.
THE CHILDREN ARE...OURS.
TOO CUTE
Hydrology Part 1
BUT... THIS ONE... IS MINE!
OH...MI HIJO... LITTLE ONE...
NO!

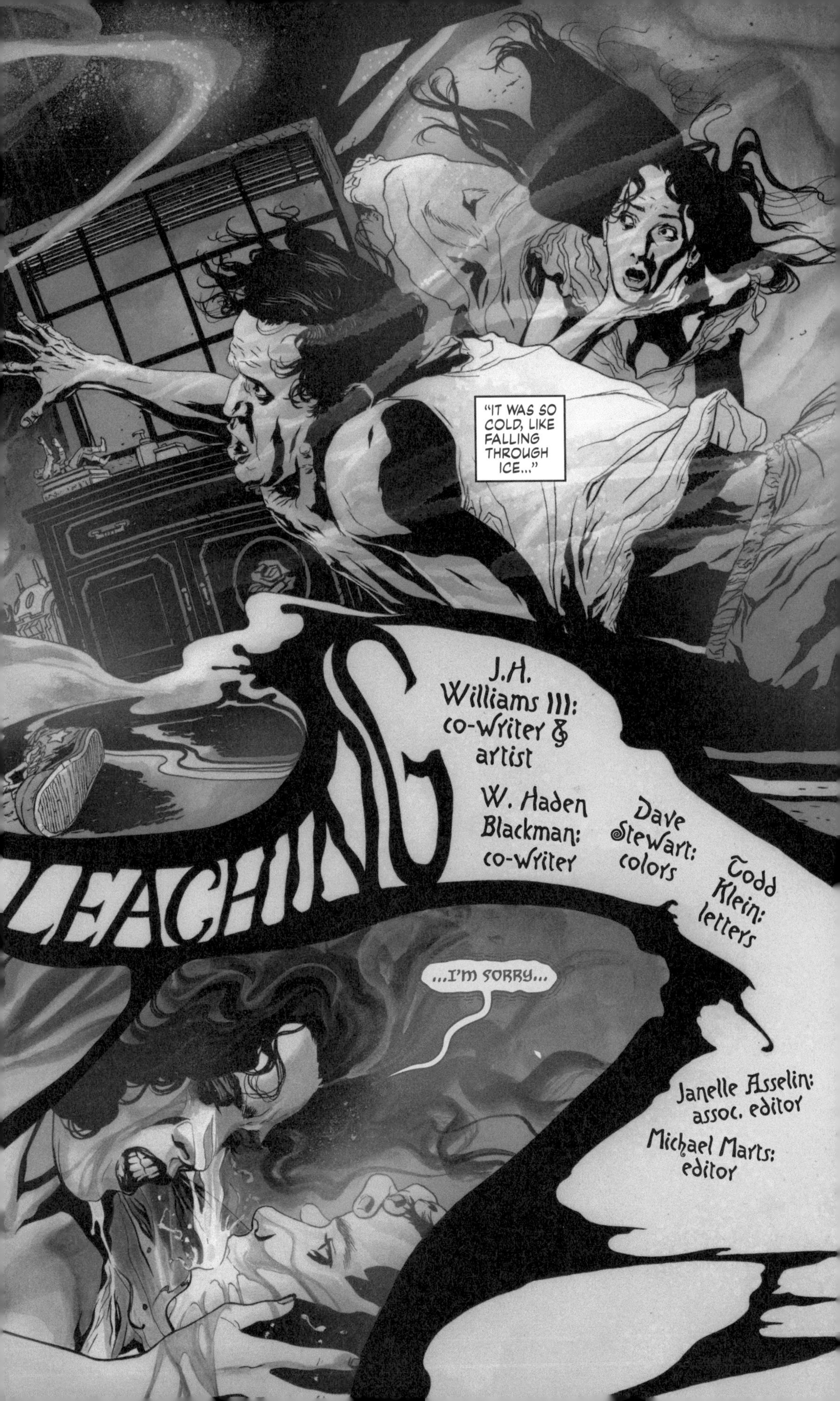
"IT WAS SO COLD, LIKE FALLING THROUGH ICE..."
LEACHING
J.H. Williams III: co-writer & artist
W. Haden Blackman: co-writer
Dave Stewart: colors
Todd Klein: letters
...I'M SORRY...
Janelle Asselin: assoc. editor
Michael Marts: editor

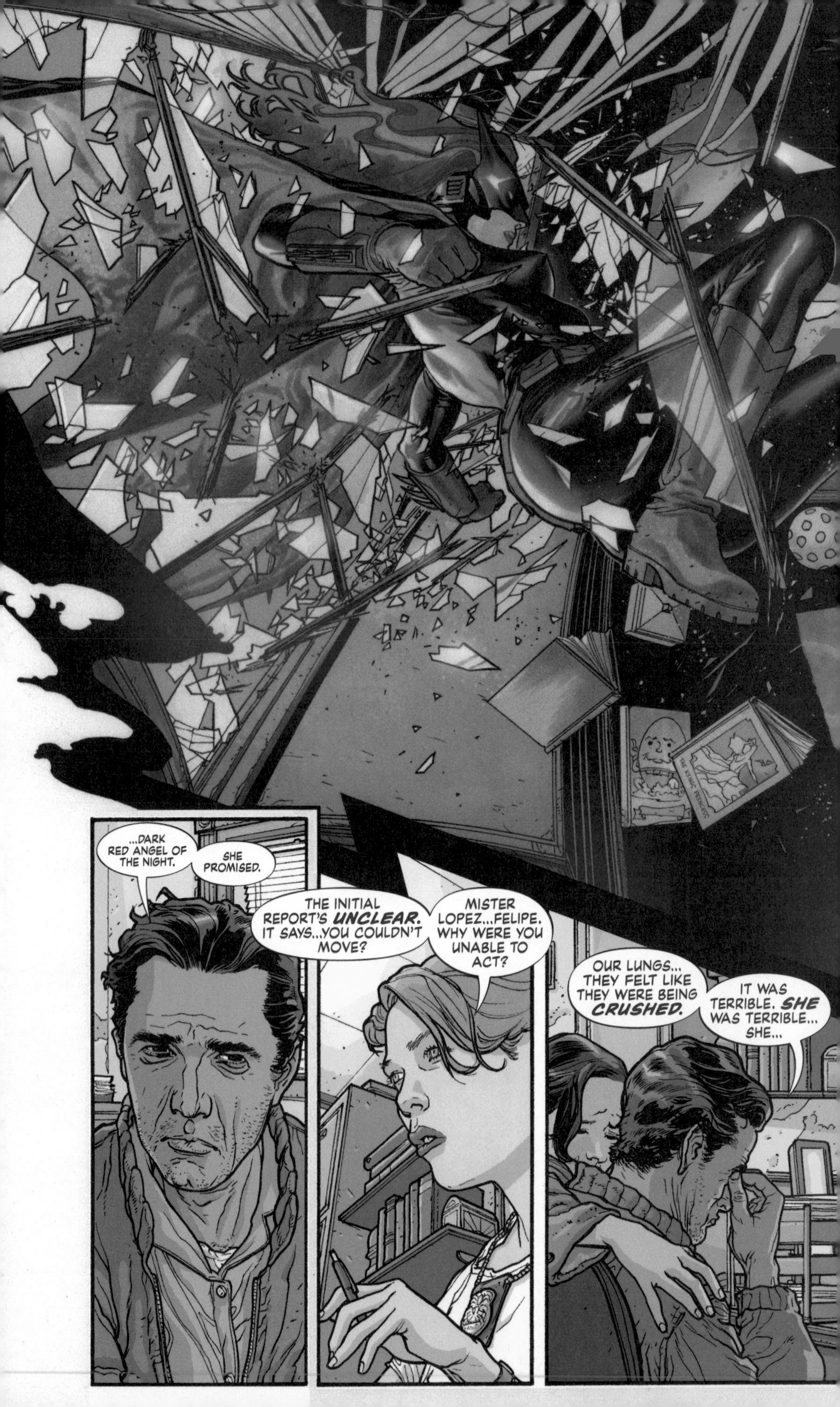

...DARK RED ANGEL OF THE NIGHT.
SHE PROMISED.
THE INITIAL REPORT'S ***UNCLEAR.*** IT SAYS...YOU COULDN'T MOVE?
MISTER LOPEZ...FELIPE. WHY WERE YOU UNABLE TO ACT?
OUR LUNGS... THEY FELT LIKE THEY WERE BEING ***CRUSHED.***
IT WAS TERRIBLE. ***SHE*** WAS TERRIBLE... SHE...

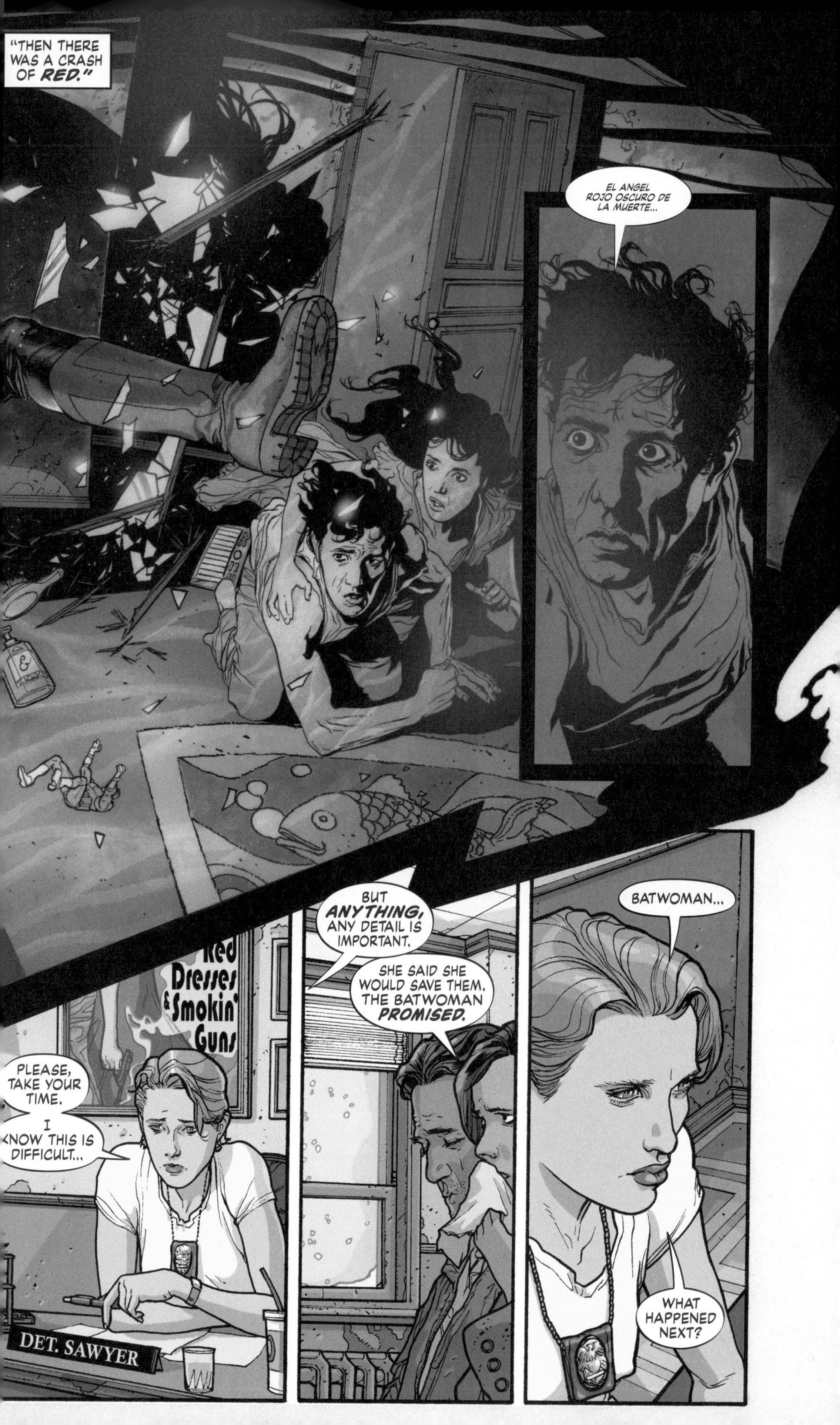
"THEN THERE WAS A CRASH OF *RED.*"
EL ANGEL ROJO OSCURO DE LA MUERTE...
BUT *ANYTHING,* ANY DETAIL IS IMPORTANT.
SHE SAID SHE WOULD SAVE THEM. THE BATWOMAN *PROMISED.*
BATWOMAN...
Red Dresses & Smokin' Guns
PLEASE, TAKE YOUR TIME.
I KNOW THIS IS DIFFICULT...
WHAT HAPPENED NEXT?
DET. SAWYER

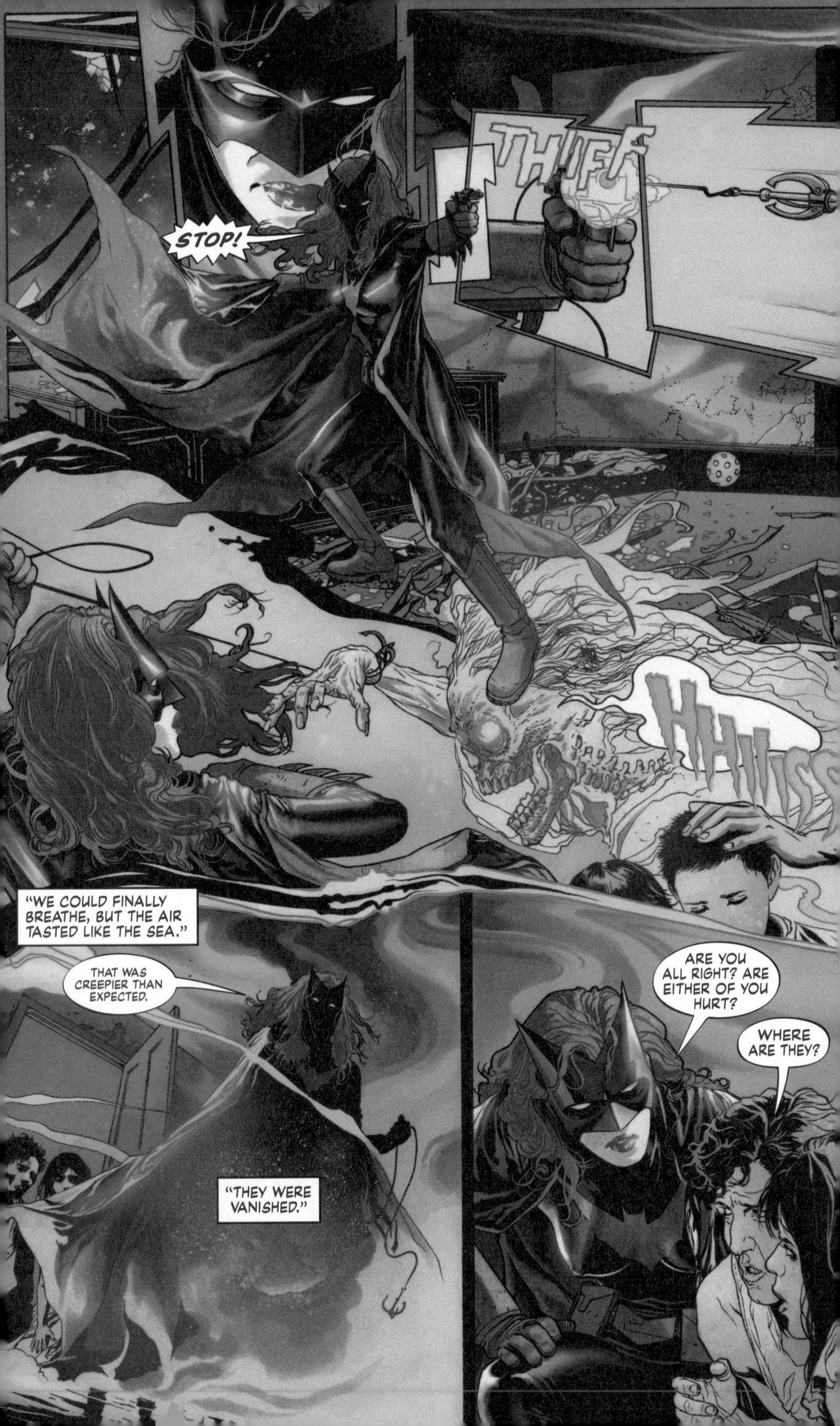

STOP!
THFFF
HHHISS
"WE COULD FINALLY BREATHE, BUT THE AIR TASTED LIKE THE SEA."
THAT WAS CREEPIER THAN EXPECTED.
"THEY WERE VANISHED."
ARE YOU ALL RIGHT? ARE EITHER OF YOU HURT?
WHERE ARE THEY?

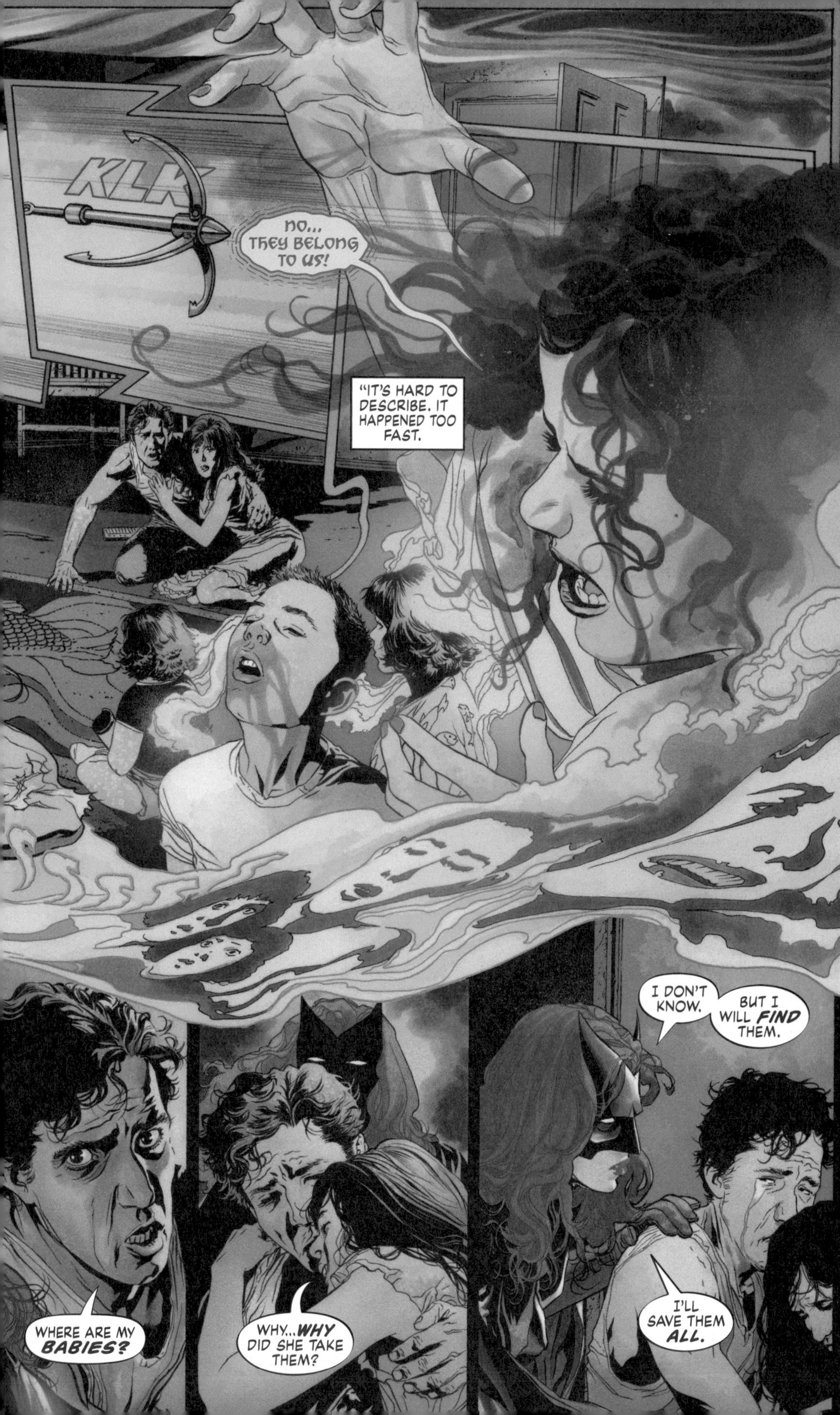
KLK
NO... THEY BELONG TO US!
"IT'S HARD TO DESCRIBE. IT HAPPENED TOO FAST.
WHERE ARE MY BABIES?
WHY...WHY DID SHE TAKE THEM?
I DON'T KNOW.
BUT I WILL FIND THEM.
I'LL SAVE THEM ALL.

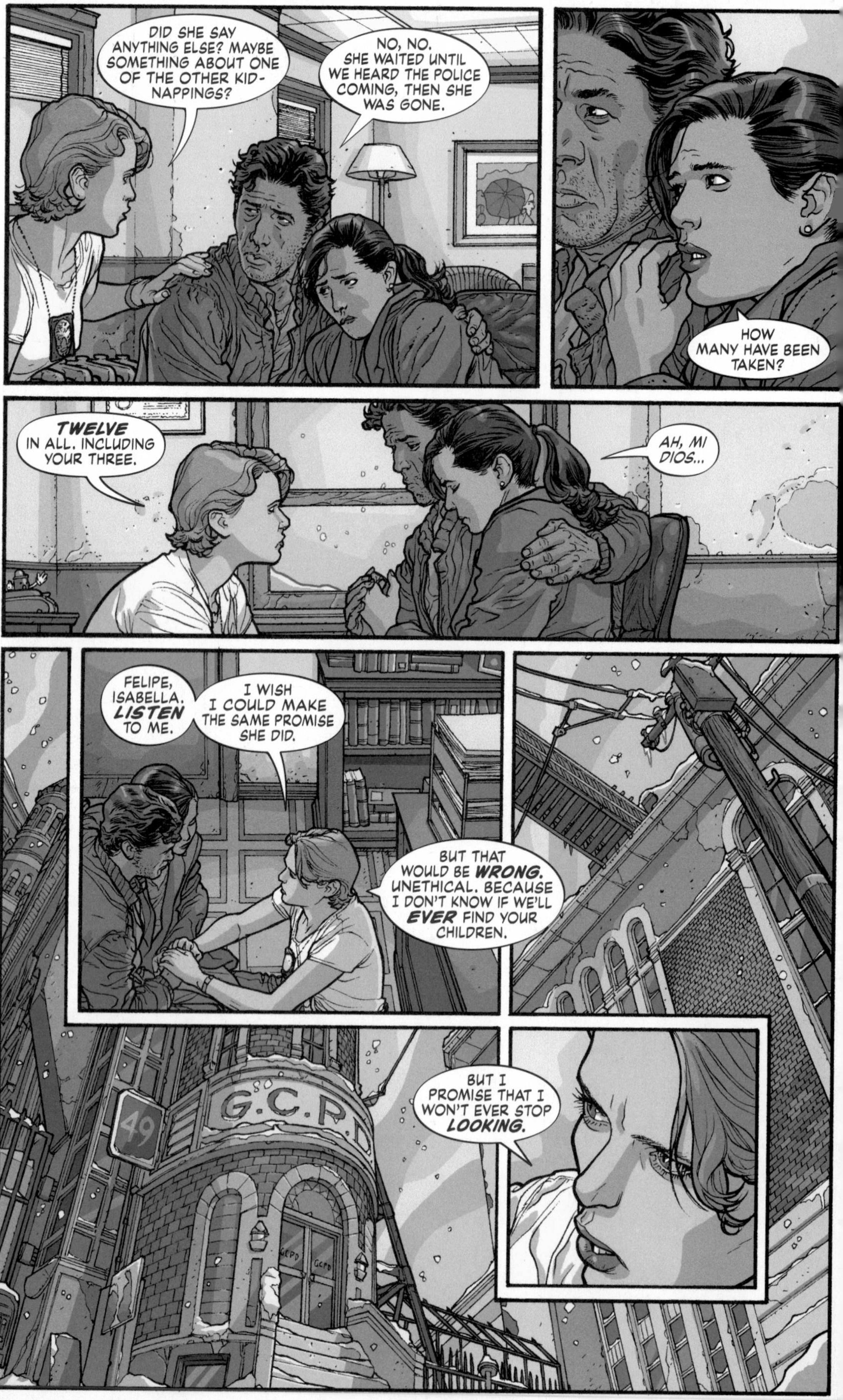
DID SHE SAY ANYTHING ELSE? MAYBE SOMETHING ABOUT ONE OF THE OTHER KID-NAPPINGS?
NO, NO. SHE WAITED UNTIL WE HEARD THE POLICE COMING, THEN SHE WAS GONE.
HOW MANY HAVE BEEN TAKEN?
TWELVE IN ALL. INCLUDING YOUR THREE.
AH, MI DIOS...
FELIPE, ISABELLA. LISTEN TO ME.
I WISH I COULD MAKE THE SAME PROMISE SHE DID.
BUT THAT WOULD BE WRONG. UNETHICAL. BECAUSE I DON'T KNOW IF WE'LL EVER FIND YOUR CHILDREN.
G.C.P.D.
49
BUT I PROMISE THAT I WON'T EVER STOP LOOKING.

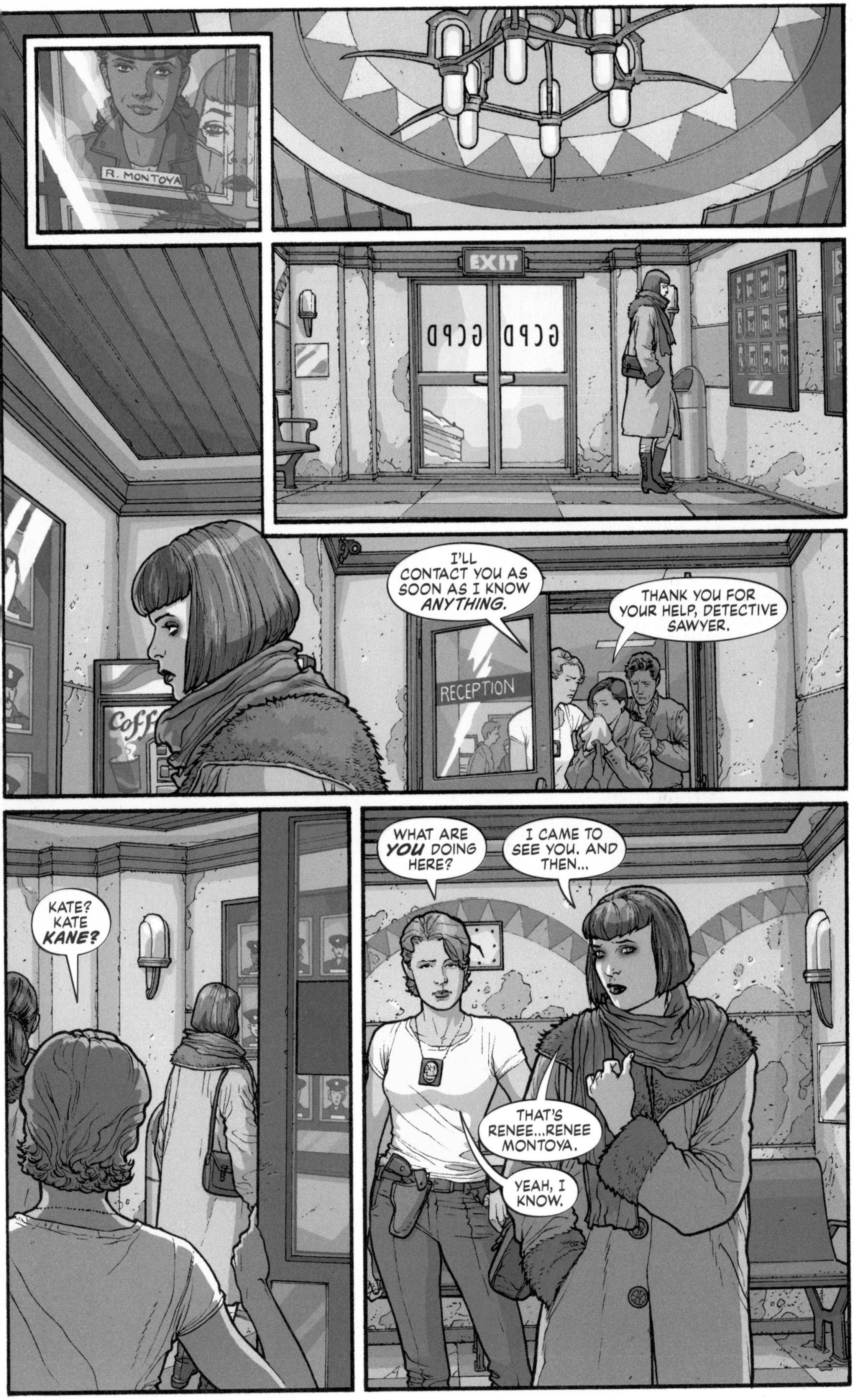
R. MONTOYA
EXIT
GCPD GCPD
I'LL CONTACT YOU AS SOON AS I KNOW ANYTHING.
THANK YOU FOR YOUR HELP, DETECTIVE SAWYER.
RECEPTION
KATE? KATE KANE?
WHAT ARE YOU DOING HERE?
I CAME TO SEE YOU. AND THEN...
THAT'S RENEE...RENEE MONTOYA.
YEAH, I KNOW.

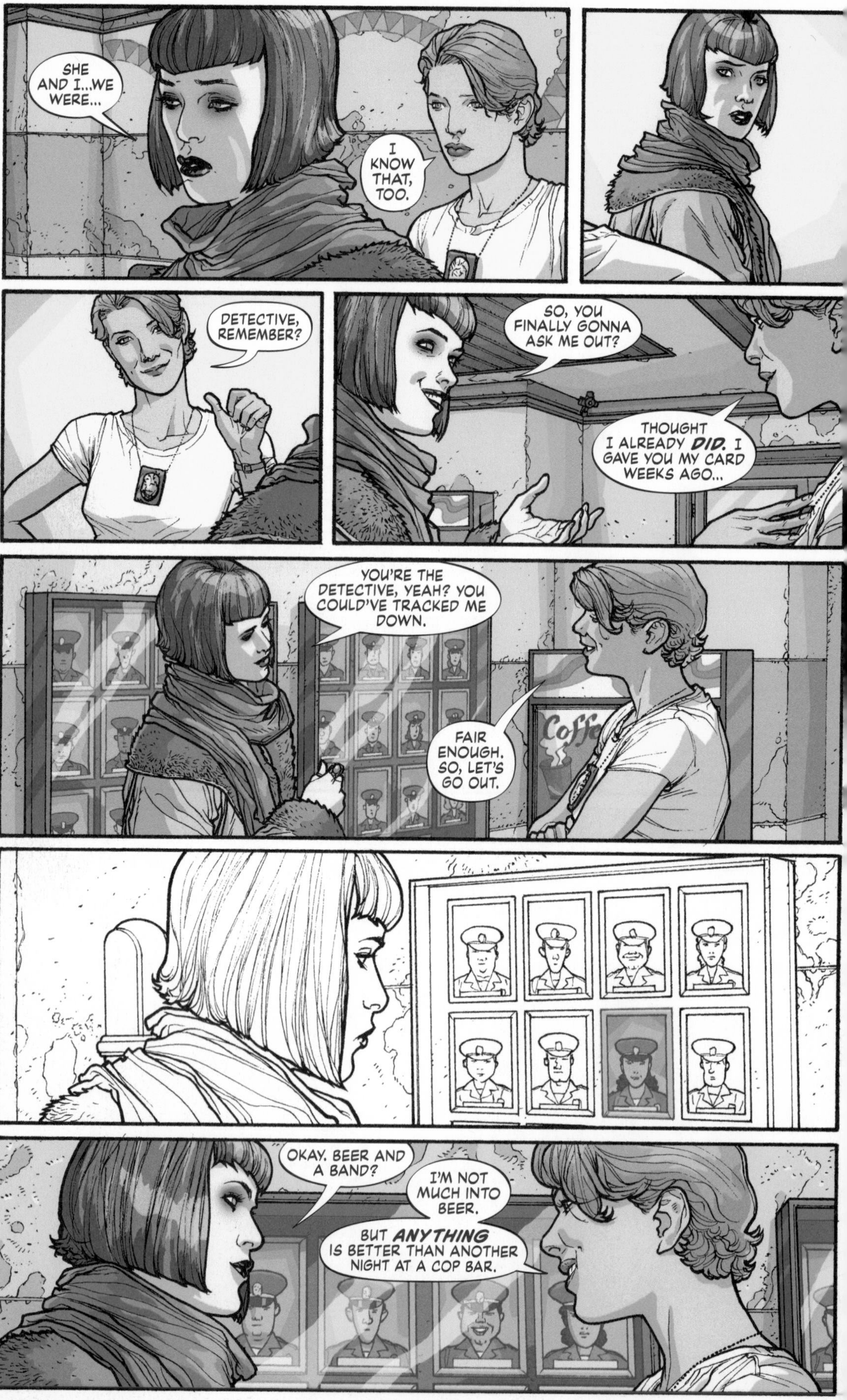

SHE AND I...WE WERE...
I KNOW THAT, TOO.
DETECTIVE, REMEMBER?
SO, YOU FINALLY GONNA ASK ME OUT?
THOUGHT I ALREADY DID. I GAVE YOU MY CARD WEEKS AGO...
YOU'RE THE DETECTIVE, YEAH? YOU COULD'VE TRACKED ME DOWN.
FAIR ENOUGH. SO, LET'S GO OUT.
Coffe
OKAY. BEER AND A BAND?
I'M NOT MUCH INTO BEER.
BUT ANYTHING IS BETTER THAN ANOTHER NIGHT AT A COP BAR.

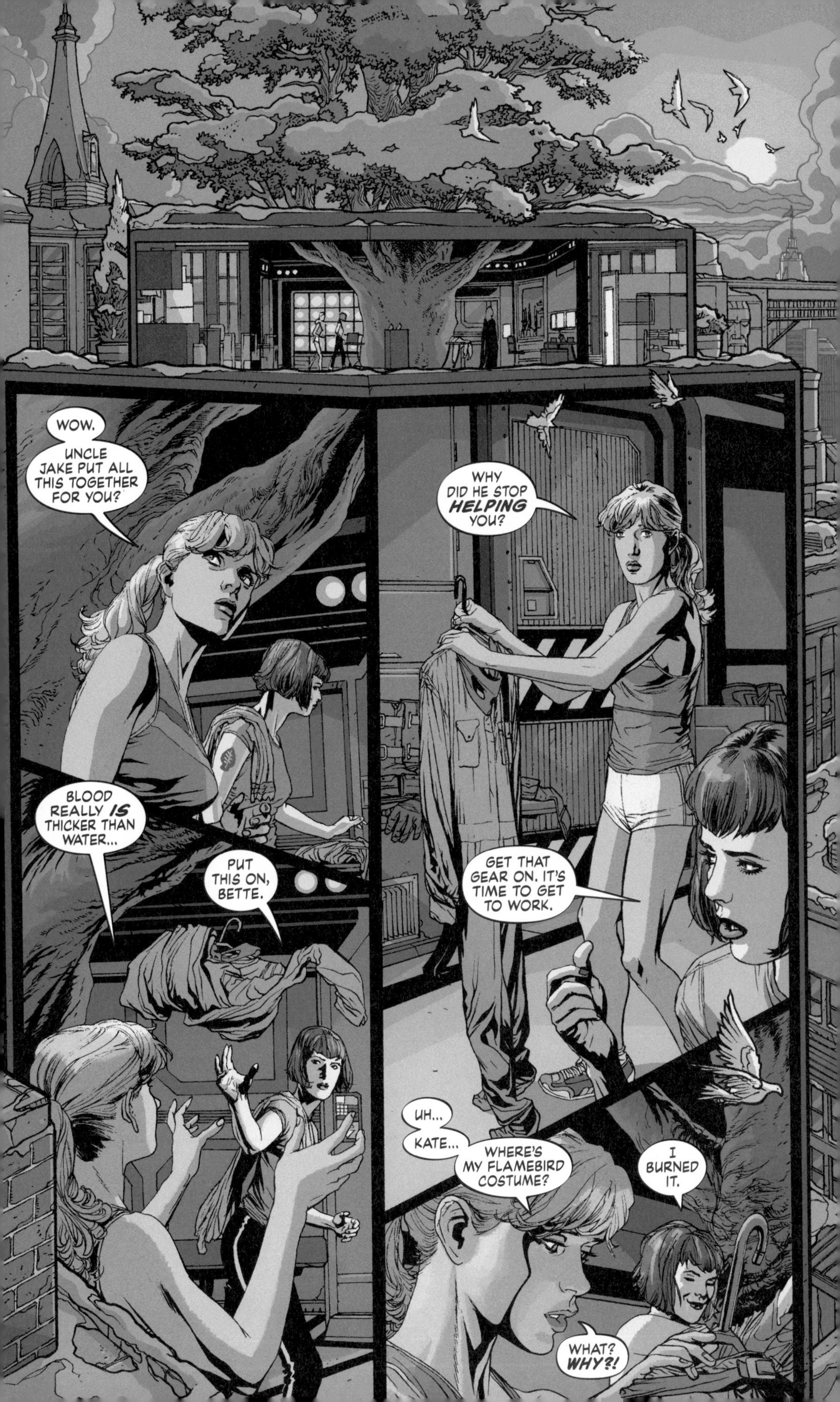
WOW.
UNCLE JAKE PUT ALL THIS TOGETHER FOR YOU?
WHY DID HE STOP HELPING YOU?
BLOOD REALLY IS THICKER THAN WATER...
PUT THIS ON, BETTE.
GET THAT GEAR ON. IT'S TIME TO GET TO WORK.
UH...
KATE...
WHERE'S MY FLAMEBIRD COSTUME?
I BURNED IT.
WHAT? WHY?!

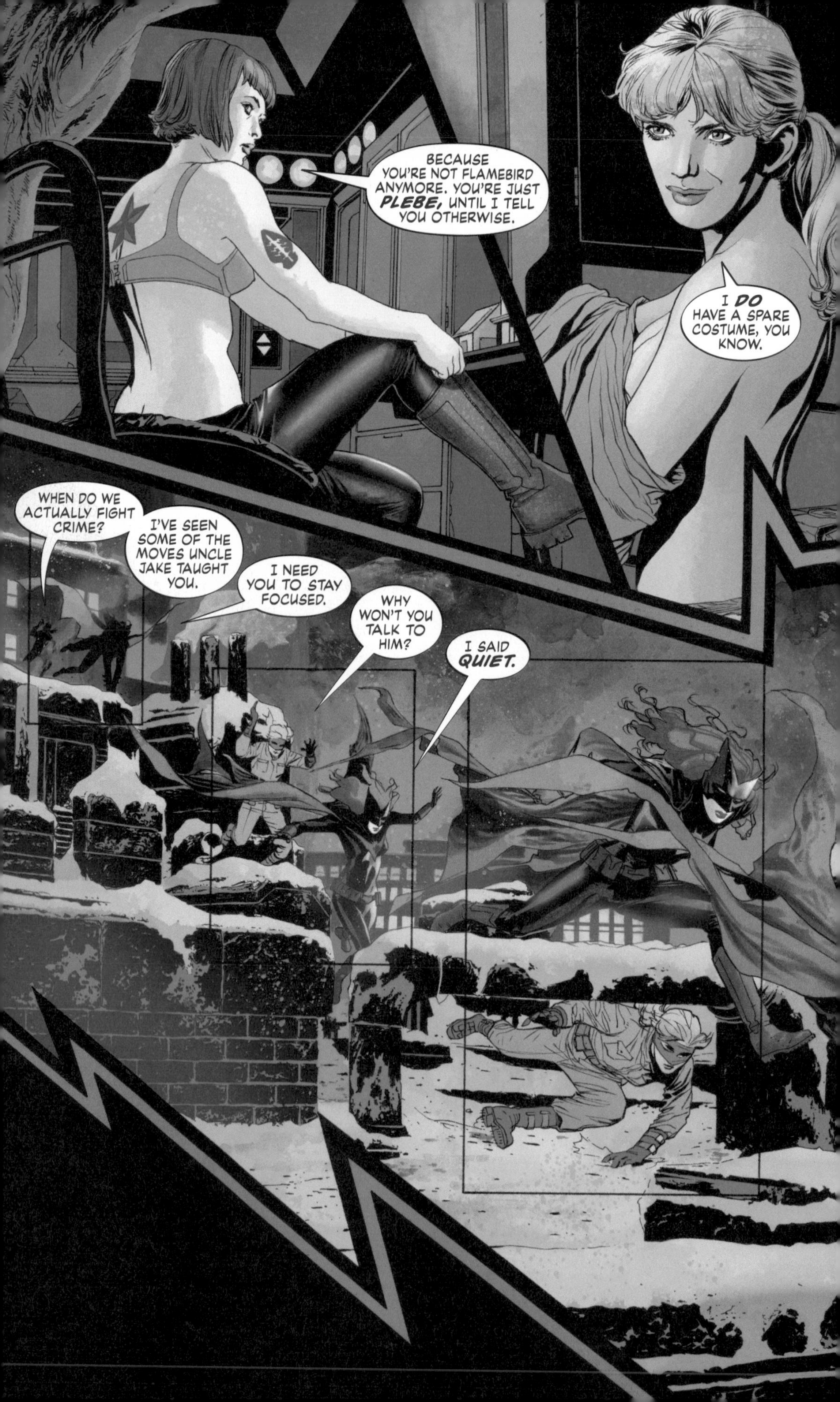
BECAUSE YOU'RE NOT FLAMEBIRD ANYMORE. YOU'RE JUST PLEBE, UNTIL I TELL YOU OTHERWISE.
I DO HAVE A SPARE COSTUME, YOU KNOW.
WHEN DO WE ACTUALLY FIGHT CRIME?
I'VE SEEN SOME OF THE MOVES UNCLE JAKE TAUGHT YOU.
I NEED YOU TO STAY FOCUSED.
WHY WON'T YOU TALK TO HIM?
I SAID QUIET.

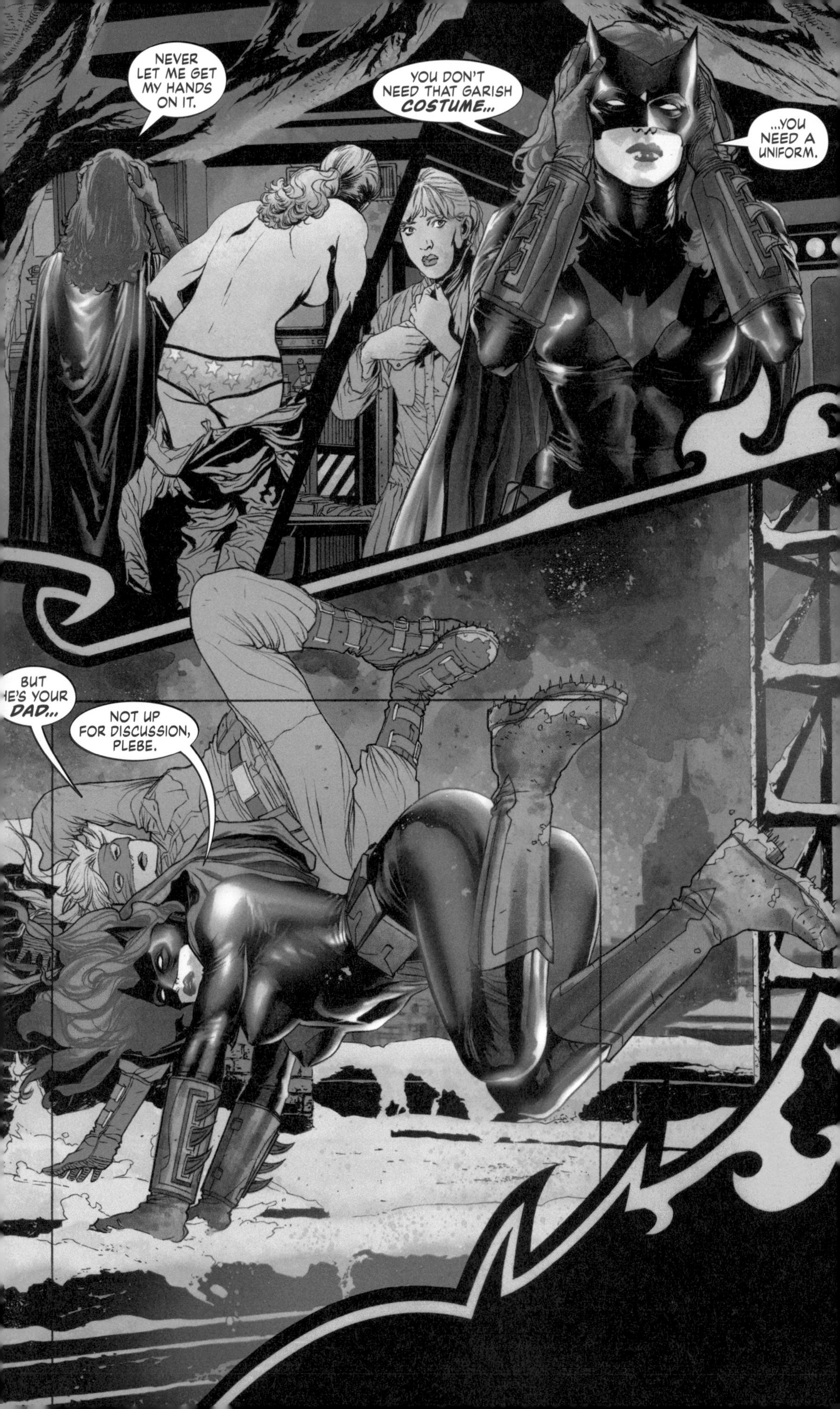
NEVER LET ME GET MY HANDS ON IT.
YOU DON'T NEED THAT GARISH *COSTUME...*
...YOU NEED A UNIFORM.
BUT HE'S YOUR *DAD...*
NOT UP FOR DISCUSSION, PLEBE.

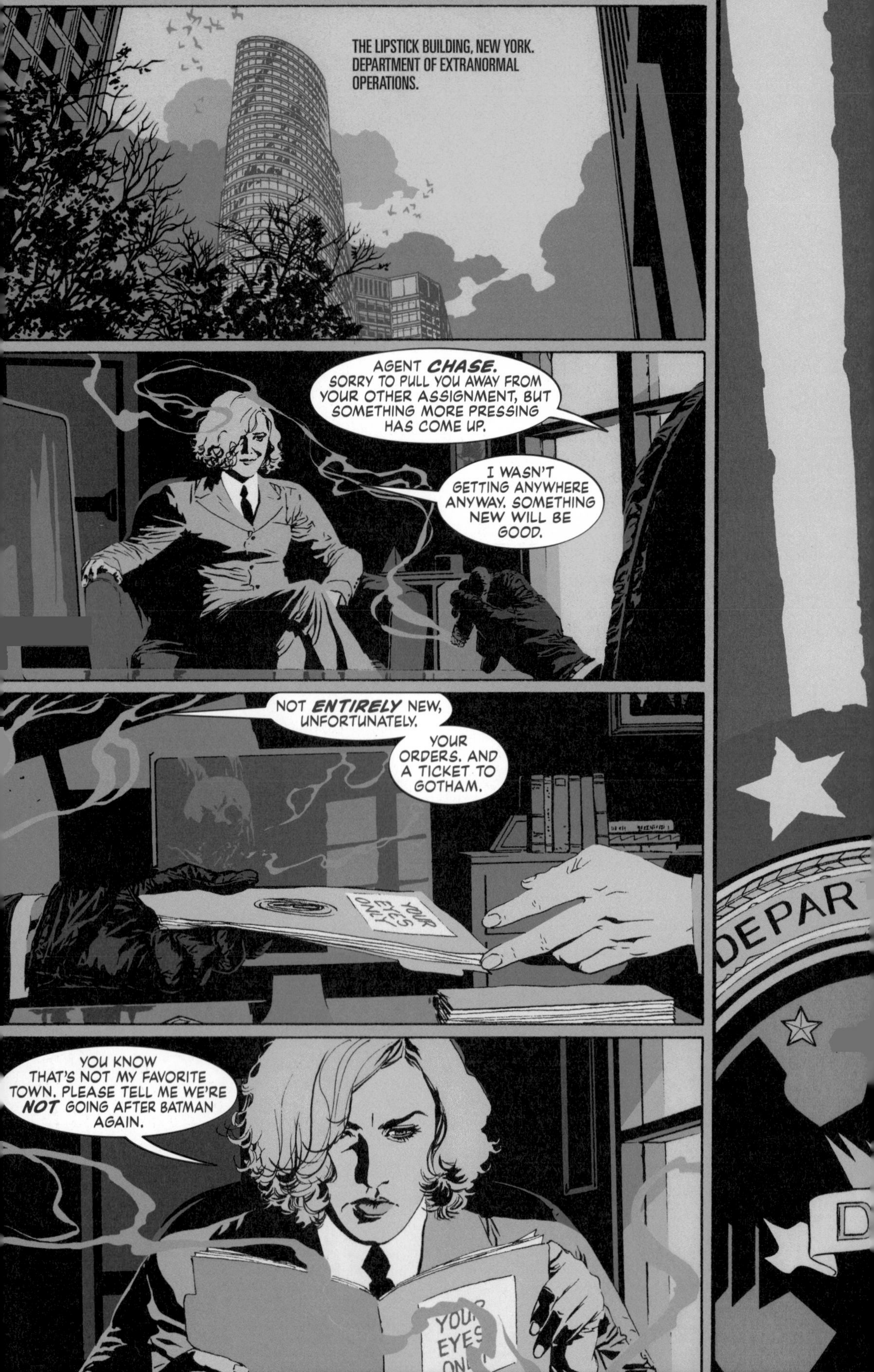
THE LIPSTICK BUILDING, NEW YORK. DEPARTMENT OF EXTRANORMAL OPERATIONS.
AGENT CHASE. SORRY TO PULL YOU AWAY FROM YOUR OTHER ASSIGNMENT, BUT SOMETHING MORE PRESSING HAS COME UP.
I WASN'T GETTING ANYWHERE ANYWAY. SOMETHING NEW WILL BE GOOD.
NOT ENTIRELY NEW, UNFORTUNATELY.
YOUR ORDERS. AND A TICKET TO GOTHAM.
YOUR EYES ONLY
YOU KNOW THAT'S NOT MY FAVORITE TOWN. PLEASE TELL ME WE'RE NOT GOING AFTER BATMAN AGAIN.
DEPAR

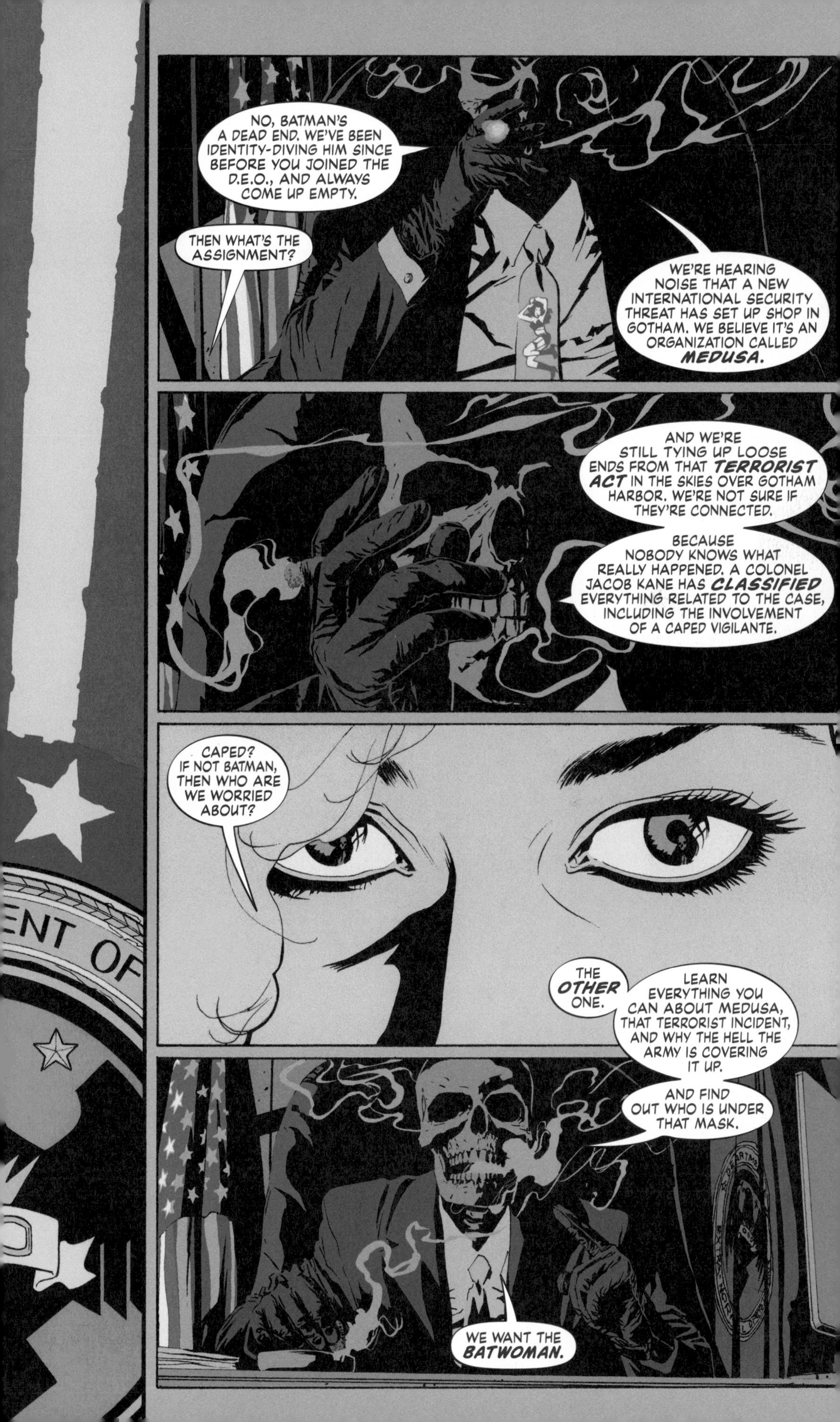
NO, BATMAN'S A DEAD END. WE'VE BEEN IDENTITY-DIVING HIM SINCE BEFORE YOU JOINED THE D.E.O., AND ALWAYS COME UP EMPTY.
THEN WHAT'S THE ASSIGNMENT?
WE'RE HEARING NOISE THAT A NEW INTERNATIONAL SECURITY THREAT HAS SET UP SHOP IN GOTHAM. WE BELIEVE IT'S AN ORGANIZATION CALLED *MEDUSA.*
AND WE'RE STILL TYING UP LOOSE ENDS FROM THAT *TERRORIST ACT* IN THE SKIES OVER GOTHAM HARBOR. WE'RE NOT SURE IF THEY'RE CONNECTED.
BECAUSE NOBODY KNOWS WHAT REALLY HAPPENED. A COLONEL JACOB KANE HAS *CLASSIFIED* EVERYTHING RELATED TO THE CASE, INCLUDING THE INVOLVEMENT OF A CAPED VIGILANTE.
CAPED? IF NOT BATMAN, THEN WHO ARE WE WORRIED ABOUT?
THE *OTHER* ONE.
LEARN EVERYTHING YOU CAN ABOUT MEDUSA, THAT TERRORIST INCIDENT, AND WHY THE HELL THE ARMY IS COVERING IT UP.
AND FIND OUT WHO IS UNDER THAT MASK.
WE WANT THE *BATWOMAN.*

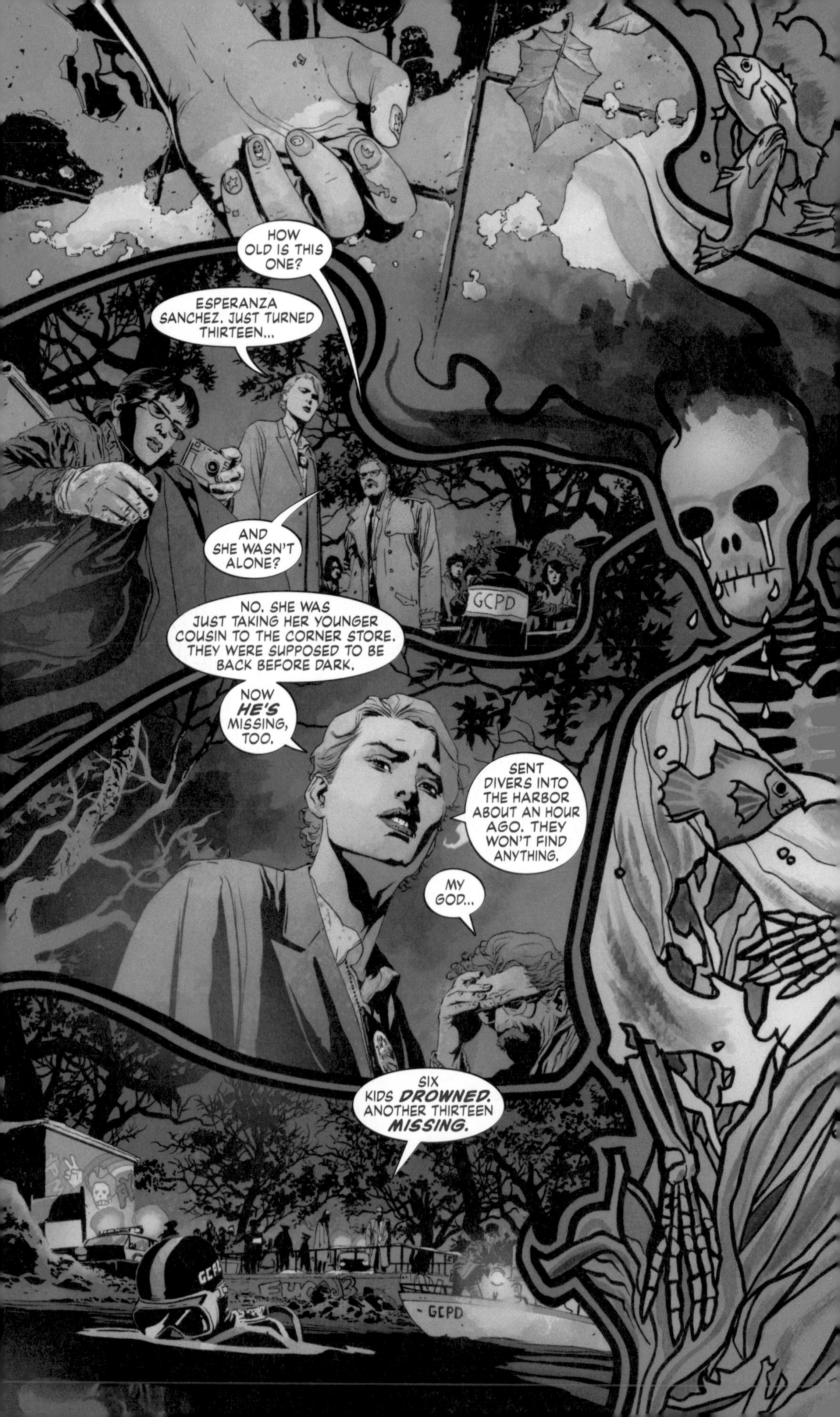

HOW OLD IS THIS ONE?
ESPERANZA SANCHEZ. JUST TURNED THIRTEEN...
AND SHE WASN'T ALONE?
NO. SHE WAS JUST TAKING HER YOUNGER COUSIN TO THE CORNER STORE. THEY WERE SUPPOSED TO BE BACK BEFORE DARK.
NOW ***HE'S*** MISSING, TOO.
SENT DIVERS INTO THE HARBOR ABOUT AN HOUR AGO. THEY WON'T FIND ANYTHING.
MY GOD...
SIX KIDS ***DROWNED.*** ANOTHER THIRTEEN ***MISSING.***
GCPD
GCPD

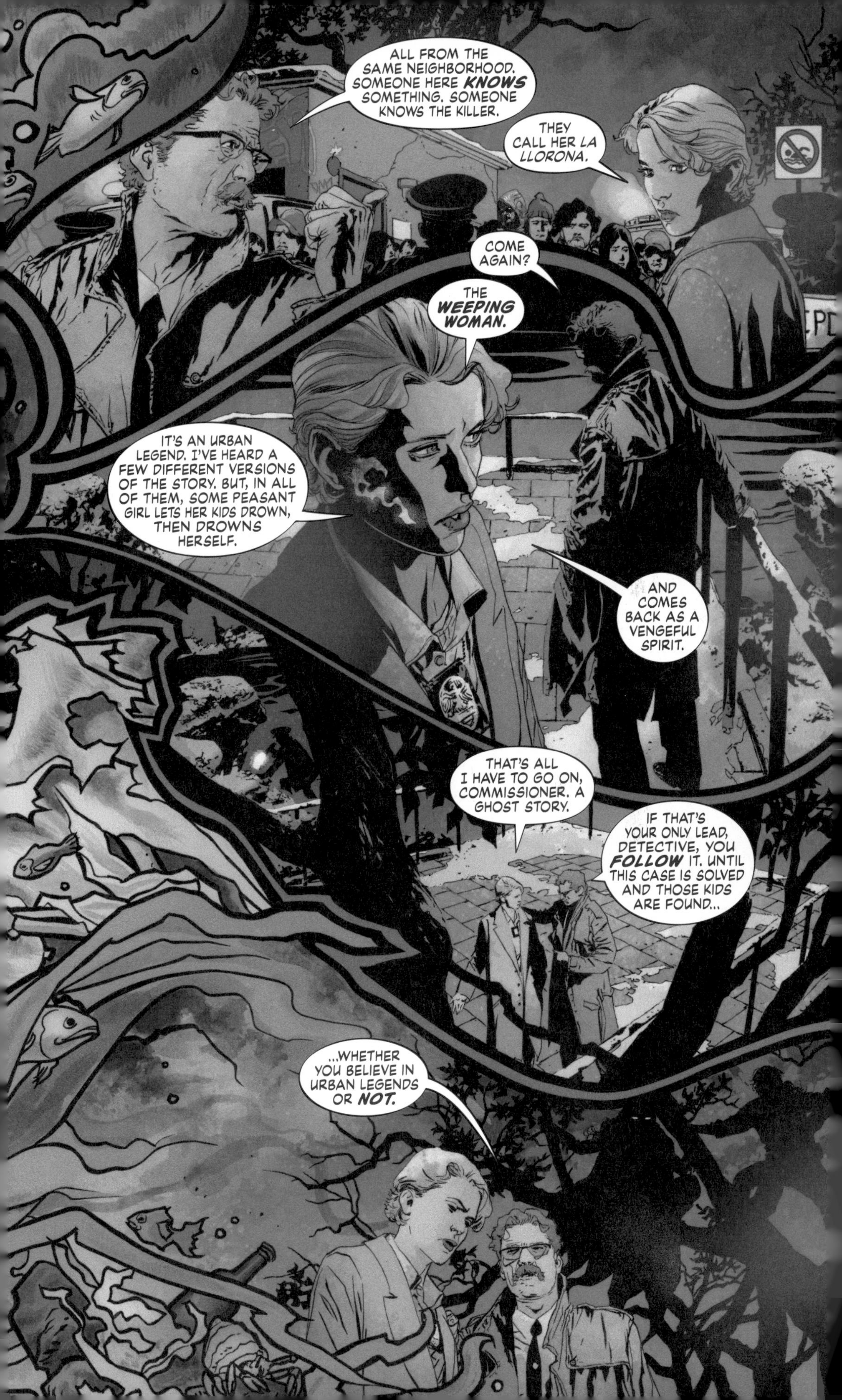

ALL FROM THE SAME NEIGHBORHOOD. SOMEONE HERE KNOWS SOMETHING. SOMEONE KNOWS THE KILLER.
THEY CALL HER LA LLORONA.
COME AGAIN?
THE WEEPING WOMAN.
IT'S AN URBAN LEGEND. I'VE HEARD A FEW DIFFERENT VERSIONS OF THE STORY. BUT, IN ALL OF THEM, SOME PEASANT GIRL LETS HER KIDS DROWN, THEN DROWNS HERSELF.
AND COMES BACK AS A VENGEFUL SPIRIT.
THAT'S ALL I HAVE TO GO ON, COMMISSIONER. A GHOST STORY.
IF THAT'S YOUR ONLY LEAD, DETECTIVE, YOU FOLLOW IT. UNTIL THIS CASE IS SOLVED AND THOSE KIDS ARE FOUND...
...WHETHER YOU BELIEVE IN URBAN LEGENDS OR NOT.

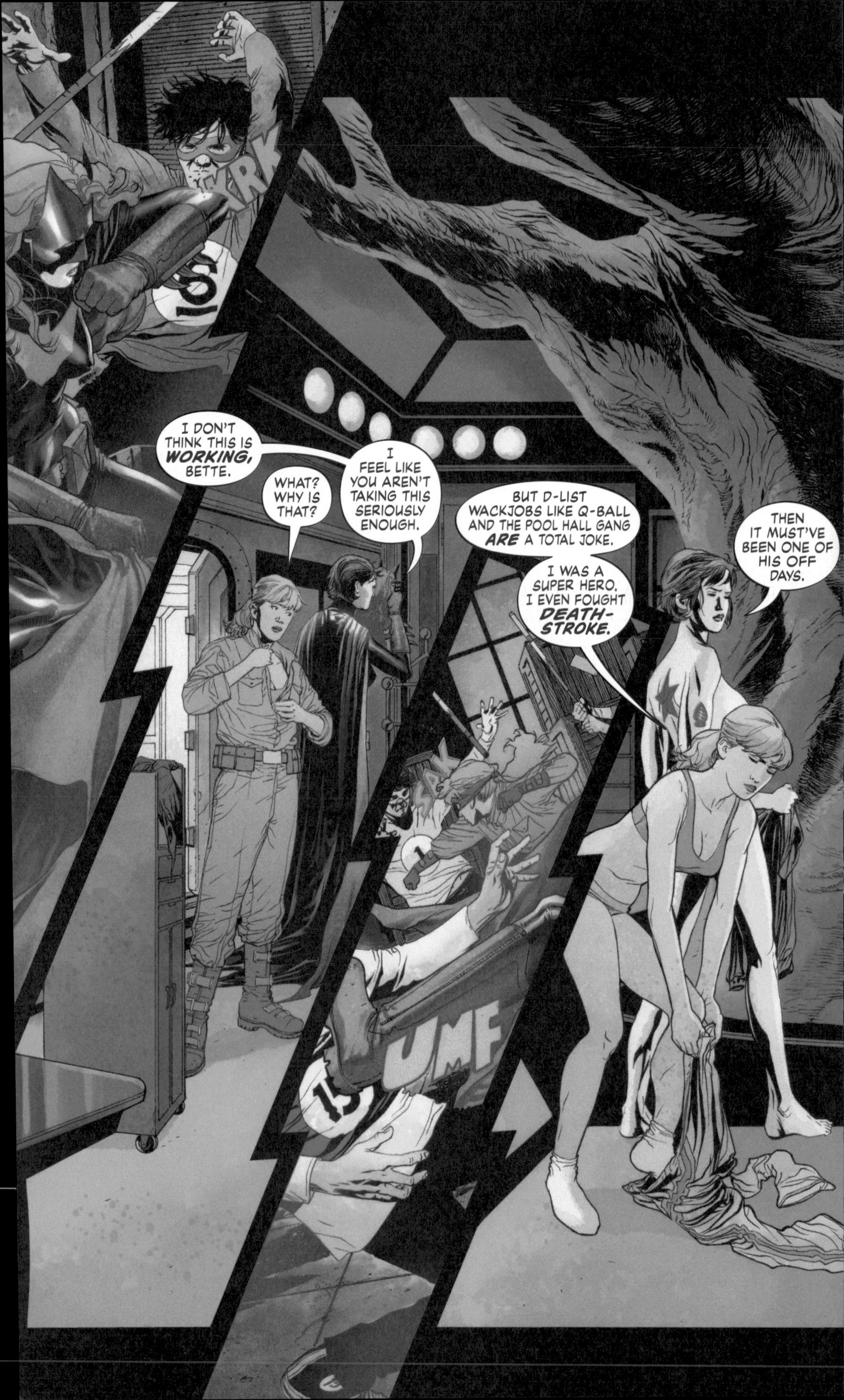

I DON'T THINK THIS IS **WORKING,** BETTE.
WHAT? WHY IS THAT?
I FEEL LIKE YOU AREN'T TAKING THIS SERIOUSLY ENOUGH.
BUT D-LIST WACKJOBS LIKE Q-BALL AND THE POOL HALL GANG **ARE** A TOTAL JOKE.
I WAS A SUPER HERO, I EVEN FOUGHT **DEATH-STROKE.**
THEN IT MUST'VE BEEN ONE OF HIS OFF DAYS.
UMF

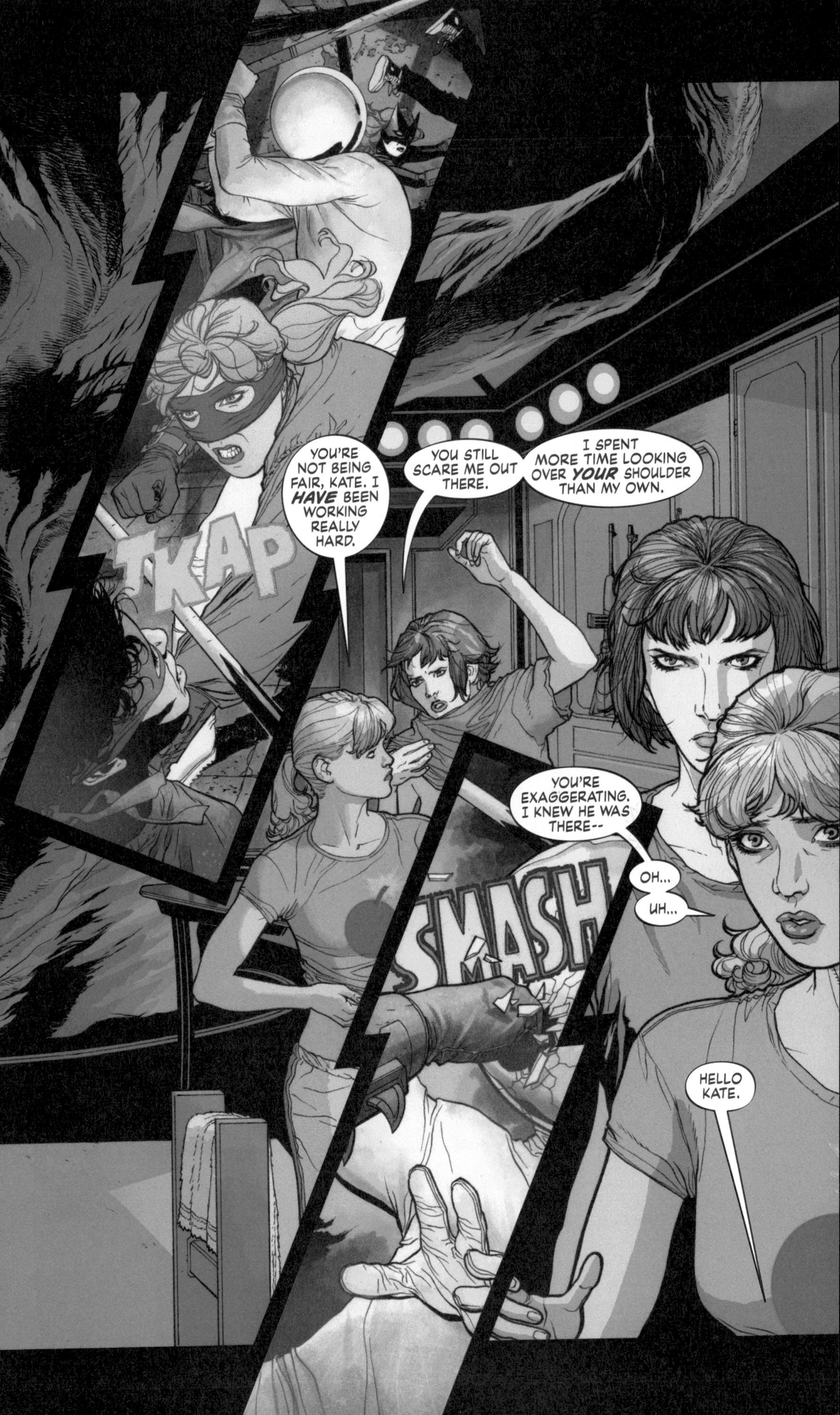
YOU'RE NOT BEING FAIR, KATE. I HAVE BEEN WORKING REALLY HARD.
TKAP
YOU STILL SCARE ME OUT THERE.
I SPENT MORE TIME LOOKING OVER YOUR SHOULDER THAN MY OWN.
YOU'RE EXAGGERATING. I KNEW HE WAS THERE--
OH...
UH...
SMASH
HELLO KATE.

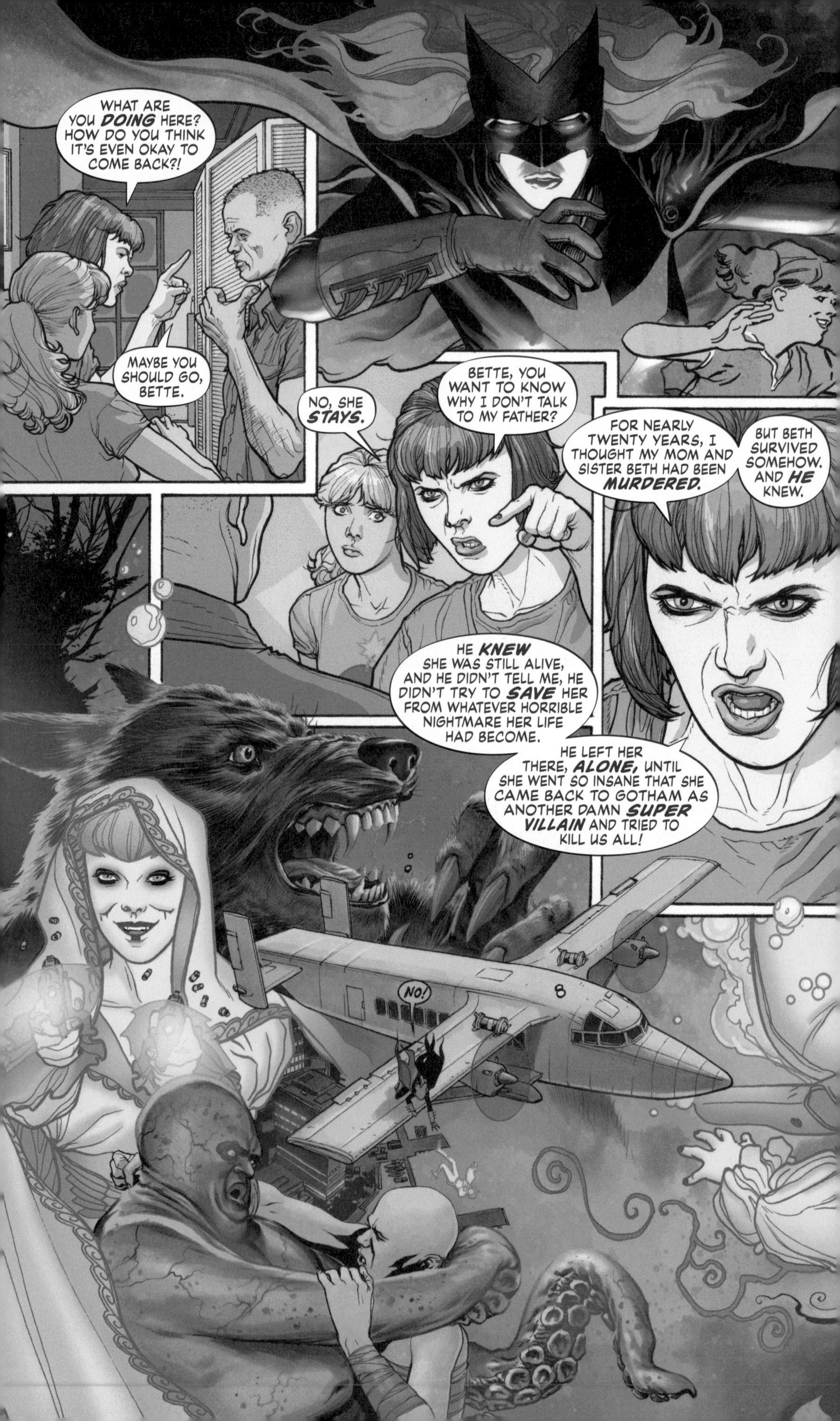
WHAT ARE YOU DOING HERE? HOW DO YOU THINK IT'S EVEN OKAY TO COME BACK?!
MAYBE YOU SHOULD GO, BETTE.
NO, SHE STAYS.
BETTE, YOU WANT TO KNOW WHY I DON'T TALK TO MY FATHER?
FOR NEARLY TWENTY YEARS, I THOUGHT MY MOM AND SISTER BETH HAD BEEN MURDERED.
BUT BETH SURVIVED SOMEHOW. AND HE KNEW.
HE KNEW SHE WAS STILL ALIVE, AND HE DIDN'T TELL ME, HE DIDN'T TRY TO SAVE HER FROM WHATEVER HORRIBLE NIGHTMARE HER LIFE HAD BECOME.
HE LEFT HER THERE, ALONE, UNTIL SHE WENT SO INSANE THAT SHE CAME BACK TO GOTHAM AS ANOTHER DAMN SUPER VILLAIN AND TRIED TO KILL US ALL!
NO!

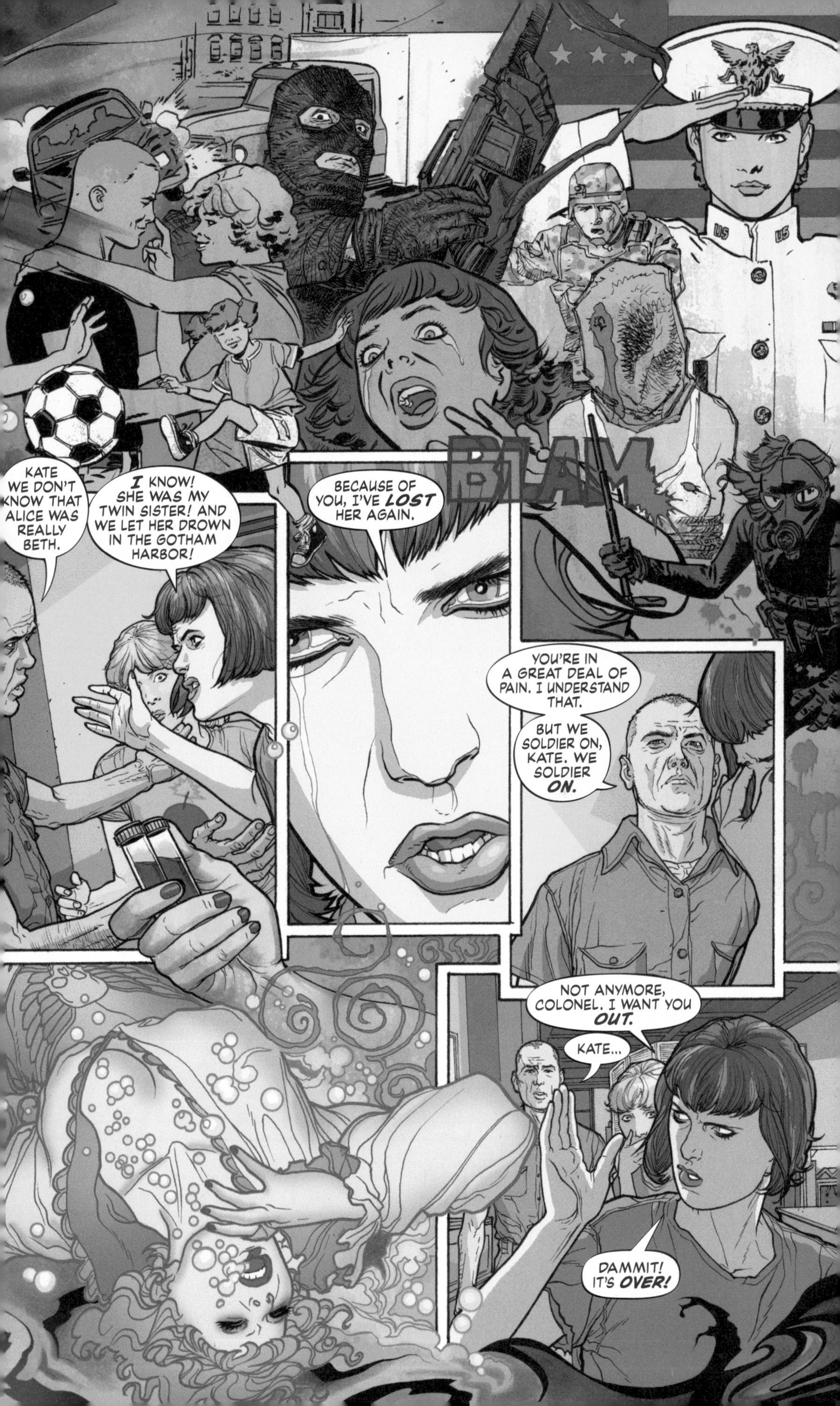

BLAM
KATE WE DON'T KNOW THAT ALICE WAS REALLY BETH.
I KNOW! SHE WAS MY TWIN SISTER! AND WE LET HER DROWN IN THE GOTHAM HARBOR!
BECAUSE OF YOU, I'VE LOST HER AGAIN.
YOU'RE IN A GREAT DEAL OF PAIN. I UNDERSTAND THAT.
BUT WE SOLDIER ON, KATE. WE SOLDIER ON.
NOT ANYMORE, COLONEL. I WANT YOU OUT.
KATE...
DAMMIT! IT'S OVER!

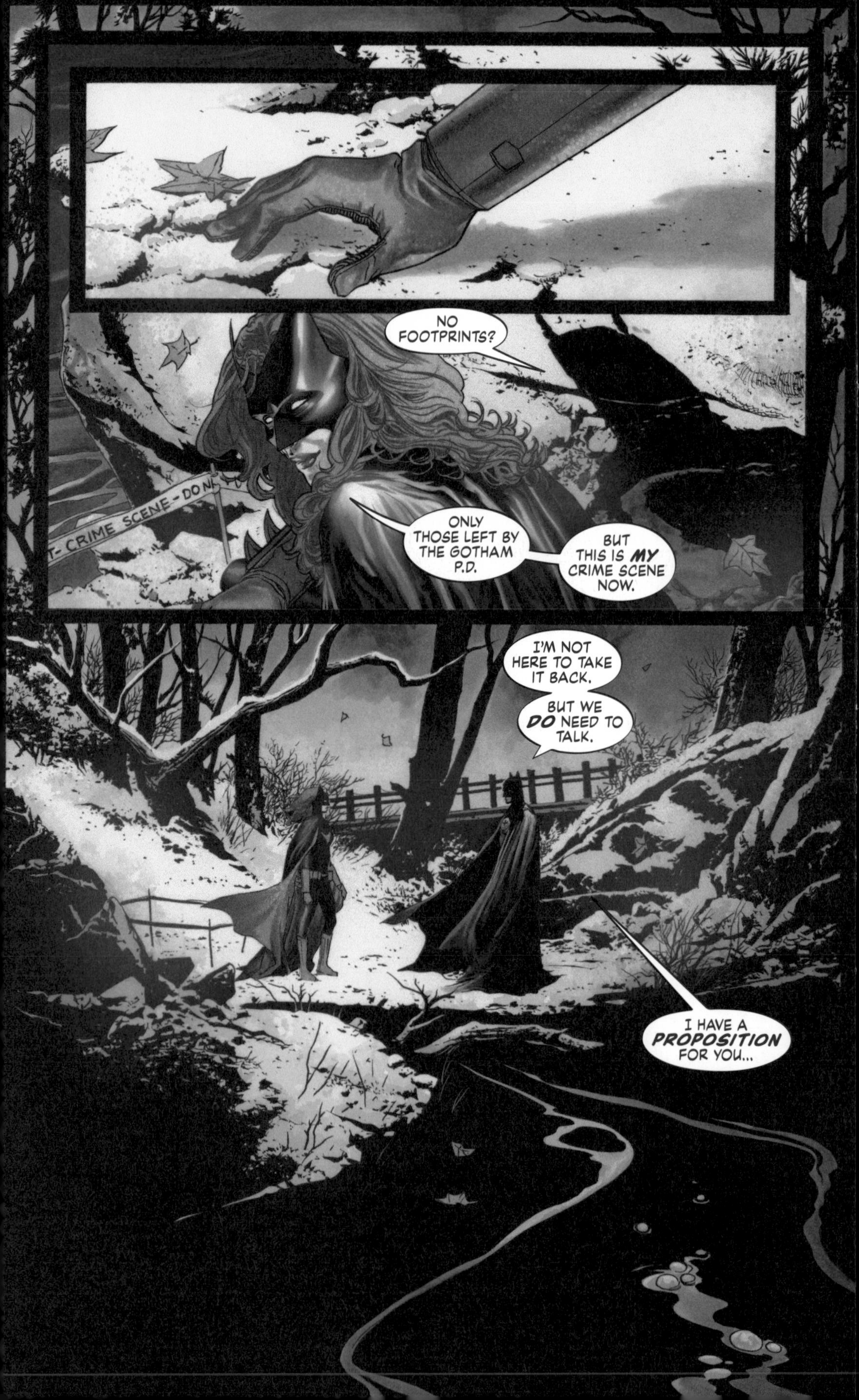

NO FOOTPRINTS?
ONLY THOSE LEFT BY THE GOTHAM P.D.
BUT THIS IS MY CRIME SCENE NOW.
CRIME SCENE-DO N
I'M NOT HERE TO TAKE IT BACK.
BUT WE DO NEED TO TALK.
I HAVE A PROPOSITION FOR YOU...

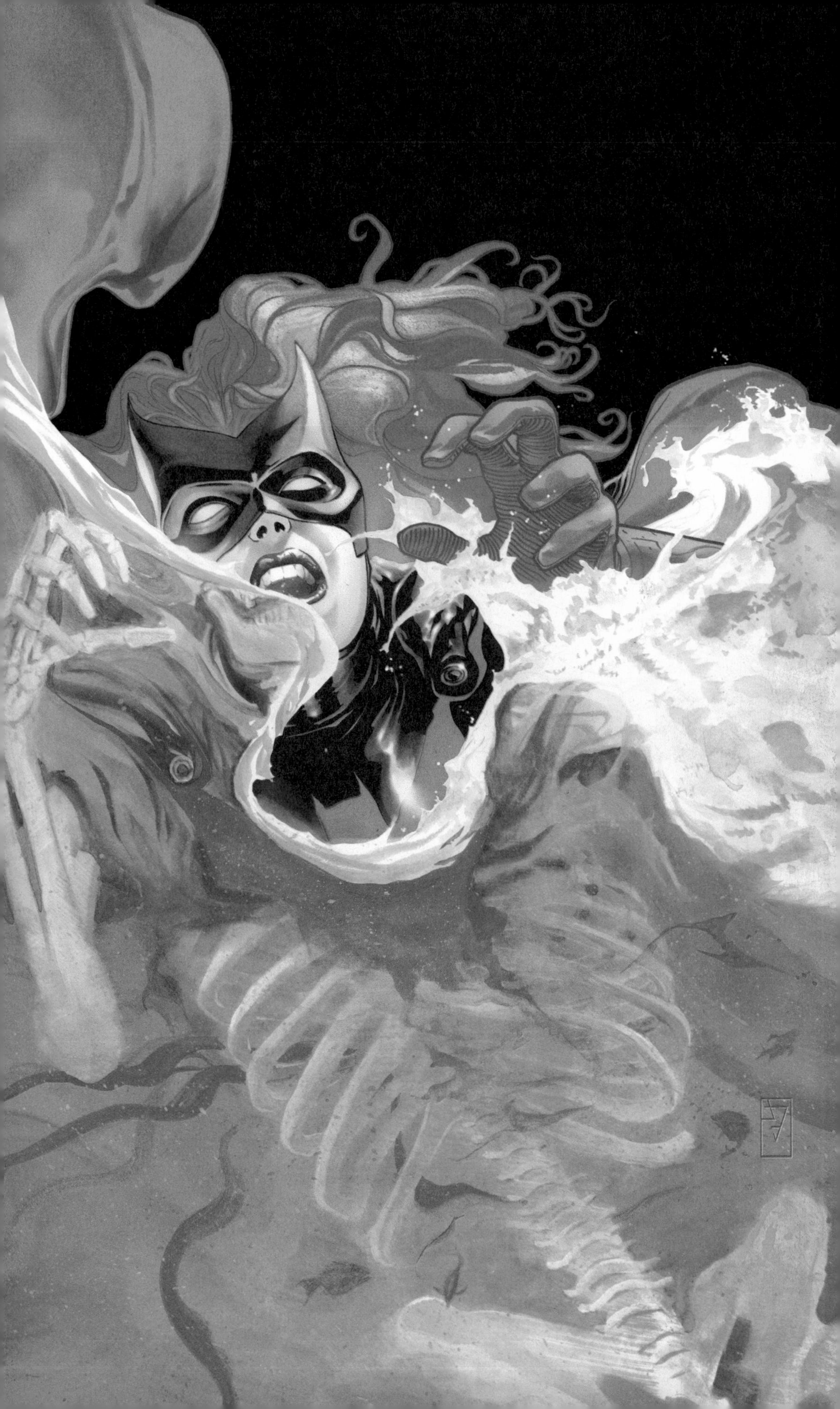

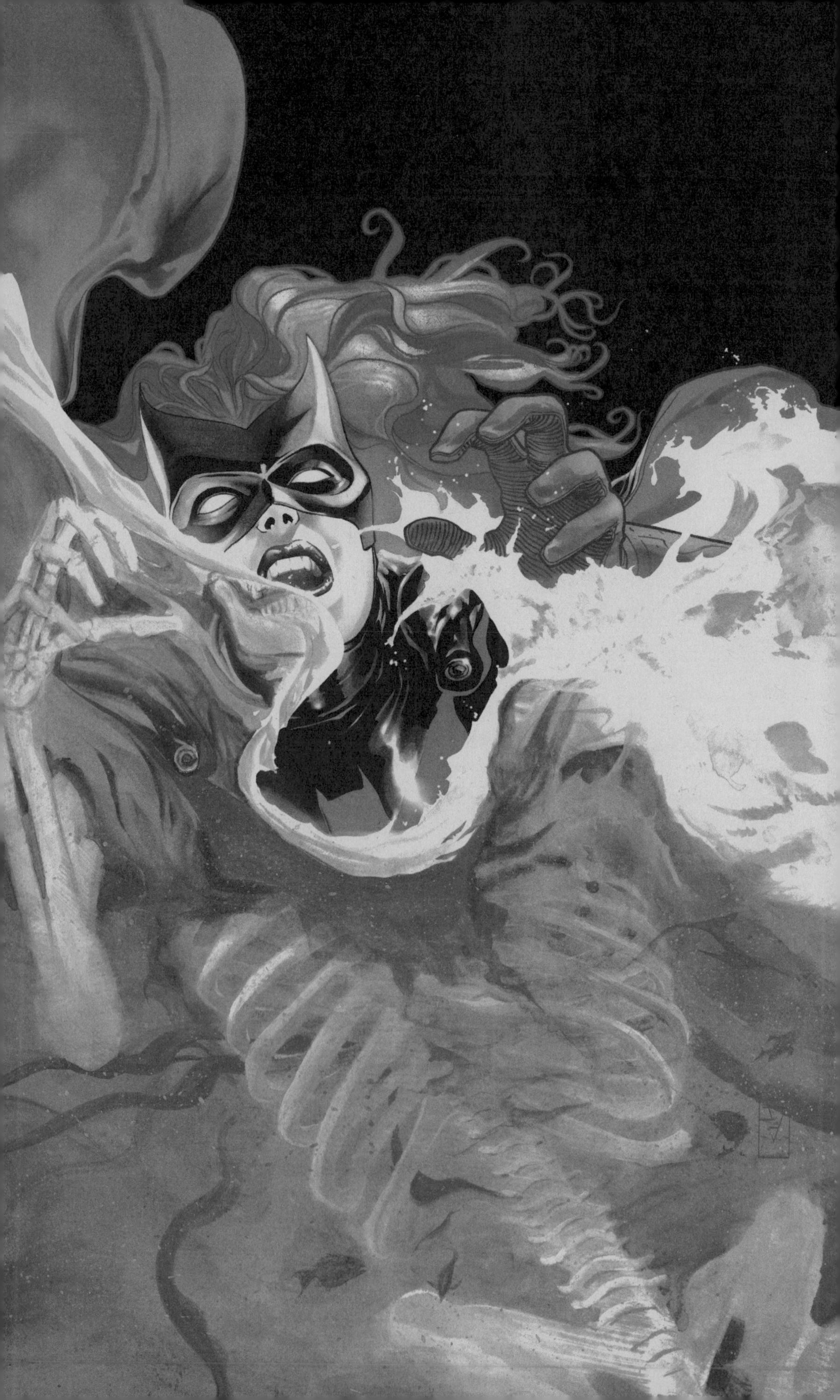

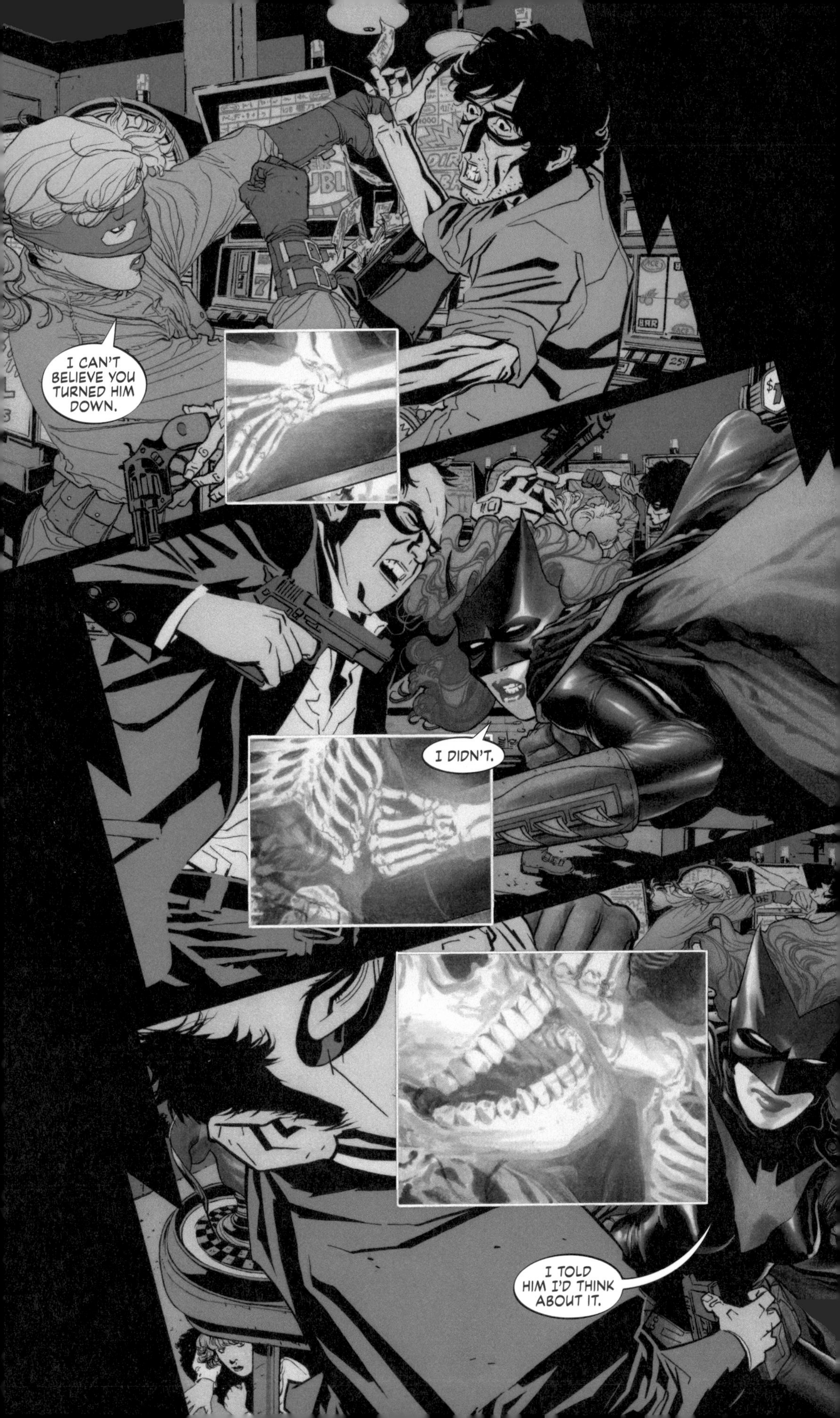
I CAN'T BELIEVE YOU TURNED HIM DOWN.
I DIDN'T.
I TOLD HIM I'D THINK ABOUT IT.

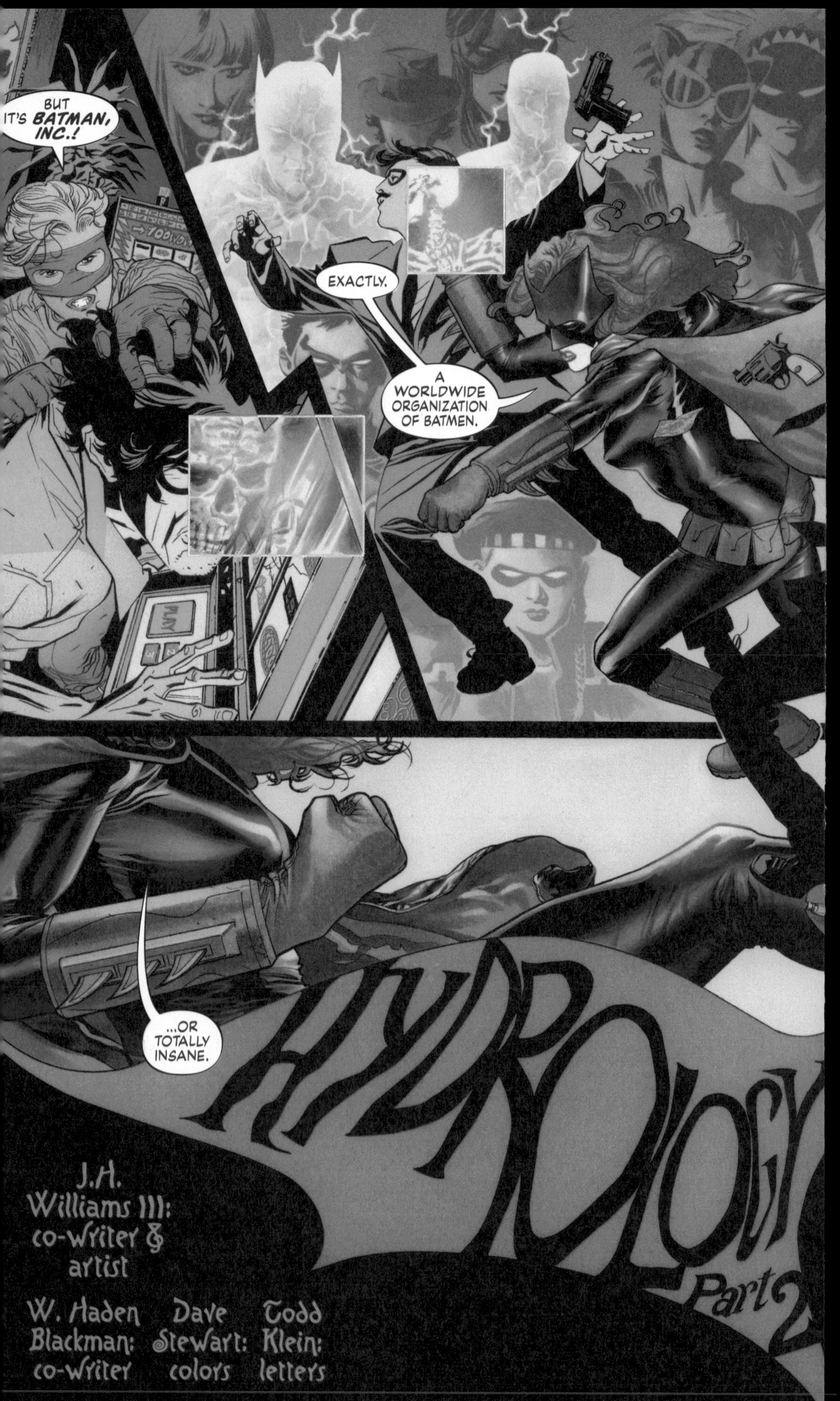

BUT IT'S BATMAN, INC.!
EXACTLY.
A WORLDWIDE ORGANIZATION OF BATMEN.
...OR TOTALLY INSANE.
HYDROLOGY Part 2
J.H. Williams III: co-writer & artist
W. Haden Blackman: co-writer
Dave Stewart: colors
Todd Klein: letters

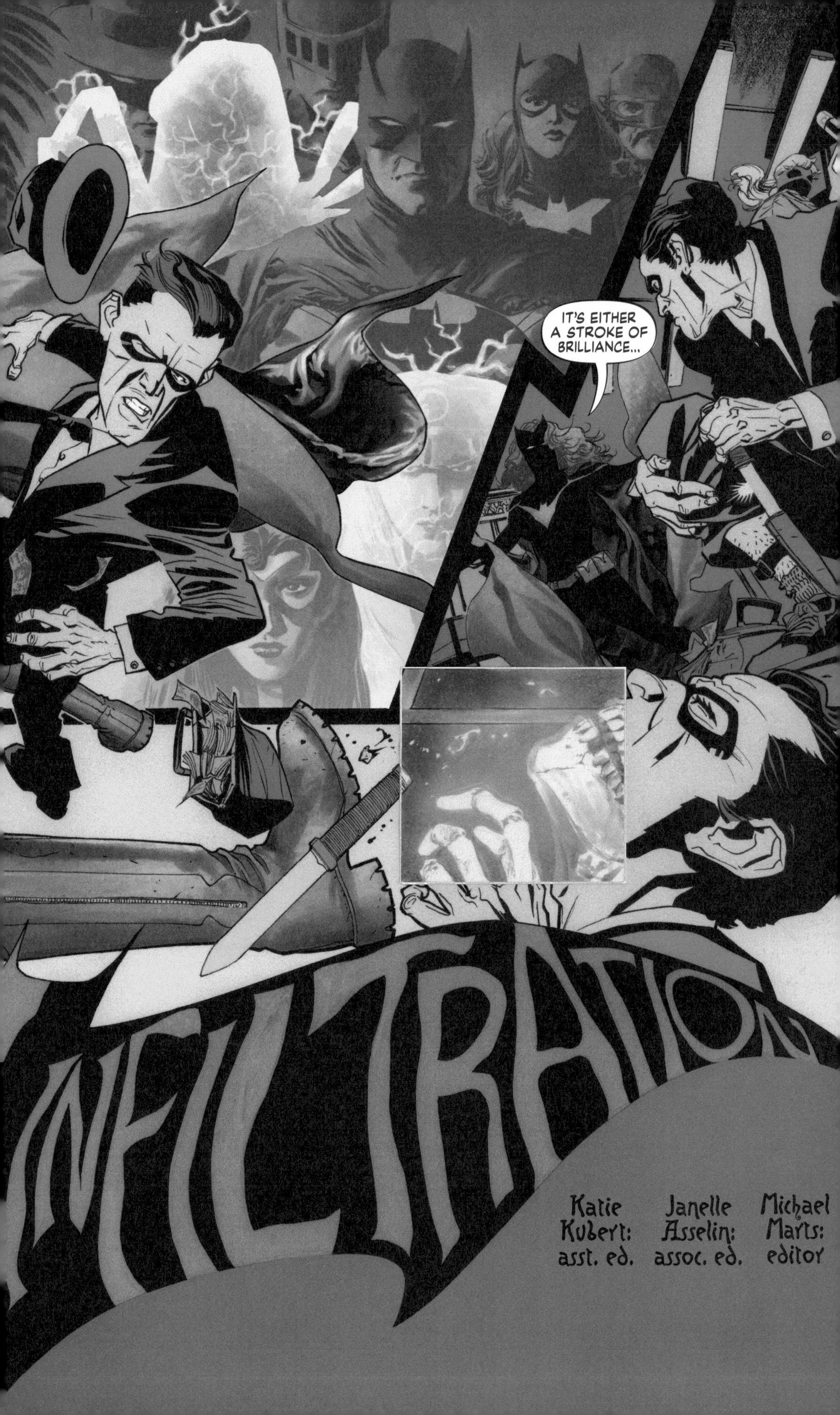
IT'S EITHER A STROKE OF BRILLIANCE...
INFILTRATION
Katie Kubert: asst. ed.
Janelle Asselin: assoc. ed.
Michael Marts: editor

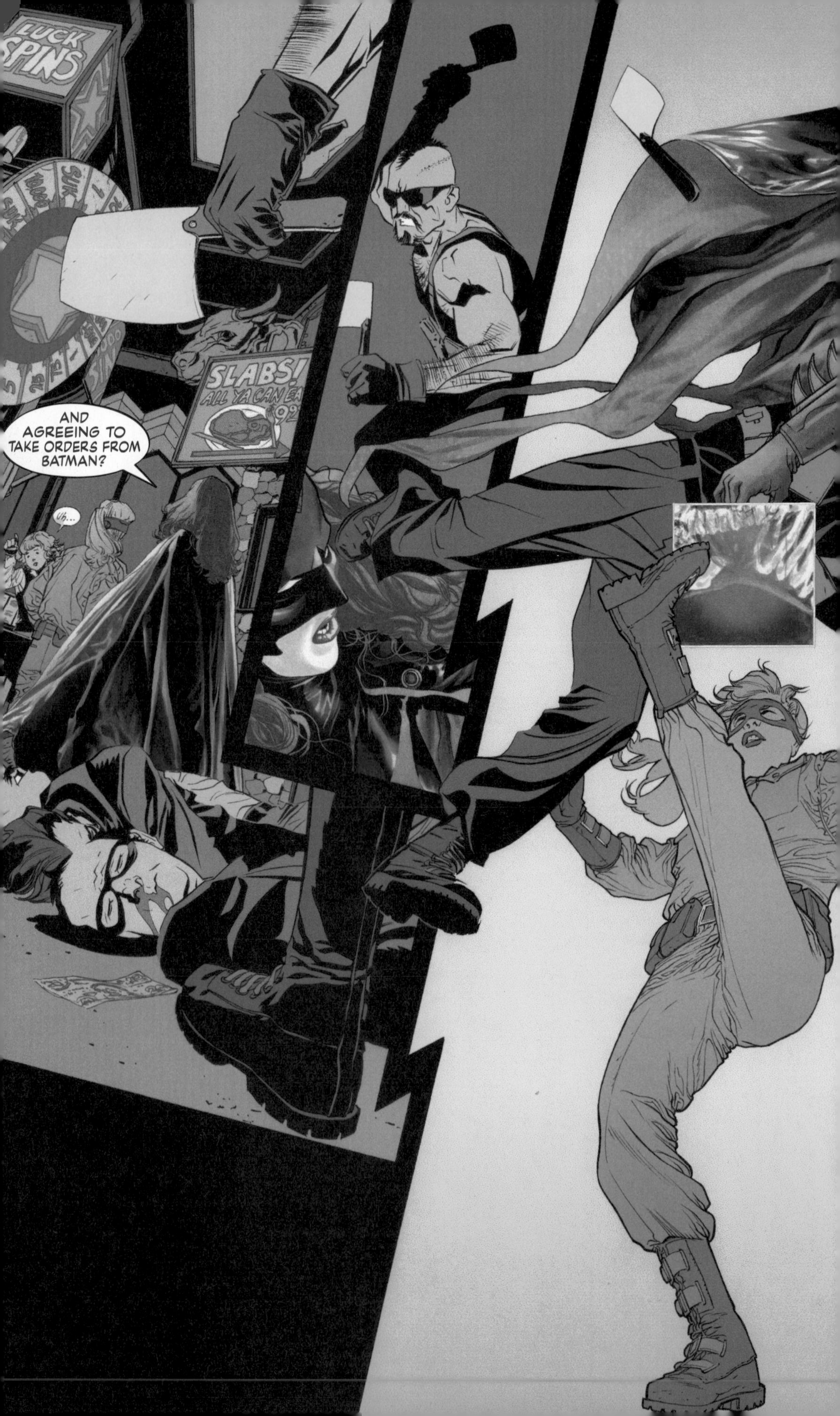
LUCK
SPINS
SLABS!
ALL YA CAN EAT
AND AGREEING TO TAKE ORDERS FROM BATMAN?
Uh...

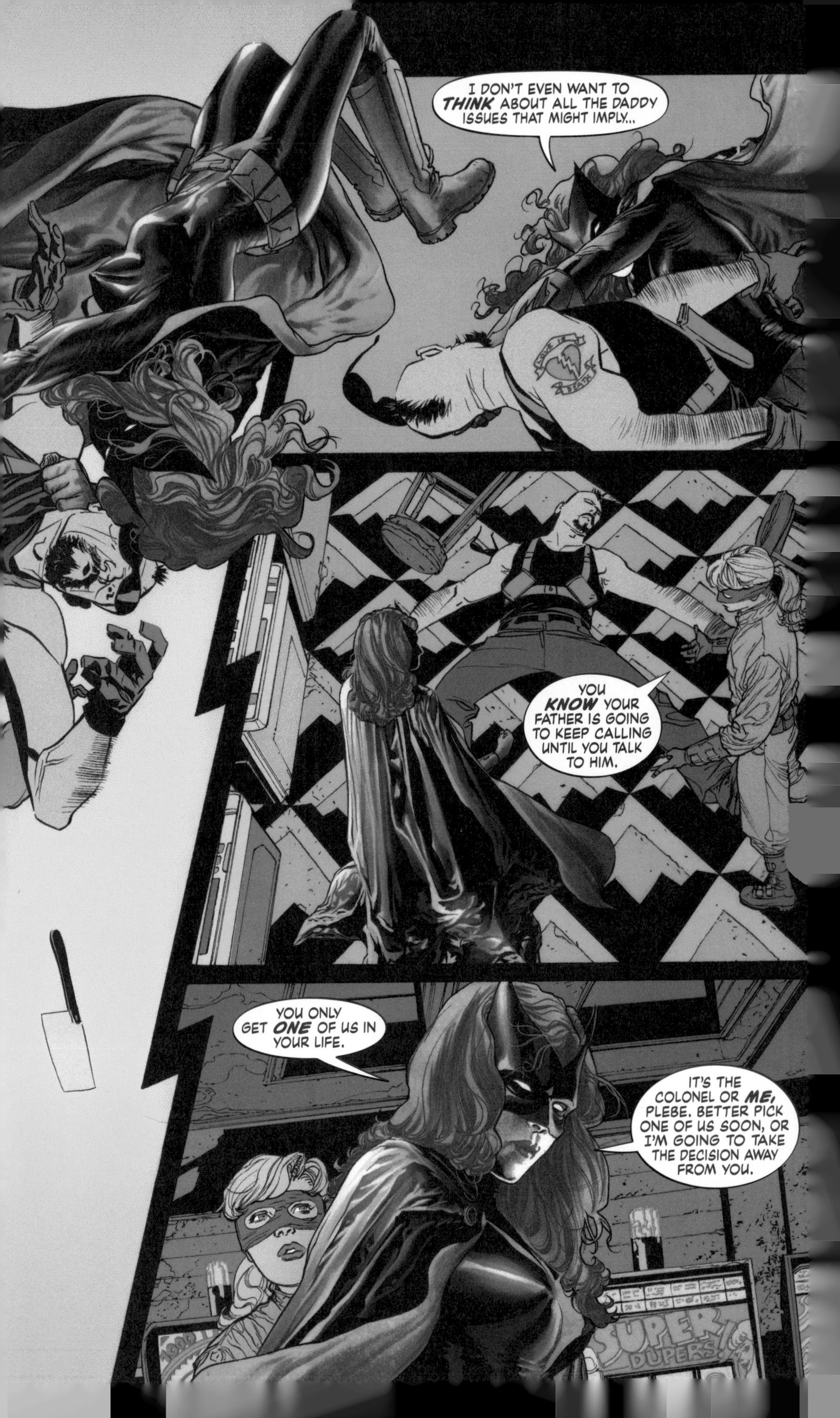

I DON'T EVEN WANT TO THINK ABOUT ALL THE DADDY ISSUES THAT MIGHT IMPLY...
YOU KNOW YOUR FATHER IS GOING TO KEEP CALLING UNTIL YOU TALK TO HIM.
YOU ONLY GET ONE OF US IN YOUR LIFE.
IT'S THE COLONEL OR ME, PLEBE. BETTER PICK ONE OF US SOON, OR I'M GOING TO TAKE THE DECISION AWAY FROM YOU.
SUPER DUPERS!

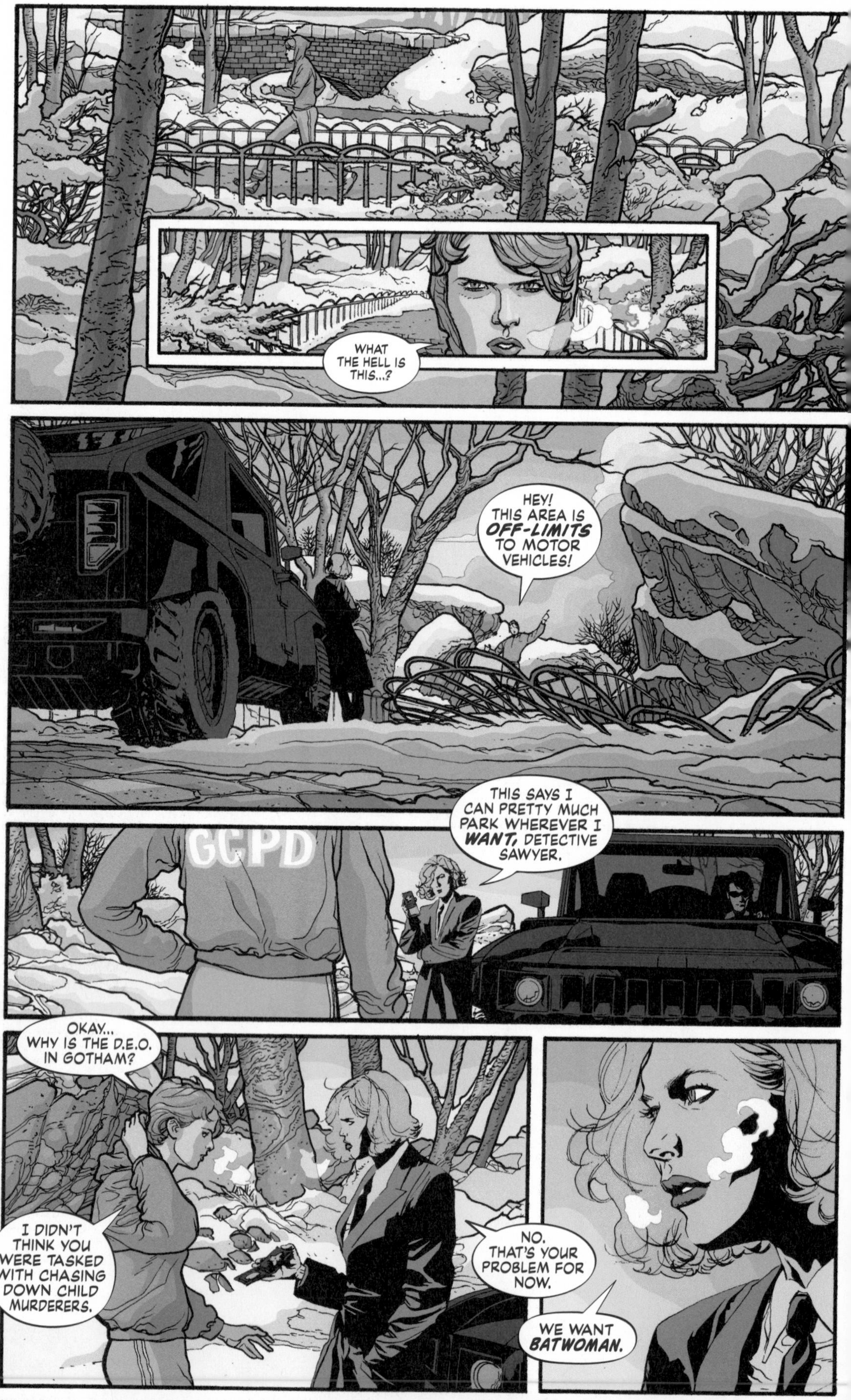
WHAT THE HELL IS THIS...?
HEY! THIS AREA IS OFF-LIMITS TO MOTOR VEHICLES!
THIS SAYS I CAN PRETTY MUCH PARK WHEREVER I WANT, DETECTIVE SAWYER.
GCPD
OKAY... WHY IS THE D.E.O. IN GOTHAM?
I DIDN'T THINK YOU WERE TASKED WITH CHASING DOWN CHILD MURDERERS.
NO. THAT'S YOUR PROBLEM FOR NOW.
WE WANT BATWOMAN.

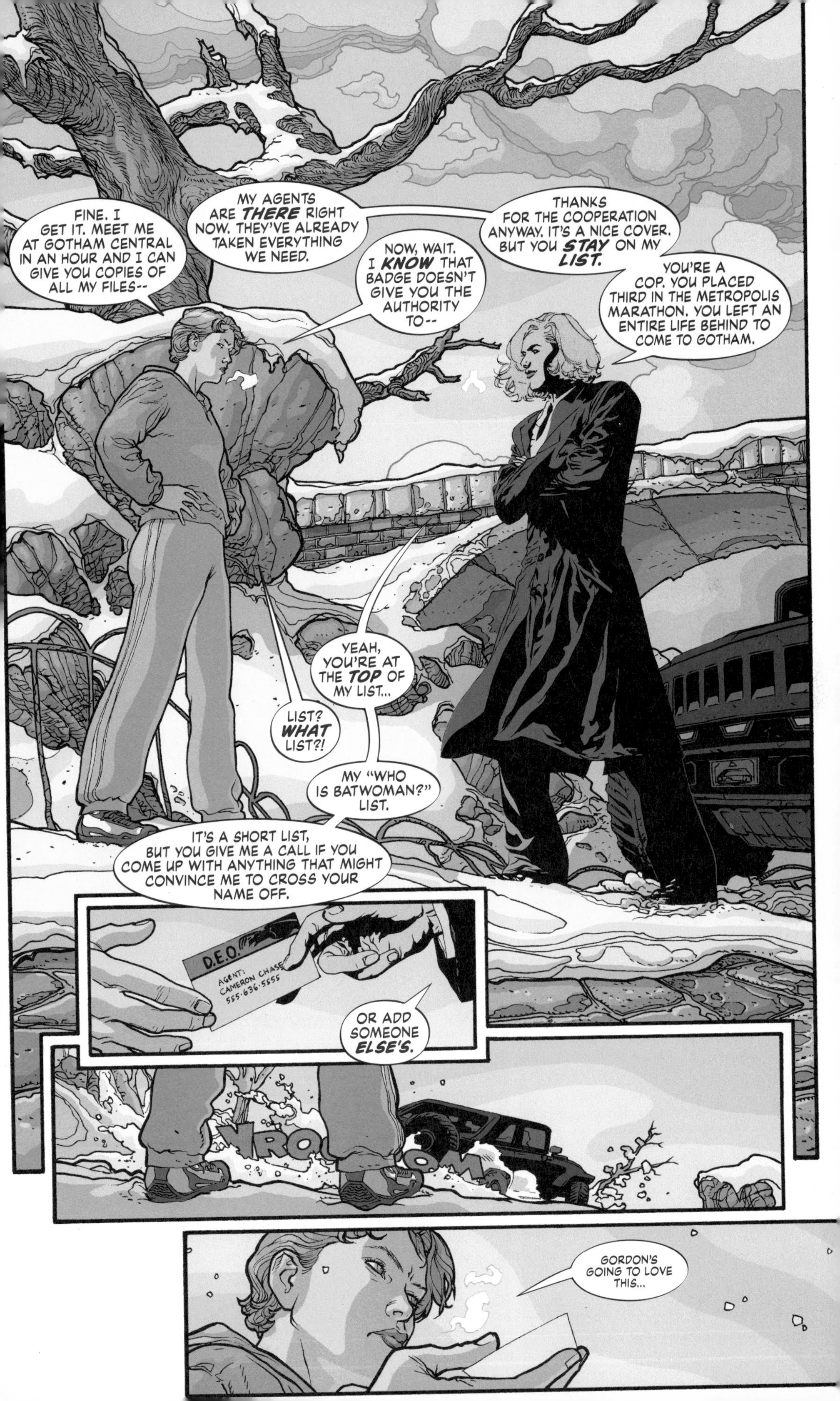

FINE. I GET IT. MEET ME AT GOTHAM CENTRAL IN AN HOUR AND I CAN GIVE YOU COPIES OF ALL MY FILES--
MY AGENTS ARE THERE RIGHT NOW. THEY'VE ALREADY TAKEN EVERYTHING WE NEED.
THANKS FOR THE COOPERATION ANYWAY. IT'S A NICE COVER. BUT YOU STAY ON MY LIST.
NOW, WAIT. I KNOW THAT BADGE DOESN'T GIVE YOU THE AUTHORITY TO--
YOU'RE A COP. YOU PLACED THIRD IN THE METROPOLIS MARATHON. YOU LEFT AN ENTIRE LIFE BEHIND TO COME TO GOTHAM.
LIST? WHAT LIST?!
YEAH, YOU'RE AT THE TOP OF MY LIST...
MY "WHO IS BATWOMAN?" LIST.
IT'S A SHORT LIST, BUT YOU GIVE ME A CALL IF YOU COME UP WITH ANYTHING THAT MIGHT CONVINCE ME TO CROSS YOUR NAME OFF.
D.E.O.
AGENT: CAMERON CHASE
555-636-5555
OR ADD SOMEONE ELSE'S.
VROOOOM
GORDON'S GOING TO LOVE THIS...

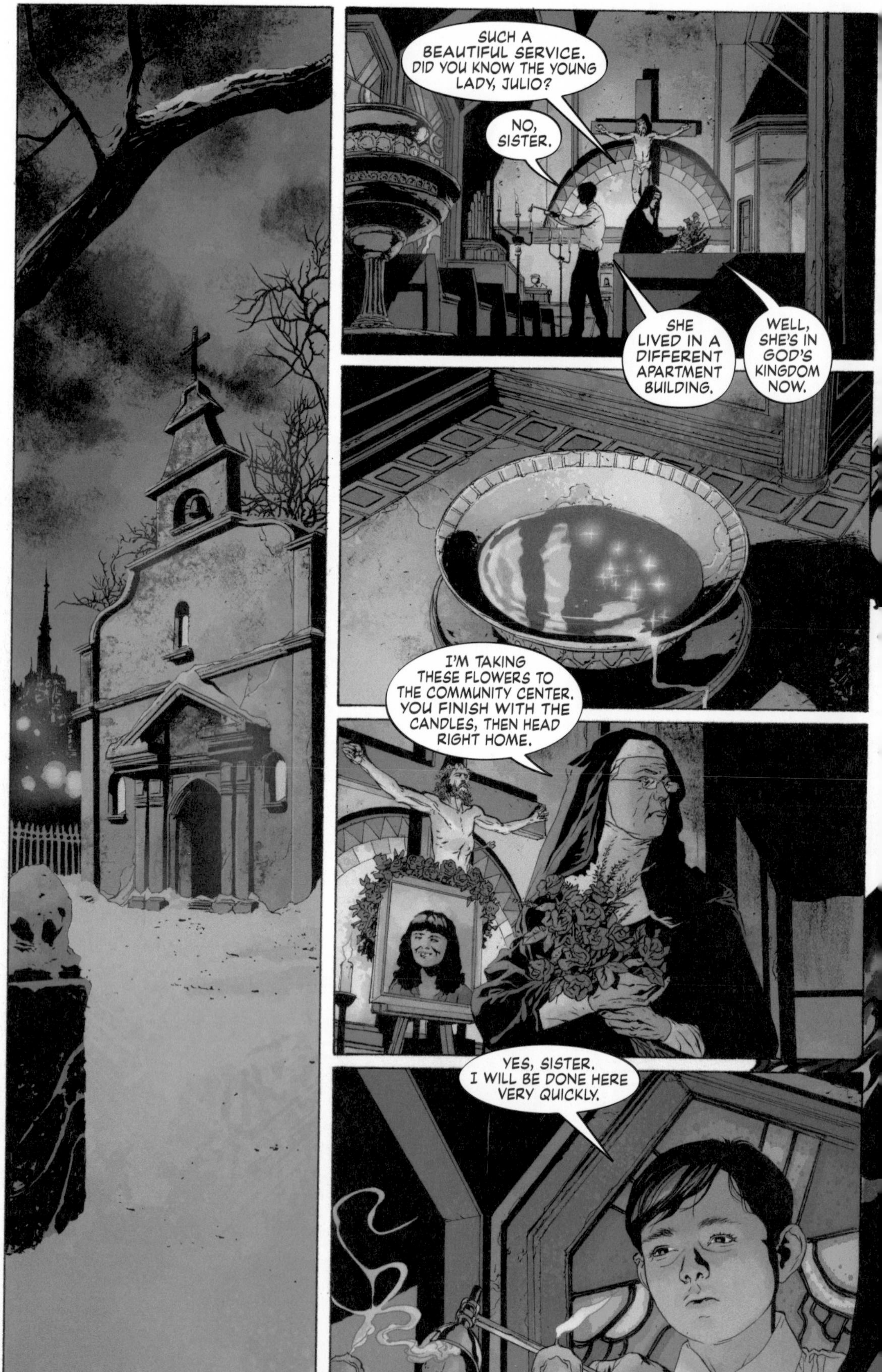
SUCH A BEAUTIFUL SERVICE. DID YOU KNOW THE YOUNG LADY, JULIO?
NO, SISTER.
SHE LIVED IN A DIFFERENT APARTMENT BUILDING.
WELL, SHE'S IN GOD'S KINGDOM NOW.
I'M TAKING THESE FLOWERS TO THE COMMUNITY CENTER. YOU FINISH WITH THE CANDLES, THEN HEAD RIGHT HOME.
YES, SISTER. I WILL BE DONE HERE VERY QUICKLY.

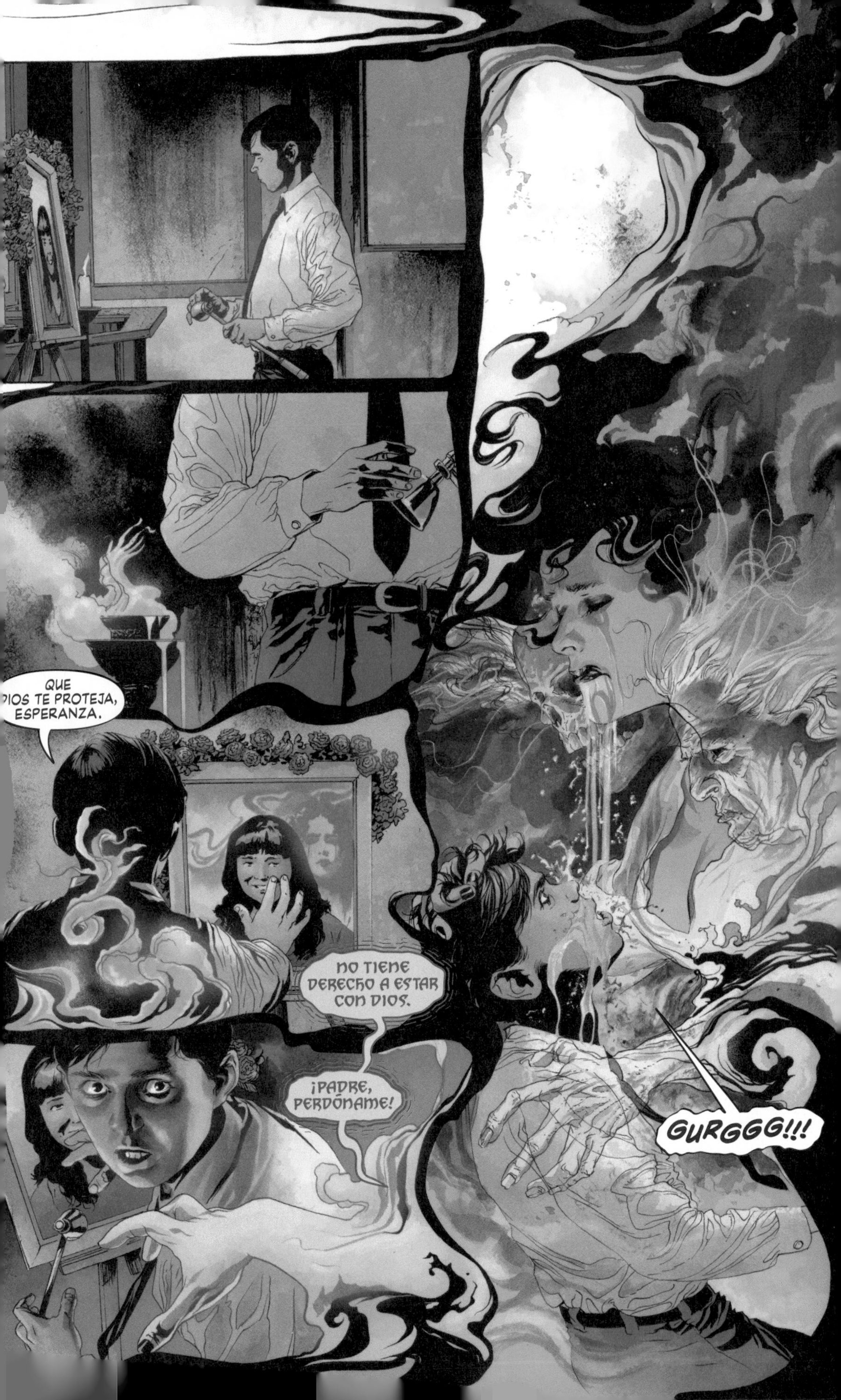
QUE DIOS TE PROTEJA, ESPERANZA.
NO TIENE DERECHO A ESTAR CON DIOS.
¡PADRE, PERDÓNAME!
GURGGG!!!

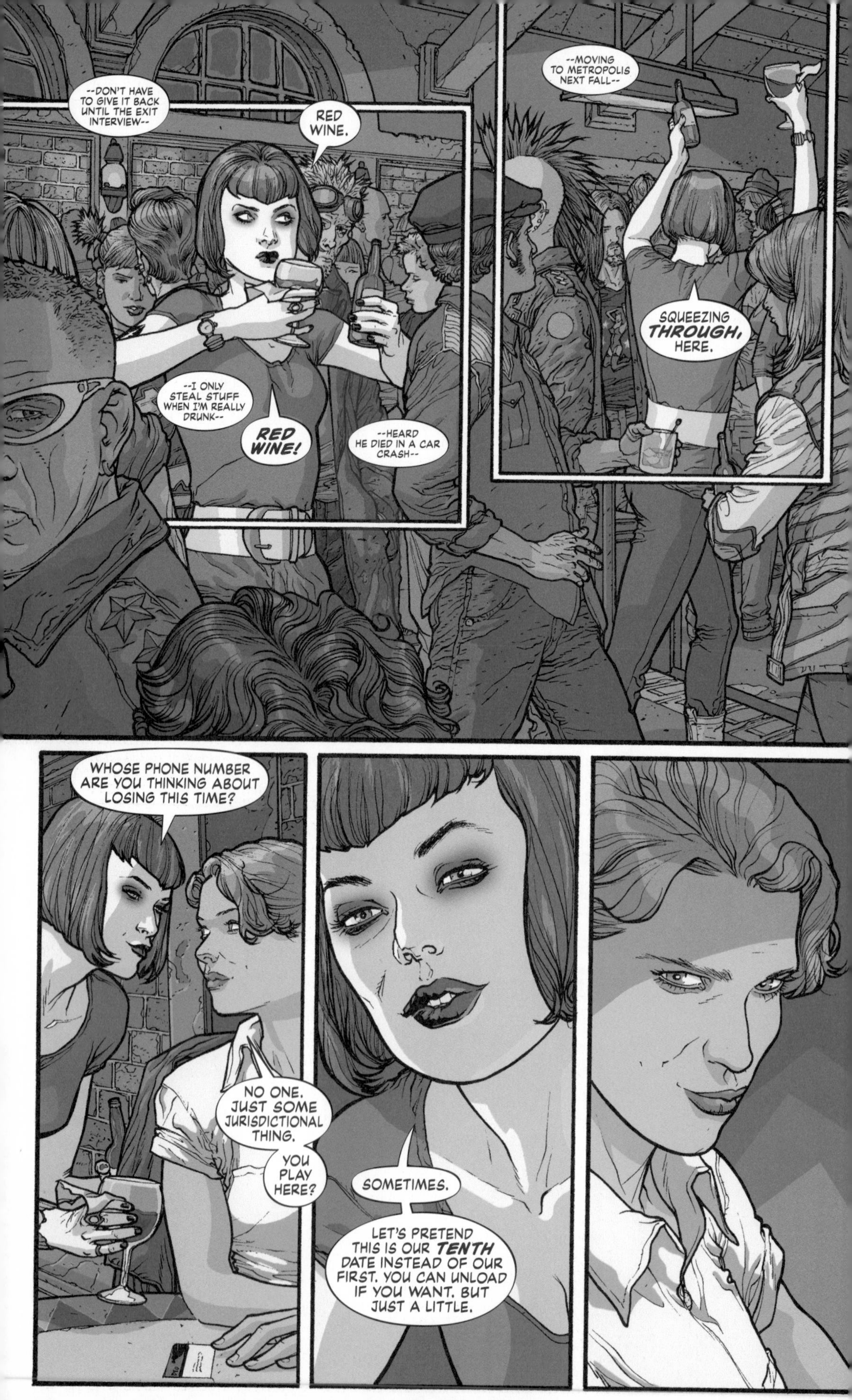
--DON'T HAVE TO GIVE IT BACK UNTIL THE EXIT INTERVIEW--
RED WINE.
--I ONLY STEAL STUFF WHEN I'M REALLY DRUNK--
RED WINE!
--HEARD HE DIED IN A CAR CRASH--
--MOVING TO METROPOLIS NEXT FALL--
SQUEEZING THROUGH, HERE.
WHOSE PHONE NUMBER ARE YOU THINKING ABOUT LOSING THIS TIME?
NO ONE. JUST SOME JURISDICTIONAL THING.
YOU PLAY HERE?
SOMETIMES.
LET'S PRETEND THIS IS OUR TENTH DATE INSTEAD OF OUR FIRST. YOU CAN UNLOAD IF YOU WANT. BUT JUST A LITTLE.

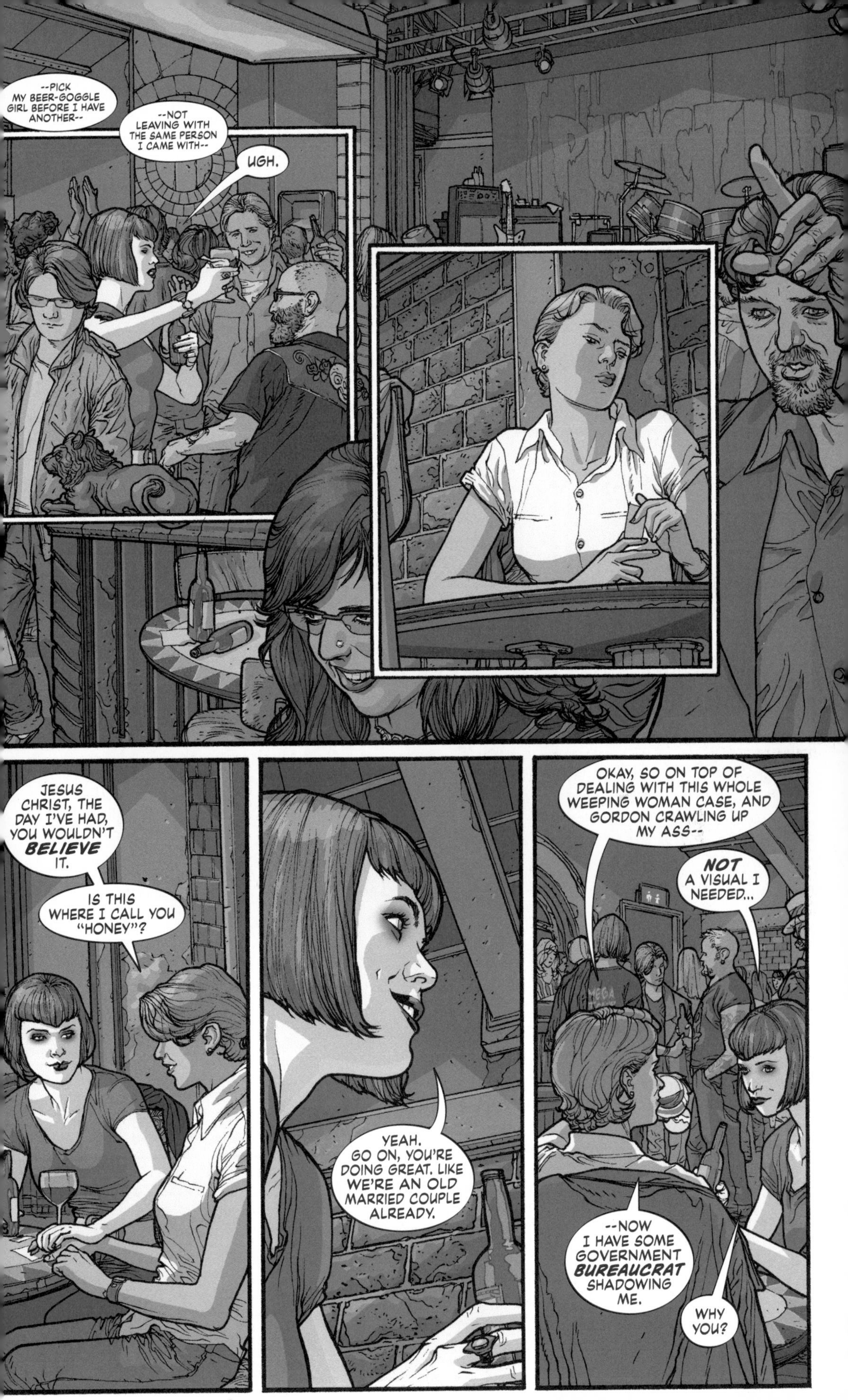
--PICK MY BEER-GOGGLE GIRL BEFORE I HAVE ANOTHER--
--NOT LEAVING WITH THE SAME PERSON I CAME WITH--
UGH.
JESUS CHRIST, THE DAY I'VE HAD, YOU WOULDN'T BELIEVE IT.
IS THIS WHERE I CALL YOU "HONEY"?
YEAH. GO ON, YOU'RE DOING GREAT. LIKE WE'RE AN OLD MARRIED COUPLE ALREADY.
OKAY, SO ON TOP OF DEALING WITH THIS WHOLE WEEPING WOMAN CASE, AND GORDON CRAWLING UP MY ASS--
NOT A VISUAL I NEEDED...
--NOW I HAVE SOME GOVERNMENT BUREAUCRAT SHADOWING ME.
WHY YOU?

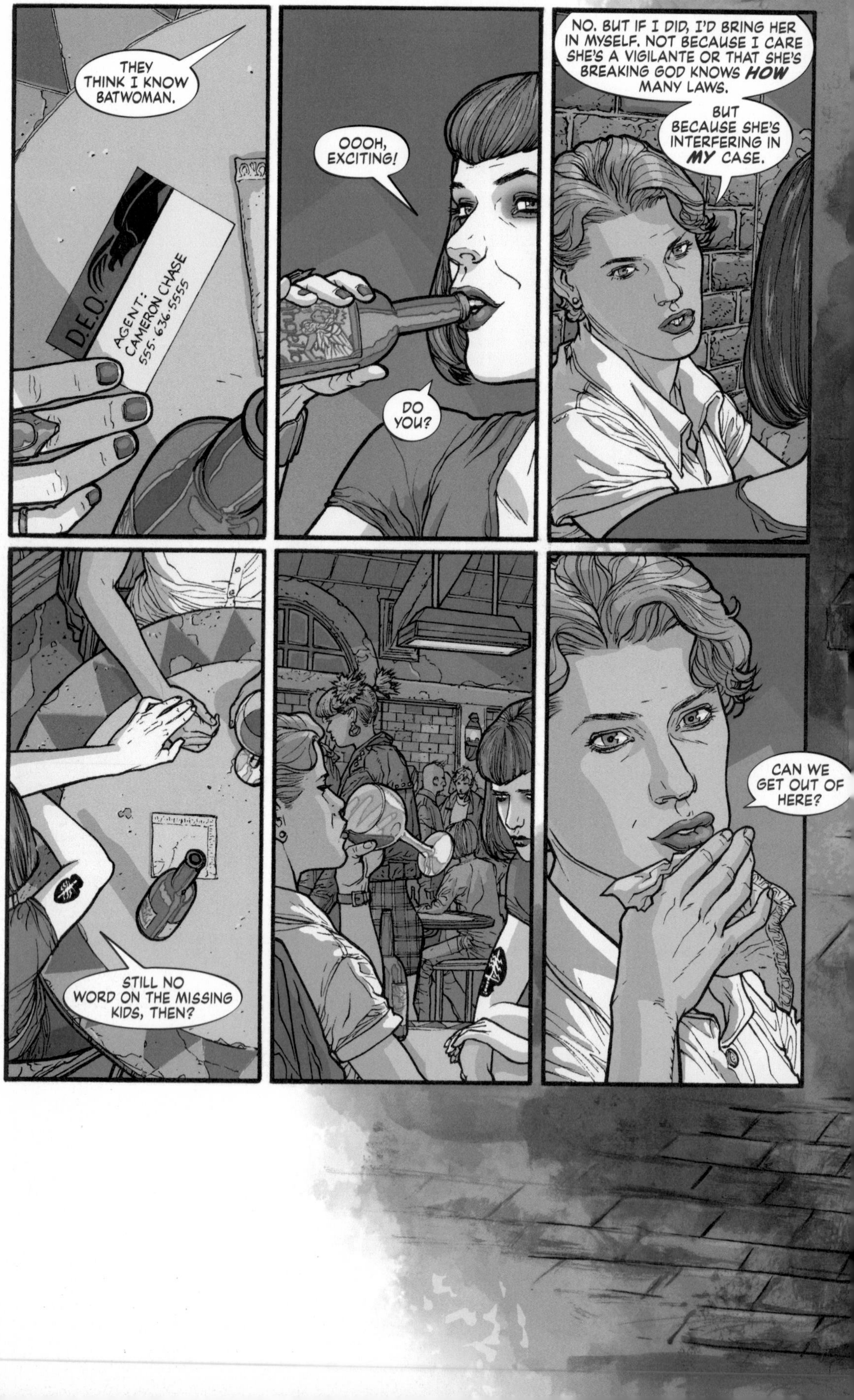
THEY THINK I KNOW BATWOMAN.
D.E.O.
AGENT: CAMERON CHASE 555·636·5555
OOOH, EXCITING!
DO YOU?
NO. BUT IF I DID, I'D BRING HER IN MYSELF. NOT BECAUSE I CARE SHE'S A VIGILANTE OR THAT SHE'S BREAKING GOD KNOWS HOW MANY LAWS.
BUT BECAUSE SHE'S INTERFERING IN MY CASE.
STILL NO WORD ON THE MISSING KIDS, THEN?
CAN WE GET OUT OF HERE?

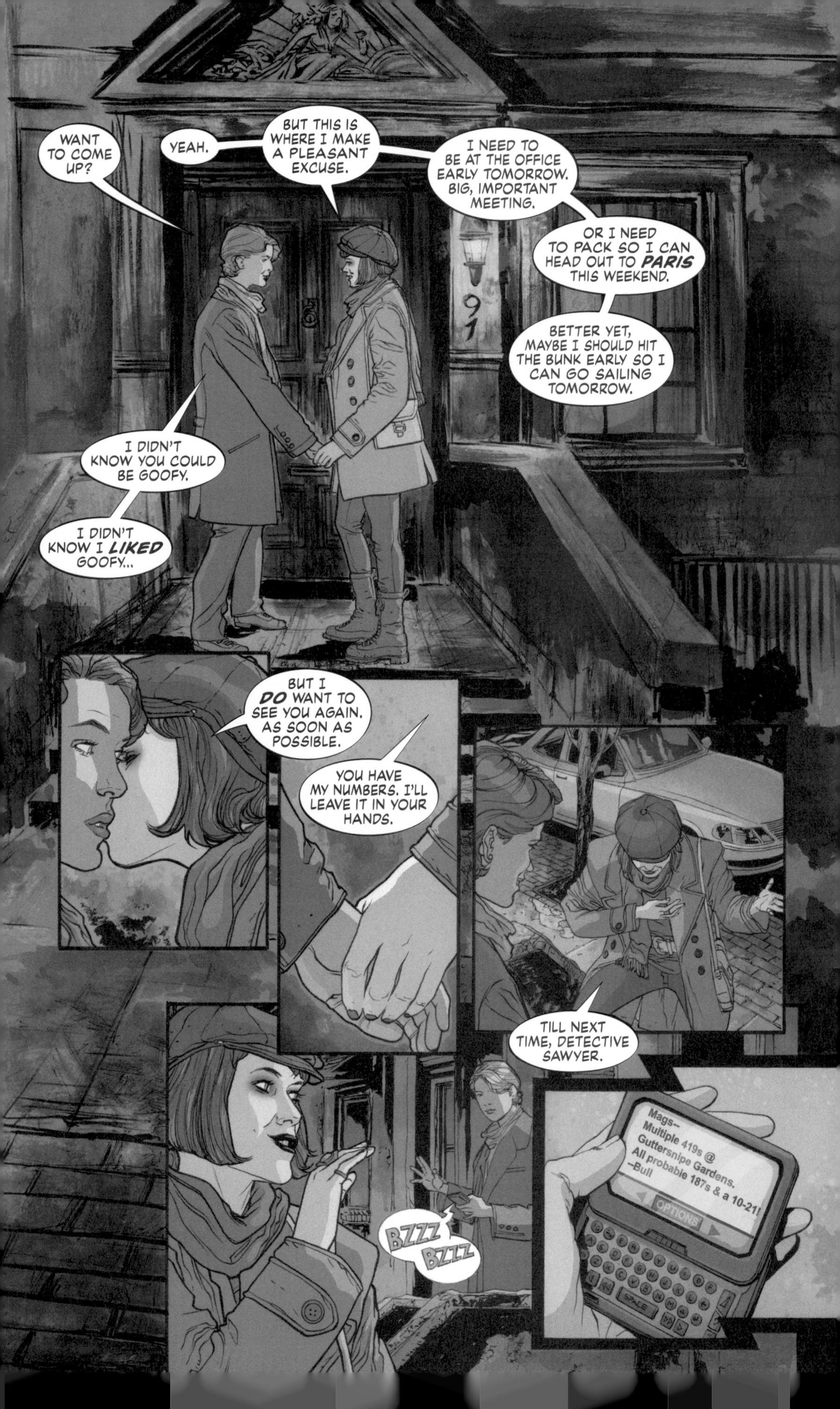
WANT TO COME UP?
YEAH.
BUT THIS IS WHERE I MAKE A PLEASANT EXCUSE.
I NEED TO BE AT THE OFFICE EARLY TOMORROW. BIG, IMPORTANT MEETING.
OR I NEED TO PACK SO I CAN HEAD OUT TO **PARIS** THIS WEEKEND.
BETTER YET, MAYBE I SHOULD HIT THE BUNK EARLY SO I CAN GO SAILING TOMORROW.
I DIDN'T KNOW YOU COULD BE GOOFY.
I DIDN'T KNOW I **LIKED** GOOFY...
BUT I **DO** WANT TO SEE YOU AGAIN. AS SOON AS POSSIBLE.
YOU HAVE MY NUMBERS. I'LL LEAVE IT IN YOUR HANDS.
TILL NEXT TIME, DETECTIVE SAWYER.
BZZZ BZZZ
Mags–
Multiple 419s @
Guttersnipe Gardens.
All probable 187s & a 10-21!
–Bull
OPTIONS

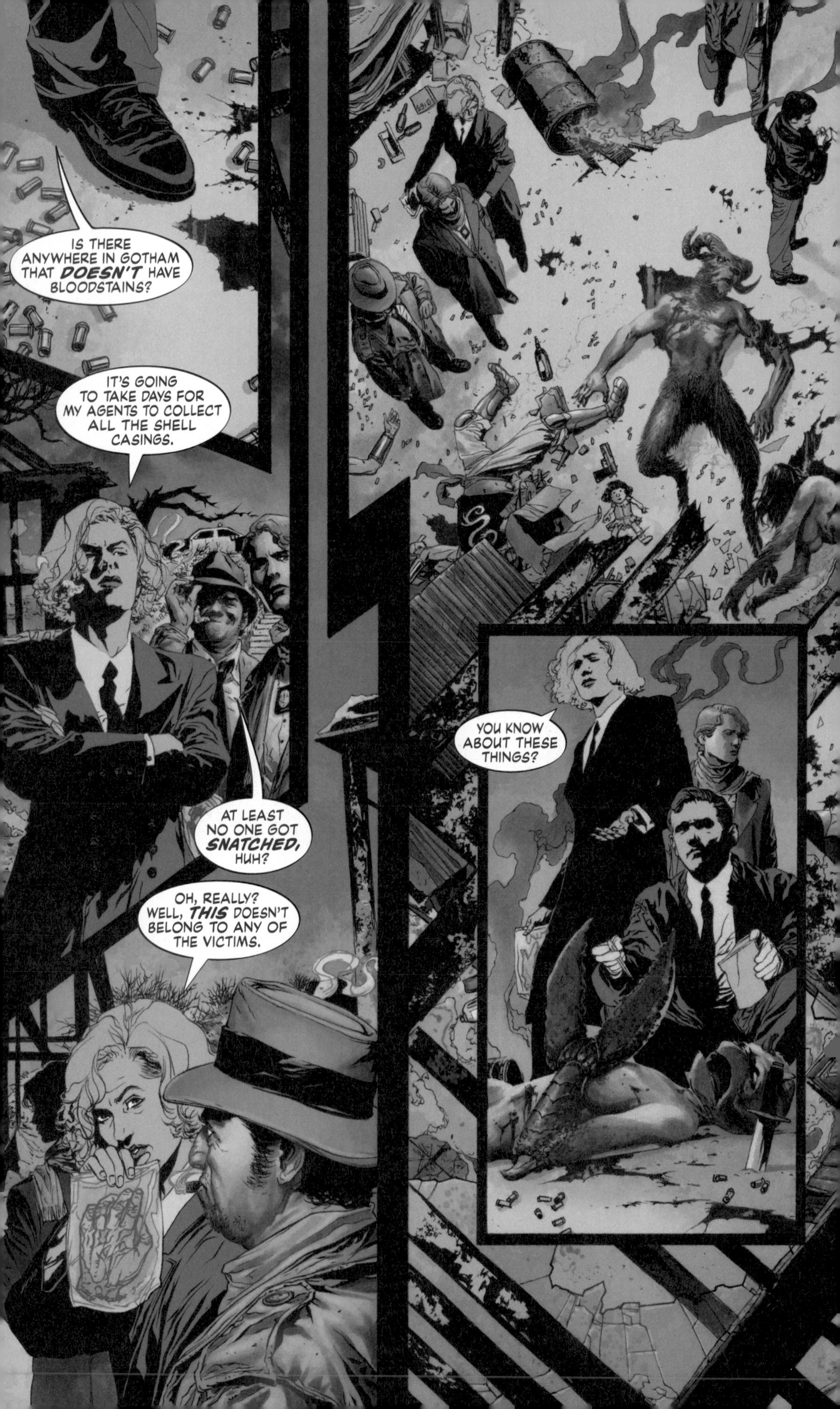
IS THERE ANYWHERE IN GOTHAM THAT DOESN'T HAVE BLOODSTAINS?
IT'S GOING TO TAKE DAYS FOR MY AGENTS TO COLLECT ALL THE SHELL CASINGS.
AT LEAST NO ONE GOT SNATCHED, HUH?
OH, REALLY? WELL, THIS DOESN'T BELONG TO ANY OF THE VICTIMS.
YOU KNOW ABOUT THESE THINGS?

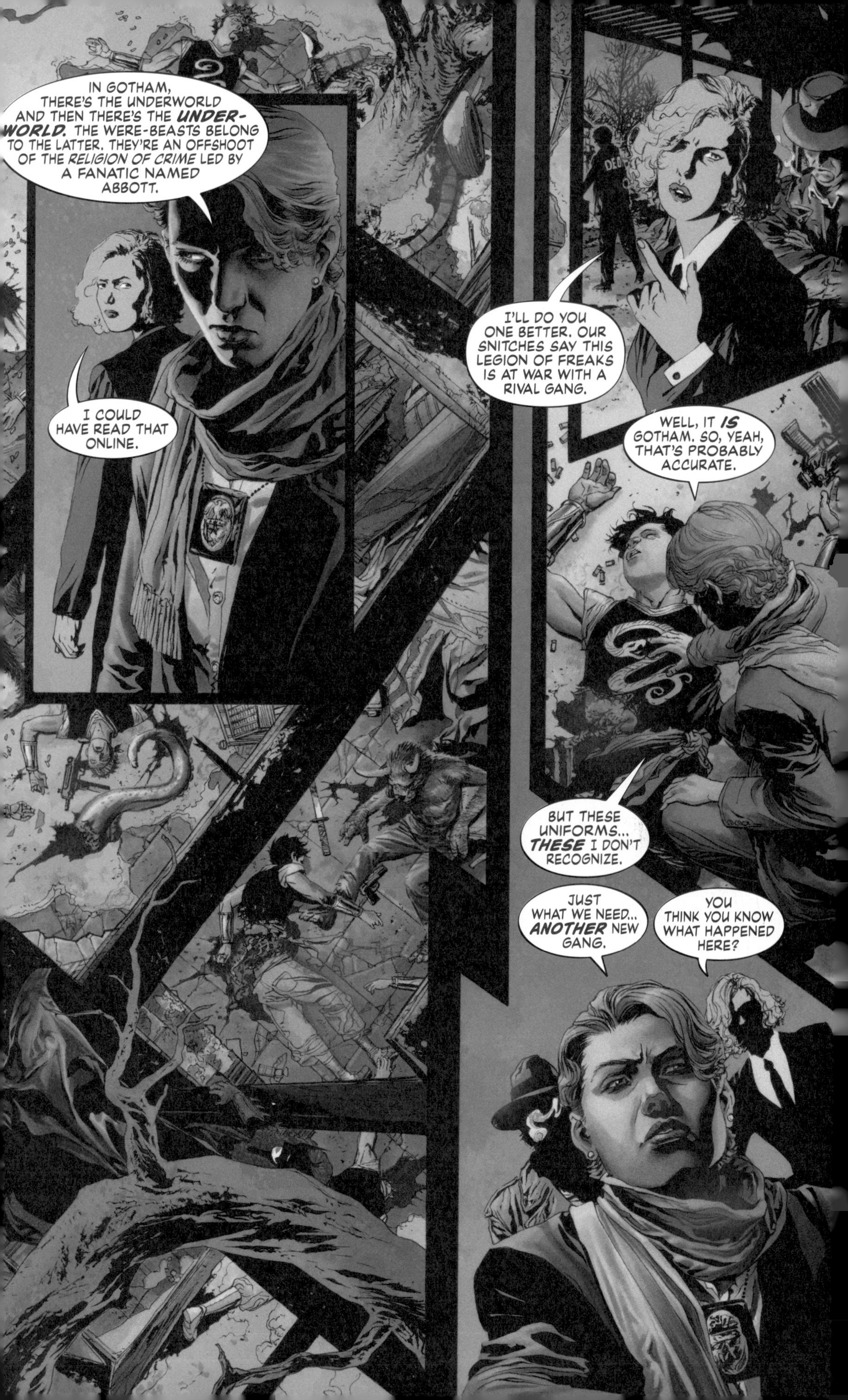
IN GOTHAM, THERE'S THE UNDERWORLD AND THEN THERE'S THE **UNDER-WORLD.** THE WERE-BEASTS BELONG TO THE LATTER. THEY'RE AN OFFSHOOT OF THE *RELIGION OF CRIME* LED BY A FANATIC NAMED ABBOTT.
I COULD HAVE READ THAT ONLINE.
I'LL DO YOU ONE BETTER. OUR SNITCHES SAY THIS LEGION OF FREAKS IS AT WAR WITH A RIVAL GANG.
WELL, IT ***IS*** GOTHAM. SO, YEAH, THAT'S PROBABLY ACCURATE.
BUT THESE UNIFORMS... ***THESE*** I DON'T RECOGNIZE.
JUST WHAT WE NEED... ***ANOTHER*** NEW GANG.
YOU THINK YOU KNOW WHAT HAPPENED HERE?

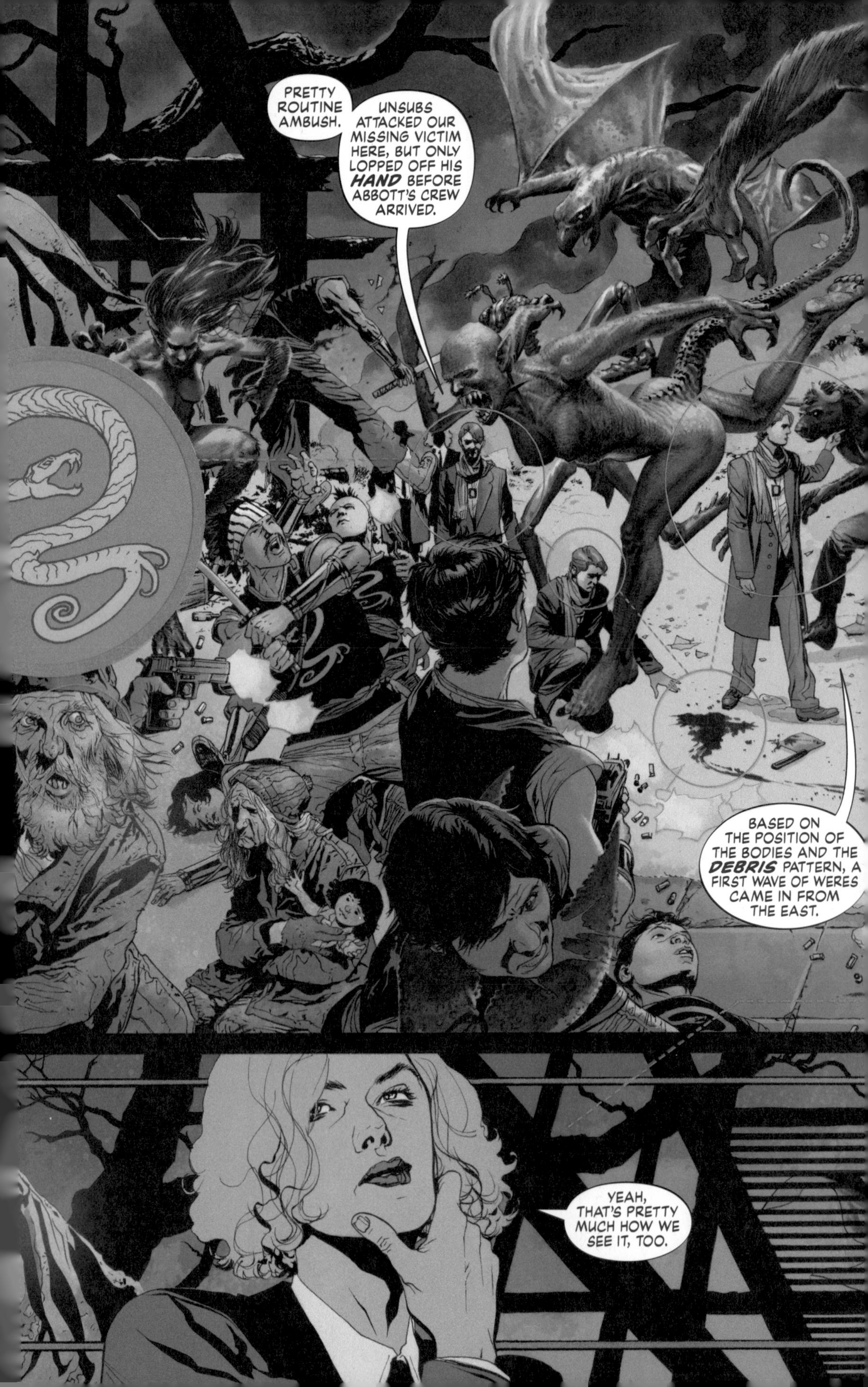
PRETTY ROUTINE AMBUSH.
UNSUBS ATTACKED OUR MISSING VICTIM HERE, BUT ONLY LOPPED OFF HIS HAND BEFORE ABBOTT'S CREW ARRIVED.
BASED ON THE POSITION OF THE BODIES AND THE DEBRIS PATTERN, A FIRST WAVE OF WERES CAME IN FROM THE EAST.
YEAH, THAT'S PRETTY MUCH HOW WE SEE IT, TOO.

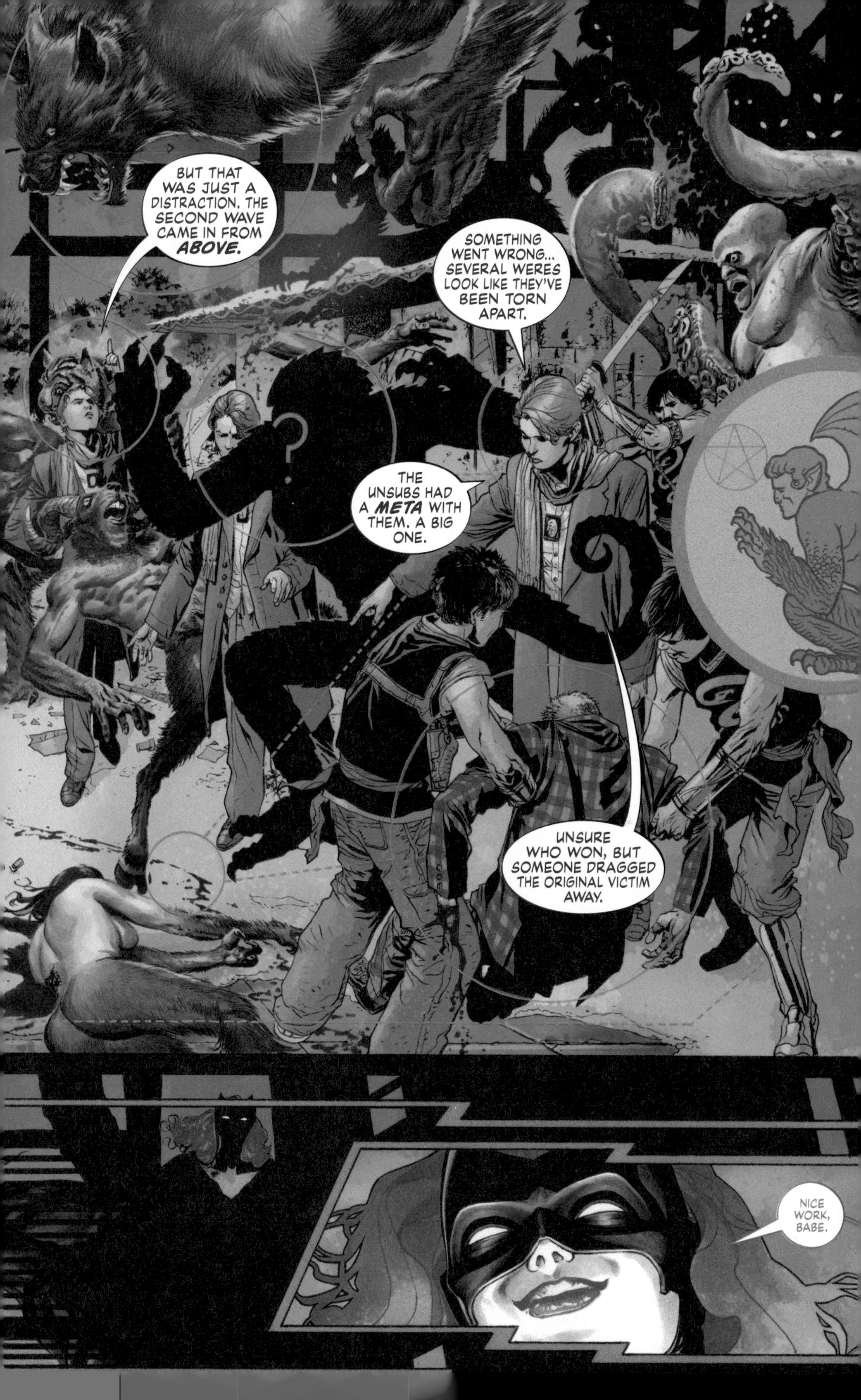
BUT THAT WAS JUST A DISTRACTION. THE SECOND WAVE CAME IN FROM ABOVE.
SOMETHING WENT WRONG... SEVERAL WERES LOOK LIKE THEY'VE BEEN TORN APART.
THE UNSUBS HAD A META WITH THEM. A BIG ONE.
UNSURE WHO WON, BUT SOMEONE DRAGGED THE ORIGINAL VICTIM AWAY.
NICE WORK, BABE.

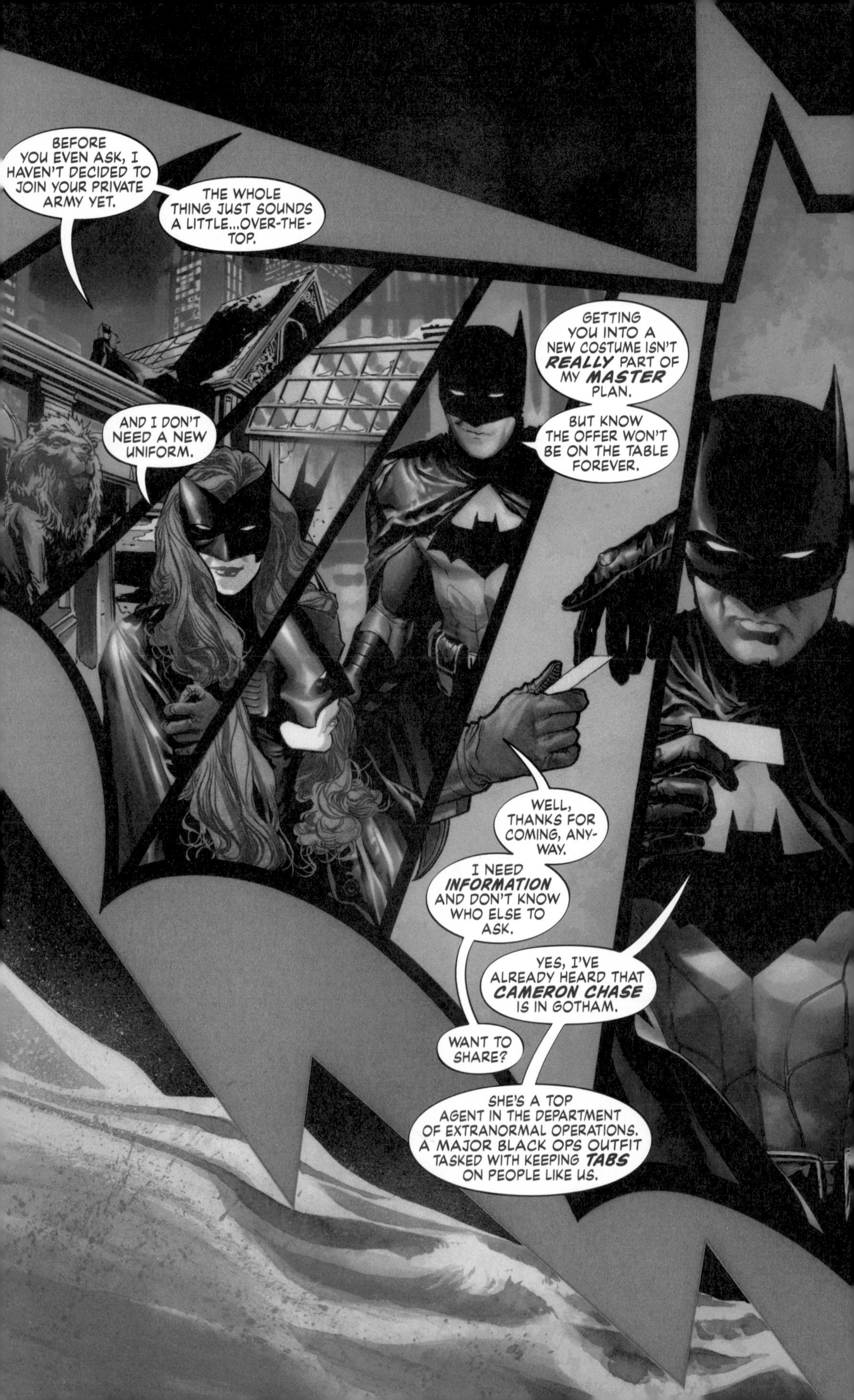
BEFORE YOU EVEN ASK, I HAVEN'T DECIDED TO JOIN YOUR PRIVATE ARMY YET.
THE WHOLE THING JUST SOUNDS A LITTLE...OVER-THE-TOP.
AND I DON'T NEED A NEW UNIFORM.
GETTING YOU INTO A NEW COSTUME ISN'T REALLY PART OF MY MASTER PLAN.
BUT KNOW THE OFFER WON'T BE ON THE TABLE FOREVER.
WELL, THANKS FOR COMING, ANY-WAY.
I NEED INFORMATION AND DON'T KNOW WHO ELSE TO ASK.
YES, I'VE ALREADY HEARD THAT CAMERON CHASE IS IN GOTHAM.
WANT TO SHARE?
SHE'S A TOP AGENT IN THE DEPARTMENT OF EXTRANORMAL OPERATIONS. A MAJOR BLACK OPS OUTFIT TASKED WITH KEEPING TABS ON PEOPLE LIKE US.

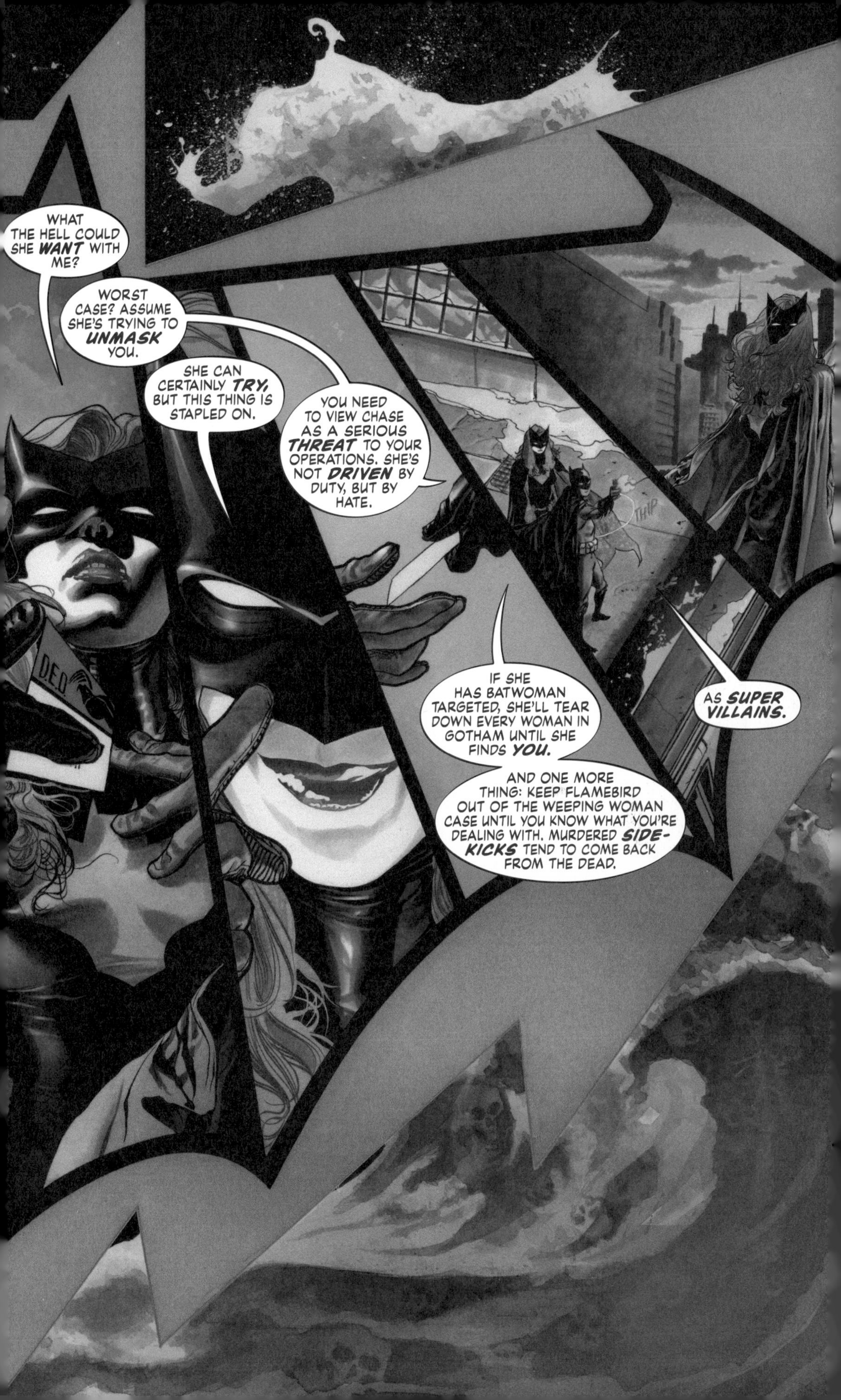
WHAT THE HELL COULD SHE WANT WITH ME?
WORST CASE? ASSUME SHE'S TRYING TO UNMASK YOU.
SHE CAN CERTAINLY TRY, BUT THIS THING IS STAPLED ON.
YOU NEED TO VIEW CHASE AS A SERIOUS THREAT TO YOUR OPERATIONS. SHE'S NOT DRIVEN BY DUTY, BUT BY HATE.
D.E.O.
THIP
IF SHE HAS BATWOMAN TARGETED, SHE'LL TEAR DOWN EVERY WOMAN IN GOTHAM UNTIL SHE FINDS YOU.
AND ONE MORE THING: KEEP FLAMEBIRD OUT OF THE WEEPING WOMAN CASE UNTIL YOU KNOW WHAT YOU'RE DEALING WITH. MURDERED SIDE-KICKS TEND TO COME BACK FROM THE DEAD.
AS SUPER VILLAINS.

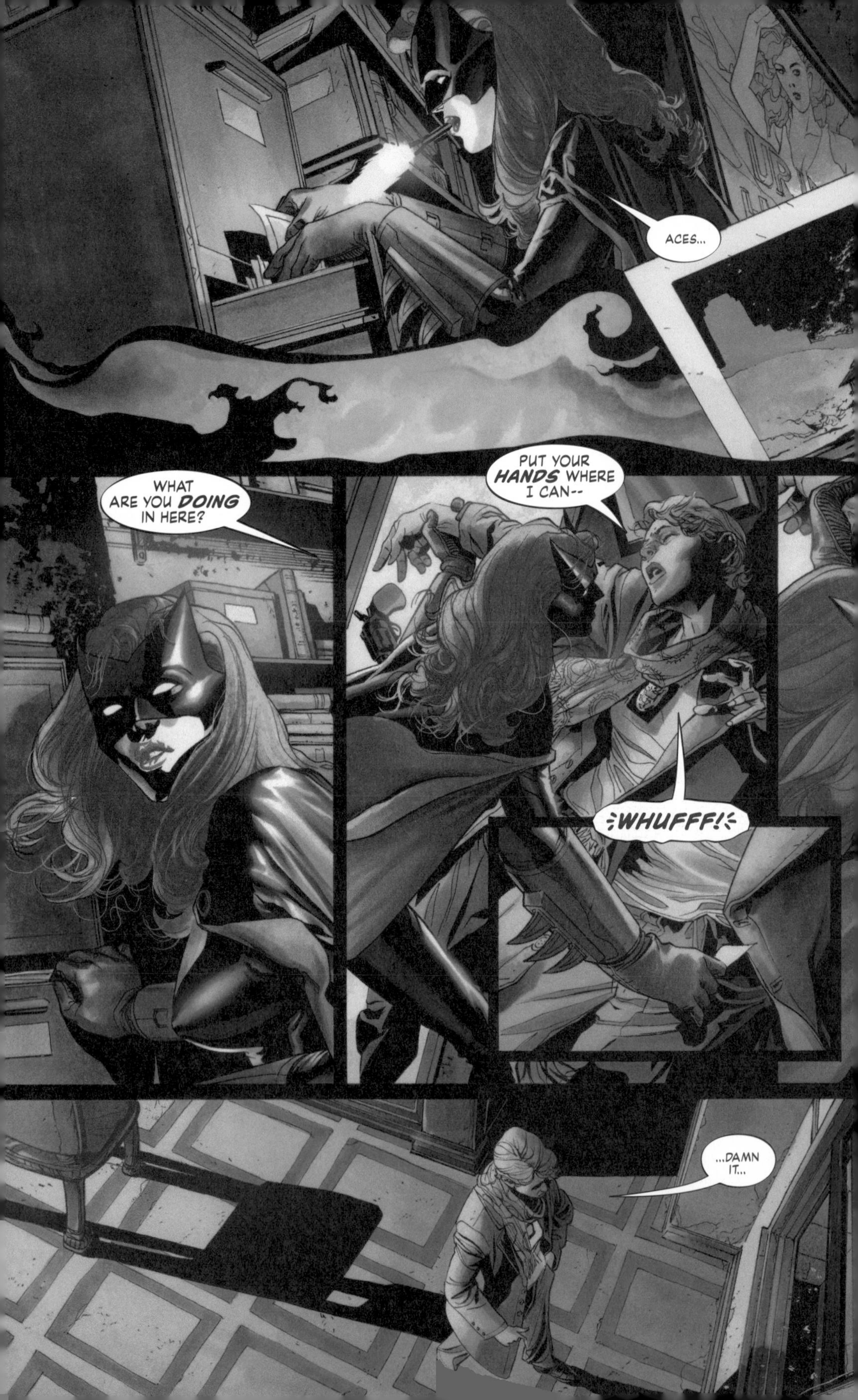
ACES...
WHAT ARE YOU DOING IN HERE?
PUT YOUR HANDS WHERE I CAN--
WHUFFF!
...DAMN IT...

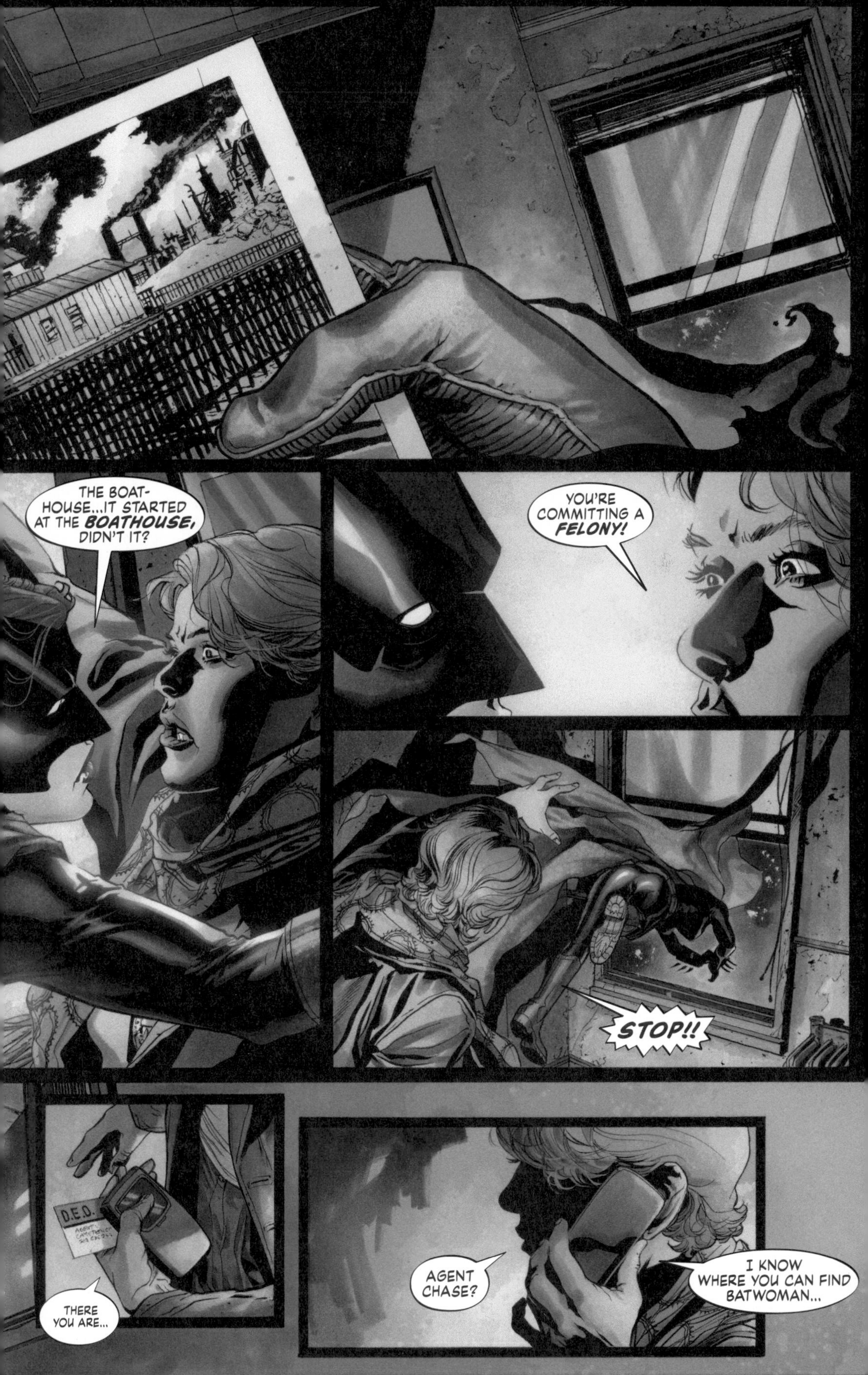
THE BOAT-HOUSE...IT STARTED AT THE BOATHOUSE, DIDN'T IT?
YOU'RE COMMITTING A FELONY!
STOP!!
D.E.O.
THERE YOU ARE...
AGENT CHASE?
I KNOW WHERE YOU CAN FIND BATWOMAN...

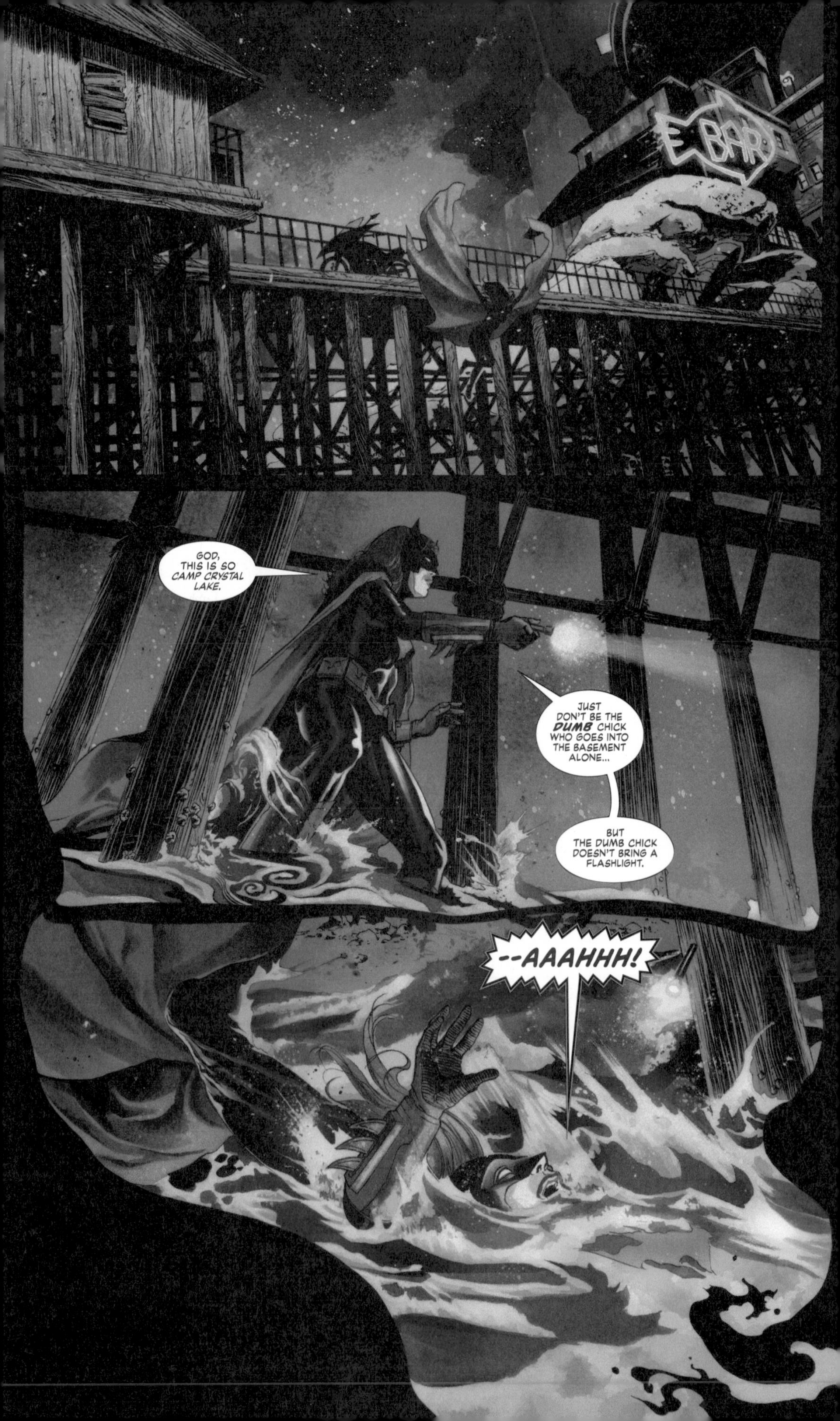
BAR
GOD, THIS IS SO CAMP CRYSTAL LAKE.
JUST DON'T BE THE DUMB CHICK WHO GOES INTO THE BASEMENT ALONE...
BUT THE DUMB CHICK DOESN'T BRING A FLASHLIGHT.
--AAAHHH!

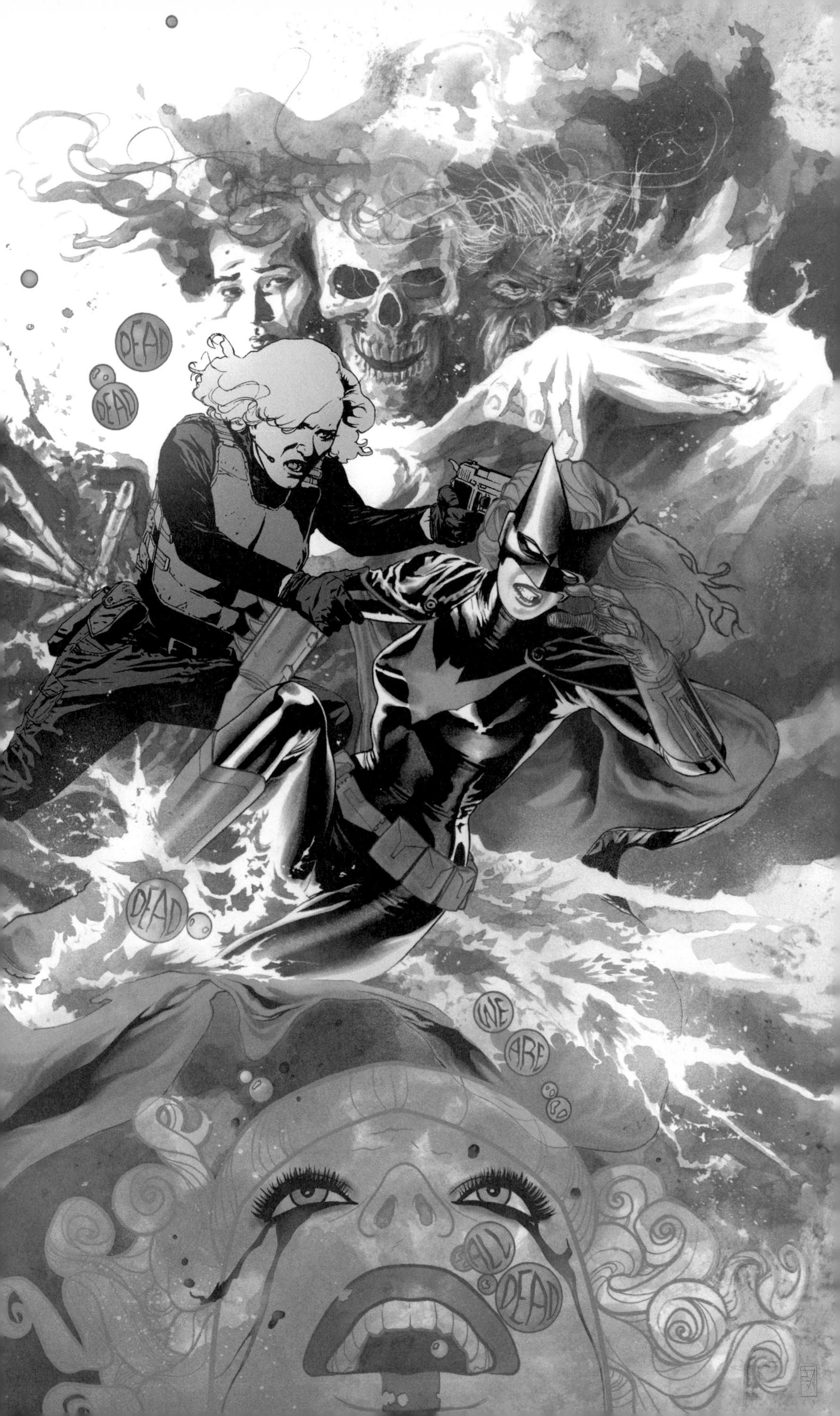

DEAD
DEAD
DEAD
WE
ARE
ALL
DEAD

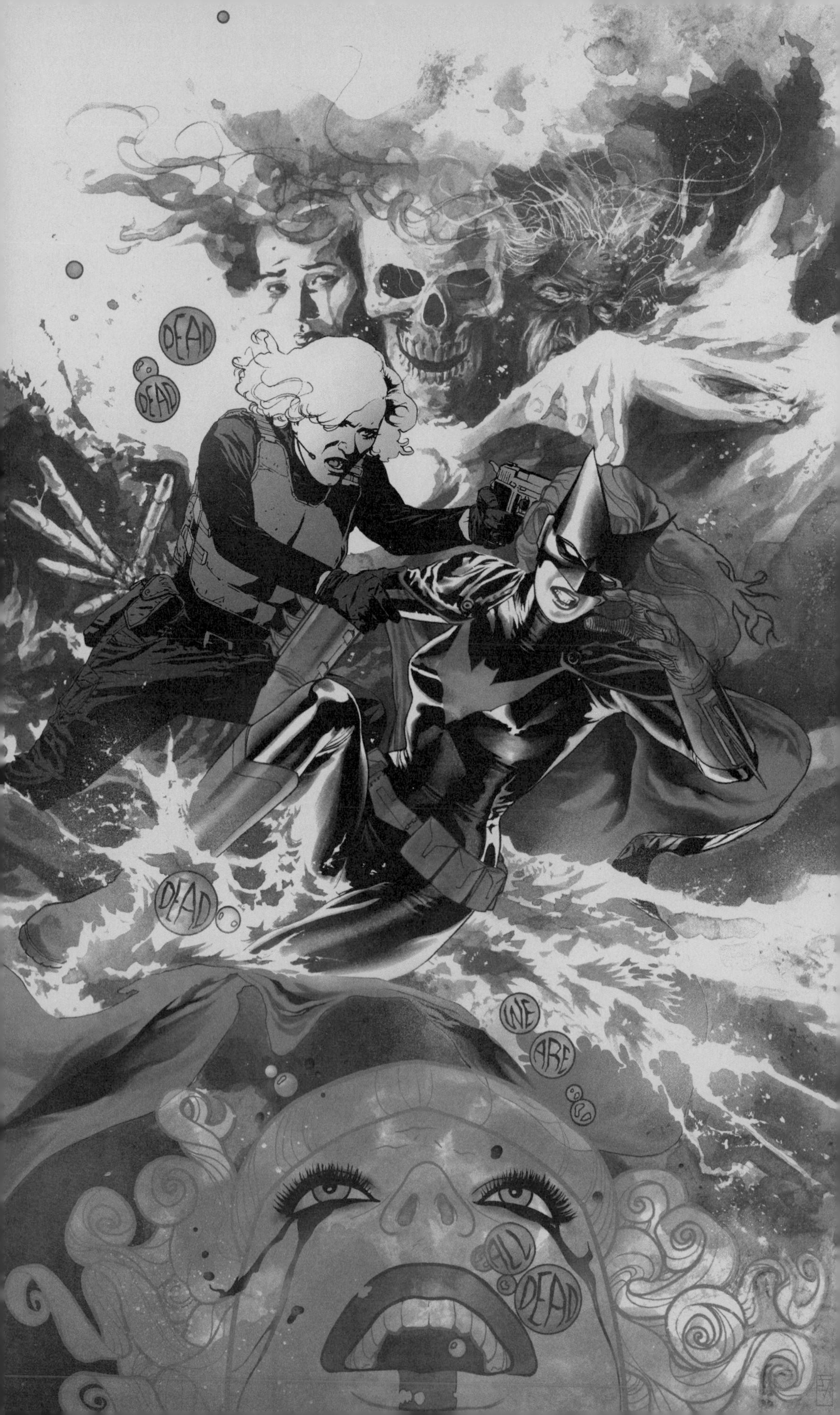
DEAD
DEAD
DEAD
WE ARE ALL DEAD

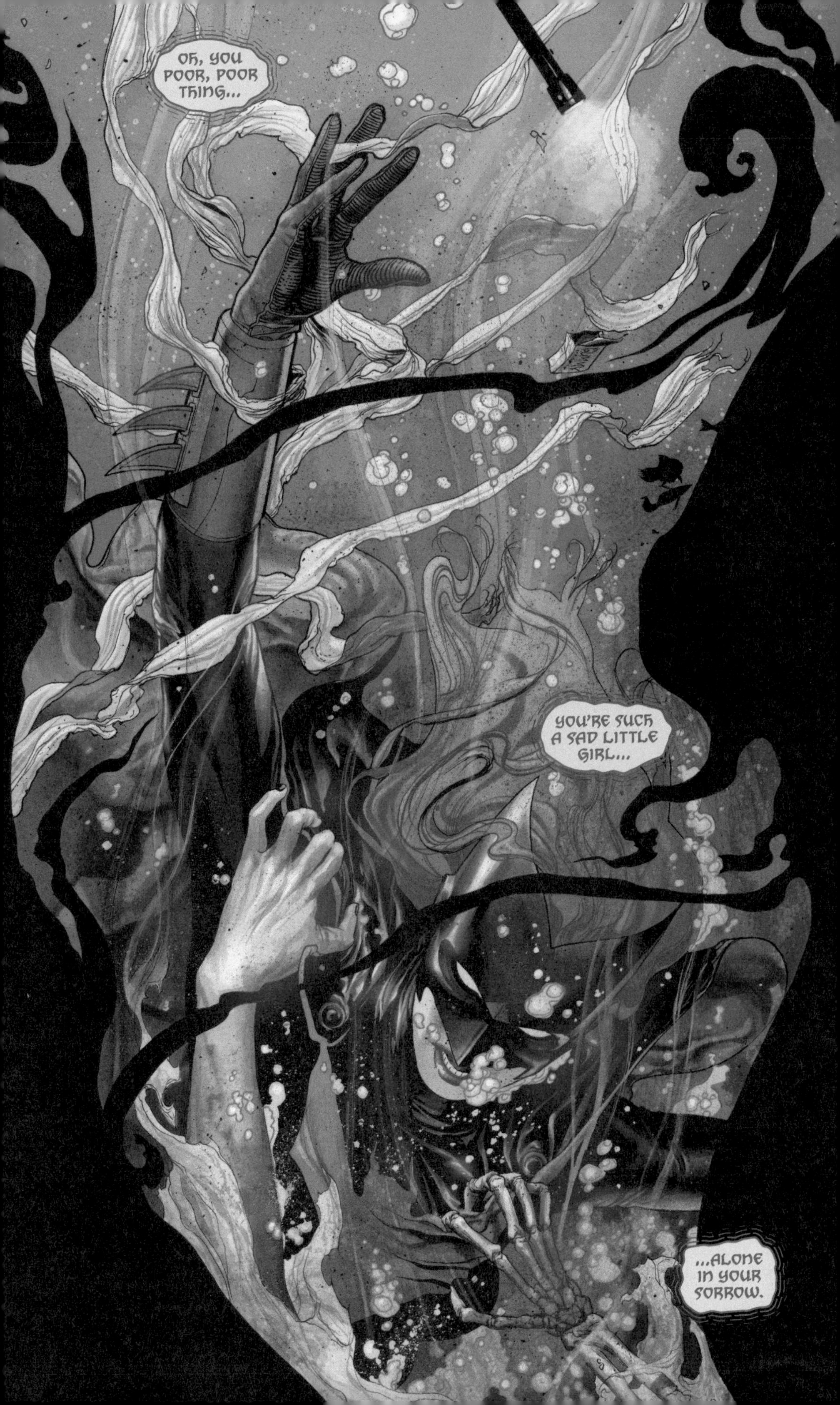
OH, YOU POOR, POOR THING...
YOU'RE SUCH A SAD LITTLE GIRL...
...ALONE IN YOUR SORROW.

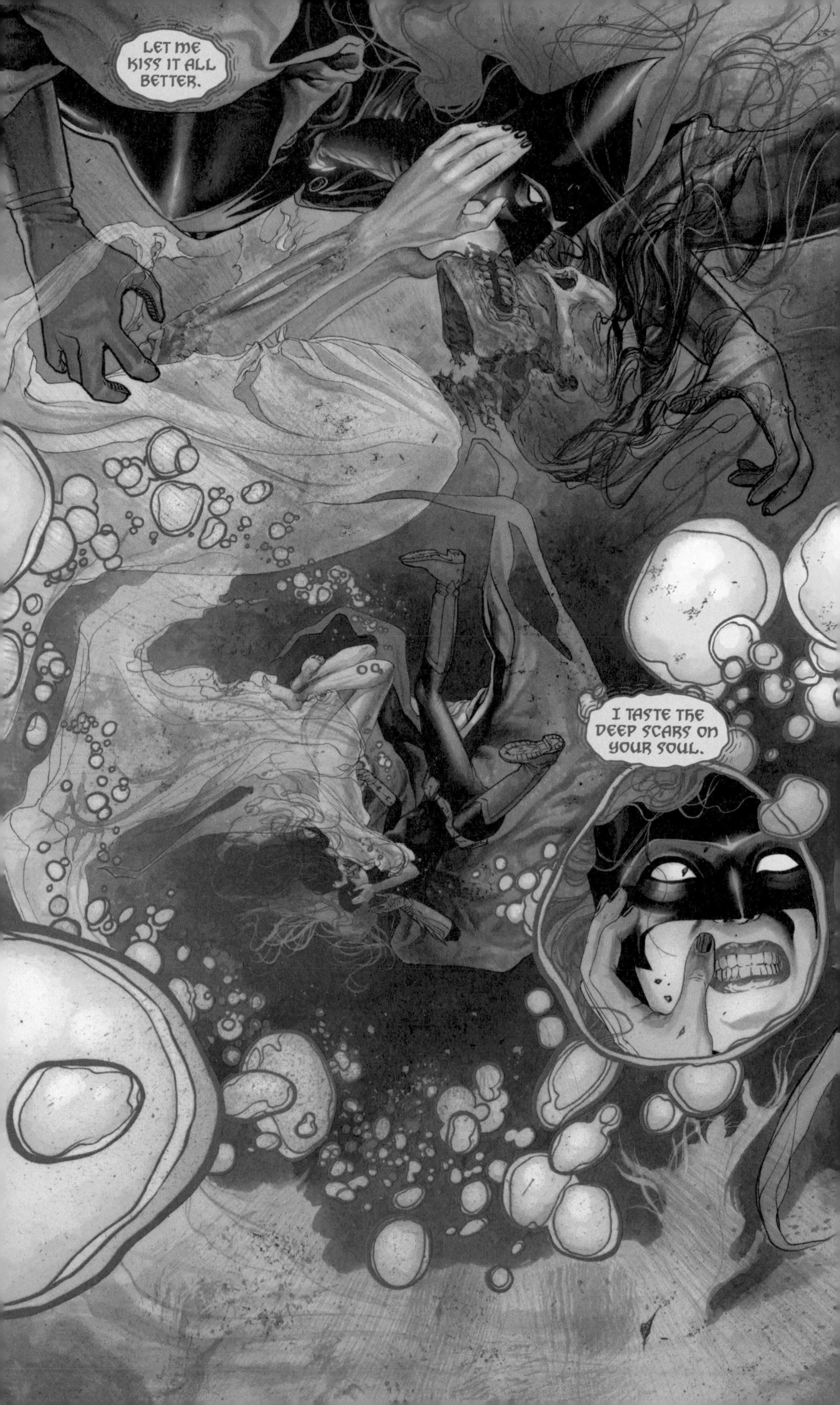
LET ME KISS IT ALL BETTER.
I TASTE THE DEEP SCARS ON YOUR SOUL.

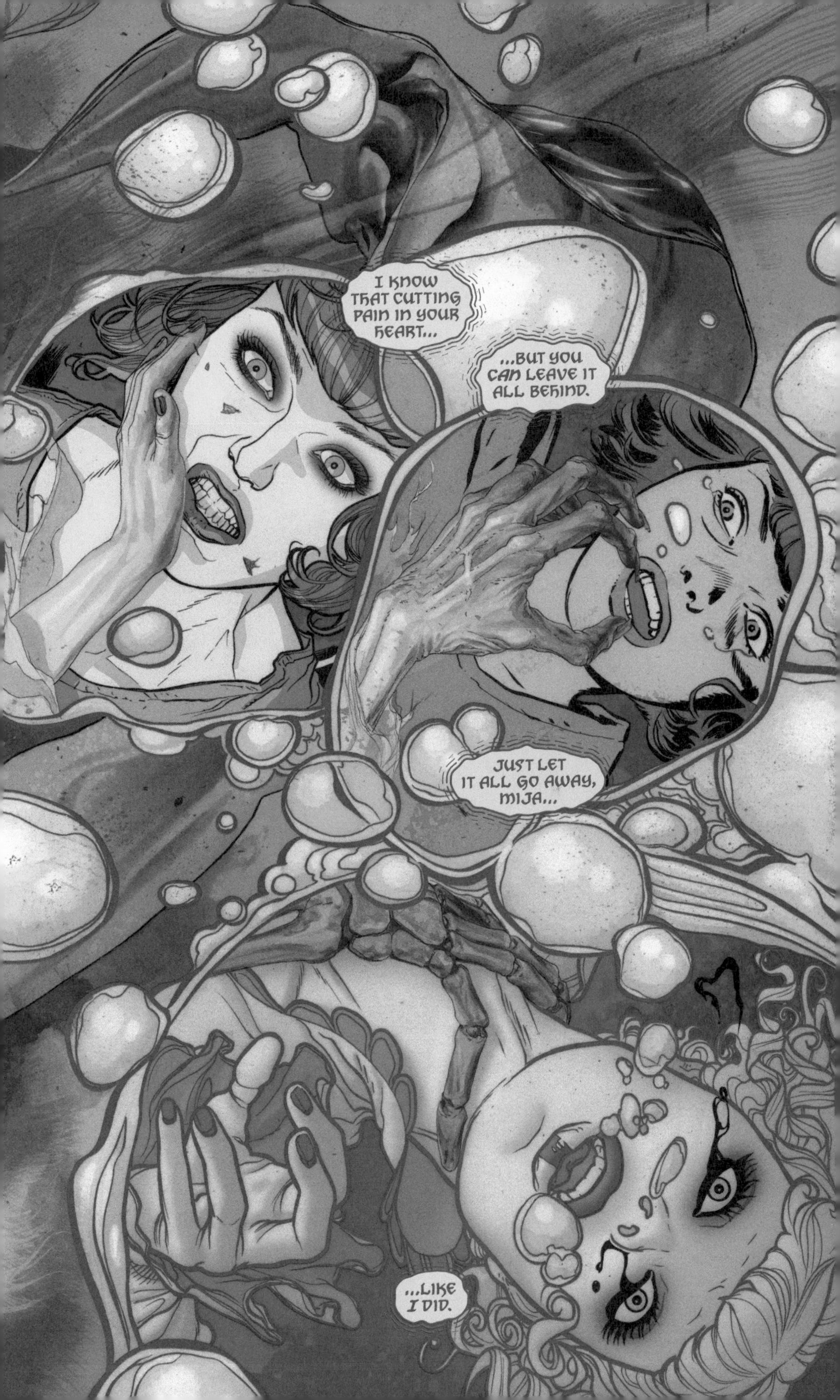
I KNOW THAT CUTTING PAIN IN YOUR HEART...
...BUT YOU CAN LEAVE IT ALL BEHIND.
JUST LET IT ALL GO AWAY, MIJA...
...LIKE I DID.

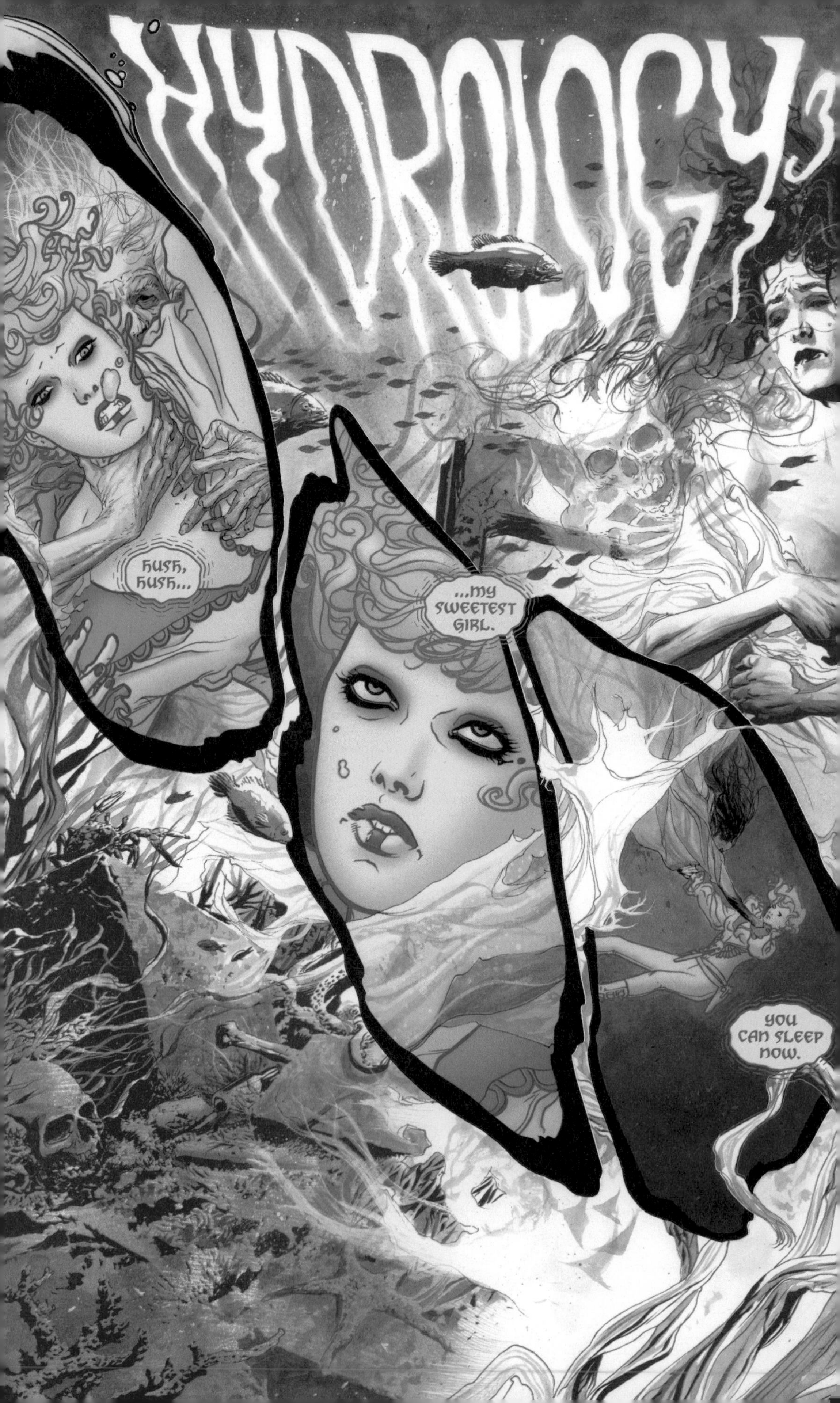
HYDROLOGY 3
HUSH, HUSH...
...MY SWEETEST GIRL.
YOU CAN SLEEP NOW.

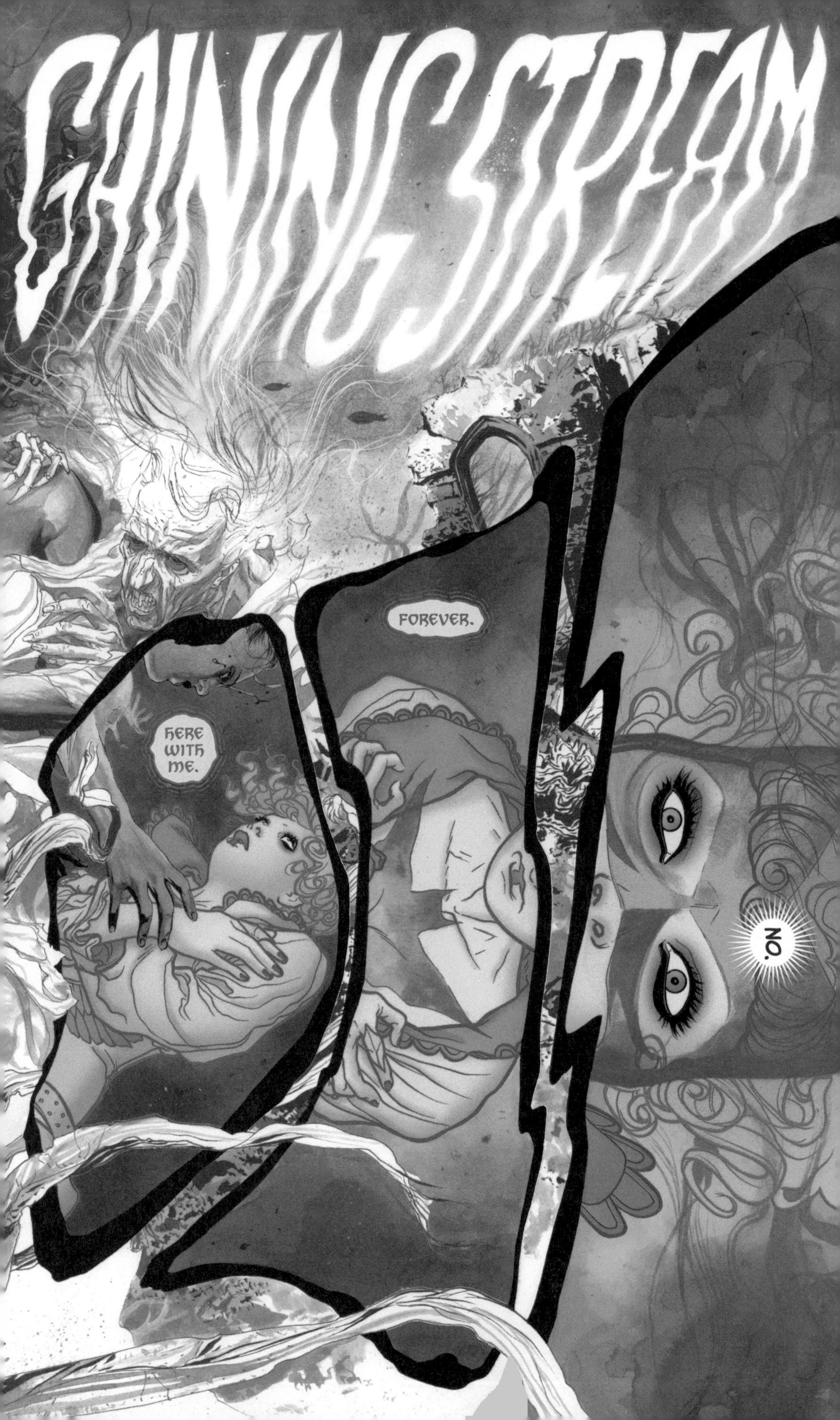
GAINING STREAM
HERE WITH ME.
FOREVER.
NO.

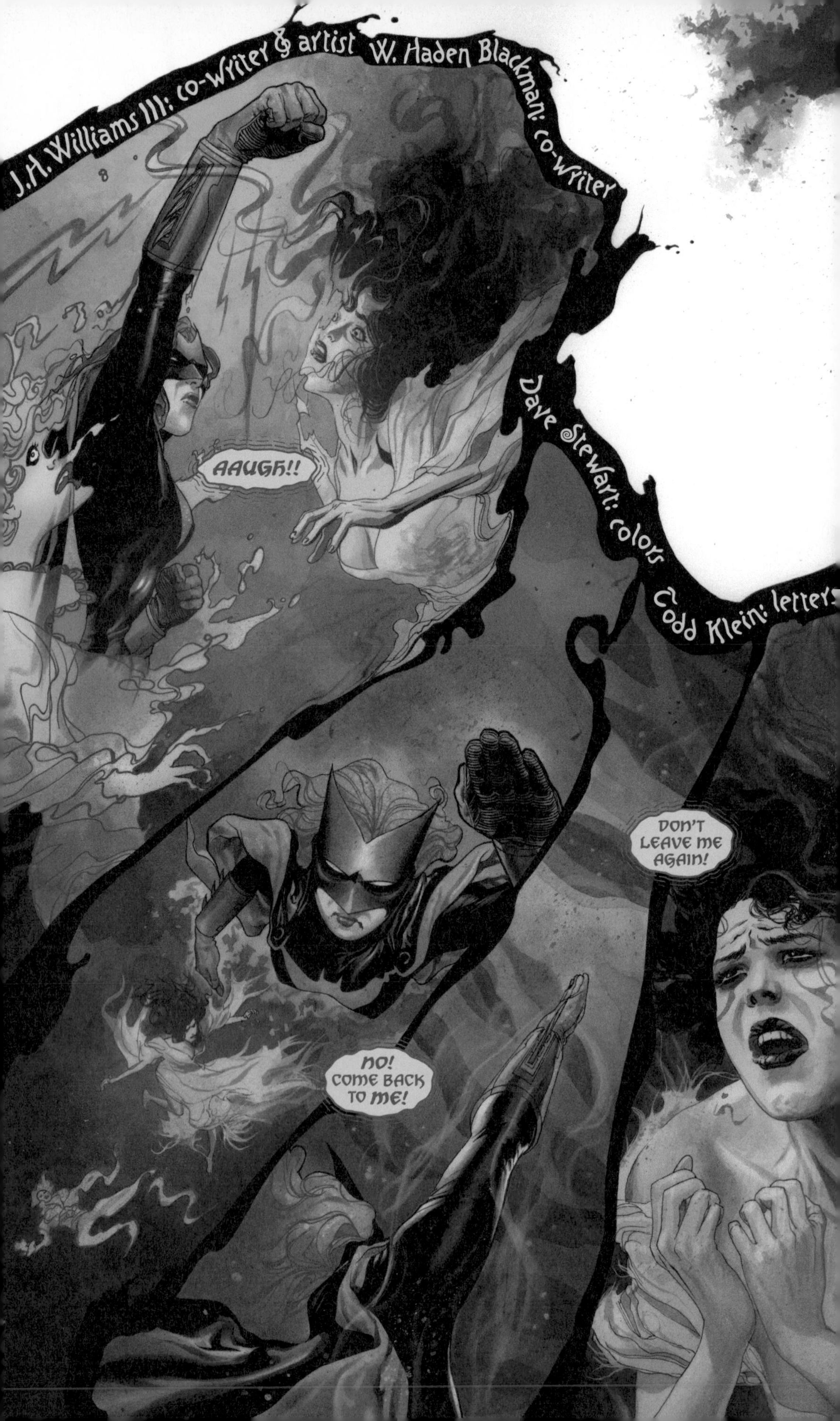
J.H. Williams III: co-writer & artist W. Haden Blackman: co-writer
Dave Stewart: colors
Todd Klein: letters
AAUGH!!
DON'T LEAVE ME AGAIN!
NO! COME BACK TO ME!

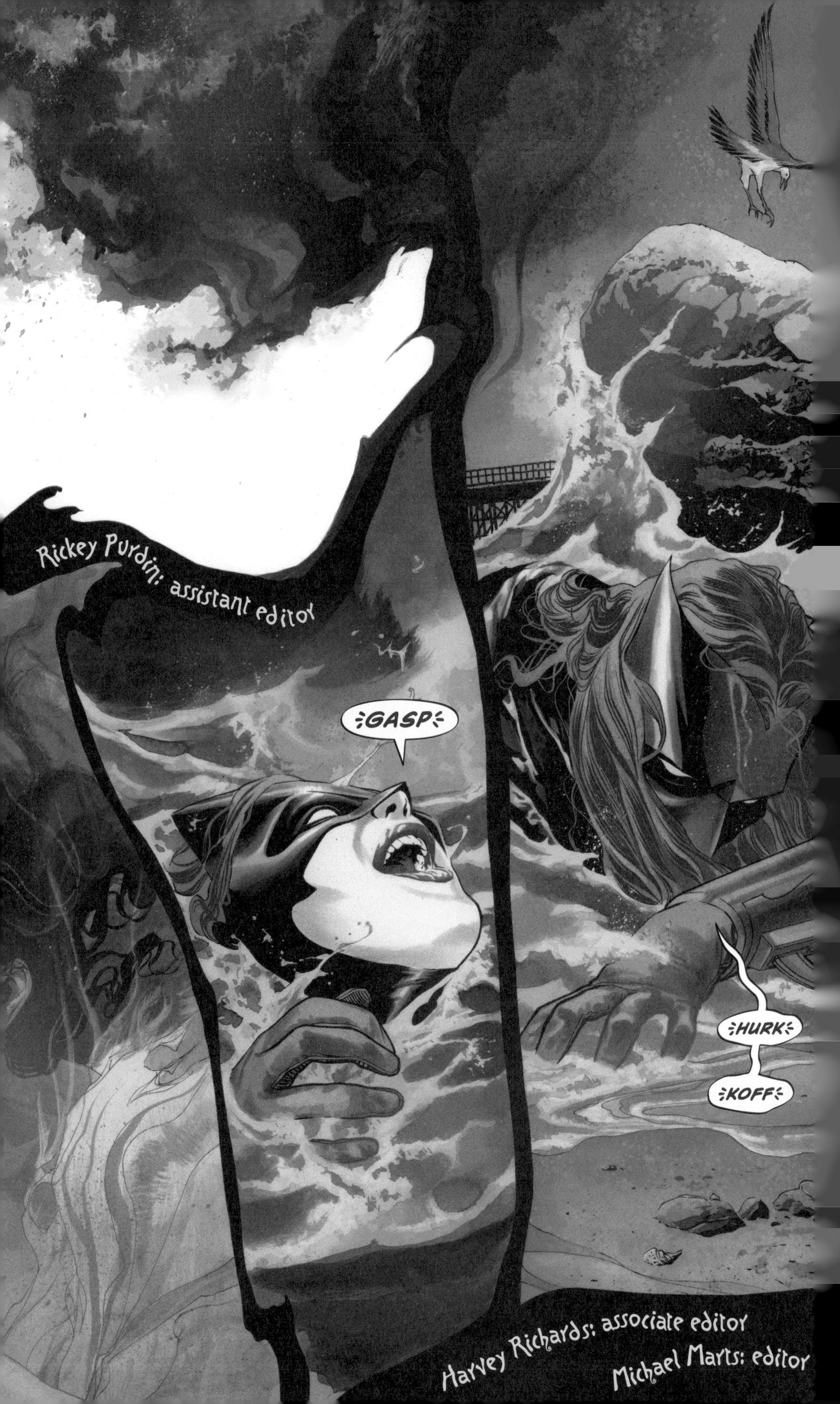
Rickey Purdin: assistant editor
GASP
HURK
KOFF
Harvey Richards: associate editor
Michael Marts: editor

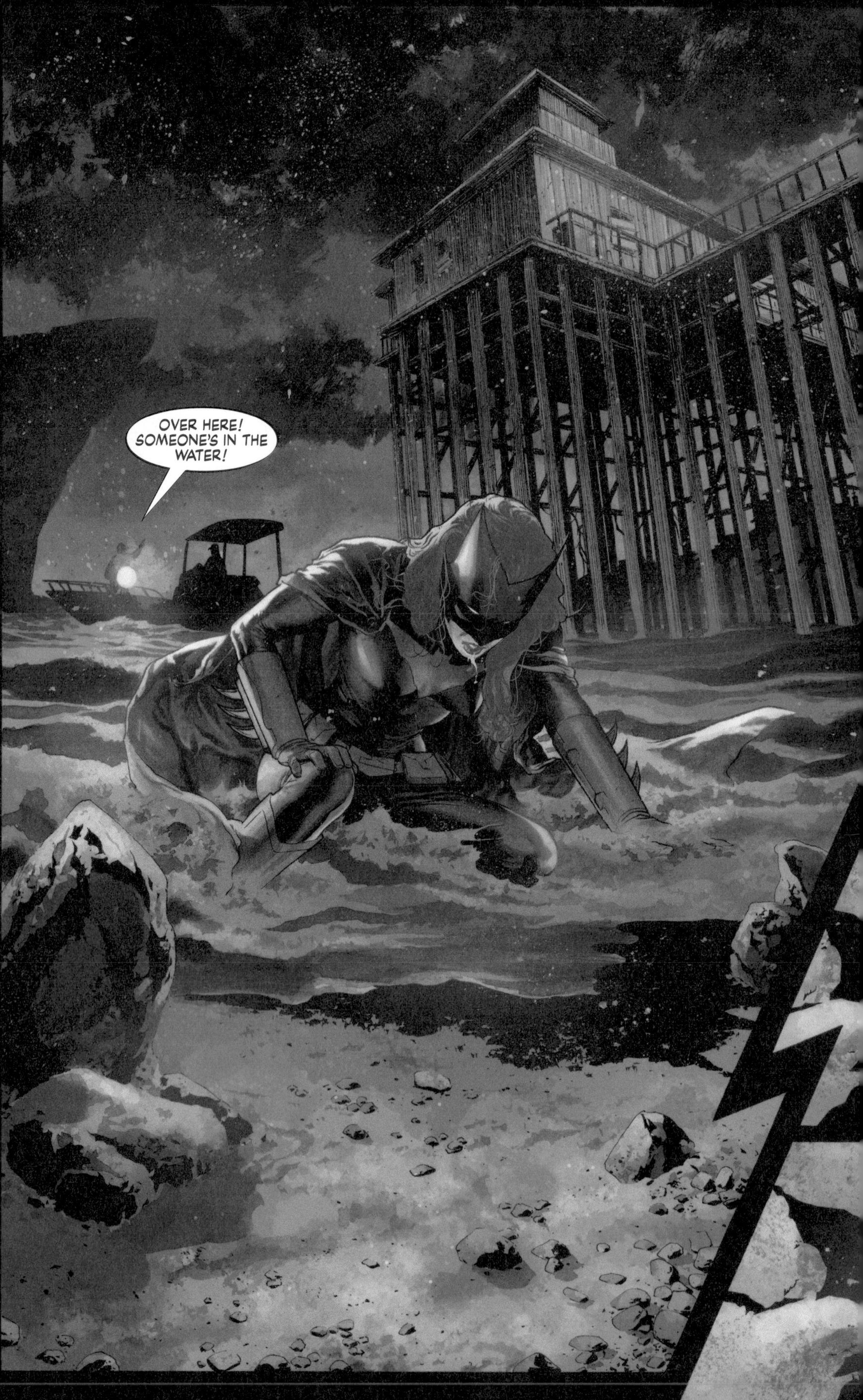
OVER HERE! SOMEONE'S IN THE WATER!

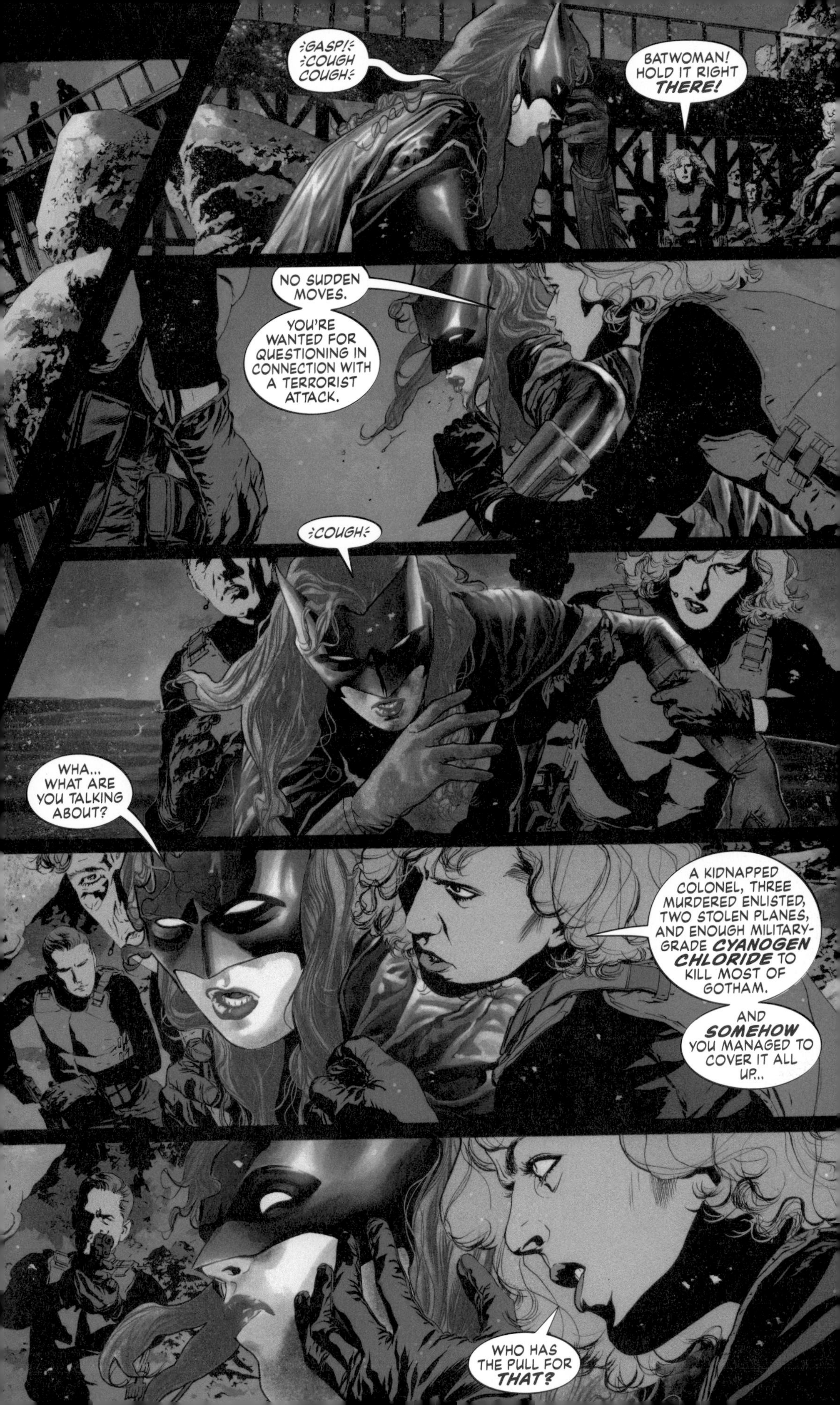

GASP! COUGH COUGH
BATWOMAN! HOLD IT RIGHT *THERE!*
NO SUDDEN MOVES.
YOU'RE WANTED FOR QUESTIONING IN CONNECTION WITH A TERRORIST ATTACK.
COUGH
WHA... WHAT ARE YOU TALKING ABOUT?
A KIDNAPPED COLONEL, THREE MURDERED ENLISTED, TWO STOLEN PLANES, AND ENOUGH MILITARY-GRADE *CYANOGEN CHLORIDE* TO KILL MOST OF GOTHAM.
AND *SOMEHOW* YOU MANAGED TO COVER IT ALL UP...
WHO HAS THE PULL FOR *THAT?*

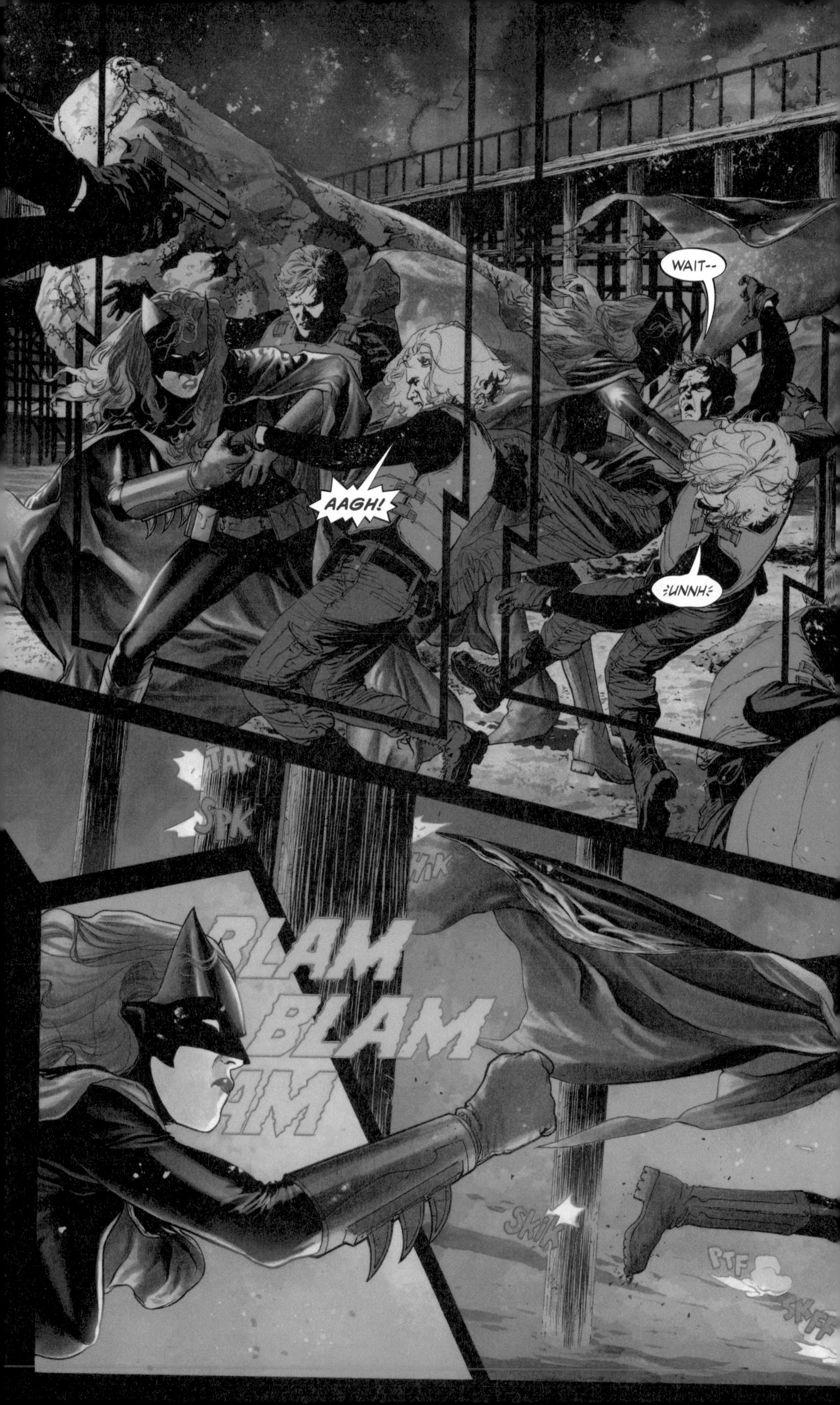
WAIT--
AAGH!
UNNH
TAK
SPK
SHIK
BLAM
BLAM
SKIK
PTF
SKFF

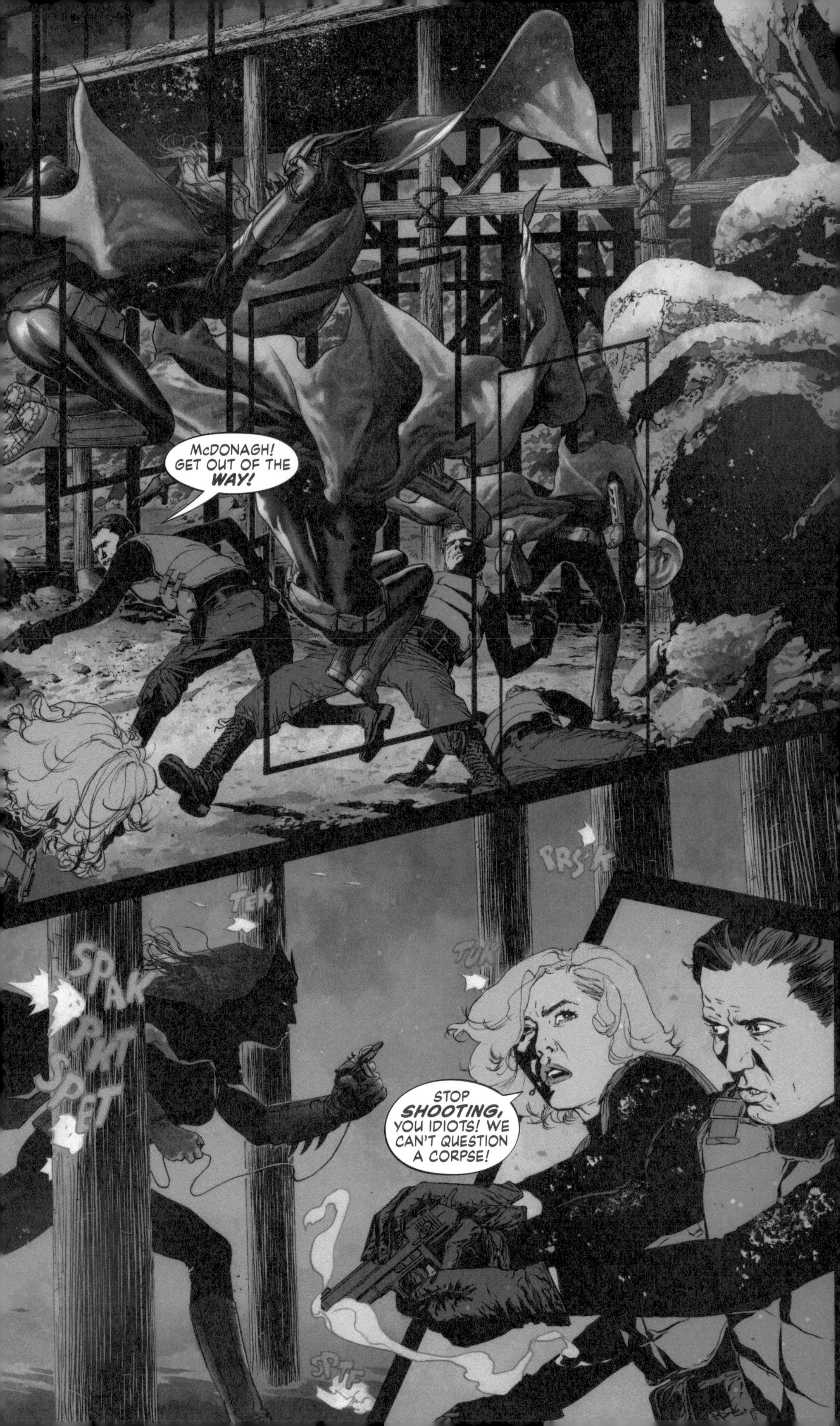
McDONAGH! GET OUT OF THE WAY!
PRS'K
TEK
TUK
SPAK
PWT
SPET
STOP SHOOTING, YOU IDIOTS! WE CAN'T QUESTION A CORPSE!
SPTF

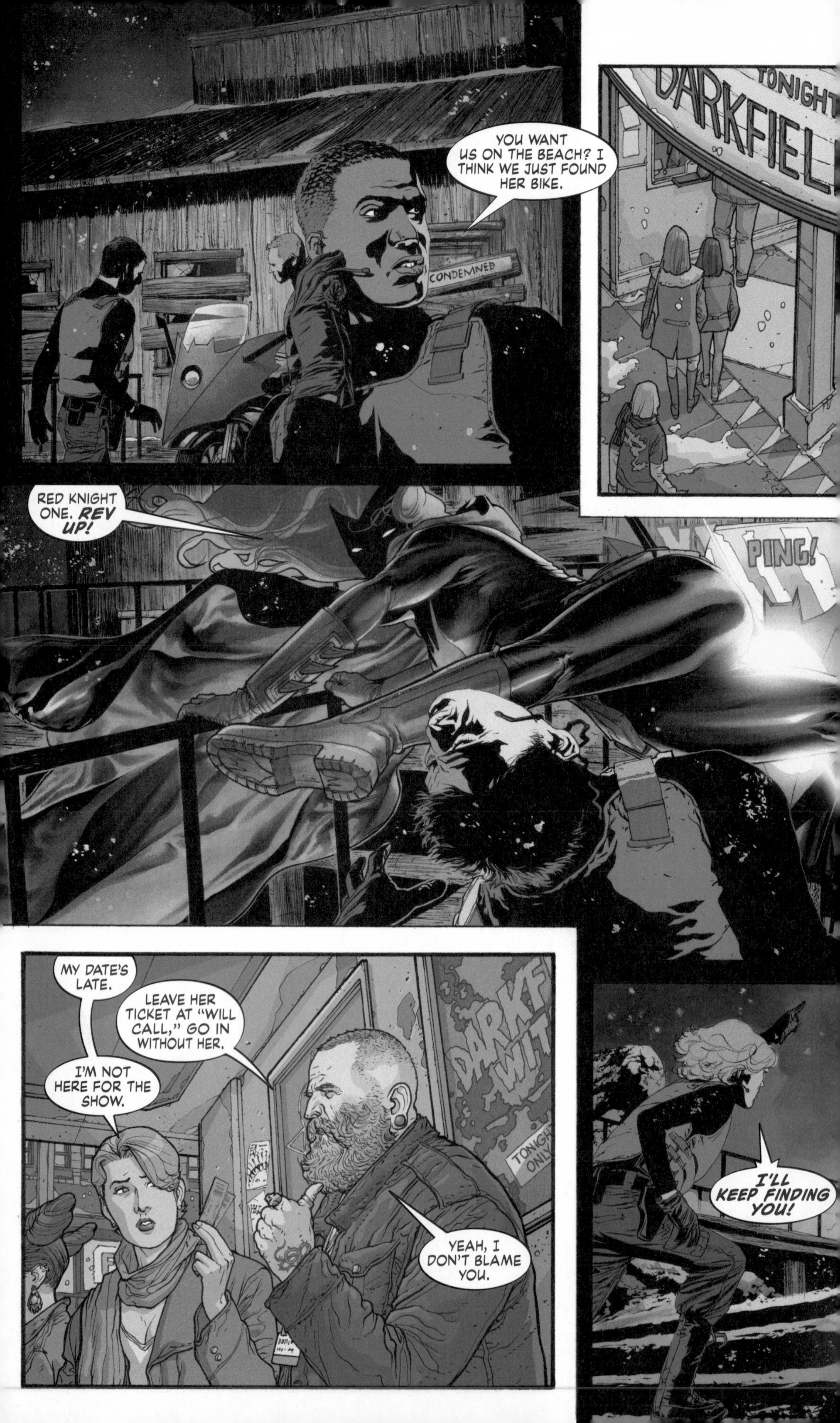

CONDEMNED
YOU WANT US ON THE BEACH? I THINK WE JUST FOUND HER BIKE.
TONIGHT
DARKFIEL
RED KNIGHT ONE. REV UP!
PING!
MY DATE'S LATE.
LEAVE HER TICKET AT "WILL CALL," GO IN WITHOUT HER.
I'M NOT HERE FOR THE SHOW.
YEAH, I DON'T BLAME YOU.
I'LL KEEP FINDING YOU!

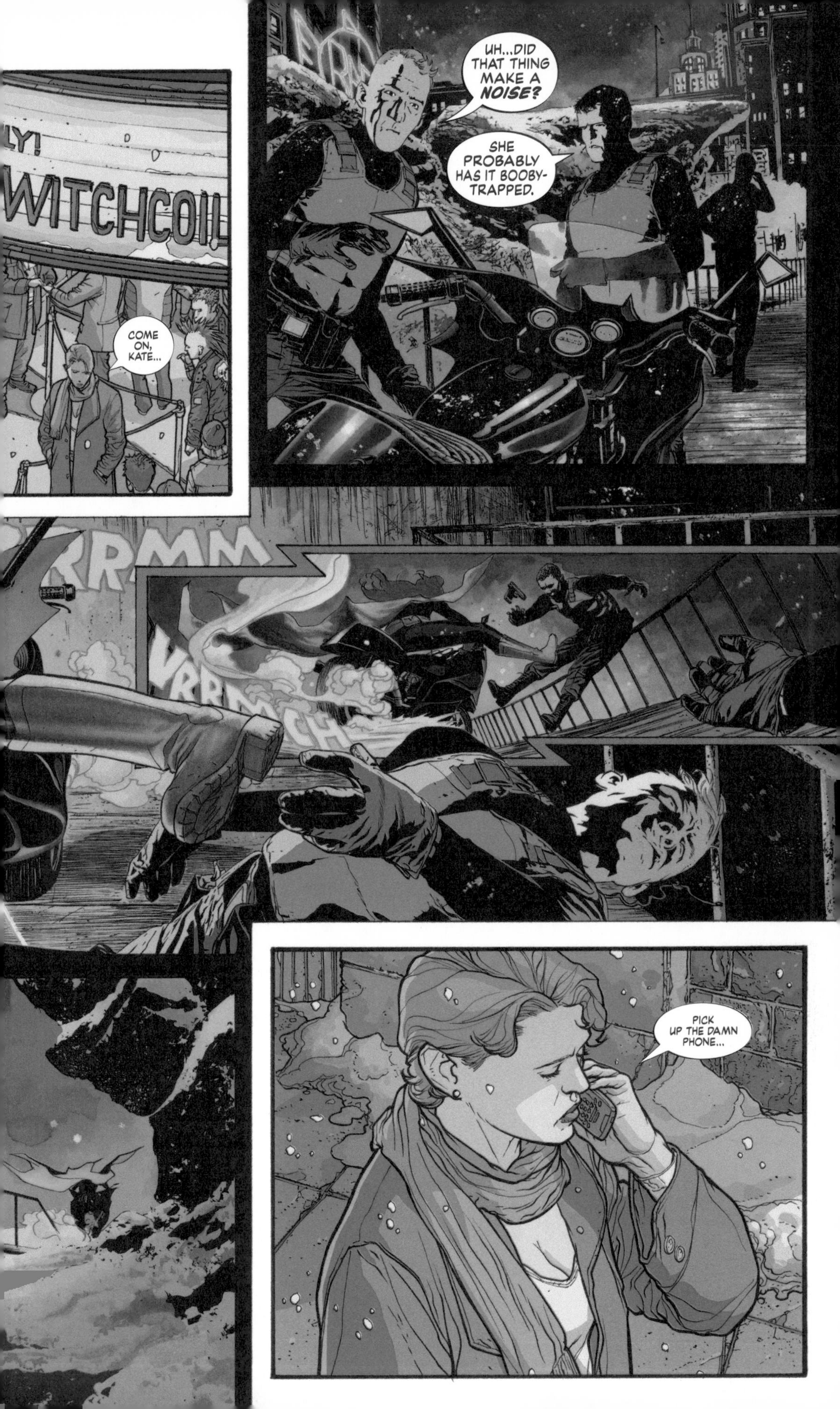

LY!
WITCHCOIL
COME ON, KATE...
UH...DID THAT THING MAKE A *NOISE?*
SHE PROBABLY HAS IT BOOBY-TRAPPED.
RRMM
VRRMCH
PICK UP THE DAMN PHONE...

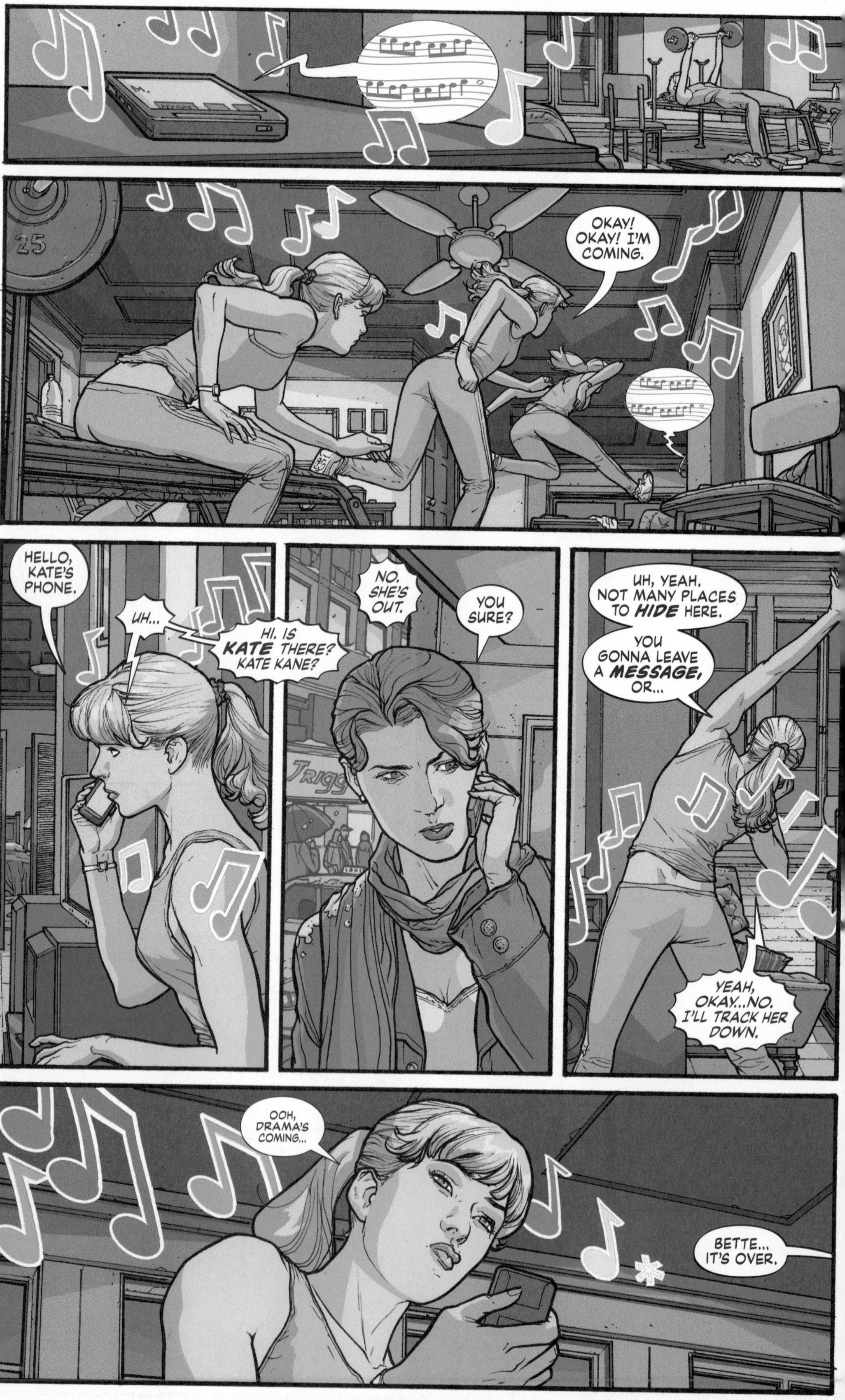
OKAY! OKAY! I'M COMING.
HELLO, KATE'S PHONE.
UH...
HI. IS KATE THERE? KATE KANE?
NO. SHE'S OUT.
YOU SURE?
UH, YEAH. NOT MANY PLACES TO HIDE HERE.
YOU GONNA LEAVE A MESSAGE, OR...
YEAH, OKAY...NO. I'LL TRACK HER DOWN.
OOH, DRAMA'S COMING...
BETTE... IT'S OVER.

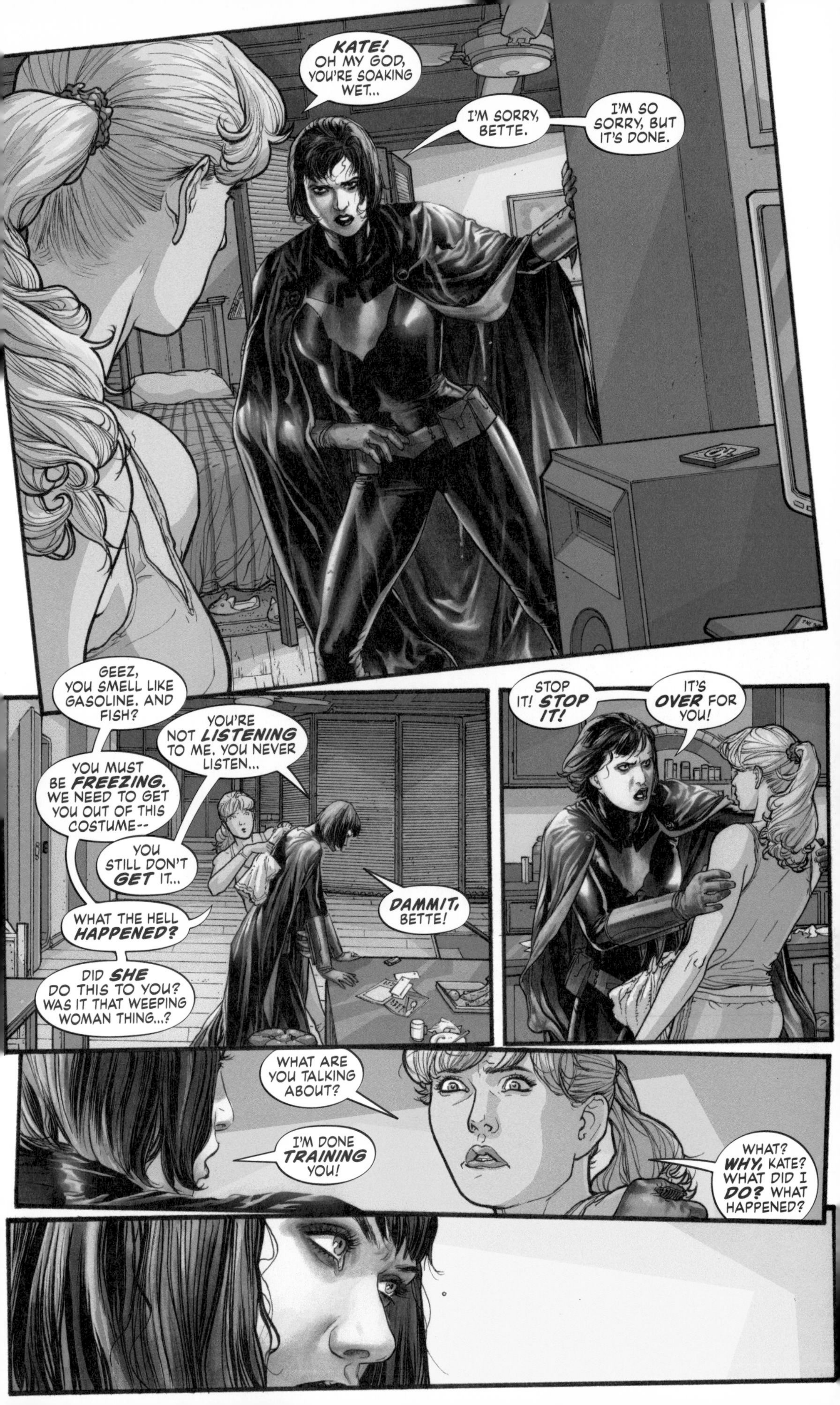
KATE! OH MY GOD, YOU'RE SOAKING WET...
I'M SORRY, BETTE.
I'M SO SORRY, BUT IT'S DONE.
GEEZ, YOU SMELL LIKE GASOLINE. AND FISH?
YOU MUST BE FREEZING. WE NEED TO GET YOU OUT OF THIS COSTUME--
YOU'RE NOT LISTENING TO ME. YOU NEVER LISTEN...
YOU STILL DON'T GET IT...
WHAT THE HELL HAPPENED?
DID SHE DO THIS TO YOU? WAS IT THAT WEEPING WOMAN THING...?
DAMMIT, BETTE!
STOP IT! STOP IT!
IT'S OVER FOR YOU!
WHAT ARE YOU TALKING ABOUT?
I'M DONE TRAINING YOU!
WHAT? WHY, KATE? WHAT DID I DO? WHAT HAPPENED?

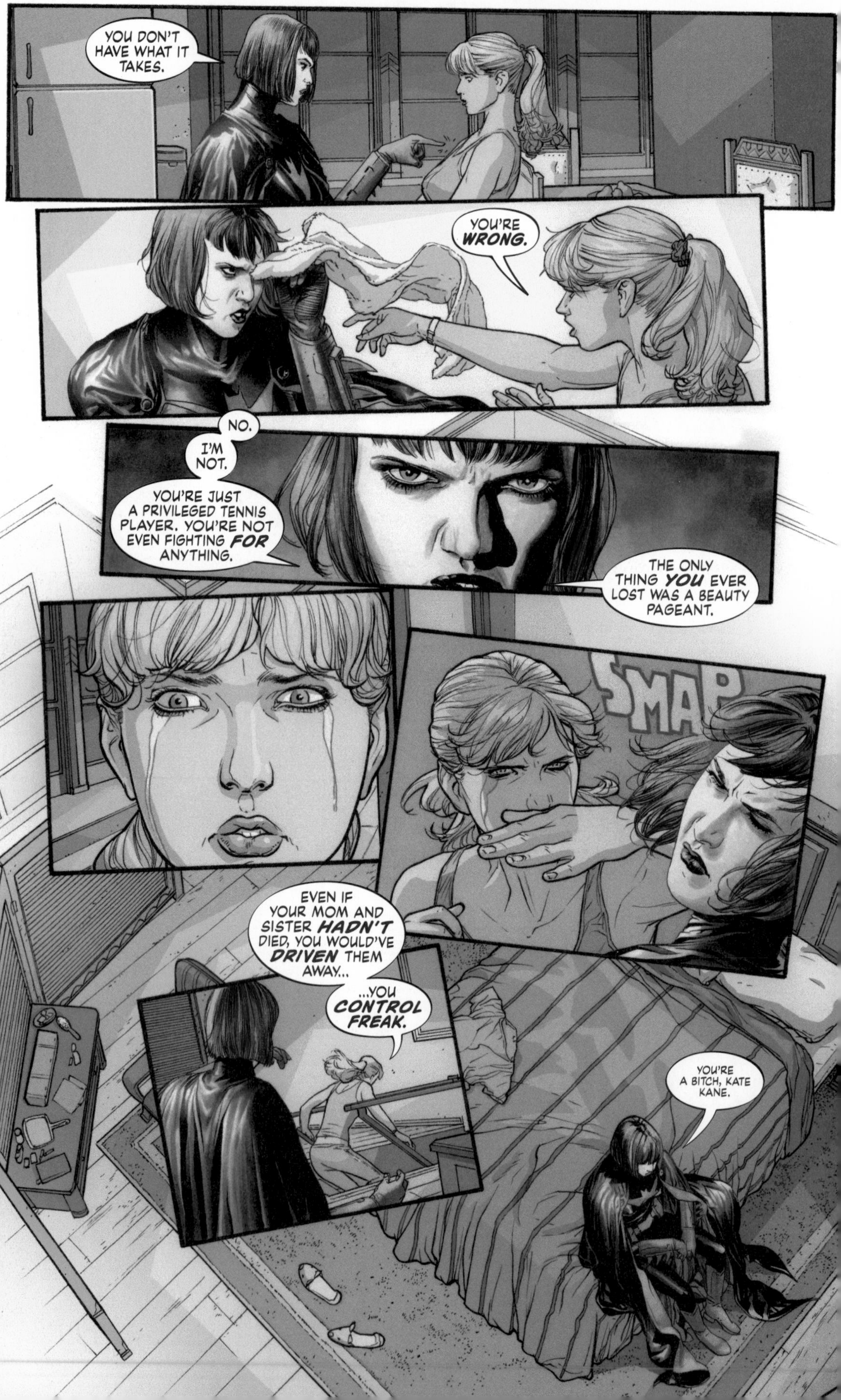
YOU DON'T HAVE WHAT IT TAKES.
YOU'RE *WRONG.*
NO.
I'M NOT.
YOU'RE JUST A PRIVILEGED TENNIS PLAYER. YOU'RE NOT EVEN FIGHTING *FOR* ANYTHING.
THE ONLY THING *YOU* EVER LOST WAS A BEAUTY PAGEANT.
SMAP
EVEN IF YOUR MOM AND SISTER *HADN'T* DIED, YOU WOULD'VE *DRIVEN* THEM AWAY...
...YOU *CONTROL FREAK.*
YOU'RE A BITCH, KATE KANE.

THIS POOL IS FOR ENLISTED ONLY, MA'AM.

MY *VICODIN* IS STARTING TO WEAR OFF, COLONEL, SO I DON'T HAVE TIME FOR YOU TO BE *CUTE* WITH ME.

JUST ANSWER MY DAMN QUESTIONS.

SIR.

WITH ALL DUE RESPECT, MA'AM, UNLESS YOU HAVE A *GENERAL* WITH YOU, I CANNOT BE COMPELLED TO TELL YOU ANYTHING.

YOU WERE KID-NAPPED A FEW MONTHS AGO BY A TERRORIST, *CORRECT?* AND *RESCUED* BY THE BATWOMAN?

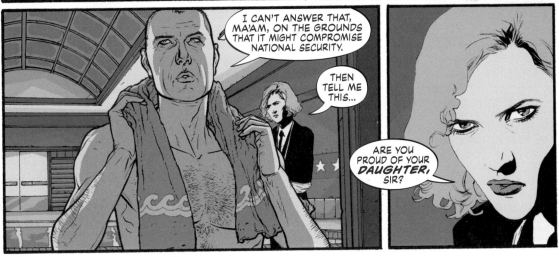

I CAN'T ANSWER THAT, MA'AM, ON THE GROUNDS THAT IT MIGHT COMPROMISE NATIONAL SECURITY.

THEN TELL ME THIS...

ARE YOU PROUD OF YOUR *DAUGHTER*, SIR?

EXCUSE ME?

SHE TRIED TO FOLLOW IN YOUR FOOTSTEPS BUT WAS **DRUMMED OUT** OF WEST POINT, RIGHT?

AND FROM WHAT I **HEAR,** SHE PARTIES ALL NIGHT, THEN SLEEPS ALL DAY IN A PENTHOUSE BUILT WITH YOUR **WIFE'S MONEY.**

NO, I GUESS NOT. NOT RIGHT **NOW.** NOT UNTIL SHE STARTS DOING SOMETHING WORTHWHILE WITH HER LIFE.

WE'RE **DONE** HERE, MA'AM.

BUT I WONDER, IF **YOUR** FATHER KNEW THIS WAS YOUR JOB...

...ASKING PEOPLE LIKE ME QUESTIONS LIKE THAT...

...WOULD HE BE PROUD OF **YOU?**

‡deet‡
deet‡
‡doot‡
‡daat
deet
deet
doot‡

YOU DONE WITH THE WARHORSE YET?

NOT QUITE. BUT HE'S DEFINITELY **NOT** GOING TO GIVE UP ANYTHING.

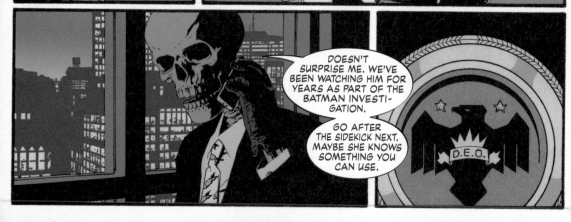

DOESN'T SURPRISE ME. WE'VE BEEN WATCHING HIM FOR YEARS AS PART OF THE BATMAN INVESTIGATION.

GO AFTER THE SIDEKICK NEXT. MAYBE SHE KNOWS SOMETHING YOU CAN USE.

D.E.O.

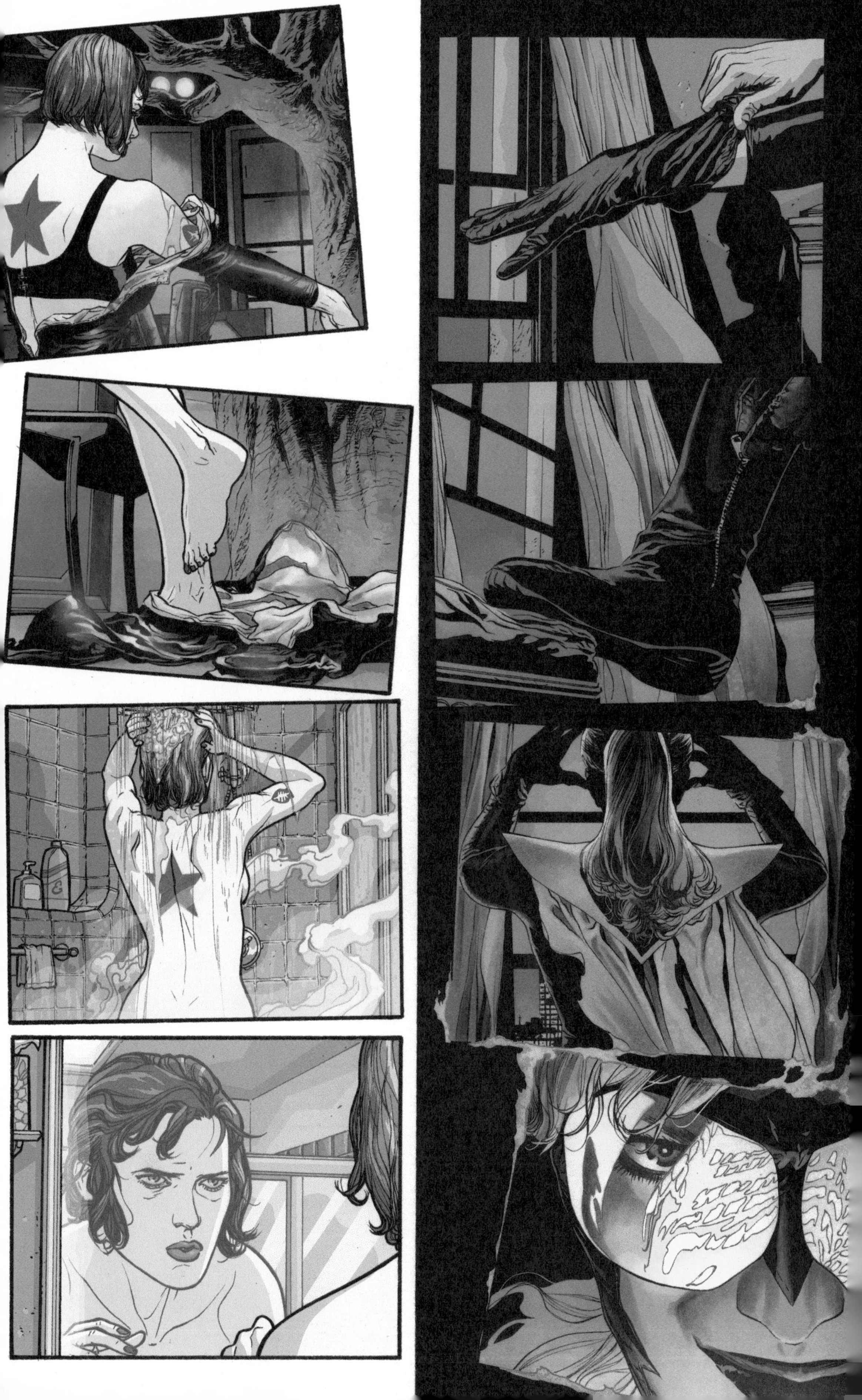

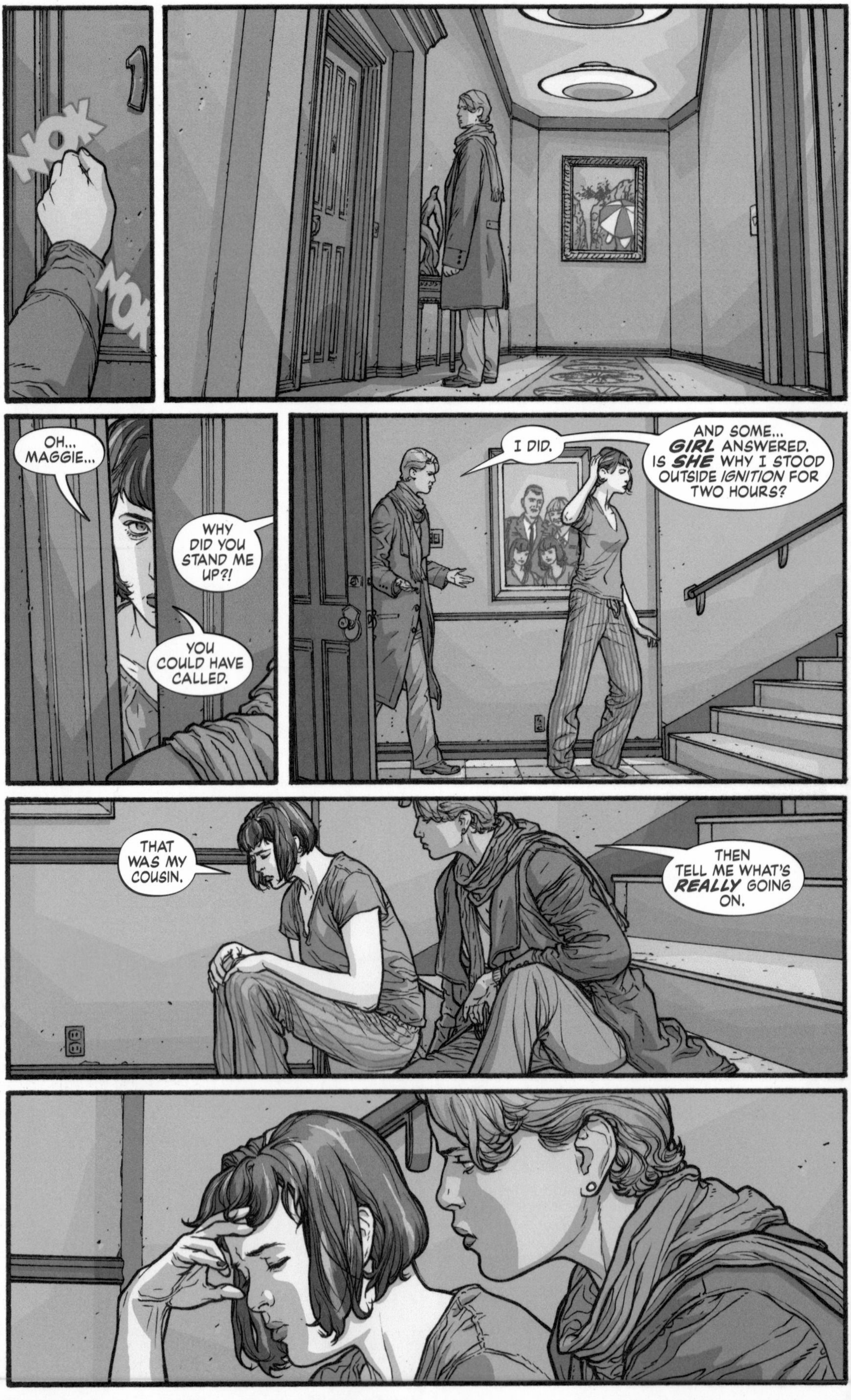
NOK
NOK
OH... MAGGIE...
WHY DID YOU STAND ME UP?!
YOU COULD HAVE CALLED.
I DID.
AND SOME... GIRL ANSWERED. IS SHE WHY I STOOD OUTSIDE IGNITION FOR TWO HOURS?
THAT WAS MY COUSIN.
THEN TELL ME WHAT'S REALLY GOING ON.

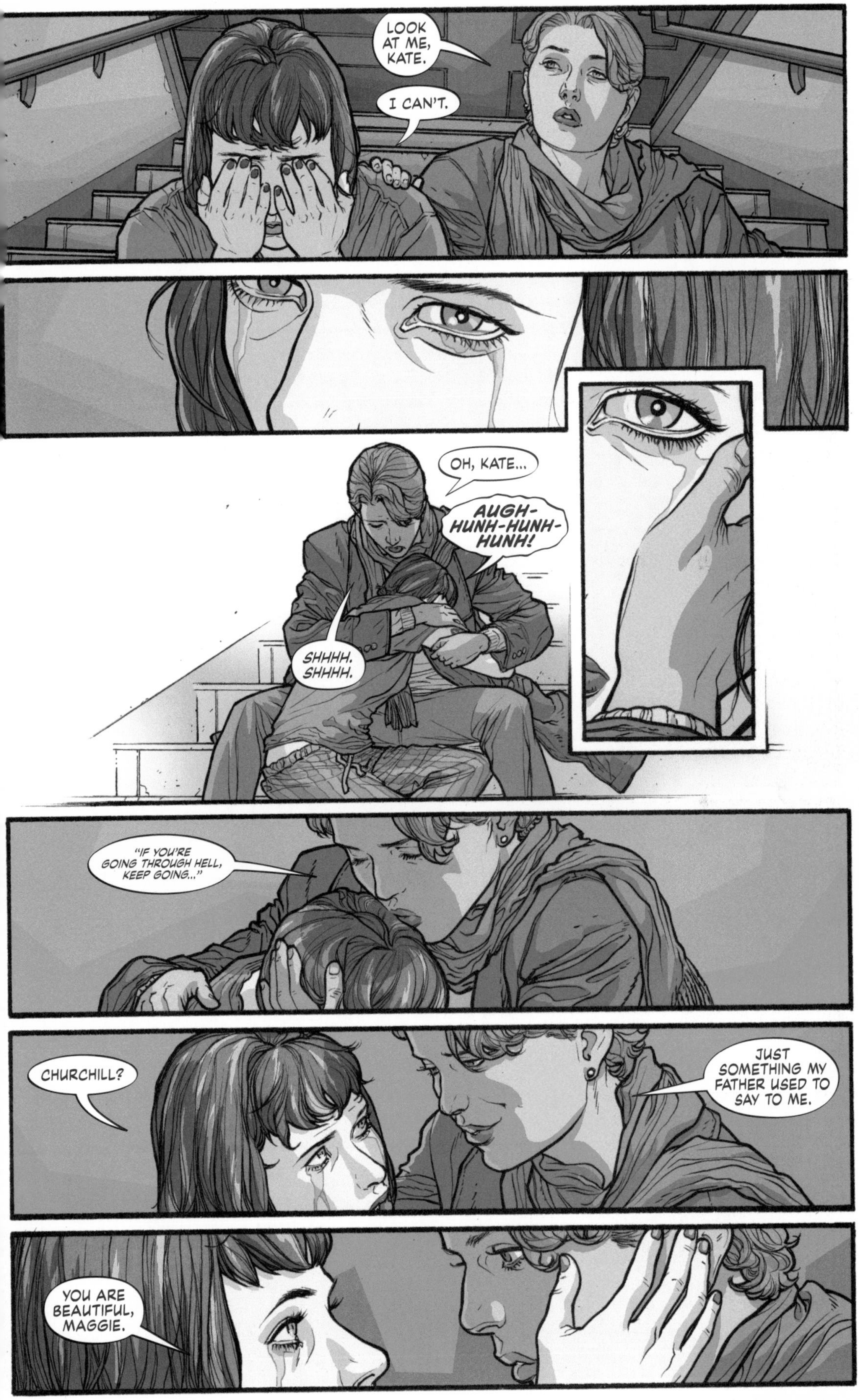
LOOK AT ME, KATE.
I CAN'T.
OH, KATE...
AUGH-HUNH-HUNH-HUNH!
SHHHH. SHHHH.
"IF YOU'RE GOING THROUGH HELL, KEEP GOING..."
CHURCHILL?
JUST SOMETHING MY FATHER USED TO SAY TO ME.
YOU ARE BEAUTIFUL, MAGGIE.

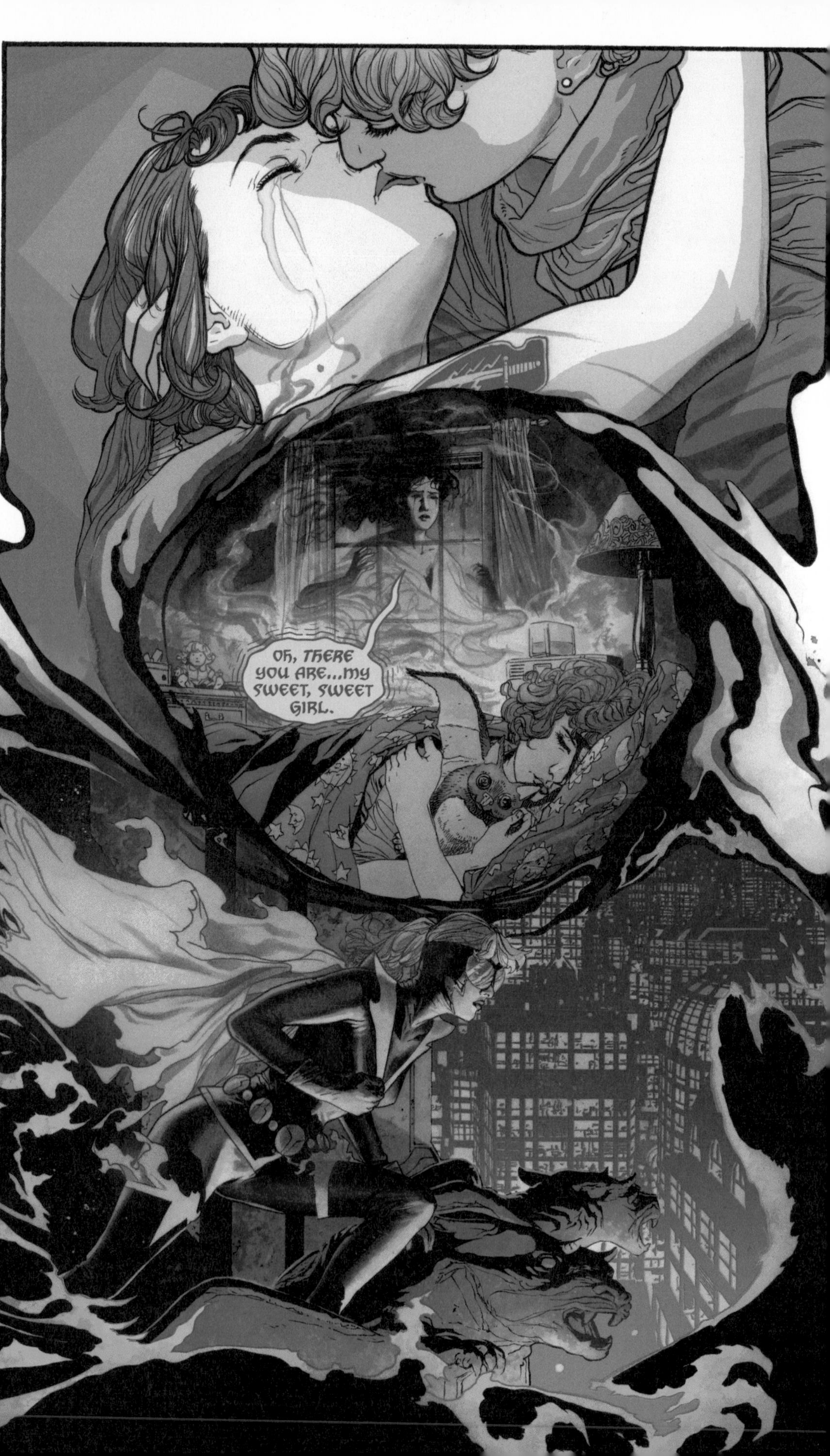
OH, THERE YOU ARE...MY SWEET, SWEET GIRL.

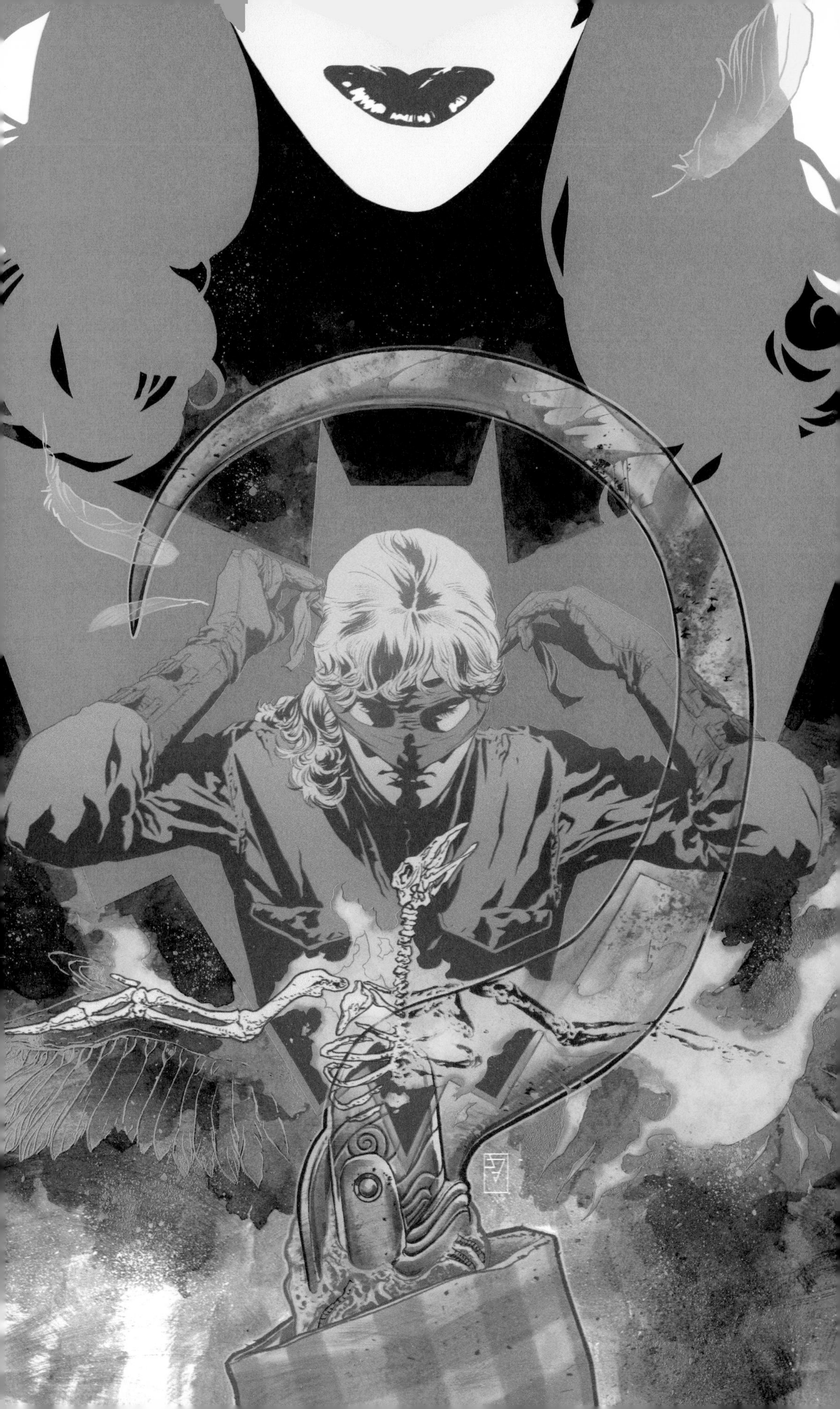

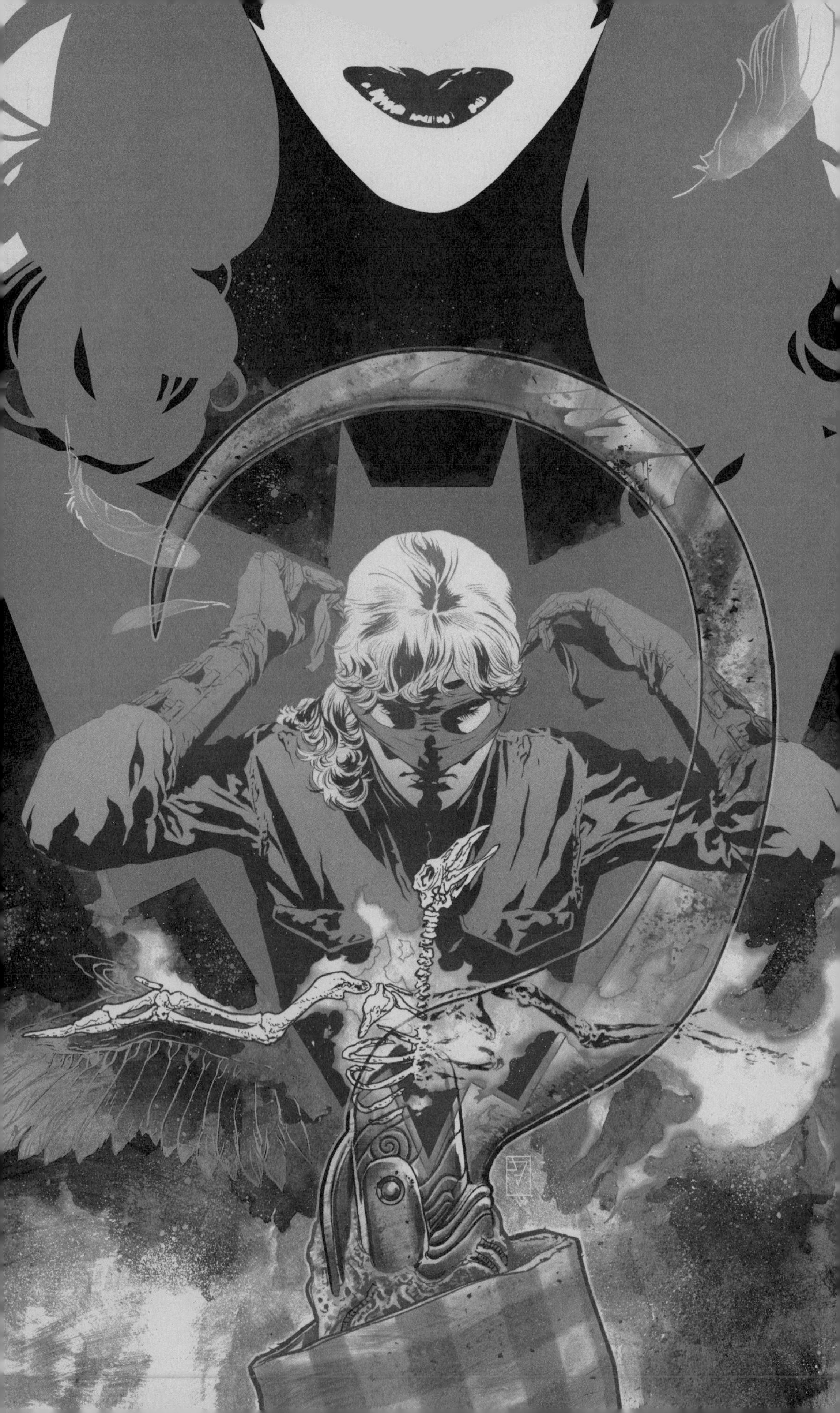

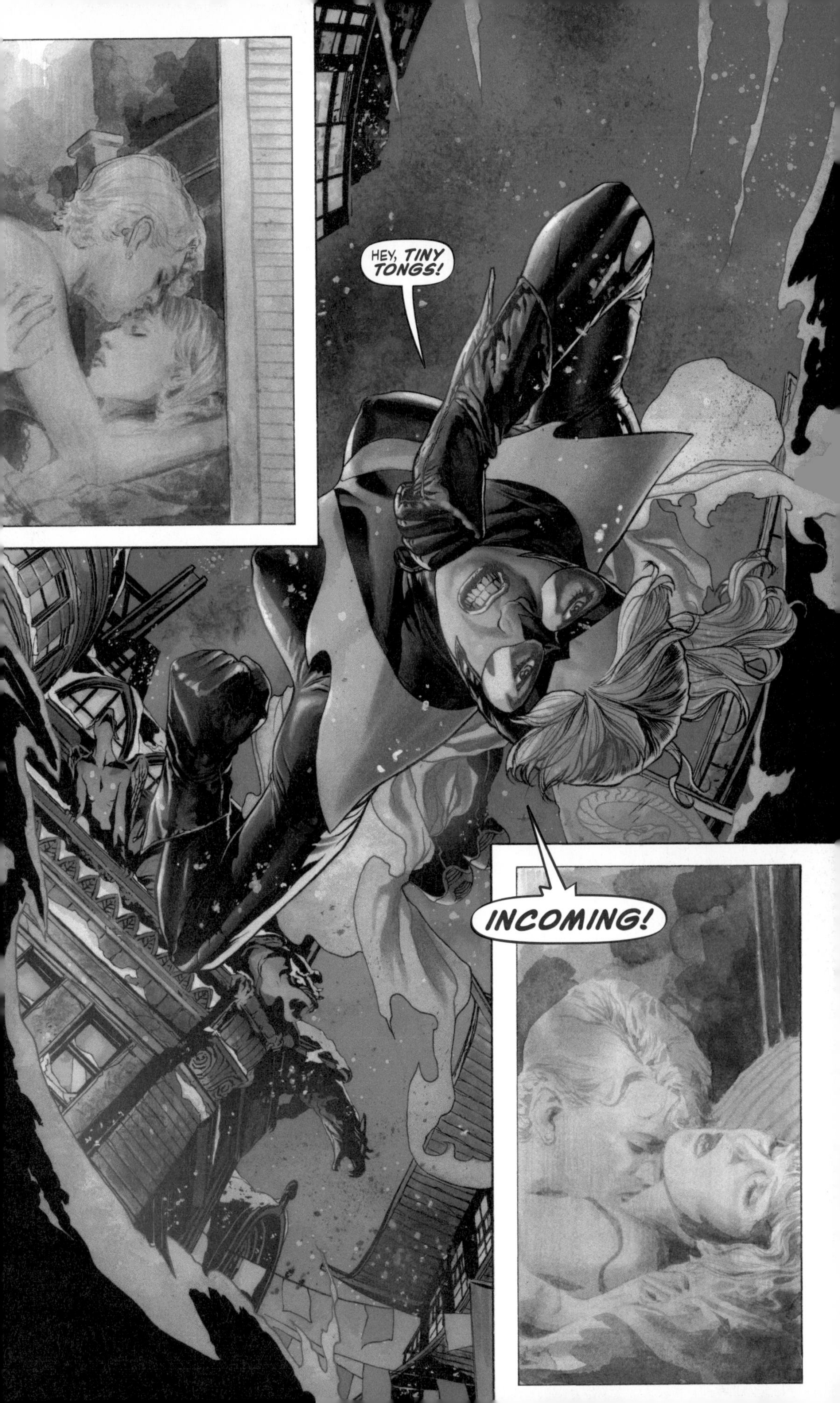
HEY, TINY TONGS!
INCOMING!

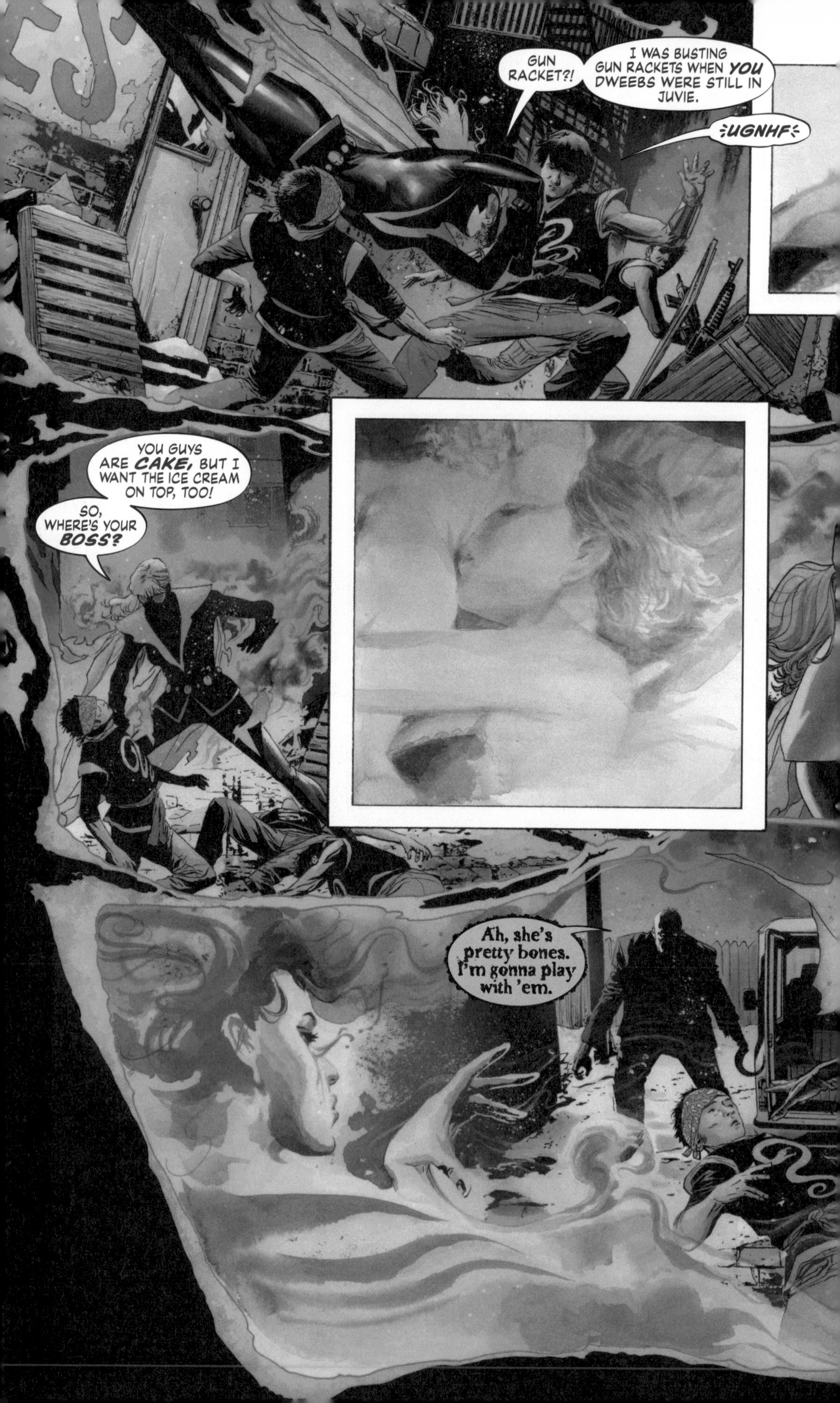
GUN RACKET?!
I WAS BUSTING GUN RACKETS WHEN YOU DWEEBS WERE STILL IN JUVIE.
UGNHF
YOU GUYS ARE CAKE, BUT I WANT THE ICE CREAM ON TOP, TOO!
SO, WHERE'S YOUR BOSS?
Ah, she's pretty bones. I'm gonna play with 'em.

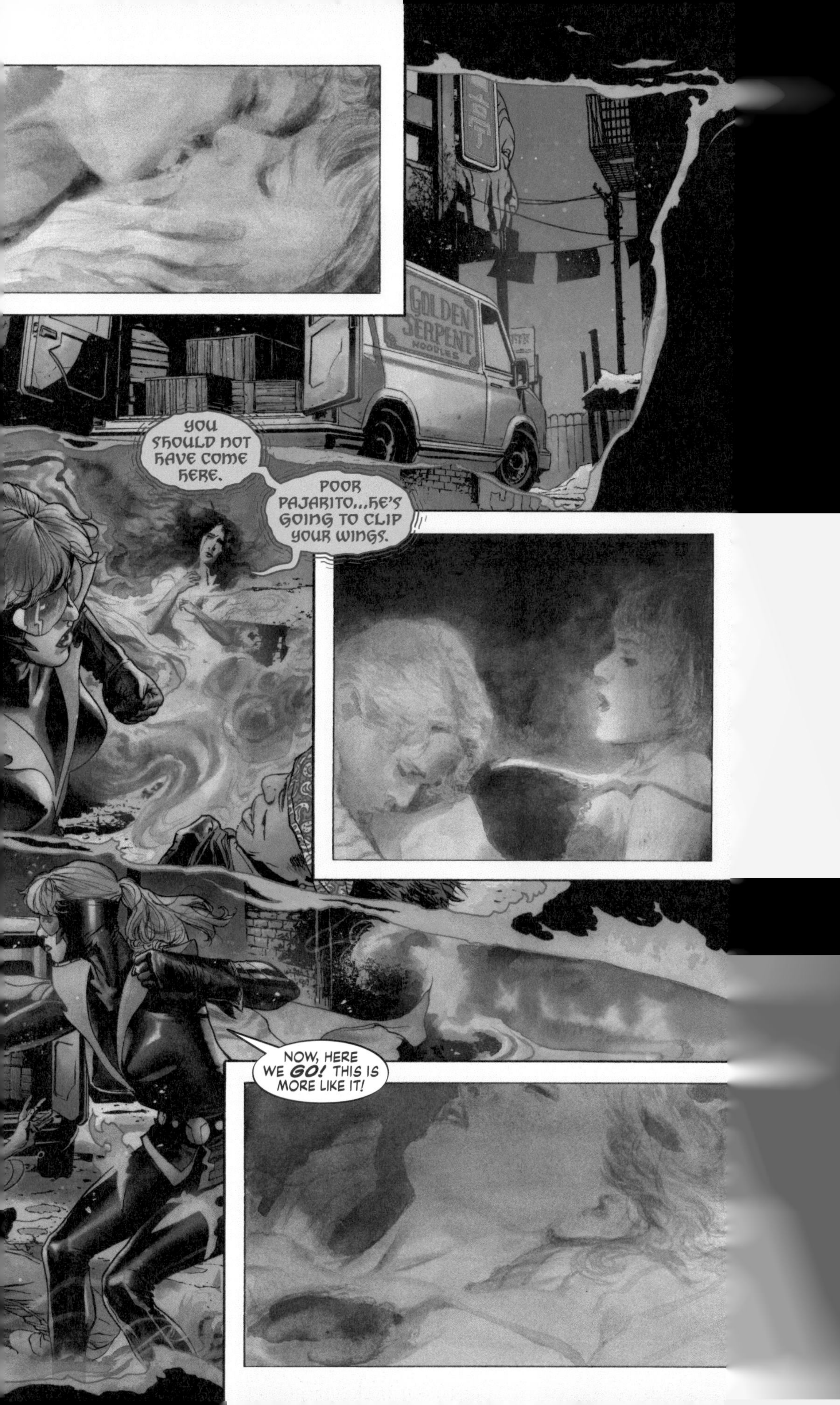

GOLDEN SERPENT NOODLES
YOU SHOULD NOT HAVE COME HERE.
POOR PAJARITO...HE'S GOING TO CLIP YOUR WINGS.
NOW, HERE WE *GO!* THIS IS MORE LIKE IT!

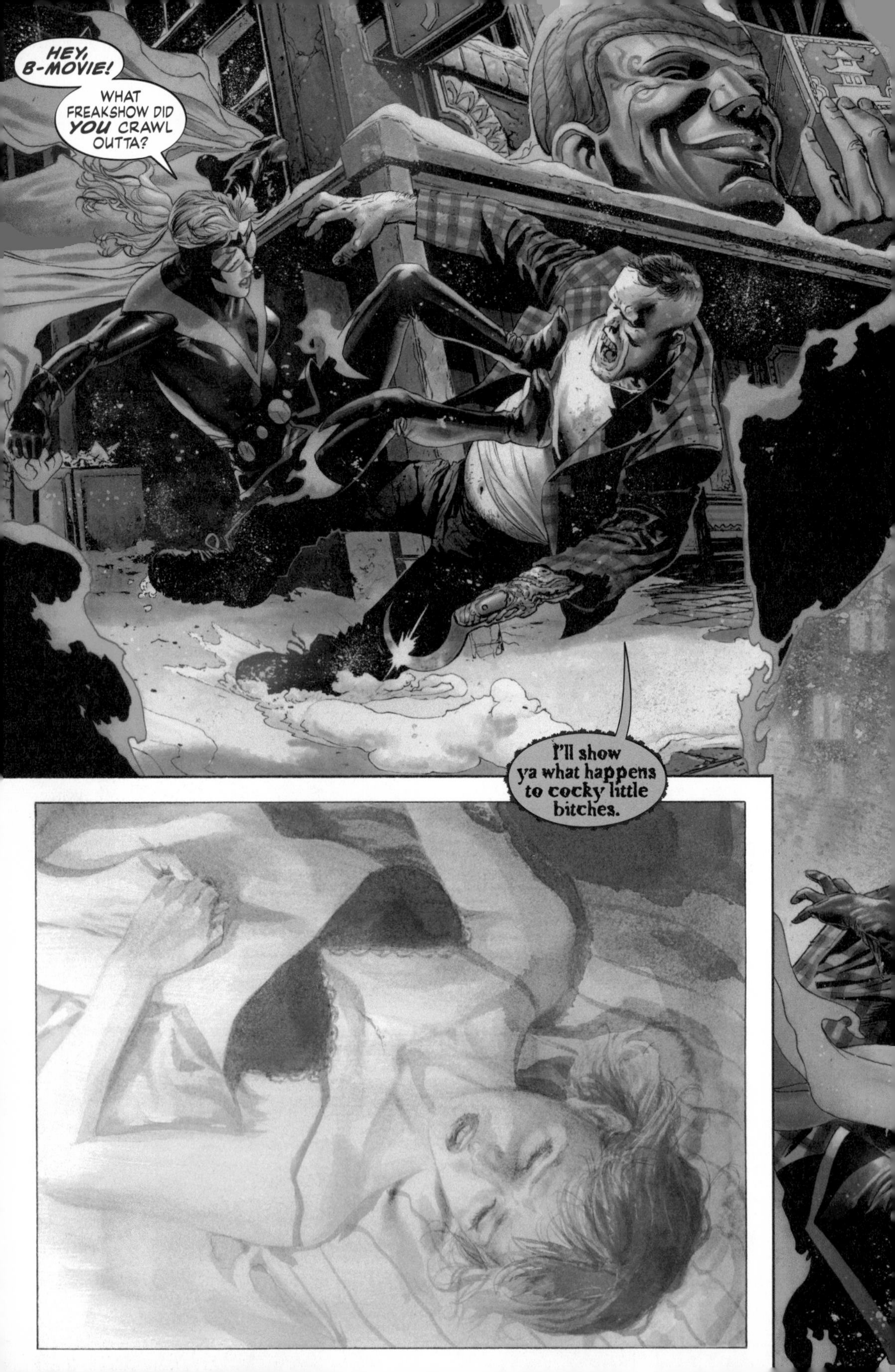
HEY, B-MOVIE!
WHAT FREAKSHOW DID YOU CRAWL OUTTA?
I'll show ya what happens to cocky little bitches.

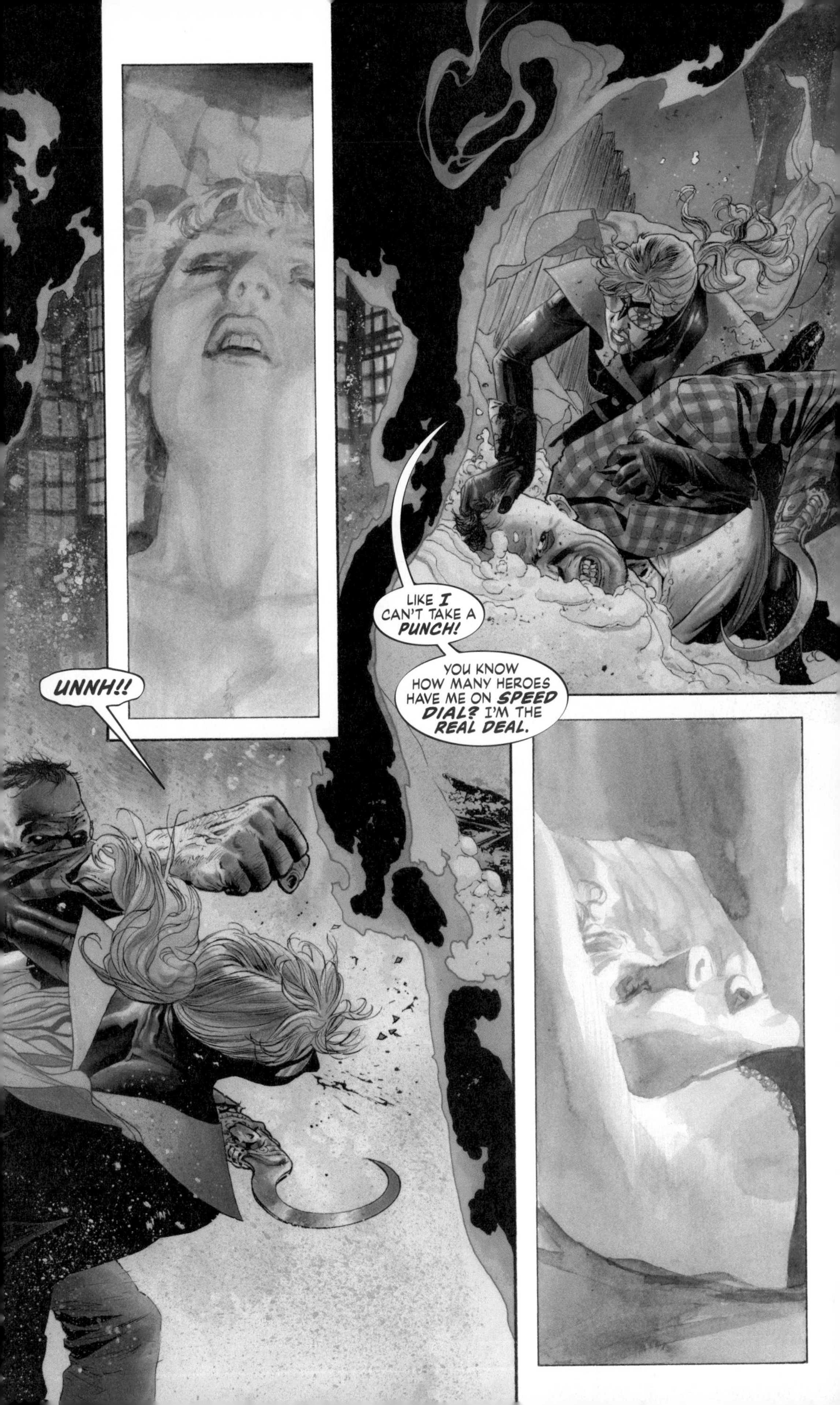
LIKE I CAN'T TAKE A PUNCH!
YOU KNOW HOW MANY HEROES HAVE ME ON SPEED DIAL? I'M THE REAL DEAL.
UNNH!!

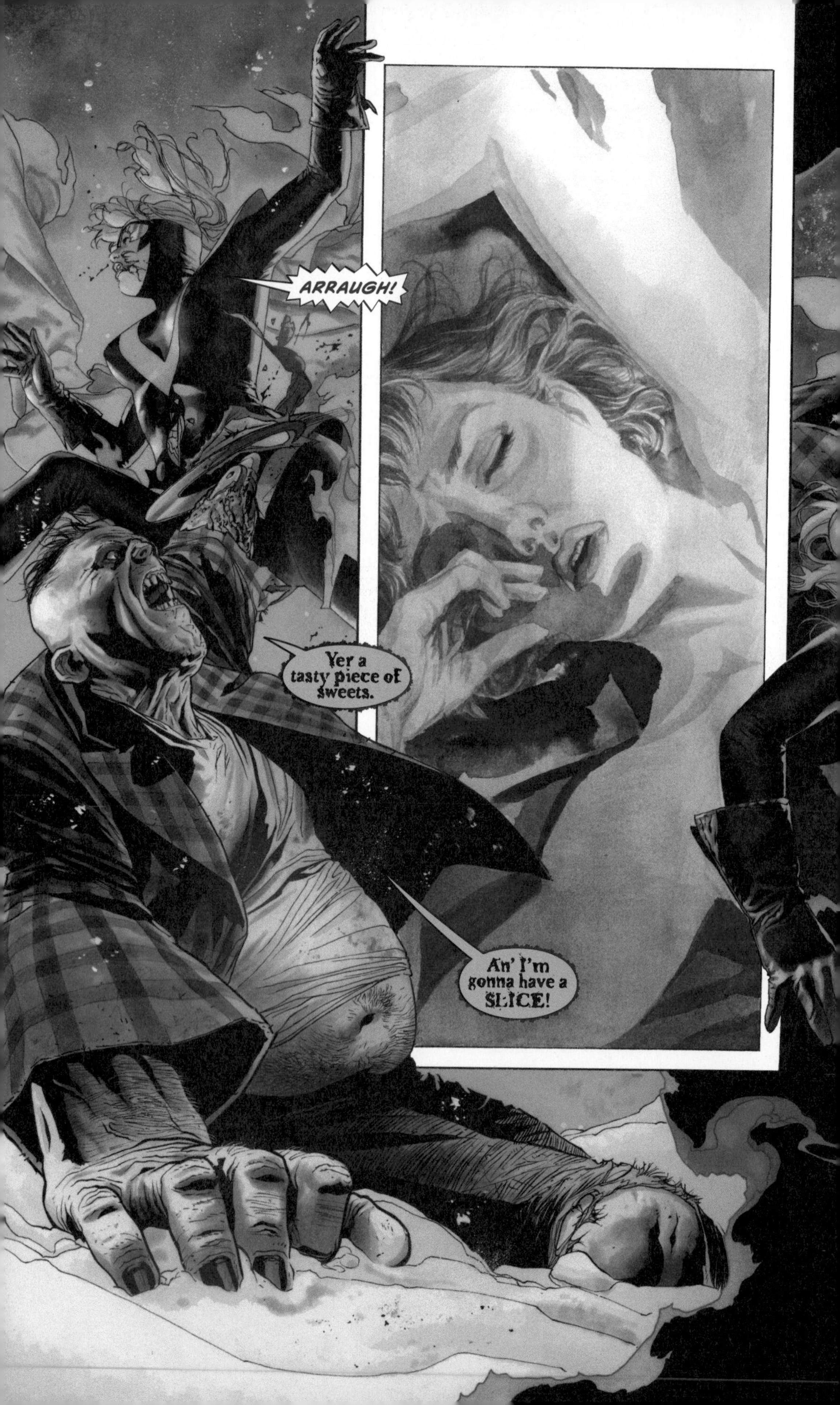
ARRAUGH!
Yer a tasty piece of sweets.
An' I'm gonna have a SLICE!

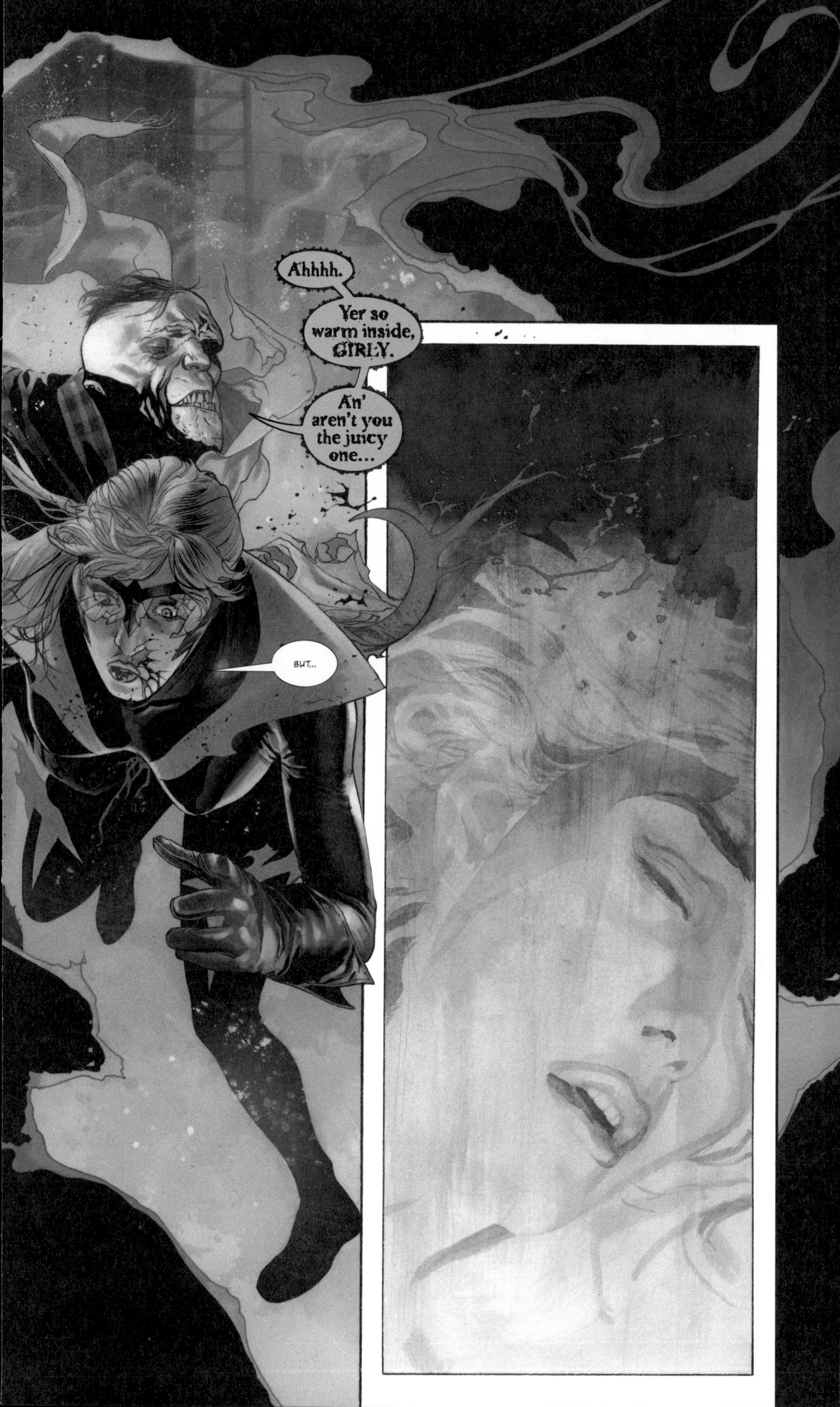
Ahhhh.
Yer so warm inside, GIRLY.
An' aren't you the juicy one...
BUT...

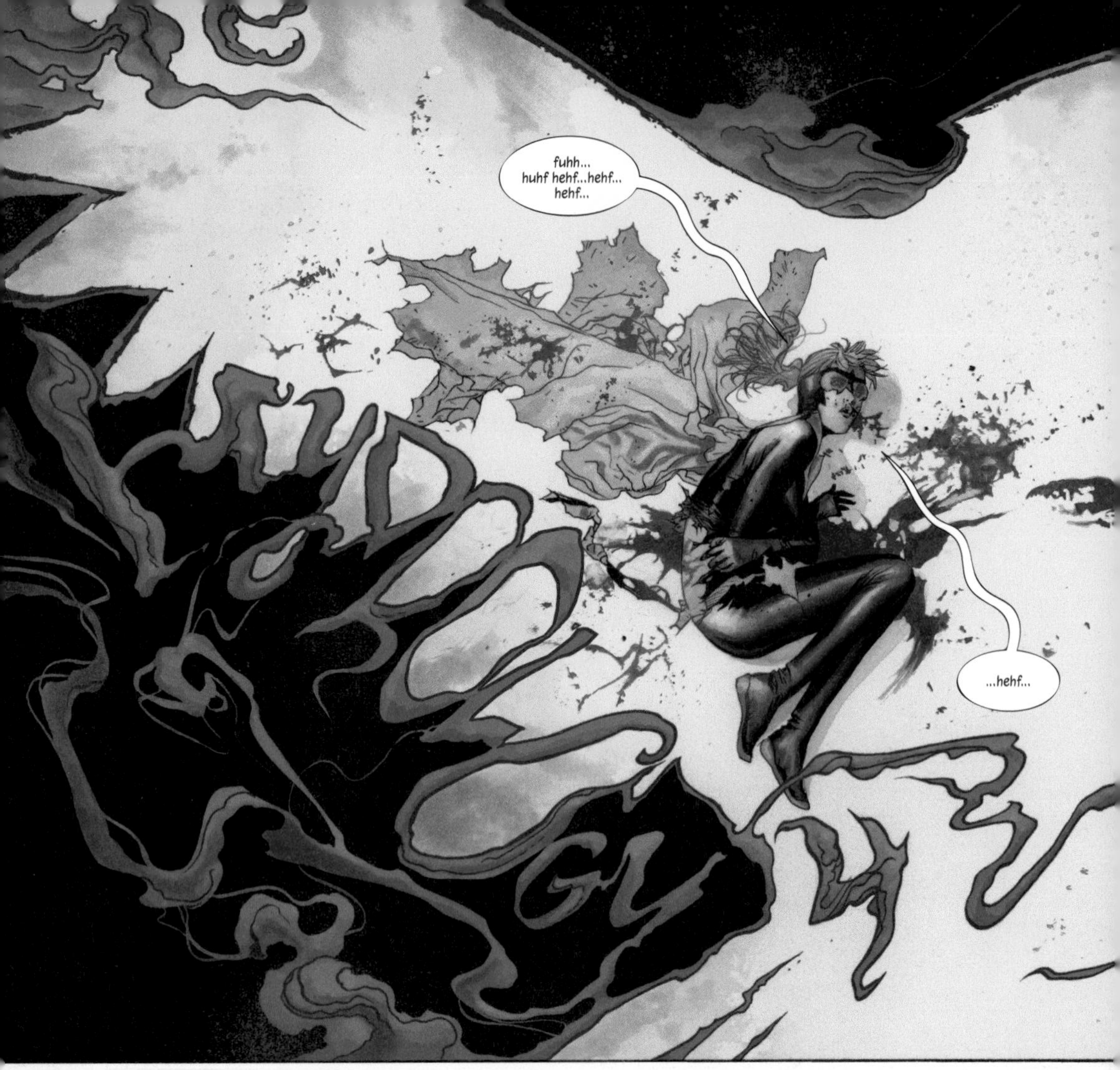
fuhh...
huhf hehf...hehf...
hehf...
...hehf...

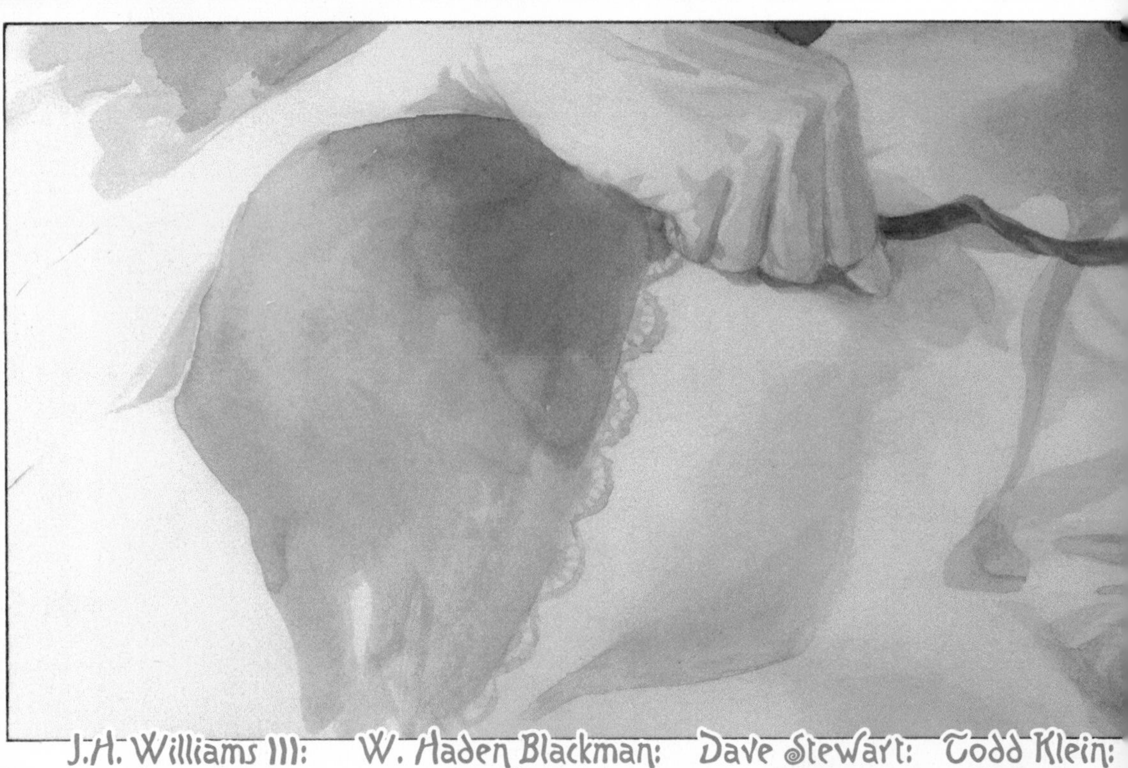

J.H. Williams III: co-writer & artist   W. Haden Blackman: co-writer   Dave Stewart: colors   Todd Klein: letters

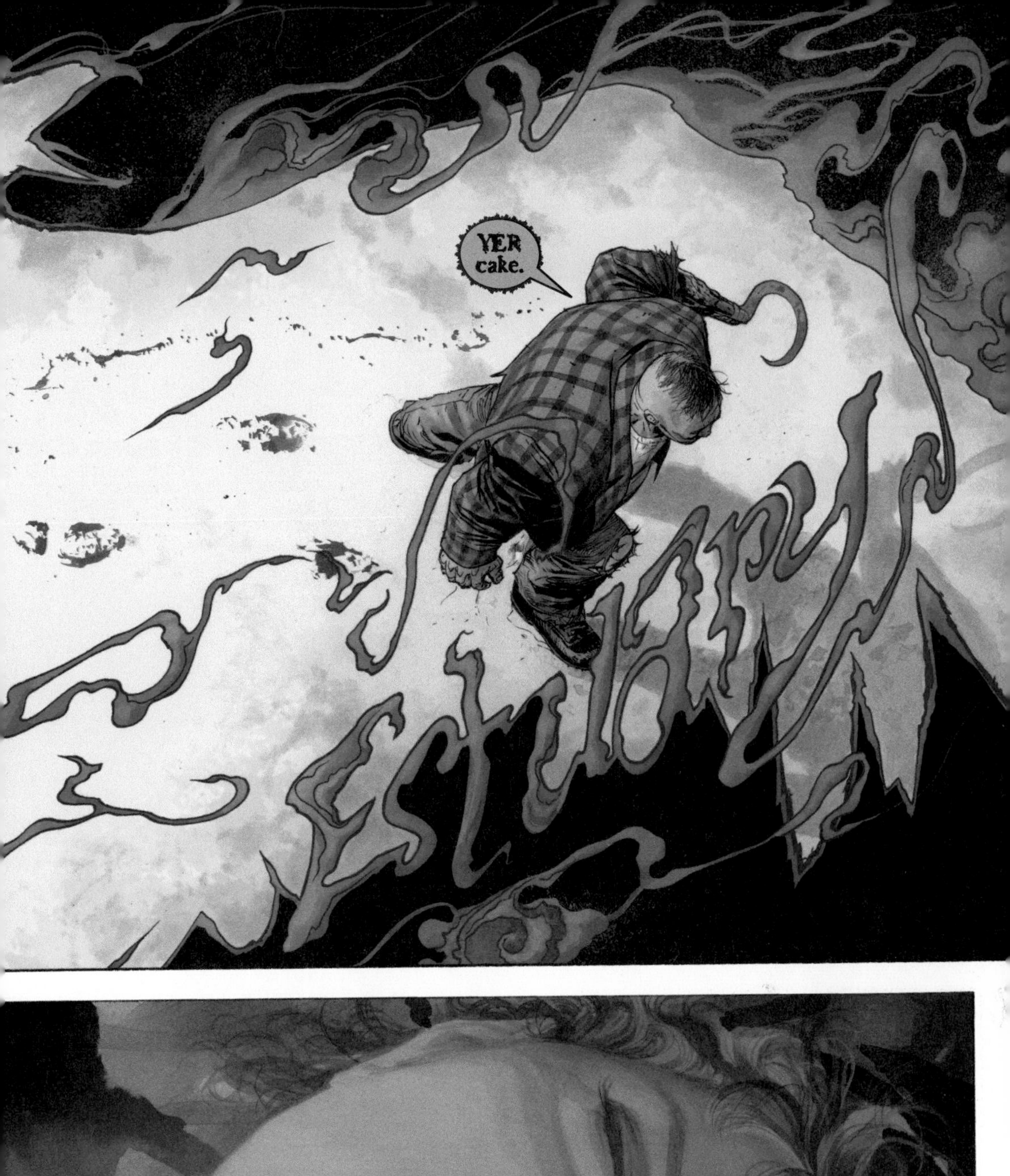
YER cake.
Estuary

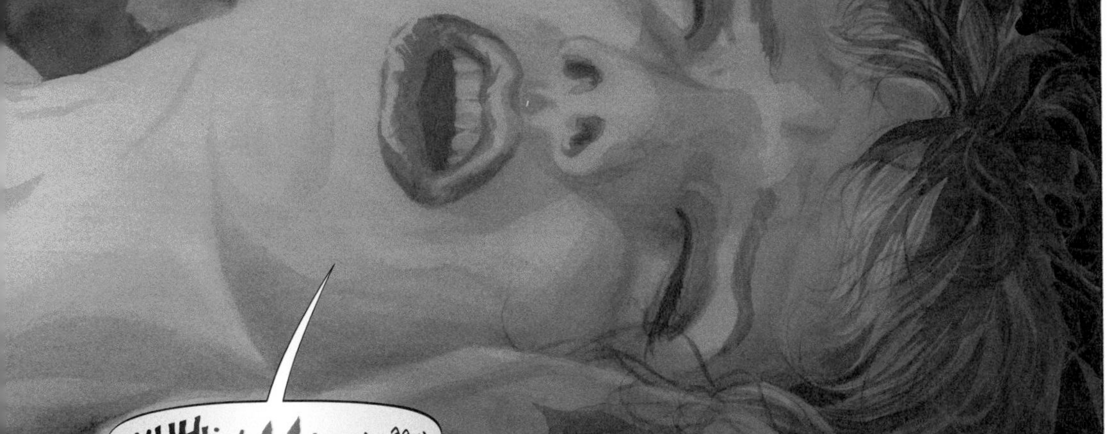
HUHlinhAAAAAAAaa...

Rickey Purdin: asst. ed.   Harvey Richards: assoc. ed.   Michael Marts: editor

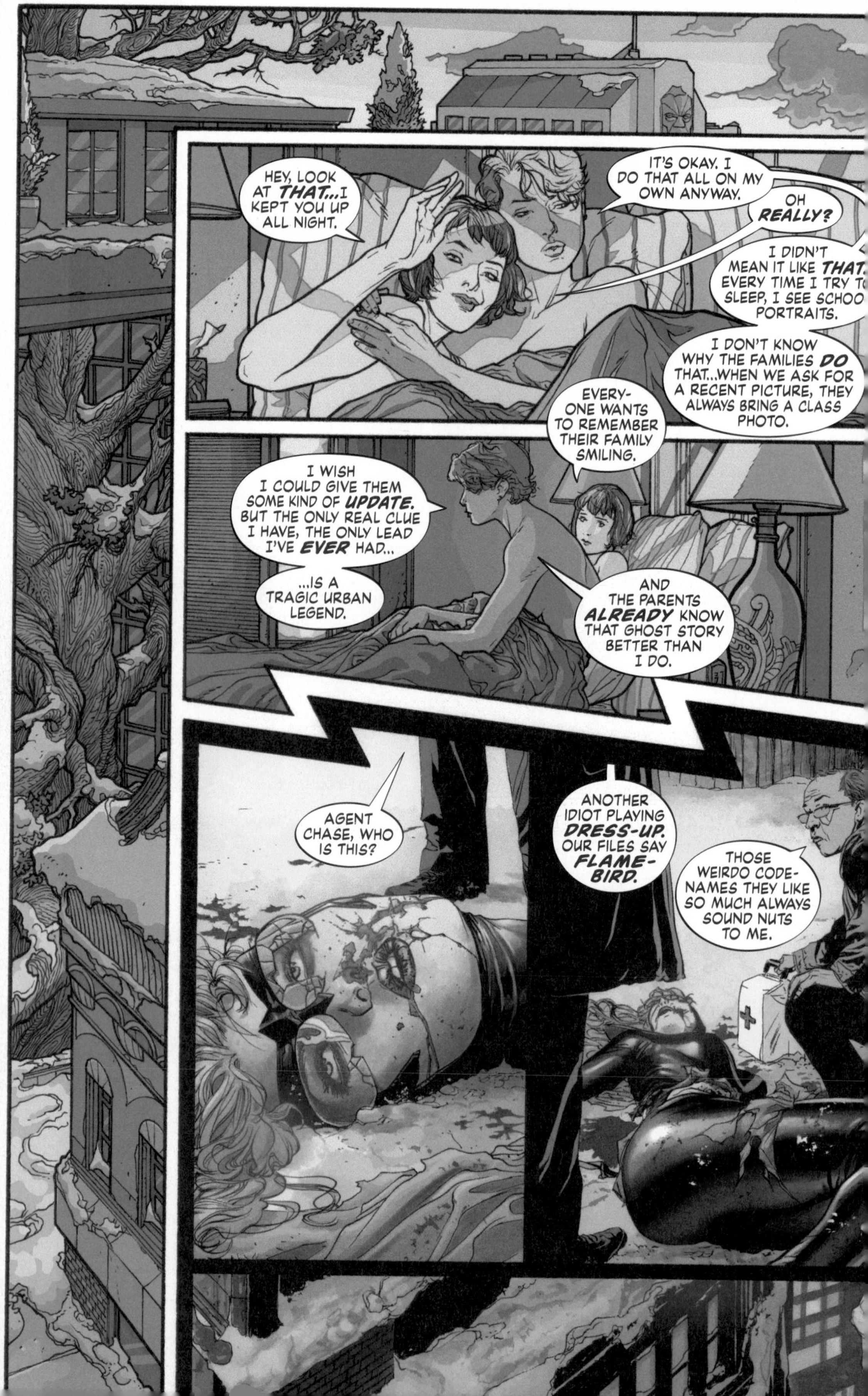
HEY, LOOK AT THAT...I KEPT YOU UP ALL NIGHT.
IT'S OKAY. I DO THAT ALL ON MY OWN ANYWAY.
OH REALLY?
I DIDN'T MEAN IT LIKE THAT. EVERY TIME I TRY TO SLEEP, I SEE SCHOOL PORTRAITS.
I DON'T KNOW WHY THE FAMILIES DO THAT...WHEN WE ASK FOR A RECENT PICTURE, THEY ALWAYS BRING A CLASS PHOTO.
EVERY-ONE WANTS TO REMEMBER THEIR FAMILY SMILING.
I WISH I COULD GIVE THEM SOME KIND OF UPDATE. BUT THE ONLY REAL CLUE I HAVE, THE ONLY LEAD I'VE EVER HAD...
...IS A TRAGIC URBAN LEGEND.
AND THE PARENTS ALREADY KNOW THAT GHOST STORY BETTER THAN I DO.
AGENT CHASE, WHO IS THIS?
ANOTHER IDIOT PLAYING DRESS-UP. OUR FILES SAY FLAME-BIRD.
THOSE WEIRDO CODE-NAMES THEY LIKE SO MUCH ALWAYS SOUND NUTS TO ME.

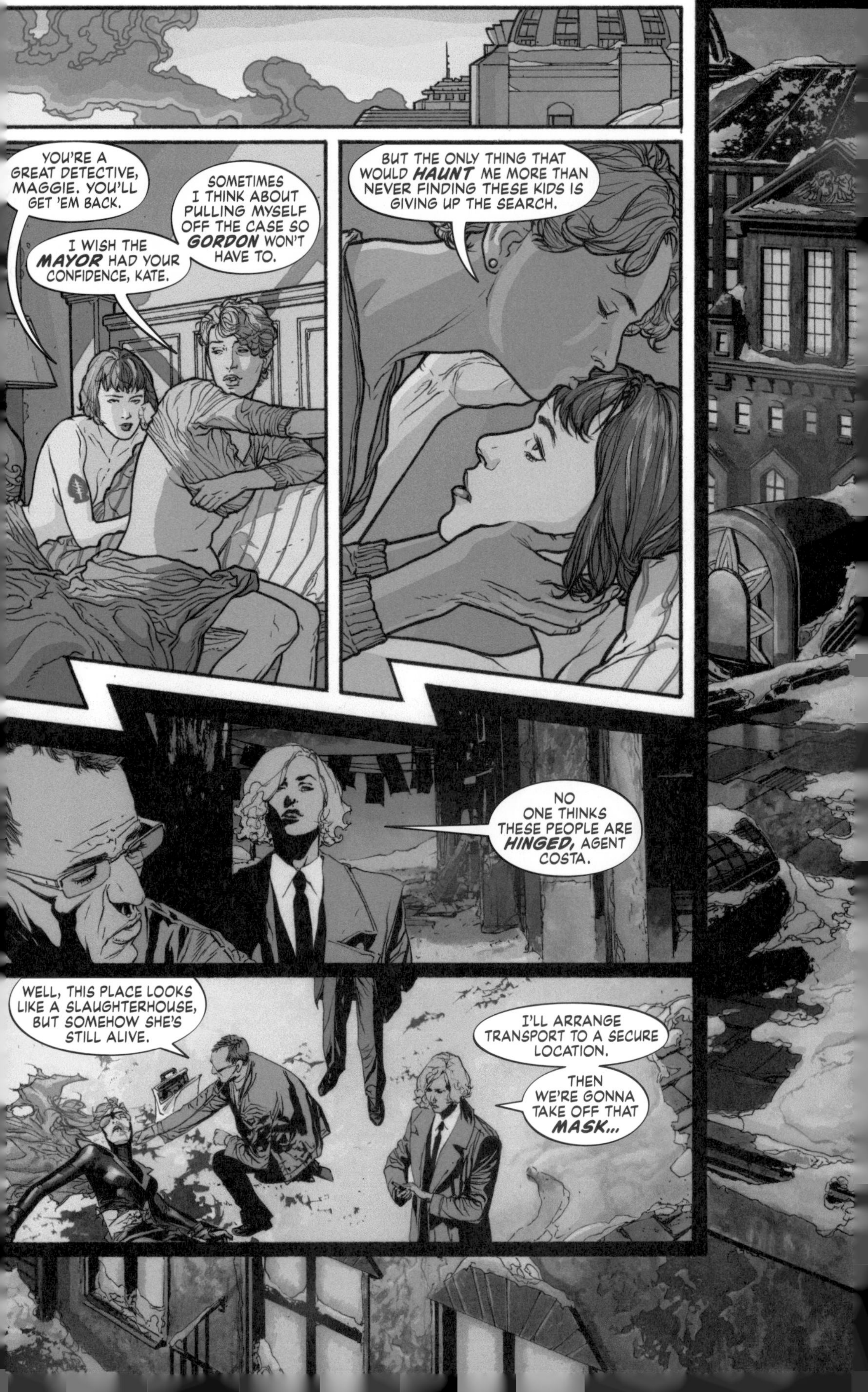
YOU'RE A GREAT DETECTIVE, MAGGIE. YOU'LL GET 'EM BACK.
I WISH THE MAYOR HAD YOUR CONFIDENCE, KATE.
SOMETIMES I THINK ABOUT PULLING MYSELF OFF THE CASE SO GORDON WON'T HAVE TO.
BUT THE ONLY THING THAT WOULD HAUNT ME MORE THAN NEVER FINDING THESE KIDS IS GIVING UP THE SEARCH.
NO ONE THINKS THESE PEOPLE ARE HINGED, AGENT COSTA.
WELL, THIS PLACE LOOKS LIKE A SLAUGHTERHOUSE, BUT SOMEHOW SHE'S STILL ALIVE.
I'LL ARRANGE TRANSPORT TO A SECURE LOCATION.
THEN WE'RE GONNA TAKE OFF THAT MASK...

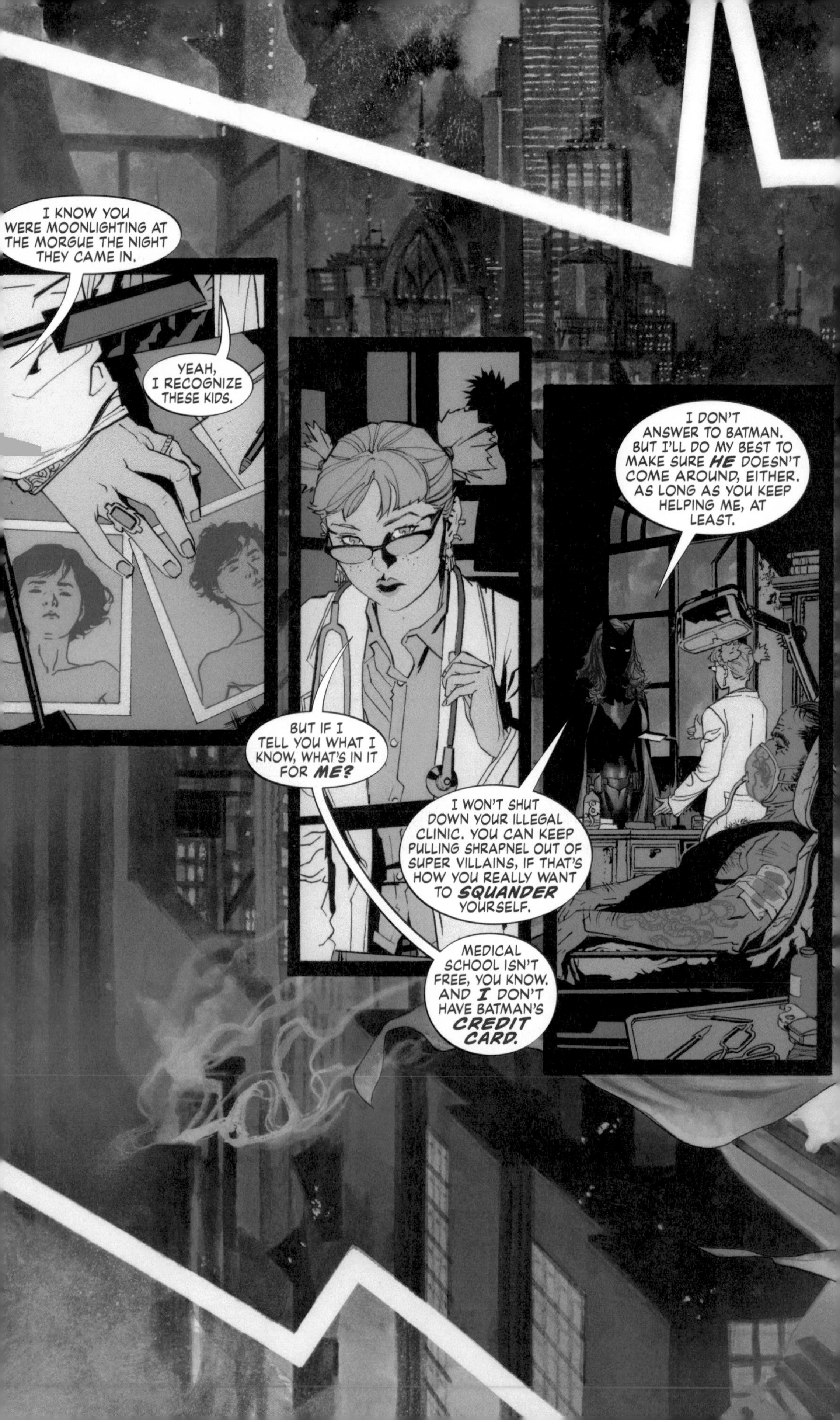
I KNOW YOU WERE MOONLIGHTING AT THE MORGUE THE NIGHT THEY CAME IN.
YEAH, I RECOGNIZE THESE KIDS.
BUT IF I TELL YOU WHAT I KNOW, WHAT'S IN IT FOR ME?
MEDICAL SCHOOL ISN'T FREE, YOU KNOW. AND I DON'T HAVE BATMAN'S CREDIT CARD.
I WON'T SHUT DOWN YOUR ILLEGAL CLINIC. YOU CAN KEEP PULLING SHRAPNEL OUT OF SUPER VILLAINS, IF THAT'S HOW YOU REALLY WANT TO SQUANDER YOURSELF.
I DON'T ANSWER TO BATMAN. BUT I'LL DO MY BEST TO MAKE SURE HE DOESN'T COME AROUND, EITHER. AS LONG AS YOU KEEP HELPING ME, AT LEAST.

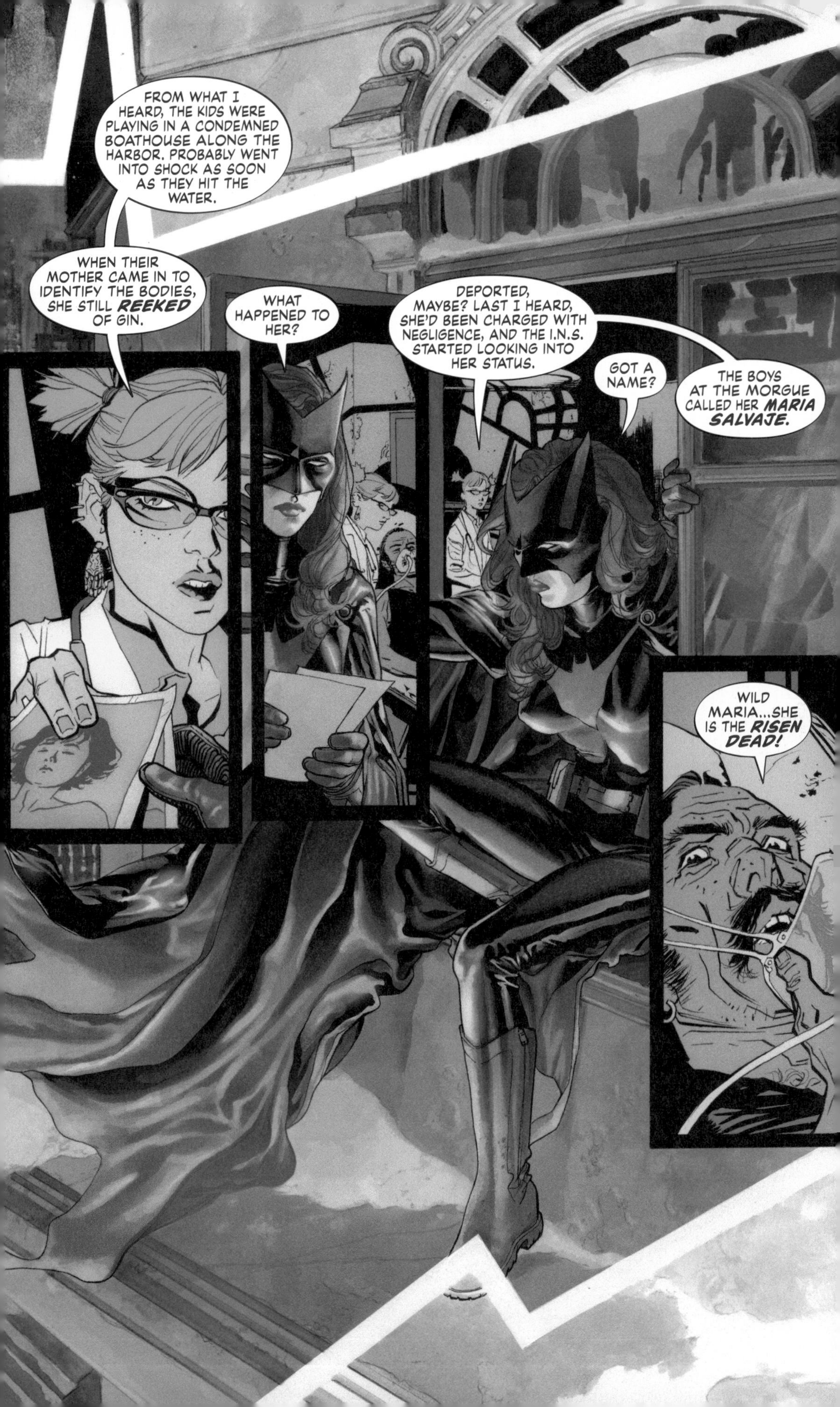
FROM WHAT I HEARD, THE KIDS WERE PLAYING IN A CONDEMNED BOATHOUSE ALONG THE HARBOR. PROBABLY WENT INTO SHOCK AS SOON AS THEY HIT THE WATER.
WHEN THEIR MOTHER CAME IN TO IDENTIFY THE BODIES, SHE STILL REEKED OF GIN.
WHAT HAPPENED TO HER?
DEPORTED, MAYBE? LAST I HEARD, SHE'D BEEN CHARGED WITH NEGLIGENCE, AND THE I.N.S. STARTED LOOKING INTO HER STATUS.
GOT A NAME?
THE BOYS AT THE MORGUE CALLED HER MARIA SALVAJE.
WILD MARIA...SHE IS THE RISEN DEAD!

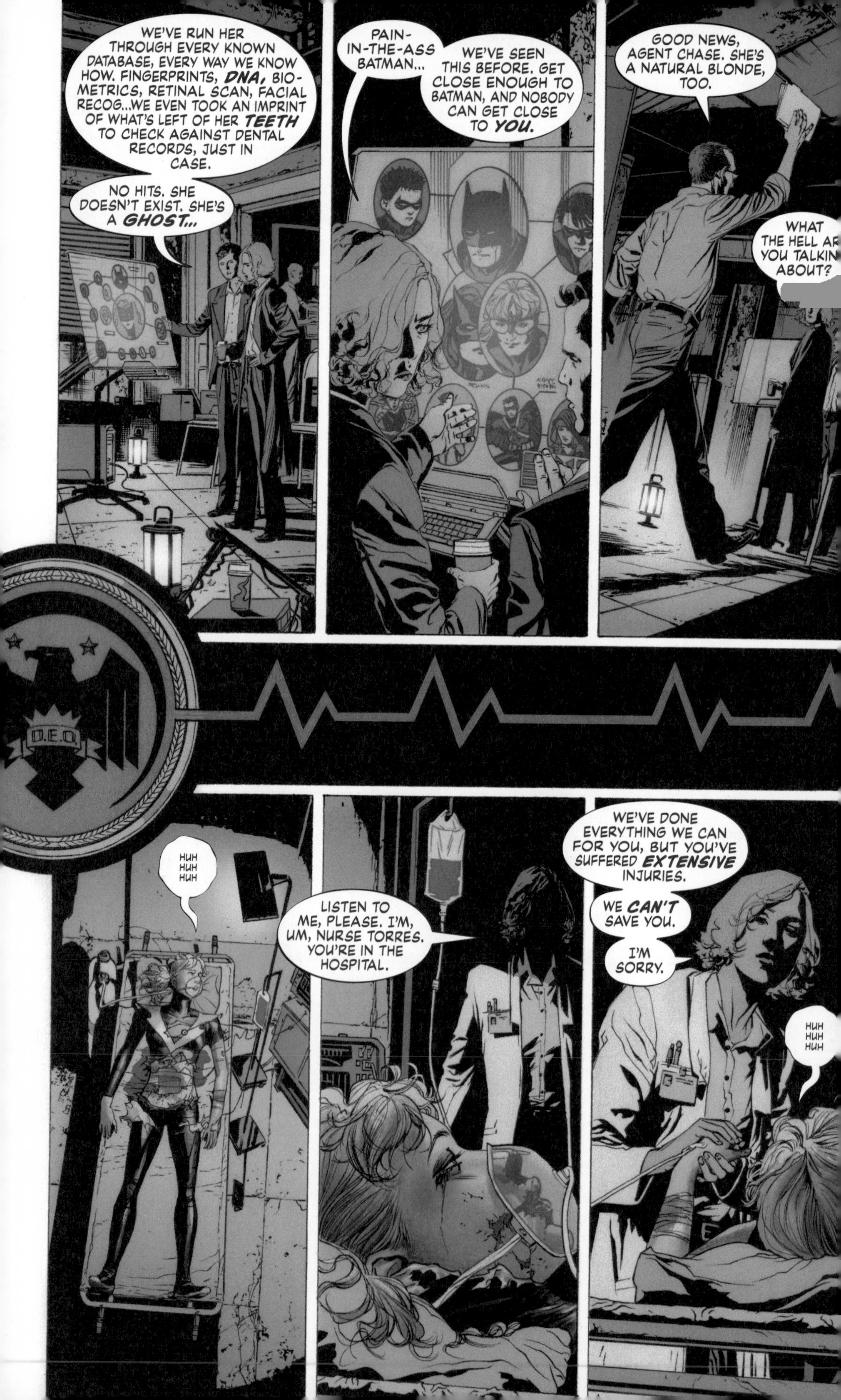
WE'VE RUN HER THROUGH EVERY KNOWN DATABASE, EVERY WAY WE KNOW HOW. FINGERPRINTS, DNA, BIO-METRICS, RETINAL SCAN, FACIAL RECOG...WE EVEN TOOK AN IMPRINT OF WHAT'S LEFT OF HER TEETH TO CHECK AGAINST DENTAL RECORDS, JUST IN CASE.
NO HITS. SHE DOESN'T EXIST. SHE'S A GHOST...
PAIN-IN-THE-ASS BATMAN...
WE'VE SEEN THIS BEFORE. GET CLOSE ENOUGH TO BATMAN, AND NOBODY CAN GET CLOSE TO YOU.
GOOD NEWS, AGENT CHASE. SHE'S A NATURAL BLONDE, TOO.
WHAT THE HELL AR YOU TALKIN ABOUT?
D.E.O.
HUH HUH HUH
LISTEN TO ME, PLEASE. I'M, UM, NURSE TORRES. YOU'RE IN THE HOSPITAL.
WE'VE DONE EVERYTHING WE CAN FOR YOU, BUT YOU'VE SUFFERED EXTENSIVE INJURIES.
WE CAN'T SAVE YOU.
I'M SORRY.
HUH HUH HUH

WE KNOW THAT BATWOMAN HAS A SIDEKICK. THE GIRL IN THAT GRAY UNIFORM WE KEEP CATCHING ON SECURITY CAMERAS? SHE'S A BLONDE.

COULD BE A WIG.

NO. WE COLLECTED BLONDE HAIRS FROM EACH OF THE SIDEKICK'S RECENT FIGHTS. THEY ALL MATCH. THEY ALL BELONG TO HER.

ONCE I REALIZED FLAMEBIRD'S *ALSO* A NATURAL BLONDE, AND ABOUT THE SAME SIZE AND AGE AS THE SIDEKICK, I COMPARED OUR SAMPLES TO HER HAIR.

ANOTHER PERFECT MATCH.

WE MAY NOT KNOW HER REAL *NAME*, BUT--

FLAMEBIRD *IS* THE BATWOMAN'S SIDEKICK.

I NEED TO CALL YOUR PARENTS, YOUR *BOYFRIEND*, ANYONE.

PLEASE, I DON'T WANT YOU TO DIE ALONE. IF YOU CAN HEAR ME, GIVE ME A NAME.

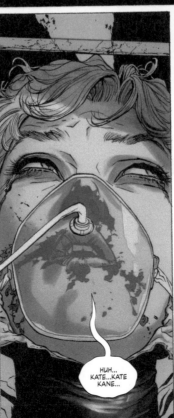

HUH... KATE...KATE KANE...

NOW THAT *CAN'T* BE A COINCIDENCE.

CHANGE HER DRESSINGS, ROLL HER OUT, AND DROP HER AT GOTHAM GENERAL.

SHE WON'T LAST THE NIGHT. NOT *HERE*, ANYWAY.

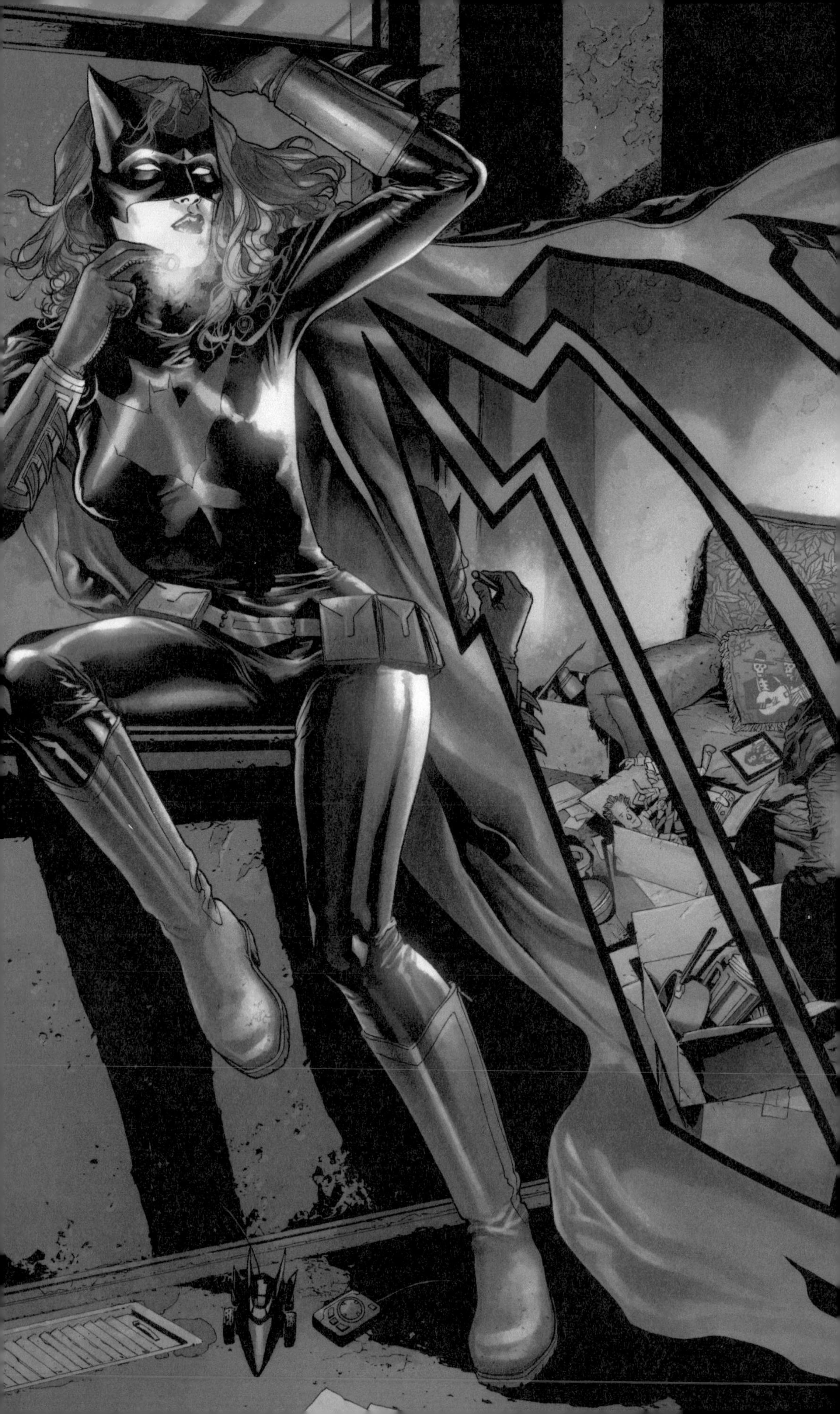

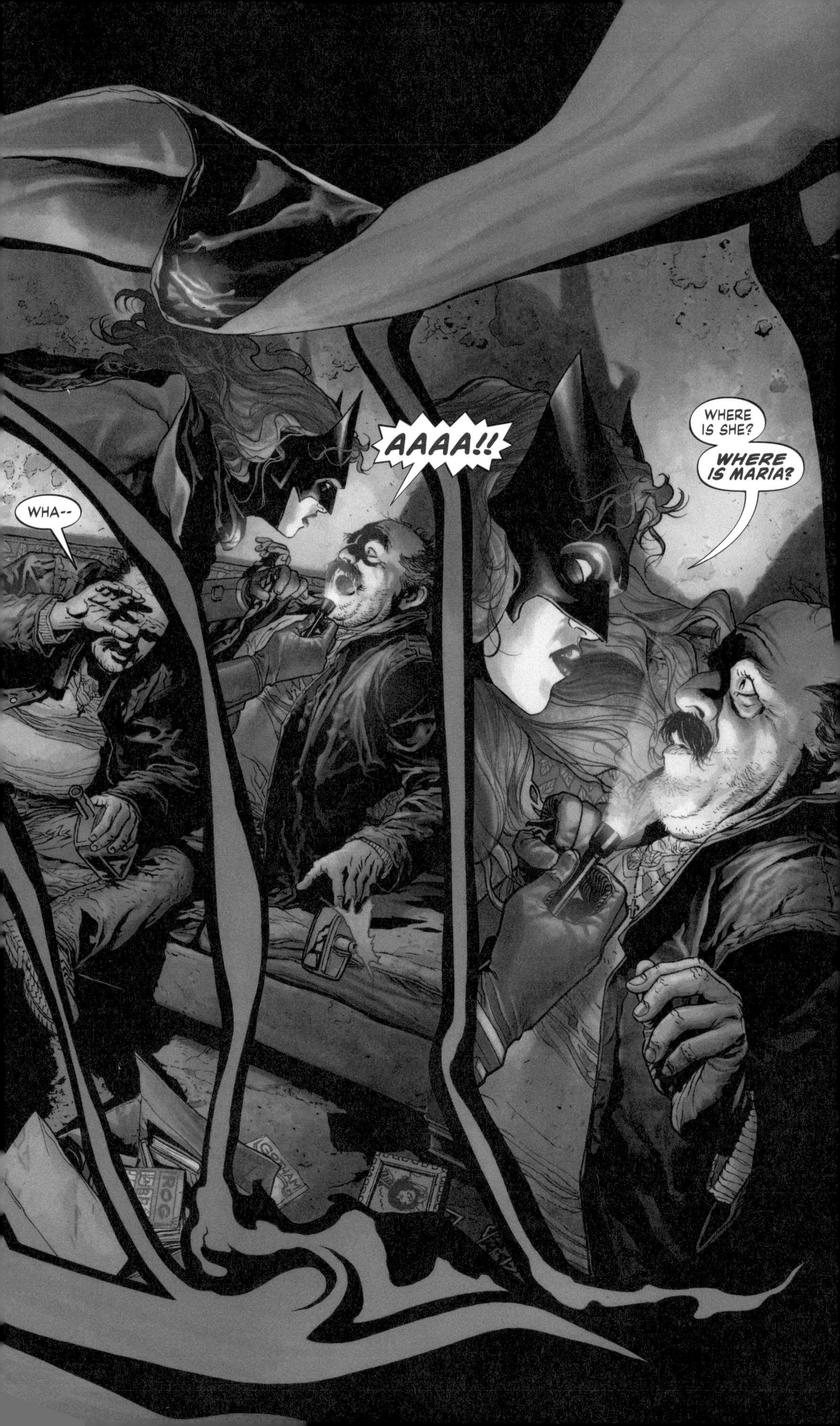
WHA--
AAAA!!
WHERE IS SHE?
WHERE IS MARIA?

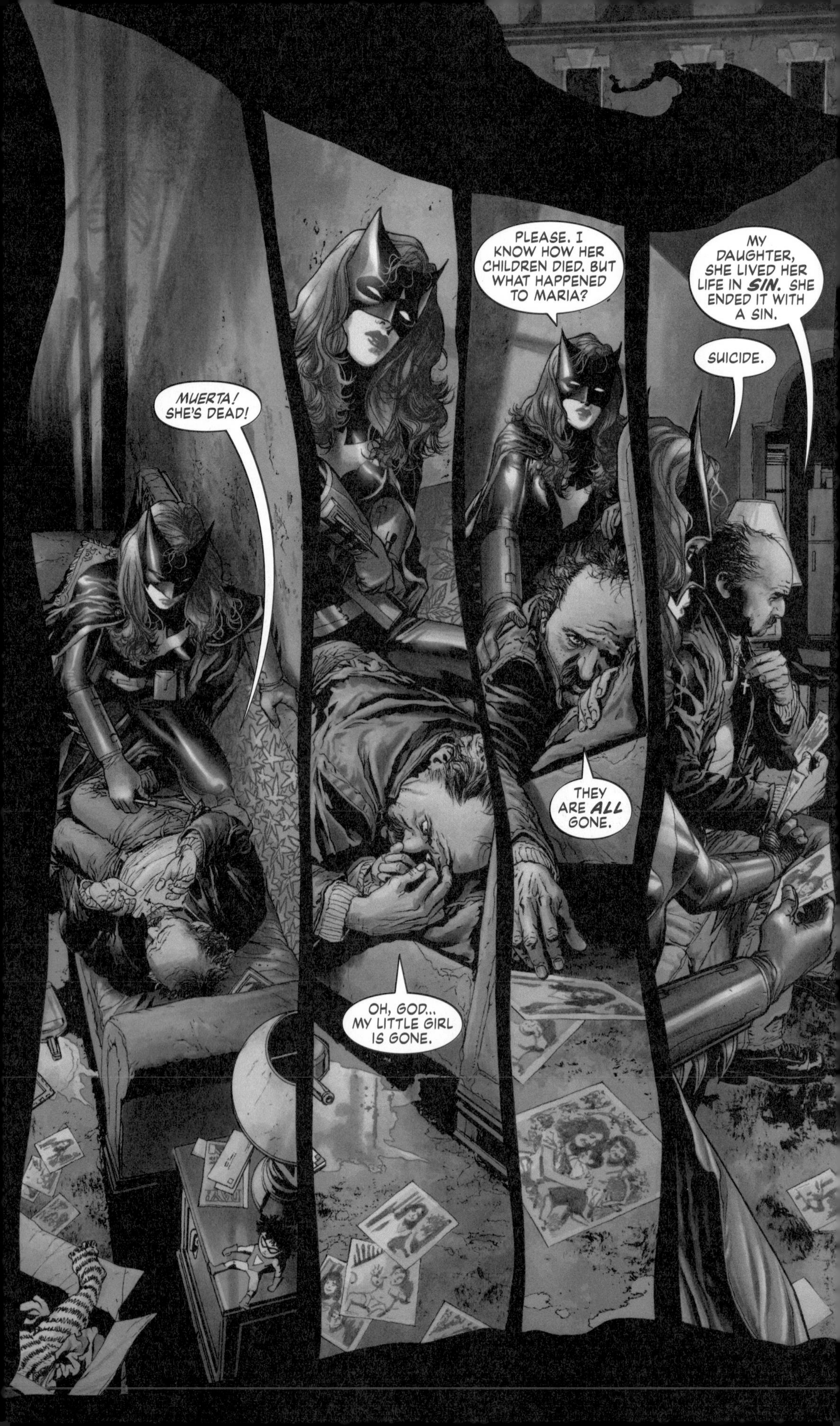
MUERTA! SHE'S DEAD!
OH, GOD... MY LITTLE GIRL IS GONE.
PLEASE. I KNOW HOW HER CHILDREN DIED. BUT WHAT HAPPENED TO MARIA?
THEY ARE ALL GONE.
MY DAUGHTER, SHE LIVED HER LIFE IN SIN. SHE ENDED IT WITH A SIN.
SUICIDE.

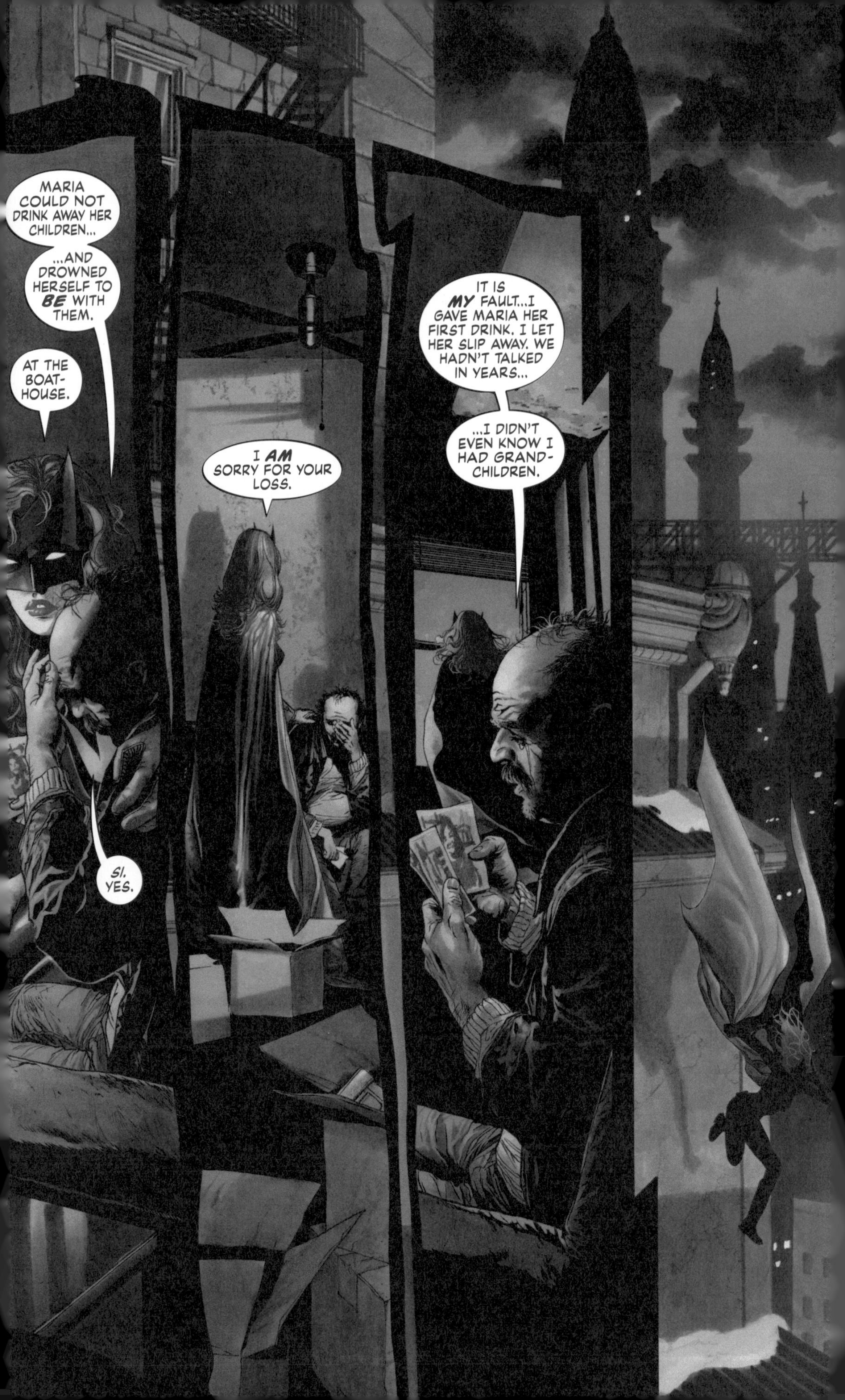

MARIA COULD NOT DRINK AWAY HER CHILDREN...
...AND DROWNED HERSELF TO BE WITH THEM.
AT THE BOAT-HOUSE.
SI. YES.
I AM SORRY FOR YOUR LOSS.
IT IS MY FAULT...I GAVE MARIA HER FIRST DRINK. I LET HER SLIP AWAY. WE HADN'T TALKED IN YEARS...
...I DIDN'T EVEN KNOW I HAD GRAND-CHILDREN.

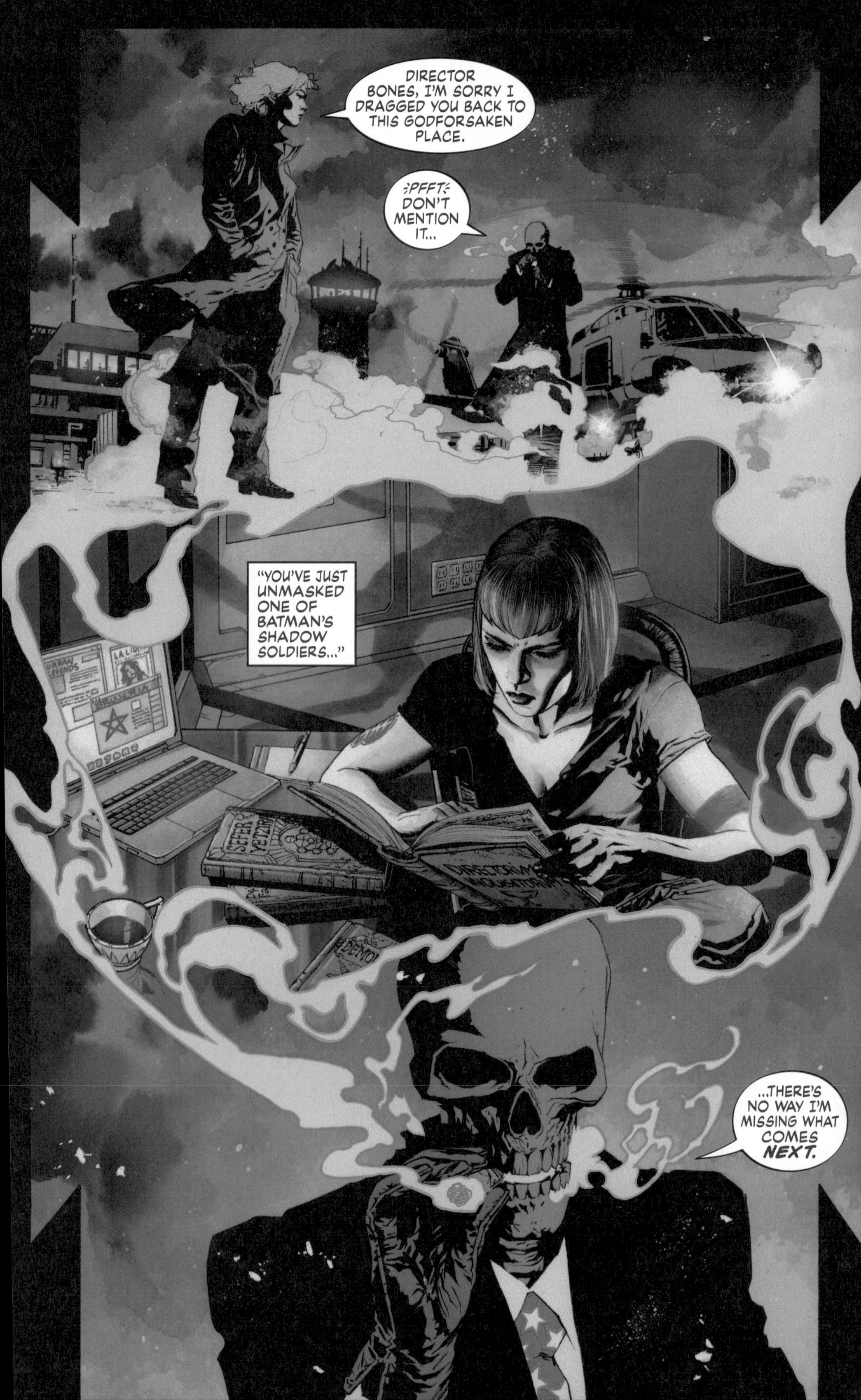
DIRECTOR BONES, I'M SORRY I DRAGGED YOU BACK TO THIS GODFORSAKEN PLACE.
PFFT DON'T MENTION IT...
"YOU'VE JUST UNMASKED ONE OF BATMAN'S SHADOW SOLDIERS..."
...THERE'S NO WAY I'M MISSING WHAT COMES *NEXT*.

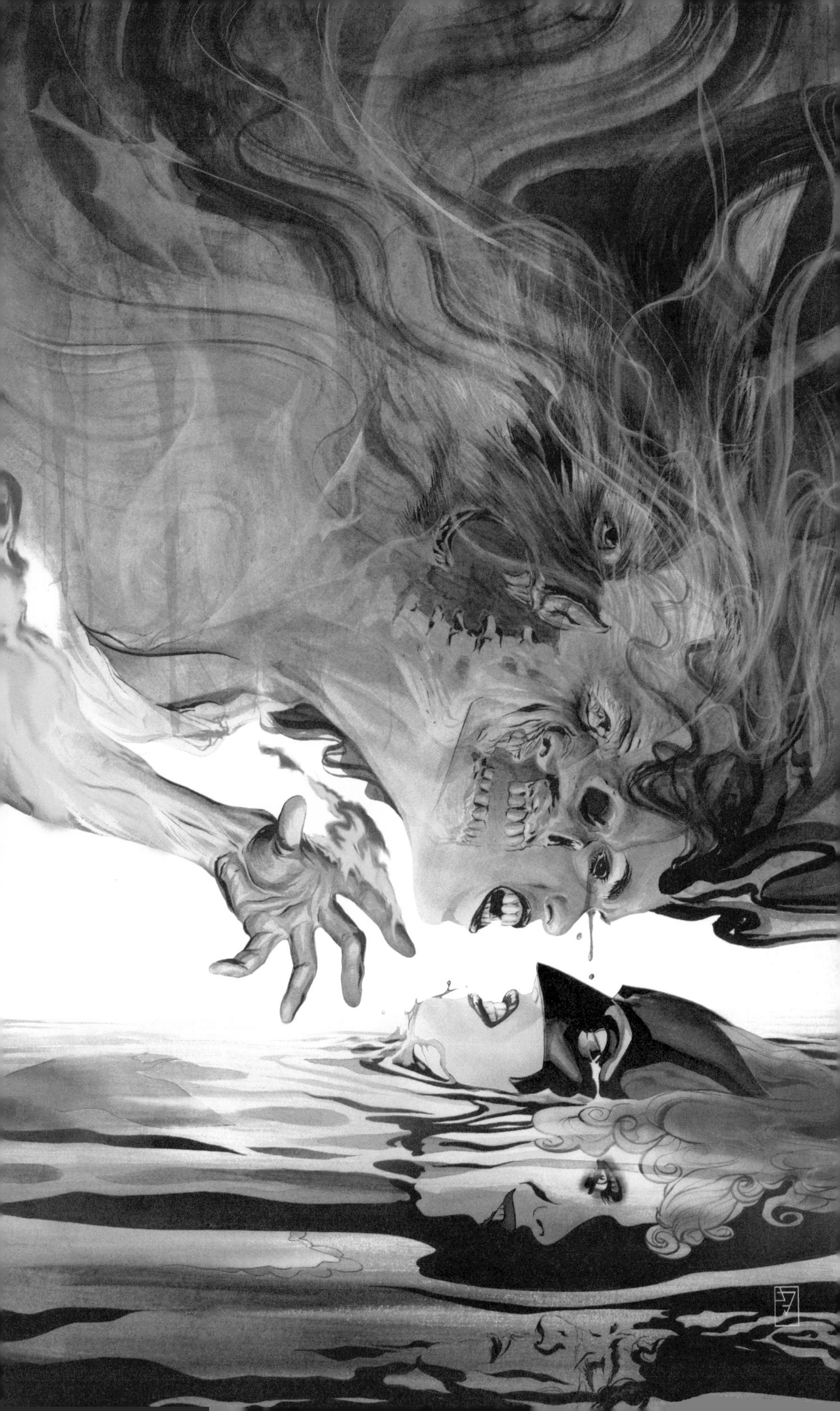

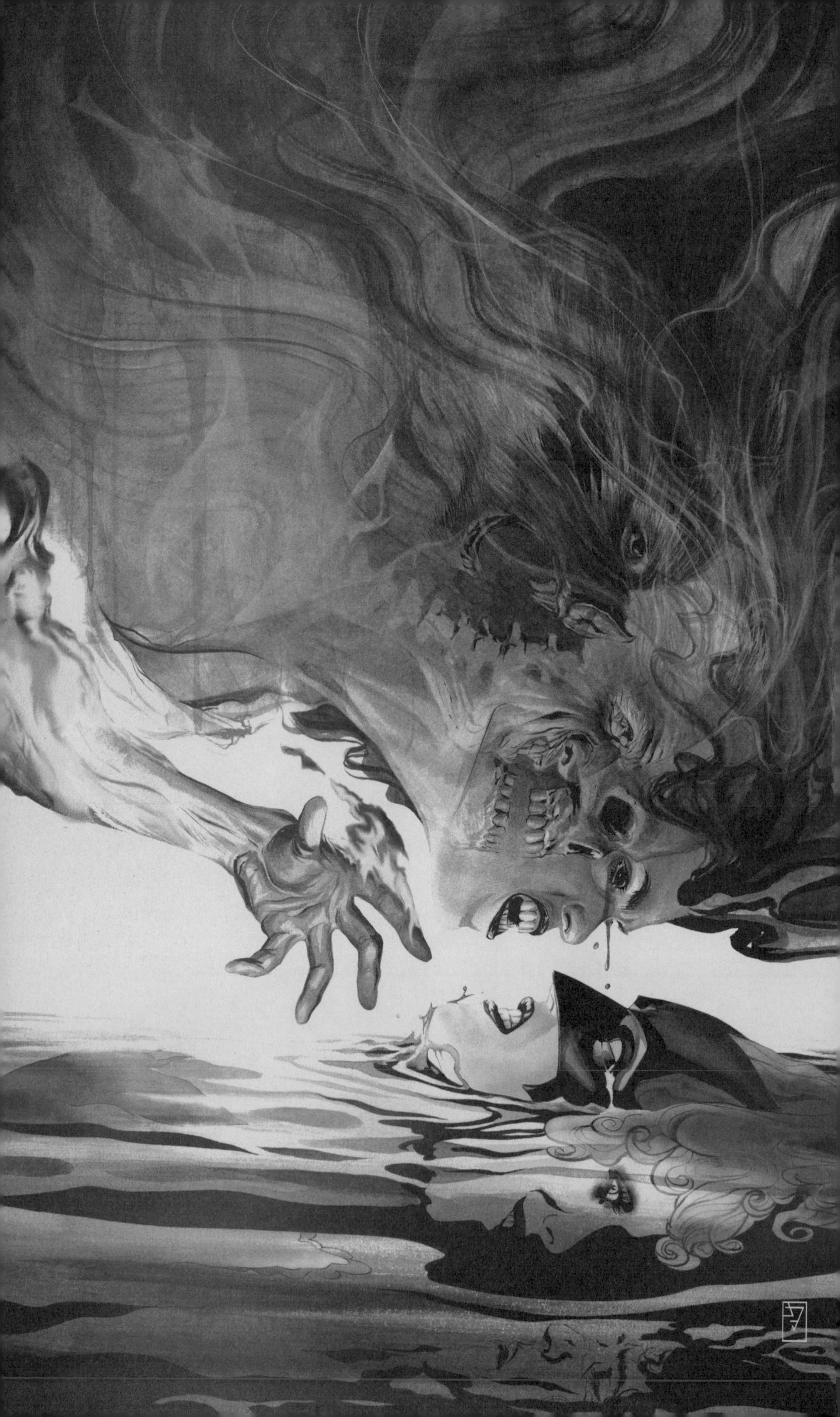

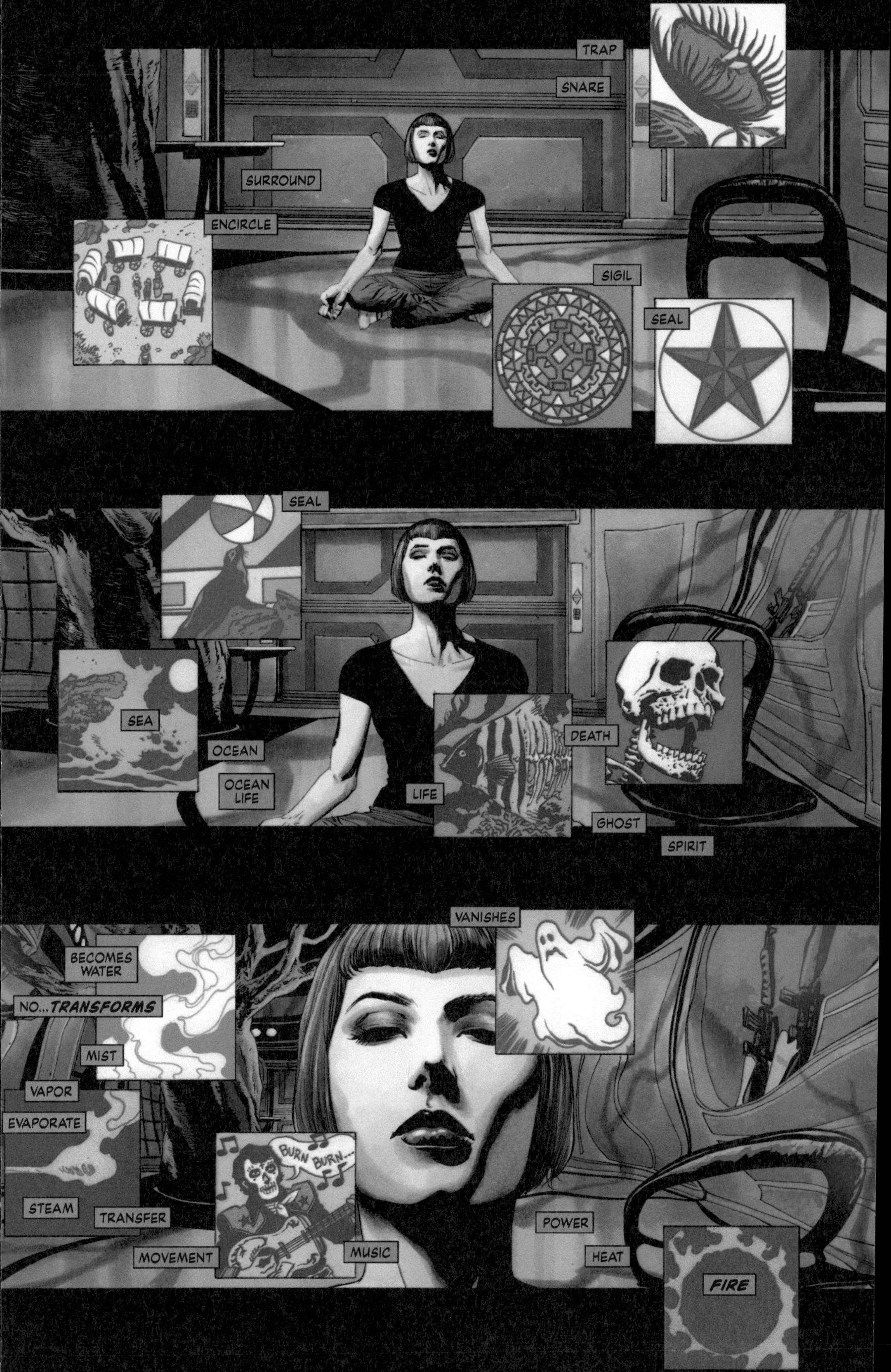

TRAP
SNARE
SURROUND
ENCIRCLE
SIGIL
SEAL
SEAL
SEA
OCEAN
OCEAN LIFE
LIFE
DEATH
GHOST
SPIRIT
VANISHES
BECOMES WATER
NO...TRANSFORMS
MIST
VAPOR
EVAPORATE
STEAM
TRANSFER
MOVEMENT
BURN BURN...
MUSIC
POWER
HEAT
FIRE

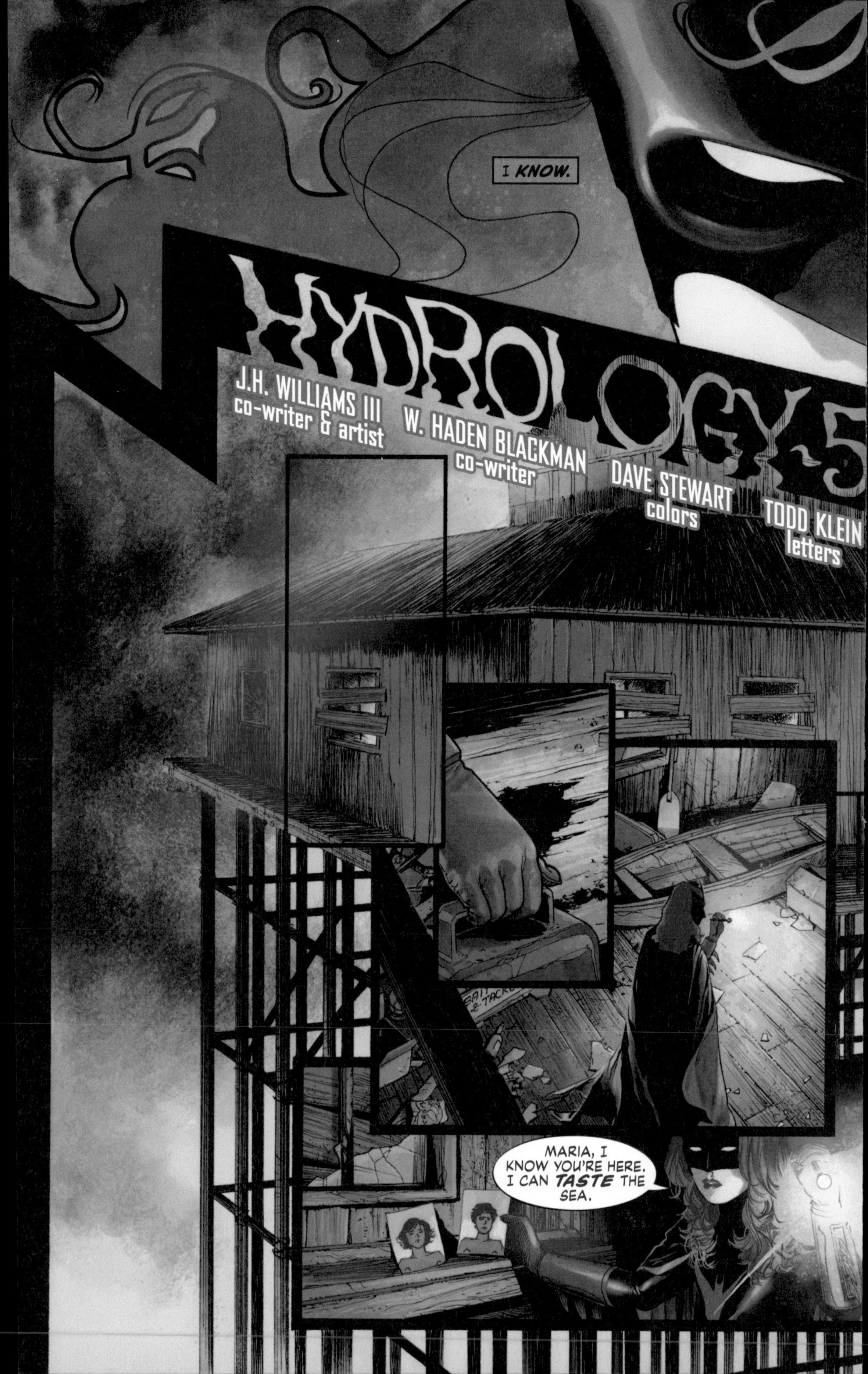
I KNOW.
HYDROLOGY 5
J.H. WILLIAMS III co-writer & artist
W. HADEN BLACKMAN co-writer
DAVE STEWART colors
TODD KLEIN letters
MARIA, I KNOW YOU'RE HERE. I CAN TASTE THE SEA.

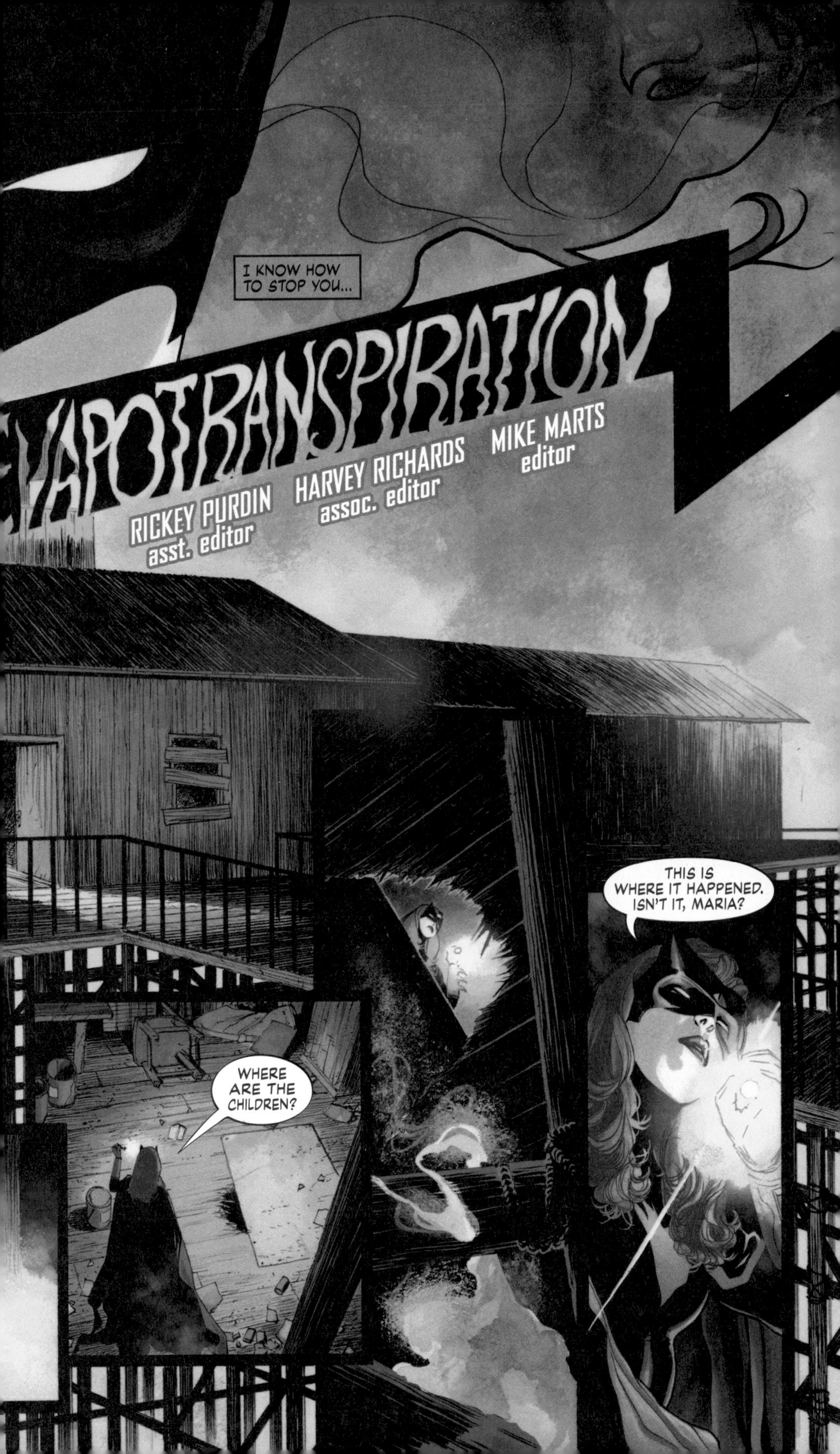
I KNOW HOW TO STOP YOU...
VAPOTRANSPIRATION
RICKEY PURDIN asst. editor
HARVEY RICHARDS assoc. editor
MIKE MARTS editor
WHERE ARE THE CHILDREN?
THIS IS WHERE IT HAPPENED. ISN'T IT, MARIA?

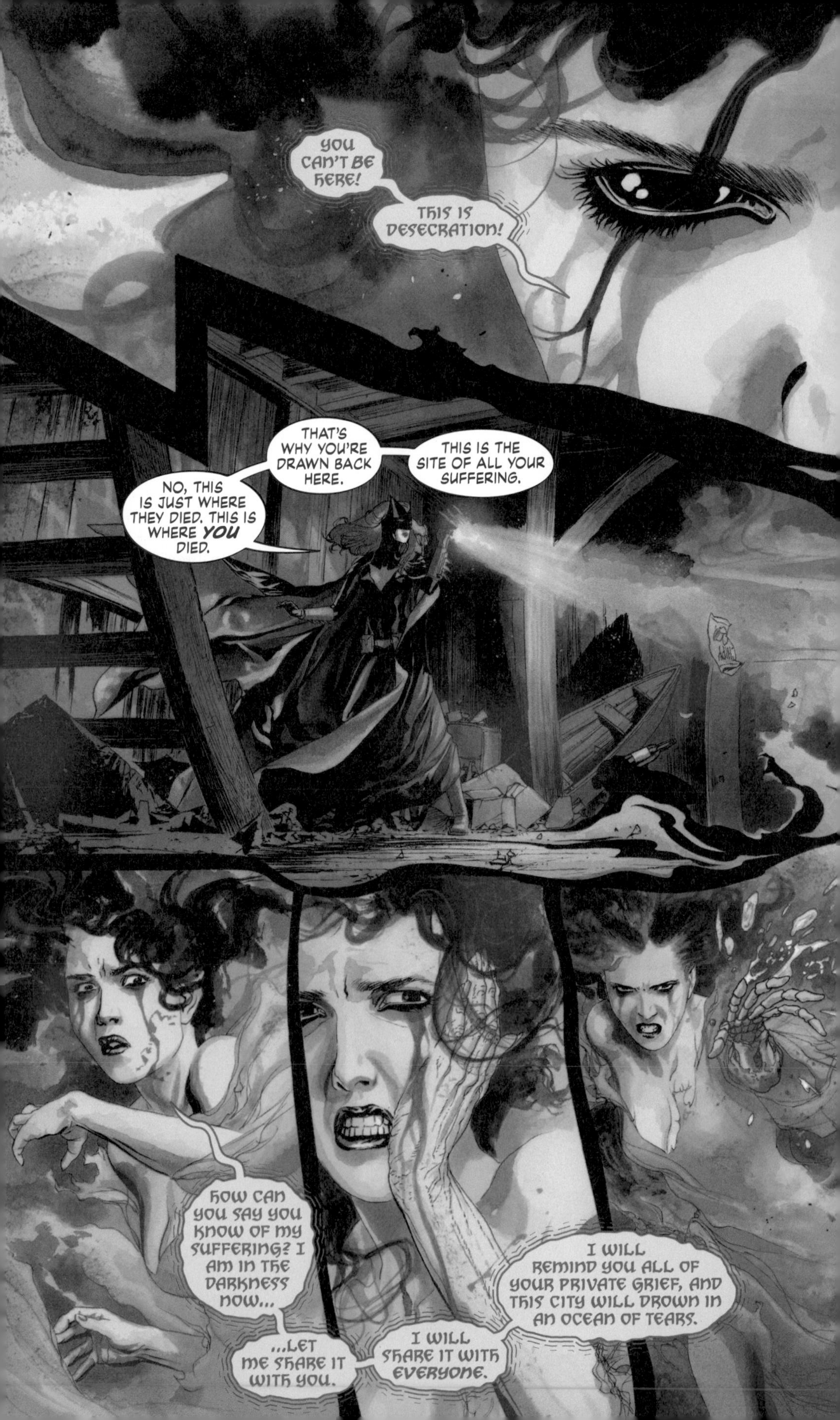
YOU CAN'T BE HERE!
THIS IS DESECRATION!
THIS IS THE SITE OF ALL YOUR SUFFERING.
THAT'S WHY YOU'RE DRAWN BACK HERE.
NO, THIS IS JUST WHERE THEY DIED. THIS IS WHERE *YOU* DIED.
HOW CAN YOU SAY YOU KNOW OF MY SUFFERING? I AM IN THE DARKNESS NOW...
...LET ME SHARE IT WITH YOU.
I WILL SHARE IT WITH EVERYONE.
I WILL REMIND YOU ALL OF YOUR PRIVATE GRIEF, AND THIS CITY WILL DROWN IN AN OCEAN OF TEARS.

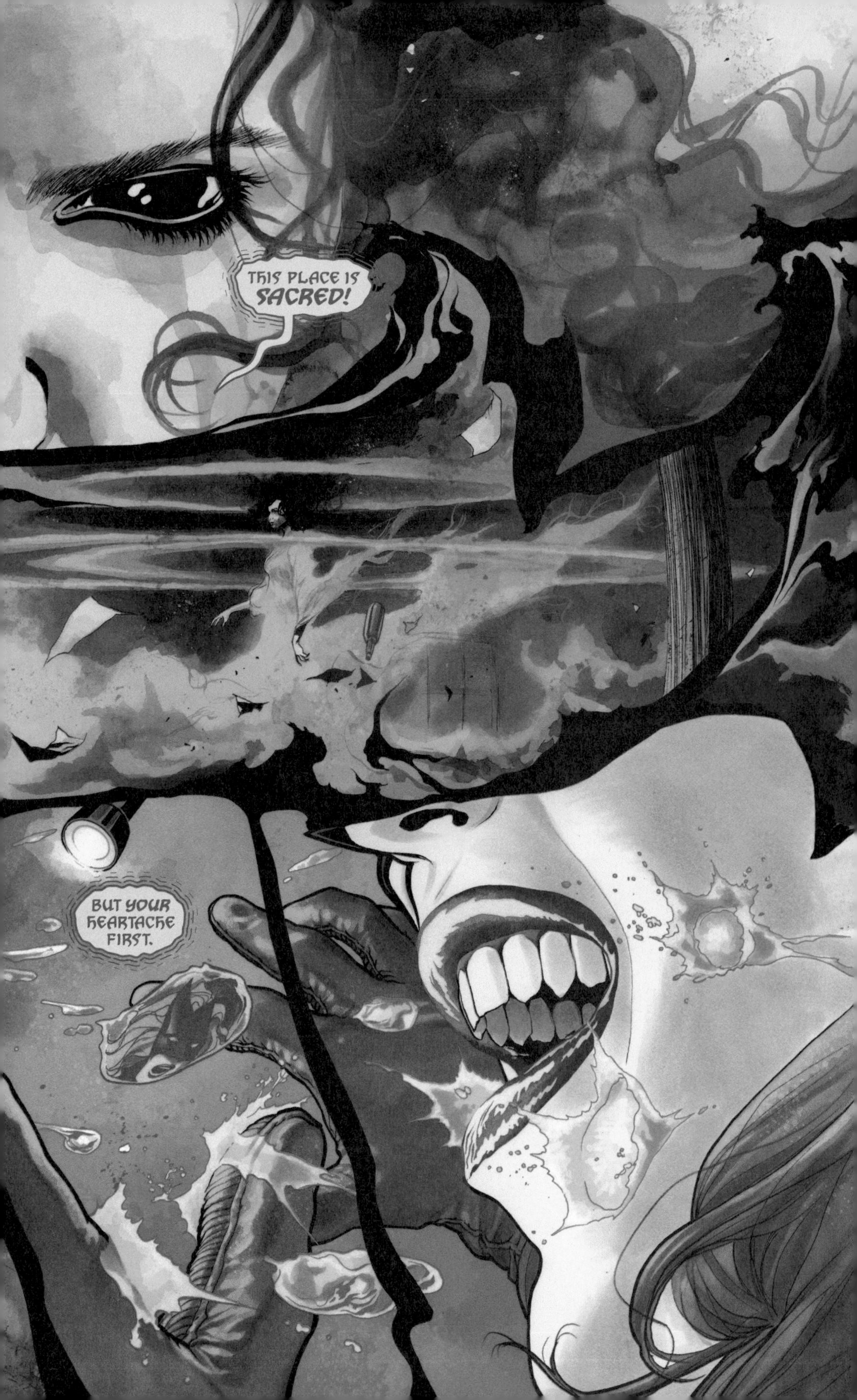
THIS PLACE IS SACRED!
BUT YOUR HEARTACHE FIRST.

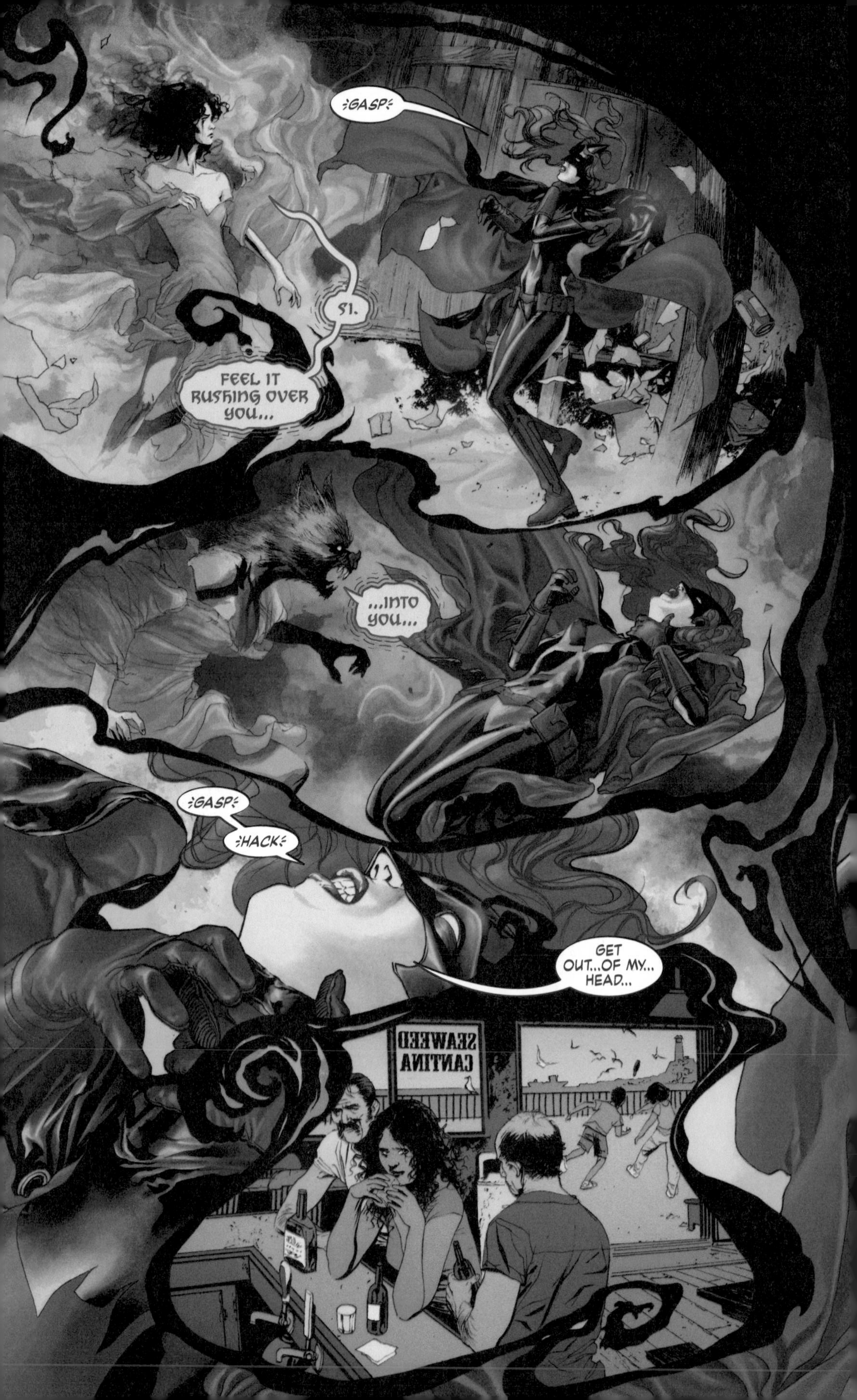
GASP
SÍ.
FEEL IT RUSHING OVER YOU...
...INTO YOU...
GASP
HACK
GET OUT...OF MY... HEAD...
SEAWEED CANTINA

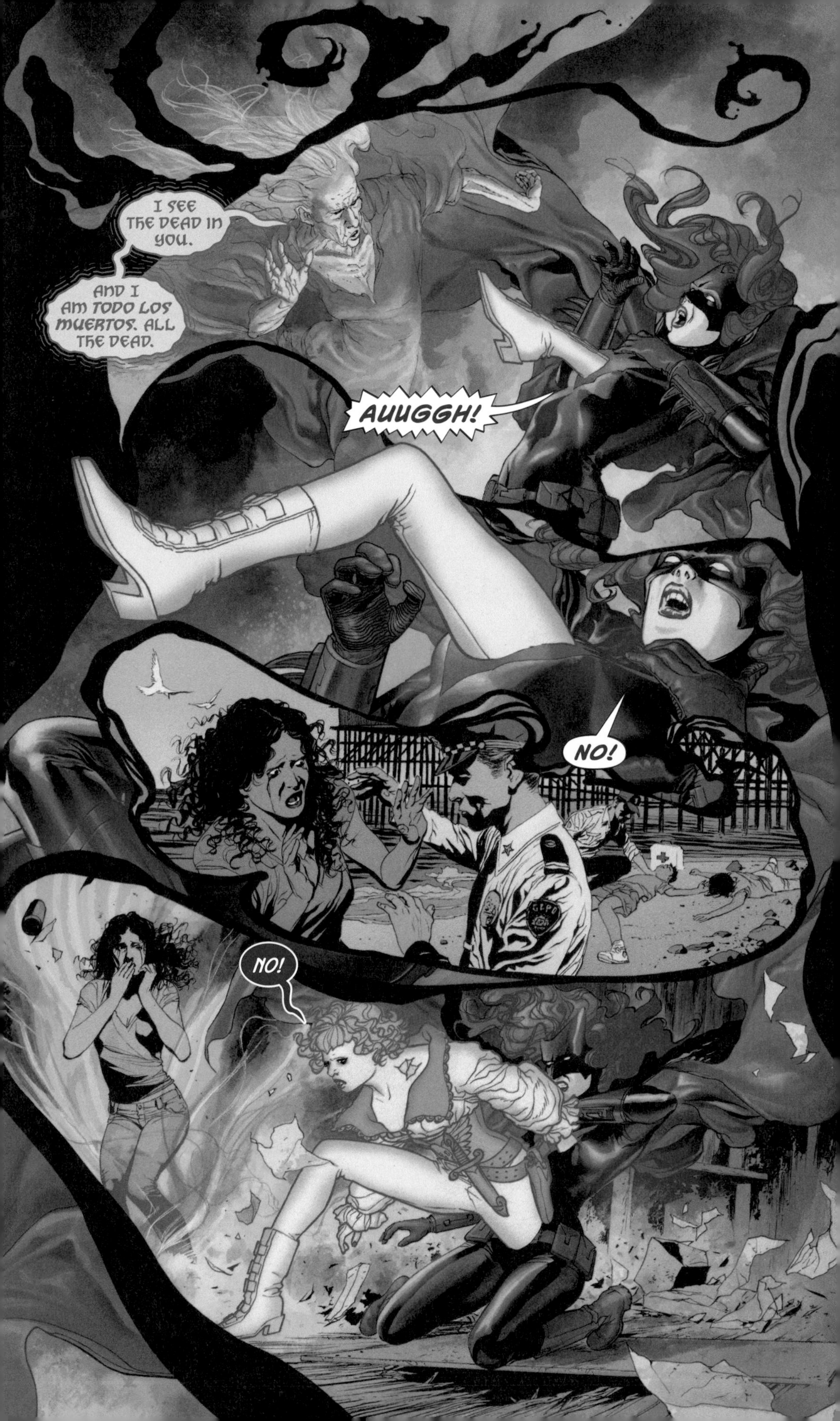
I SEE THE DEAD IN YOU.
AND I AM TODO LOS MUERTOS. ALL THE DEAD.
AUUGGH!
NO!
NO!

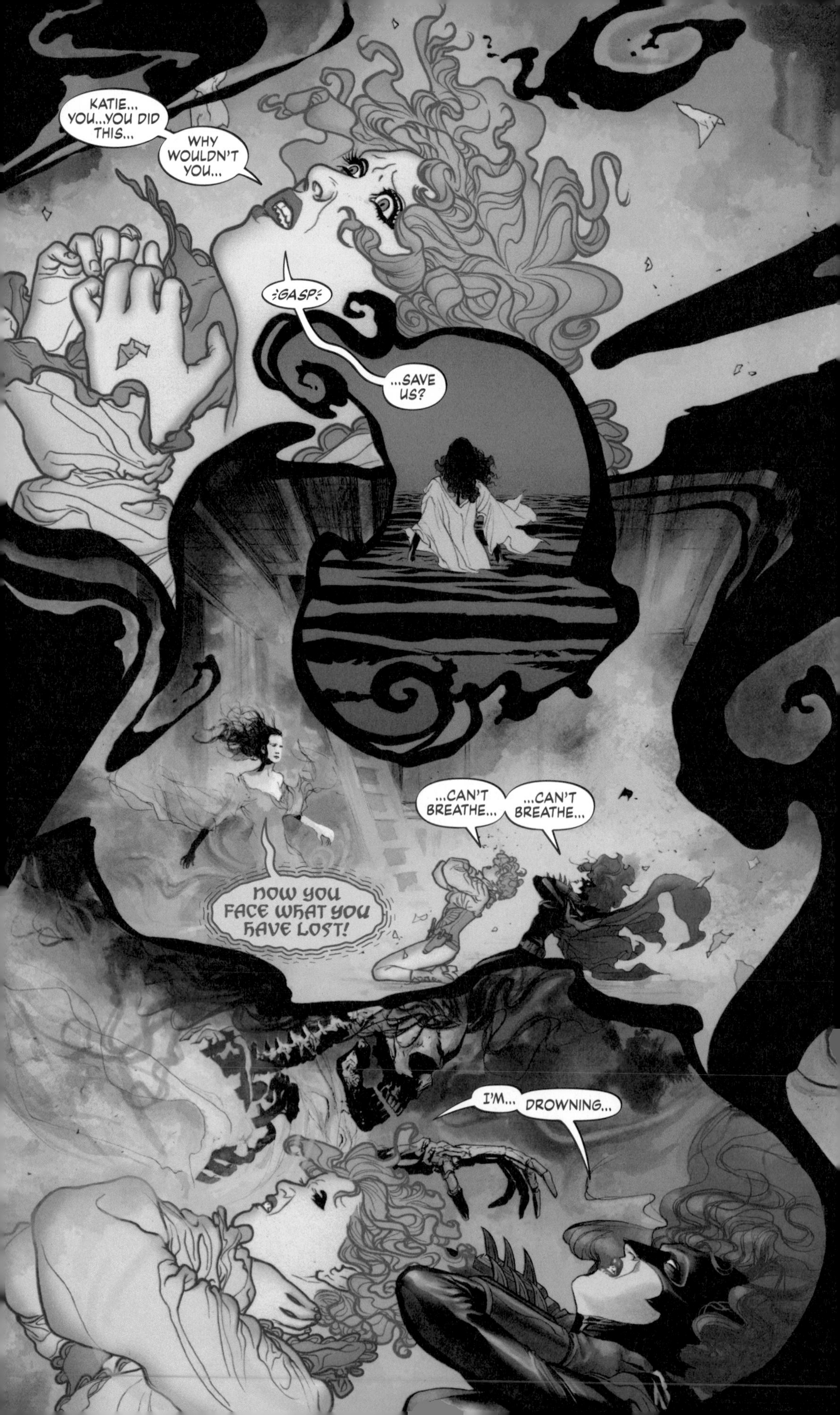
KATIE... YOU...YOU DID THIS...
WHY WOULDN'T YOU...
GASP
...SAVE US?
...CAN'T BREATHE...
...CAN'T BREATHE...
NOW YOU FACE WHAT YOU HAVE LOST!
I'M...
DROWNING...

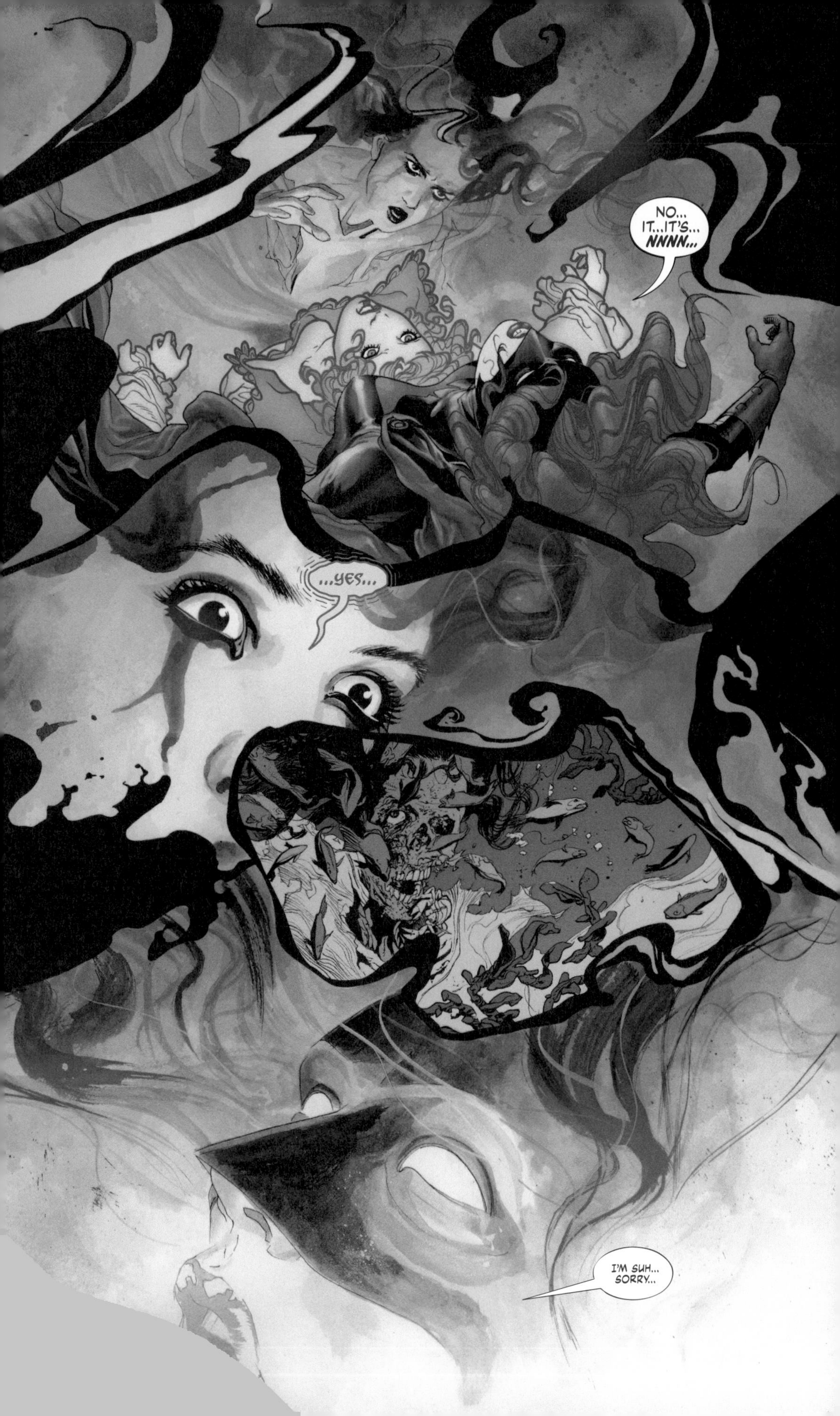
NO... IT...IT'S... NNNN...
...YES...
I'M SUH... SORRY...

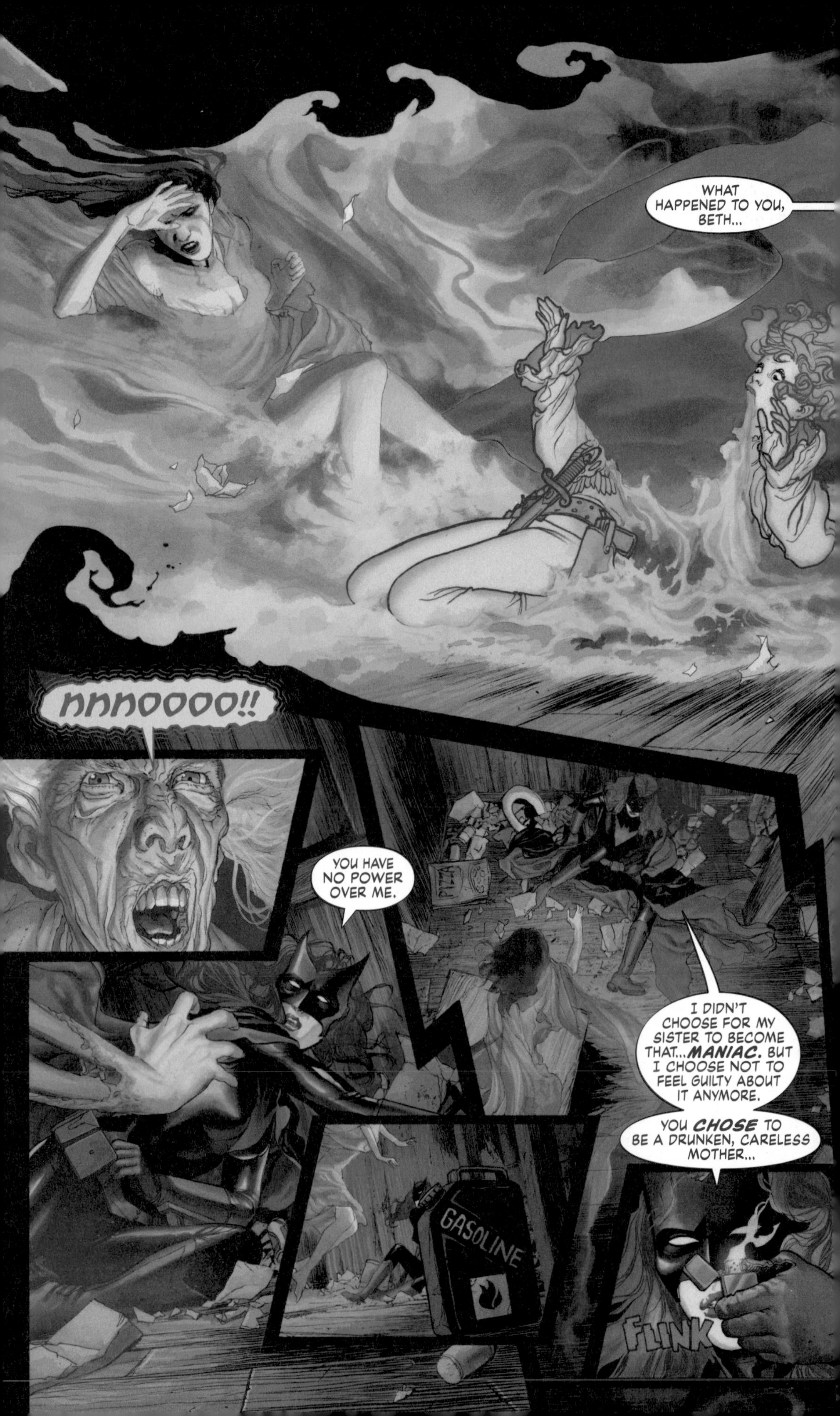
WHAT HAPPENED TO YOU, BETH...
NNNOOOO!!
YOU HAVE NO POWER OVER ME.
I DIDN'T CHOOSE FOR MY SISTER TO BECOME THAT...MANIAC. BUT I CHOOSE NOT TO FEEL GUILTY ABOUT IT ANYMORE.
YOU CHOSE TO BE A DRUNKEN, CARELESS MOTHER...
GASOLINE
FLINK

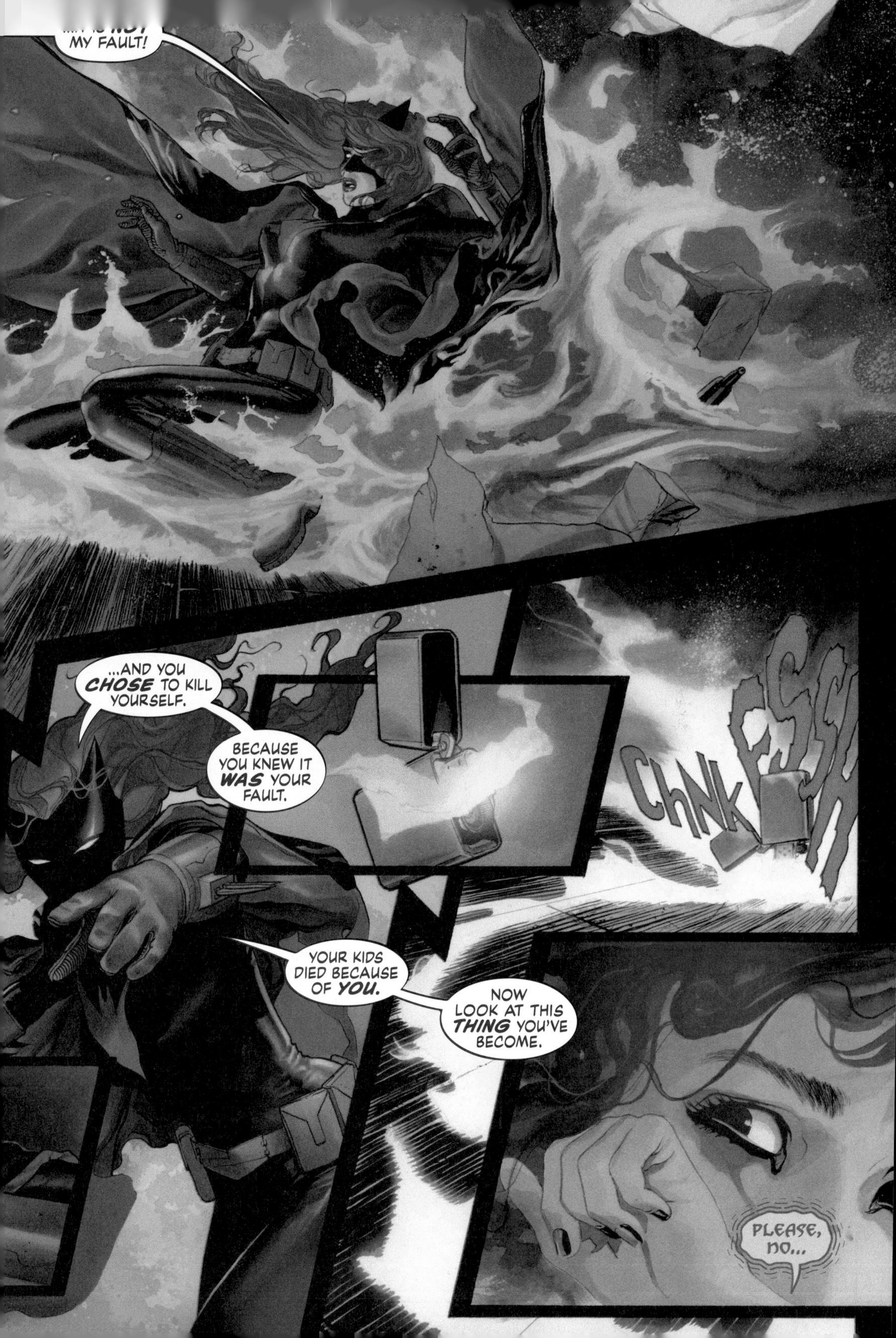
MY FAULT!
...AND YOU CHOSE TO KILL YOURSELF.
BECAUSE YOU KNEW IT WAS YOUR FAULT.
ChNK
FSSH
YOUR KIDS DIED BECAUSE OF YOU.
NOW LOOK AT THIS THING YOU'VE BECOME.
PLEASE, NO...

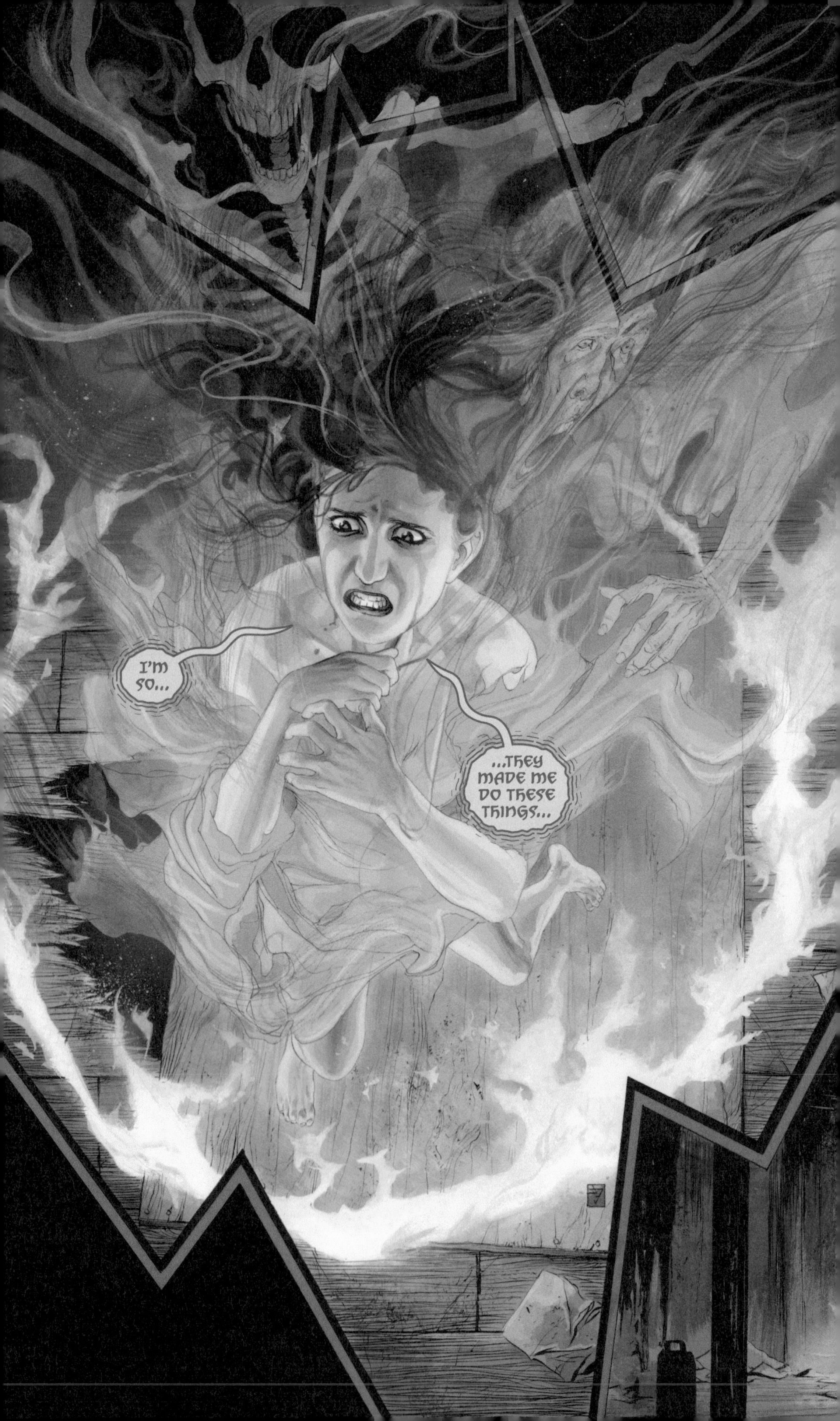
I'M SO...
...THEY MADE ME DO THESE THINGS...

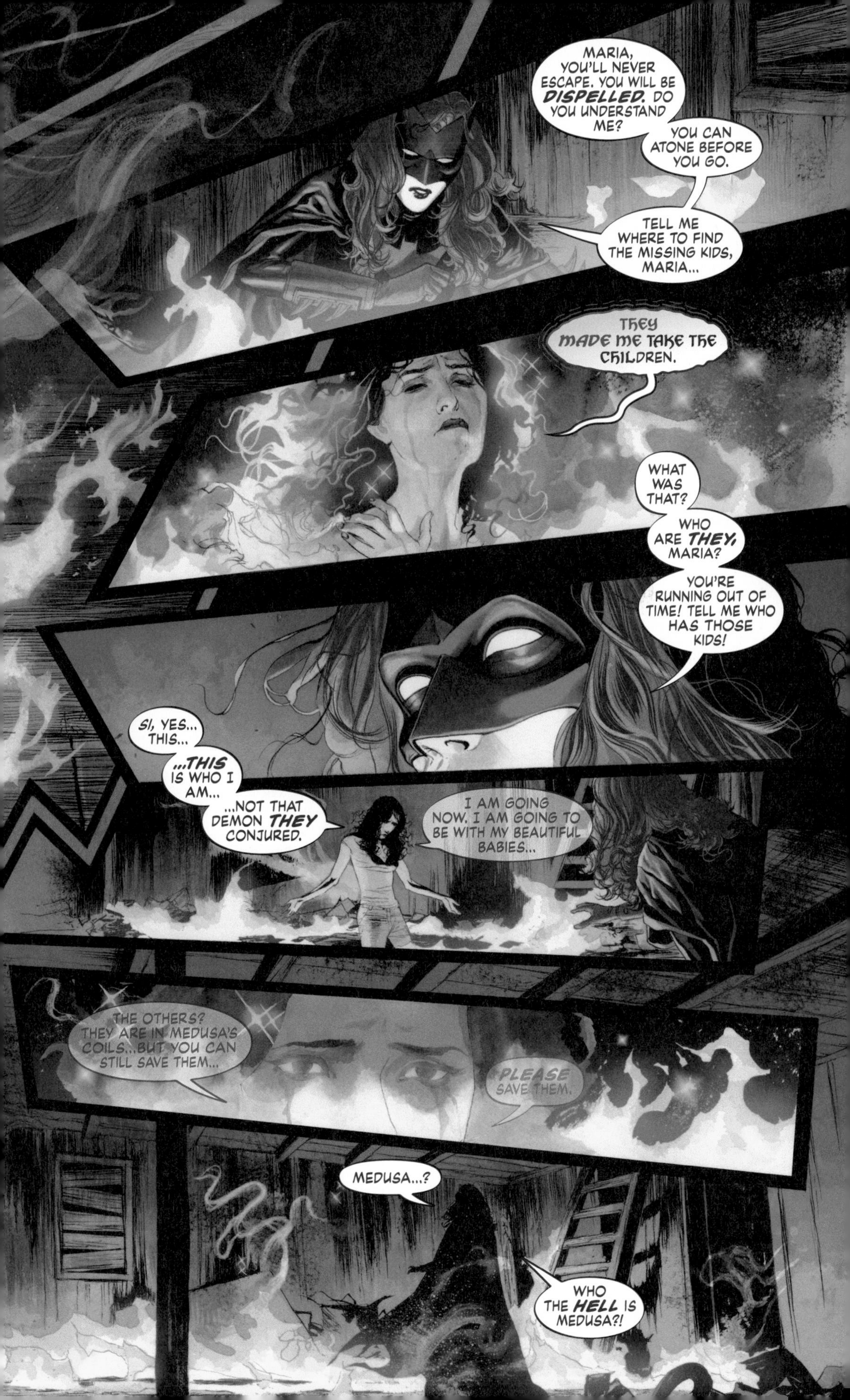
MARIA, YOU'LL NEVER ESCAPE. YOU WILL BE DISPELLED. DO YOU UNDERSTAND ME?
YOU CAN ATONE BEFORE YOU GO.
TELL ME WHERE TO FIND THE MISSING KIDS, MARIA...
THEY MADE ME TAKE THE CHILDREN.
WHAT WAS THAT?
WHO ARE THEY, MARIA?
YOU'RE RUNNING OUT OF TIME! TELL ME WHO HAS THOSE KIDS!
SI, YES... THIS...
...THIS IS WHO I AM...
...NOT THAT DEMON THEY CONJURED.
I AM GOING NOW. I AM GOING TO BE WITH MY BEAUTIFUL BABIES...
THE OTHERS? THEY ARE IN MEDUSA'S COILS...BUT YOU CAN STILL SAVE THEM...
PLEASE SAVE THEM.
MEDUSA...?
WHO THE HELL IS MEDUSA?!

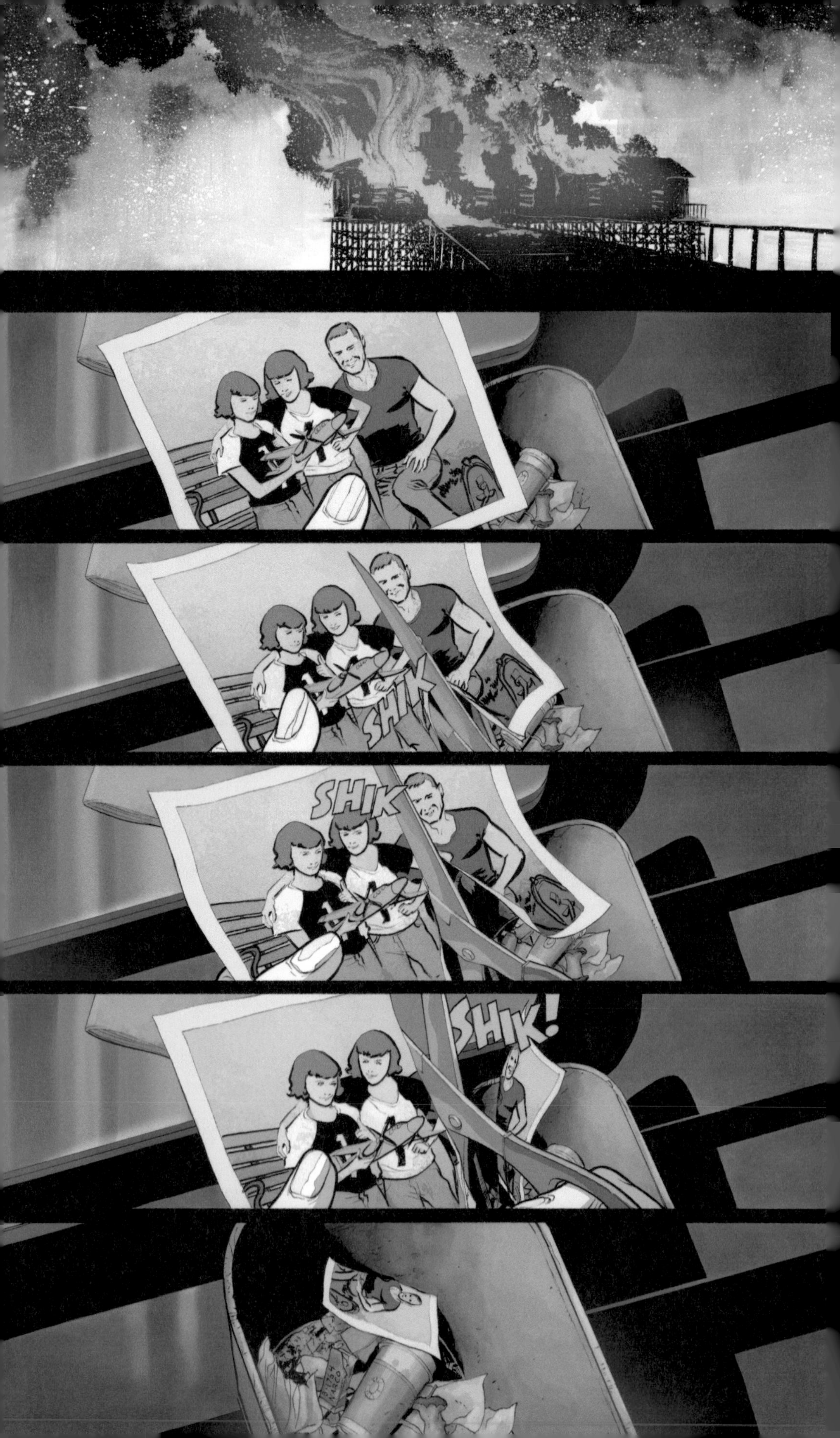
SHIK
SHIK
SHIK!

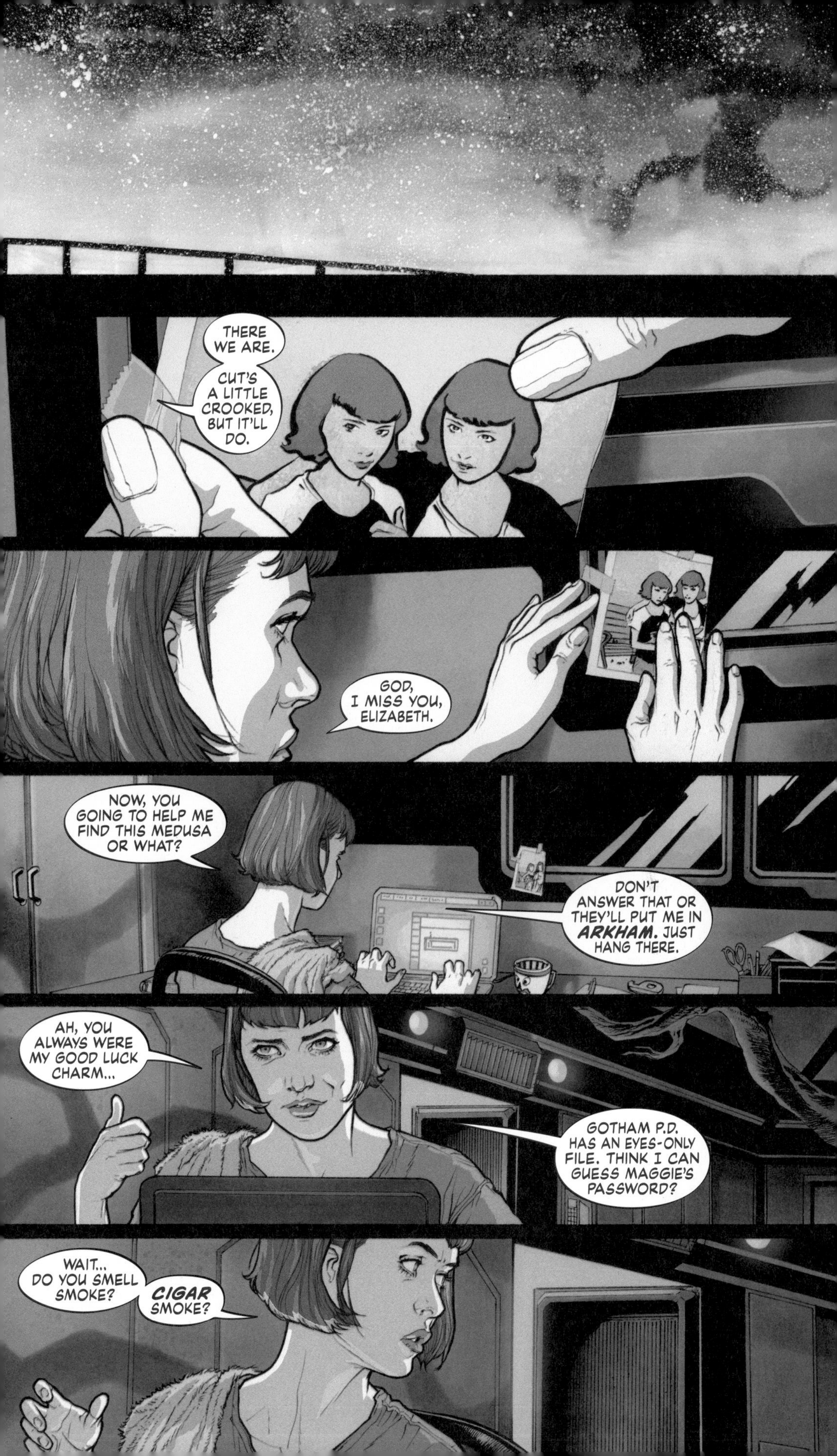
THERE WE ARE.
CUT'S A LITTLE CROOKED, BUT IT'LL DO.
GOD, I MISS YOU, ELIZABETH.
NOW, YOU GOING TO HELP ME FIND THIS MEDUSA OR WHAT?
DON'T ANSWER THAT OR THEY'LL PUT ME IN ARKHAM. JUST HANG THERE.
AH, YOU ALWAYS WERE MY GOOD LUCK CHARM...
GOTHAM P.D. HAS AN EYES-ONLY FILE. THINK I CAN GUESS MAGGIE'S PASSWORD?
WAIT... DO YOU SMELL SMOKE?
CIGAR SMOKE?

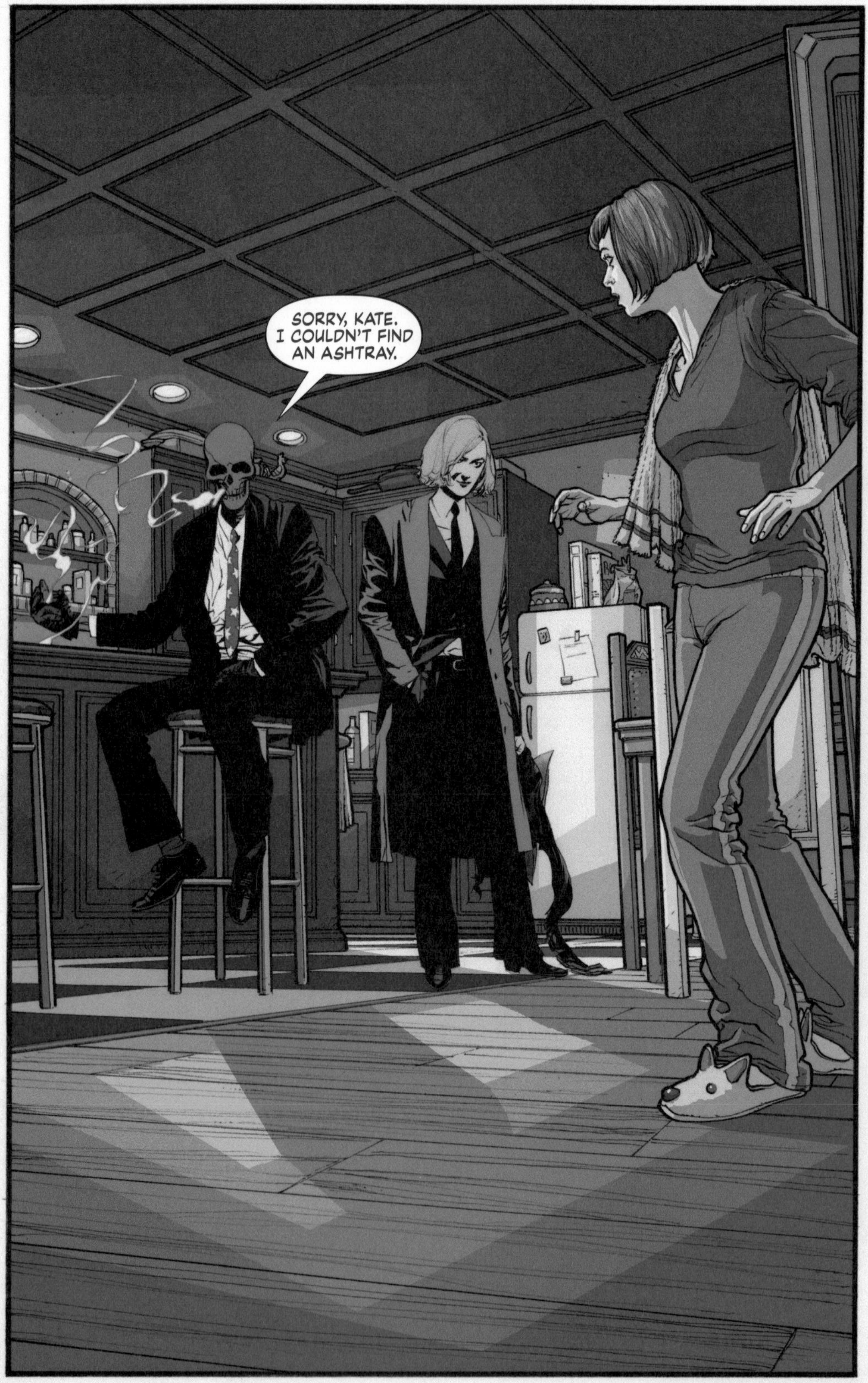
SORRY, KATE. I COULDN'T FIND AN ASHTRAY.

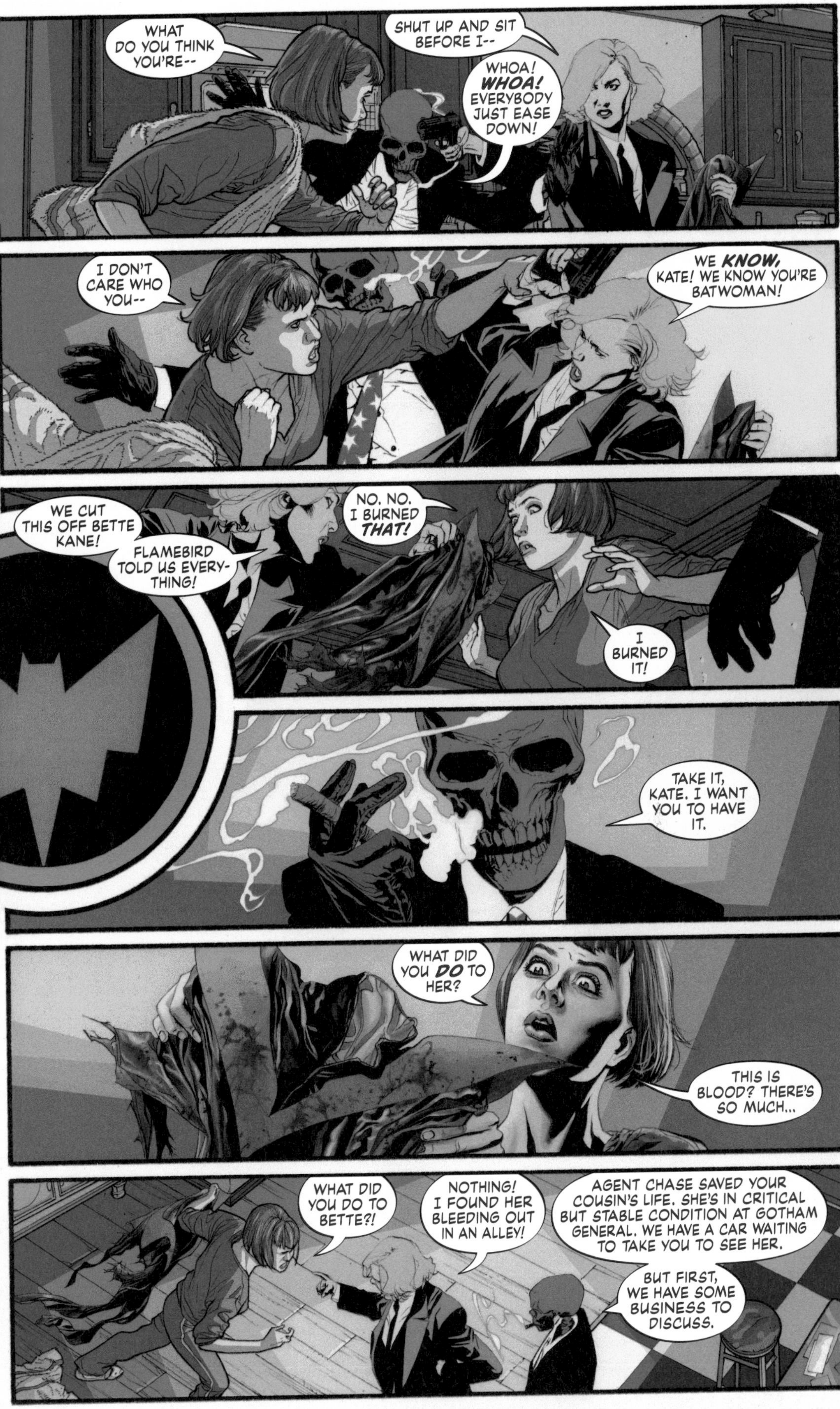
WHAT DO YOU THINK YOU'RE--
SHUT UP AND SIT BEFORE I--
WHOA! WHOA! EVERYBODY JUST EASE DOWN!
I DON'T CARE WHO YOU--
WE KNOW, KATE! WE KNOW YOU'RE BATWOMAN!
WE CUT THIS OFF BETTE KANE!
FLAMEBIRD TOLD US EVERYTHING!
NO. NO. I BURNED THAT!
I BURNED IT!
TAKE IT, KATE. I WANT YOU TO HAVE IT.
WHAT DID YOU DO TO HER?
THIS IS BLOOD? THERE'S SO MUCH...
WHAT DID YOU DO TO BETTE?!
NOTHING! I FOUND HER BLEEDING OUT IN AN ALLEY!
AGENT CHASE SAVED YOUR COUSIN'S LIFE. SHE'S IN CRITICAL BUT STABLE CONDITION AT GOTHAM GENERAL. WE HAVE A CAR WAITING TO TAKE YOU TO SEE HER.
BUT FIRST, WE HAVE SOME BUSINESS TO DISCUSS.

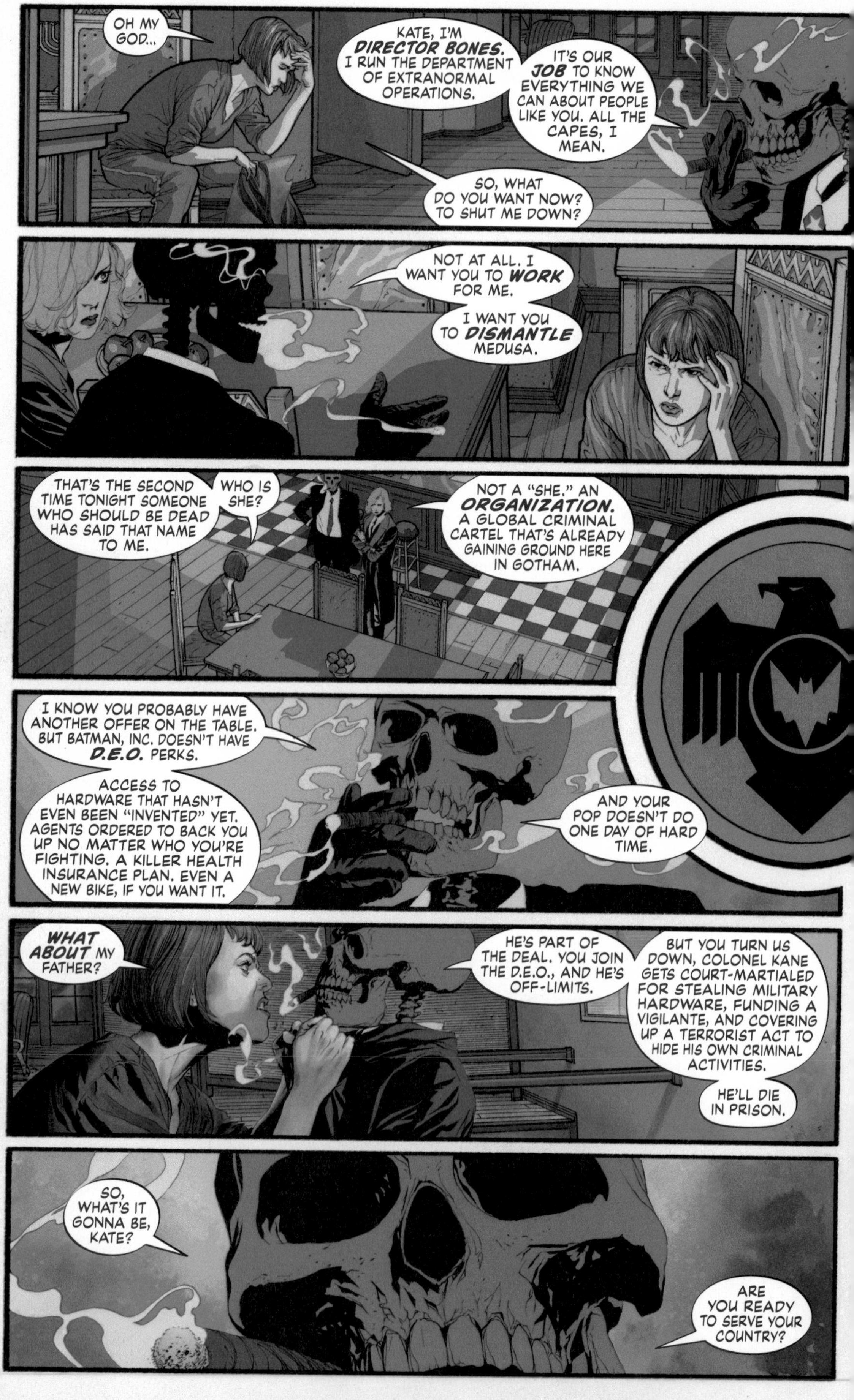
OH MY GOD...
KATE, I'M DIRECTOR BONES. I RUN THE DEPARTMENT OF EXTRANORMAL OPERATIONS.
IT'S OUR JOB TO KNOW EVERYTHING WE CAN ABOUT PEOPLE LIKE YOU. ALL THE CAPES, I MEAN.
SO, WHAT DO YOU WANT NOW? TO SHUT ME DOWN?
NOT AT ALL. I WANT YOU TO WORK FOR ME.
I WANT YOU TO DISMANTLE MEDUSA.
WHO IS SHE?
NOT A "SHE." AN ORGANIZATION. A GLOBAL CRIMINAL CARTEL THAT'S ALREADY GAINING GROUND HERE IN GOTHAM.
THAT'S THE SECOND TIME TONIGHT SOMEONE WHO SHOULD BE DEAD HAS SAID THAT NAME TO ME.
I KNOW YOU PROBABLY HAVE ANOTHER OFFER ON THE TABLE. BUT BATMAN, INC. DOESN'T HAVE D.E.O. PERKS.
ACCESS TO HARDWARE THAT HASN'T EVEN BEEN "INVENTED" YET. AGENTS ORDERED TO BACK YOU UP NO MATTER WHO YOU'RE FIGHTING. A KILLER HEALTH INSURANCE PLAN. EVEN A NEW BIKE, IF YOU WANT IT.
AND YOUR POP DOESN'T DO ONE DAY OF HARD TIME.
WHAT ABOUT MY FATHER?
HE'S PART OF THE DEAL. YOU JOIN THE D.E.O., AND HE'S OFF-LIMITS.
BUT YOU TURN US DOWN, COLONEL KANE GETS COURT-MARTIALED FOR STEALING MILITARY HARDWARE, FUNDING A VIGILANTE, AND COVERING UP A TERRORIST ACT TO HIDE HIS OWN CRIMINAL ACTIVITIES.
HE'LL DIE IN PRISON.
SO, WHAT'S IT GONNA BE, KATE?
ARE YOU READY TO SERVE YOUR COUNTRY?

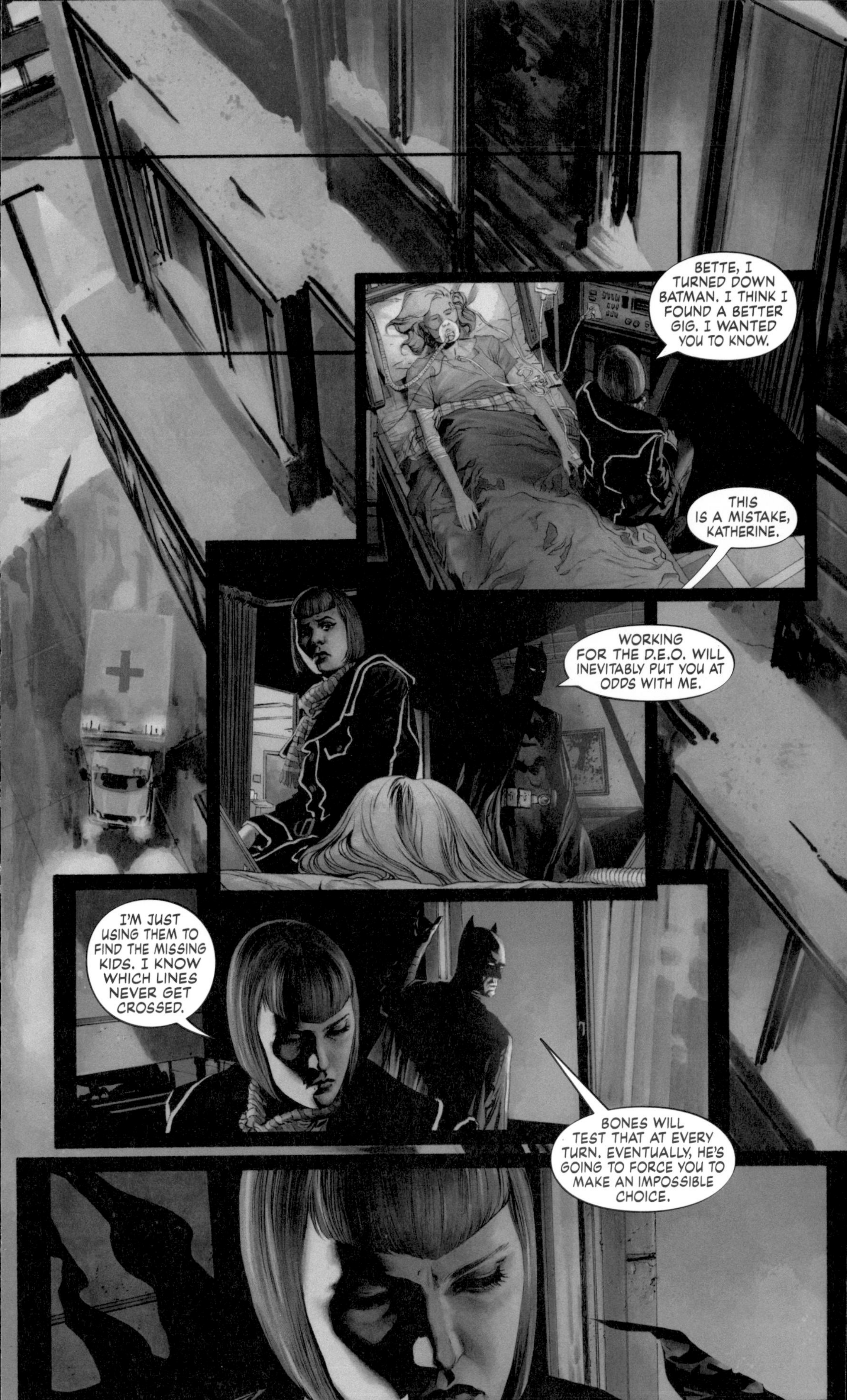
BETTE, I TURNED DOWN BATMAN. I THINK I FOUND A BETTER GIG. I WANTED YOU TO KNOW.
THIS IS A MISTAKE, KATHERINE.
WORKING FOR THE D.E.O. WILL INEVITABLY PUT YOU AT ODDS WITH ME.
I'M JUST USING THEM TO FIND THE MISSING KIDS. I KNOW WHICH LINES NEVER GET CROSSED.
BONES WILL TEST THAT AT EVERY TURN. EVENTUALLY, HE'S GOING TO FORCE YOU TO MAKE AN IMPOSSIBLE CHOICE.

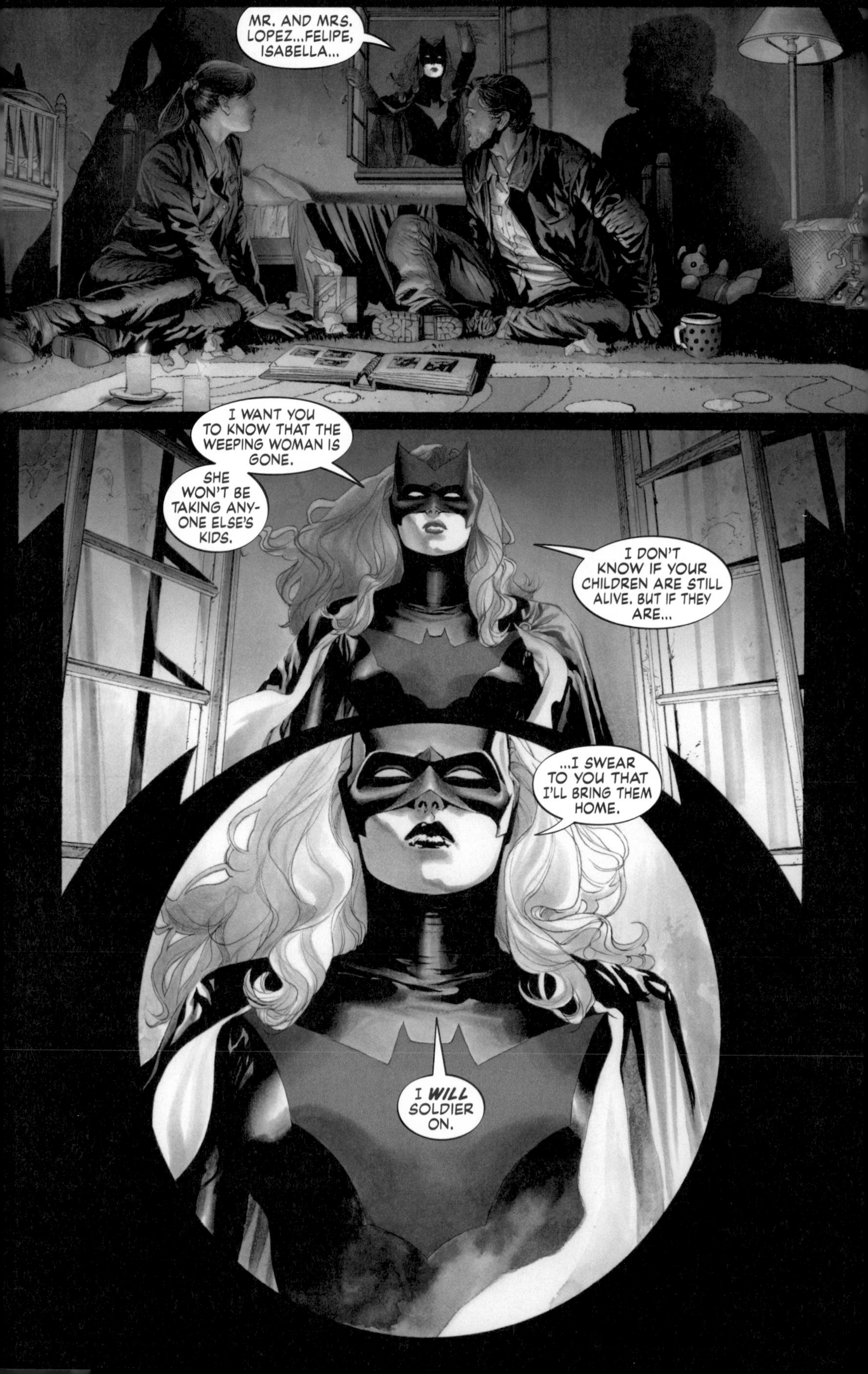
MR. AND MRS. LOPEZ...FELIPE, ISABELLA...
I WANT YOU TO KNOW THAT THE WEEPING WOMAN IS GONE.
SHE WON'T BE TAKING ANYONE ELSE'S KIDS.
I DON'T KNOW IF YOUR CHILDREN ARE STILL ALIVE. BUT IF THEY ARE...
...I SWEAR TO YOU THAT I'LL BRING THEM HOME.
I *WILL* SOLDIER ON.

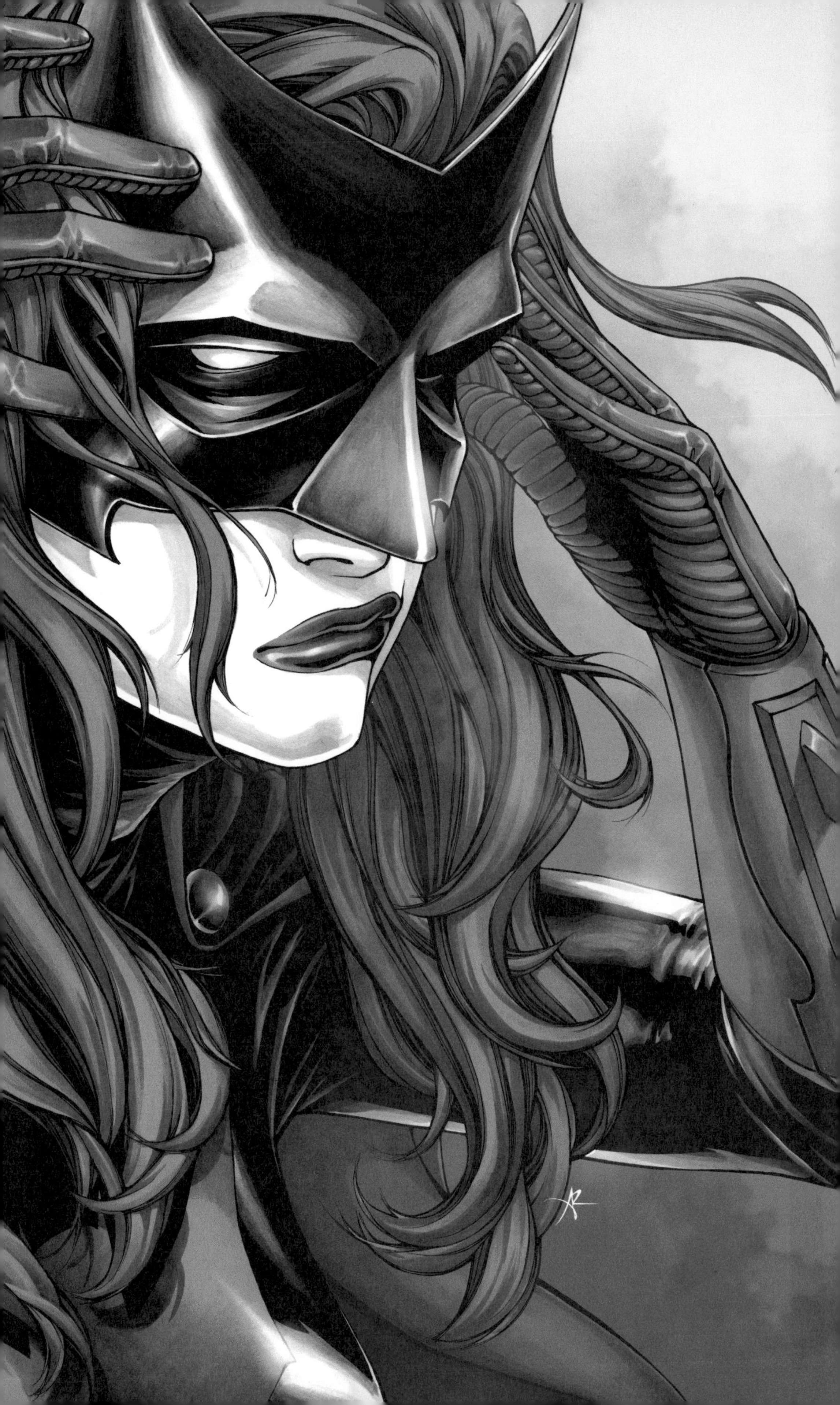

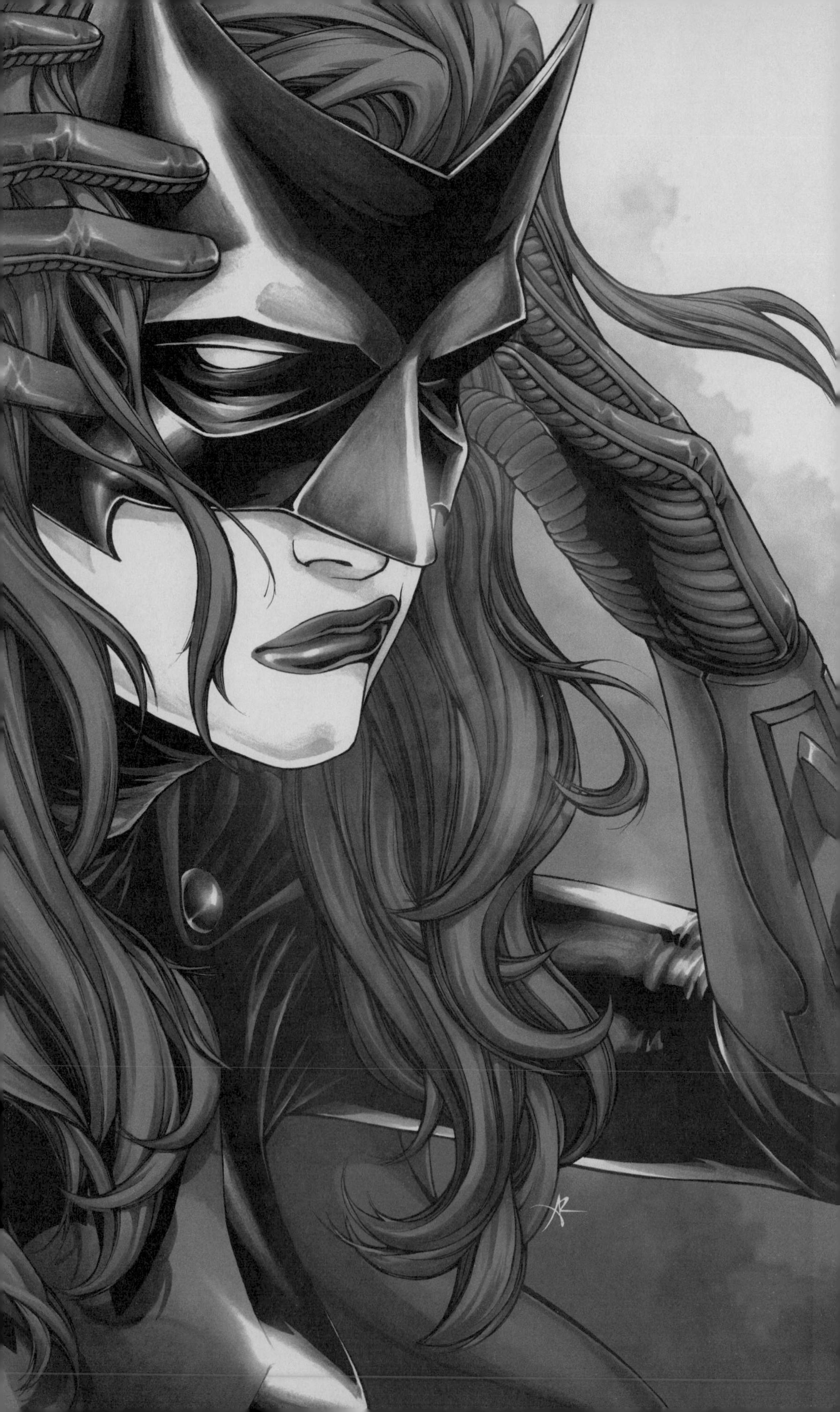

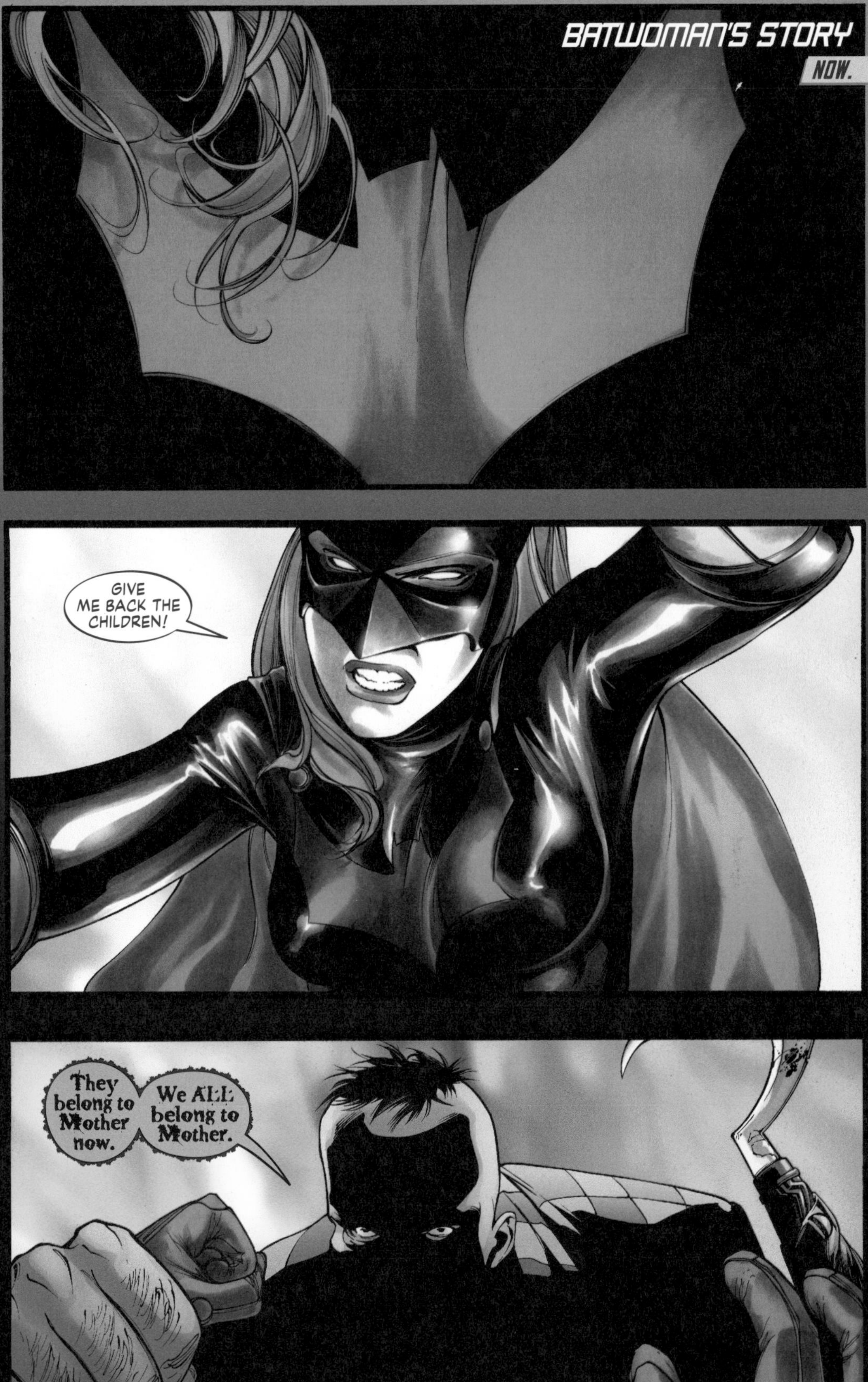
BATWOMAN'S STORY
NOW.
GIVE ME BACK THE CHILDREN!
They belong to Mother now.
We ALL belong to Mother.

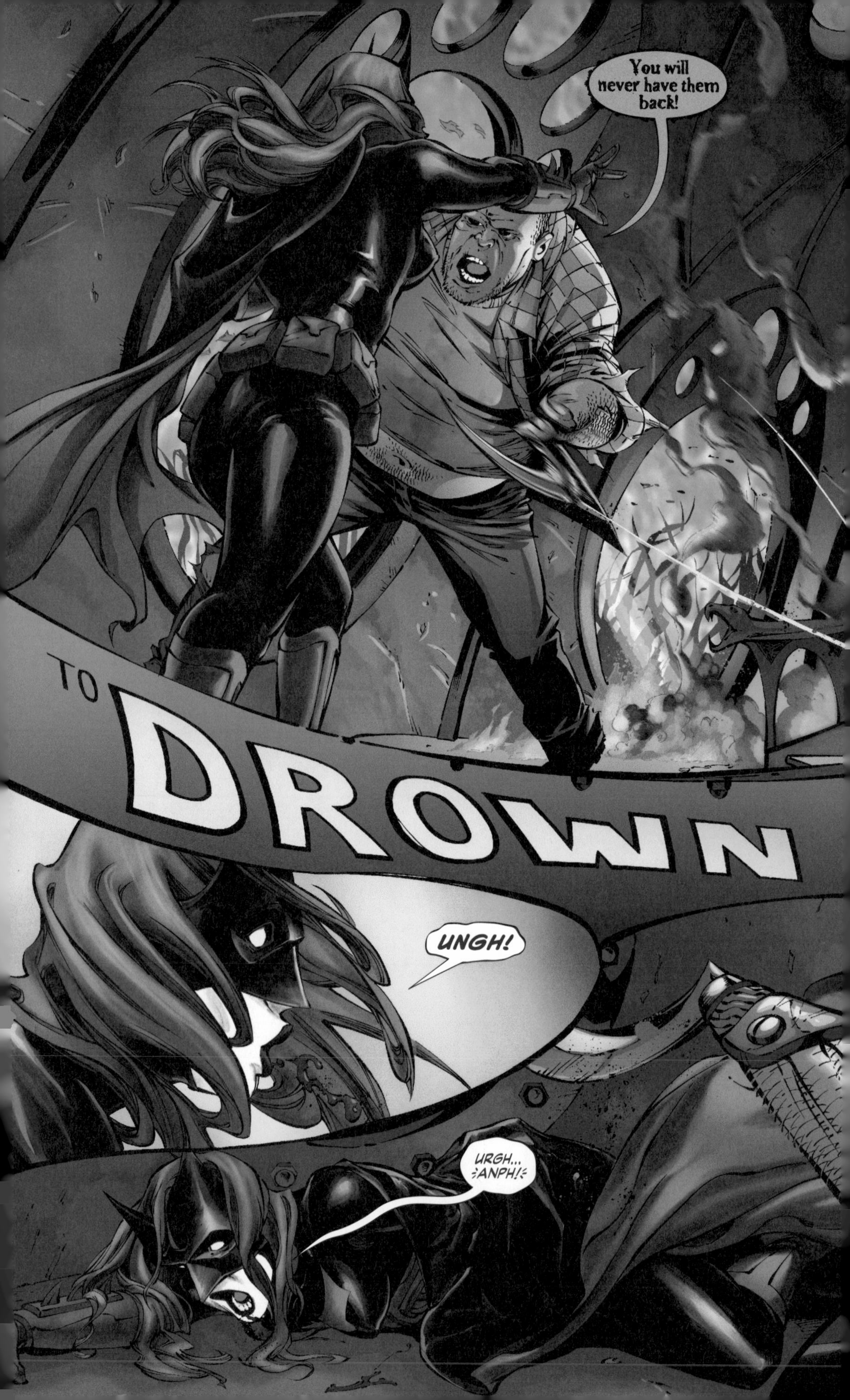
You will never have them back!
TO
DROWN
UNGH!
URGH... ANPH!

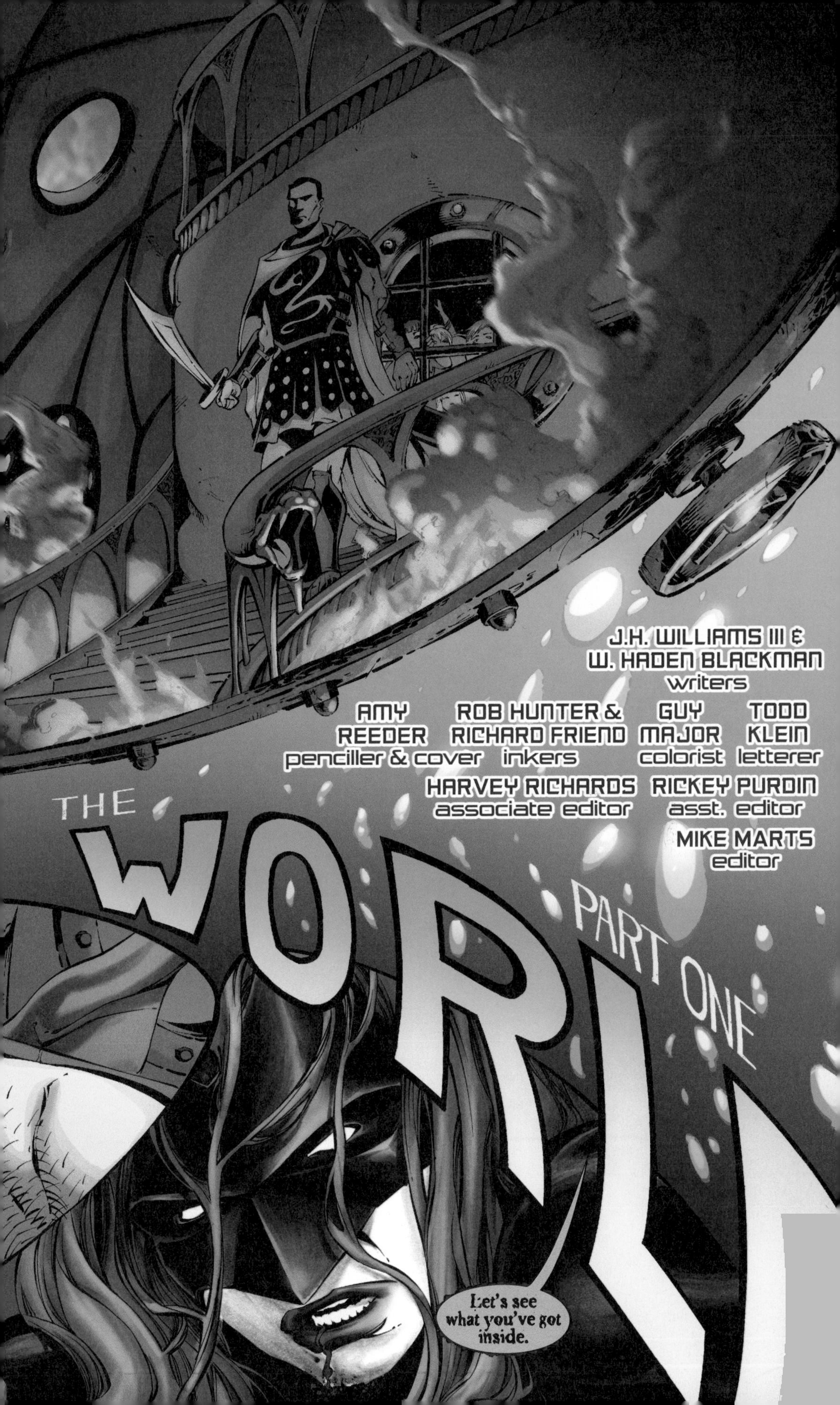
J.H. WILLIAMS III & W. HADEN BLACKMAN writers
AMY REEDER penciller & cover
ROB HUNTER & RICHARD FRIEND inkers
GUY MAJOR colorist
TODD KLEIN letterer
HARVEY RICHARDS associate editor
RICKEY PURDIN asst. editor
MIKE MARTS editor
THE WORL
PART ONE
Let's see what you've got inside.

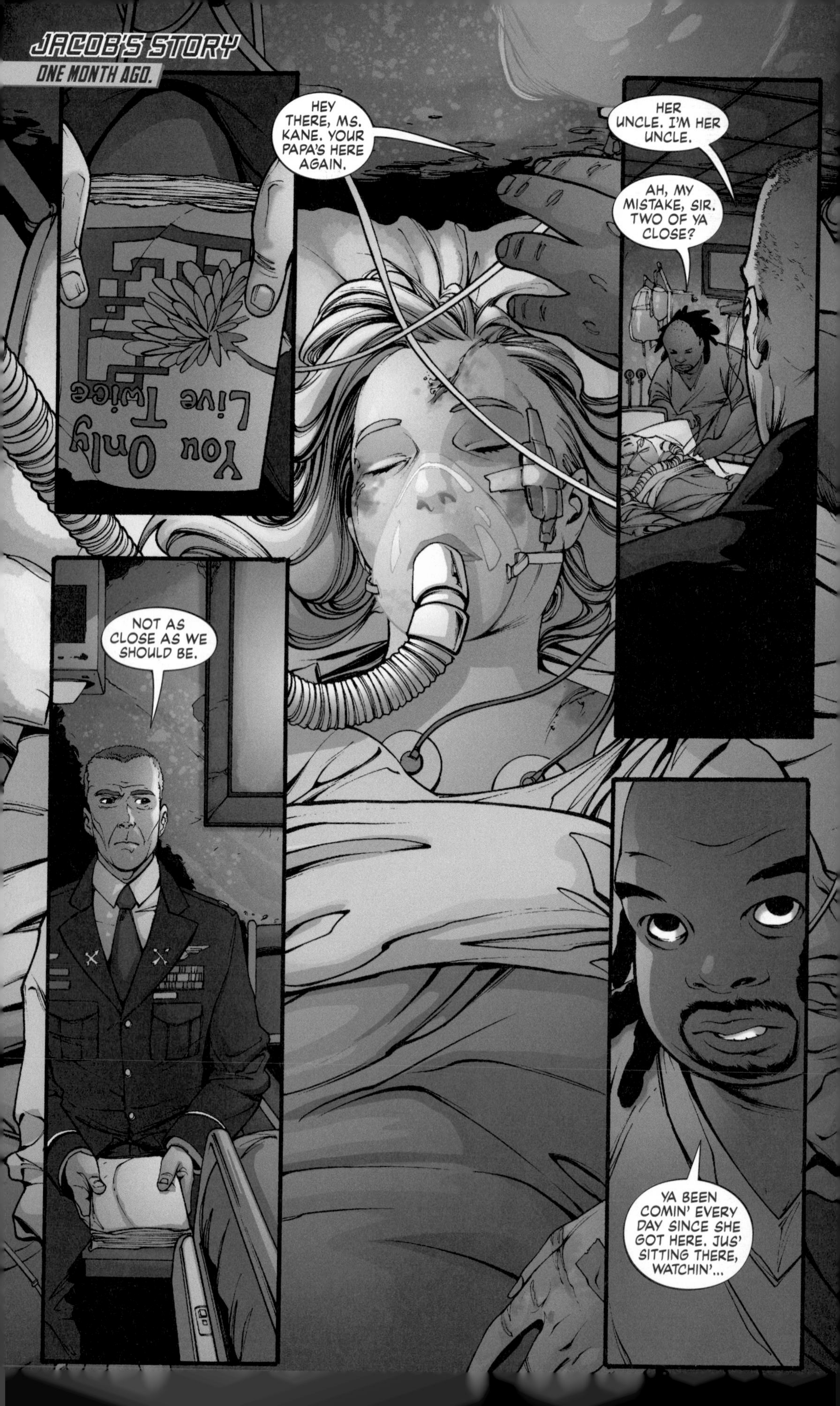
JACOB'S STORY
ONE MONTH AGO.
You Only Live Twice
HEY THERE, MS. KANE. YOUR PAPA'S HERE AGAIN.
HER UNCLE. I'M HER UNCLE.
AH, MY MISTAKE, SIR. TWO OF YA CLOSE?
NOT AS CLOSE AS WE SHOULD BE.
YA BEEN COMIN' EVERY DAY SINCE SHE GOT HERE. JUS' SITTING THERE, WATCHIN'...

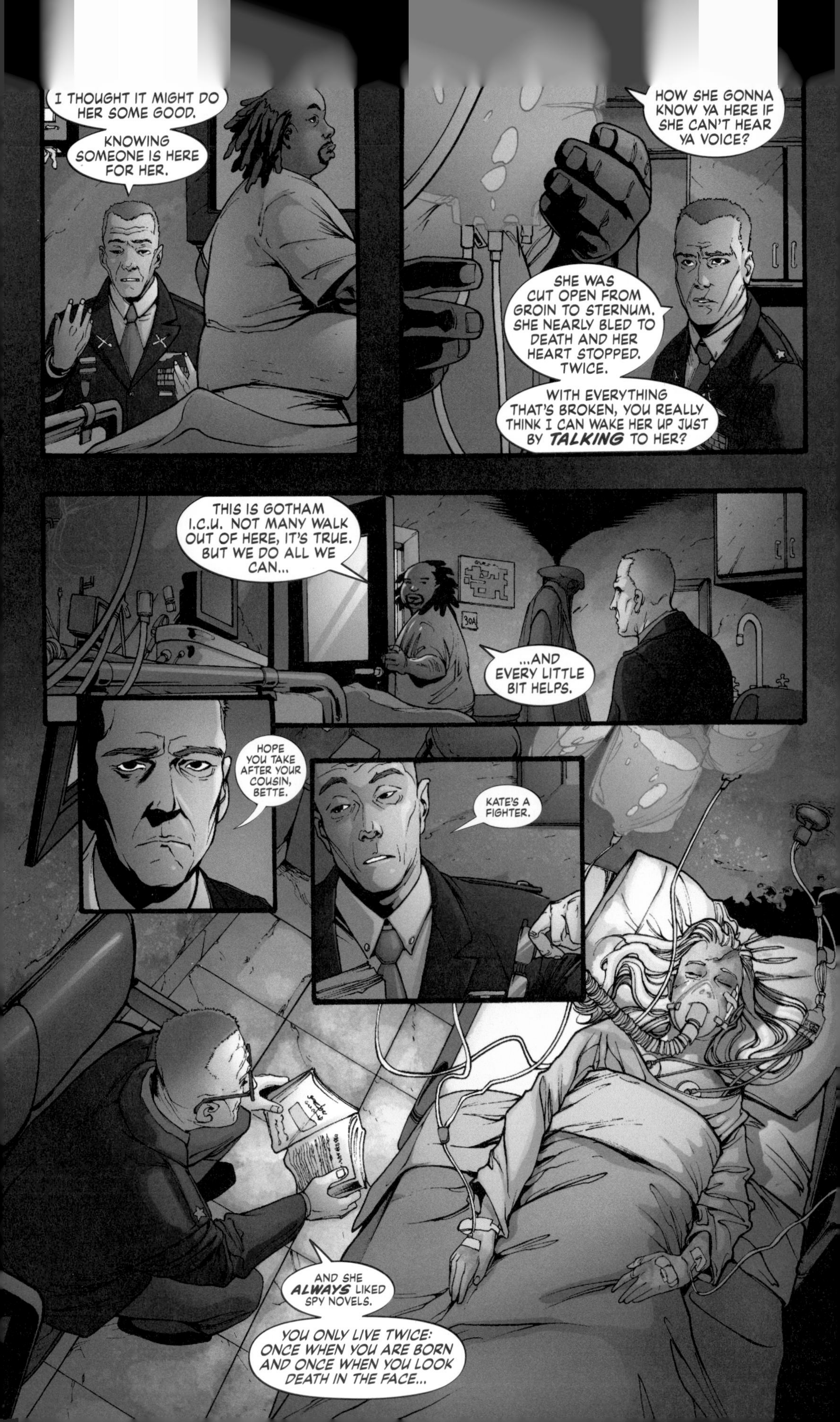
I THOUGHT IT MIGHT DO HER SOME GOOD.
KNOWING SOMEONE IS HERE FOR HER.
HOW SHE GONNA KNOW YA HERE IF SHE CAN'T HEAR YA VOICE?
SHE WAS CUT OPEN FROM GROIN TO STERNUM. SHE NEARLY BLED TO DEATH AND HER HEART STOPPED. TWICE.
WITH EVERYTHING THAT'S BROKEN, YOU REALLY THINK I CAN WAKE HER UP JUST BY TALKING TO HER?
THIS IS GOTHAM I.C.U. NOT MANY WALK OUT OF HERE, IT'S TRUE. BUT WE DO ALL WE CAN...
...AND EVERY LITTLE BIT HELPS.
HOPE YOU TAKE AFTER YOUR COUSIN, BETTE.
KATE'S A FIGHTER.
AND SHE ALWAYS LIKED SPY NOVELS.
YOU ONLY LIVE TWICE: ONCE WHEN YOU ARE BORN AND ONCE WHEN YOU LOOK DEATH IN THE FACE...

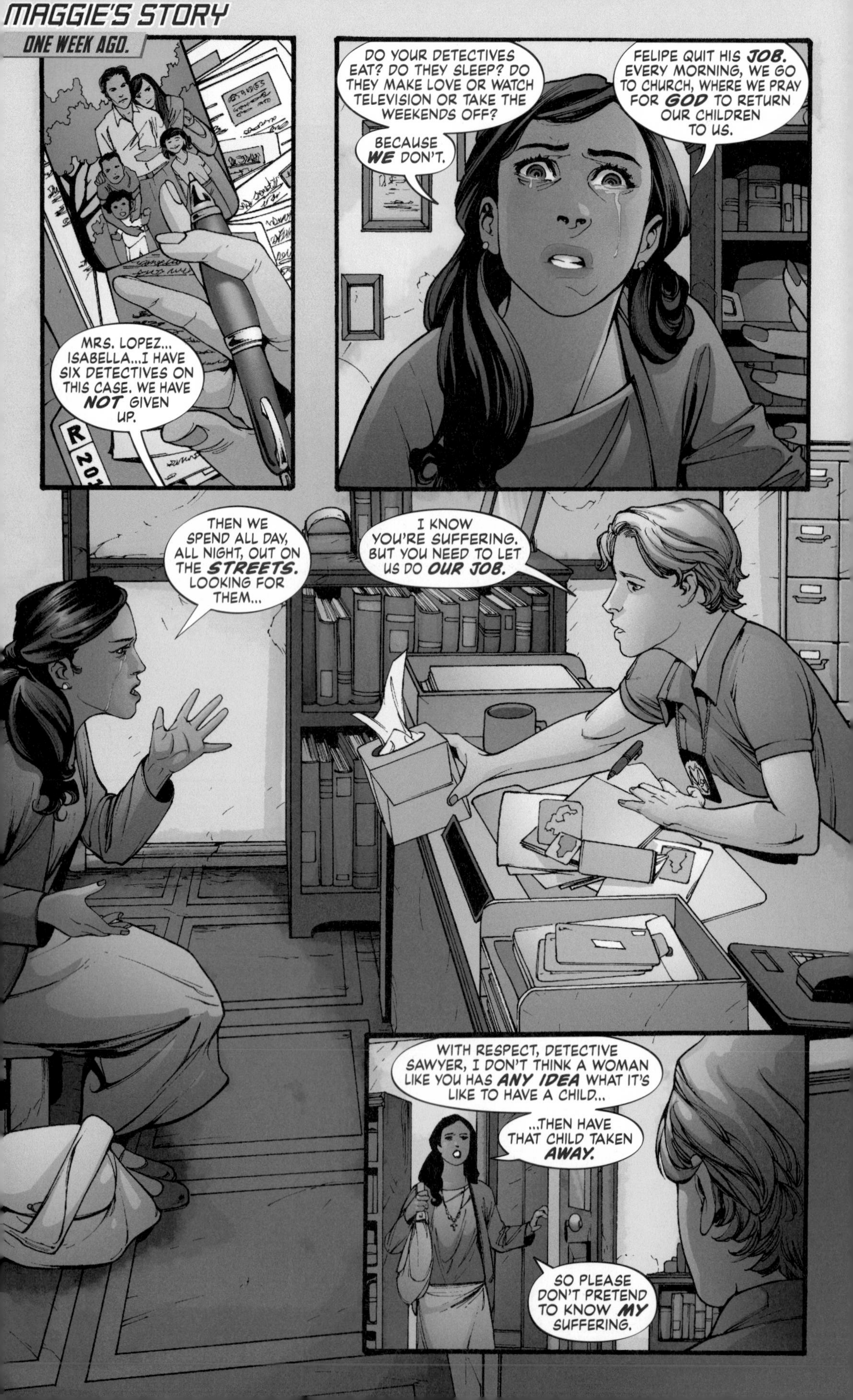

MAGGIE'S STORY
ONE WEEK AGO.
MRS. LOPEZ... ISABELLA...I HAVE SIX DETECTIVES ON THIS CASE. WE HAVE NOT GIVEN UP.
DO YOUR DETECTIVES EAT? DO THEY SLEEP? DO THEY MAKE LOVE OR WATCH TELEVISION OR TAKE THE WEEKENDS OFF?
BECAUSE WE DON'T.
FELIPE QUIT HIS JOB. EVERY MORNING, WE GO TO CHURCH, WHERE WE PRAY FOR GOD TO RETURN OUR CHILDREN TO US.
THEN WE SPEND ALL DAY, ALL NIGHT, OUT ON THE STREETS. LOOKING FOR THEM...
I KNOW YOU'RE SUFFERING. BUT YOU NEED TO LET US DO OUR JOB.
WITH RESPECT, DETECTIVE SAWYER, I DON'T THINK A WOMAN LIKE YOU HAS ANY IDEA WHAT IT'S LIKE TO HAVE A CHILD...
...THEN HAVE THAT CHILD TAKEN AWAY.
SO PLEASE DON'T PRETEND TO KNOW MY SUFFERING.

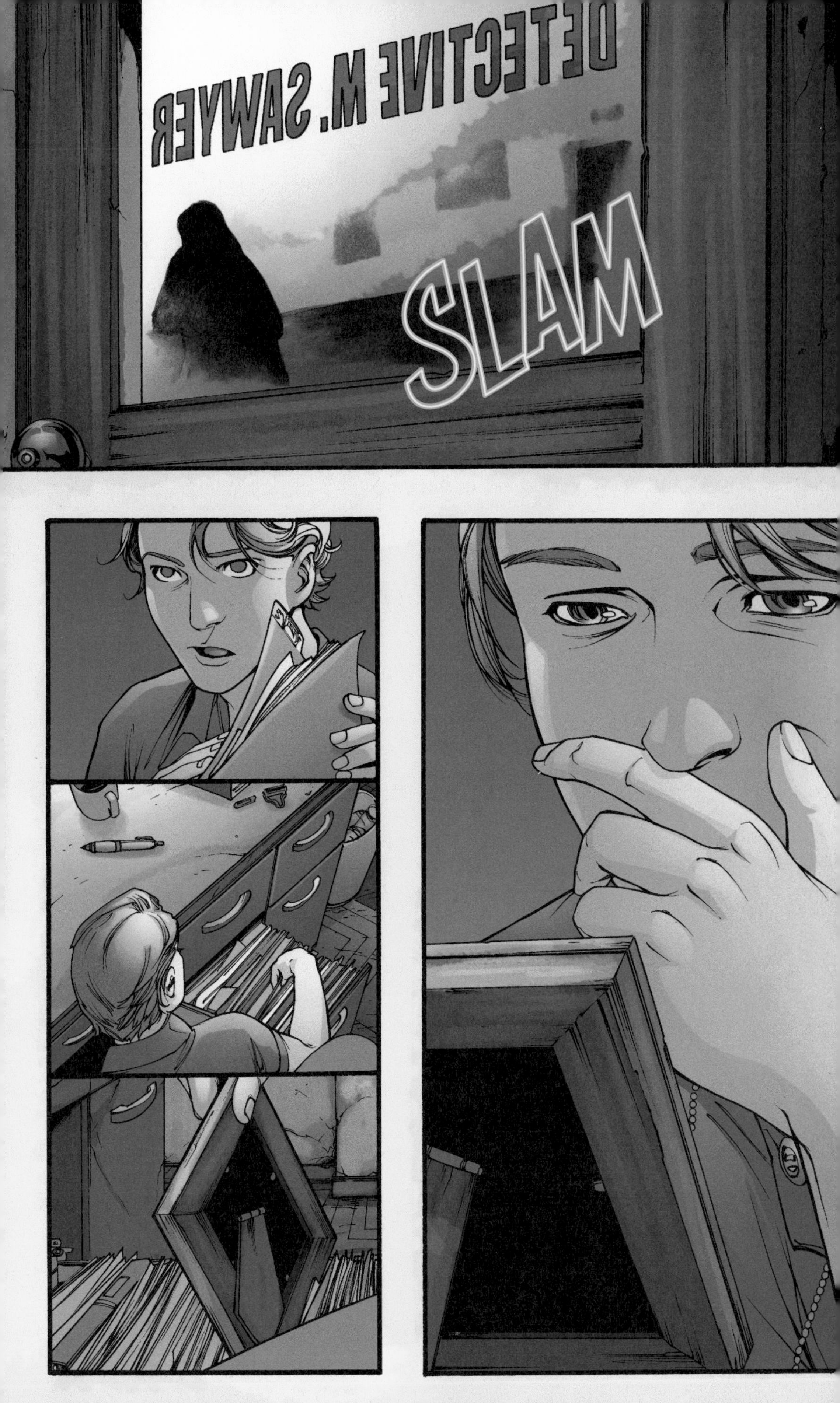
DETECTIVE M. SAWYER
SLAM

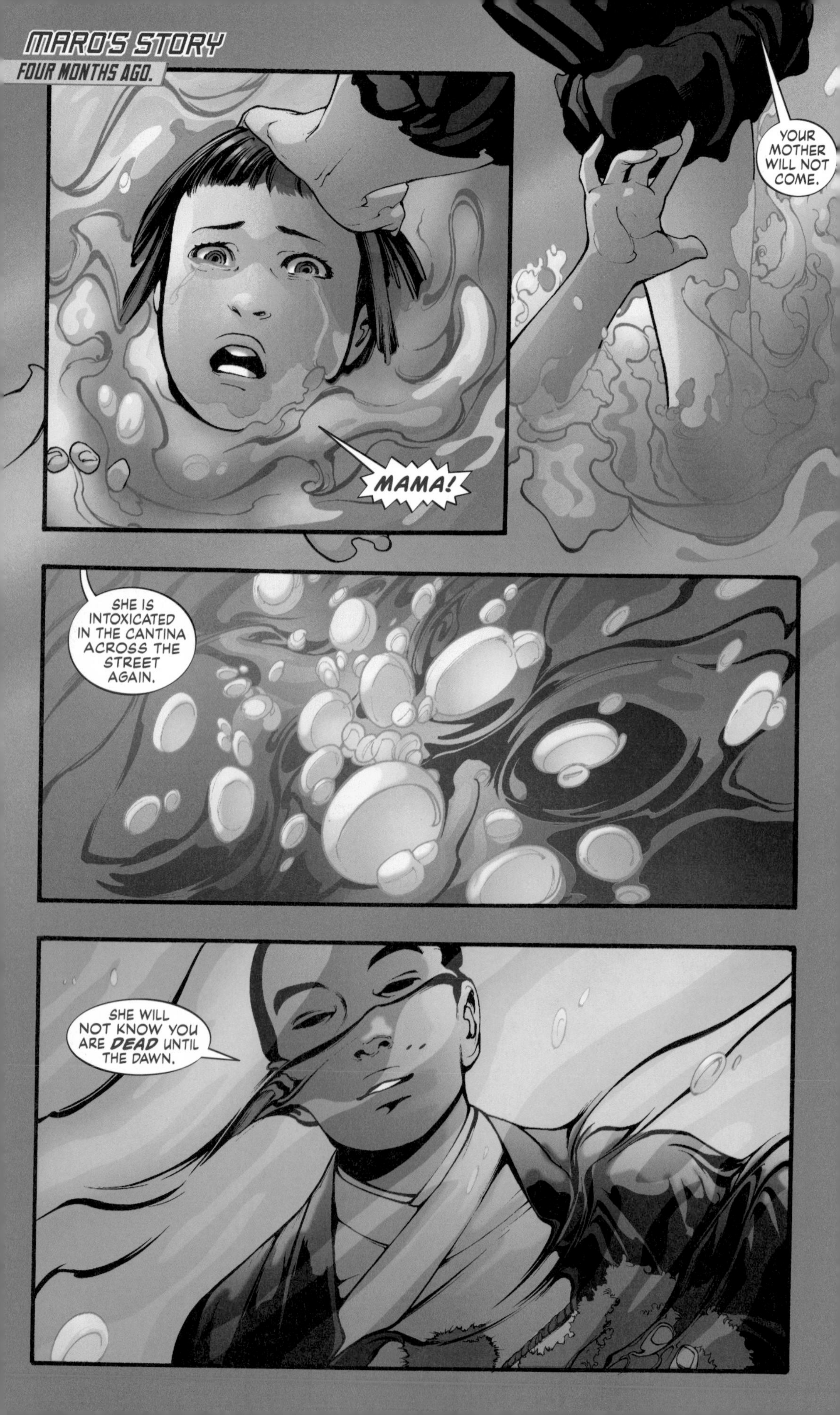
MARO'S STORY
FOUR MONTHS AGO.
MAMA!
YOUR MOTHER WILL NOT COME.
SHE IS INTOXICATED IN THE CANTINA ACROSS THE STREET AGAIN.
SHE WILL NOT KNOW YOU ARE DEAD UNTIL THE DAWN.

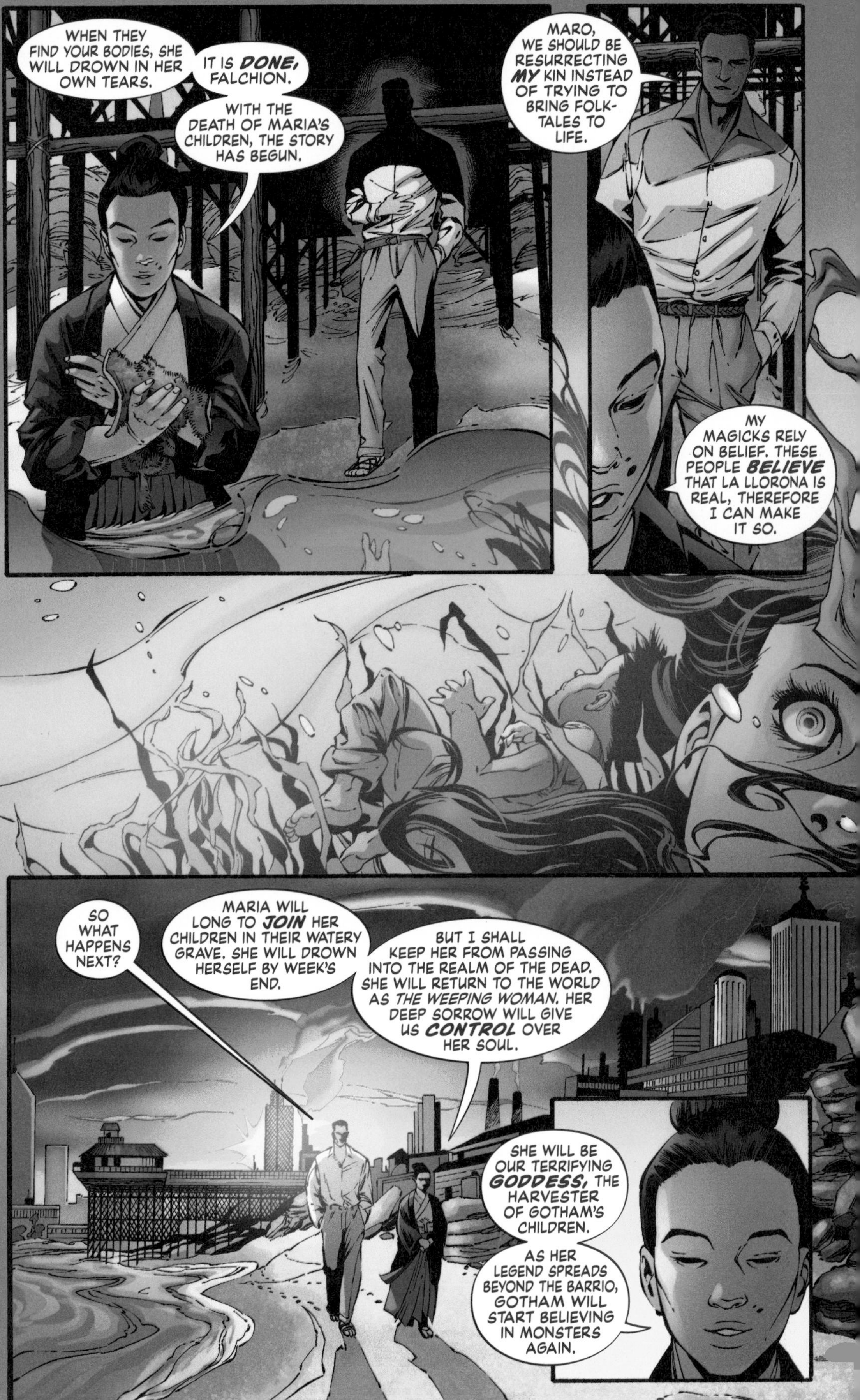
WHEN THEY FIND YOUR BODIES, SHE WILL DROWN IN HER OWN TEARS.
IT IS DONE, FALCHION.
WITH THE DEATH OF MARIA'S CHILDREN, THE STORY HAS BEGUN.
MARO, WE SHOULD BE RESURRECTING MY KIN INSTEAD OF TRYING TO BRING FOLK-TALES TO LIFE.
MY MAGICKS RELY ON BELIEF. THESE PEOPLE BELIEVE THAT LA LLORONA IS REAL, THEREFORE I CAN MAKE IT SO.
SO WHAT HAPPENS NEXT?
MARIA WILL LONG TO JOIN HER CHILDREN IN THEIR WATERY GRAVE. SHE WILL DROWN HERSELF BY WEEK'S END.
BUT I SHALL KEEP HER FROM PASSING INTO THE REALM OF THE DEAD. SHE WILL RETURN TO THE WORLD AS THE WEEPING WOMAN. HER DEEP SORROW WILL GIVE US CONTROL OVER HER SOUL.
SHE WILL BE OUR TERRIFYING GODDESS, THE HARVESTER OF GOTHAM'S CHILDREN.
AS HER LEGEND SPREADS BEYOND THE BARRIO, GOTHAM WILL START BELIEVING IN MONSTERS AGAIN.

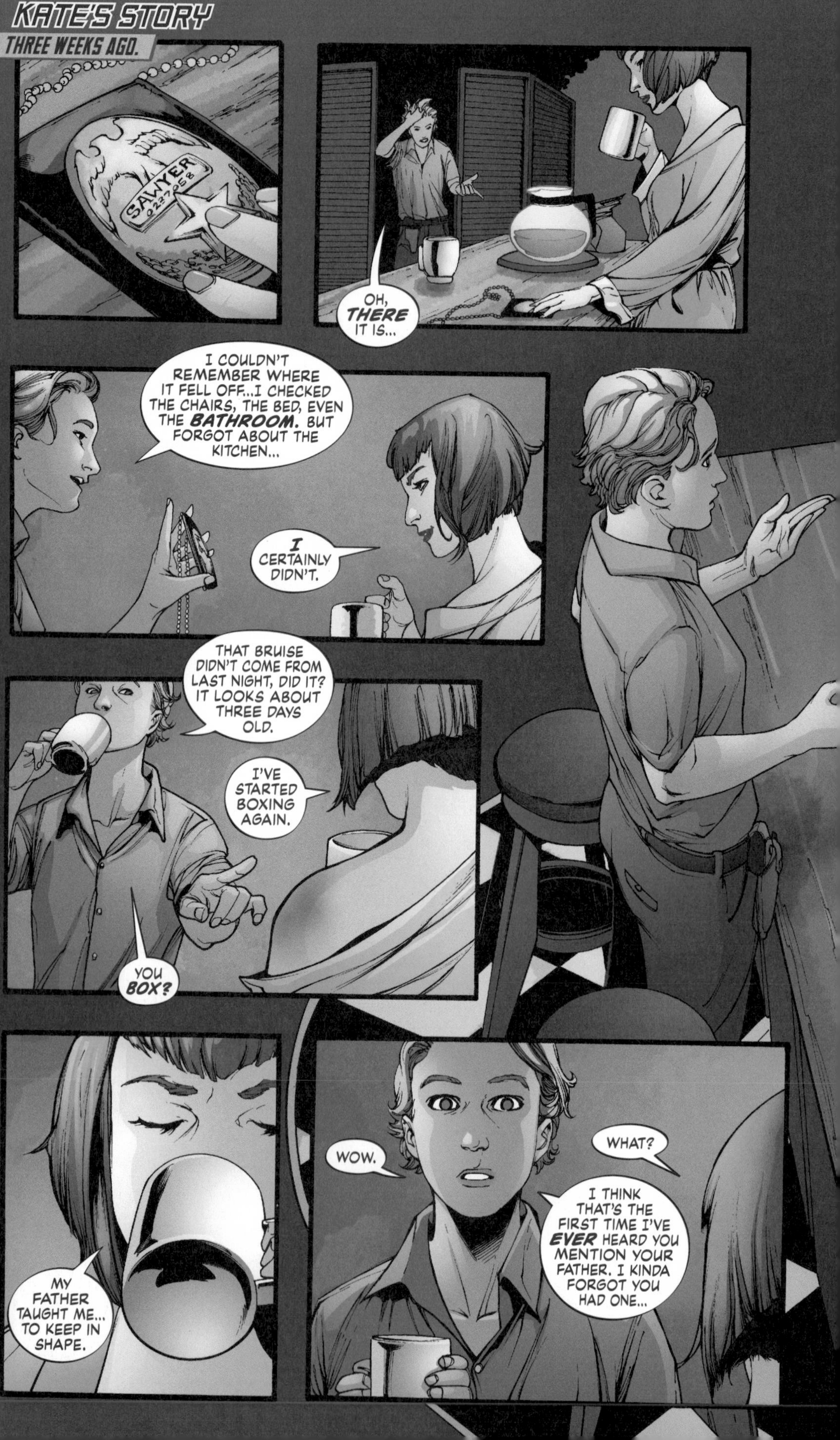
KATE'S STORY
THREE WEEKS AGO.
SAWYER
OH, THERE IT IS...
I COULDN'T REMEMBER WHERE IT FELL OFF...I CHECKED THE CHAIRS, THE BED, EVEN THE BATHROOM. BUT FORGOT ABOUT THE KITCHEN...
I CERTAINLY DIDN'T.
THAT BRUISE DIDN'T COME FROM LAST NIGHT, DID IT? IT LOOKS ABOUT THREE DAYS OLD.
I'VE STARTED BOXING AGAIN.
YOU BOX?
MY FATHER TAUGHT ME... TO KEEP IN SHAPE.
WOW.
WHAT?
I THINK THAT'S THE FIRST TIME I'VE EVER HEARD YOU MENTION YOUR FATHER. I KINDA FORGOT YOU HAD ONE...

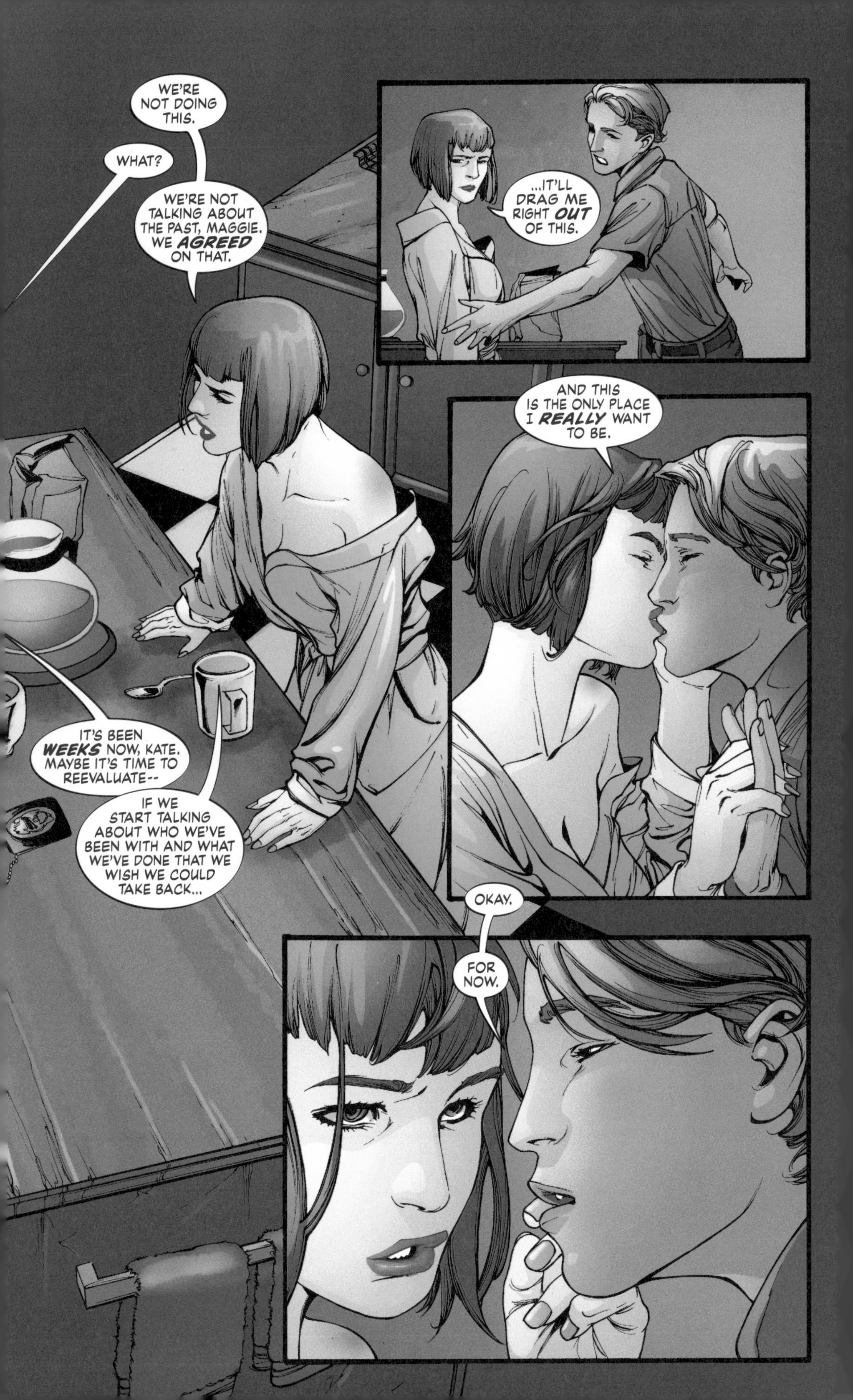
WE'RE NOT DOING THIS.
WHAT?
WE'RE NOT TALKING ABOUT THE PAST, MAGGIE. WE AGREED ON THAT.
...IT'LL DRAG ME RIGHT OUT OF THIS.
AND THIS IS THE ONLY PLACE I REALLY WANT TO BE.
IT'S BEEN WEEKS NOW, KATE. MAYBE IT'S TIME TO REEVALUATE--
IF WE START TALKING ABOUT WHO WE'VE BEEN WITH AND WHAT WE'VE DONE THAT WE WISH WE COULD TAKE BACK...
OKAY.
FOR NOW.

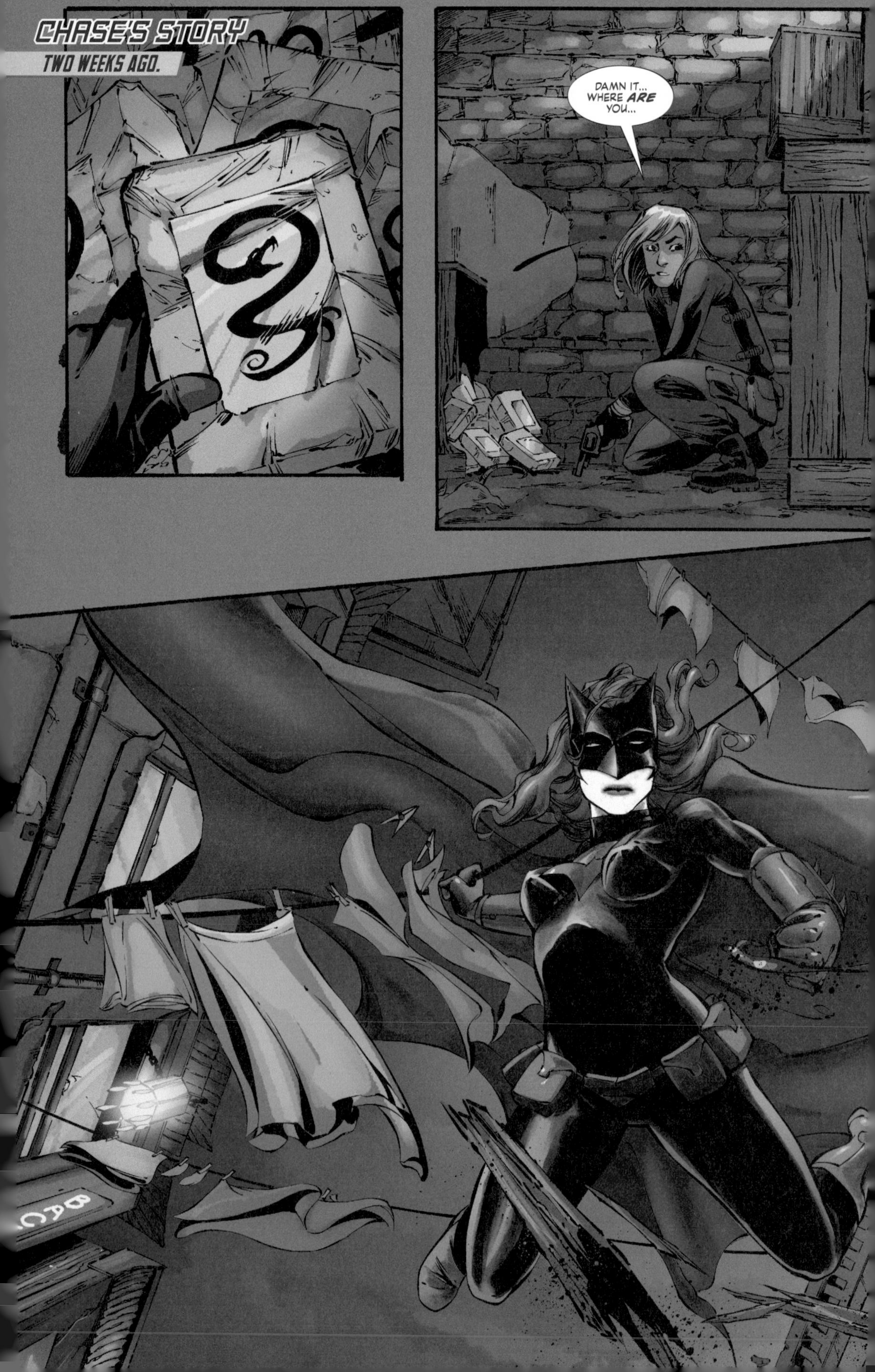
CHASE'S STORY
TWO WEEKS AGO.
DAMN IT... WHERE ARE YOU...

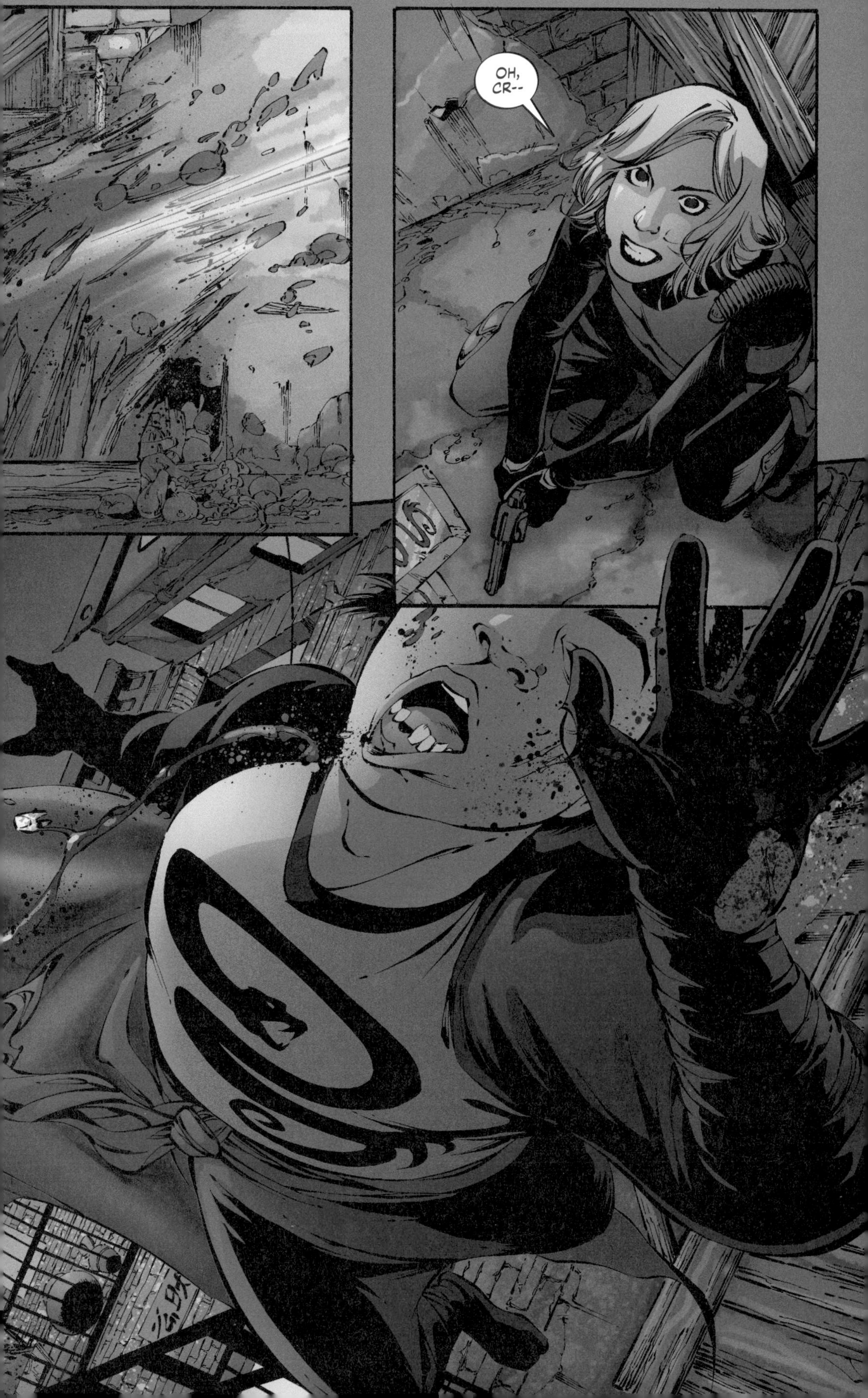
OH, CR--

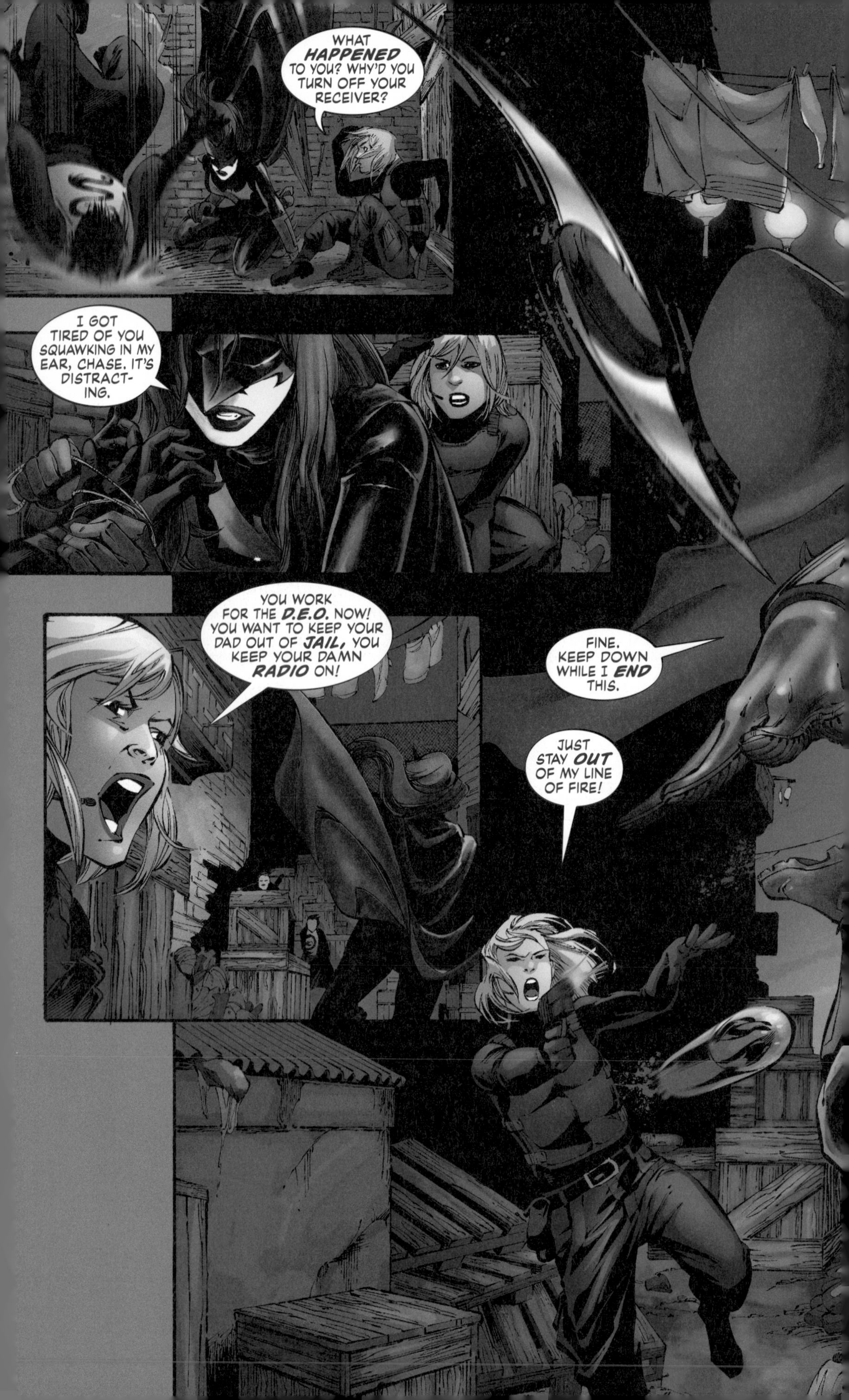
WHAT HAPPENED TO YOU? WHY'D YOU TURN OFF YOUR RECEIVER?
I GOT TIRED OF YOU SQUAWKING IN MY EAR, CHASE. IT'S DISTRACTING.
YOU WORK FOR THE D.E.O. NOW! YOU WANT TO KEEP YOUR DAD OUT OF JAIL, YOU KEEP YOUR DAMN RADIO ON!
FINE. KEEP DOWN WHILE I END THIS.
JUST STAY OUT OF MY LINE OF FIRE!

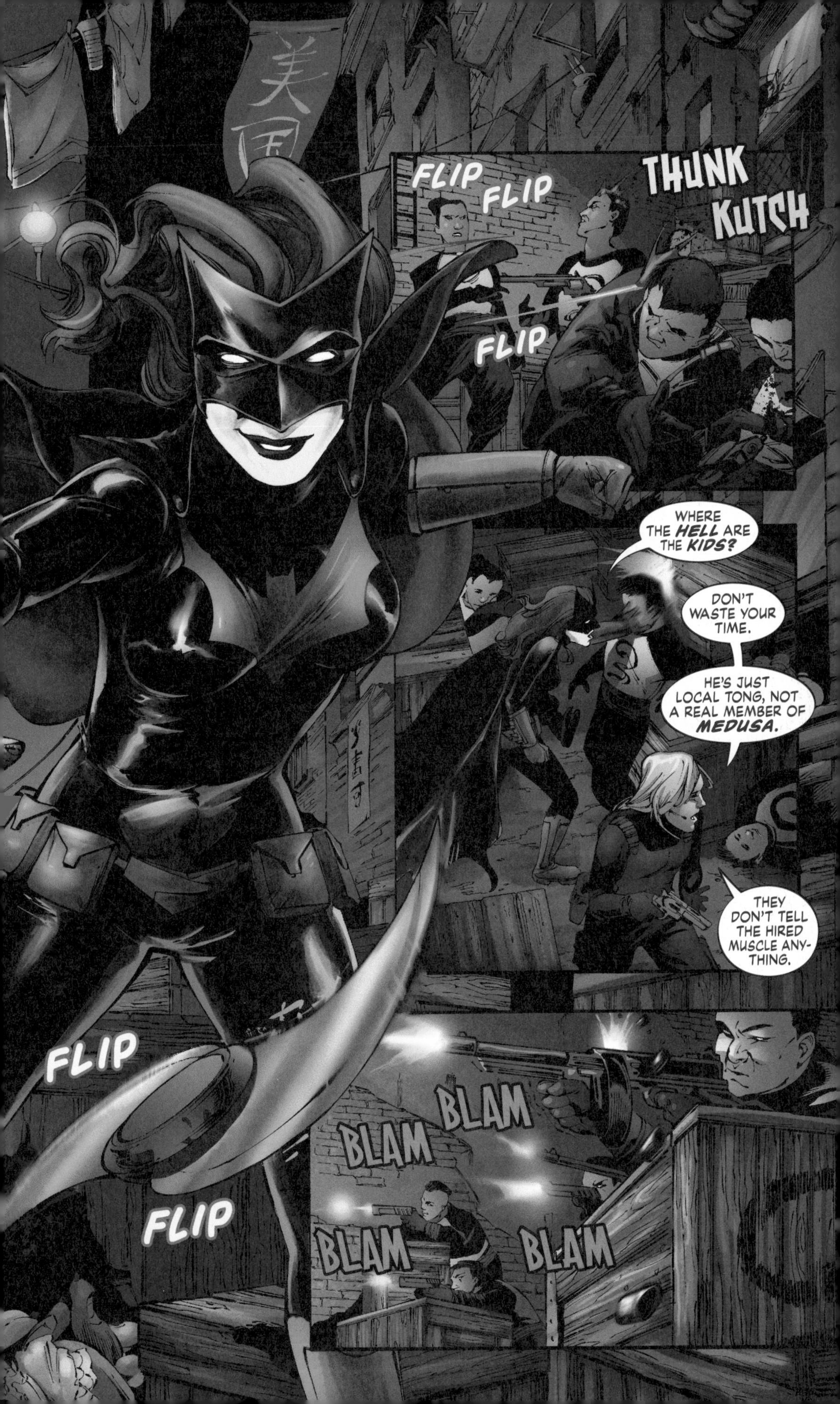

FLIP
FLIP
THUNK
KUTCH
FLIP
WHERE THE HELL ARE THE KIDS?
DON'T WASTE YOUR TIME.
HE'S JUST LOCAL TONG, NOT A REAL MEMBER OF MEDUSA.
THEY DON'T TELL THE HIRED MUSCLE ANY-THING.
FLIP
FLIP
BLAM
BLAM
BLAM
BLAM

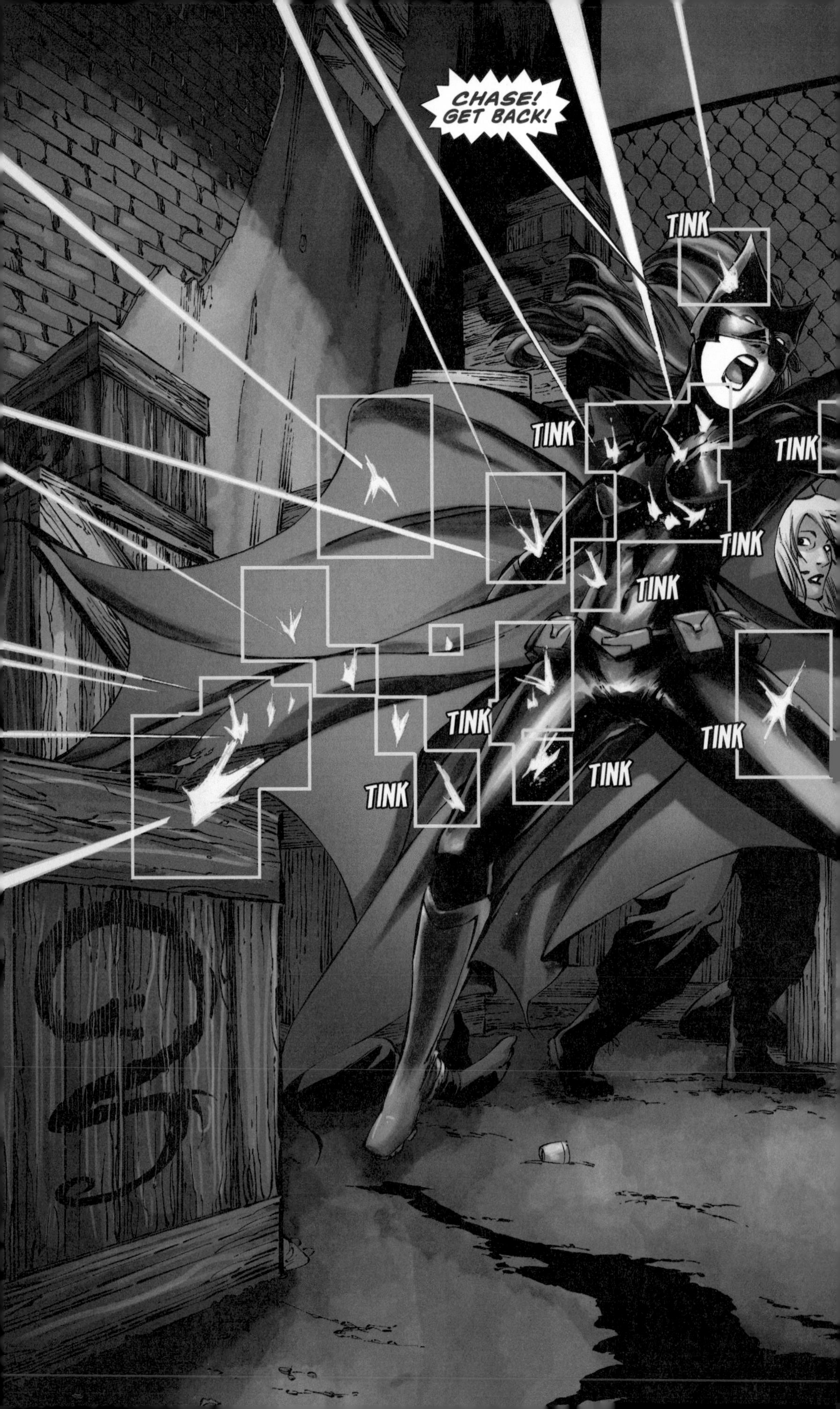

CHASE! GET BACK!
TINK
TINK
TINK
TINK
TINK
TINK
TINK
TINK
TINK

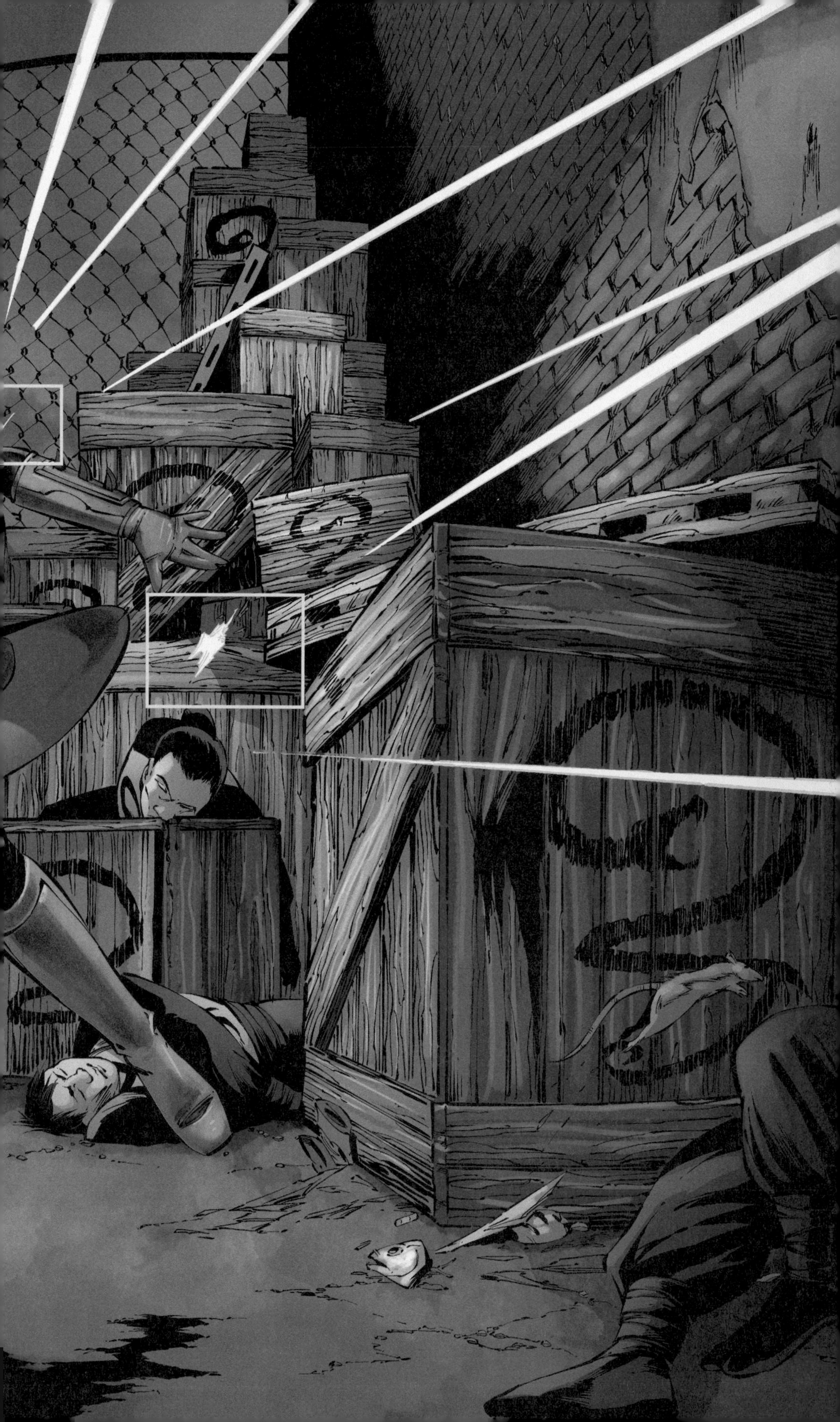

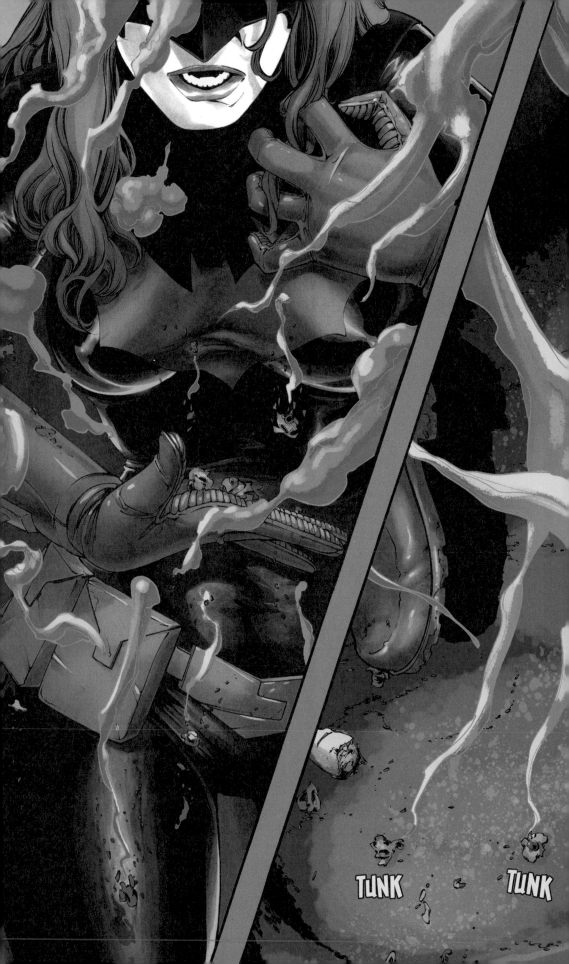

TUNK   TUNK

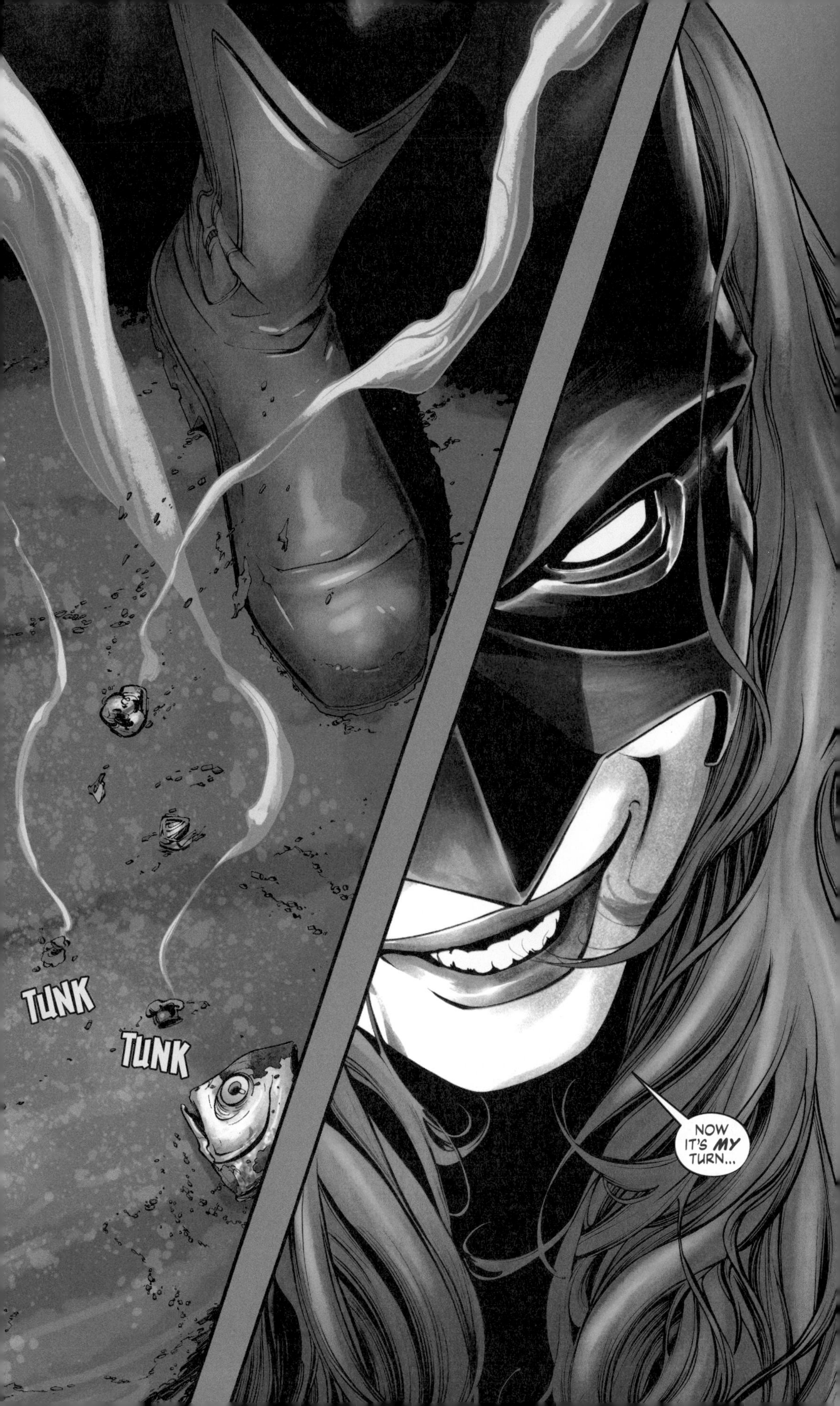
TUNK
TUNK
NOW IT'S *MY* TURN...

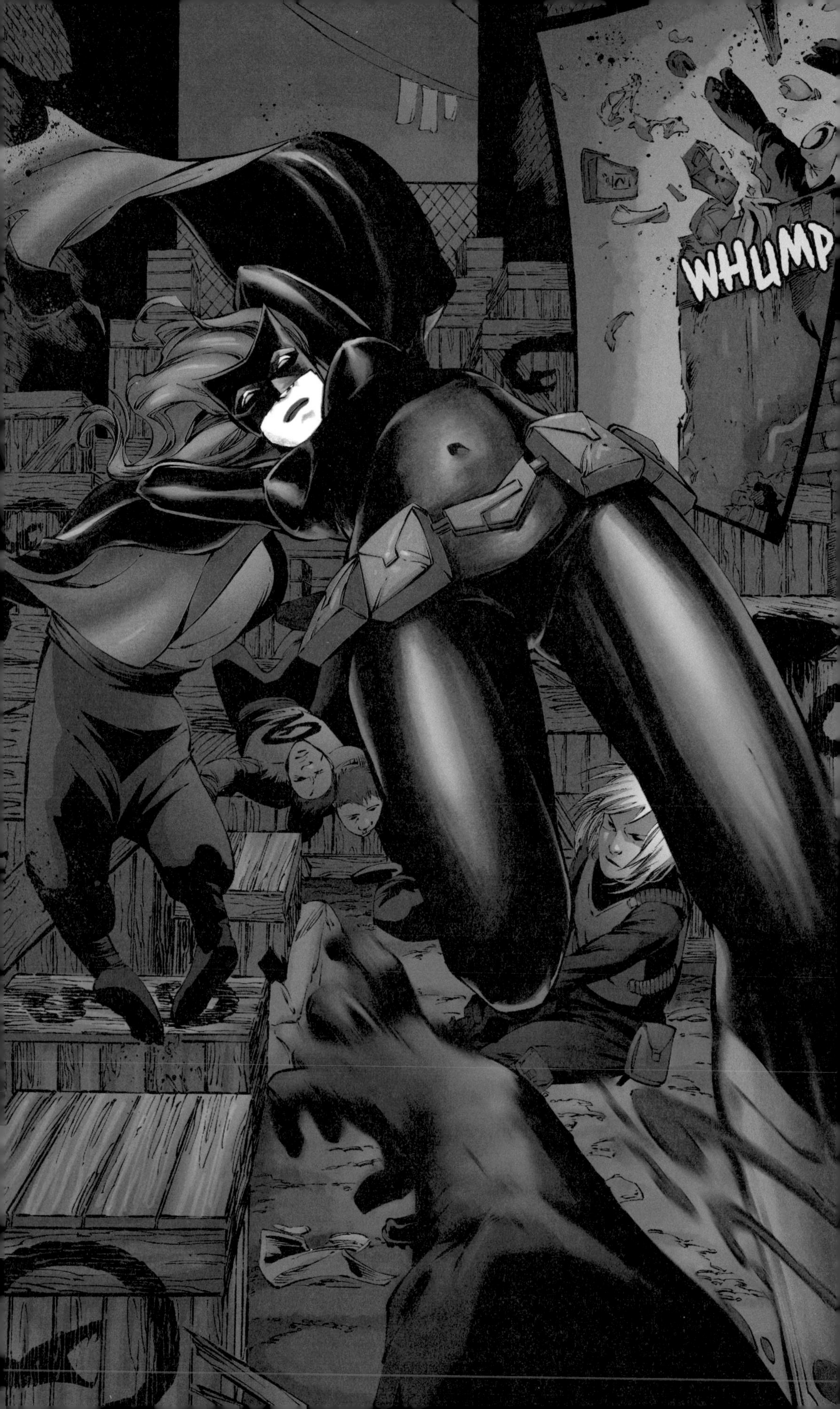
WHUMP

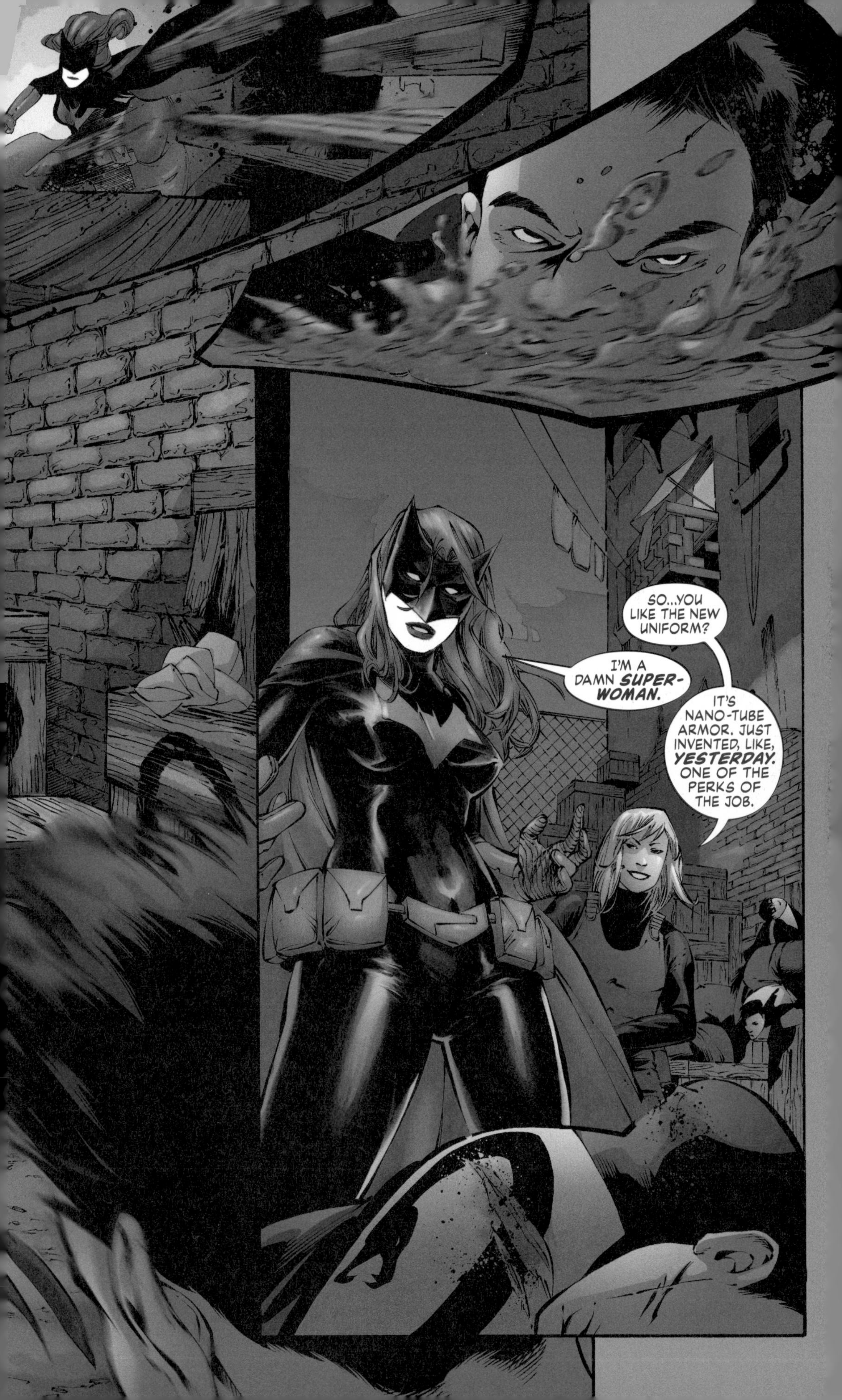

SO...YOU LIKE THE NEW UNIFORM?
I'M A DAMN SUPER-WOMAN.
IT'S NANO-TUBE ARMOR. JUST INVENTED, LIKE, YESTERDAY. ONE OF THE PERKS OF THE JOB.

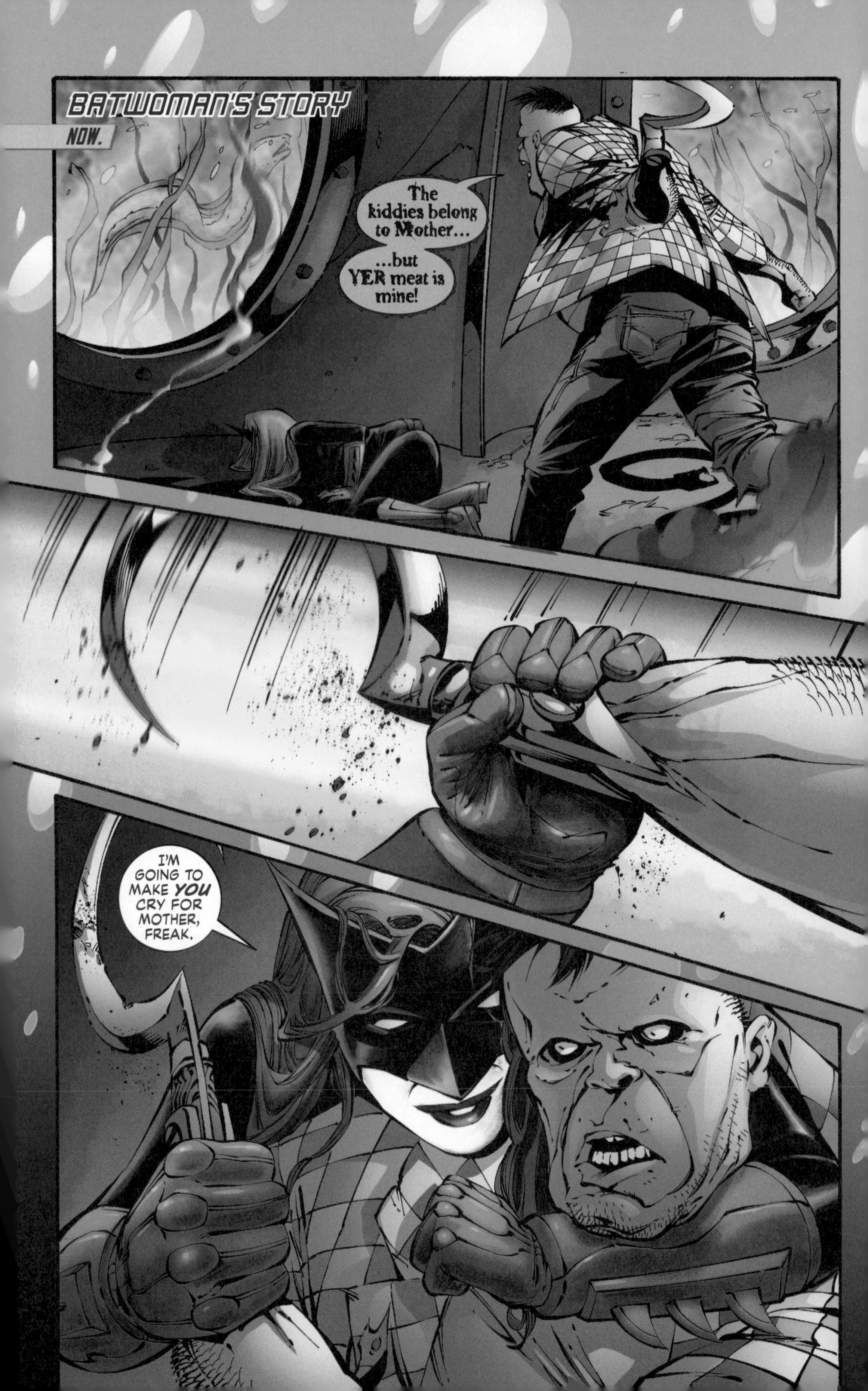
BATWOMAN'S STORY
NOW.
The kiddies belong to Mother...
...but YER meat is mine!
I'M GOING TO MAKE YOU CRY FOR MOTHER, FREAK.

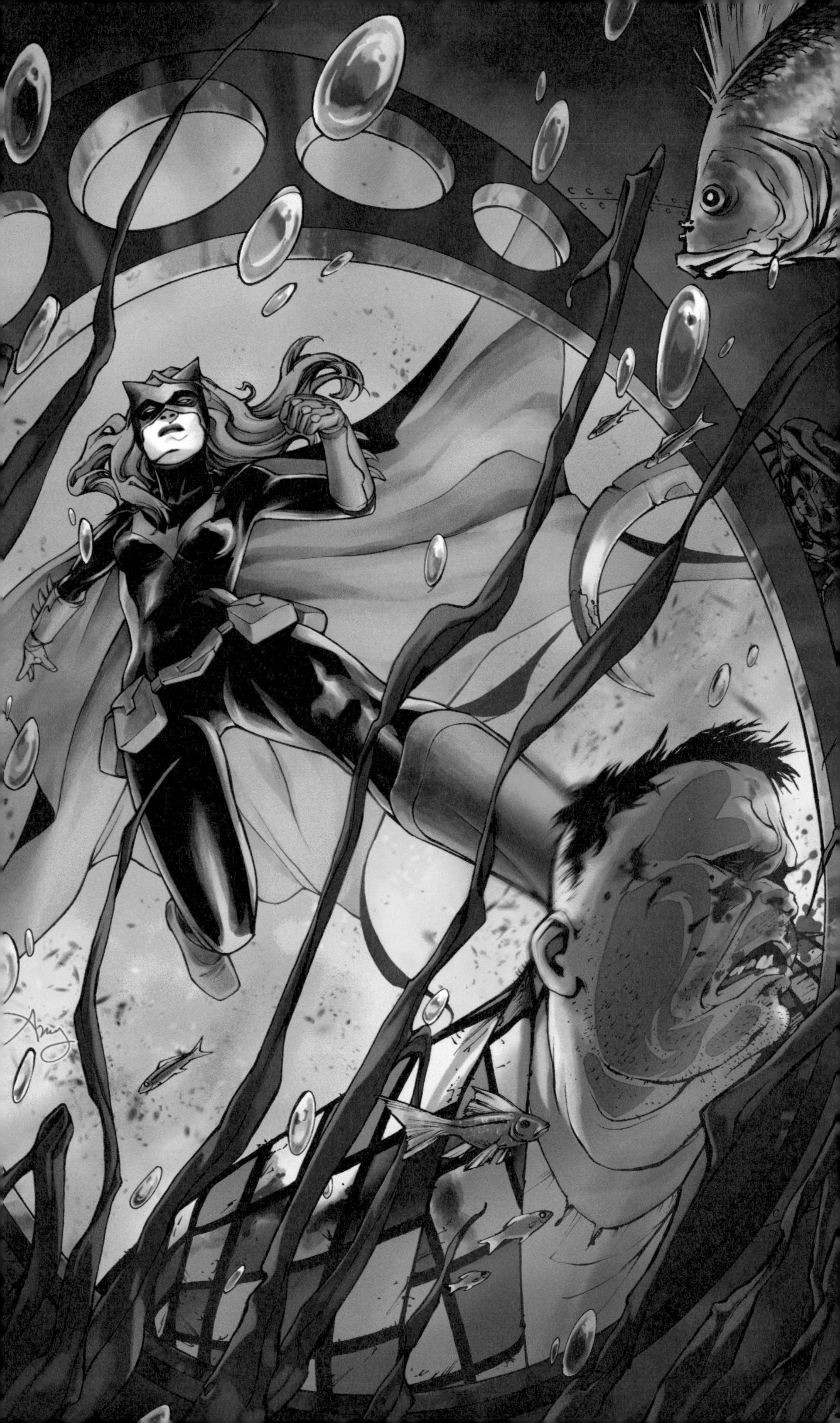

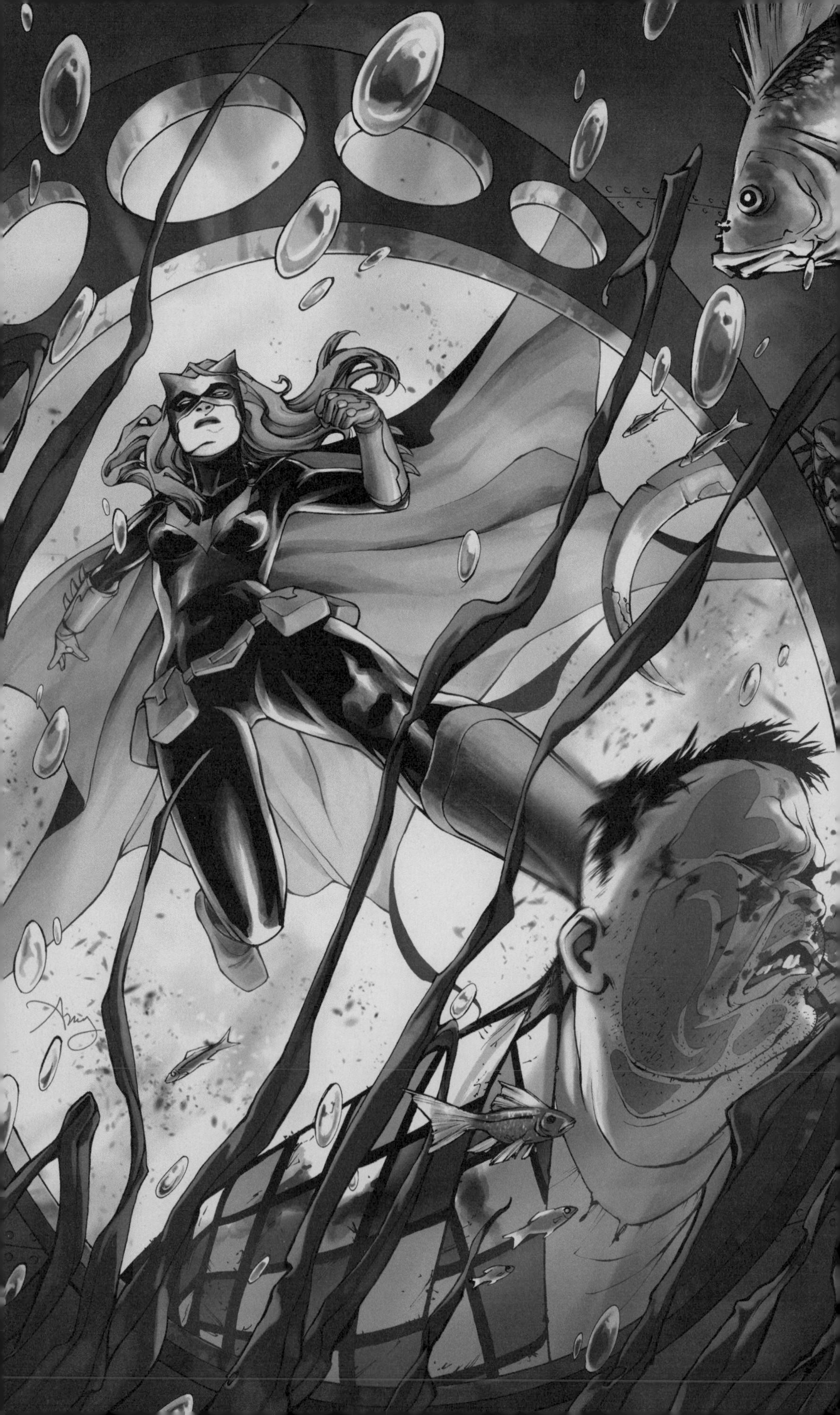

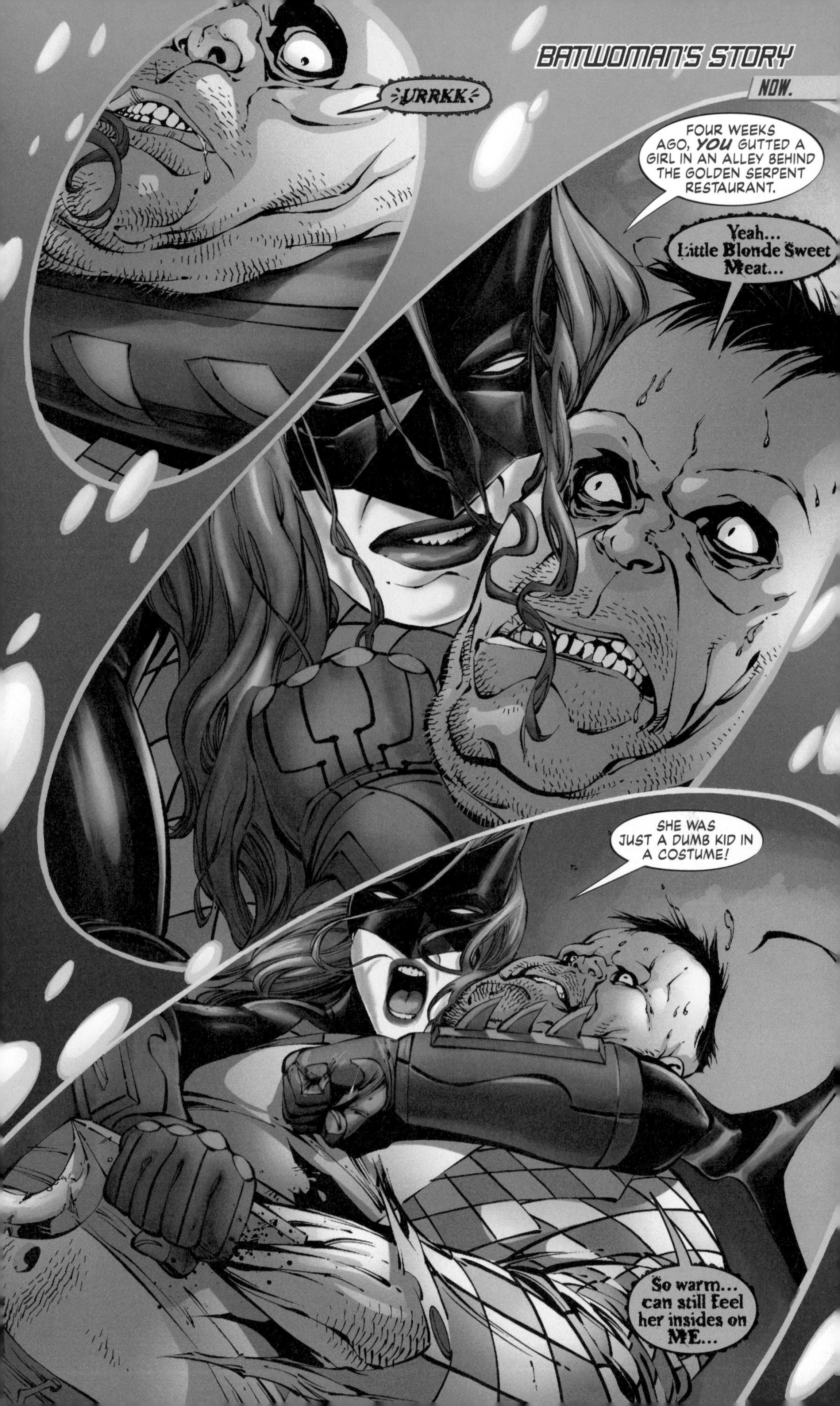

BATWOMAN'S STORY
NOW.
URRKK
FOUR WEEKS AGO, YOU GUTTED A GIRL IN AN ALLEY BEHIND THE GOLDEN SERPENT RESTAURANT.
Yeah... Little Blonde Sweet Meat...
SHE WAS JUST A DUMB KID IN A COSTUME!
So warm... can still feel her insides on ME...

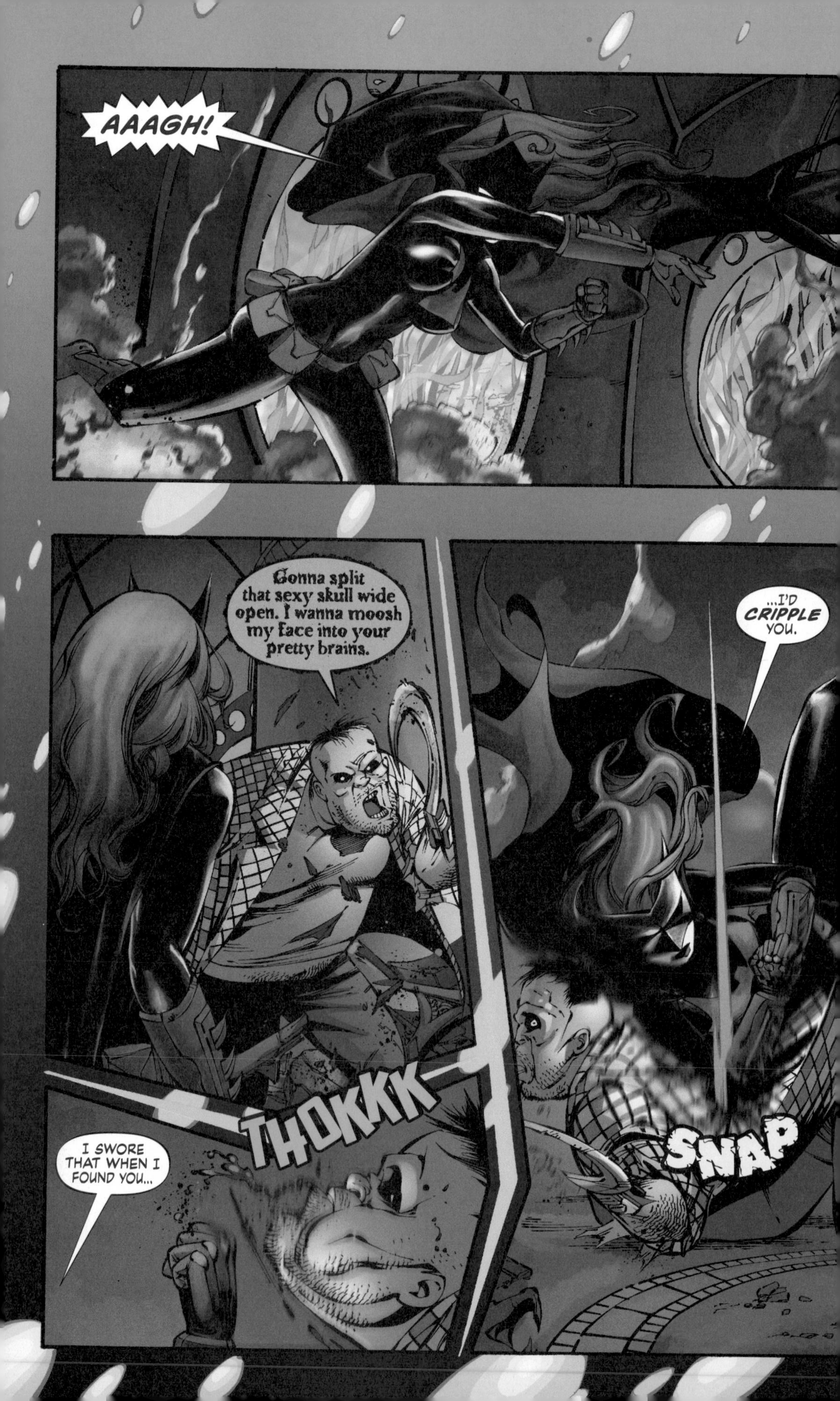
AAAGH!
Gonna split that sexy skull wide open. I wanna moosh my face into your pretty brains.
THOKKK
I SWORE THAT WHEN I FOUND YOU...
...I'D CRIPPLE YOU.
SNAP

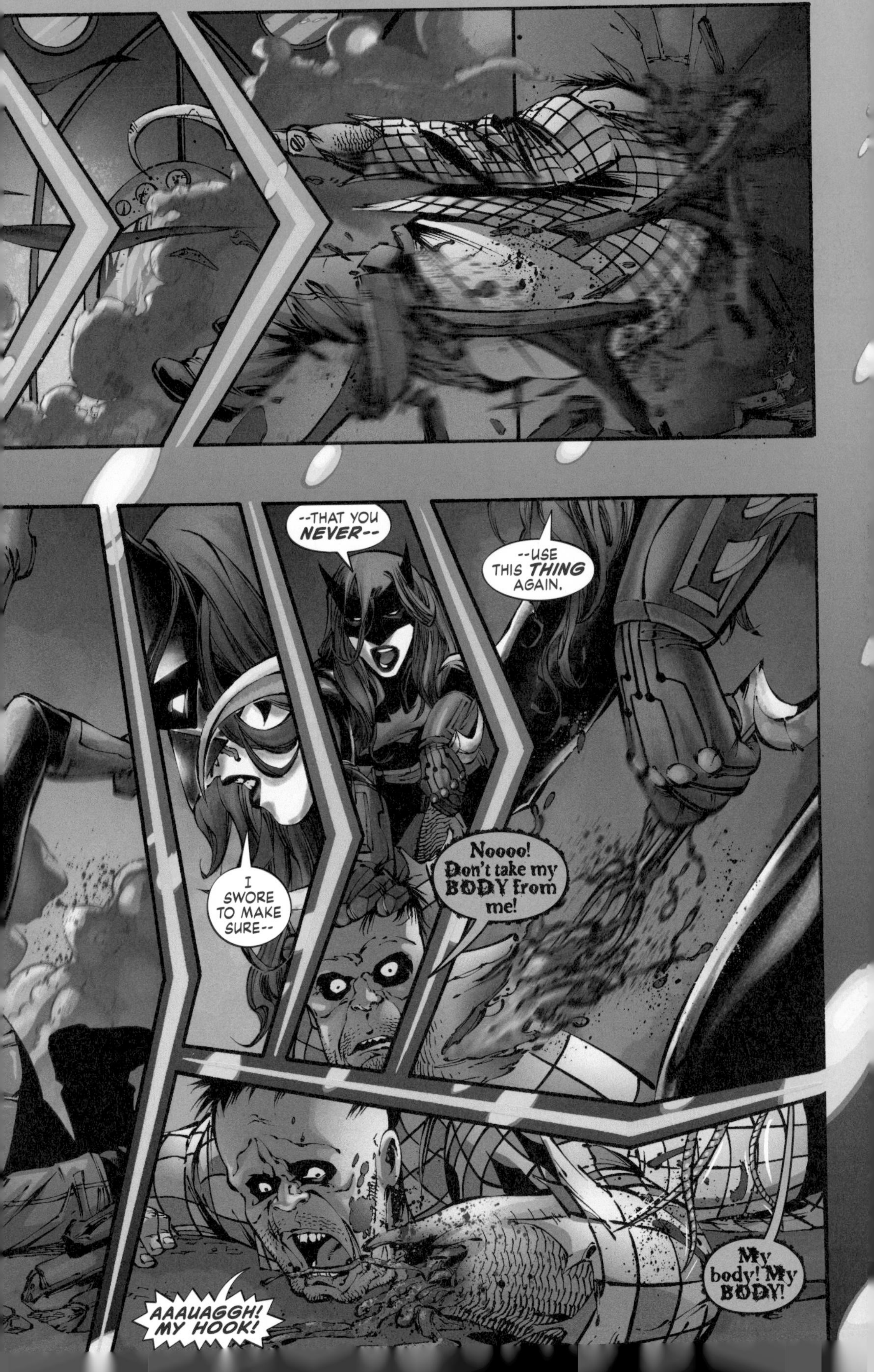
--THAT YOU NEVER--
--USE THIS THING AGAIN.
I SWORE TO MAKE SURE--
Noooo! Don't take my BODY from me!
AAAUAGGH! MY HOOK!
My body! My BODY!

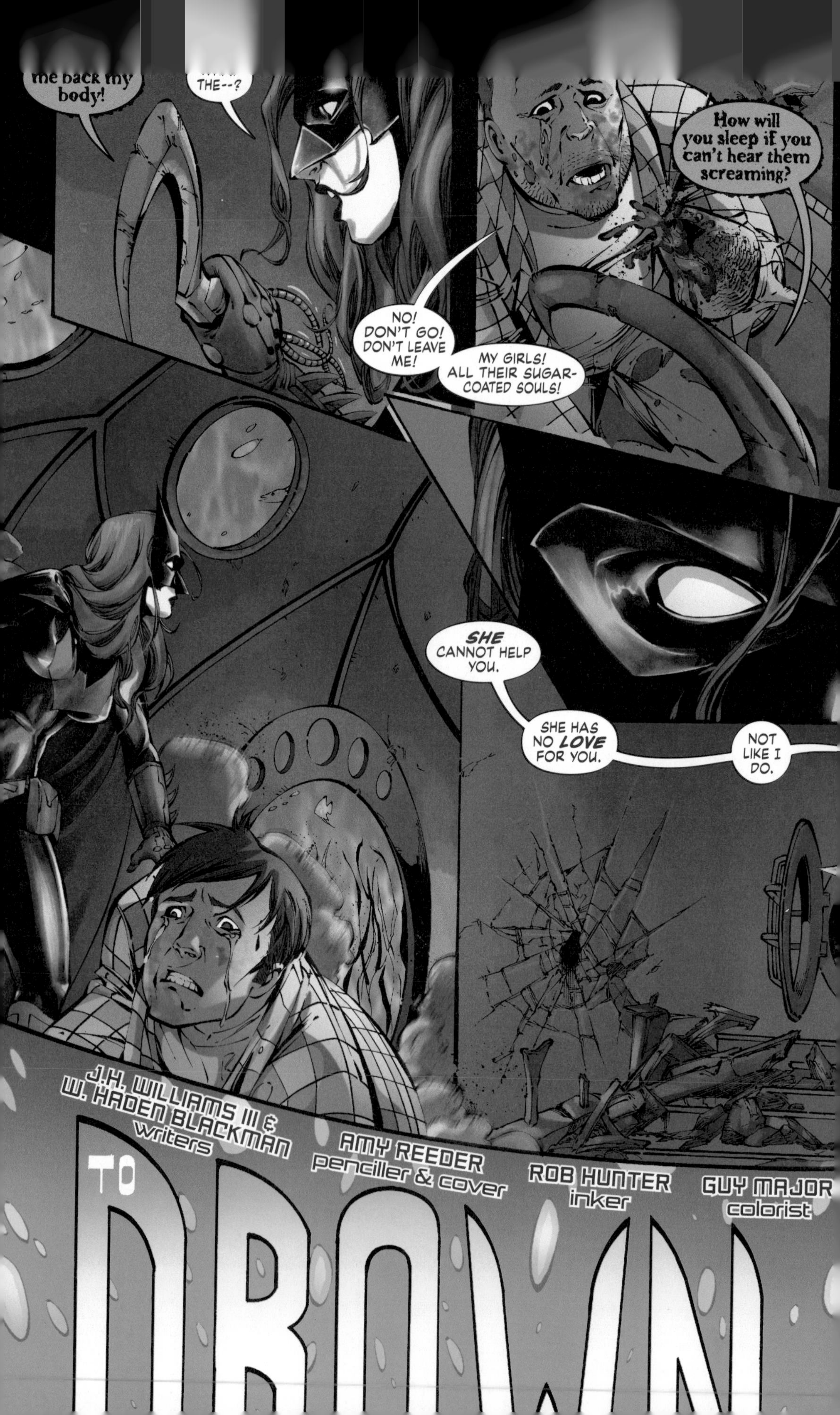
me back my body!
THE--?
How will you sleep if you can't hear them screaming?
NO! DON'T GO! DON'T LEAVE ME!
MY GIRLS! ALL THEIR SUGAR-COATED SOULS!
SHE CANNOT HELP YOU.
SHE HAS NO LOVE FOR YOU.
NOT LIKE I DO.
J.H. WILLIAMS III & W. HADEN BLACKMAN writers
AMY REEDER penciller & cover
ROB HUNTER inker
GUY MAJOR colorist
TO DROWN

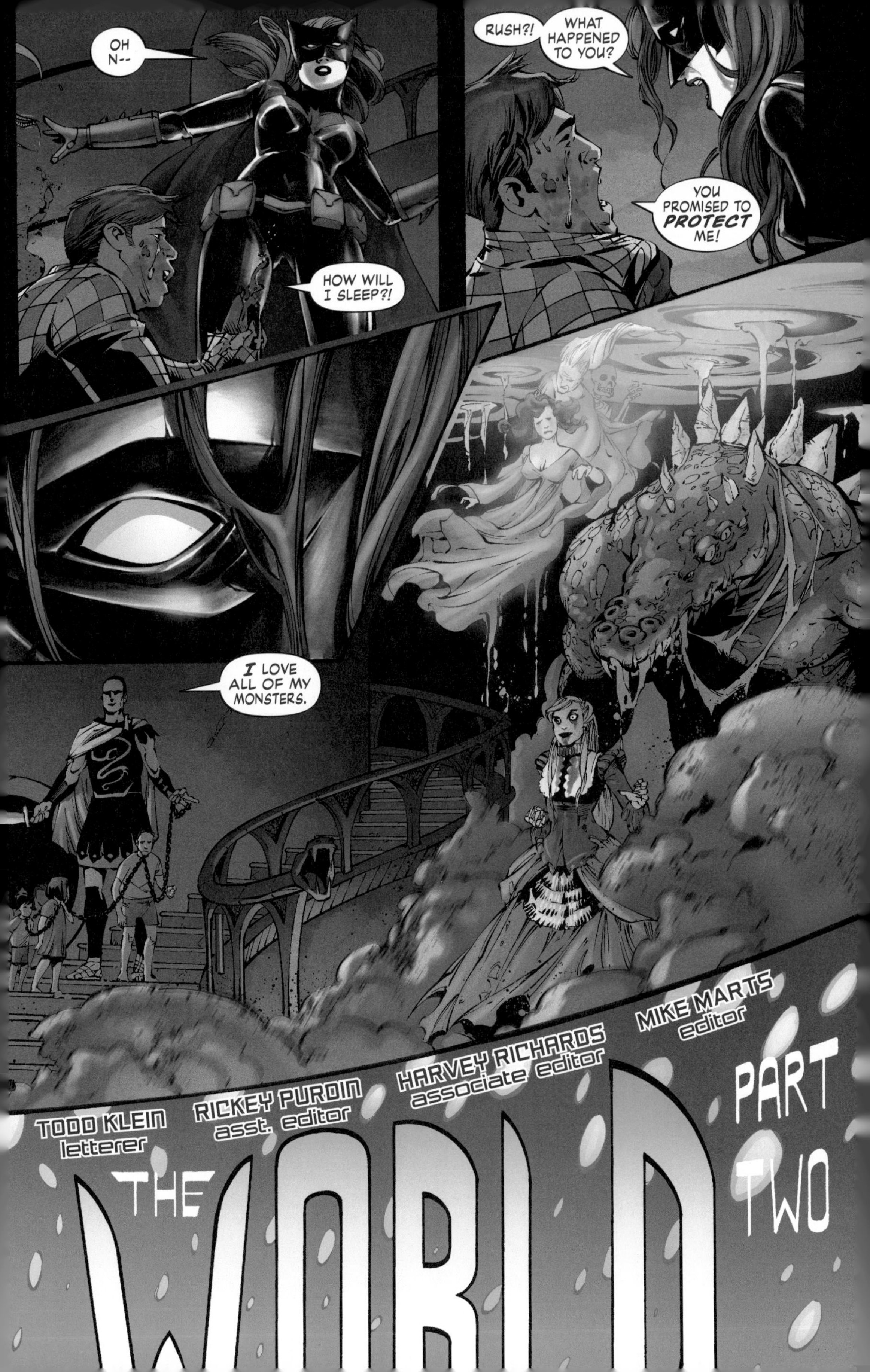

OH N--
HOW WILL I SLEEP?!
RUSH?!
WHAT HAPPENED TO YOU?
YOU PROMISED TO PROTECT ME!
I LOVE ALL OF MY MONSTERS.
TODD KLEIN letterer
RICKEY PURDIN asst. editor
HARVEY RICHARDS associate editor
MIKE MARTS editor
THE WORLD PART TWO

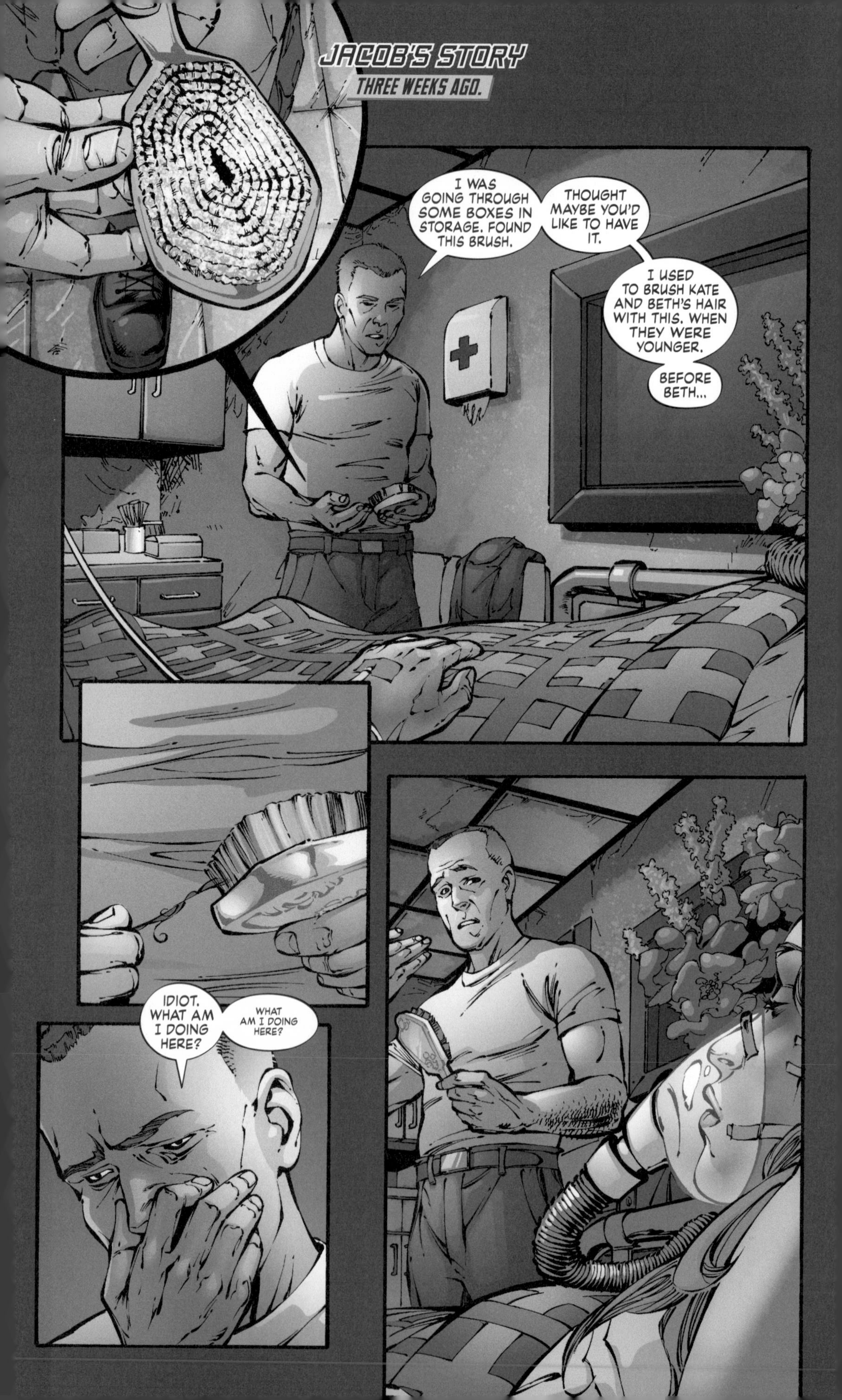

JACOB'S STORY
THREE WEEKS AGO.
I WAS GOING THROUGH SOME BOXES IN STORAGE. FOUND THIS BRUSH.
THOUGHT MAYBE YOU'D LIKE TO HAVE IT.
I USED TO BRUSH KATE AND BETH'S HAIR WITH THIS. WHEN THEY WERE YOUNGER.
BEFORE BETH...
IDIOT. WHAT AM I DOING HERE?
WHAT AM I DOING HERE?

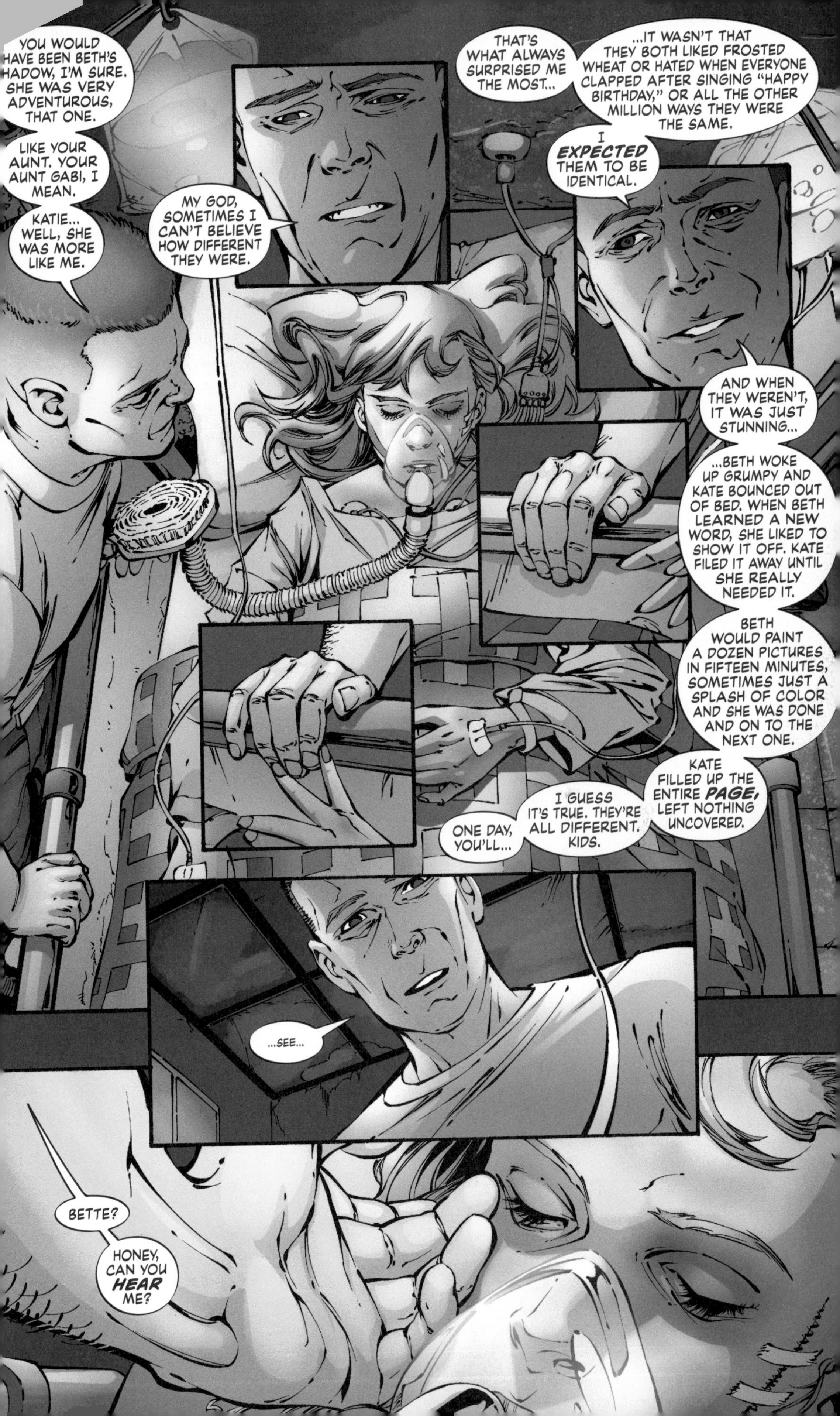
YOU WOULD HAVE BEEN BETH'S SHADOW, I'M SURE. SHE WAS VERY ADVENTUROUS, THAT ONE.
LIKE YOUR AUNT. YOUR AUNT GABI, I MEAN.
KATIE... WELL, SHE WAS MORE LIKE ME.
MY GOD, SOMETIMES I CAN'T BELIEVE HOW DIFFERENT THEY WERE.
THAT'S WHAT ALWAYS SURPRISED ME THE MOST...
...IT WASN'T THAT THEY BOTH LIKED FROSTED WHEAT OR HATED WHEN EVERYONE CLAPPED AFTER SINGING "HAPPY BIRTHDAY," OR ALL THE OTHER MILLION WAYS THEY WERE THE SAME.
I EXPECTED THEM TO BE IDENTICAL.
AND WHEN THEY WEREN'T, IT WAS JUST STUNNING...
...BETH WOKE UP GRUMPY AND KATE BOUNCED OUT OF BED. WHEN BETH LEARNED A NEW WORD, SHE LIKED TO SHOW IT OFF. KATE FILED IT AWAY UNTIL SHE REALLY NEEDED IT.
BETH WOULD PAINT A DOZEN PICTURES IN FIFTEEN MINUTES, SOMETIMES JUST A SPLASH OF COLOR AND SHE WAS DONE AND ON TO THE NEXT ONE.
KATE FILLED UP THE ENTIRE PAGE, LEFT NOTHING UNCOVERED.
I GUESS IT'S TRUE. THEY'RE ALL DIFFERENT. KIDS.
ONE DAY, YOU'LL...
...SEE...
BETTE?
HONEY, CAN YOU HEAR ME?

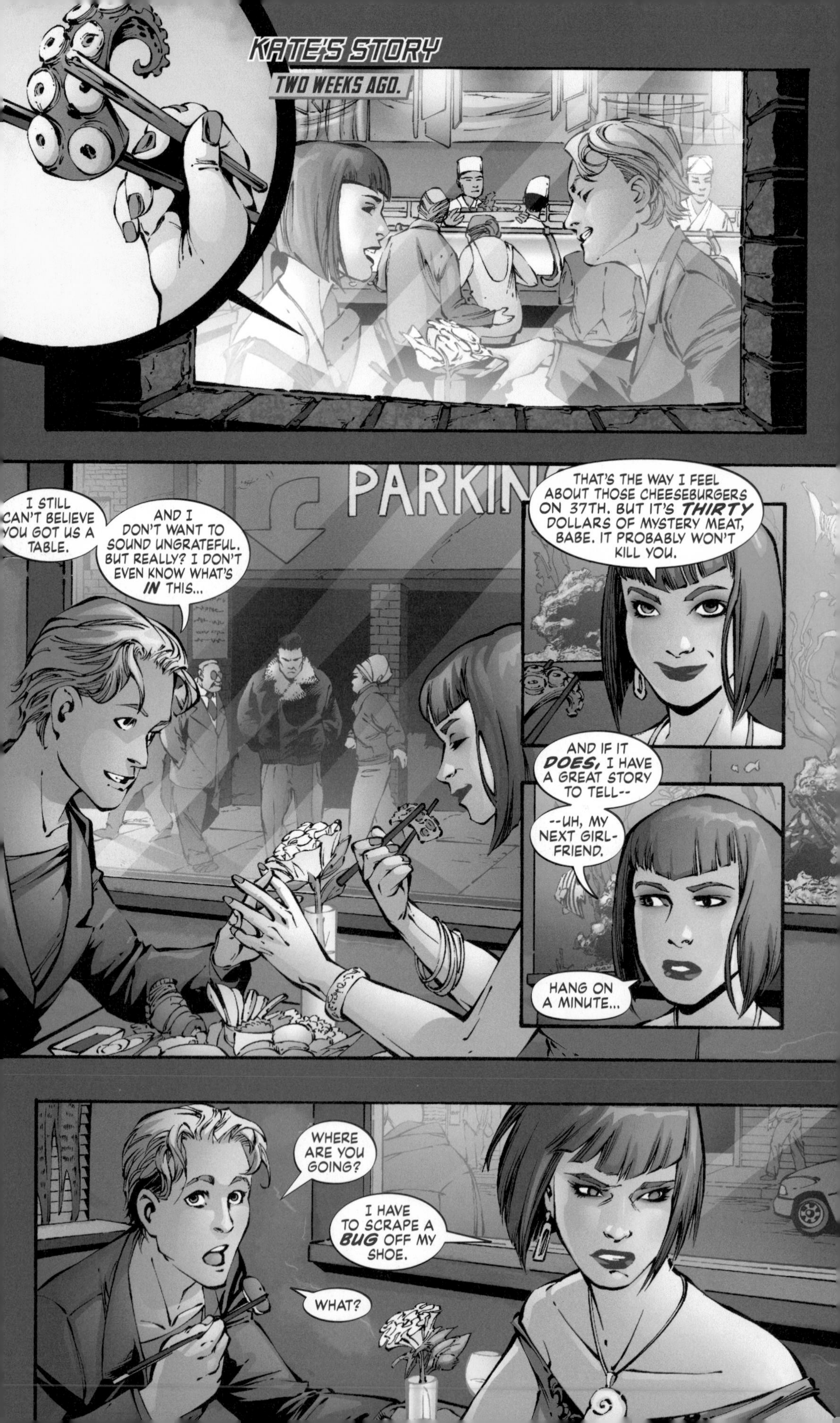

KATE'S STORY
TWO WEEKS AGO.
PARKIN
I STILL CAN'T BELIEVE YOU GOT US A TABLE.
AND I DON'T WANT TO SOUND UNGRATEFUL. BUT REALLY? I DON'T EVEN KNOW WHAT'S IN THIS...
THAT'S THE WAY I FEEL ABOUT THOSE CHEESEBURGERS ON 37TH. BUT IT'S THIRTY DOLLARS OF MYSTERY MEAT, BABE. IT PROBABLY WON'T KILL YOU.
AND IF IT DOES, I HAVE A GREAT STORY TO TELL--
--UH, MY NEXT GIRL-FRIEND.
HANG ON A MINUTE...
WHERE ARE YOU GOING?
I HAVE TO SCRAPE A BUG OFF MY SHOE.
WHAT?

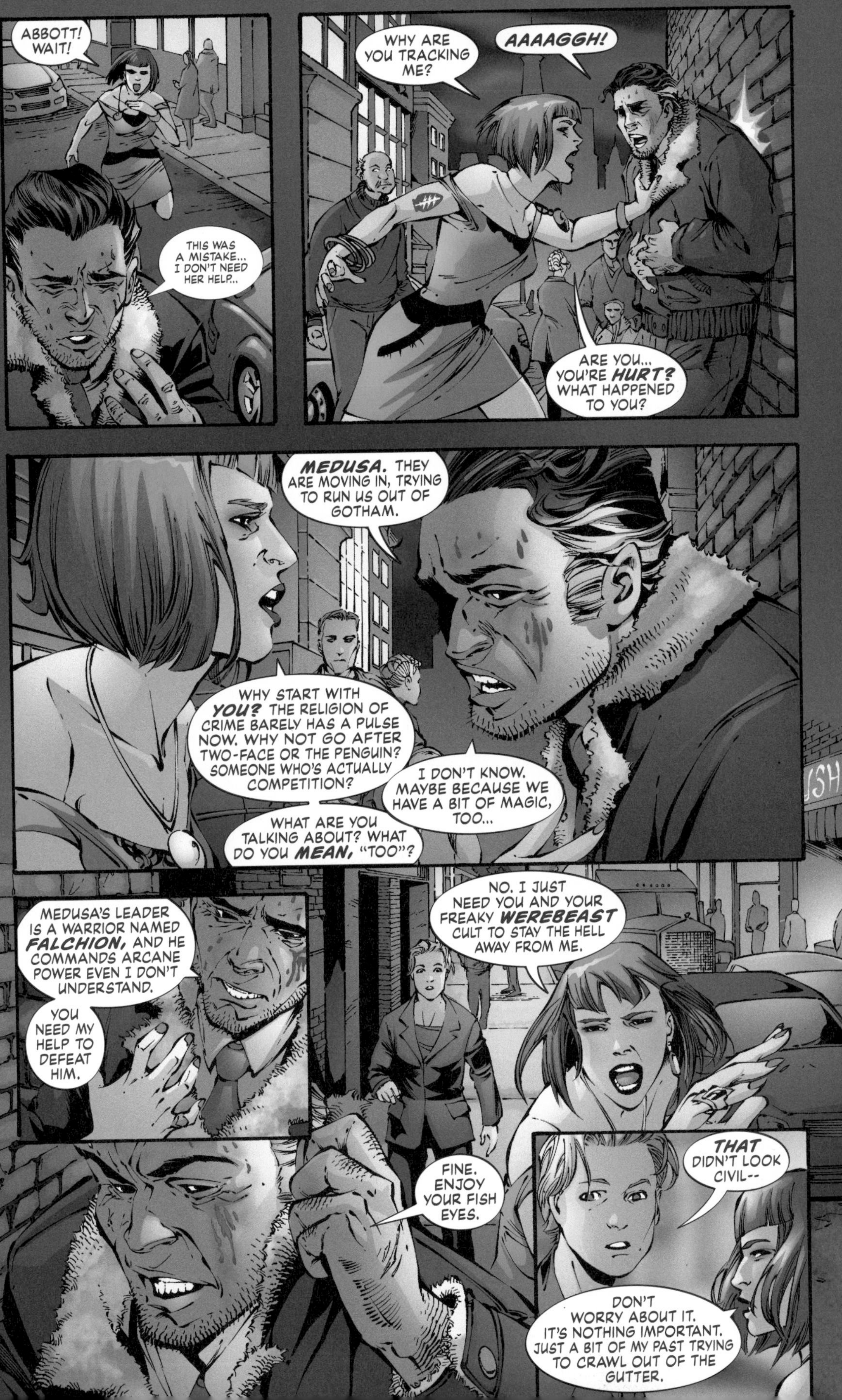

ABBOTT! WAIT!
THIS WAS A MISTAKE... I DON'T NEED HER HELP..
WHY ARE YOU TRACKING ME?
AAAAGGH!
ARE YOU... YOU'RE HURT? WHAT HAPPENED TO YOU?
MEDUSA. THEY ARE MOVING IN, TRYING TO RUN US OUT OF GOTHAM.
WHY START WITH YOU? THE RELIGION OF CRIME BARELY HAS A PULSE NOW. WHY NOT GO AFTER TWO-FACE OR THE PENGUIN? SOMEONE WHO'S ACTUALLY COMPETITION?
I DON'T KNOW. MAYBE BECAUSE WE HAVE A BIT OF MAGIC, TOO...
WHAT ARE YOU TALKING ABOUT? WHAT DO YOU MEAN, "TOO"?
SUSHI
MEDUSA'S LEADER IS A WARRIOR NAMED FALCHION, AND HE COMMANDS ARCANE POWER EVEN I DON'T UNDERSTAND.
YOU NEED MY HELP TO DEFEAT HIM.
NO. I JUST NEED YOU AND YOUR FREAKY WEREBEAST CULT TO STAY THE HELL AWAY FROM ME.
FINE. ENJOY YOUR FISH EYES.
THAT DIDN'T LOOK CIVIL--
DON'T WORRY ABOUT IT. IT'S NOTHING IMPORTANT. JUST A BIT OF MY PAST TRYING TO CRAWL OUT OF THE GUTTER.

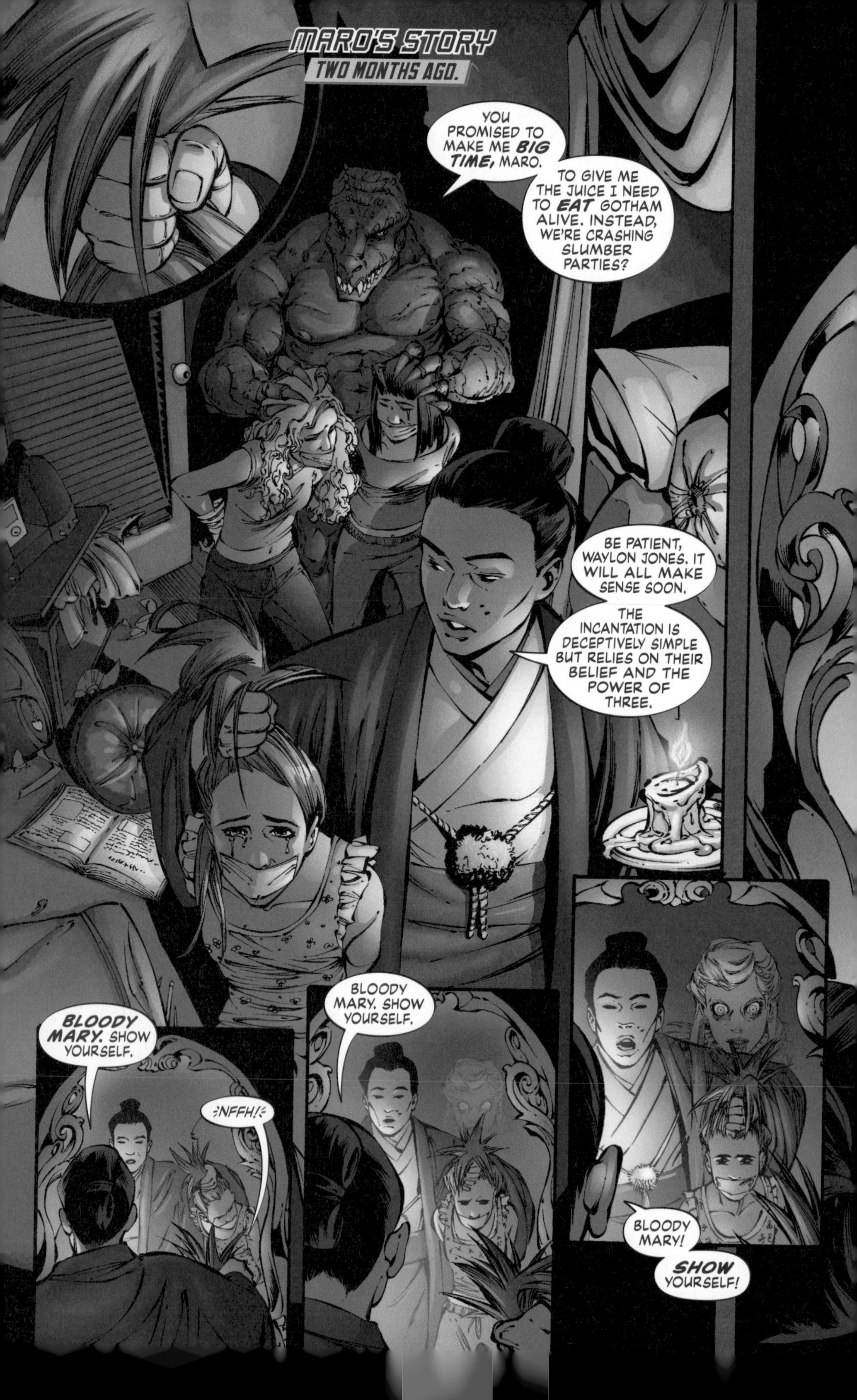
MARO'S STORY
TWO MONTHS AGO.
YOU PROMISED TO MAKE ME BIG TIME, MARO.
TO GIVE ME THE JUICE I NEED TO EAT GOTHAM ALIVE. INSTEAD, WE'RE CRASHING SLUMBER PARTIES?
BE PATIENT, WAYLON JONES. IT WILL ALL MAKE SENSE SOON.
THE INCANTATION IS DECEPTIVELY SIMPLE BUT RELIES ON THEIR BELIEF AND THE POWER OF THREE.
BLOODY MARY. SHOW YOURSELF.
NFFH!
BLOODY MARY. SHOW YOURSELF.
BLOODY MARY!
SHOW YOURSELF!

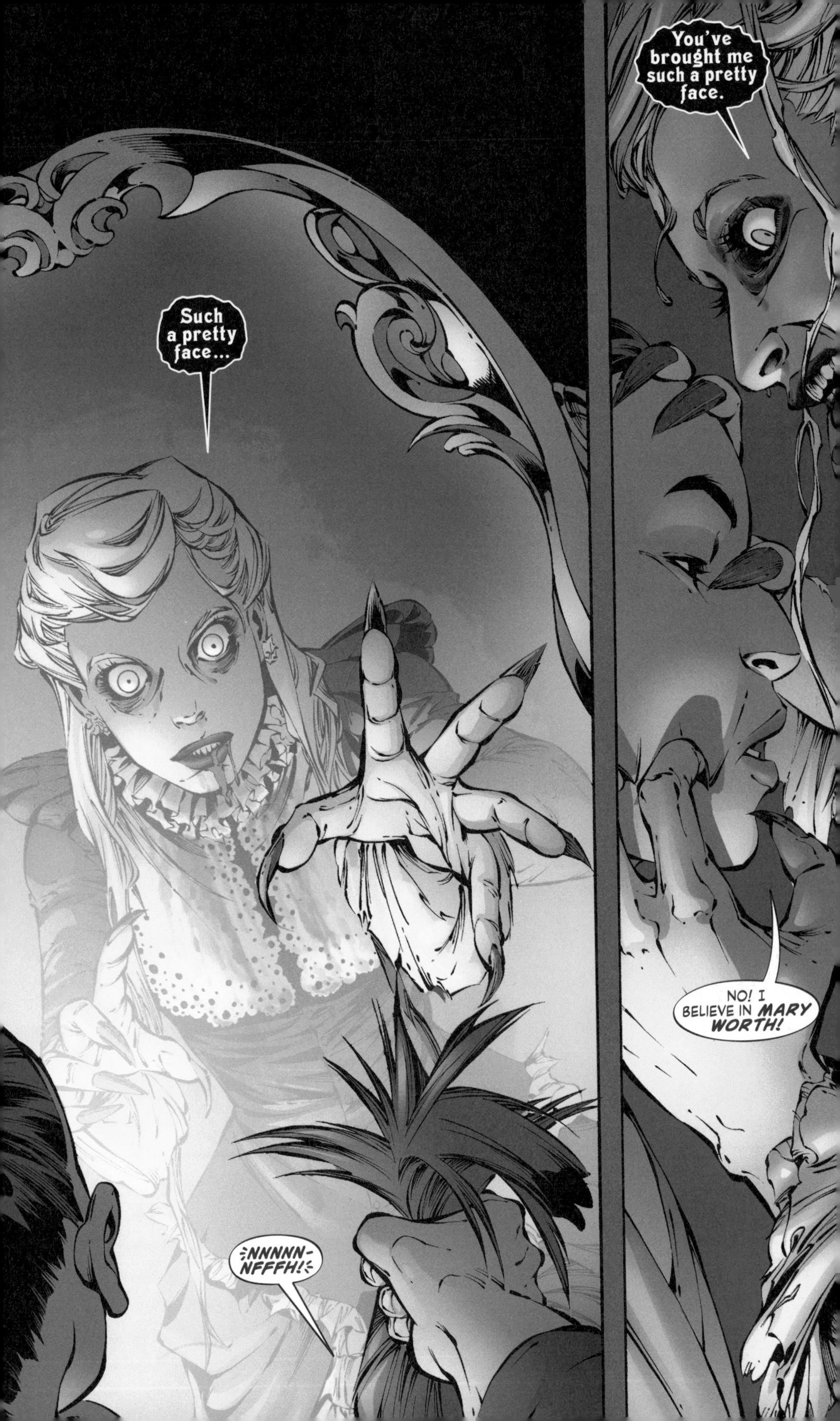
Such a pretty face...
ᵃNNNNN-NFFFH!ᵃ
You've brought me such a pretty face.
NO! I BELIEVE IN MARY WORTH!

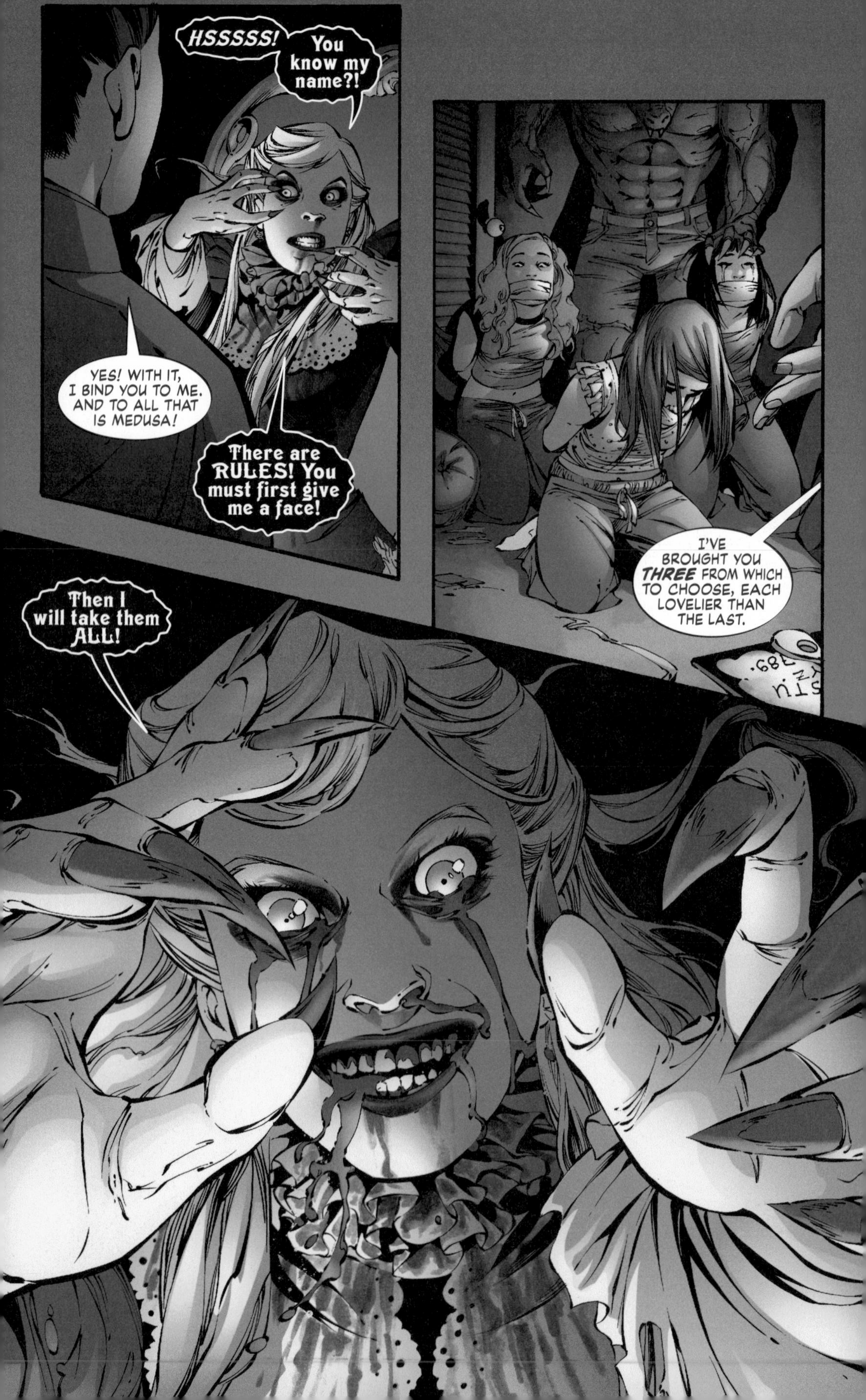
HSSSSS!
You know my name?!
YES! WITH IT, I BIND YOU TO ME. AND TO ALL THAT IS MEDUSA!
There are RULES! You must first give me a face!
I'VE BROUGHT YOU THREE FROM WHICH TO CHOOSE, EACH LOVELIER THAN THE LAST.
Then I will take them ALL!

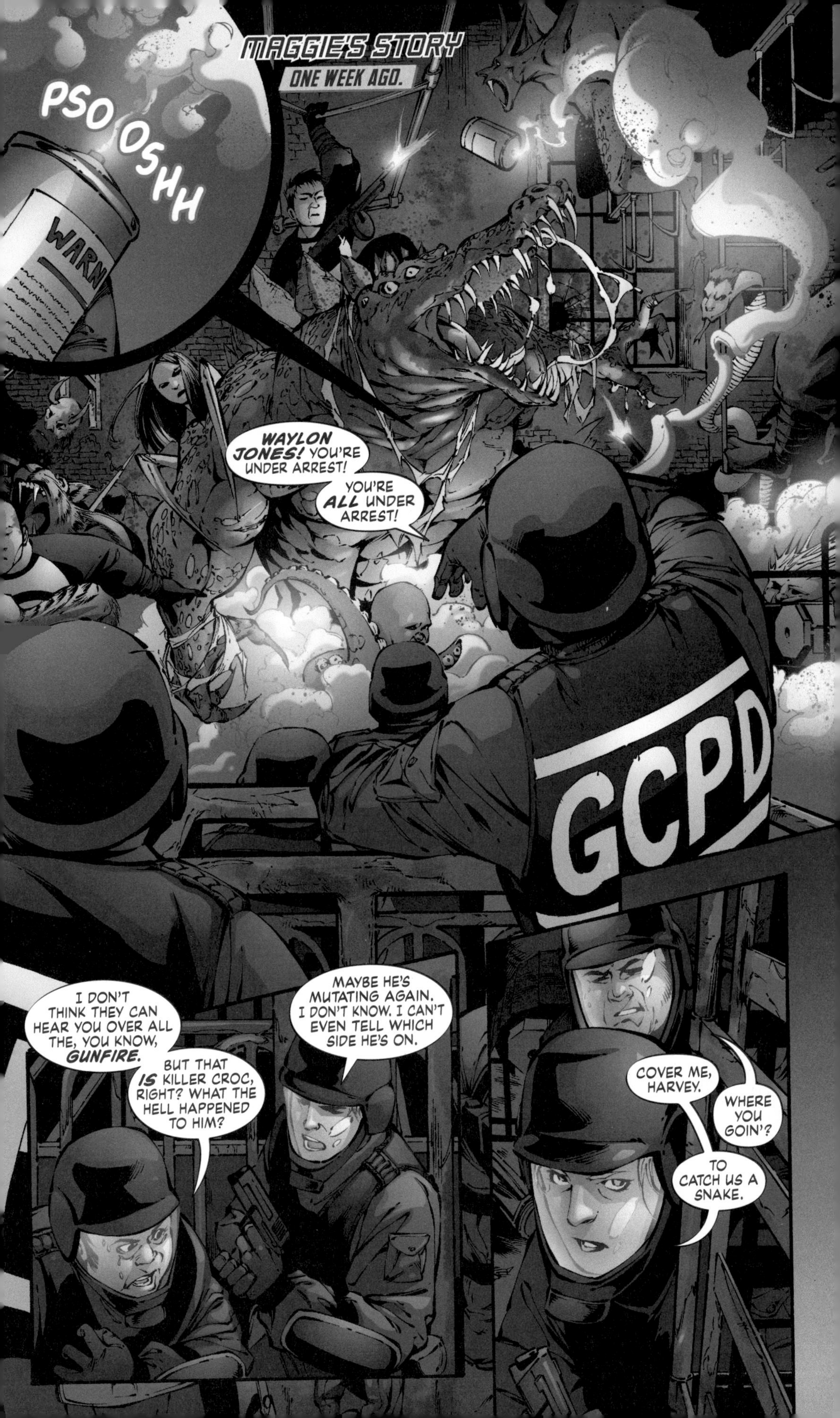
MAGGIE'S STORY
ONE WEEK AGO.
PSOOSHH
WARN
WAYLON JONES! YOU'RE UNDER ARREST!
YOU'RE ALL UNDER ARREST!
GCPD
I DON'T THINK THEY CAN HEAR YOU OVER ALL THE, YOU KNOW, GUNFIRE.
BUT THAT IS KILLER CROC, RIGHT? WHAT THE HELL HAPPENED TO HIM?
MAYBE HE'S MUTATING AGAIN. I DON'T KNOW. I CAN'T EVEN TELL WHICH SIDE HE'S ON.
COVER ME, HARVEY.
WHERE YOU GOIN'?
TO CATCH US A SNAKE.

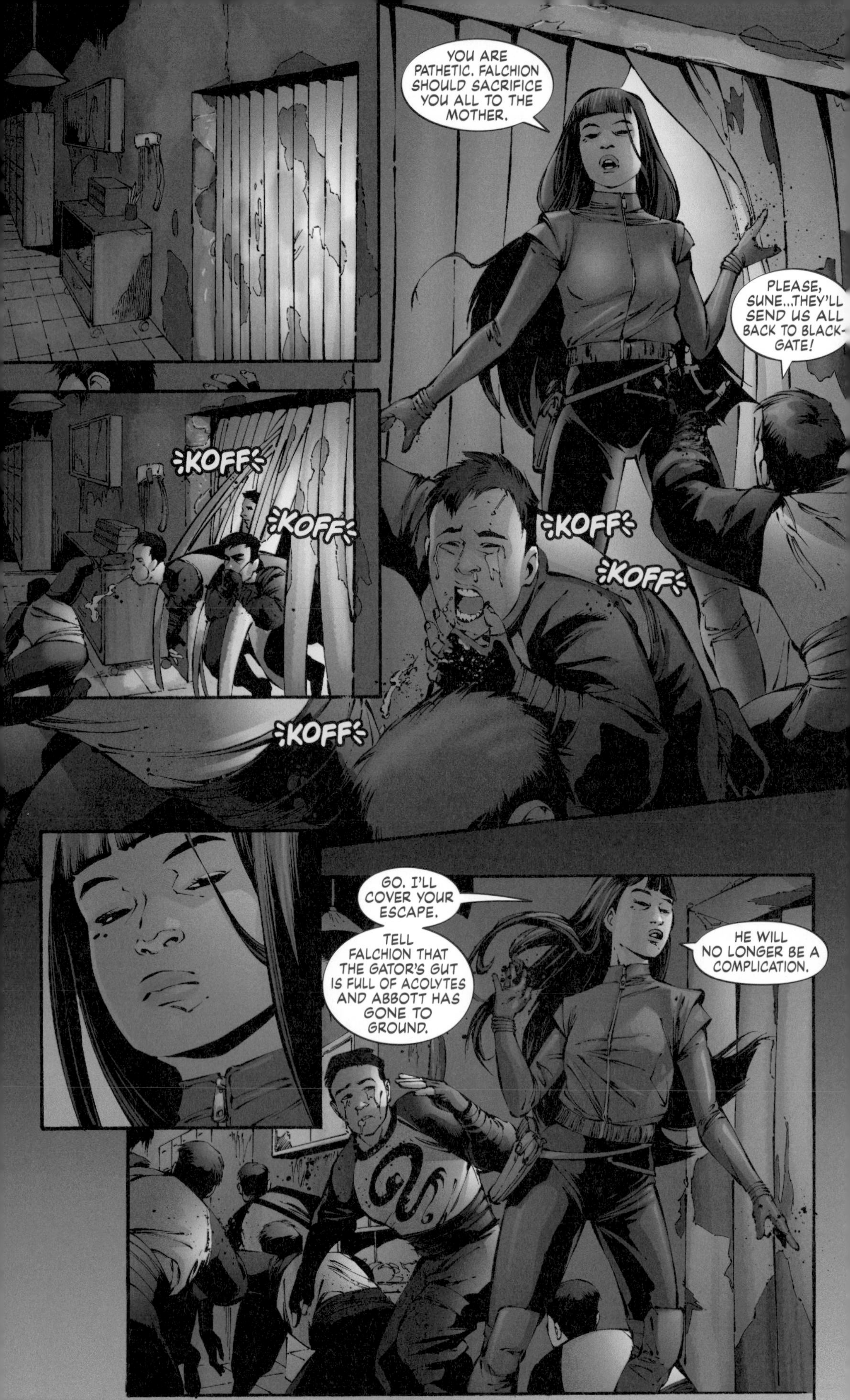
YOU ARE PATHETIC. FALCHION SHOULD SACRIFICE YOU ALL TO THE MOTHER.
PLEASE, SUNE...THEY'LL SEND US ALL BACK TO BLACK-GATE!
KOFF
KOFF
KOFF
KOFF
KOFF
GO. I'LL COVER YOUR ESCAPE.
TELL FALCHION THAT THE GATOR'S GUT IS FULL OF ACOLYTES AND ABBOTT HAS GONE TO GROUND.
HE WILL NO LONGER BE A COMPLICATION.

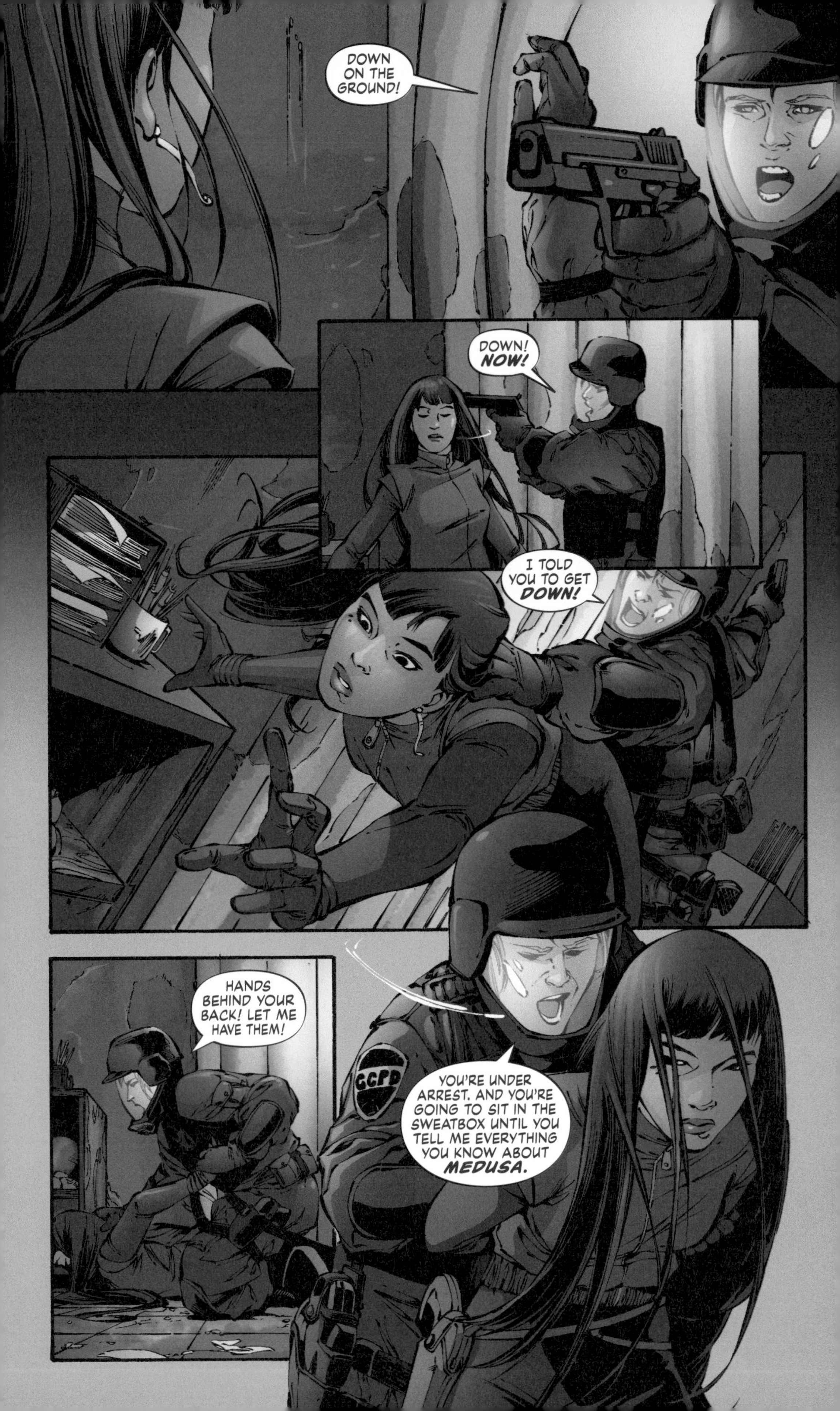
DOWN ON THE GROUND!
DOWN! NOW!
I TOLD YOU TO GET DOWN!
HANDS BEHIND YOUR BACK! LET ME HAVE THEM!
GCPD
YOU'RE UNDER ARREST. AND YOU'RE GOING TO SIT IN THE SWEATBOX UNTIL YOU TELL ME EVERYTHING YOU KNOW ABOUT MEDUSA.

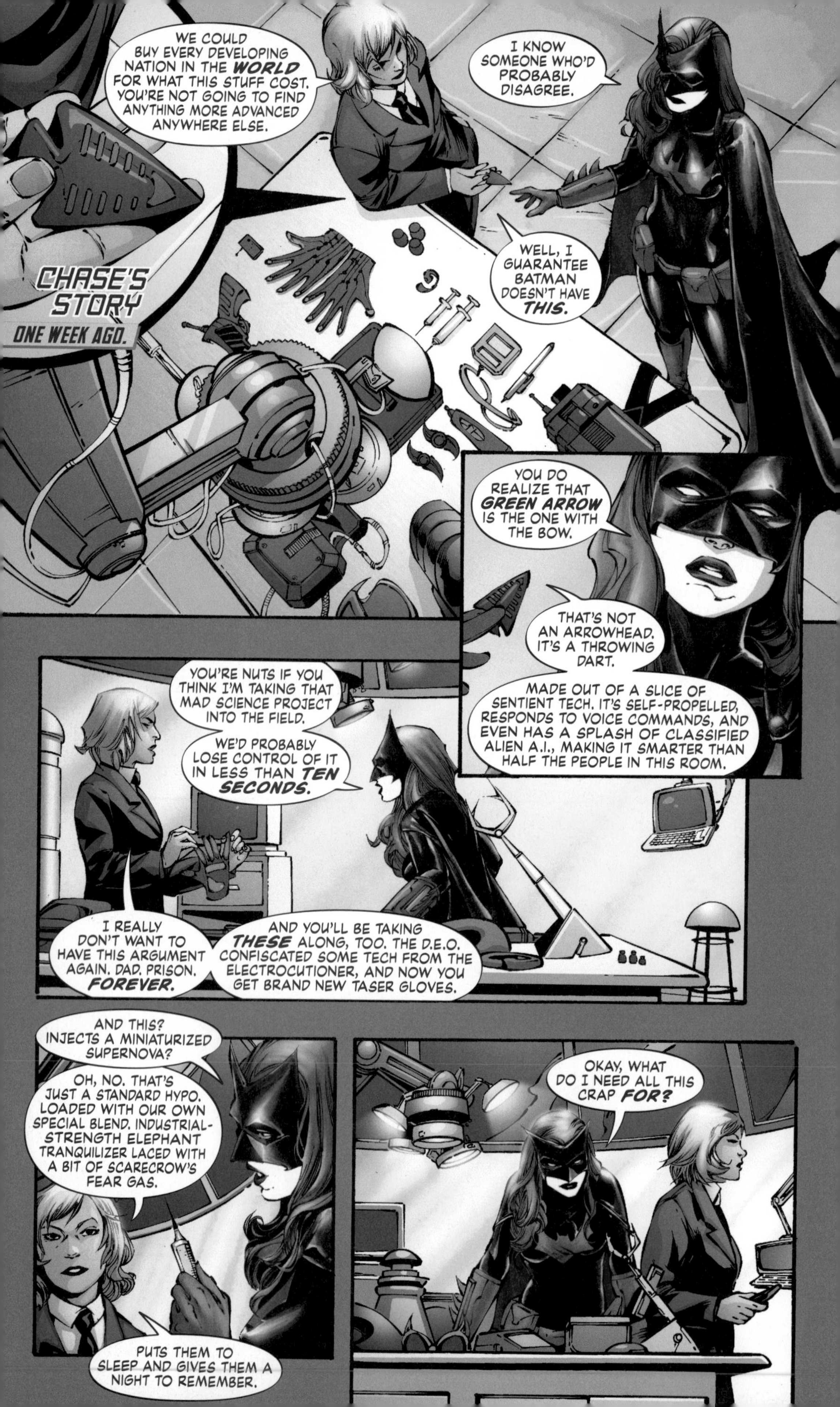
WE COULD BUY EVERY DEVELOPING NATION IN THE **WORLD** FOR WHAT THIS STUFF COST. YOU'RE NOT GOING TO FIND ANYTHING MORE ADVANCED ANYWHERE ELSE.
I KNOW SOMEONE WHO'D PROBABLY DISAGREE.
CHASE'S STORY
ONE WEEK AGO.
WELL, I GUARANTEE BATMAN DOESN'T HAVE **THIS.**
YOU DO REALIZE THAT **GREEN ARROW** IS THE ONE WITH THE BOW.
THAT'S NOT AN ARROWHEAD. IT'S A THROWING DART.
MADE OUT OF A SLICE OF SENTIENT TECH. IT'S SELF-PROPELLED, RESPONDS TO VOICE COMMANDS, AND EVEN HAS A SPLASH OF CLASSIFIED ALIEN A.I., MAKING IT SMARTER THAN HALF THE PEOPLE IN THIS ROOM.
YOU'RE NUTS IF YOU THINK I'M TAKING THAT MAD SCIENCE PROJECT INTO THE FIELD.
WE'D PROBABLY LOSE CONTROL OF IT IN LESS THAN **TEN SECONDS.**
I REALLY DON'T WANT TO HAVE THIS ARGUMENT AGAIN. DAD. PRISON. **FOREVER.**
AND YOU'LL BE TAKING **THESE** ALONG, TOO. THE D.E.O. CONFISCATED SOME TECH FROM THE ELECTROCUTIONER, AND NOW YOU GET BRAND NEW TASER GLOVES.
AND THIS? INJECTS A MINIATURIZED SUPERNOVA?
OH, NO. THAT'S JUST A STANDARD HYPO. LOADED WITH OUR OWN SPECIAL BLEND. INDUSTRIAL-STRENGTH ELEPHANT TRANQUILIZER LACED WITH A BIT OF SCARECROW'S FEAR GAS.
PUTS THEM TO SLEEP AND GIVES THEM A NIGHT TO REMEMBER.
OKAY, WHAT DO I NEED ALL THIS CRAP **FOR?**

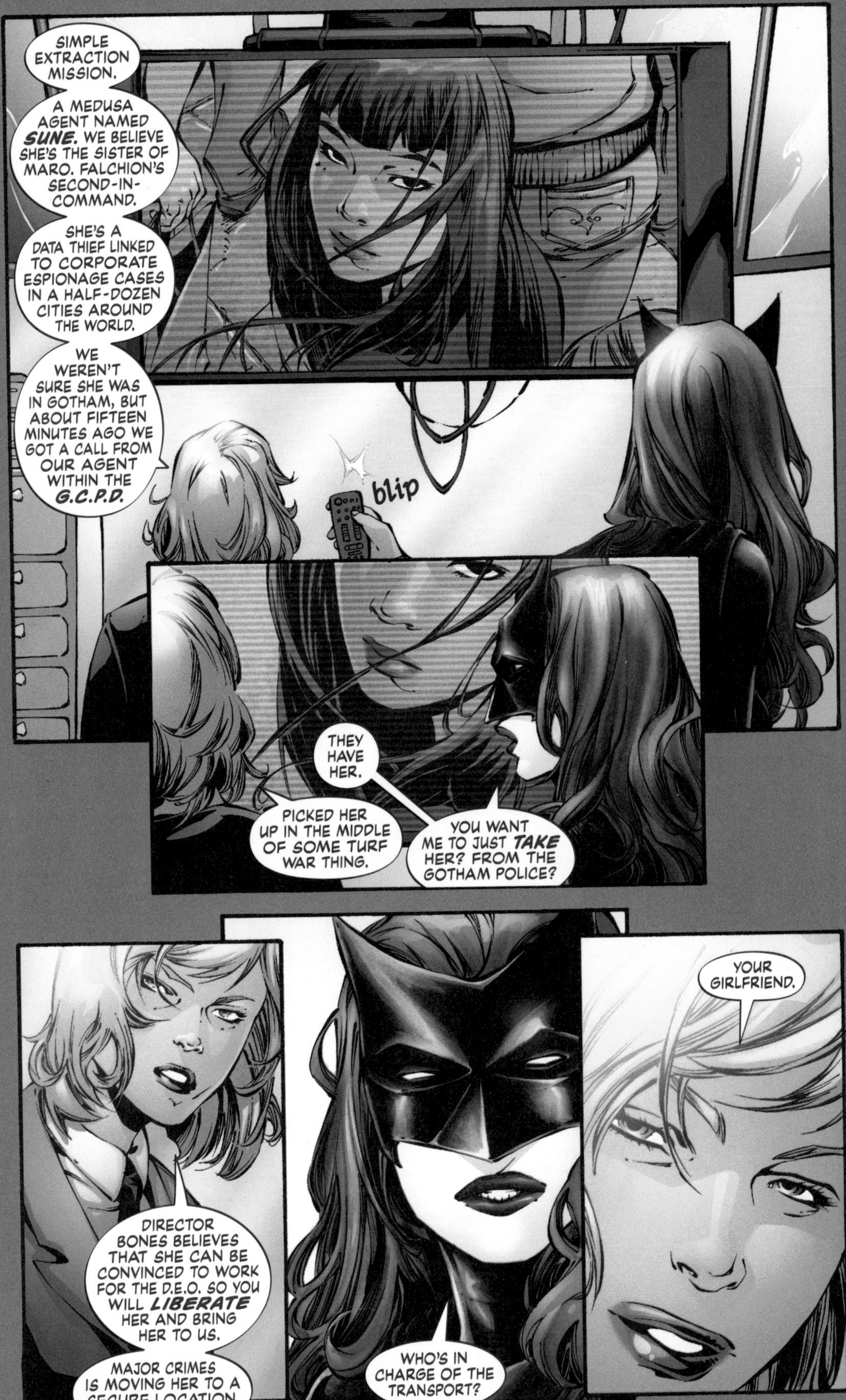

SIMPLE EXTRACTION MISSION.
A MEDUSA AGENT NAMED SUNE. WE BELIEVE SHE'S THE SISTER OF MARO. FALCHION'S SECOND-IN-COMMAND.
SHE'S A DATA THIEF LINKED TO CORPORATE ESPIONAGE CASES IN A HALF-DOZEN CITIES AROUND THE WORLD.
WE WEREN'T SURE SHE WAS IN GOTHAM, BUT ABOUT FIFTEEN MINUTES AGO WE GOT A CALL FROM OUR AGENT WITHIN THE G.C.P.D.
blip
THEY HAVE HER.
PICKED HER UP IN THE MIDDLE OF SOME TURF WAR THING.
YOU WANT ME TO JUST TAKE HER? FROM THE GOTHAM POLICE?
DIRECTOR BONES BELIEVES THAT SHE CAN BE CONVINCED TO WORK FOR THE D.E.O. SO YOU WILL LIBERATE HER AND BRING HER TO US.
MAJOR CRIMES IS MOVING HER TO A SECURE LOCATION. TONIGHT.
WHO'S IN CHARGE OF THE TRANSPORT?
YOUR GIRLFRIEND.

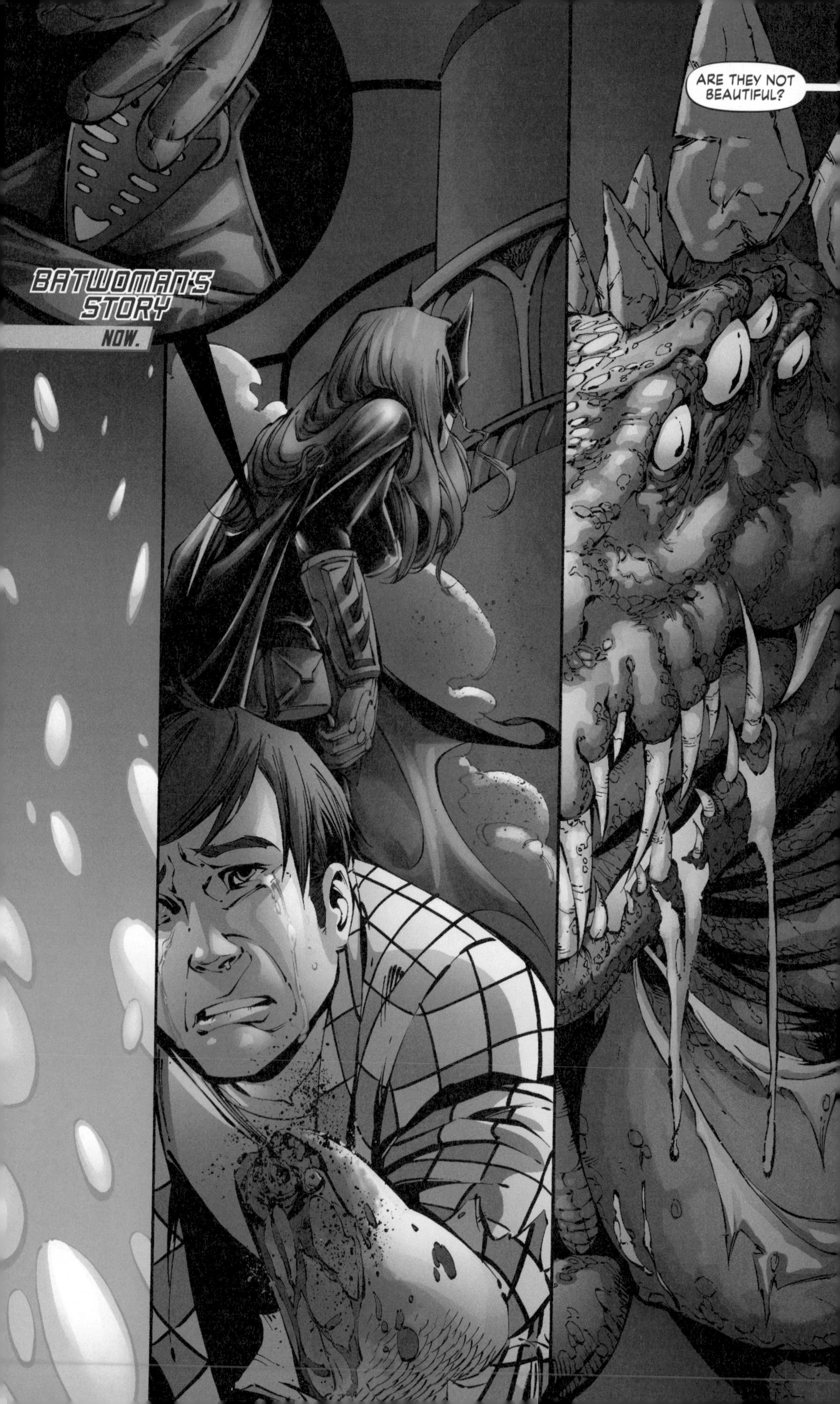
BATWOMAN'S STORY
NOW.
ARE THEY NOT BEAUTIFUL?

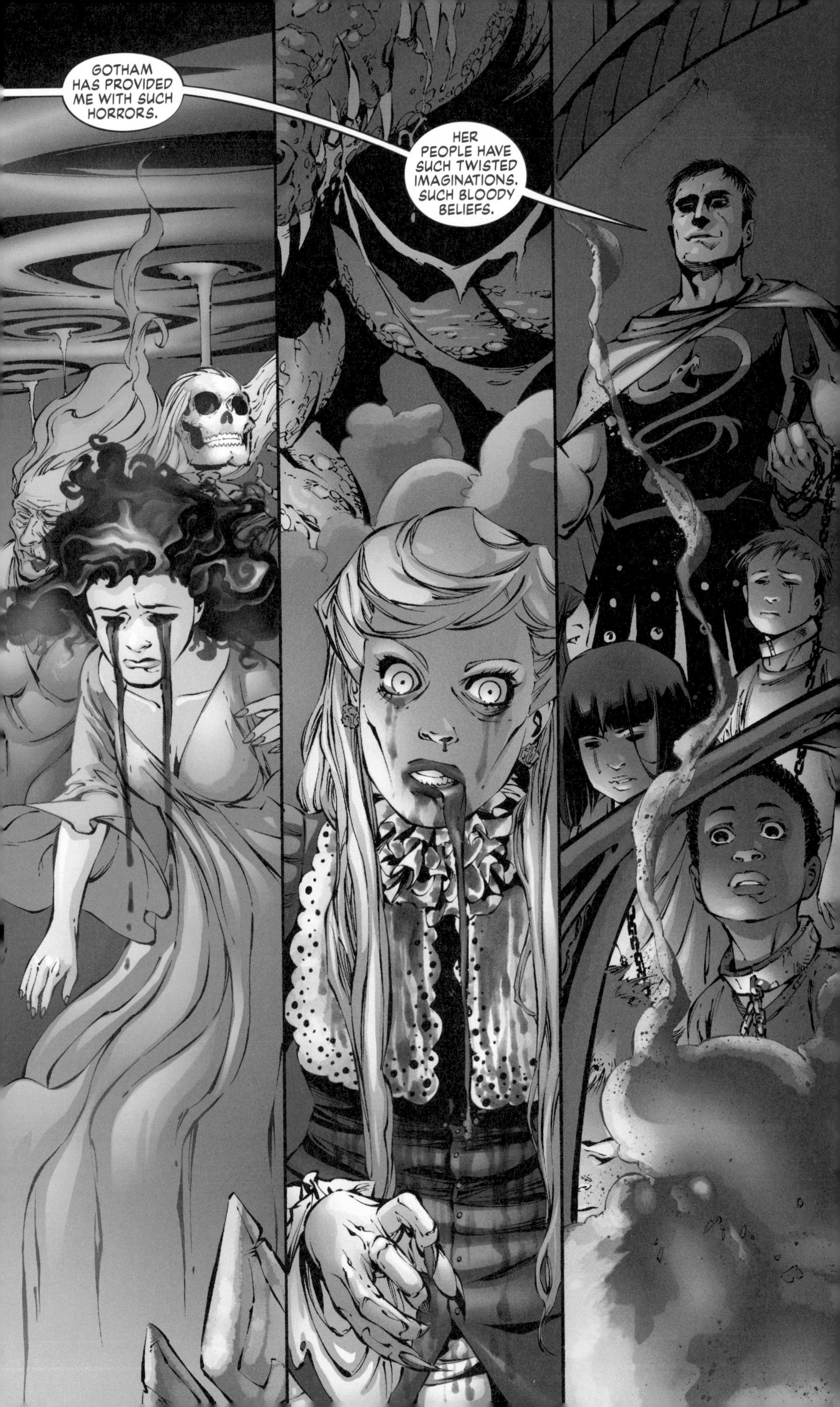

GOTHAM HAS PROVIDED ME WITH SUCH HORRORS.
HER PEOPLE HAVE SUCH TWISTED IMAGINATIONS. SUCH BLOODY BELIEFS.

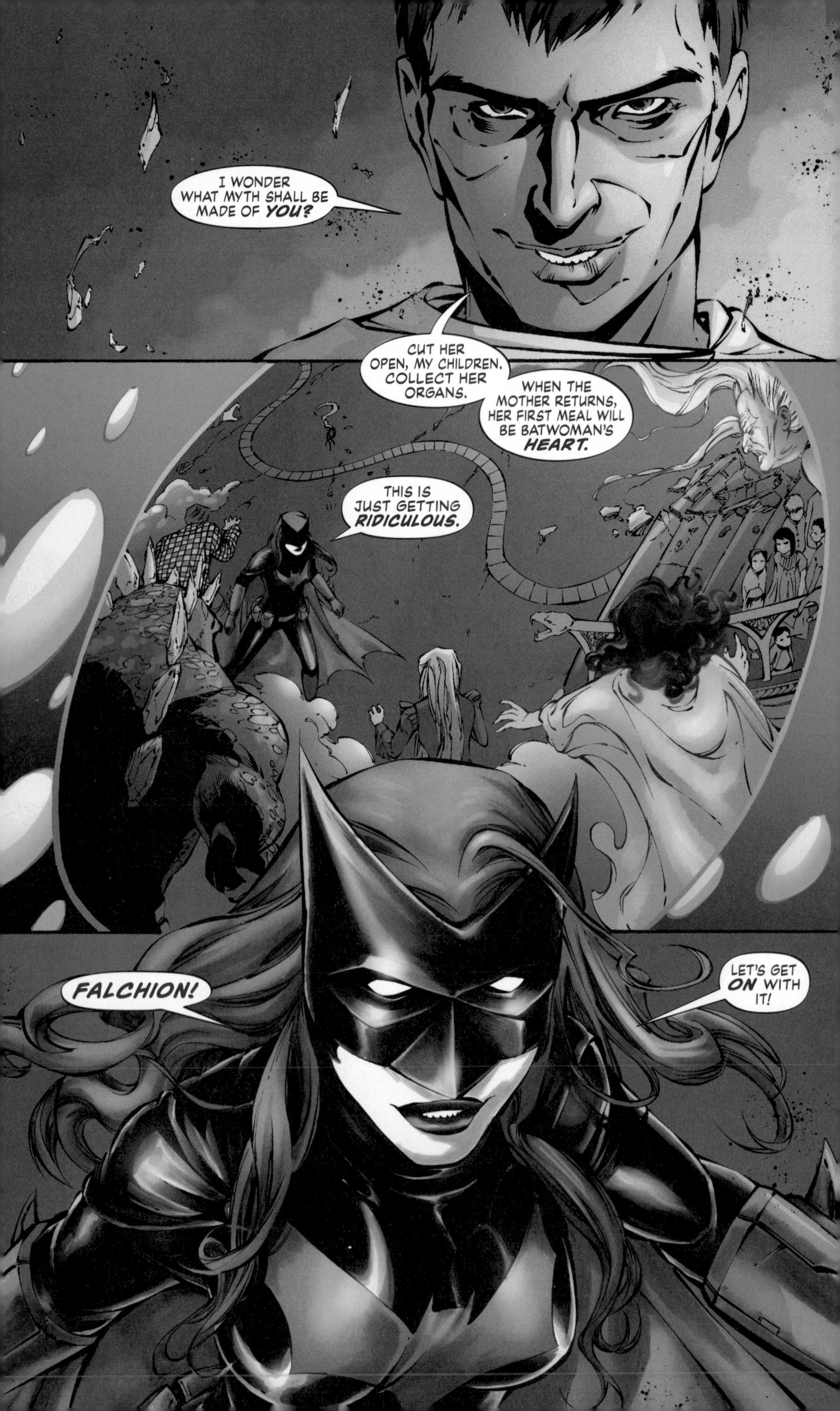
I WONDER WHAT MYTH SHALL BE MADE OF YOU?
CUT HER OPEN, MY CHILDREN. COLLECT HER ORGANS.
WHEN THE MOTHER RETURNS, HER FIRST MEAL WILL BE BATWOMAN'S HEART.
THIS IS JUST GETTING RIDICULOUS.
FALCHION!
LET'S GET ON WITH IT!

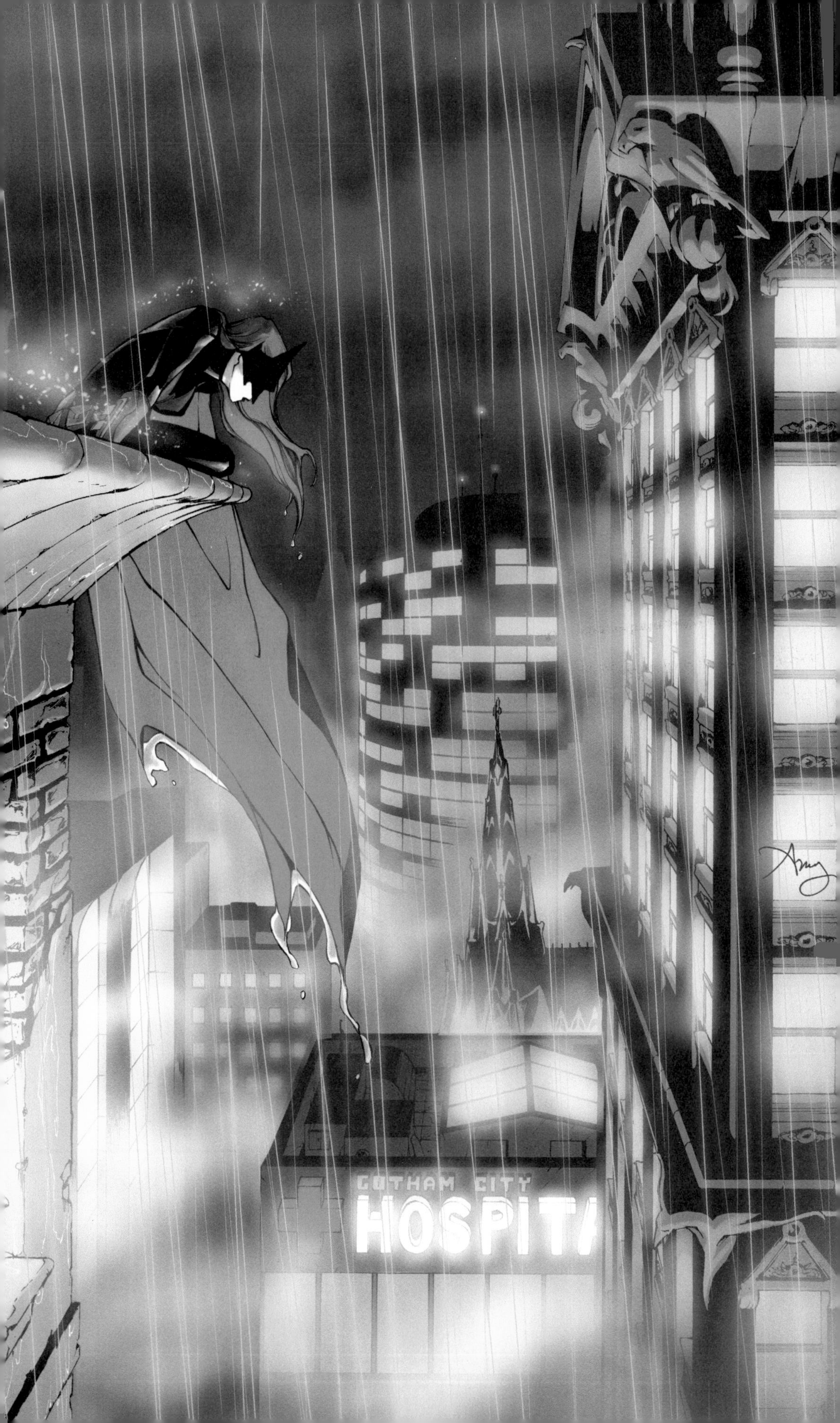

GOTHAM CITY
HOSPIT

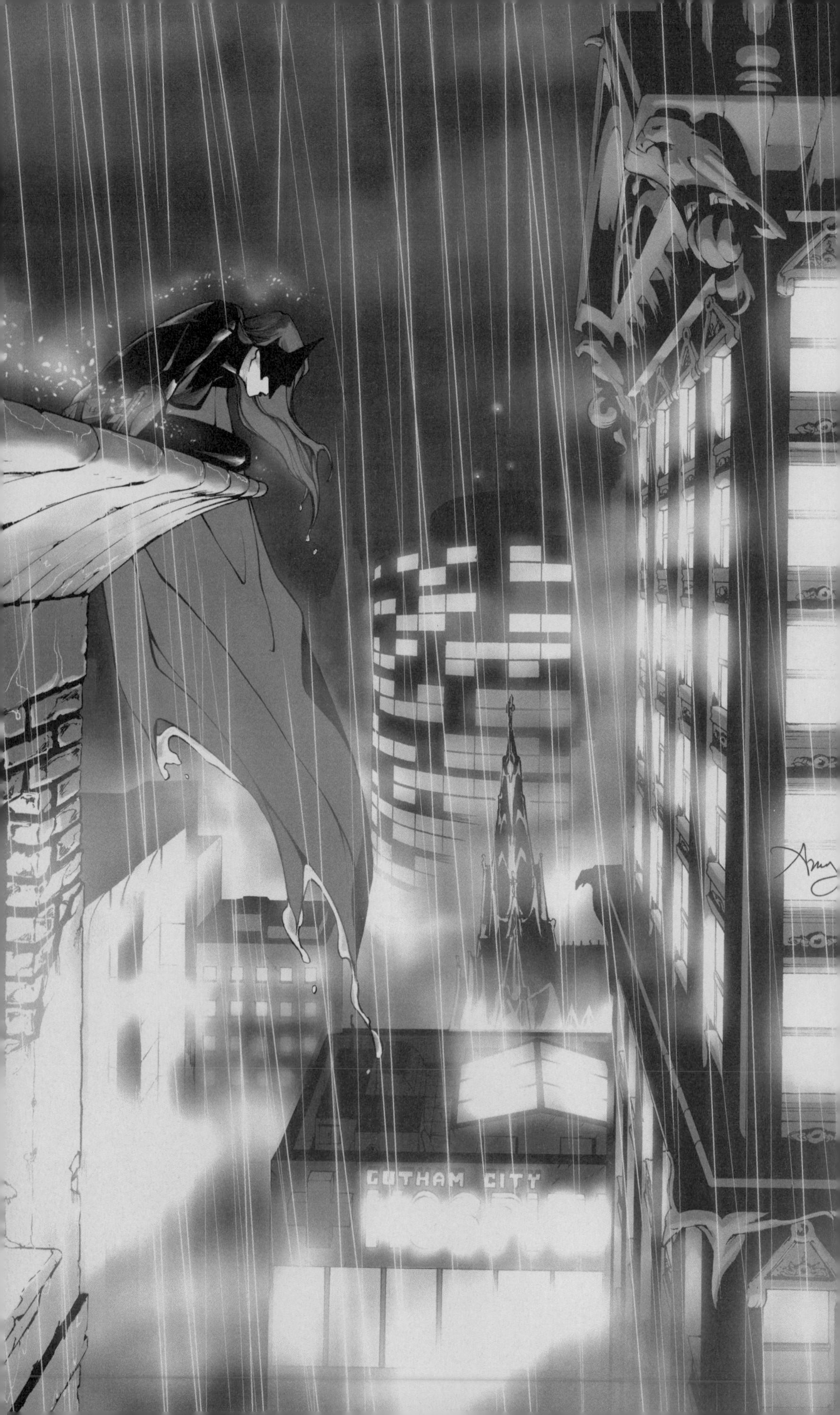
GOTHAM CITY

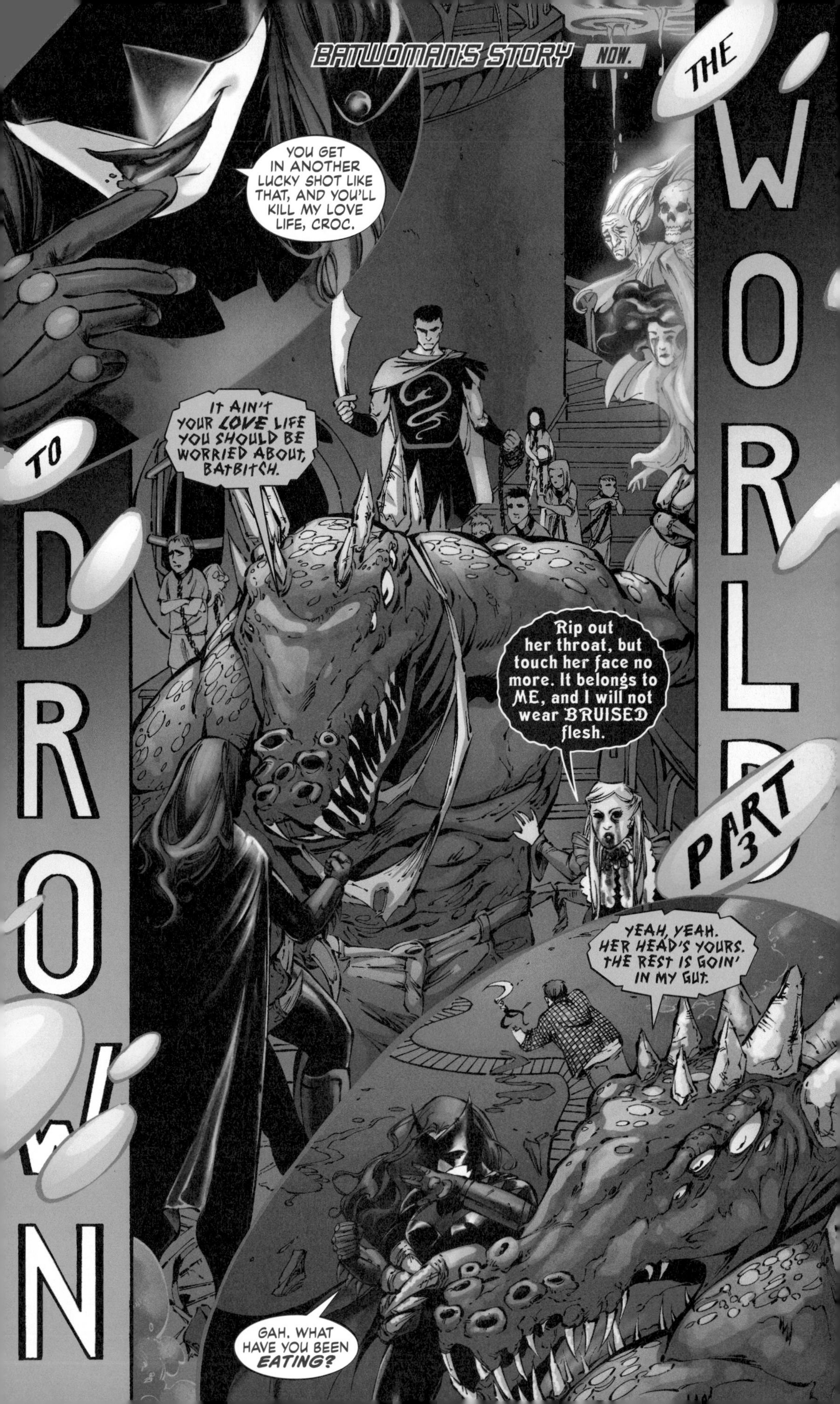
BATWOMAN'S STORY NOW.
THE WORLD TO DROWN PART 3
YOU GET IN ANOTHER LUCKY SHOT LIKE THAT, AND YOU'LL KILL MY LOVE LIFE, CROC.
IT AIN'T YOUR LOVE LIFE YOU SHOULD BE WORRIED ABOUT, BATBITCH.
Rip out her throat, but touch her face no more. It belongs to ME, and I will not wear BRUISED flesh.
YEAH, YEAH. HER HEAD'S YOURS. THE REST IS GOIN' IN MY GUT.
GAH. WHAT HAVE YOU BEEN EATING?

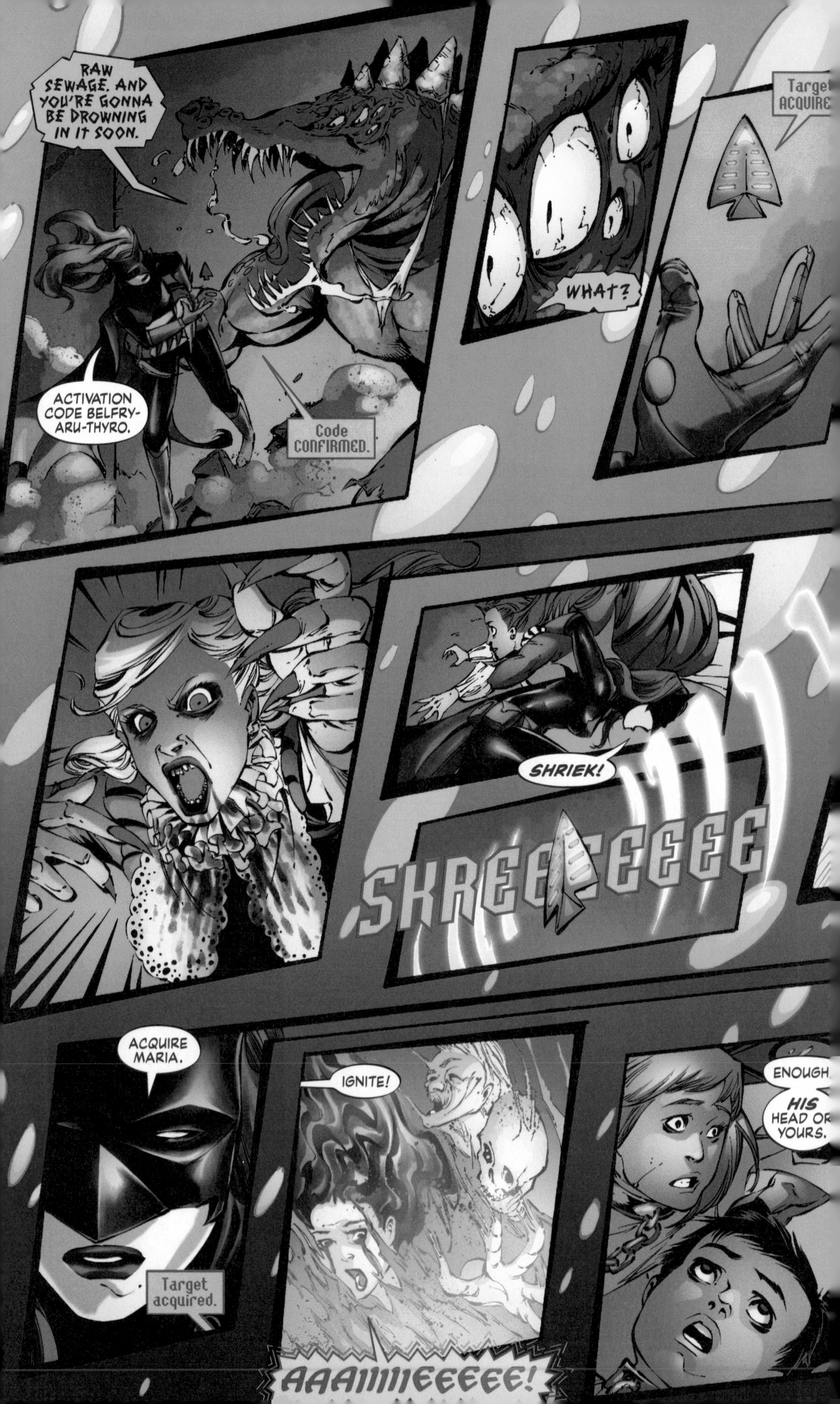
RAW SEWAGE. AND YOU'RE GONNA BE DROWNING IN IT SOON.
ACTIVATION CODE BELFRY-ARU-THYRO.
Code CONFIRMED.
WHAT?
Target ACQUIRE
SHRIEK!
SKREE EEEEE
ACQUIRE MARIA.
Target acquired.
IGNITE!
ENOUGH. HIS HEAD OR YOURS.
AAAIIIIIEEEEE!

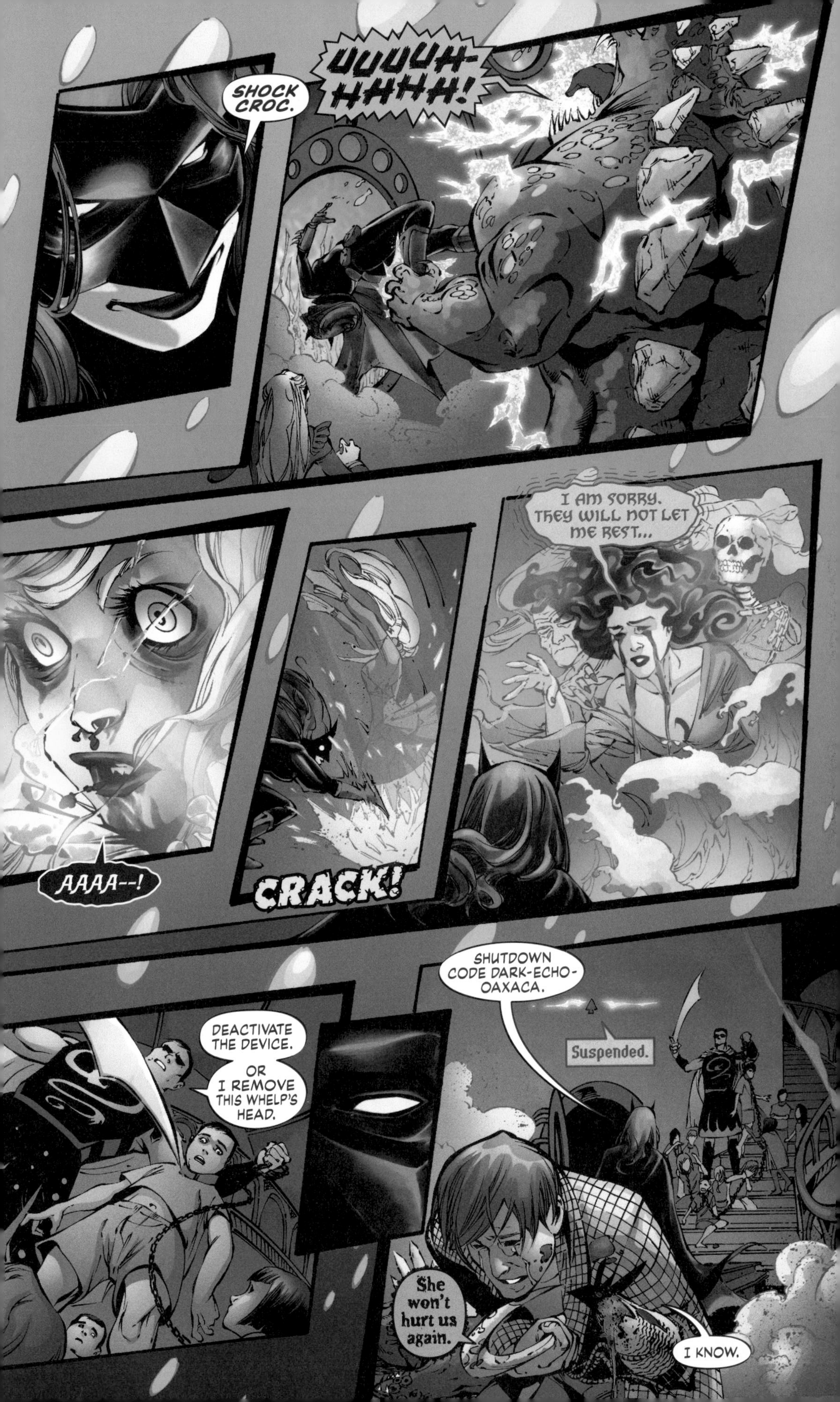
SHOCK CROC.
UUUUH-HHHH!
AAAA--!
CRACK!
I AM SORRY. THEY WILL NOT LET ME REST...
DEACTIVATE THE DEVICE.
OR I REMOVE THIS WHELP'S HEAD.
SHUTDOWN CODE DARK-ECHO-OAXACA.
Suspended.
She won't hurt us again.
I KNOW.

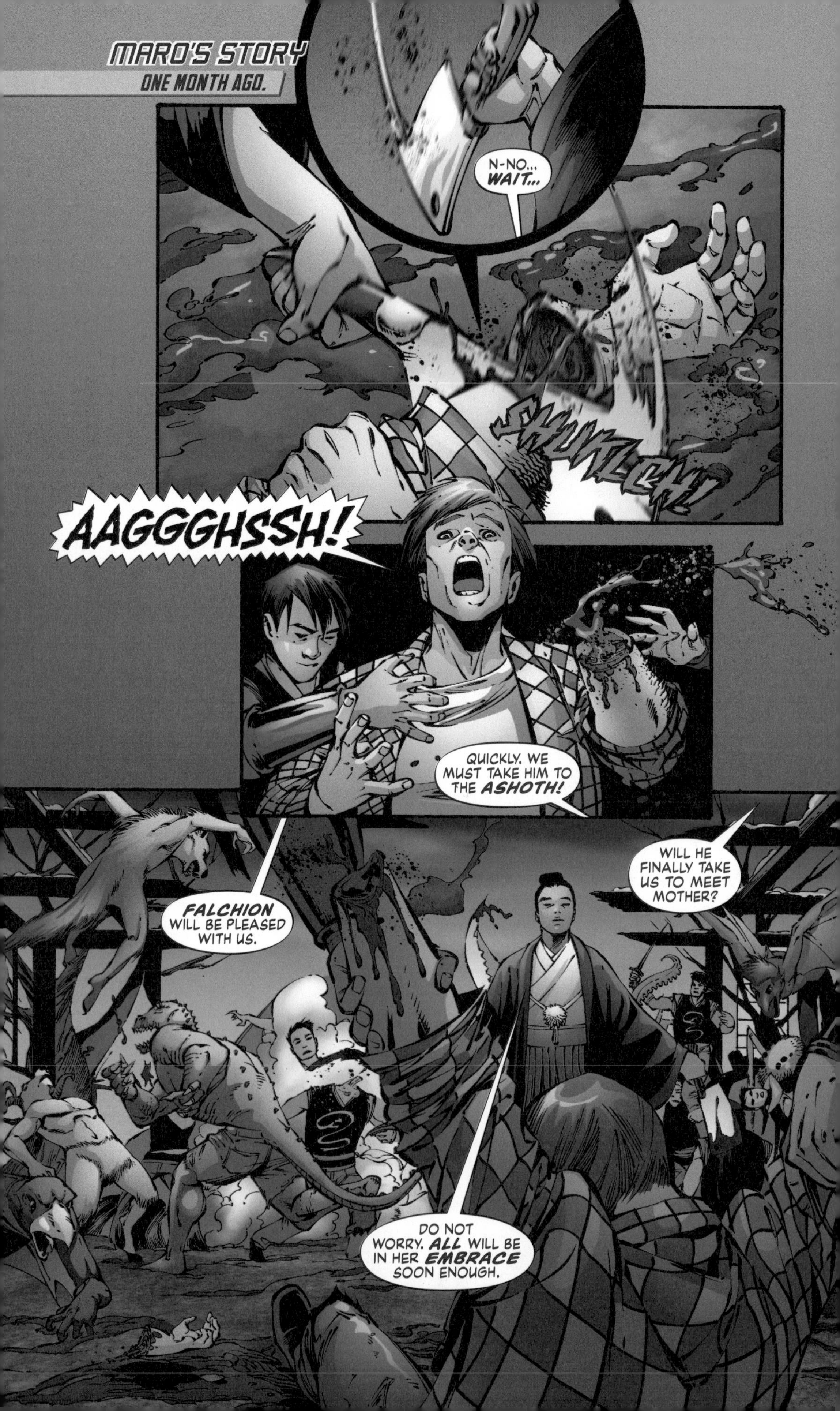
MARO'S STORY
ONE MONTH AGO.
N-NO... WAIT...
SHUKLCH!
AAGGGHSSH!
QUICKLY. WE MUST TAKE HIM TO THE ASHOTH!
FALCHION WILL BE PLEASED WITH US.
WILL HE FINALLY TAKE US TO MEET MOTHER?
DO NOT WORRY. ALL WILL BE IN HER EMBRACE SOON ENOUGH.

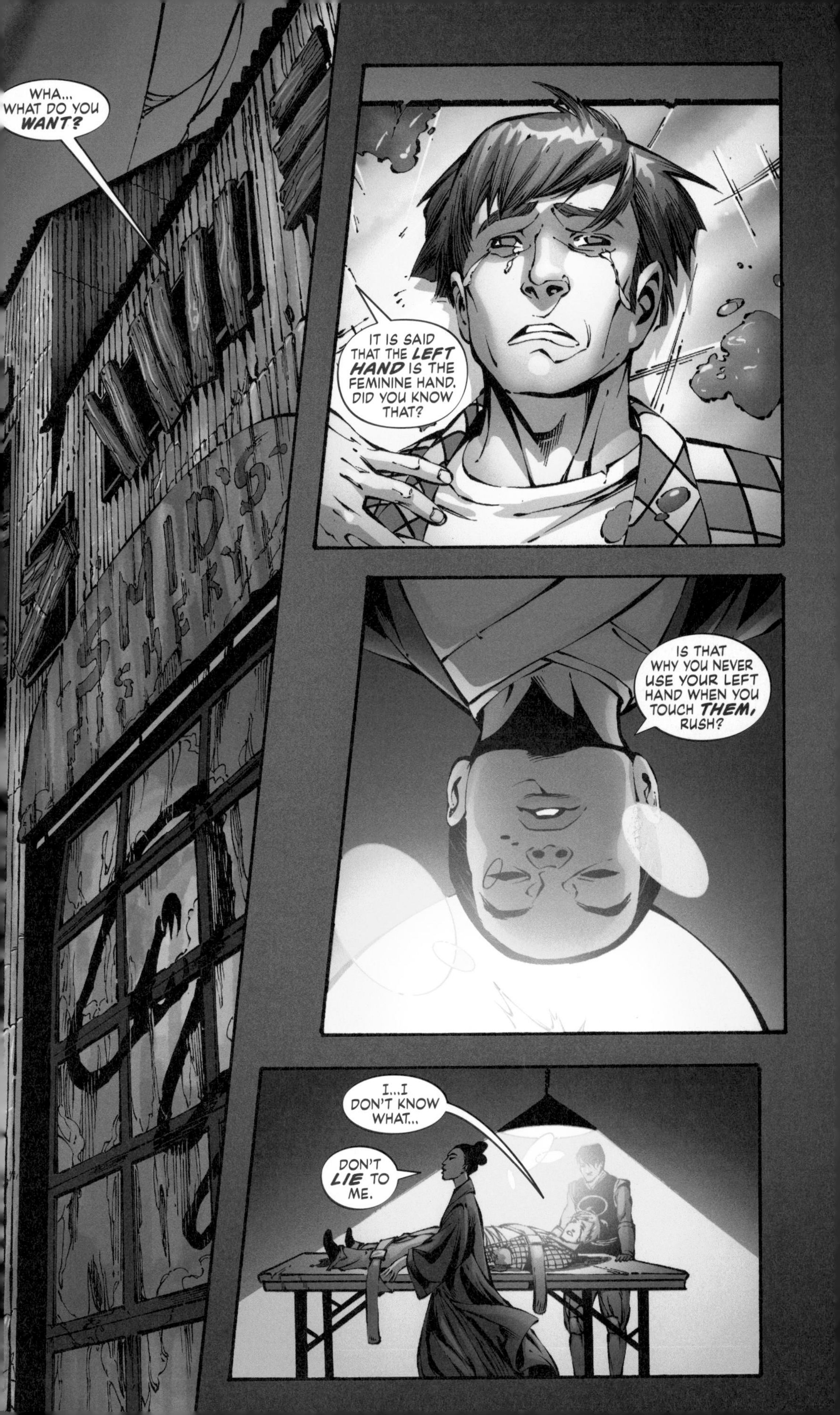
WHA... WHAT DO YOU WANT?
IT IS SAID THAT THE LEFT HAND IS THE FEMININE HAND. DID YOU KNOW THAT?
IS THAT WHY YOU NEVER USE YOUR LEFT HAND WHEN YOU TOUCH THEM, RUSH?
I...I DON'T KNOW WHAT...
DON'T LIE TO ME.

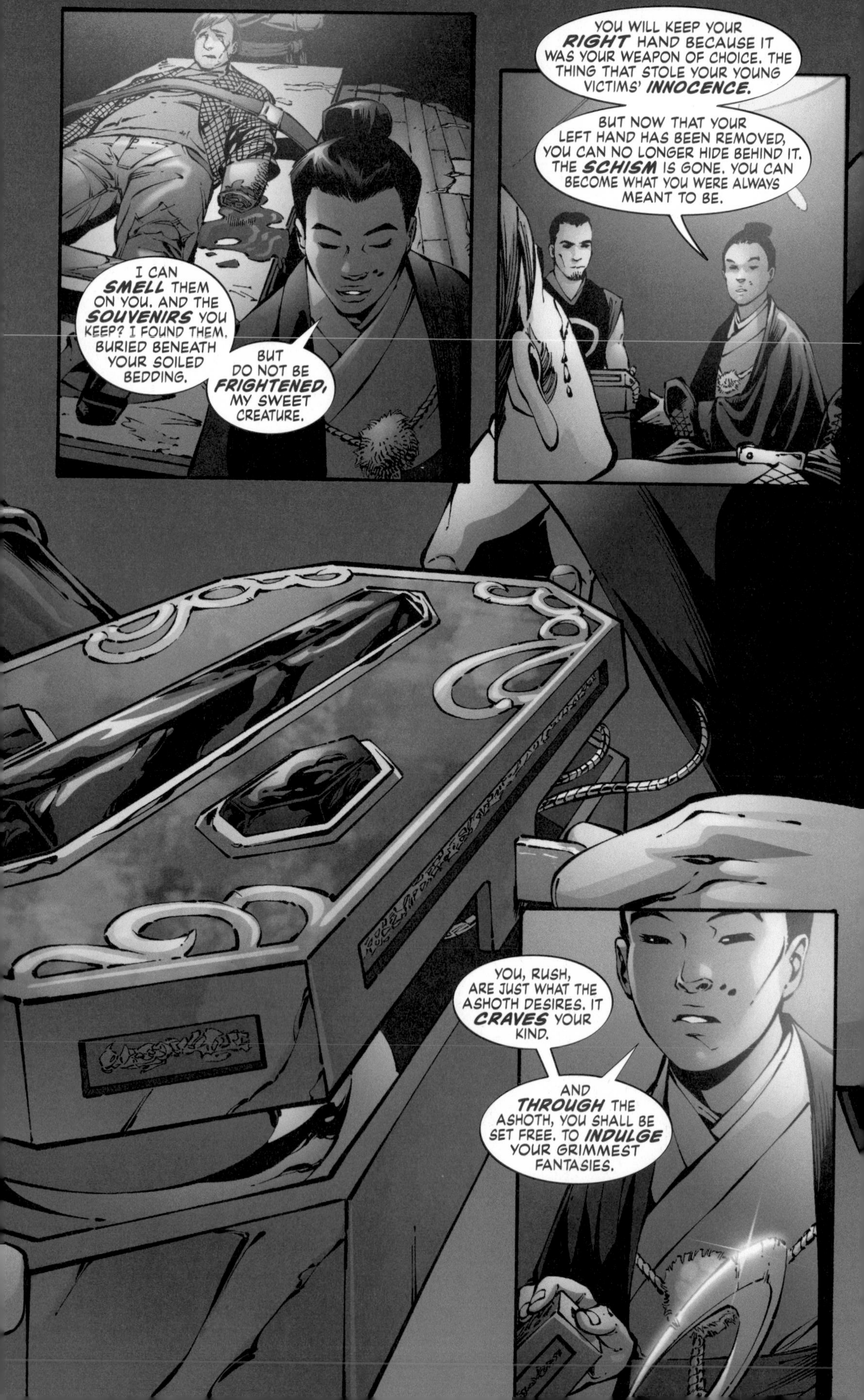
I CAN SMELL THEM ON YOU. AND THE SOUVENIRS YOU KEEP? I FOUND THEM. BURIED BENEATH YOUR SOILED BEDDING.
BUT DO NOT BE FRIGHTENED, MY SWEET CREATURE.
YOU WILL KEEP YOUR RIGHT HAND BECAUSE IT WAS YOUR WEAPON OF CHOICE. THE THING THAT STOLE YOUR YOUNG VICTIMS' INNOCENCE.
BUT NOW THAT YOUR LEFT HAND HAS BEEN REMOVED, YOU CAN NO LONGER HIDE BEHIND IT. THE SCHISM IS GONE. YOU CAN BECOME WHAT YOU WERE ALWAYS MEANT TO BE.
YOU, RUSH, ARE JUST WHAT THE ASHOTH DESIRES. IT CRAVES YOUR KIND.
AND THROUGH THE ASHOTH, YOU SHALL BE SET FREE. TO INDULGE YOUR GRIMMEST FANTASIES.

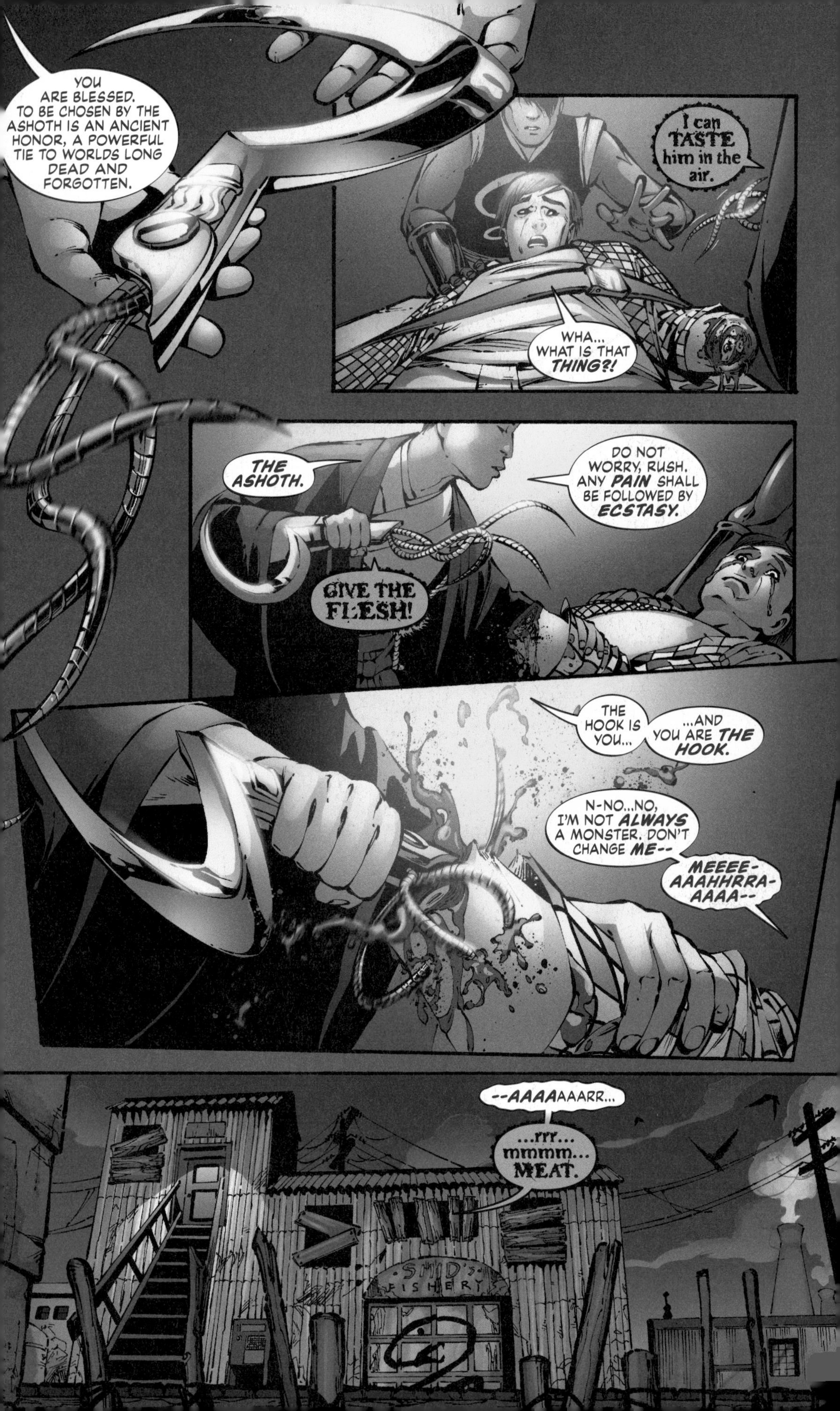

YOU ARE BLESSED. TO BE CHOSEN BY THE ASHOTH IS AN ANCIENT HONOR, A POWERFUL TIE TO WORLDS LONG DEAD AND FORGOTTEN.
I can TASTE him in the air.
WHA... WHAT IS THAT THING?!
THE ASHOTH.
DO NOT WORRY, RUSH. ANY PAIN SHALL BE FOLLOWED BY ECSTASY.
GIVE THE FLESH!
THE HOOK IS YOU...
...AND YOU ARE THE HOOK.
N-NO...NO, I'M NOT ALWAYS A MONSTER. DON'T CHANGE ME--
MEEEE-AAAHHRRA-AAAA--
--AAAAAAARR...
...rrr... mmmm... MEAT.
SMID'S FISHERY

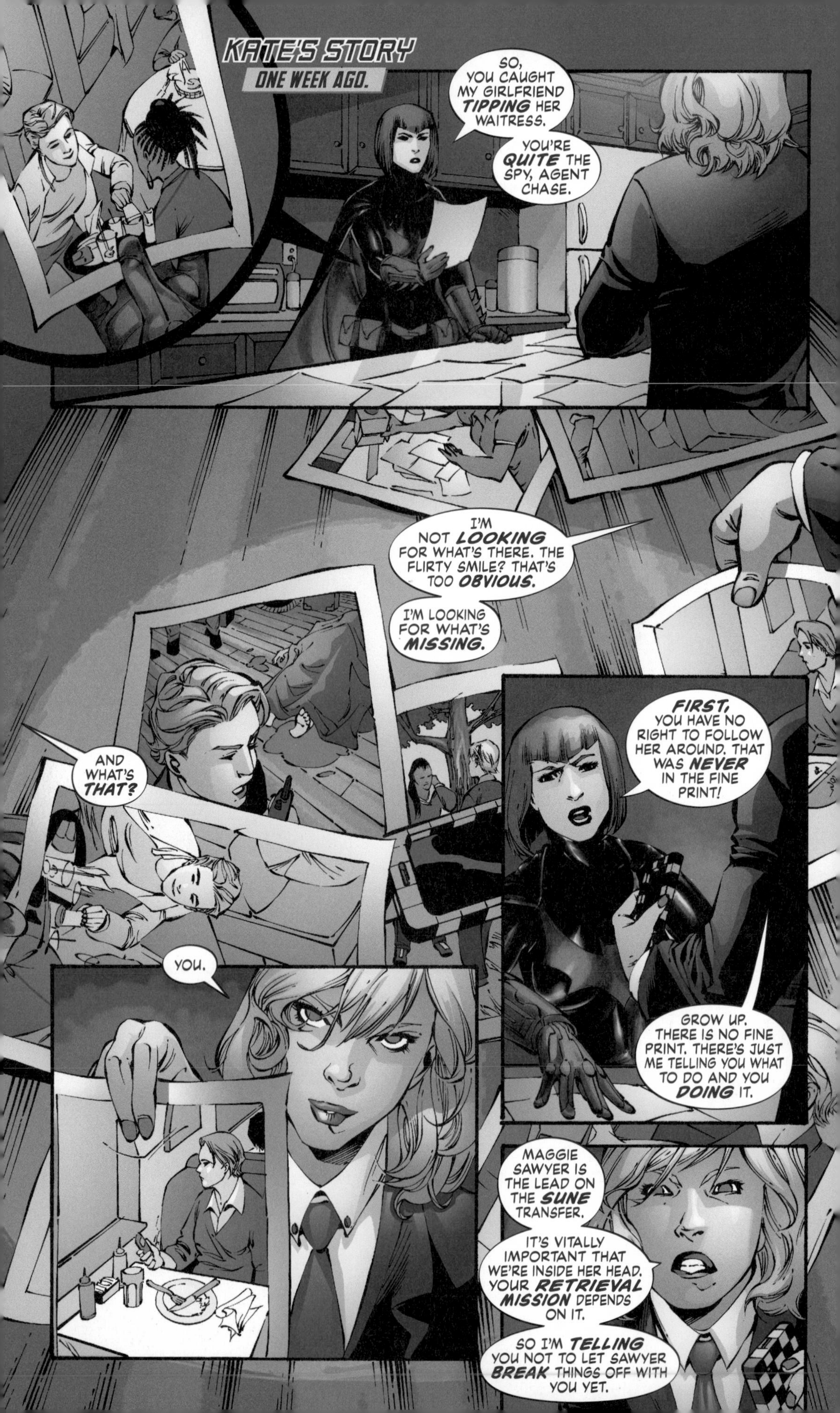
KATE'S STORY
ONE WEEK AGO.
SO, YOU CAUGHT MY GIRLFRIEND TIPPING HER WAITRESS.
YOU'RE QUITE THE SPY, AGENT CHASE.
I'M NOT LOOKING FOR WHAT'S THERE. THE FLIRTY SMILE? THAT'S TOO OBVIOUS.
I'M LOOKING FOR WHAT'S MISSING.
AND WHAT'S THAT?
YOU.
FIRST, YOU HAVE NO RIGHT TO FOLLOW HER AROUND. THAT WAS NEVER IN THE FINE PRINT!
GROW UP. THERE IS NO FINE PRINT. THERE'S JUST ME TELLING YOU WHAT TO DO AND YOU DOING IT.
MAGGIE SAWYER IS THE LEAD ON THE SUNE TRANSFER.
IT'S VITALLY IMPORTANT THAT WE'RE INSIDE HER HEAD. YOUR RETRIEVAL MISSION DEPENDS ON IT.
SO I'M TELLING YOU NOT TO LET SAWYER BREAK THINGS OFF WITH YOU YET.

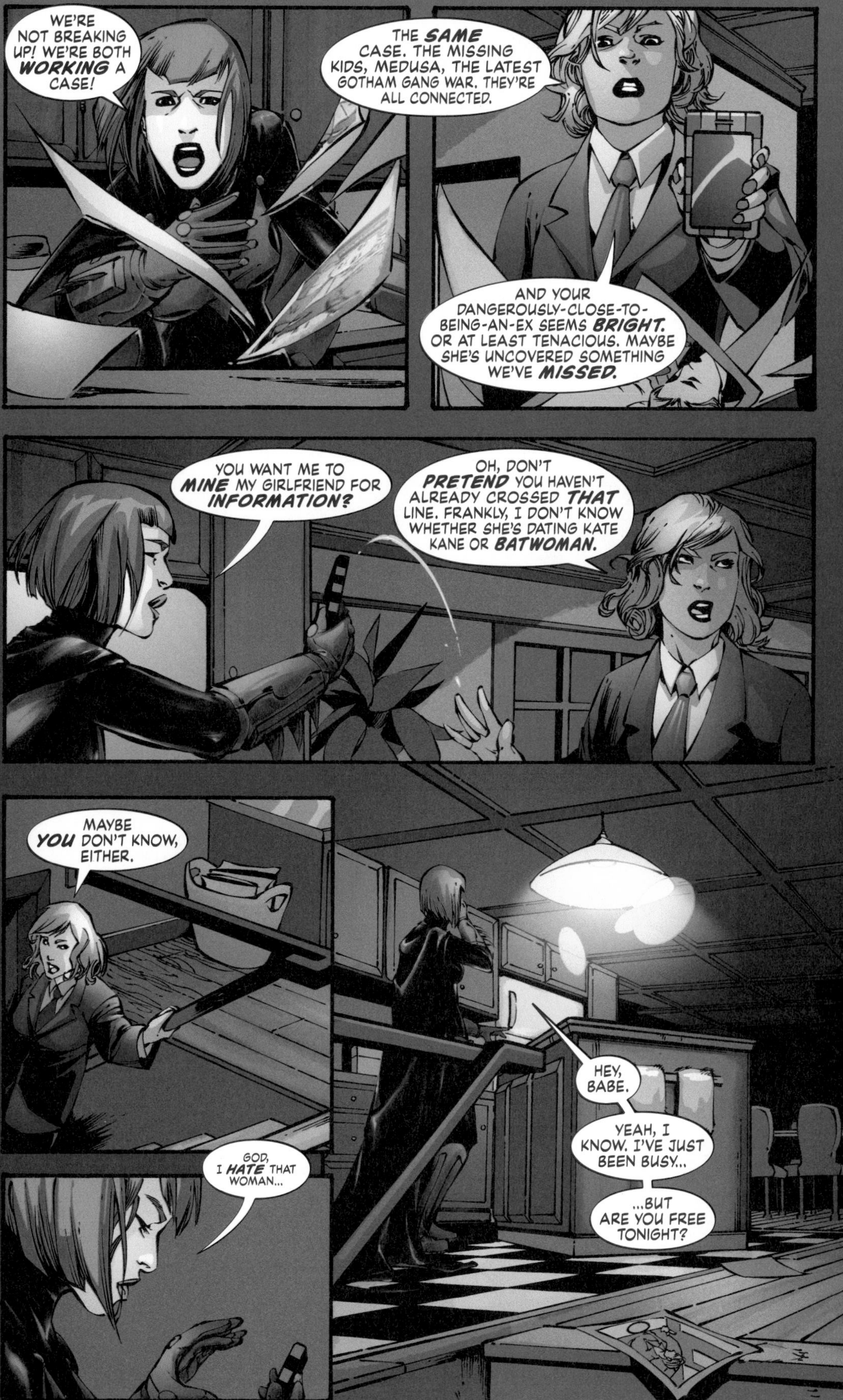
WE'RE NOT BREAKING UP! WE'RE BOTH WORKING A CASE!
THE SAME CASE. THE MISSING KIDS, MEDUSA, THE LATEST GOTHAM GANG WAR. THEY'RE ALL CONNECTED.
AND YOUR DANGEROUSLY-CLOSE-TO-BEING-AN-EX SEEMS BRIGHT. OR AT LEAST TENACIOUS. MAYBE SHE'S UNCOVERED SOMETHING WE'VE MISSED.
YOU WANT ME TO MINE MY GIRLFRIEND FOR INFORMATION?
OH, DON'T PRETEND YOU HAVEN'T ALREADY CROSSED THAT LINE. FRANKLY, I DON'T KNOW WHETHER SHE'S DATING KATE KANE OR BATWOMAN.
MAYBE YOU DON'T KNOW, EITHER.
GOD, I HATE THAT WOMAN...
HEY, BABE.
YEAH, I KNOW. I'VE JUST BEEN BUSY...
...BUT ARE YOU FREE TONIGHT?

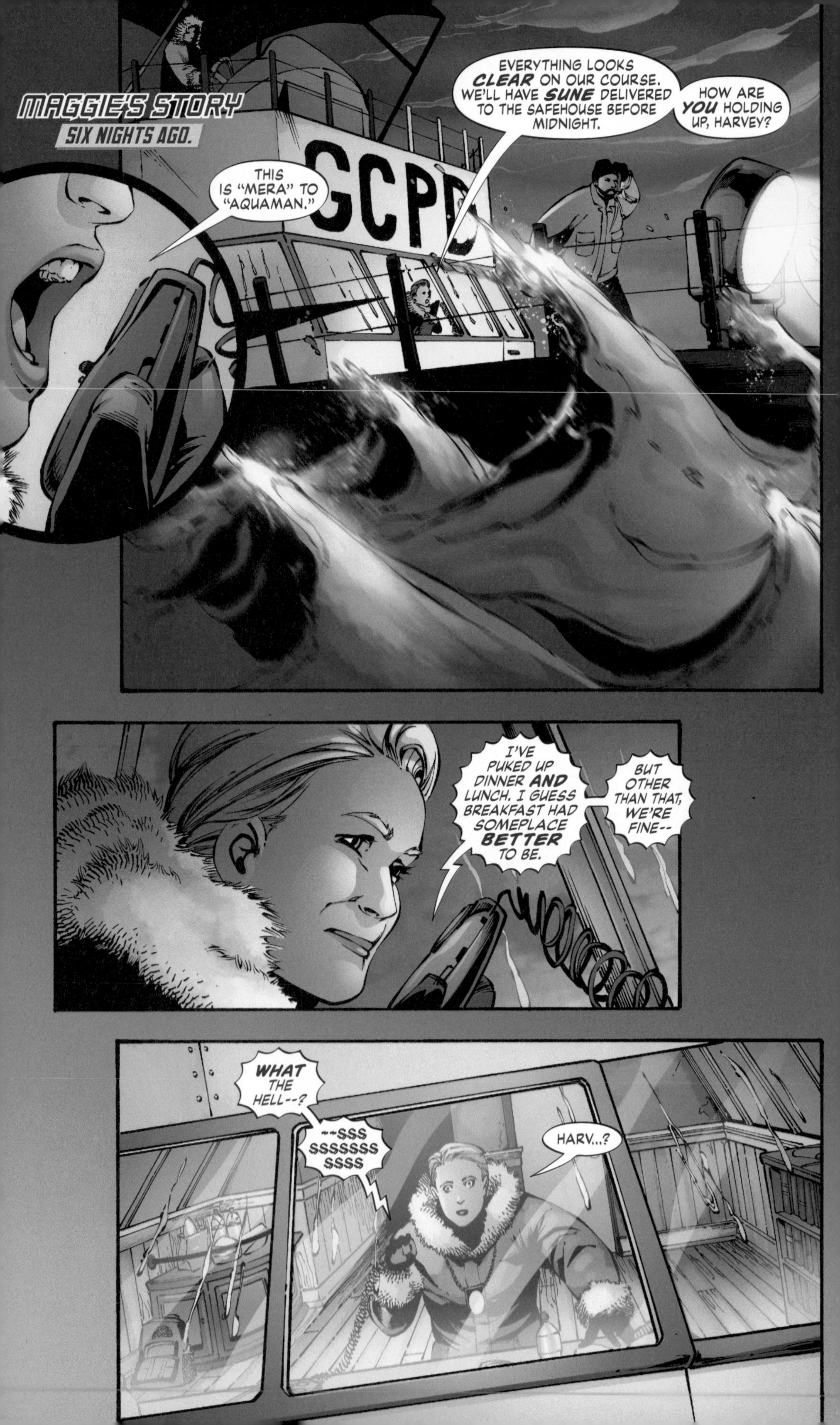
MAGGIE'S STORY
SIX NIGHTS AGO.
EVERYTHING LOOKS CLEAR ON OUR COURSE. WE'LL HAVE SUNE DELIVERED TO THE SAFEHOUSE BEFORE MIDNIGHT.
HOW ARE YOU HOLDING UP, HARVEY?
THIS IS "MERA" TO "AQUAMAN."
GCPD
I'VE PUKED UP DINNER AND LUNCH. I GUESS BREAKFAST HAD SOMEPLACE BETTER TO BE.
BUT OTHER THAN THAT, WE'RE FINE--
WHAT THE HELL--?
--SSS SSSSSSS SSSS
HARV...?

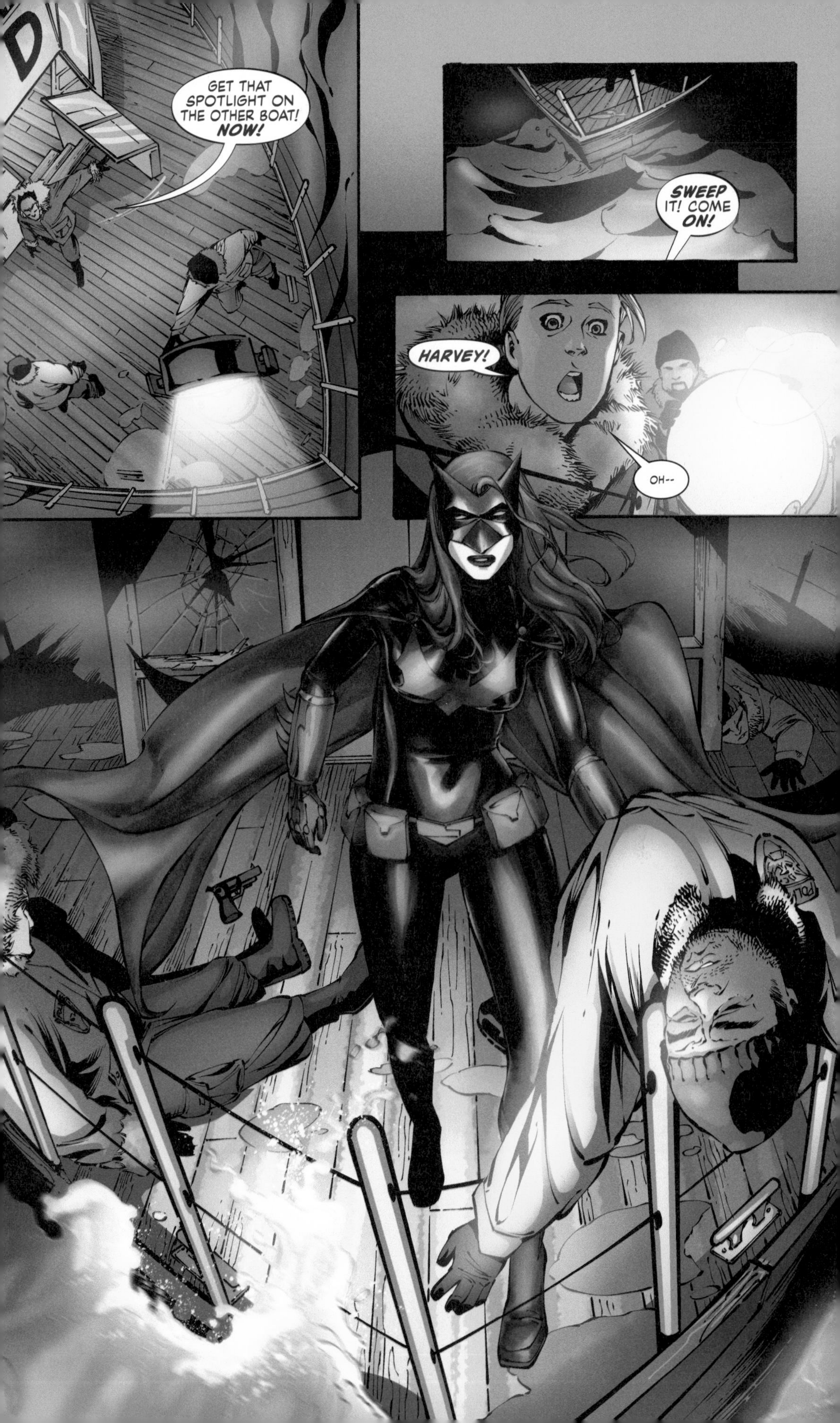
GET THAT SPOTLIGHT ON THE OTHER BOAT! NOW!
SWEEP IT! COME ON!
HARVEY!
OH--

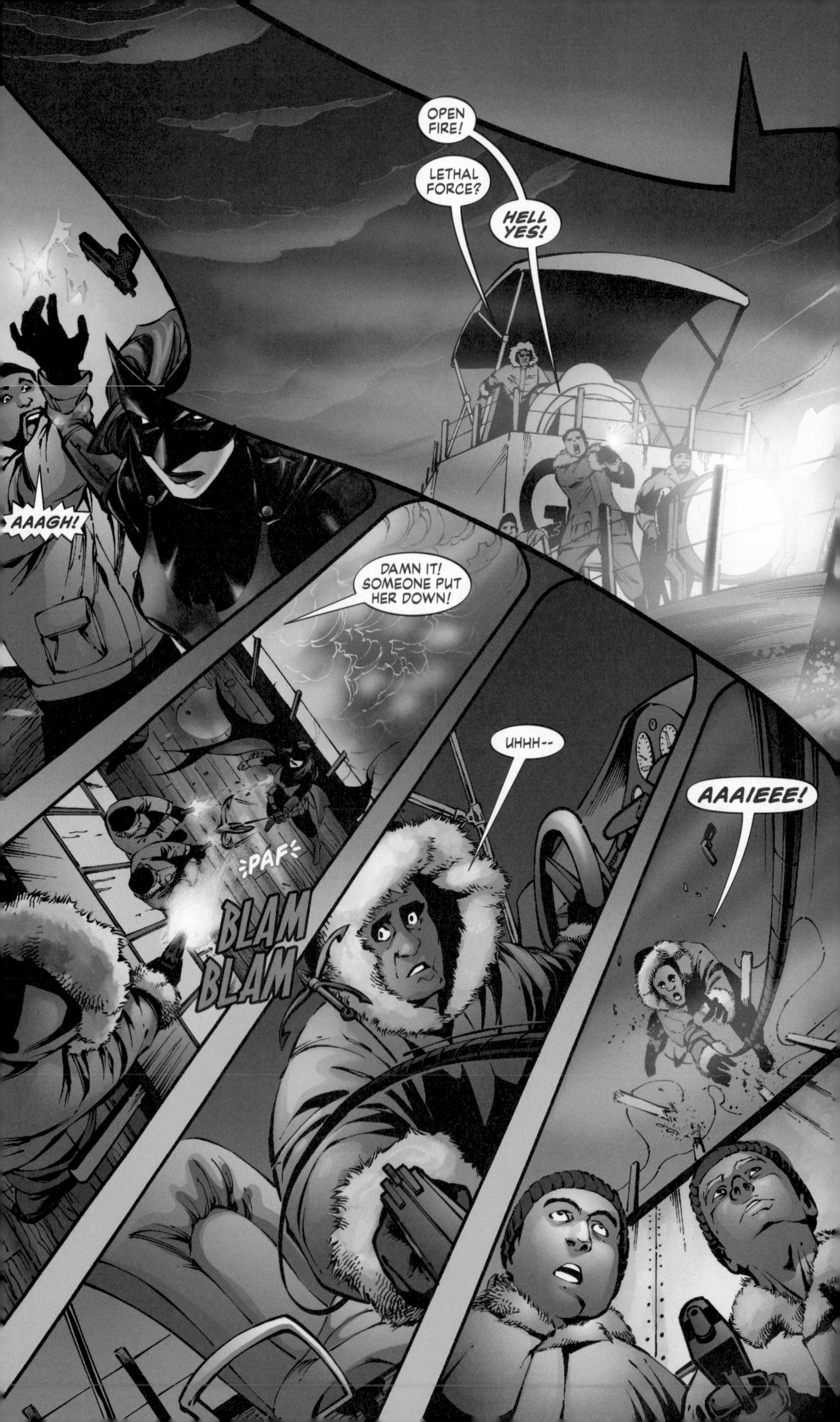

OPEN FIRE!
LETHAL FORCE?
HELL YES!
AAAGH!
DAMN IT! SOMEONE PUT HER DOWN!
PAF
BLAM BLAM
UHHH--
AAAIEEE!

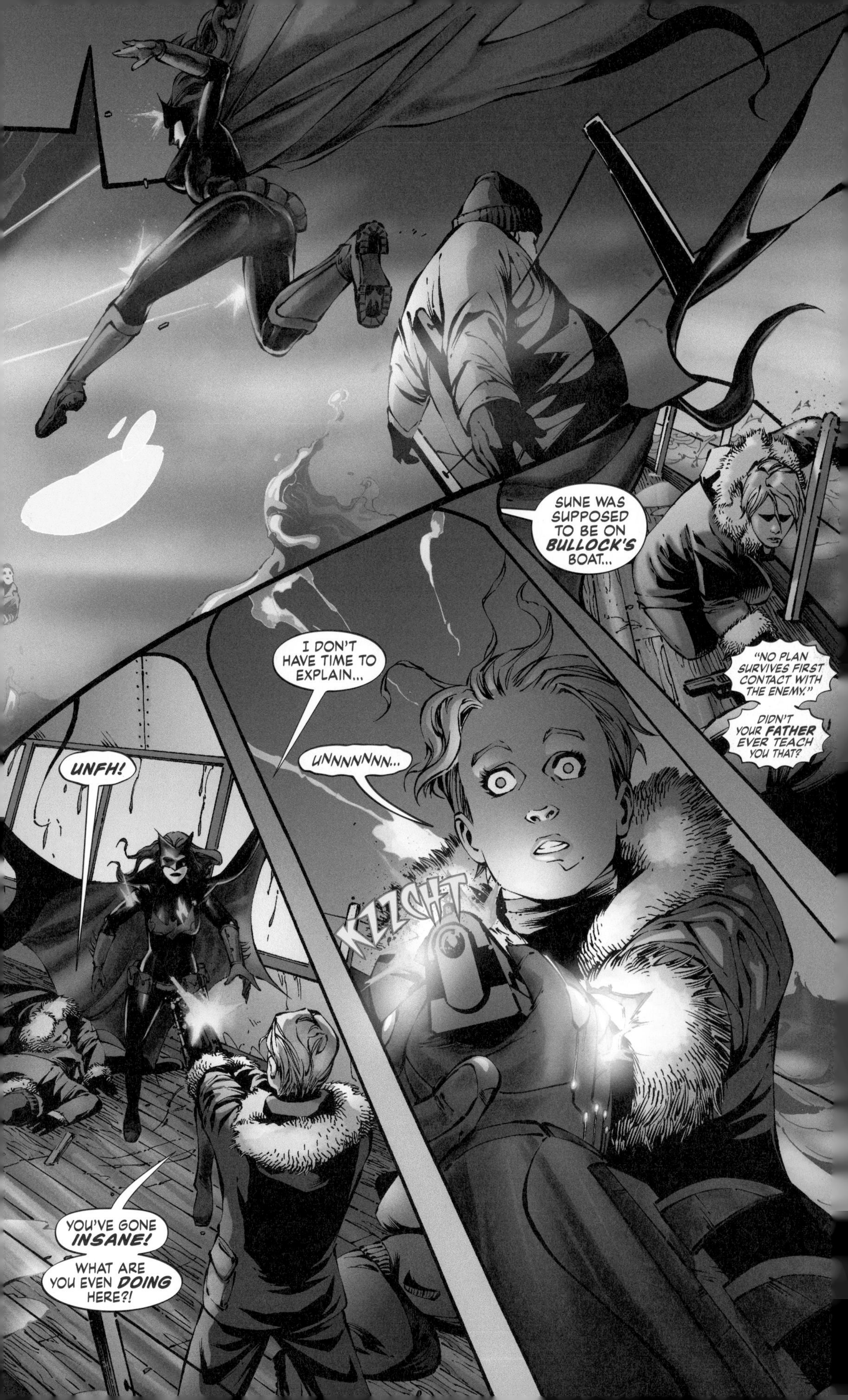
SUNE WAS SUPPOSED TO BE ON BULLOCK'S BOAT...
"NO PLAN SURVIVES FIRST CONTACT WITH THE ENEMY."
DIDN'T YOUR FATHER EVER TEACH YOU THAT?
I DON'T HAVE TIME TO EXPLAIN...
UNNNNNNN...
KZZCHT
UNFH!
YOU'VE GONE INSANE!
WHAT ARE YOU EVEN DOING HERE?!

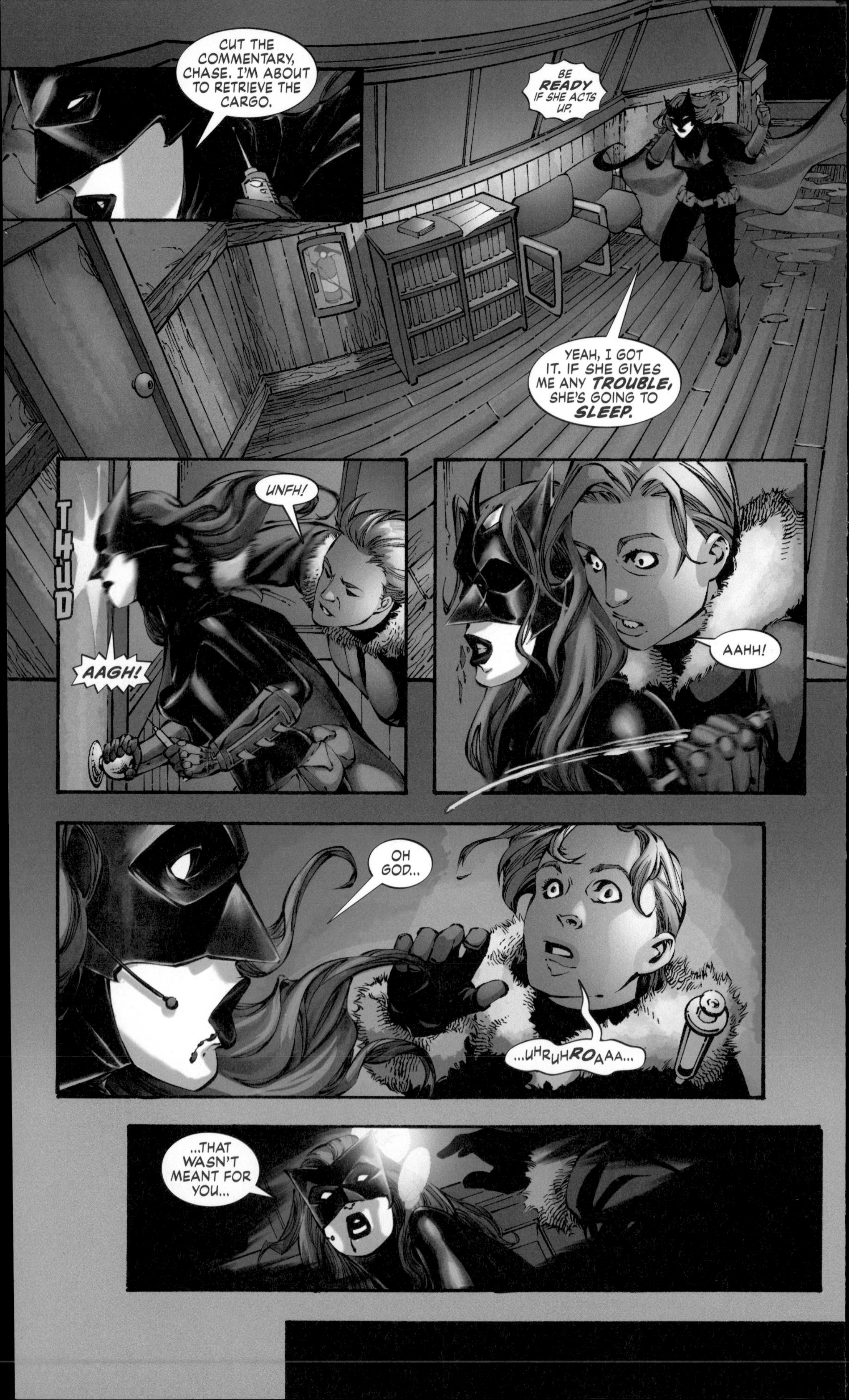

CUT THE COMMENTARY, CHASE. I'M ABOUT TO RETRIEVE THE CARGO.
BE READY IF SHE ACTS UP.
YEAH, I GOT IT. IF SHE GIVES ME ANY TROUBLE, SHE'S GOING TO SLEEP.
UNFH!
THUD
AAGH!
AAHH!
OH GOD...
...UHRUHROAAA...
...THAT WASN'T MEANT FOR YOU...

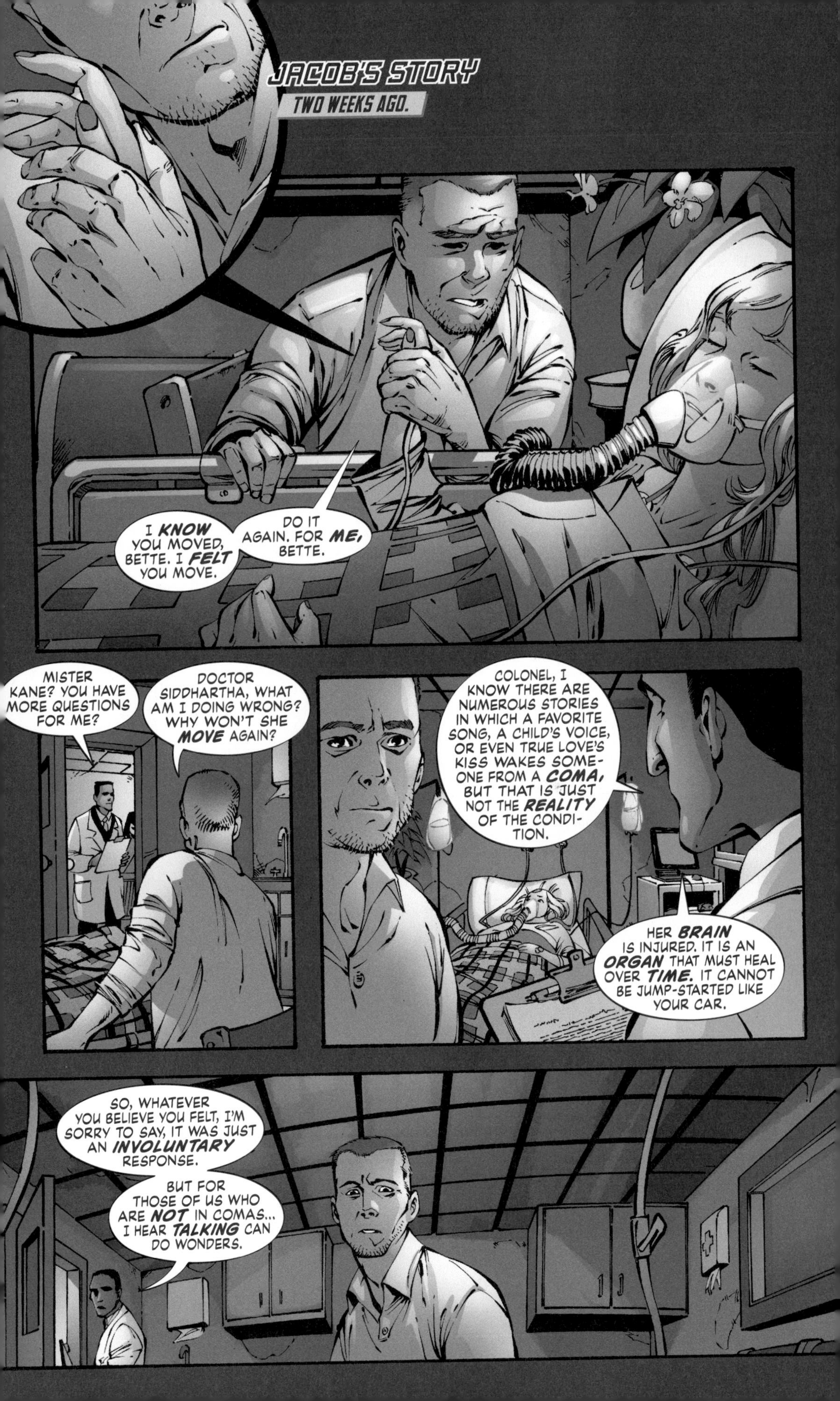
JACOB'S STORY
TWO WEEKS AGO.
I KNOW YOU MOVED, BETTE. I FELT YOU MOVE.
DO IT AGAIN. FOR ME, BETTE.
MISTER KANE? YOU HAVE MORE QUESTIONS FOR ME?
DOCTOR SIDDHARTHA, WHAT AM I DOING WRONG? WHY WON'T SHE MOVE AGAIN?
COLONEL, I KNOW THERE ARE NUMEROUS STORIES IN WHICH A FAVORITE SONG, A CHILD'S VOICE, OR EVEN TRUE LOVE'S KISS WAKES SOME-ONE FROM A COMA, BUT THAT IS JUST NOT THE REALITY OF THE CONDI-TION.
HER BRAIN IS INJURED. IT IS AN ORGAN THAT MUST HEAL OVER TIME. IT CANNOT BE JUMP-STARTED LIKE YOUR CAR.
SO, WHATEVER YOU BELIEVE YOU FELT, I'M SORRY TO SAY, IT WAS JUST AN INVOLUNTARY RESPONSE.
BUT FOR THOSE OF US WHO ARE NOT IN COMAS... I HEAR TALKING CAN DO WONDERS.

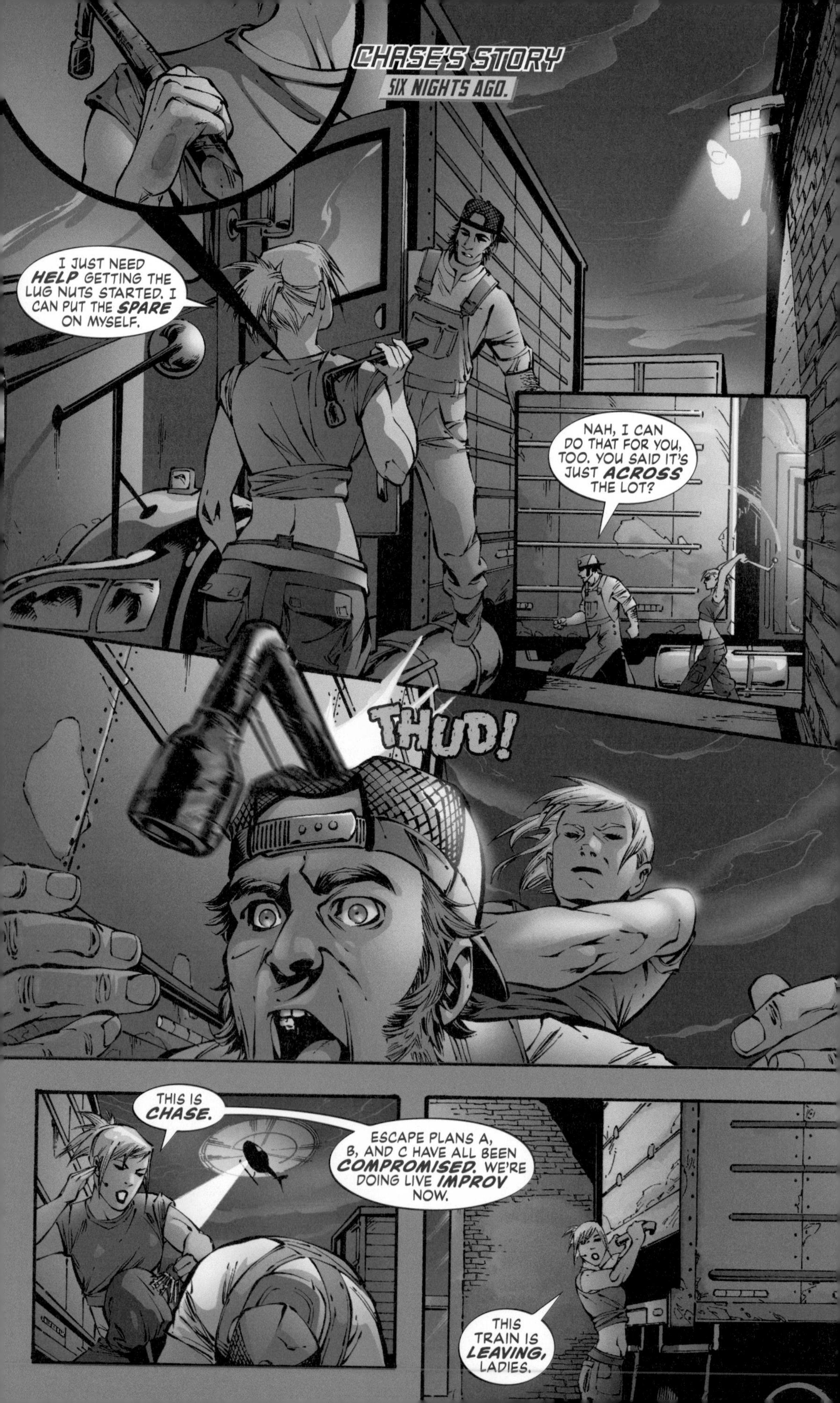
CHASE'S STORY
SIX NIGHTS AGO.
I JUST NEED HELP GETTING THE LUG NUTS STARTED. I CAN PUT THE SPARE ON MYSELF.
NAH, I CAN DO THAT FOR YOU, TOO. YOU SAID IT'S JUST ACROSS THE LOT?
THUD!
THIS IS CHASE.
ESCAPE PLANS A, B, AND C HAVE ALL BEEN COMPROMISED. WE'RE DOING LIVE IMPROV NOW.
THIS TRAIN IS LEAVING, LADIES.

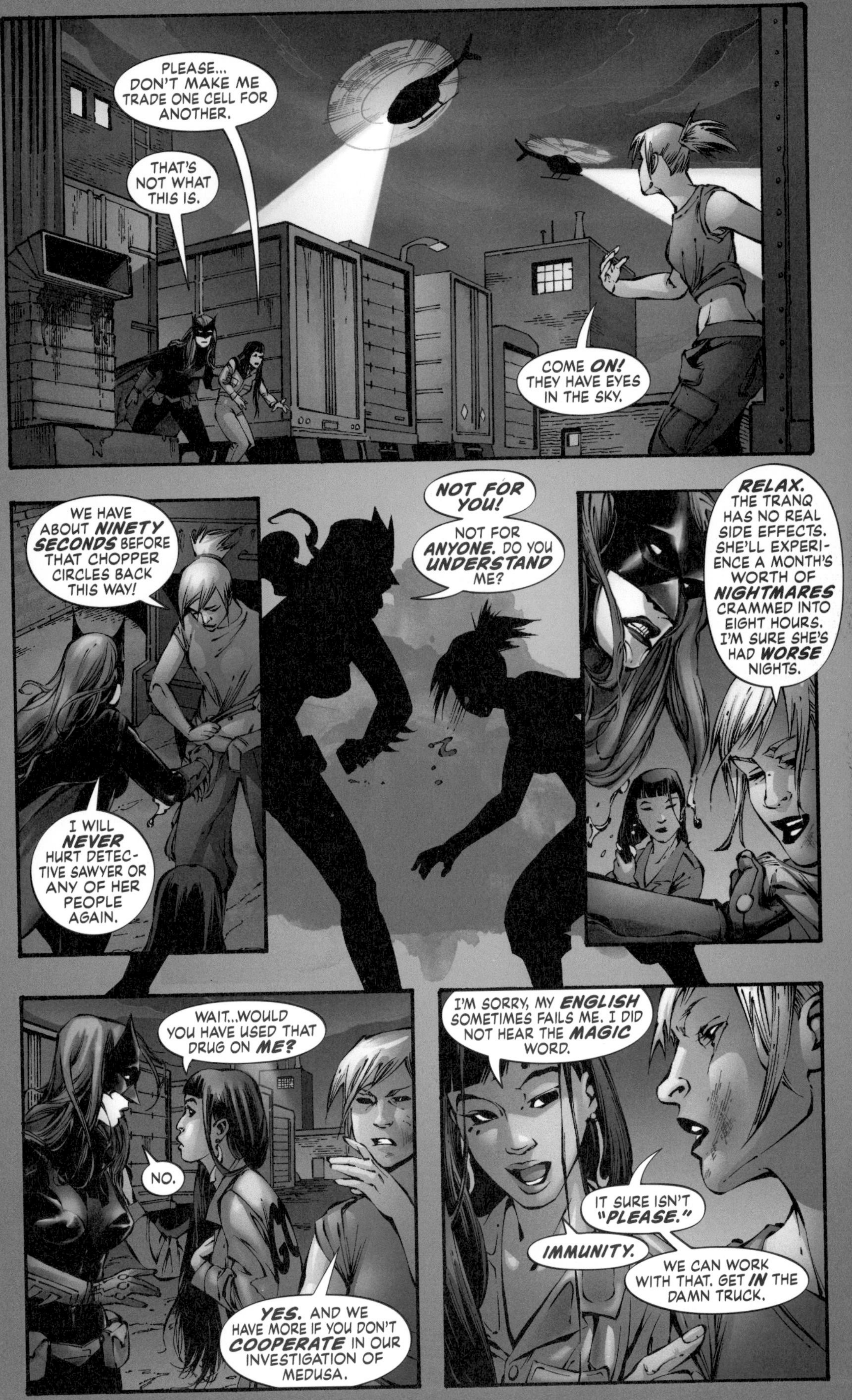
PLEASE... DON'T MAKE ME TRADE ONE CELL FOR ANOTHER.
THAT'S NOT WHAT THIS IS.
COME ON! THEY HAVE EYES IN THE SKY.
WE HAVE ABOUT NINETY SECONDS BEFORE THAT CHOPPER CIRCLES BACK THIS WAY!
I WILL NEVER HURT DETECTIVE SAWYER OR ANY OF HER PEOPLE AGAIN.
NOT FOR YOU!
NOT FOR ANYONE. DO YOU UNDERSTAND ME?
RELAX. THE TRANQ HAS NO REAL SIDE EFFECTS. SHE'LL EXPERIENCE A MONTH'S WORTH OF NIGHTMARES CRAMMED INTO EIGHT HOURS. I'M SURE SHE'S HAD WORSE NIGHTS.
WAIT..WOULD YOU HAVE USED THAT DRUG ON ME?
NO.
YES. AND WE HAVE MORE IF YOU DON'T COOPERATE IN OUR INVESTIGATION OF MEDUSA.
I'M SORRY, MY ENGLISH SOMETIMES FAILS ME. I DID NOT HEAR THE MAGIC WORD.
IT SURE ISN'T "PLEASE."
IMMUNITY.
WE CAN WORK WITH THAT. GET IN THE DAMN TRUCK.

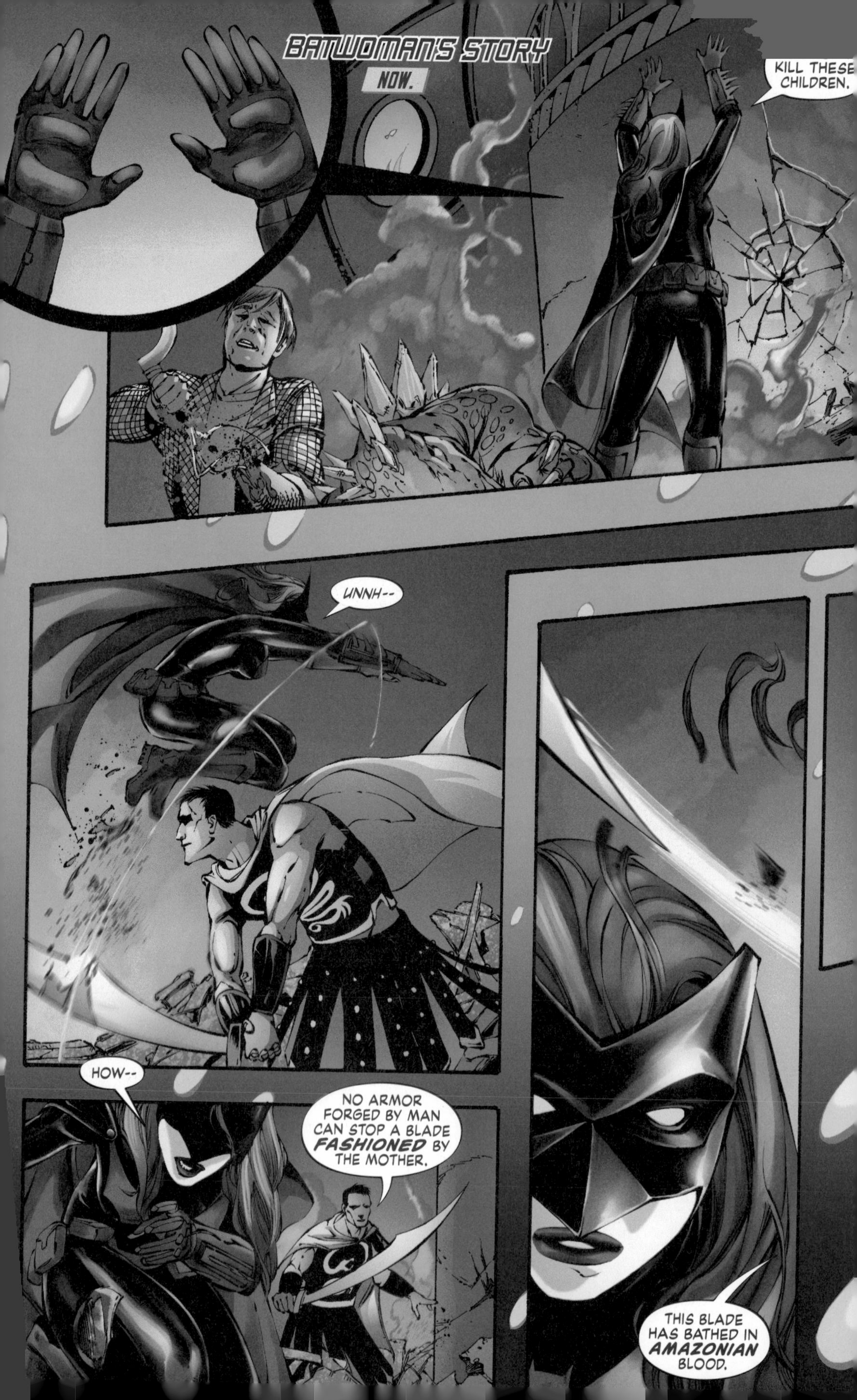
BATWOMAN'S STORY
NOW.
KILL THESE CHILDREN.
UNNH--
HOW--
NO ARMOR FORGED BY MAN CAN STOP A BLADE FASHIONED BY THE MOTHER.
THIS BLADE HAS BATHED IN AMAZONIAN BLOOD.

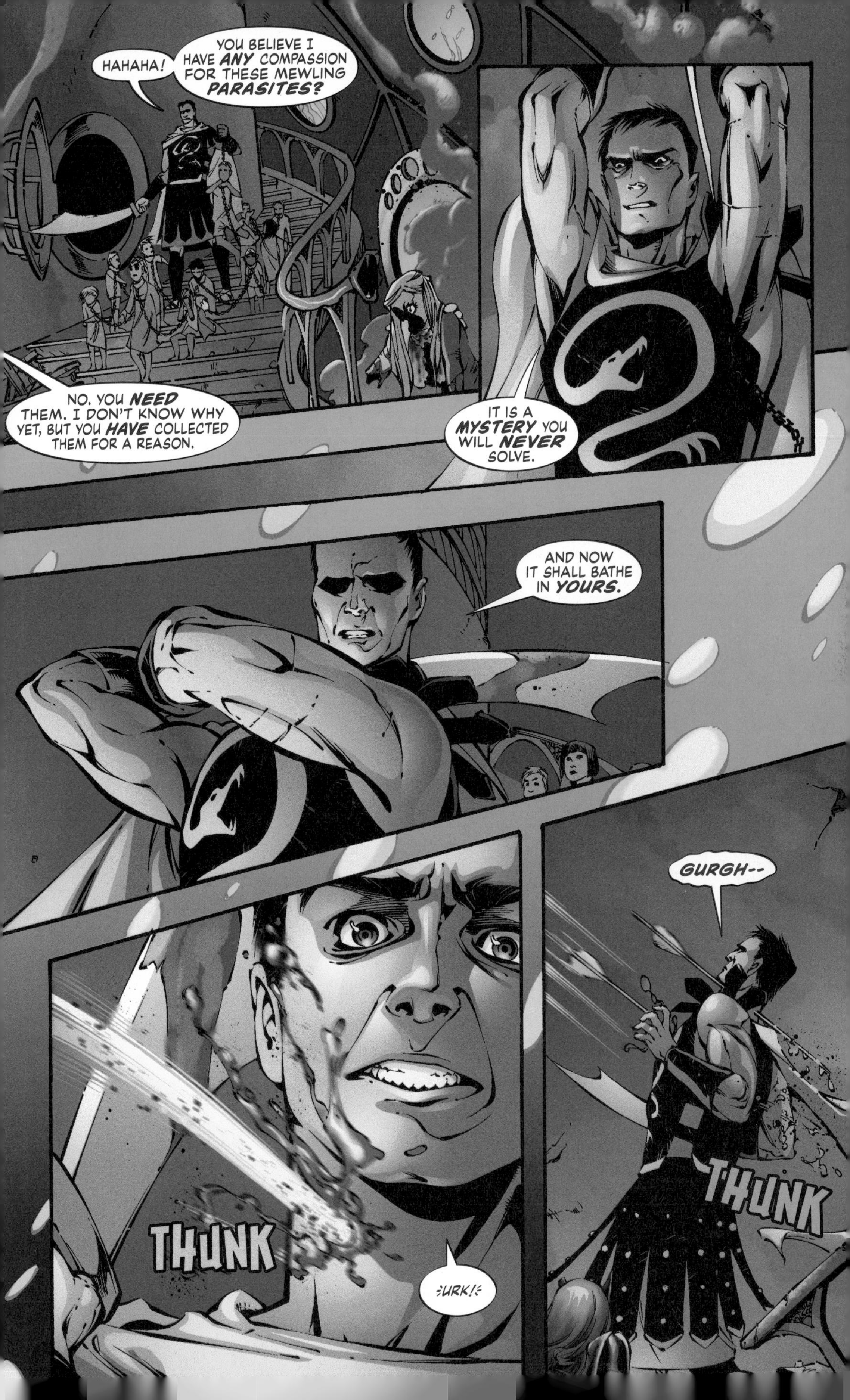
HAHAHA!
YOU BELIEVE I HAVE ANY COMPASSION FOR THESE MEWLING PARASITES?
NO. YOU NEED THEM. I DON'T KNOW WHY YET, BUT YOU HAVE COLLECTED THEM FOR A REASON.
IT IS A MYSTERY YOU WILL NEVER SOLVE.
AND NOW IT SHALL BATHE IN YOURS.
THUNK
URK!
GURGH--
THUNK

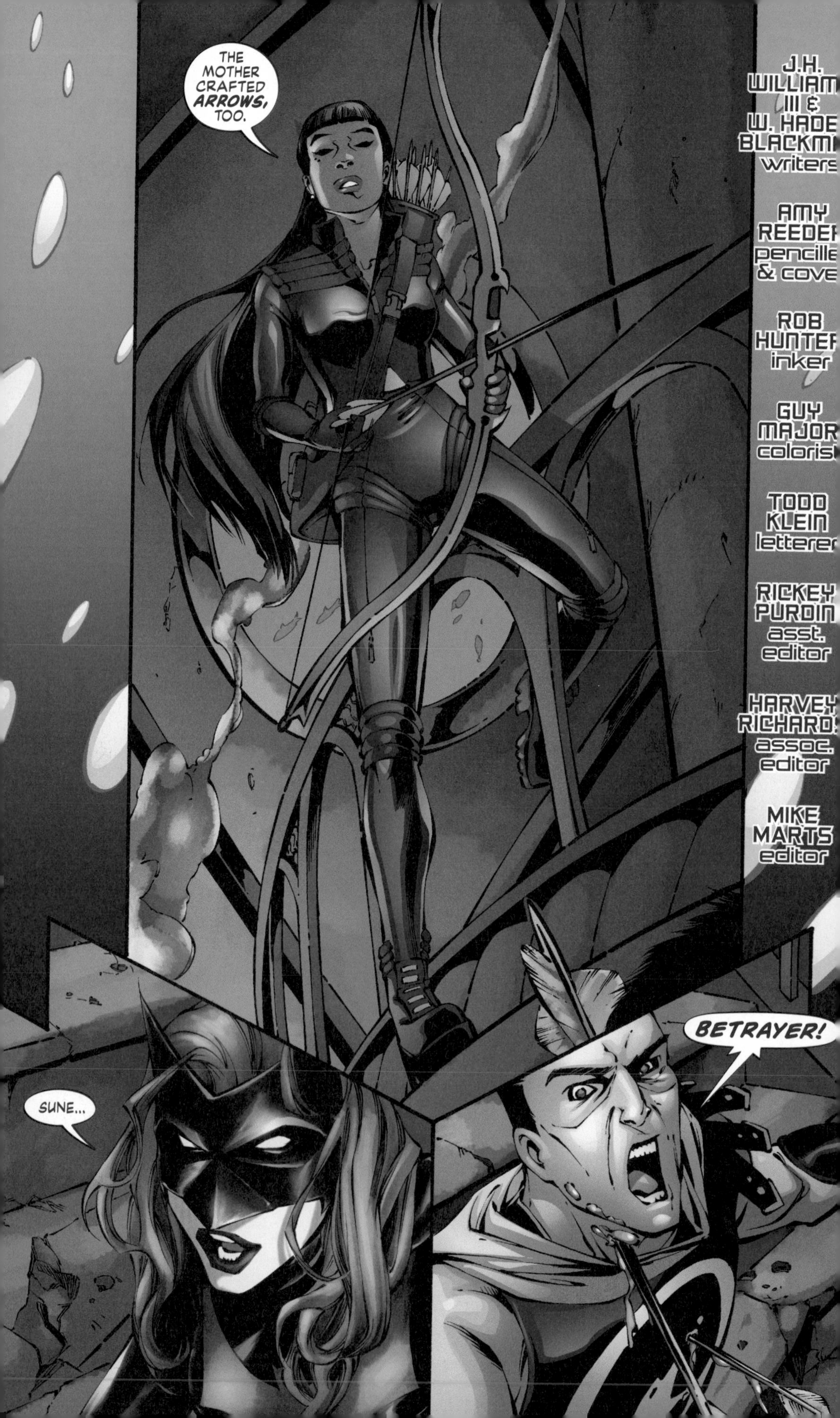
THE MOTHER CRAFTED ARROWS, TOO.
SUNE...
BETRAYER!
J.H. WILLIAMS III & W. HADEN BLACKMAN writers
AMY REEDER penciller & cover
ROB HUNTER inker
GUY MAJOR colorist
TODD KLEIN letterer
RICKEY PURDIN asst. editor
HARVEY RICHARDS assoc. editor
MIKE MARTS editor

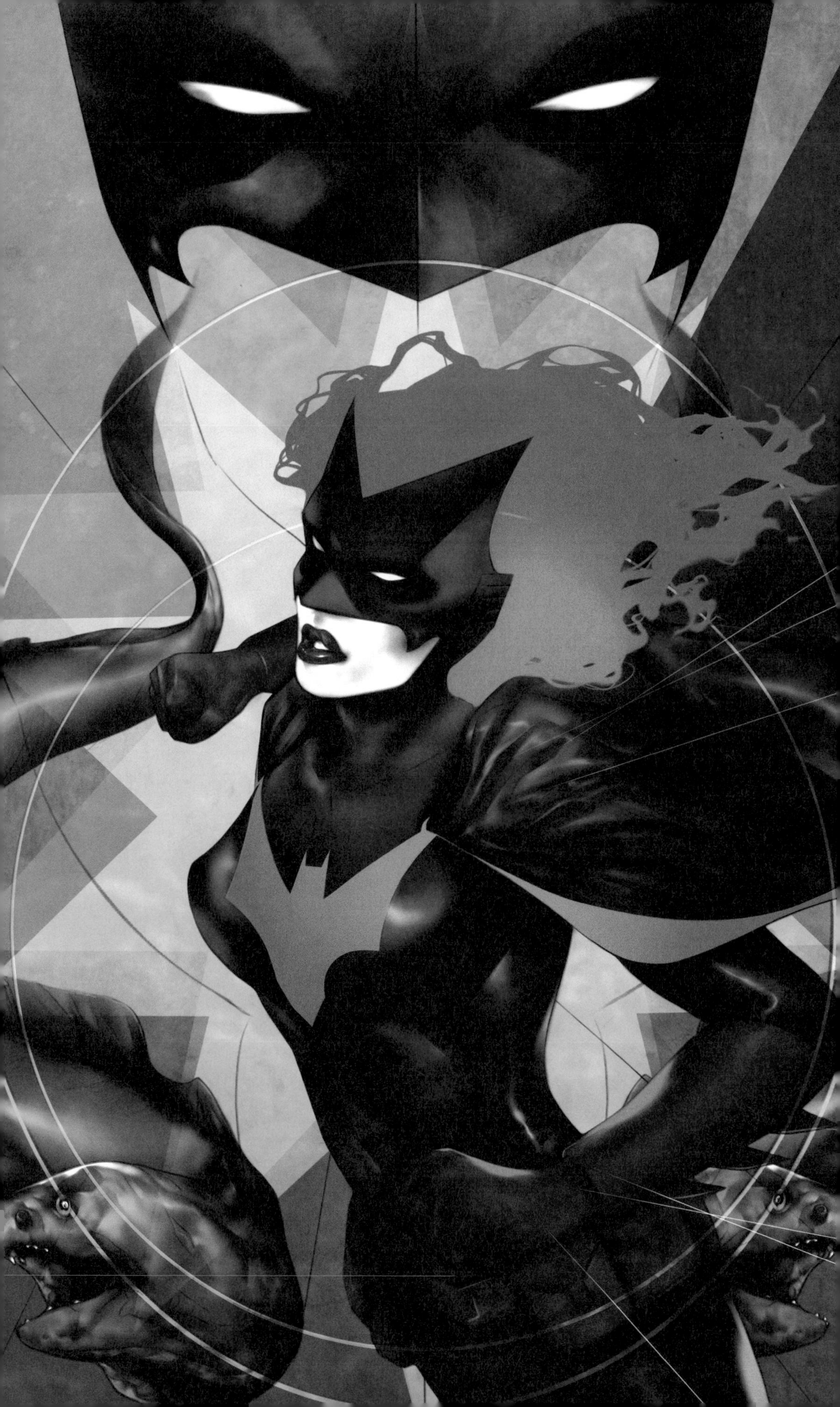

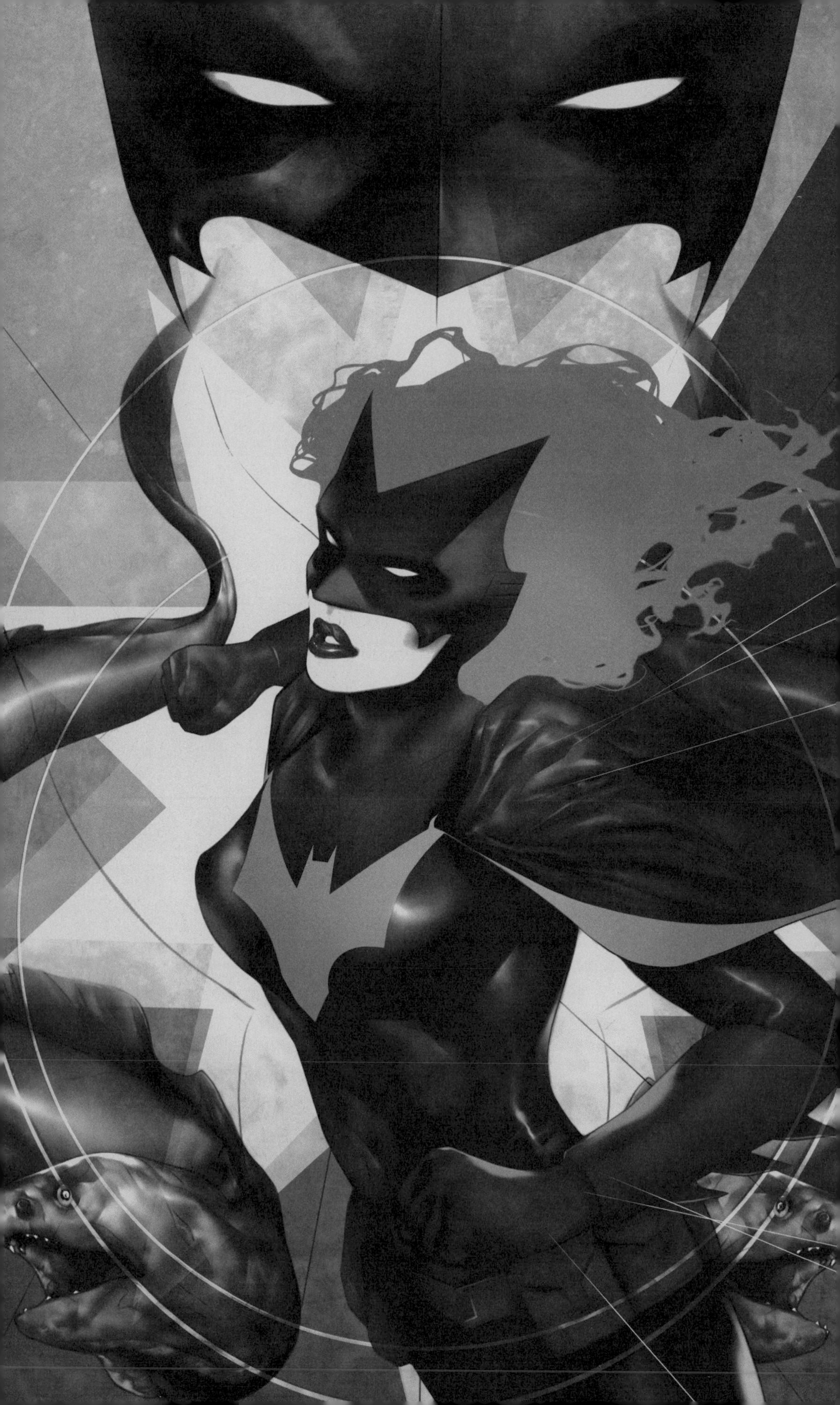

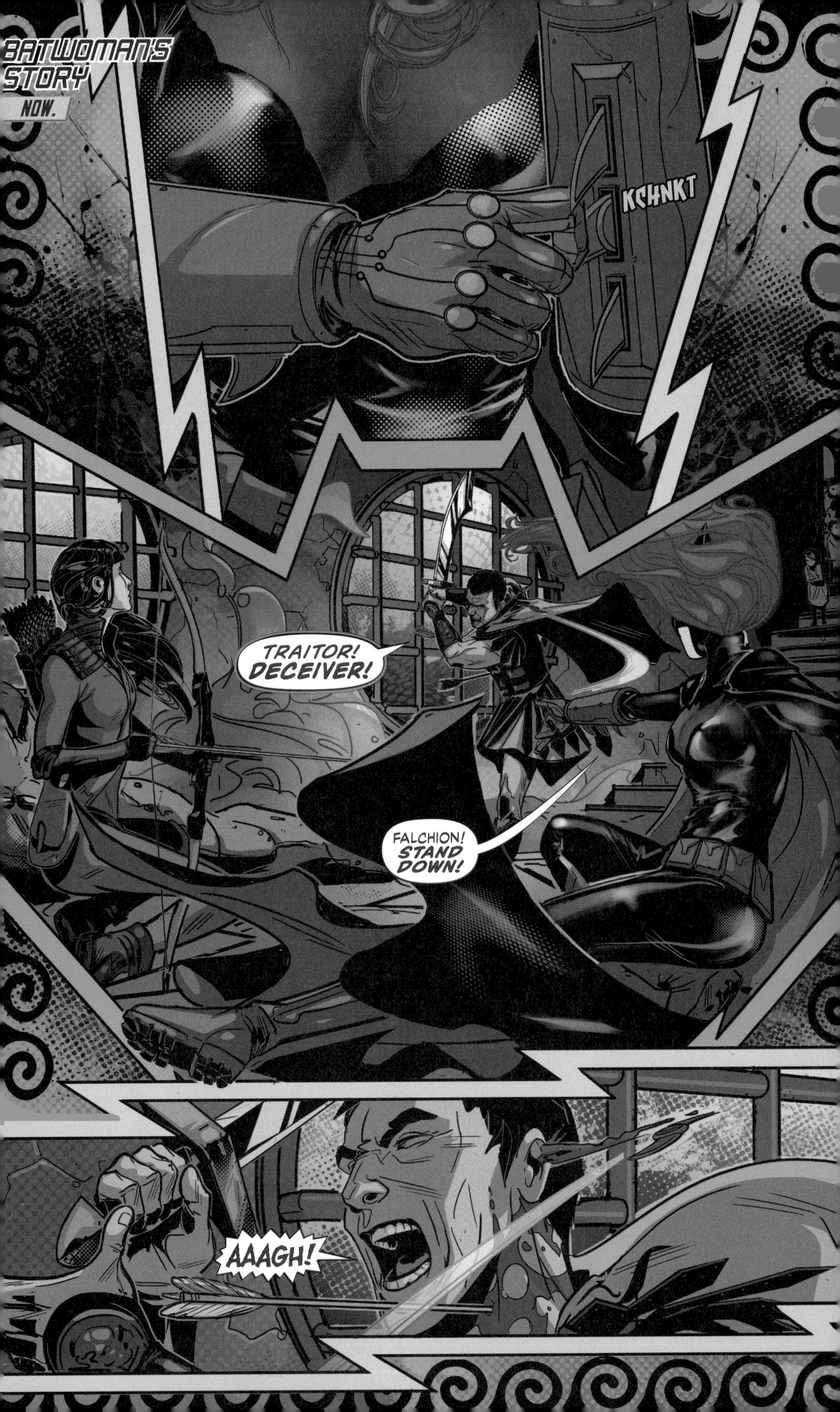
BATWOMAN'S STORY
NOW.
KCHNKT
TRAITOR! DECEIVER!
FALCHION! STAND DOWN!
AAAGH!

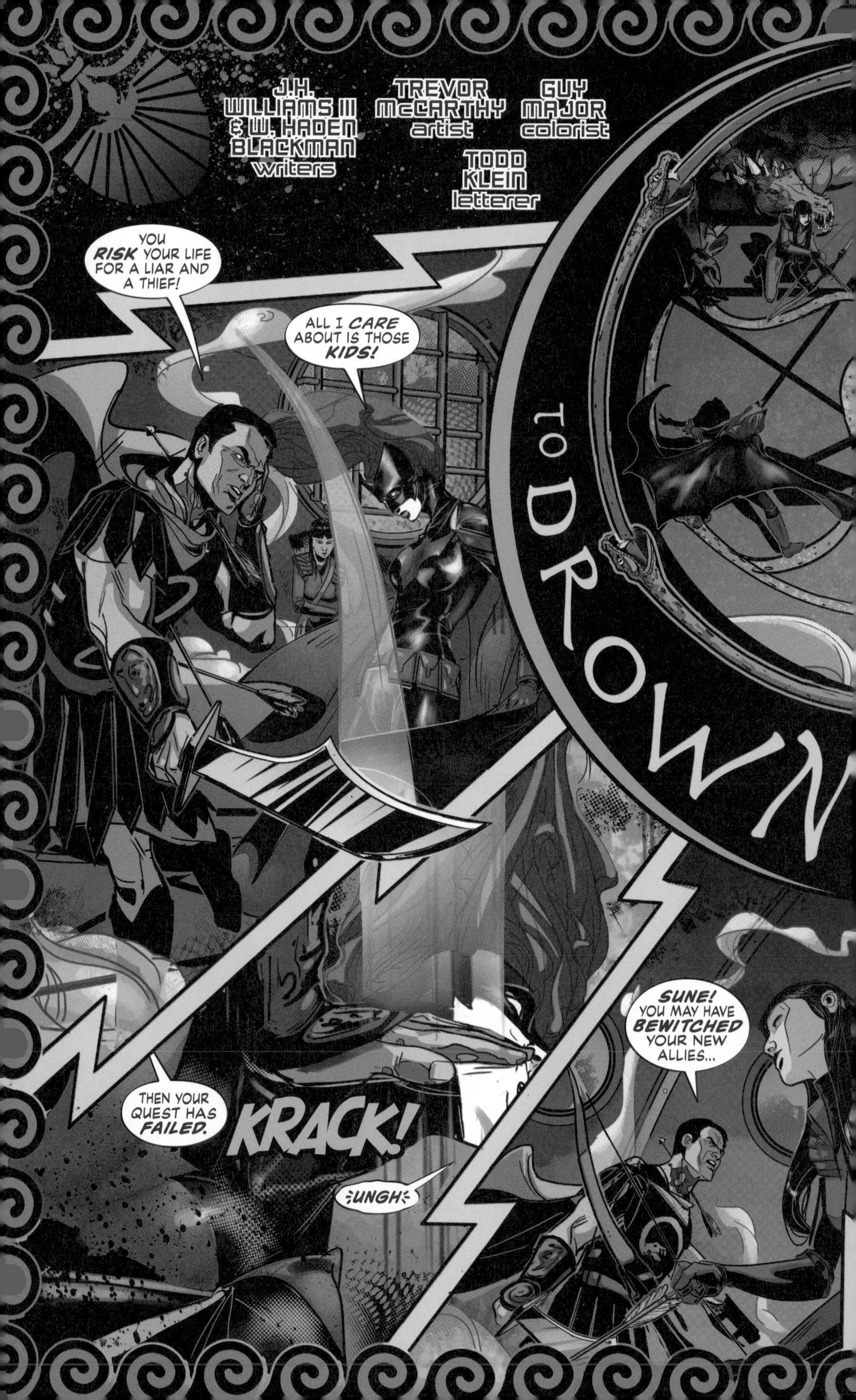

J.H. WILLIAMS III & W. HADEN BLACKMAN writers
TREVOR McCARTHY artist
GUY MAJOR colorist
TODD KLEIN letterer
YOU RISK YOUR LIFE FOR A LIAR AND A THIEF!
ALL I CARE ABOUT IS THOSE KIDS!
TO DROWN
THEN YOUR QUEST HAS FAILED.
KRACK!
UNGH
SUNE! YOU MAY HAVE BEWITCHED YOUR NEW ALLIES...

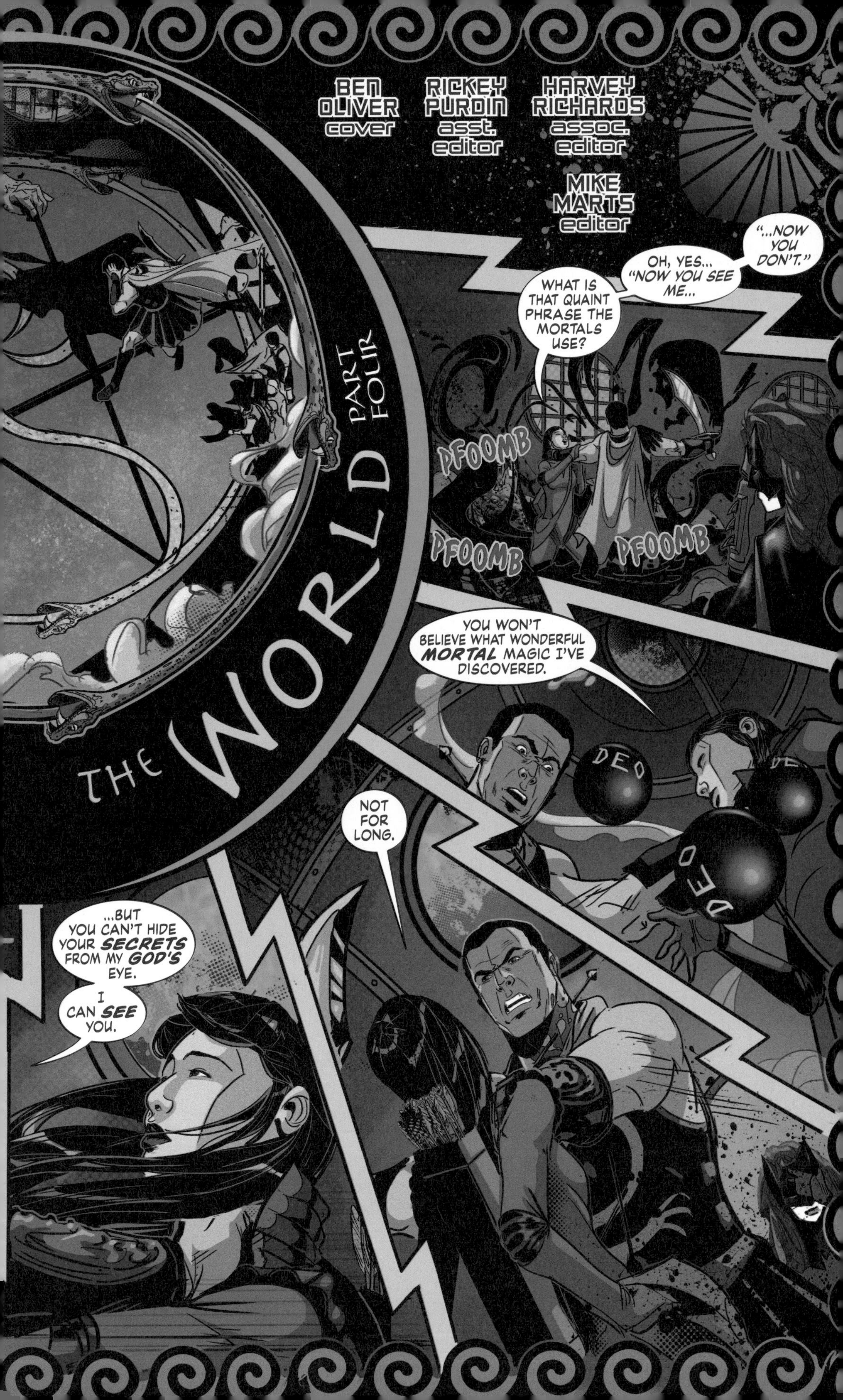
BEN OLIVER cover
RICKEY PURDIN asst. editor
HARVEY RICHARDS assoc. editor
MIKE MARTS editor
THE WORLD PART FOUR
WHAT IS THAT QUAINT PHRASE THE MORTALS USE?
OH, YES... "NOW YOU SEE ME...
"...NOW YOU DON'T."
PFOOMB
PFOOMB
PFOOMB
YOU WON'T BELIEVE WHAT WONDERFUL MORTAL MAGIC I'VE DISCOVERED.
DEO
DEO
NOT FOR LONG.
...BUT YOU CAN'T HIDE YOUR SECRETS FROM MY GOD'S EYE.
I CAN SEE YOU.

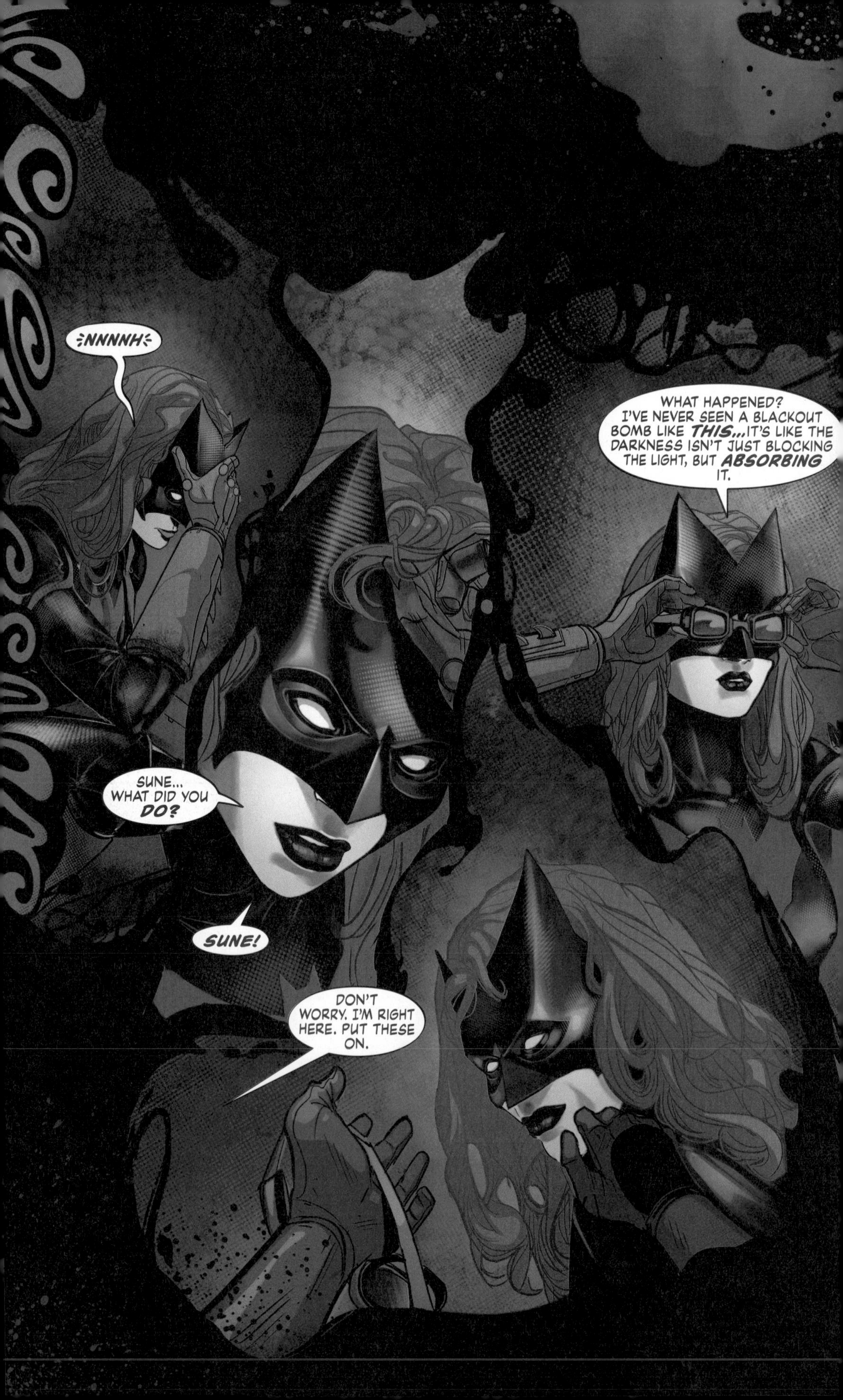
NNNNH
WHAT HAPPENED? I'VE NEVER SEEN A BLACKOUT BOMB LIKE THIS...IT'S LIKE THE DARKNESS ISN'T JUST BLOCKING THE LIGHT, BUT ABSORBING IT.
SUNE... WHAT DID YOU DO?
SUNE!
DON'T WORRY. I'M RIGHT HERE. PUT THESE ON.

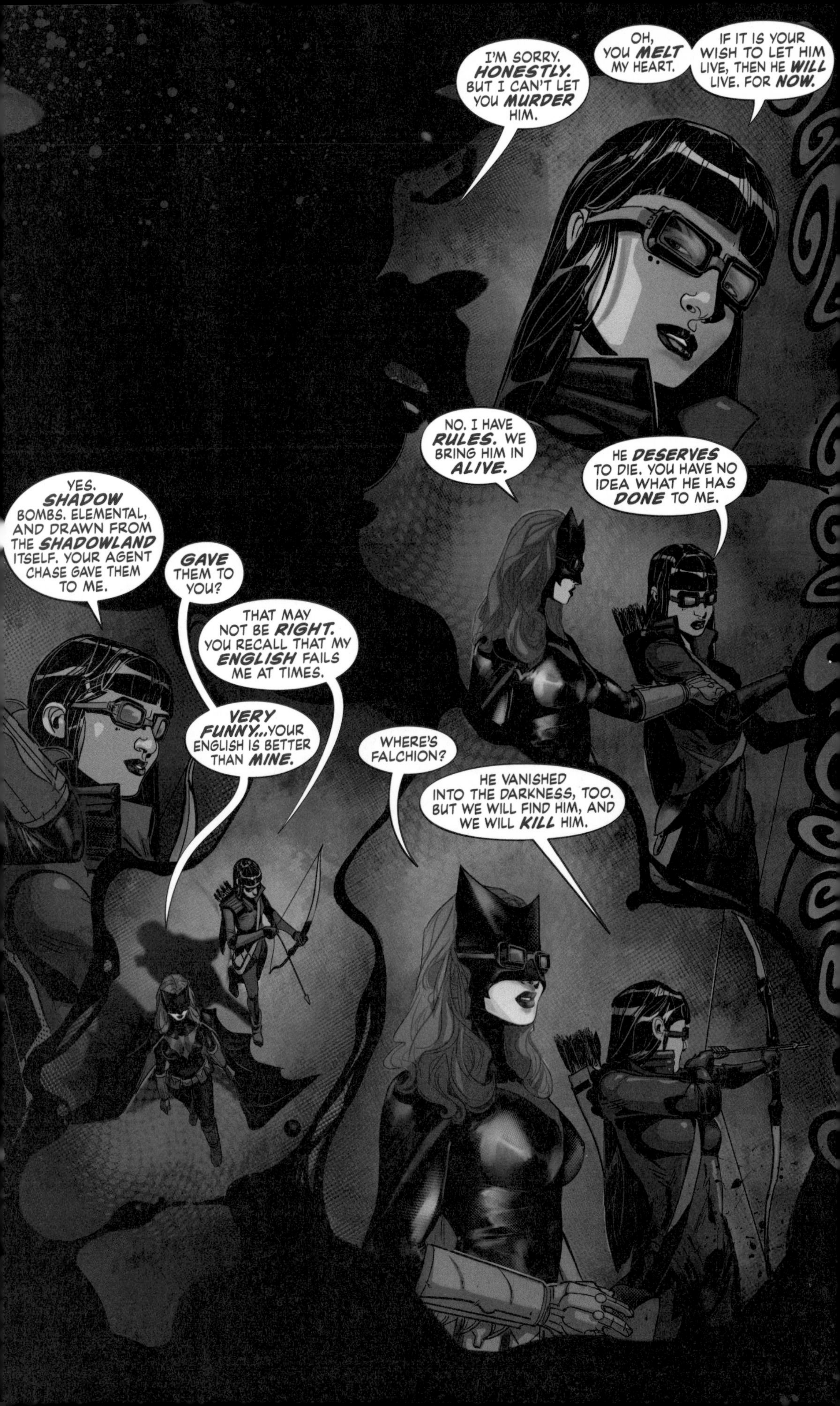
I'M SORRY. HONESTLY. BUT I CAN'T LET YOU MURDER HIM.
OH, YOU MELT MY HEART.
IF IT IS YOUR WISH TO LET HIM LIVE, THEN HE WILL LIVE. FOR NOW.
NO. I HAVE RULES. WE BRING HIM IN ALIVE.
HE DESERVES TO DIE. YOU HAVE NO IDEA WHAT HE HAS DONE TO ME.
YES. SHADOW BOMBS. ELEMENTAL, AND DRAWN FROM THE SHADOWLAND ITSELF. YOUR AGENT CHASE GAVE THEM TO ME.
GAVE THEM TO YOU?
THAT MAY NOT BE RIGHT. YOU RECALL THAT MY ENGLISH FAILS ME AT TIMES.
VERY FUNNY...YOUR ENGLISH IS BETTER THAN MINE.
WHERE'S FALCHION?
HE VANISHED INTO THE DARKNESS, TOO. BUT WE WILL FIND HIM, AND WE WILL KILL HIM.

eeeeeeeeeeeeeeeeeeeeeeeeeeeeeeeeeeeeeeeeeeeeeee

OH MY GOD!

WE NEED YOU TO LEAVE THE ROOM, SIR! SOMEBODY HELP ME GET HIM OUT OF HERE!

BETTE, YOU CAN'T *DO* THIS!

eeeeeeeeeeeeeeeeeeeeeeeeeeeeeeeeeeeeeeeeeeeeeee

SIR, YOU HAVE TO LEAVE THE ROOM *NOW!*

BETTE, BE STRONG! THINK OF KATE! BE LIKE *KATE* NOW, YOU ALWAYS WANTED TO BE LIKE HER!

SHOW ME YOU CAN BE LIKE HER!

eeeeeeeeeeeeeeeeeeeeeeeeeeeeeeeeeeeeeeeeeeeeeee

PLEASE, SIR...

GET YOUR DAMN HANDS OFF ME! THAT'S MY BETTE!

BETTE! FIGHT, DAMN YOU! FIGHT!

SIR! DON'T MAKE US CALL SECURITY...

USMA

eeeeeeeeeeeeeeeeeeeeeeeeeeeeeeeeeeeeeeeeeeeeeee

NO!

BETTE! I'M HERE, BETTE! DON'T GO!

SECURITY!

eeeeeeeeeeeeeeeeeeeeeeeeeeeeeeeeeeeeeeeeeeeeeee

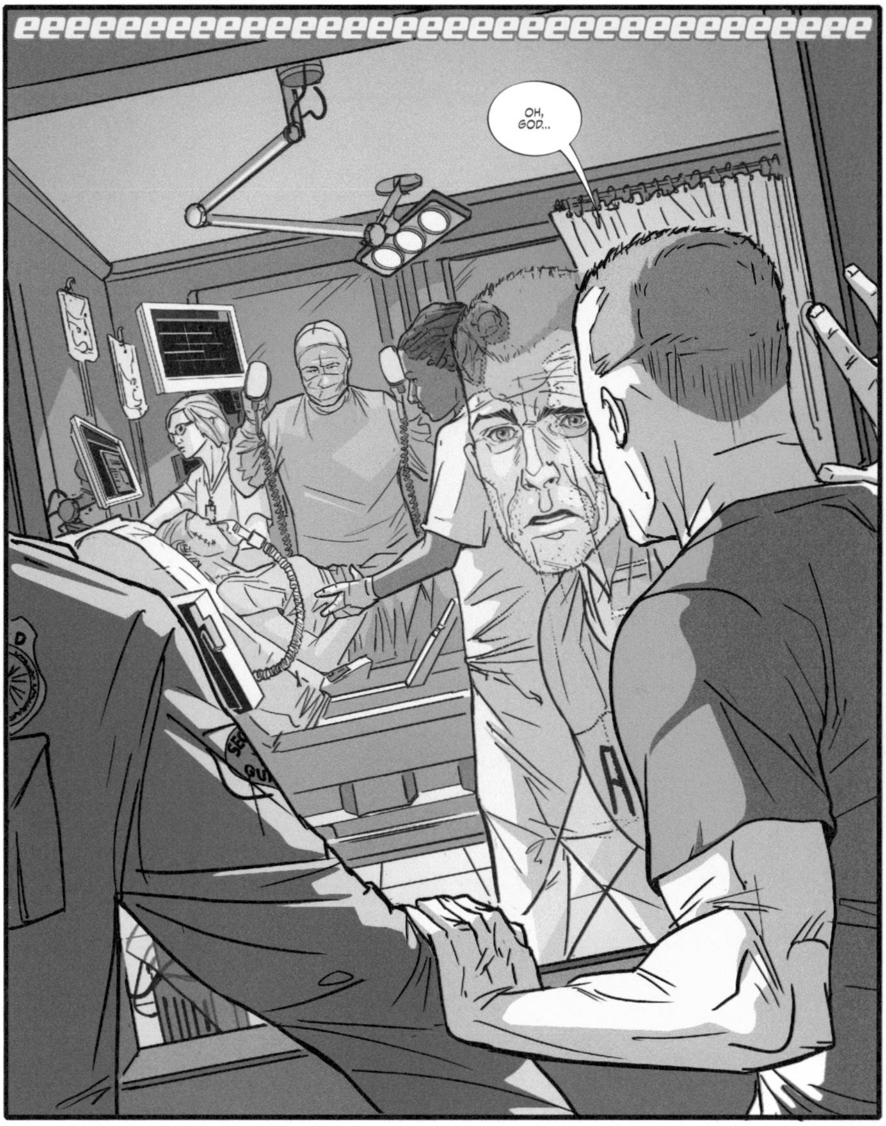
EEEEEEEEEEEEEEEEEEEEEEEEEEEEEEEEEEEEEEEEEE
OH, GOD...

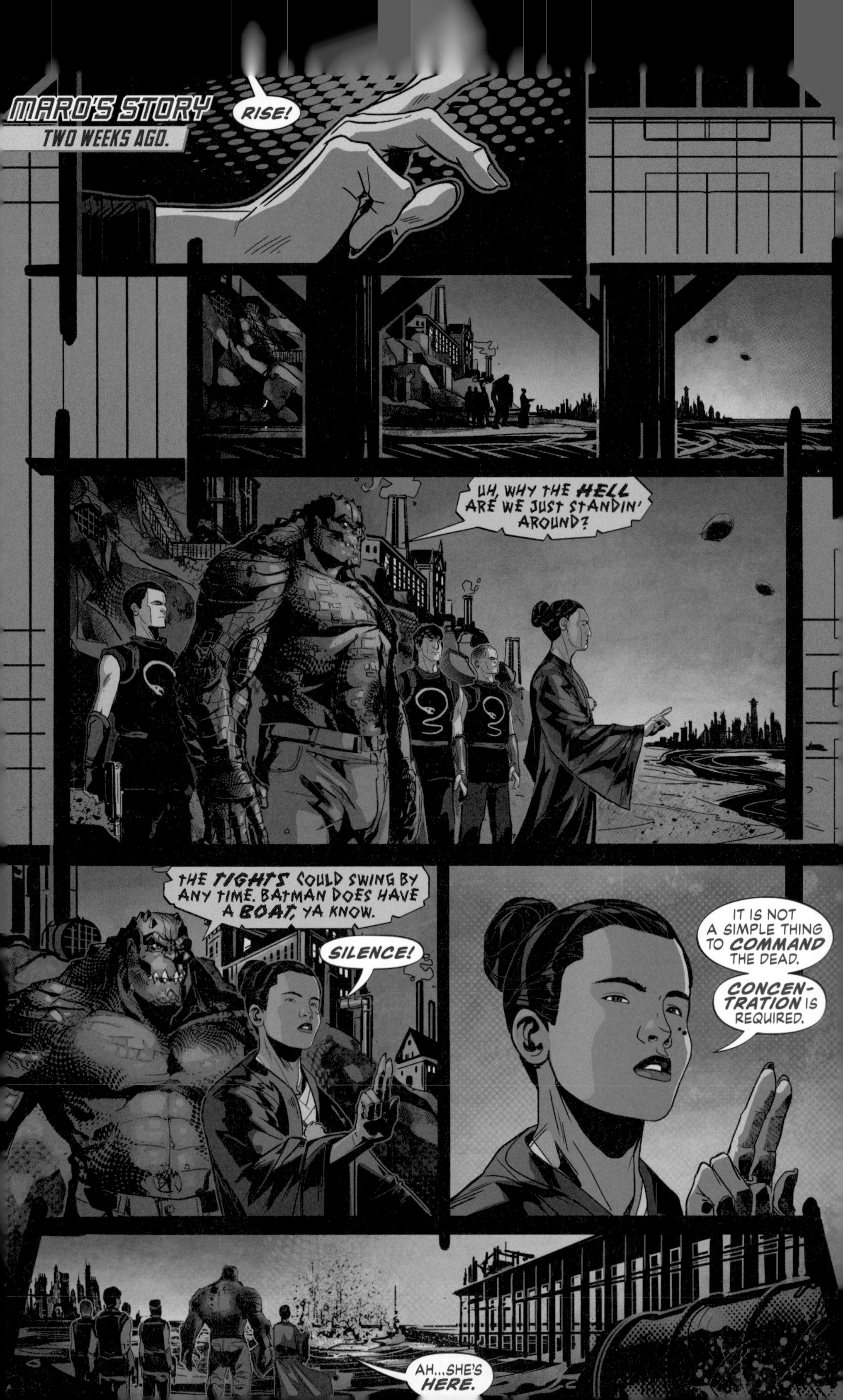
MARO'S STORY
TWO WEEKS AGO.
RISE!
UH, WHY THE HELL ARE WE JUST STANDIN' AROUND?
THE TIGHTS COULD SWING BY ANY TIME. BATMAN DOES HAVE A BOAT, YA KNOW.
SILENCE!
IT IS NOT A SIMPLE THING TO COMMAND THE DEAD.
CONCEN-TRATION IS REQUIRED.
AH...SHE'S HERE.

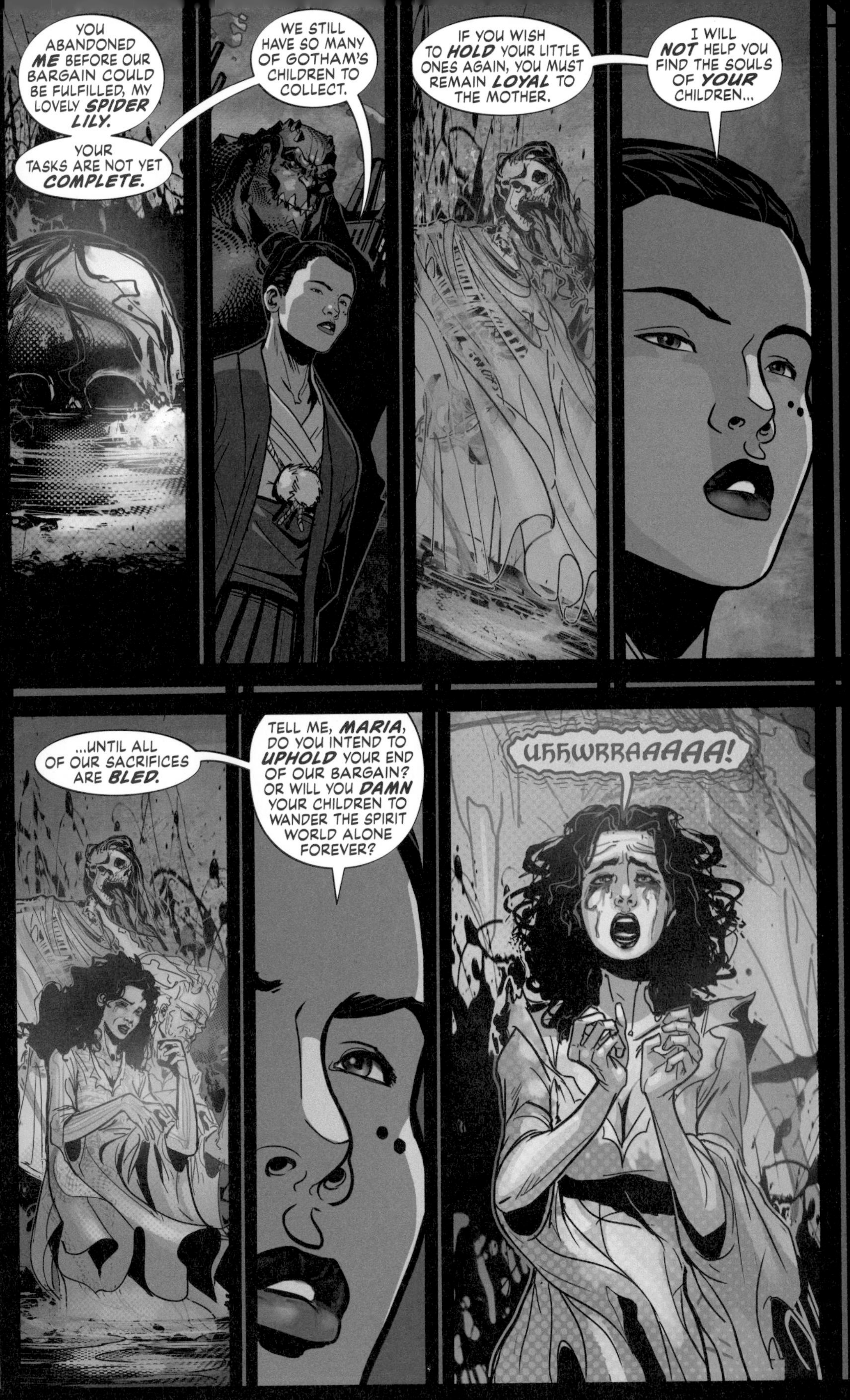
YOU ABANDONED ME BEFORE OUR BARGAIN COULD BE FULFILLED, MY LOVELY SPIDER LILY.
YOUR TASKS ARE NOT YET COMPLETE.
WE STILL HAVE SO MANY OF GOTHAM'S CHILDREN TO COLLECT.
IF YOU WISH TO HOLD YOUR LITTLE ONES AGAIN, YOU MUST REMAIN LOYAL TO THE MOTHER.
I WILL NOT HELP YOU FIND THE SOULS OF YOUR CHILDREN...
...UNTIL ALL OF OUR SACRIFICES ARE BLED.
TELL ME, MARIA, DO YOU INTEND TO UPHOLD YOUR END OF OUR BARGAIN? OR WILL YOU DAMN YOUR CHILDREN TO WANDER THE SPIRIT WORLD ALONE FOREVER?
UHHWRRAAAAA!

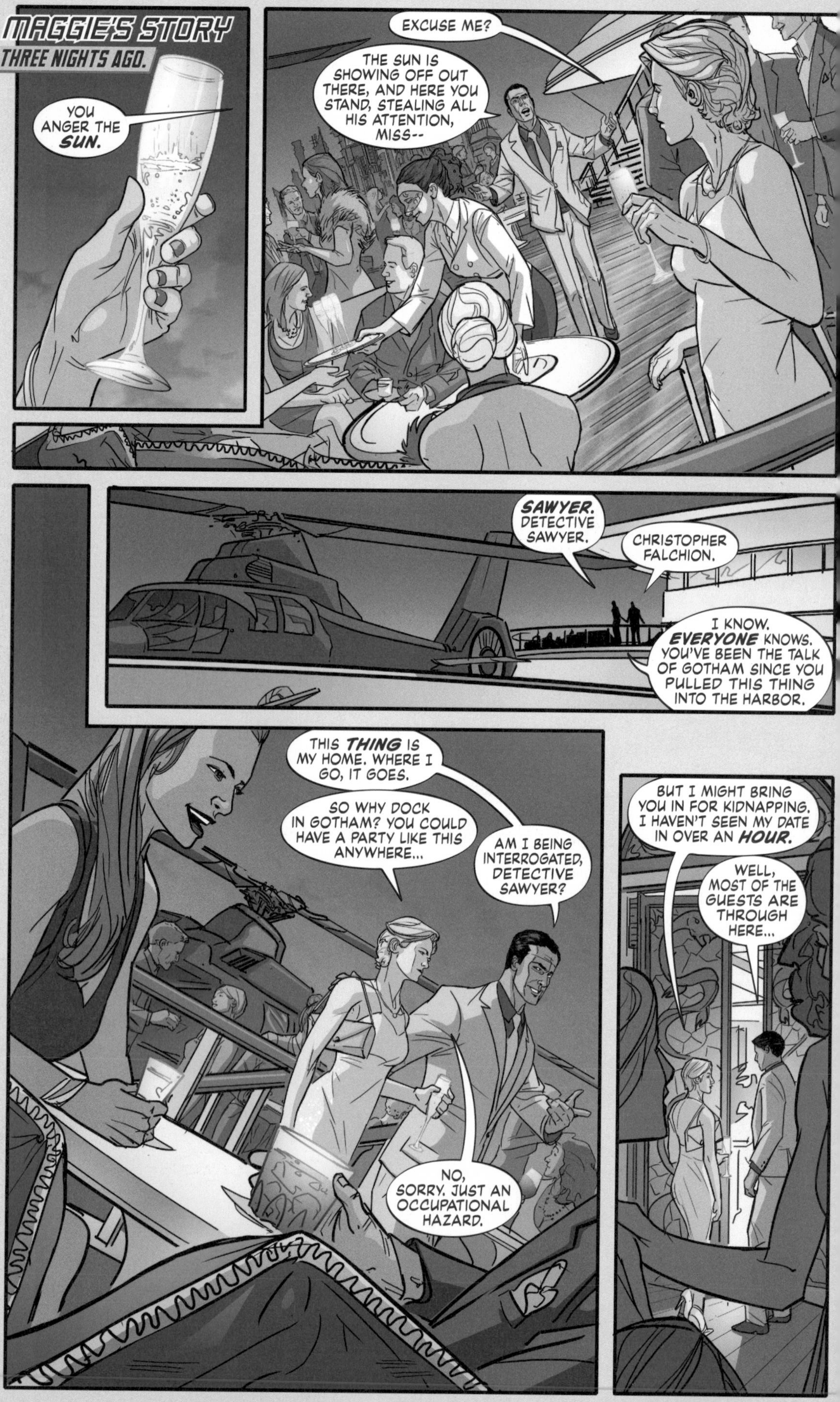
MAGGIE'S STORY
THREE NIGHTS AGO.
YOU ANGER THE SUN.
EXCUSE ME?
THE SUN IS SHOWING OFF OUT THERE, AND HERE YOU STAND, STEALING ALL HIS ATTENTION, MISS--
SAWYER. DETECTIVE SAWYER.
CHRISTOPHER FALCHION.
I KNOW. EVERYONE KNOWS. YOU'VE BEEN THE TALK OF GOTHAM SINCE YOU PULLED THIS THING INTO THE HARBOR.
THIS THING IS MY HOME. WHERE I GO, IT GOES.
SO WHY DOCK IN GOTHAM? YOU COULD HAVE A PARTY LIKE THIS ANYWHERE...
AM I BEING INTERROGATED, DETECTIVE SAWYER?
NO, SORRY. JUST AN OCCUPATIONAL HAZARD.
BUT I MIGHT BRING YOU IN FOR KIDNAPPING. I HAVEN'T SEEN MY DATE IN OVER AN HOUR.
WELL, MOST OF THE GUESTS ARE THROUGH HERE...

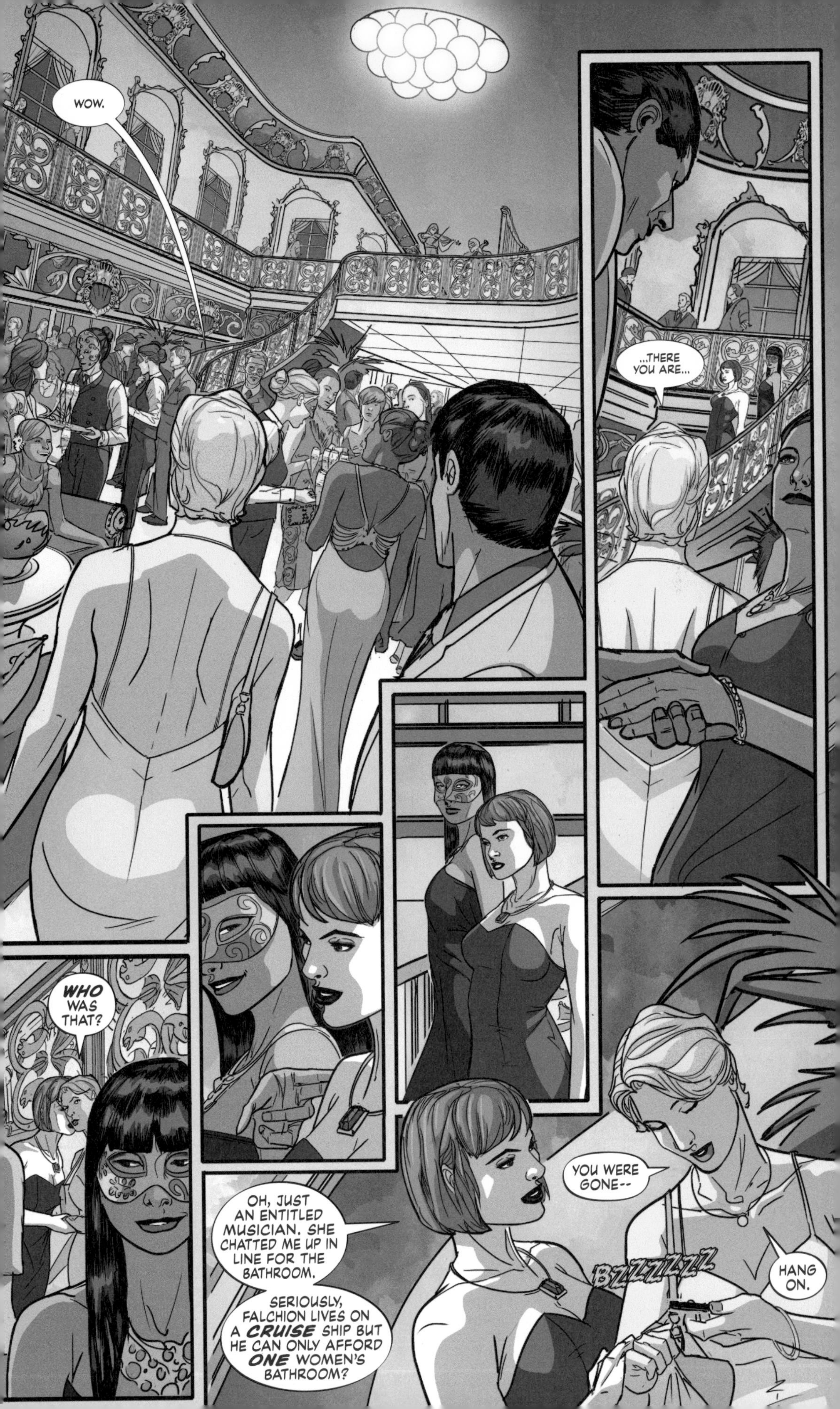
WOW.
...THERE YOU ARE...
WHO WAS THAT?
OH, JUST AN ENTITLED MUSICIAN. SHE CHATTED ME UP IN LINE FOR THE BATHROOM.
SERIOUSLY, FALCHION LIVES ON A CRUISE SHIP BUT HE CAN ONLY AFFORD ONE WOMEN'S BATHROOM?
YOU WERE GONE--
BZZZZZZ
HANG ON.

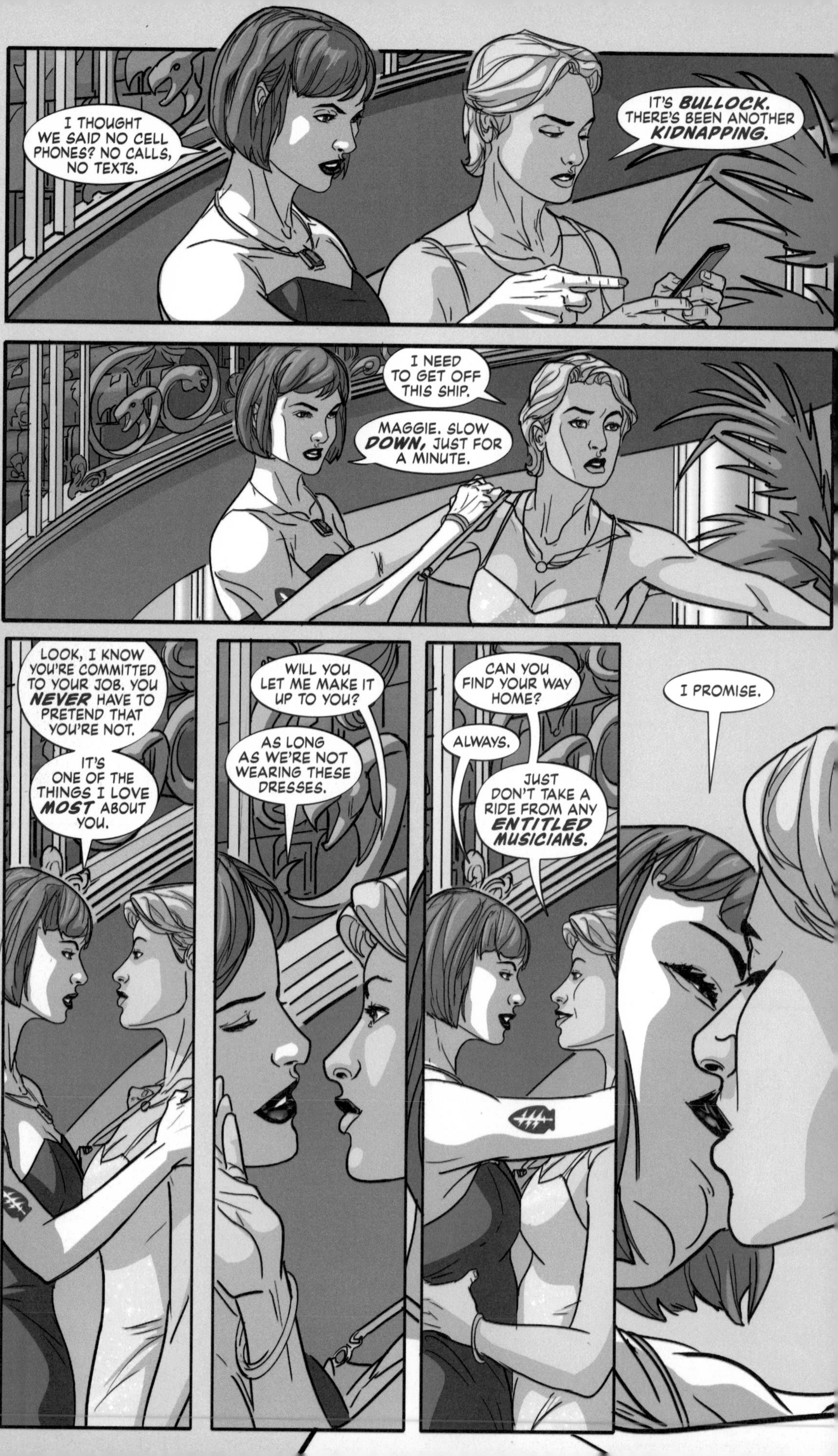
I THOUGHT WE SAID NO CELL PHONES? NO CALLS, NO TEXTS.
IT'S **BULLOCK.** THERE'S BEEN ANOTHER **KIDNAPPING.**
I NEED TO GET OFF THIS SHIP.
MAGGIE. SLOW **DOWN,** JUST FOR A MINUTE.
LOOK, I KNOW YOU'RE COMMITTED TO YOUR JOB. YOU **NEVER** HAVE TO PRETEND THAT YOU'RE NOT.
IT'S ONE OF THE THINGS I LOVE **MOST** ABOUT YOU.
WILL YOU LET ME MAKE IT UP TO YOU?
AS LONG AS WE'RE NOT WEARING THESE DRESSES.
CAN YOU FIND YOUR WAY HOME?
ALWAYS.
JUST DON'T TAKE A RIDE FROM ANY **ENTITLED MUSICIANS.**
I PROMISE.

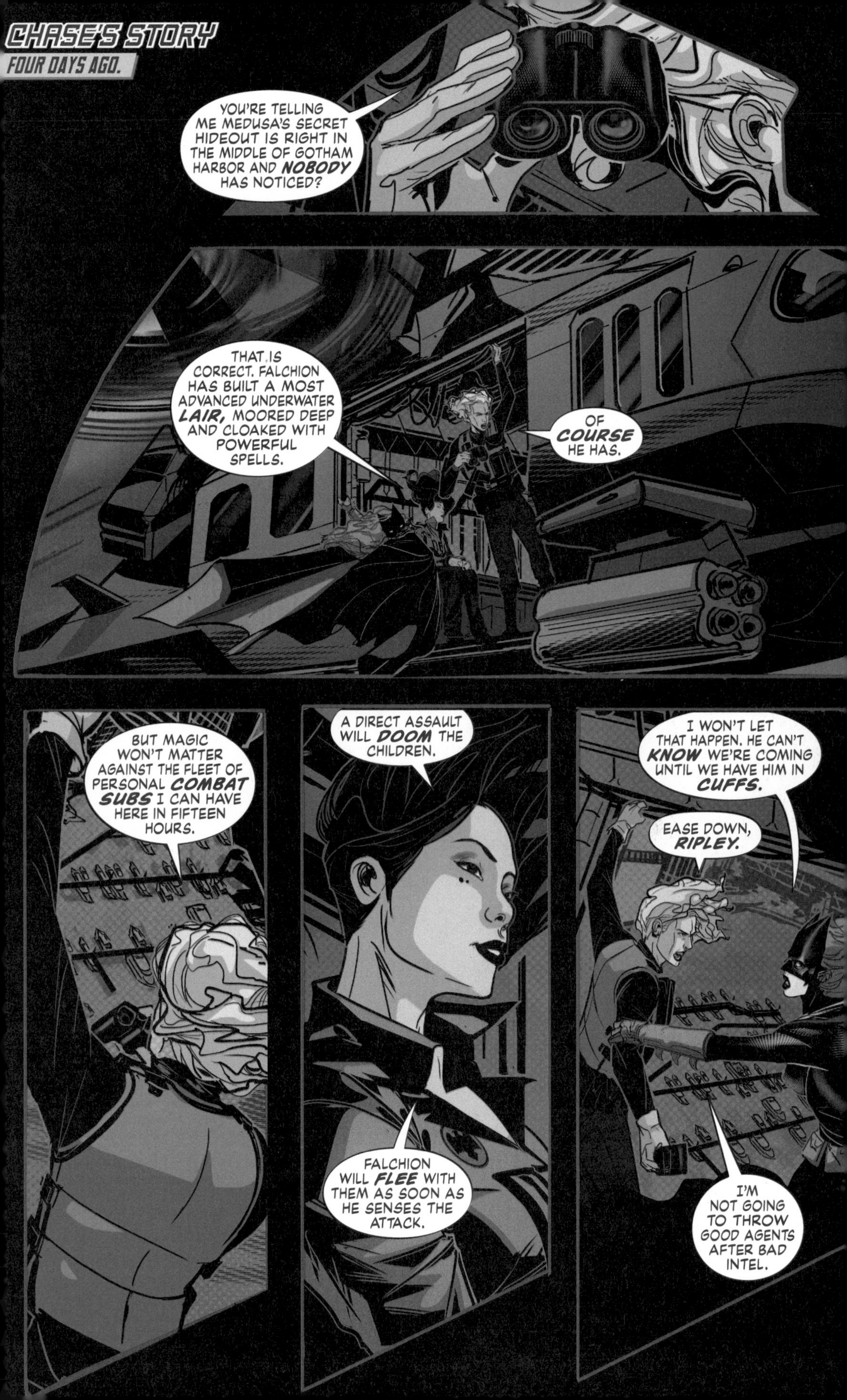
CHASE'S STORY
FOUR DAYS AGO.
YOU'RE TELLING ME MEDUSA'S SECRET HIDEOUT IS RIGHT IN THE MIDDLE OF GOTHAM HARBOR AND NOBODY HAS NOTICED?
THAT IS CORRECT. FALCHION HAS BUILT A MOST ADVANCED UNDERWATER LAIR, MOORED DEEP AND CLOAKED WITH POWERFUL SPELLS.
OF COURSE HE HAS.
BUT MAGIC WON'T MATTER AGAINST THE FLEET OF PERSONAL COMBAT SUBS I CAN HAVE HERE IN FIFTEEN HOURS.
A DIRECT ASSAULT WILL DOOM THE CHILDREN.
FALCHION WILL FLEE WITH THEM AS SOON AS HE SENSES THE ATTACK.
I WON'T LET THAT HAPPEN. HE CAN'T KNOW WE'RE COMING UNTIL WE HAVE HIM IN CUFFS.
EASE DOWN, RIPLEY.
I'M NOT GOING TO THROW GOOD AGENTS AFTER BAD INTEL.

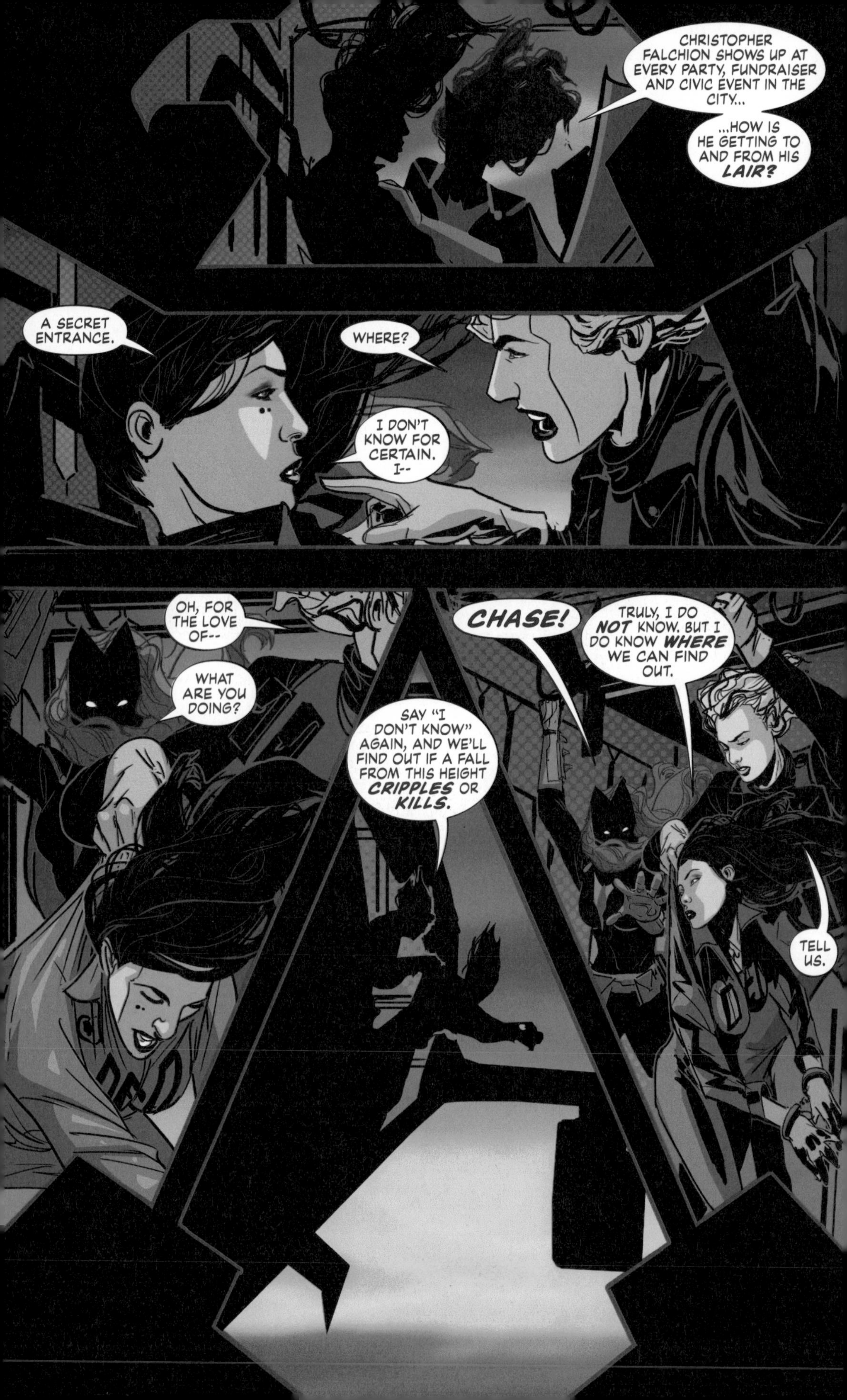
CHRISTOPHER FALCHION SHOWS UP AT EVERY PARTY, FUNDRAISER AND CIVIC EVENT IN THE CITY...
...HOW IS HE GETTING TO AND FROM HIS *LAIR?*
A SECRET ENTRANCE.
WHERE?
I DON'T KNOW FOR CERTAIN. I--
OH, FOR THE LOVE OF--
WHAT ARE YOU DOING?
SAY "I DON'T KNOW" AGAIN, AND WE'LL FIND OUT IF A FALL FROM THIS HEIGHT *CRIPPLES* OR *KILLS.*
CHASE!
TRULY, I DO *NOT* KNOW. BUT I DO KNOW *WHERE* WE CAN FIND OUT.
TELL US.

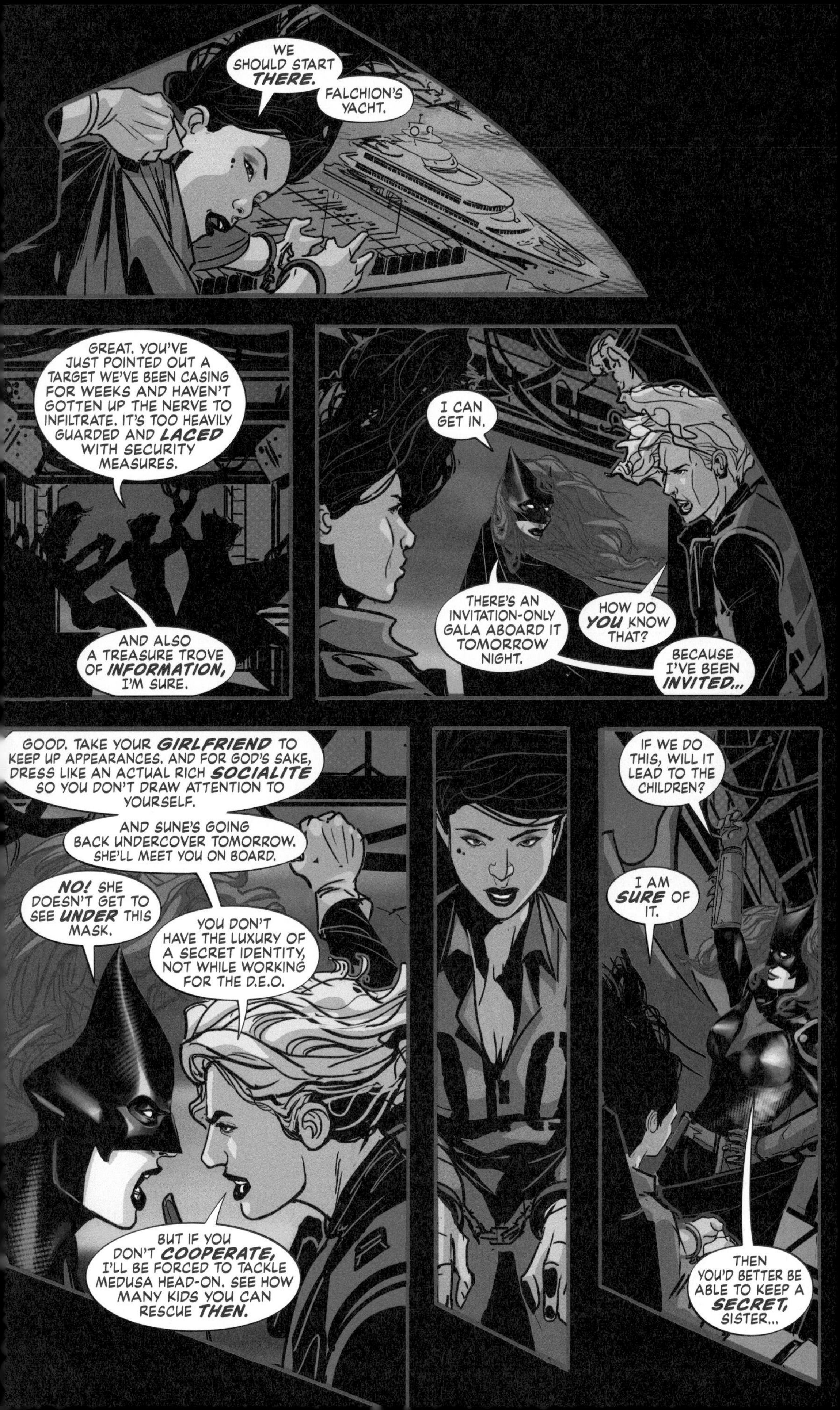
WE SHOULD START THERE.
FALCHION'S YACHT.
GREAT. YOU'VE JUST POINTED OUT A TARGET WE'VE BEEN CASING FOR WEEKS AND HAVEN'T GOTTEN UP THE NERVE TO INFILTRATE. IT'S TOO HEAVILY GUARDED AND LACED WITH SECURITY MEASURES.
AND ALSO A TREASURE TROVE OF INFORMATION, I'M SURE.
I CAN GET IN.
HOW DO YOU KNOW THAT?
THERE'S AN INVITATION-ONLY GALA ABOARD IT TOMORROW NIGHT.
BECAUSE I'VE BEEN INVITED...
GOOD. TAKE YOUR GIRLFRIEND TO KEEP UP APPEARANCES. AND FOR GOD'S SAKE, DRESS LIKE AN ACTUAL RICH SOCIALITE SO YOU DON'T DRAW ATTENTION TO YOURSELF.
AND SUNE'S GOING BACK UNDERCOVER TOMORROW. SHE'LL MEET YOU ON BOARD.
NO! SHE DOESN'T GET TO SEE UNDER THIS MASK.
YOU DON'T HAVE THE LUXURY OF A SECRET IDENTITY, NOT WHILE WORKING FOR THE D.E.O.
BUT IF YOU DON'T COOPERATE, I'LL BE FORCED TO TACKLE MEDUSA HEAD-ON. SEE HOW MANY KIDS YOU CAN RESCUE THEN.
IF WE DO THIS, WILL IT LEAD TO THE CHILDREN?
I AM SURE OF IT.
THEN YOU'D BETTER BE ABLE TO KEEP A SECRET, SISTER...

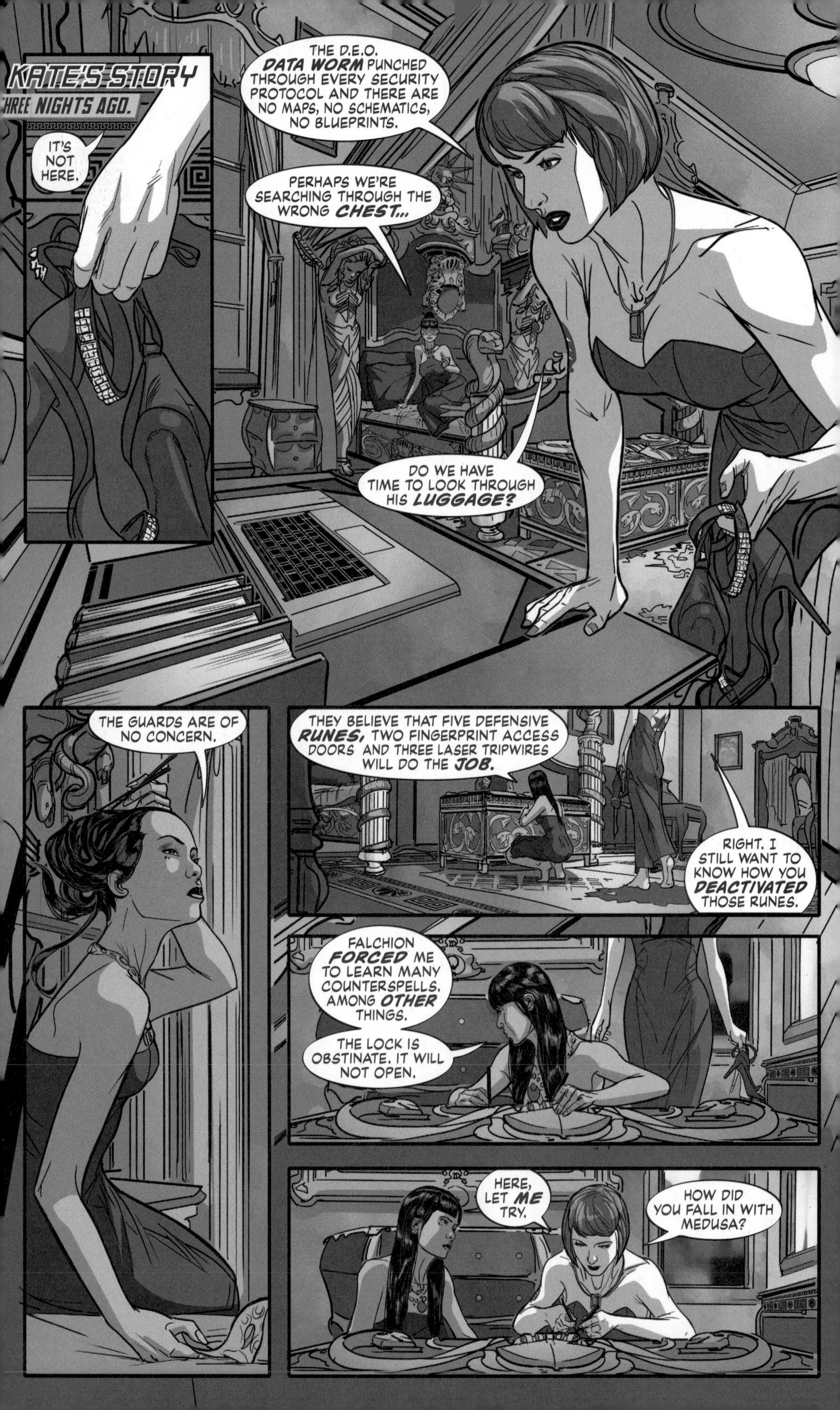

KATE'S STORY
THREE NIGHTS AGO.
IT'S NOT HERE.
THE D.E.O. DATA WORM PUNCHED THROUGH EVERY SECURITY PROTOCOL AND THERE ARE NO MAPS, NO SCHEMATICS, NO BLUEPRINTS.
PERHAPS WE'RE SEARCHING THROUGH THE WRONG CHEST...
DO WE HAVE TIME TO LOOK THROUGH HIS LUGGAGE?
THE GUARDS ARE OF NO CONCERN.
THEY BELIEVE THAT FIVE DEFENSIVE RUNES, TWO FINGERPRINT ACCESS DOORS AND THREE LASER TRIPWIRES WILL DO THE JOB.
RIGHT. I STILL WANT TO KNOW HOW YOU DEACTIVATED THOSE RUNES.
FALCHION FORCED ME TO LEARN MANY COUNTERSPELLS, AMONG OTHER THINGS.
THE LOCK IS OBSTINATE. IT WILL NOT OPEN.
HERE, LET ME TRY.
HOW DID YOU FALL IN WITH MEDUSA?

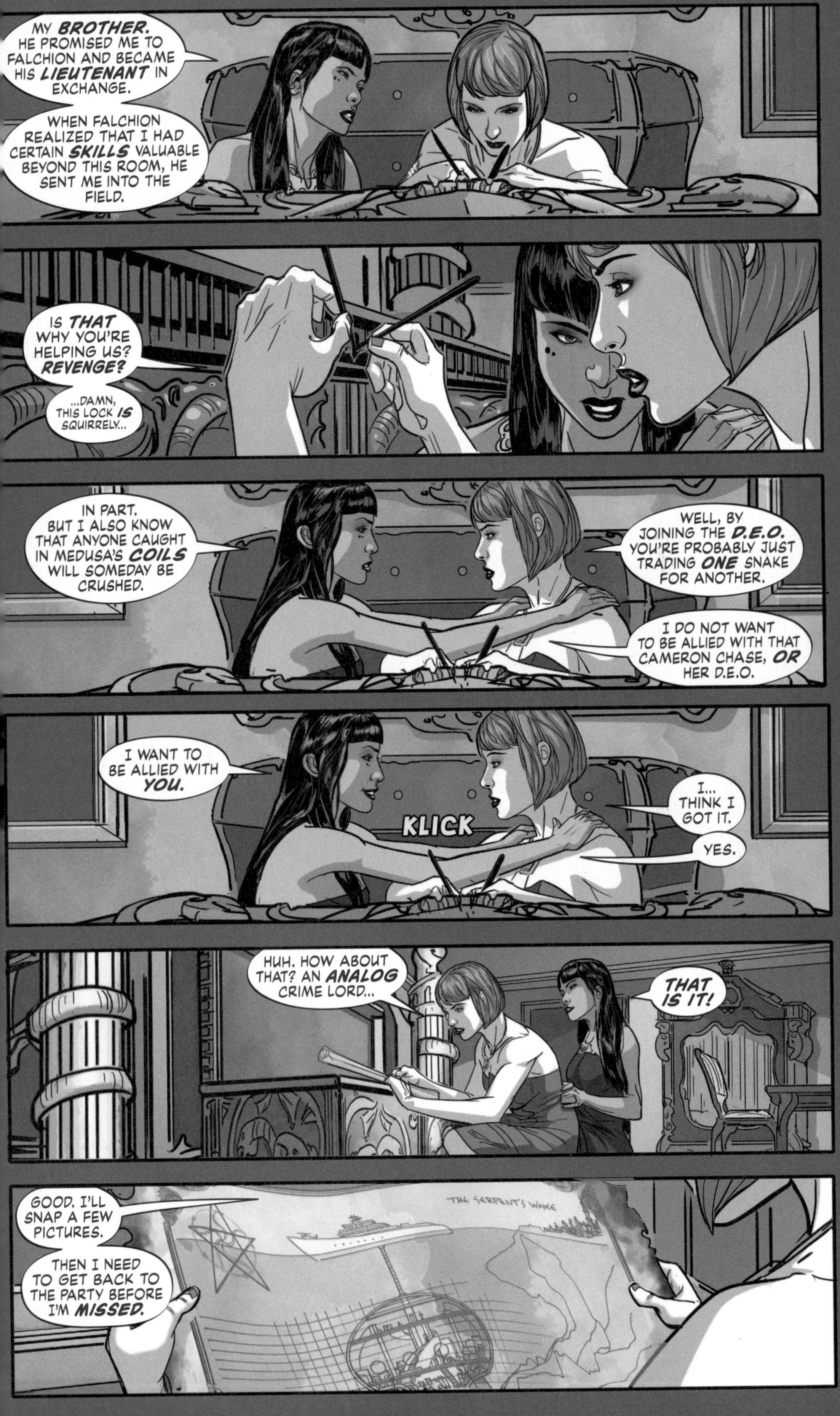

MY BROTHER. HE PROMISED ME TO FALCHION AND BECAME HIS LIEUTENANT IN EXCHANGE.
WHEN FALCHION REALIZED THAT I HAD CERTAIN SKILLS VALUABLE BEYOND THIS ROOM, HE SENT ME INTO THE FIELD.
IS THAT WHY YOU'RE HELPING US? REVENGE?
...DAMN, THIS LOCK IS SQUIRRELY...
IN PART. BUT I ALSO KNOW THAT ANYONE CAUGHT IN MEDUSA'S COILS WILL SOMEDAY BE CRUSHED.
WELL, BY JOINING THE D.E.O. YOU'RE PROBABLY JUST TRADING ONE SNAKE FOR ANOTHER.
I DO NOT WANT TO BE ALLIED WITH THAT CAMERON CHASE, OR HER D.E.O.
I WANT TO BE ALLIED WITH YOU.
KLICK
I... THINK I GOT IT.
YES.
HUH. HOW ABOUT THAT? AN ANALOG CRIME LORD...
THAT IS IT!
GOOD. I'LL SNAP A FEW PICTURES.
THEN I NEED TO GET BACK TO THE PARTY BEFORE I'M MISSED.
THE SERPENT'S WAKE

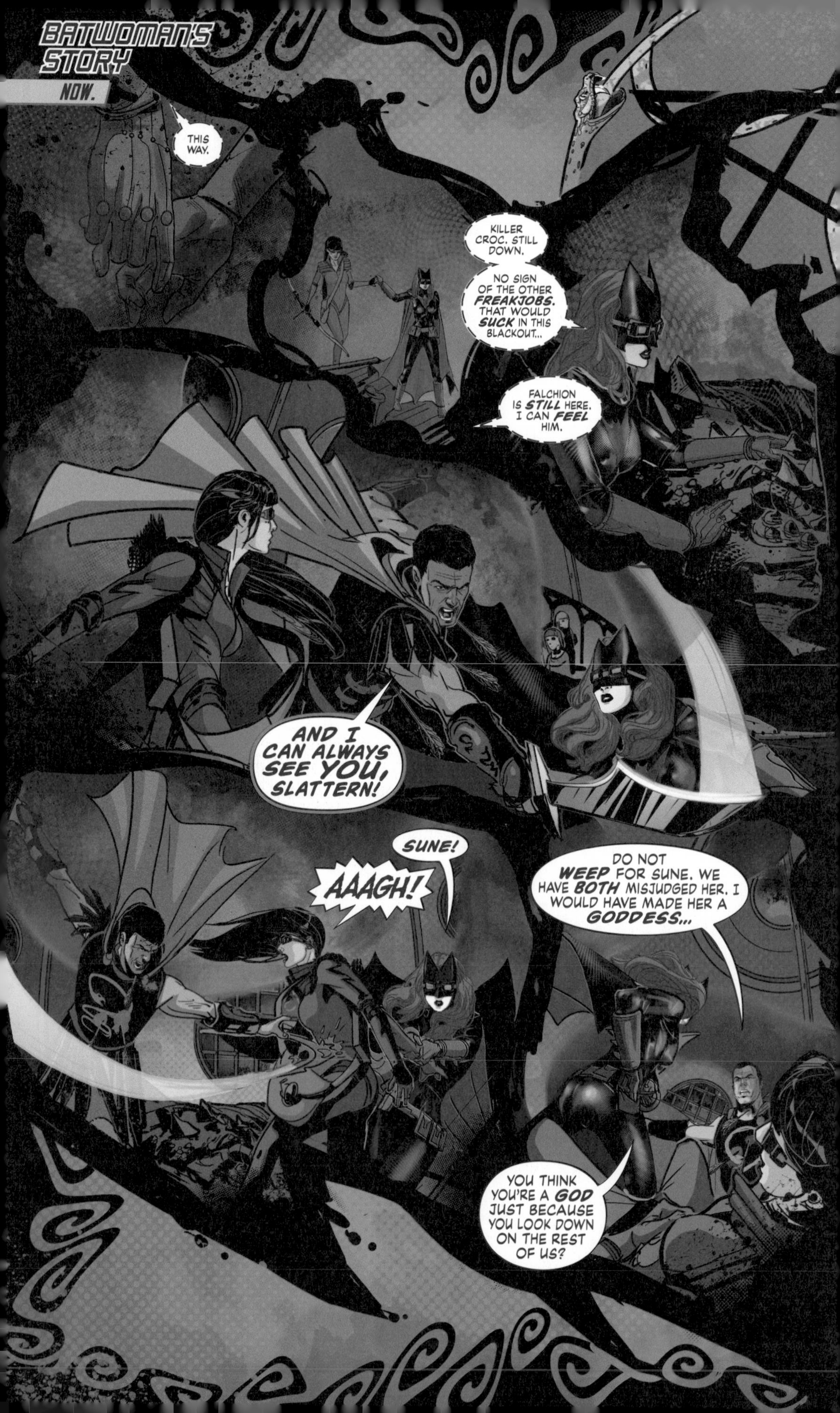
BATWOMAN'S STORY
NOW.
THIS WAY.
KILLER CROC. STILL DOWN.
NO SIGN OF THE OTHER FREAKJOBS. THAT WOULD SUCK IN THIS BLACKOUT...
FALCHION IS STILL HERE. I CAN FEEL HIM.
AND I CAN ALWAYS SEE YOU, SLATTERN!
SUNE!
AAAGH!
DO NOT WEEP FOR SUNE. WE HAVE BOTH MISJUDGED HER. I WOULD HAVE MADE HER A GODDESS...
YOU THINK YOU'RE A GOD JUST BECAUSE YOU LOOK DOWN ON THE REST OF US?

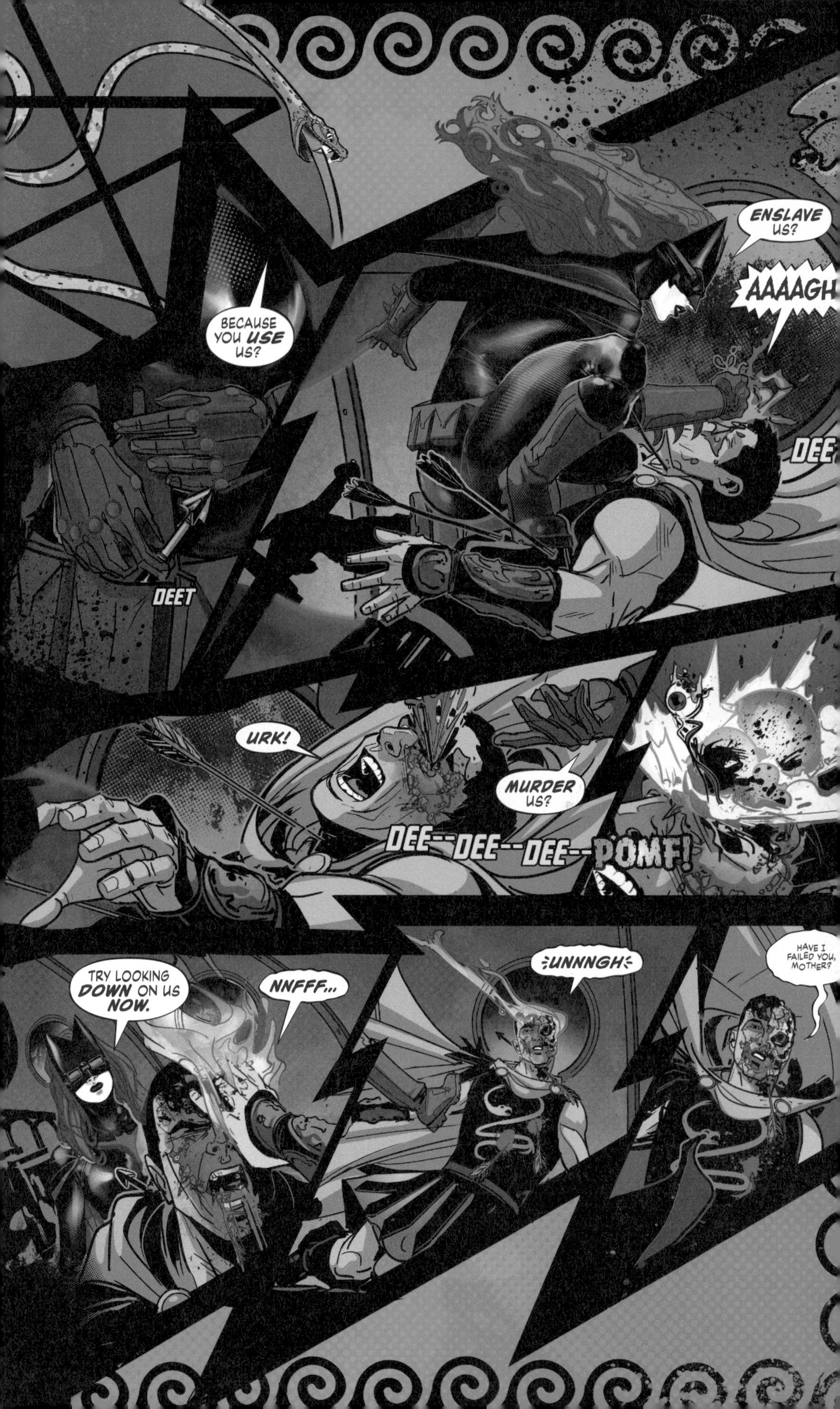
BECAUSE YOU USE US?
DEET
ENSLAVE US?
AAAAGH
DEE
URK!
MURDER US?
DEE--DEE--DEE--POMF!
TRY LOOKING DOWN ON US NOW.
NNFFF...
UNNNGH
HAVE I FAILED YOU, MOTHER?

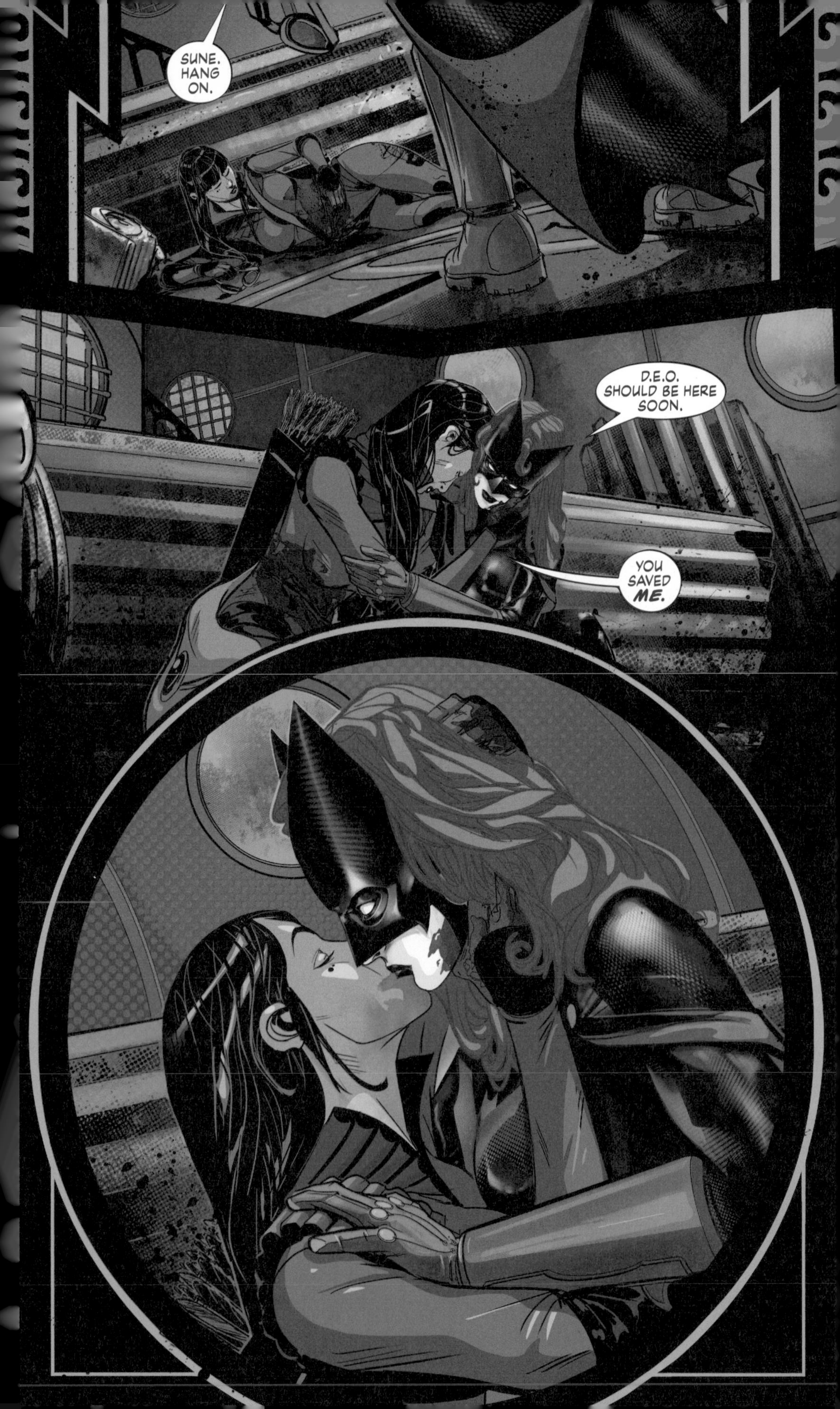
SUNE. HANG ON.
D.E.O. SHOULD BE HERE SOON.
YOU SAVED ***ME.***

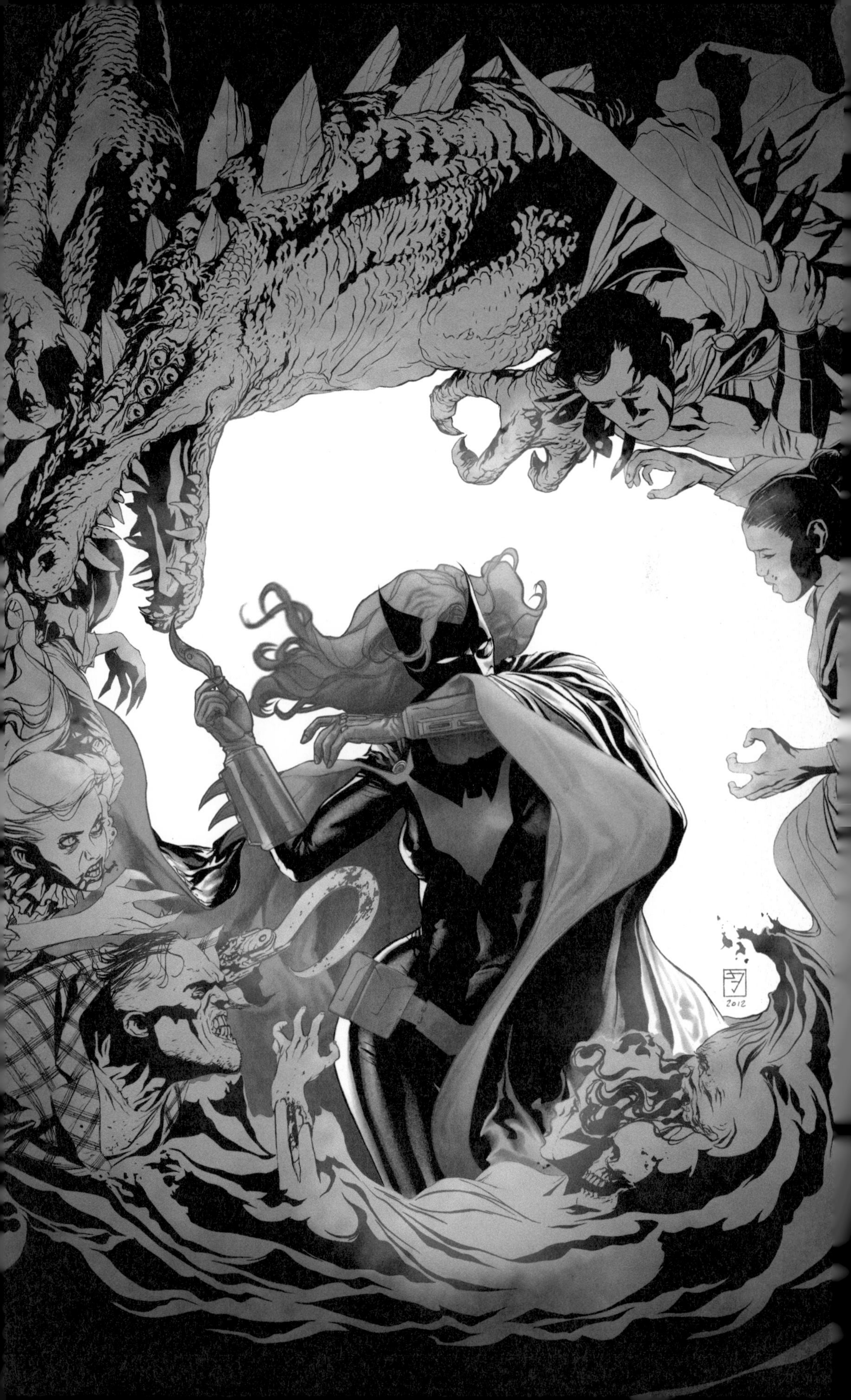
2012

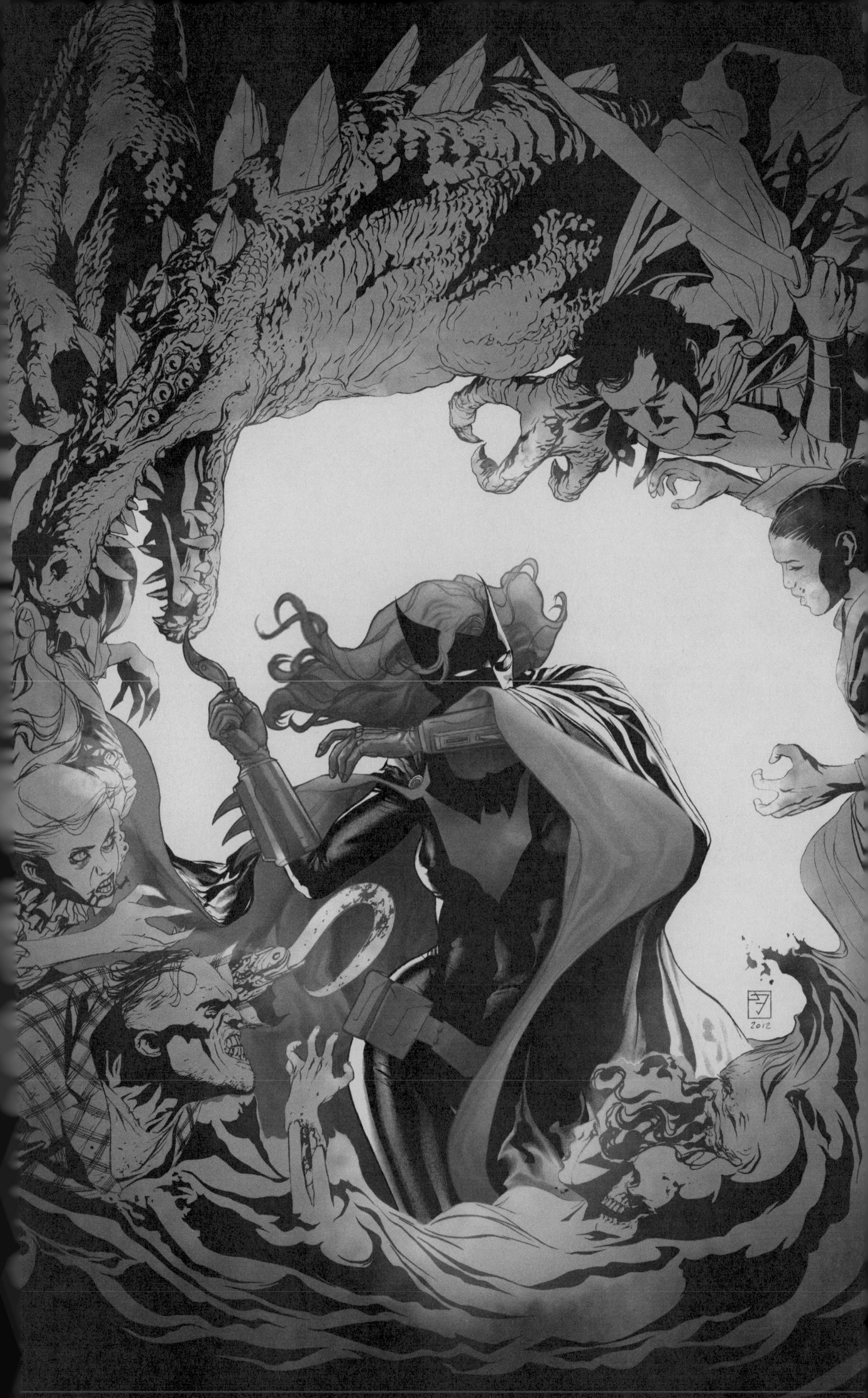

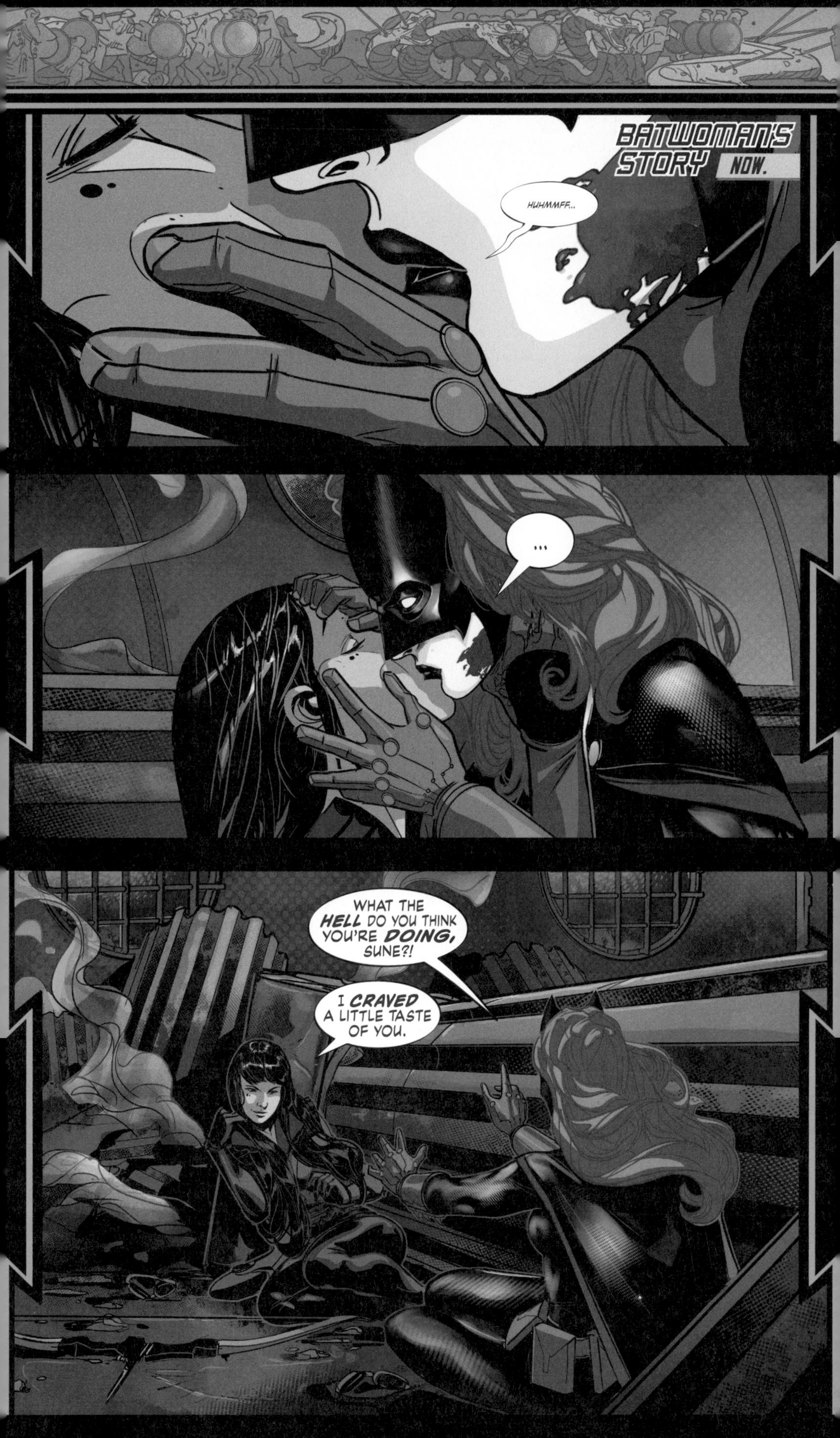
BATWOMAN'S STORY NOW.
HUHMMFF...
...
WHAT THE HELL DO YOU THINK YOU'RE DOING, SUNE?!
I CRAVED A LITTLE TASTE OF YOU.

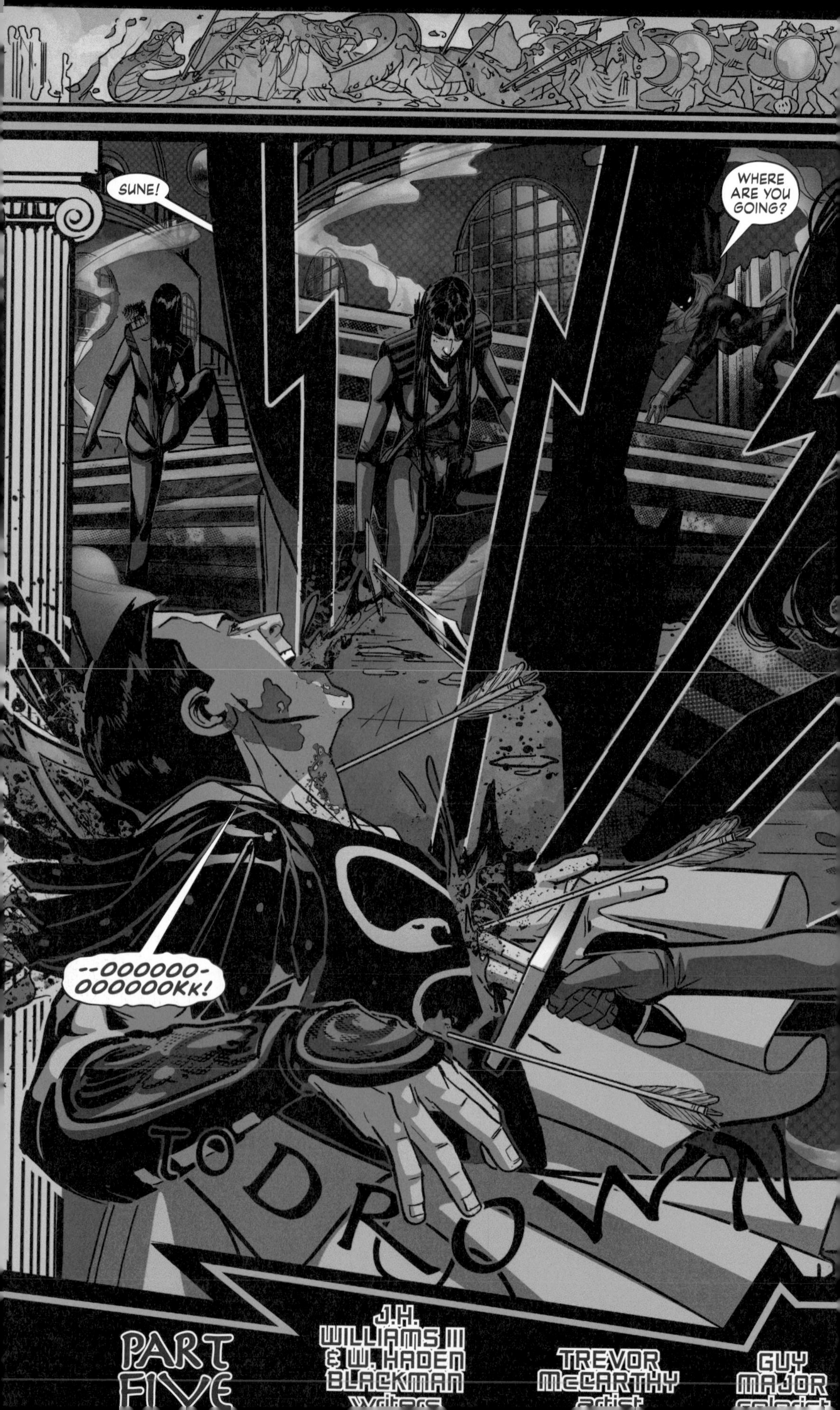
SUNE!
WHERE ARE YOU GOING?
--OOOOOO-OOOOOOKK!
TO DROWN
PART FIVE
J.H. WILLIAMS III & W. HADEN BLACKMAN
TREVOR McCARTHY
GUY MAJOR

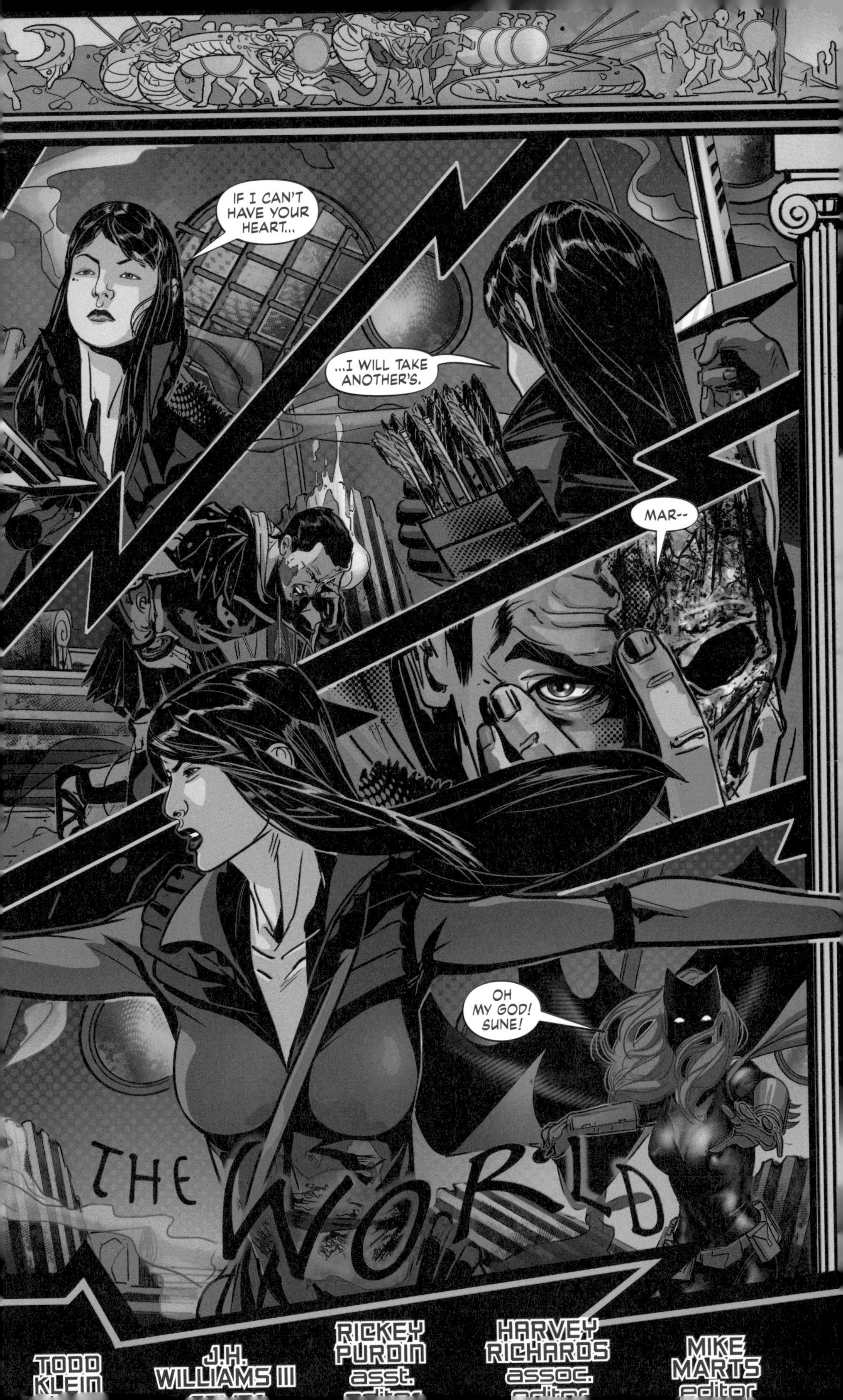

IF I CAN'T HAVE YOUR HEART...
...I WILL TAKE ANOTHER'S.
MAR--
OH MY GOD! SUNE!
THE WORLD
TODD KLEIN
J.H. WILLIAMS III
RICKEY PURDIN asst.
HARVEY RICHARDS assoc.
MIKE MARTS

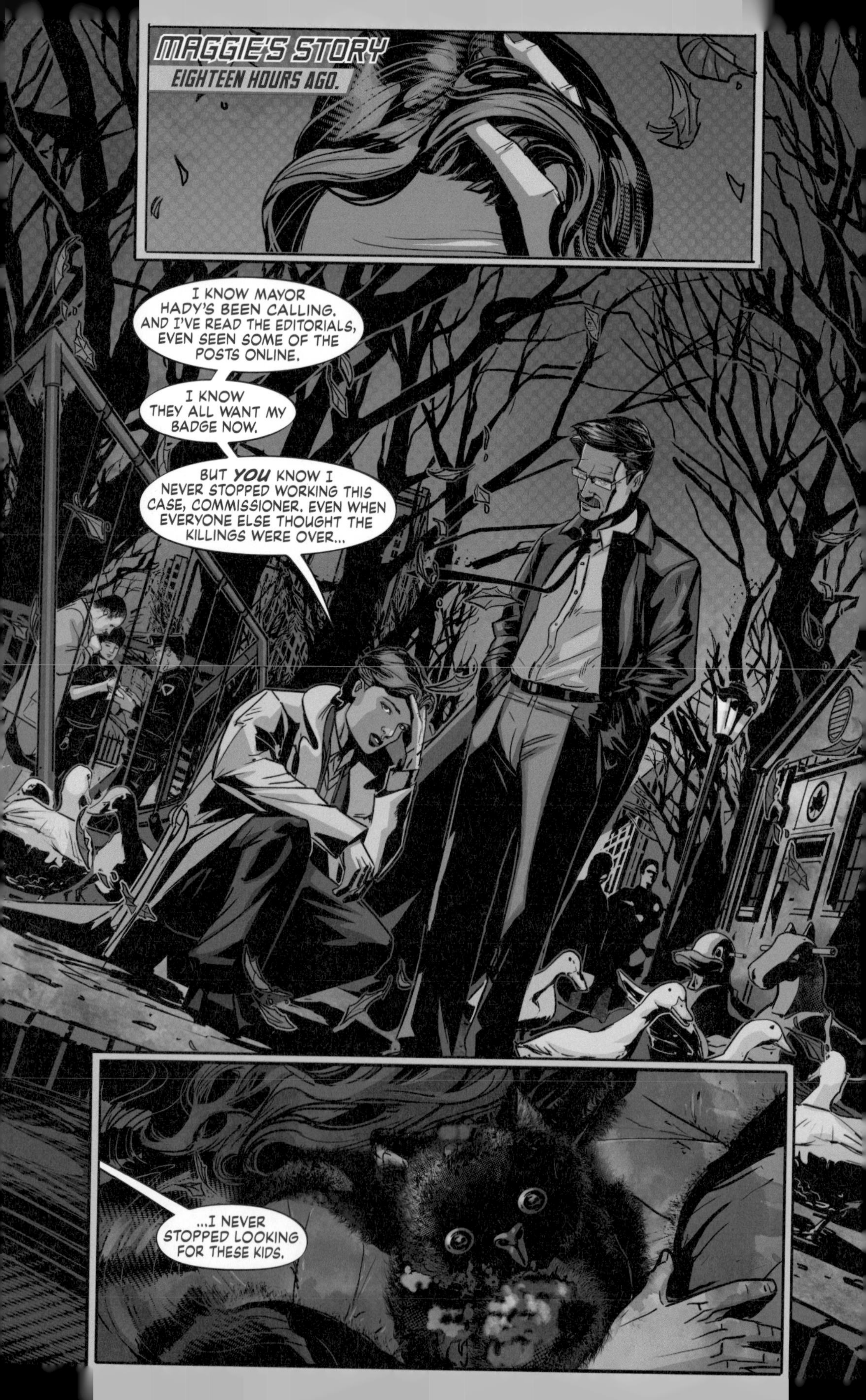
MAGGIE'S STORY
EIGHTEEN HOURS AGO.
I KNOW MAYOR HADY'S BEEN CALLING. AND I'VE READ THE EDITORIALS, EVEN SEEN SOME OF THE POSTS ONLINE.
I KNOW THEY ALL WANT MY BADGE NOW.
BUT YOU KNOW I NEVER STOPPED WORKING THIS CASE, COMMISSIONER. EVEN WHEN EVERYONE ELSE THOUGHT THE KILLINGS WERE OVER...
...I NEVER STOPPED LOOKING FOR THESE KIDS.

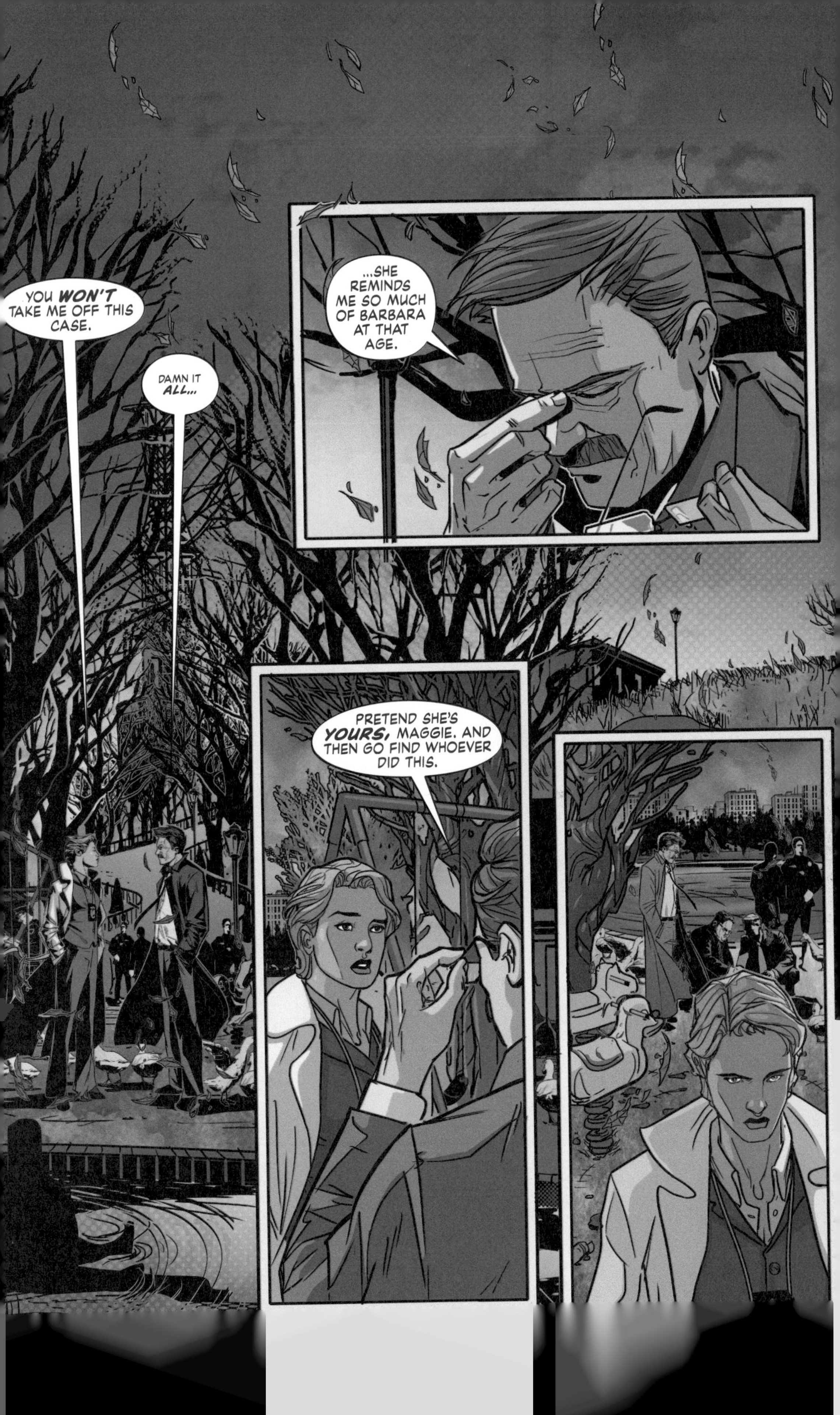
...SHE REMINDS ME SO MUCH OF BARBARA AT THAT AGE.
YOU **WON'T** TAKE ME OFF THIS CASE.
DAMN IT **ALL...**
PRETEND SHE'S **YOURS,** MAGGIE. AND THEN GO FIND WHOEVER DID THIS.

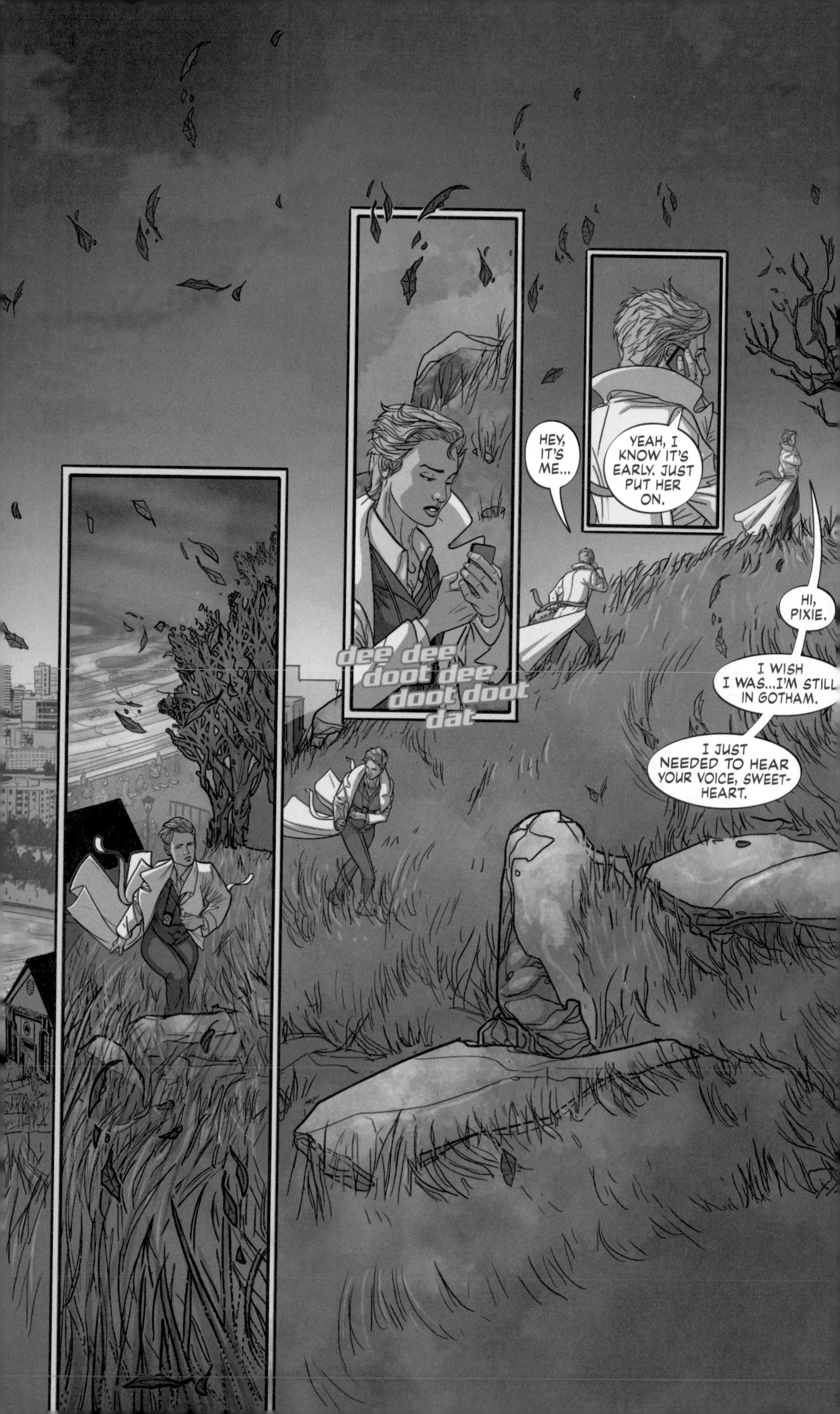
dee dee doot dee doot doot dat
HEY, IT'S ME...
YEAH, I KNOW IT'S EARLY. JUST PUT HER ON.
HI, PIXIE.
I WISH I WAS...I'M STILL IN GOTHAM.
I JUST NEEDED TO HEAR YOUR VOICE, SWEET-HEART.

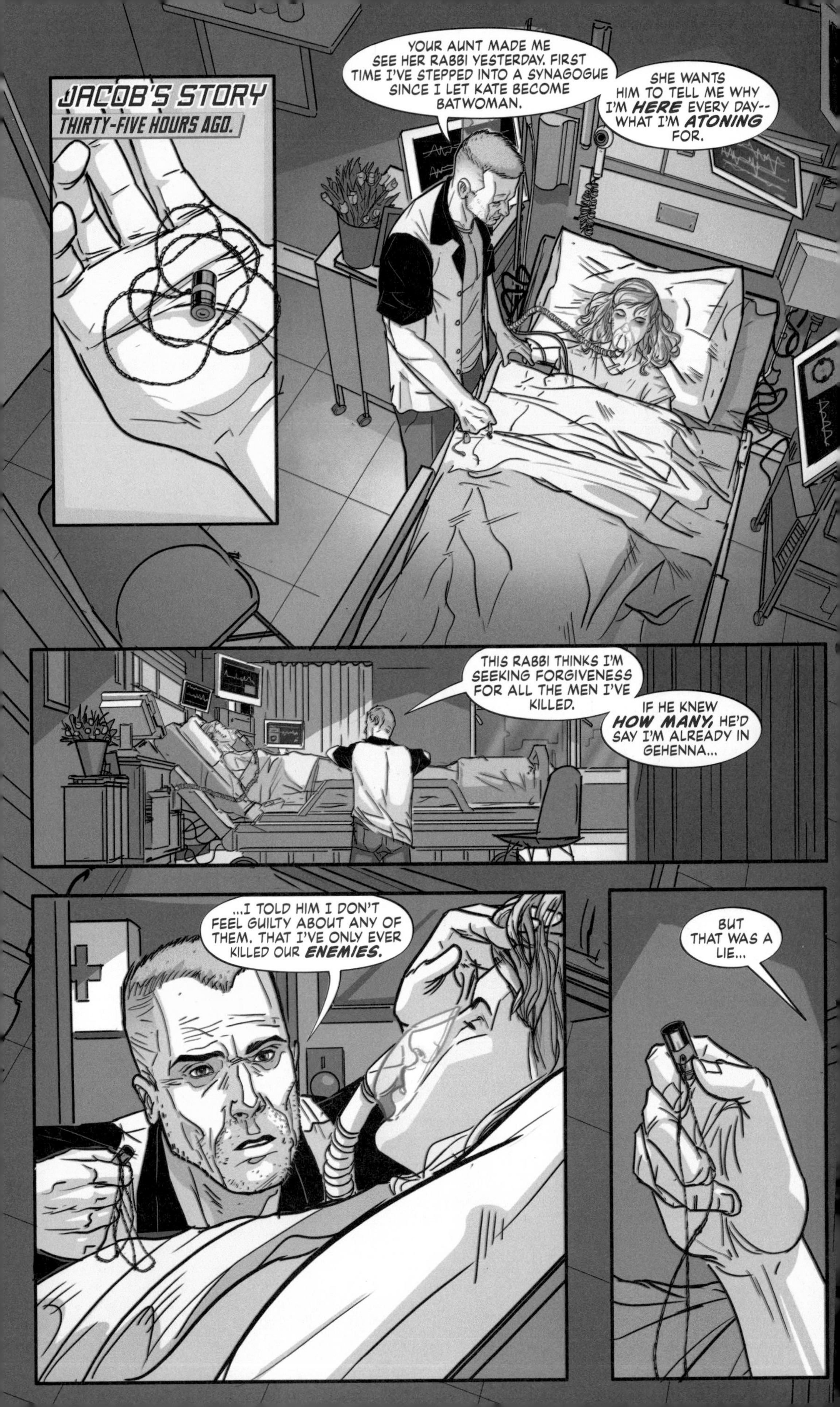
JACOB'S STORY
THIRTY-FIVE HOURS AGO.
YOUR AUNT MADE ME SEE HER RABBI YESTERDAY. FIRST TIME I'VE STEPPED INTO A SYNAGOGUE SINCE I LET KATE BECOME BATWOMAN.
SHE WANTS HIM TO TELL ME WHY I'M HERE EVERY DAY-- WHAT I'M ATONING FOR.
THIS RABBI THINKS I'M SEEKING FORGIVENESS FOR ALL THE MEN I'VE KILLED.
IF HE KNEW HOW MANY, HE'D SAY I'M ALREADY IN GEHENNA...
...I TOLD HIM I DON'T FEEL GUILTY ABOUT ANY OF THEM. THAT I'VE ONLY EVER KILLED OUR ENEMIES.
BUT THAT WAS A LIE...

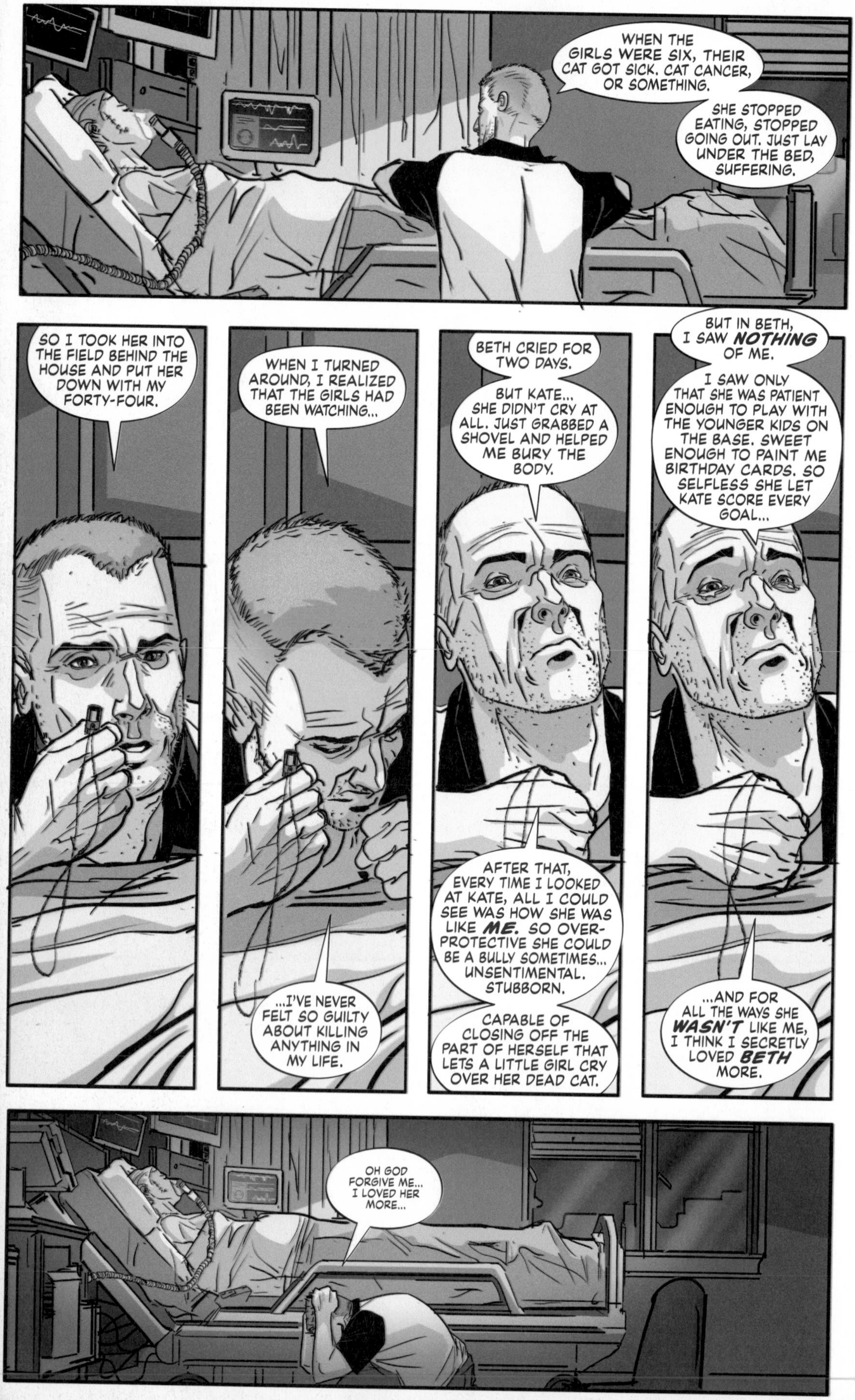
WHEN THE GIRLS WERE SIX, THEIR CAT GOT SICK. CAT CANCER, OR SOMETHING.
SHE STOPPED EATING, STOPPED GOING OUT. JUST LAY UNDER THE BED, SUFFERING.
SO I TOOK HER INTO THE FIELD BEHIND THE HOUSE AND PUT HER DOWN WITH MY FORTY-FOUR.
WHEN I TURNED AROUND, I REALIZED THAT THE GIRLS HAD BEEN WATCHING...
...I'VE NEVER FELT SO GUILTY ABOUT KILLING ANYTHING IN MY LIFE.
BETH CRIED FOR TWO DAYS.
BUT KATE... SHE DIDN'T CRY AT ALL. JUST GRABBED A SHOVEL AND HELPED ME BURY THE BODY.
AFTER THAT, EVERY TIME I LOOKED AT KATE, ALL I COULD SEE WAS HOW SHE WAS LIKE ME. SO OVER-PROTECTIVE SHE COULD BE A BULLY SOMETIMES... UNSENTIMENTAL. STUBBORN.
CAPABLE OF CLOSING OFF THE PART OF HERSELF THAT LETS A LITTLE GIRL CRY OVER HER DEAD CAT.
BUT IN BETH, I SAW NOTHING OF ME.
I SAW ONLY THAT SHE WAS PATIENT ENOUGH TO PLAY WITH THE YOUNGER KIDS ON THE BASE. SWEET ENOUGH TO PAINT ME BIRTHDAY CARDS. SO SELFLESS SHE LET KATE SCORE EVERY GOAL...
...AND FOR ALL THE WAYS SHE WASN'T LIKE ME, I THINK I SECRETLY LOVED BETH MORE.
OH GOD FORGIVE ME... I LOVED HER MORE...

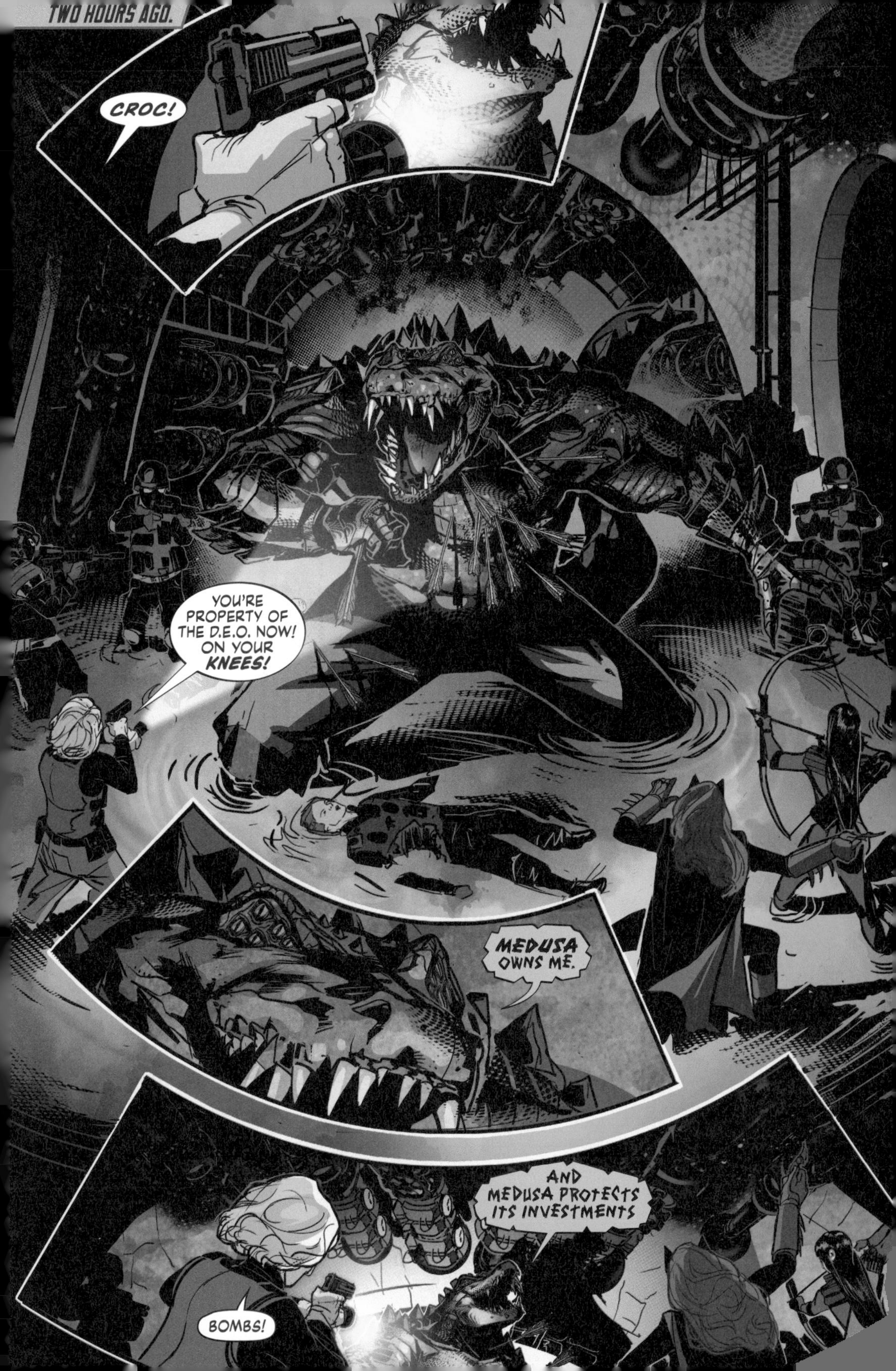
TWO HOURS AGO.
CROC!
YOU'RE PROPERTY OF THE D.E.O. NOW! ON YOUR KNEES!
MEDUSA OWNS ME.
AND MEDUSA PROTECTS ITS INVESTMENTS
BOMBS!

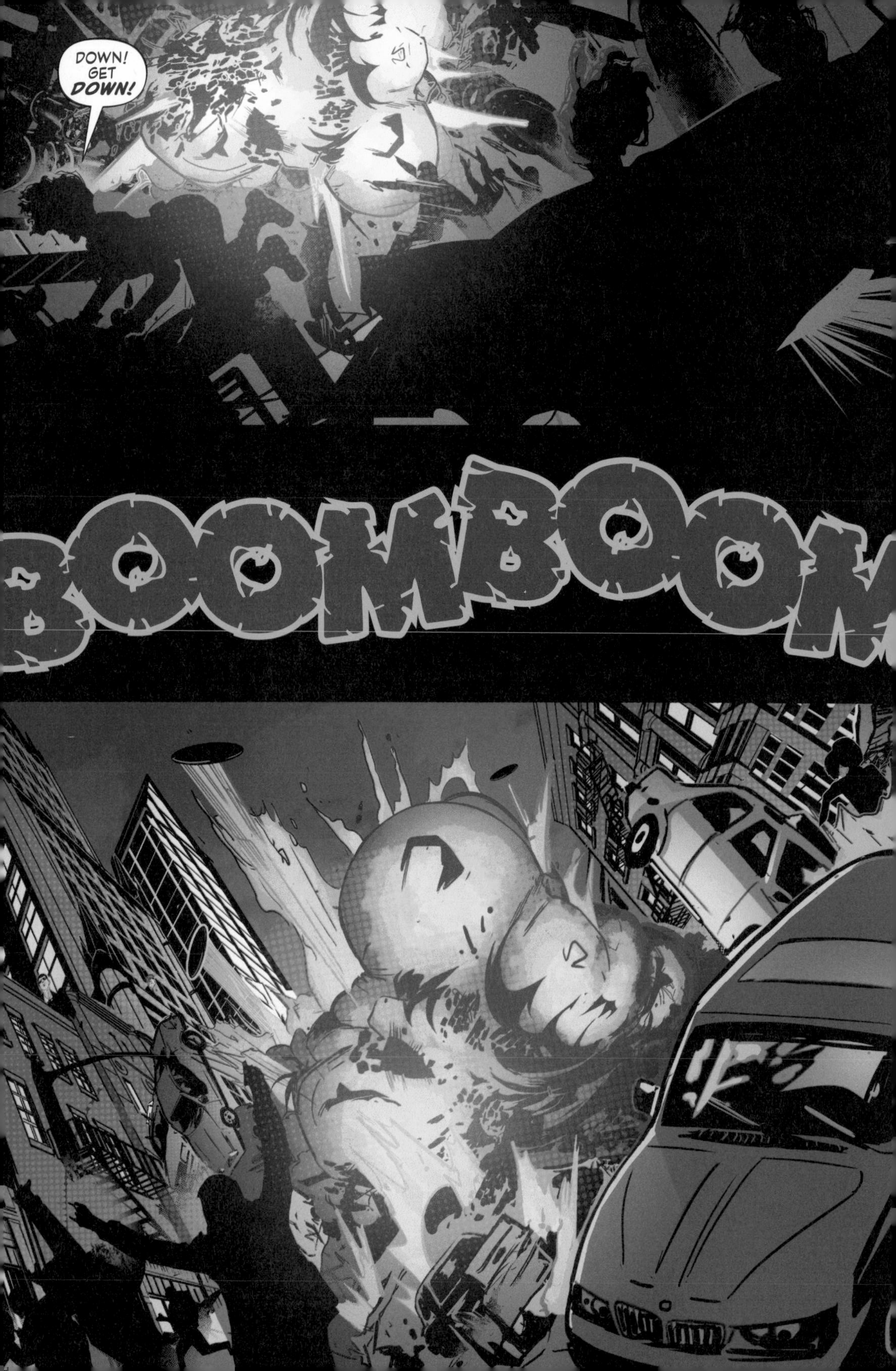
DOWN! GET DOWN!
BOOMBOOM

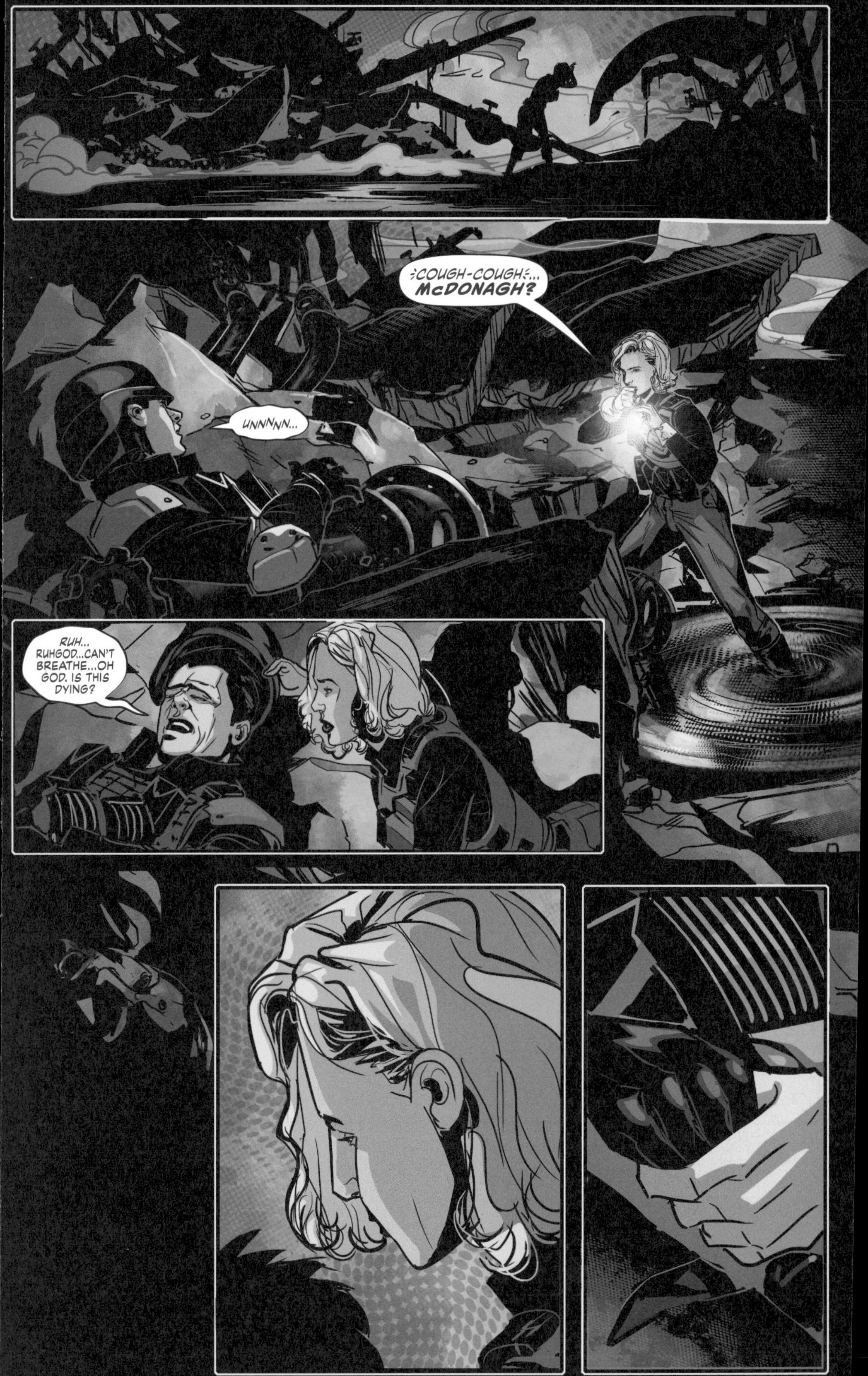

COUGH-COUGH... McDONAGH?
UNNNNN...
RUH... RUHGOD...CAN'T BREATHE...OH GOD, IS THIS DYING?

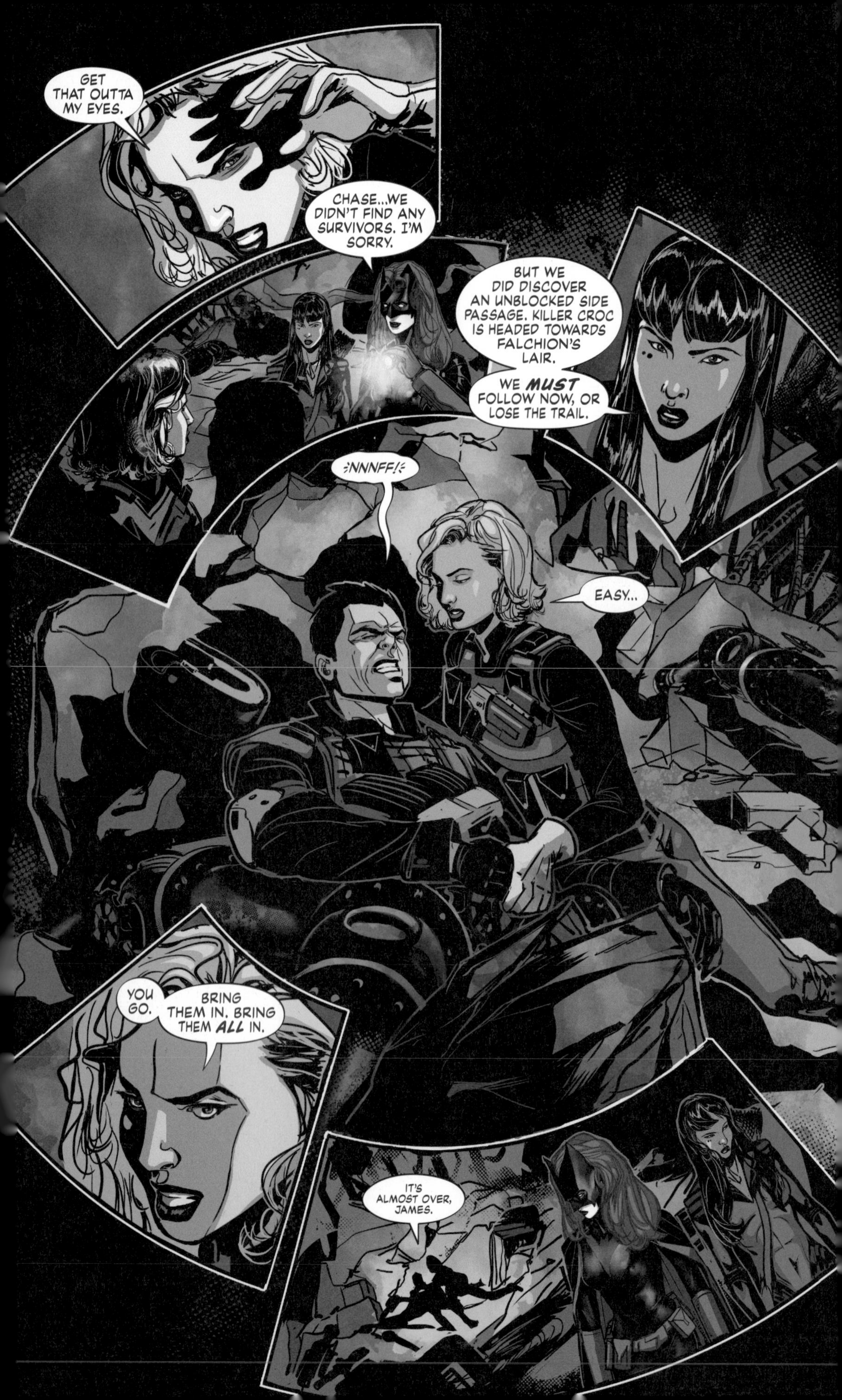
GET THAT OUTTA MY EYES.
CHASE...WE DIDN'T FIND ANY SURVIVORS. I'M SORRY.
BUT WE DID DISCOVER AN UNBLOCKED SIDE PASSAGE. KILLER CROC IS HEADED TOWARDS FALCHION'S LAIR.
WE MUST FOLLOW NOW, OR LOSE THE TRAIL.
NNNFF!
EASY...
YOU GO.
BRING THEM IN. BRING THEM ALL IN.
IT'S ALMOST OVER, JAMES.

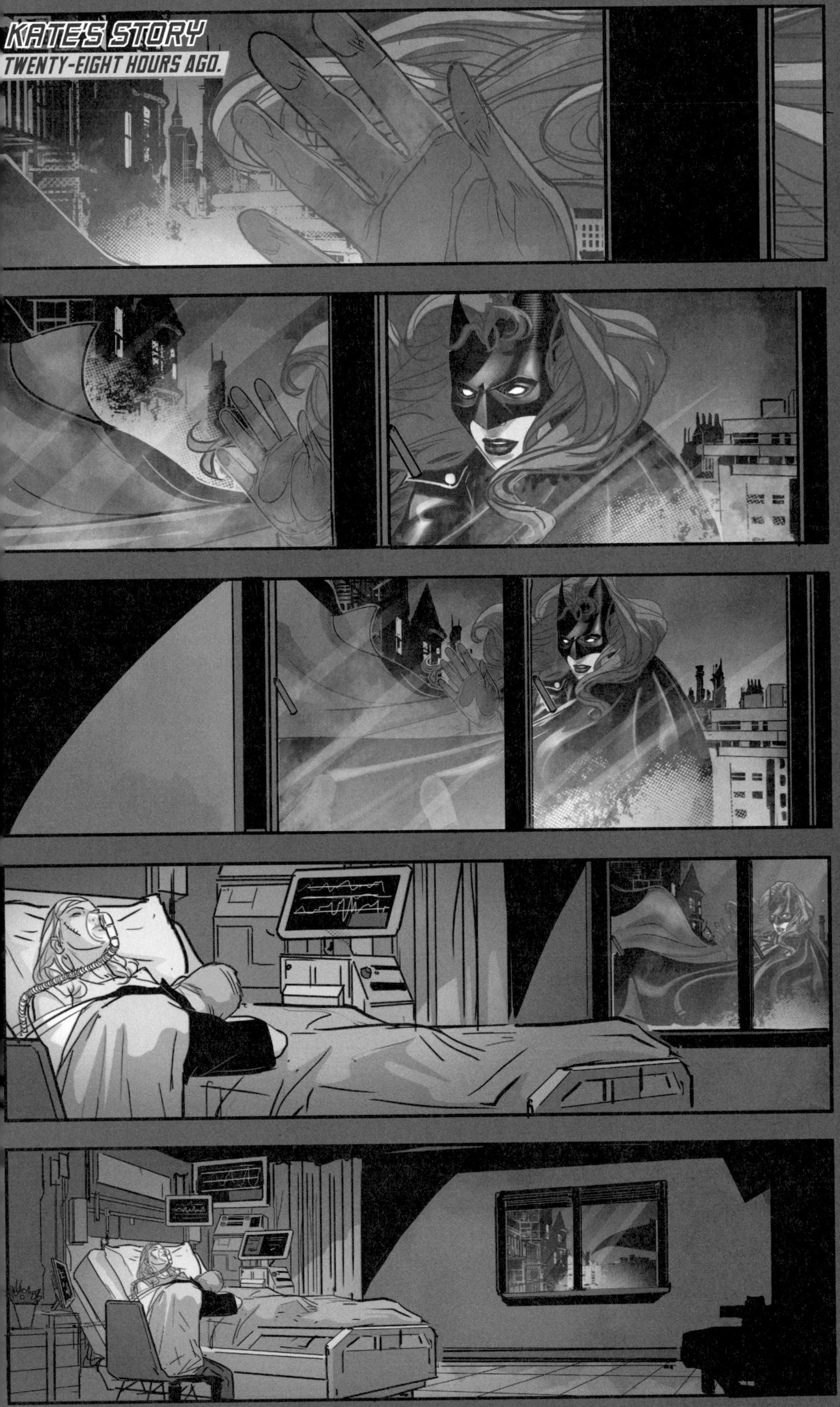
KATE'S STORY
TWENTY-EIGHT HOURS AGO.

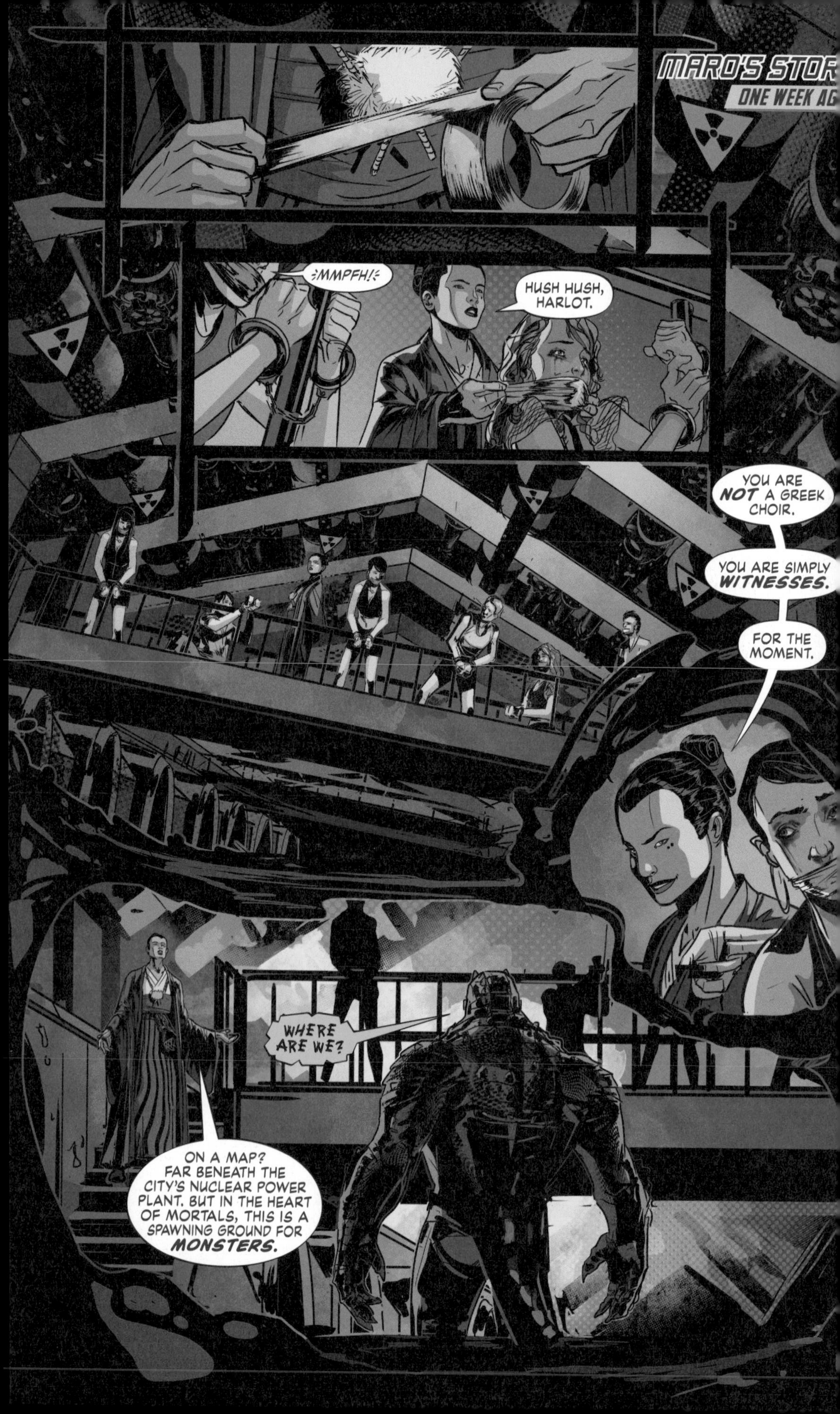
MARO'S STOR
ONE WEEK AG
MMPFH!
HUSH HUSH, HARLOT.
YOU ARE NOT A GREEK CHOIR.
YOU ARE SIMPLY WITNESSES.
FOR THE MOMENT.
WHERE ARE WE?
ON A MAP? FAR BENEATH THE CITY'S NUCLEAR POWER PLANT. BUT IN THE HEART OF MORTALS, THIS IS A SPAWNING GROUND FOR MONSTERS.

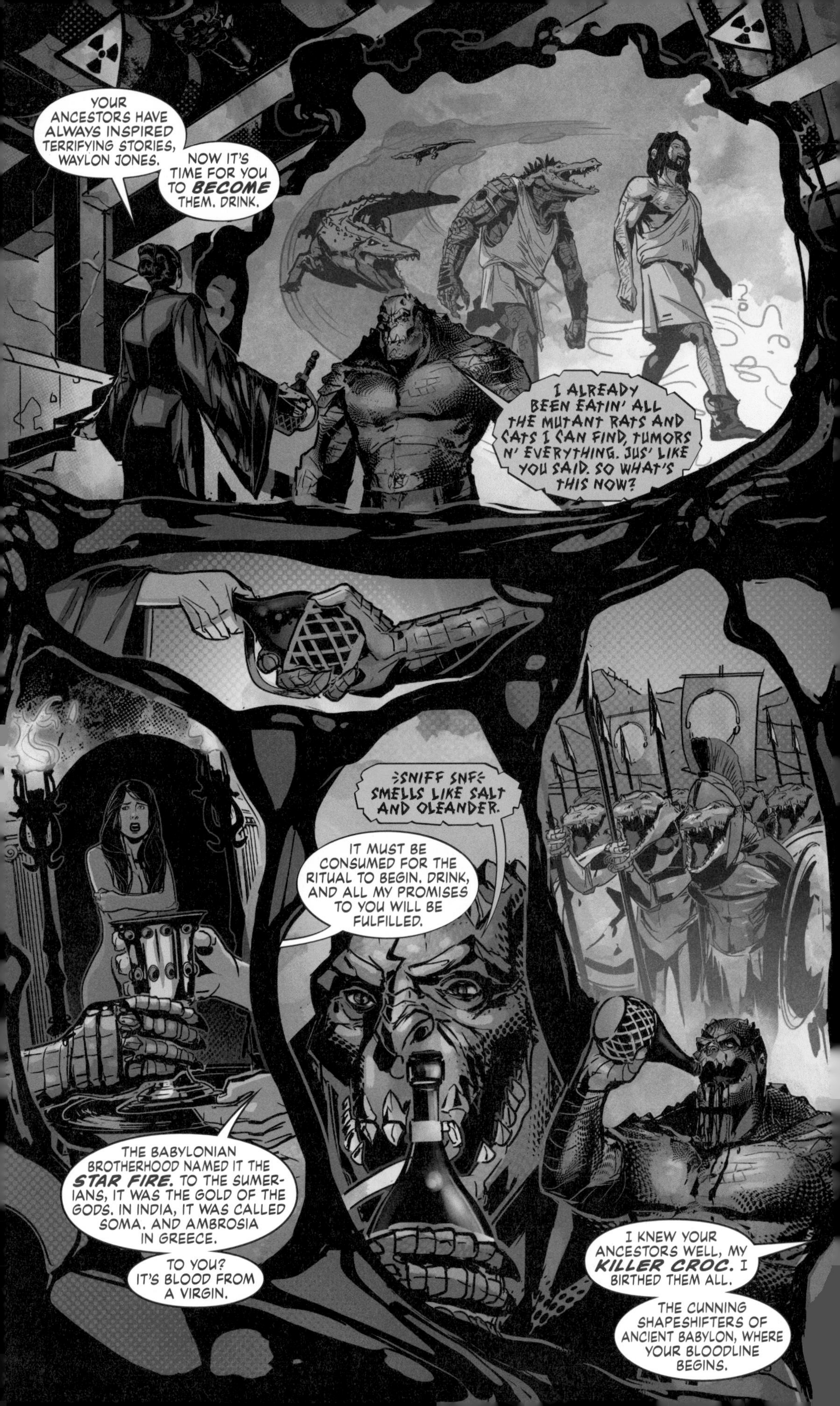
YOUR ANCESTORS HAVE ALWAYS INSPIRED TERRIFYING STORIES, WAYLON JONES.
NOW IT'S TIME FOR YOU TO BECOME THEM. DRINK.
I ALREADY BEEN EATIN' ALL THE MUTANT RATS AND CATS I CAN FIND, TUMORS N' EVERYTHING. JUS' LIKE YOU SAID. SO WHAT'S THIS NOW?
THE BABYLONIAN BROTHERHOOD NAMED IT THE STAR FIRE. TO THE SUMER-IANS, IT WAS THE GOLD OF THE GODS. IN INDIA, IT WAS CALLED SOMA. AND AMBROSIA IN GREECE.
TO YOU? IT'S BLOOD FROM A VIRGIN.
SNIFF SNF SMELLS LIKE SALT AND OLEANDER.
IT MUST BE CONSUMED FOR THE RITUAL TO BEGIN. DRINK, AND ALL MY PROMISES TO YOU WILL BE FULFILLED.
I KNEW YOUR ANCESTORS WELL, MY KILLER CROC. I BIRTHED THEM ALL.
THE CUNNING SHAPESHIFTERS OF ANCIENT BABYLON, WHERE YOUR BLOODLINE BEGINS.

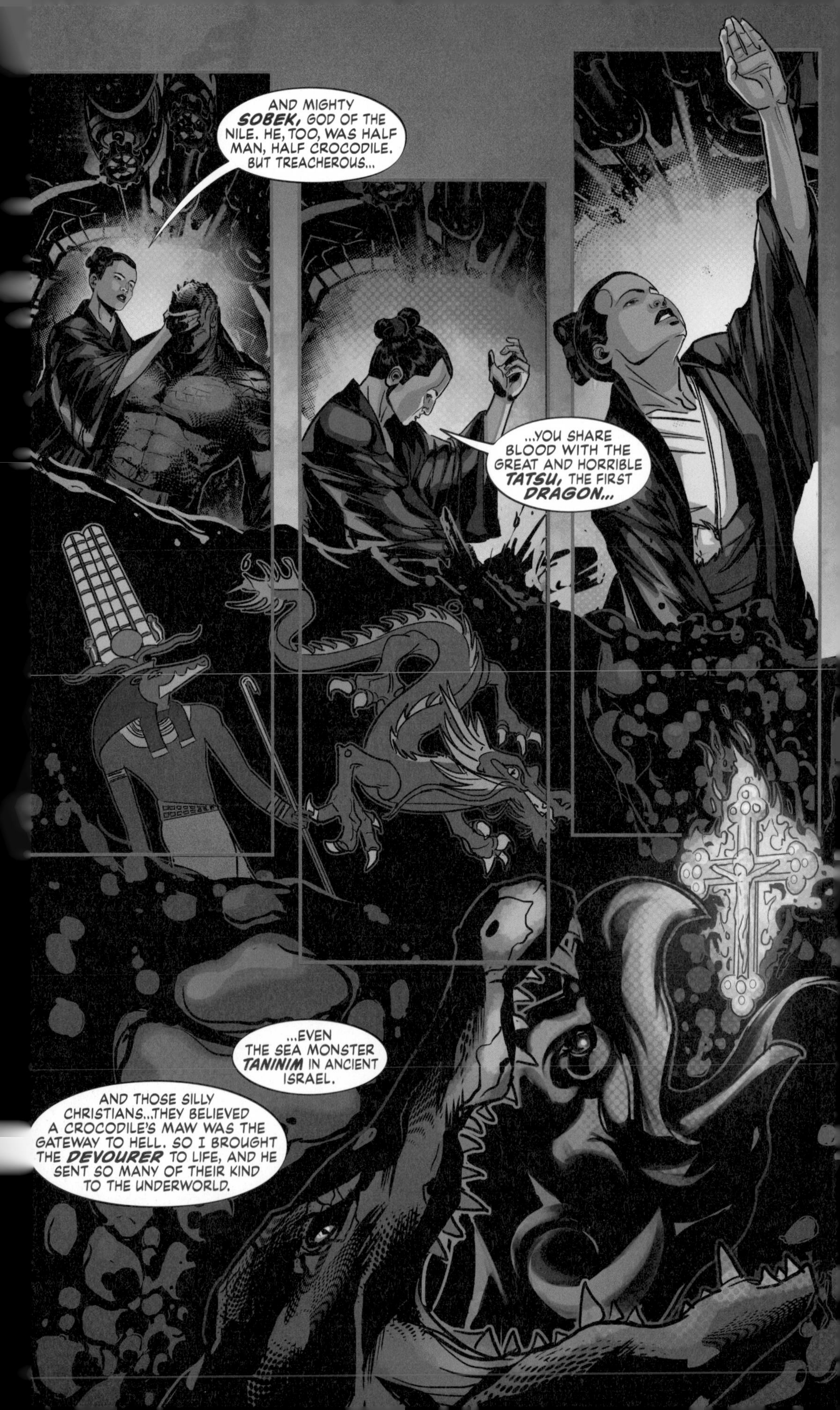
AND MIGHTY SOBEK, GOD OF THE NILE. HE, TOO, WAS HALF MAN, HALF CROCODILE. BUT TREACHEROUS...
...YOU SHARE BLOOD WITH THE GREAT AND HORRIBLE TATSU, THE FIRST DRAGON...
...EVEN THE SEA MONSTER TANINIM IN ANCIENT ISRAEL.
AND THOSE SILLY CHRISTIANS...THEY BELIEVED A CROCODILE'S MAW WAS THE GATEWAY TO HELL. SO I BROUGHT THE DEVOURER TO LIFE, AND HE SENT SO MANY OF THEIR KIND TO THE UNDERWORLD.

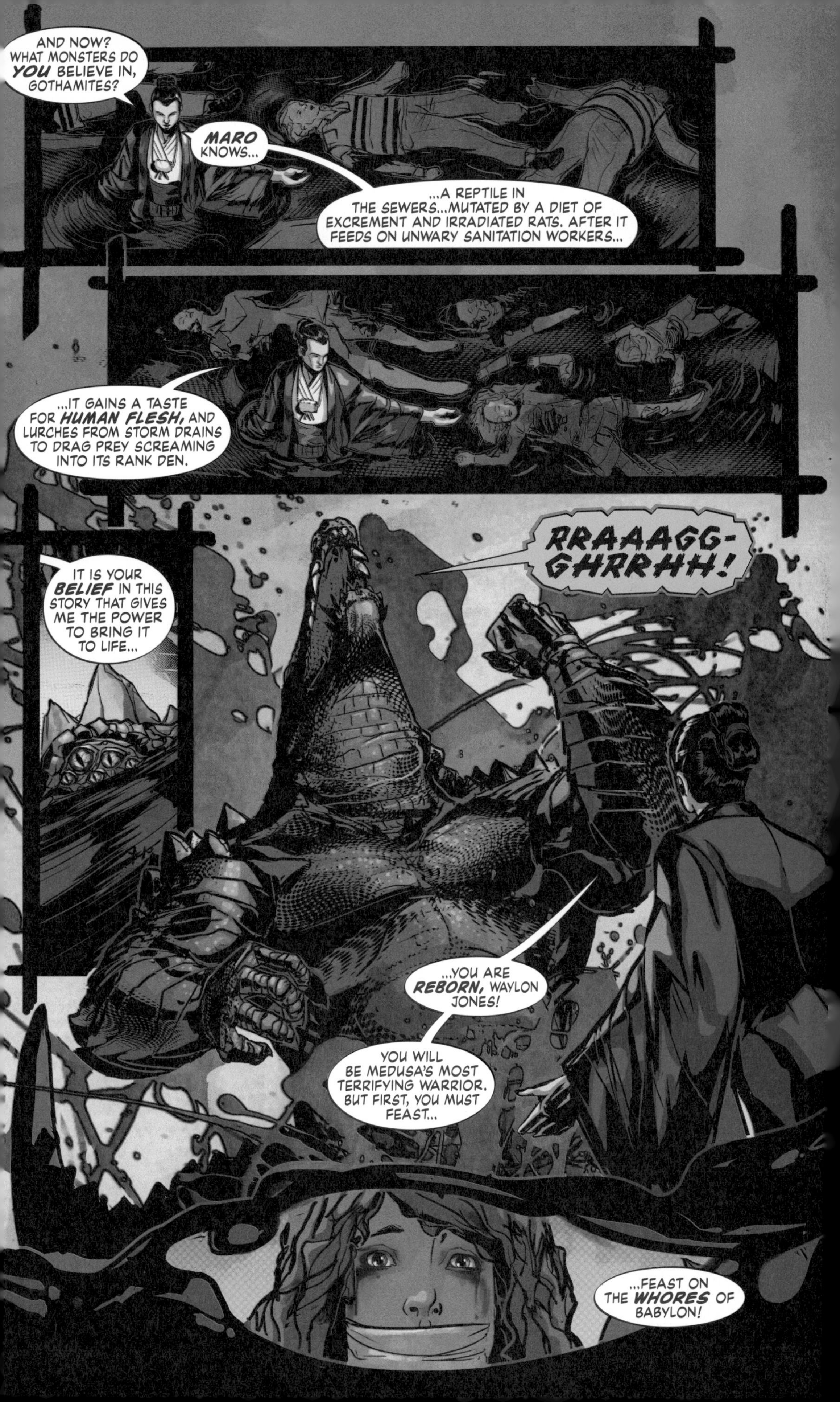
AND NOW? WHAT MONSTERS DO *YOU* BELIEVE IN, GOTHAMITES?
MARO KNOWS...
...A REPTILE IN THE SEWERS...MUTATED BY A DIET OF EXCREMENT AND IRRADIATED RATS. AFTER IT FEEDS ON UNWARY SANITATION WORKERS...
...IT GAINS A TASTE FOR *HUMAN FLESH,* AND LURCHES FROM STORM DRAINS TO DRAG PREY SCREAMING INTO ITS RANK DEN.
IT IS YOUR *BELIEF* IN THIS STORY THAT GIVES ME THE POWER TO BRING IT TO LIFE...
RRAAAGG-GHRRHH!
...YOU ARE *REBORN,* WAYLON JONES!
YOU WILL BE MEDUSA'S MOST TERRIFYING WARRIOR. BUT FIRST, YOU MUST FEAST...
...FEAST ON THE *WHORES* OF BABYLON!

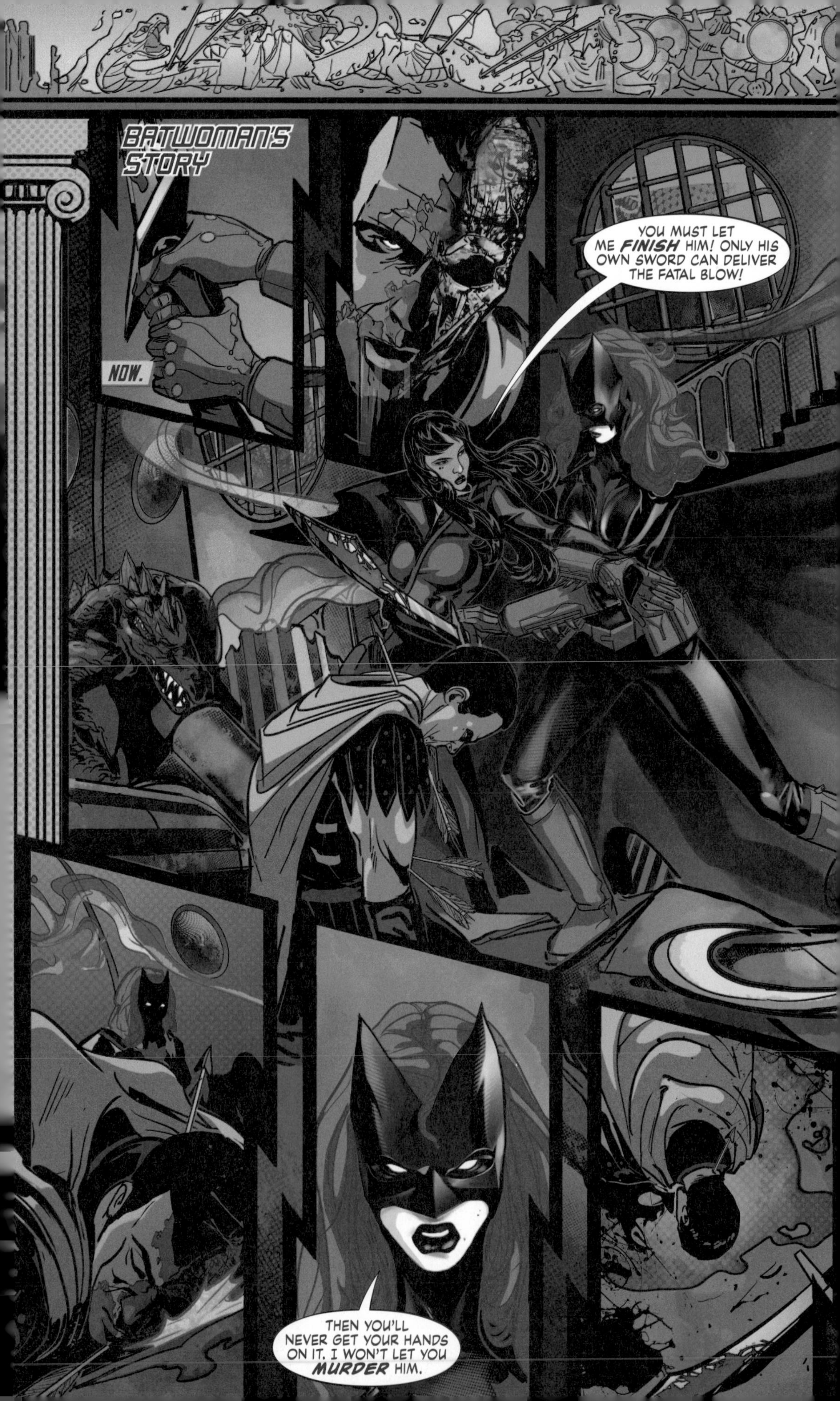
BATWOMAN'S STORY
NOW.
YOU MUST LET ME FINISH HIM! ONLY HIS OWN SWORD CAN DELIVER THE FATAL BLOW!
THEN YOU'LL NEVER GET YOUR HANDS ON IT. I WON'T LET YOU MURDER HIM.

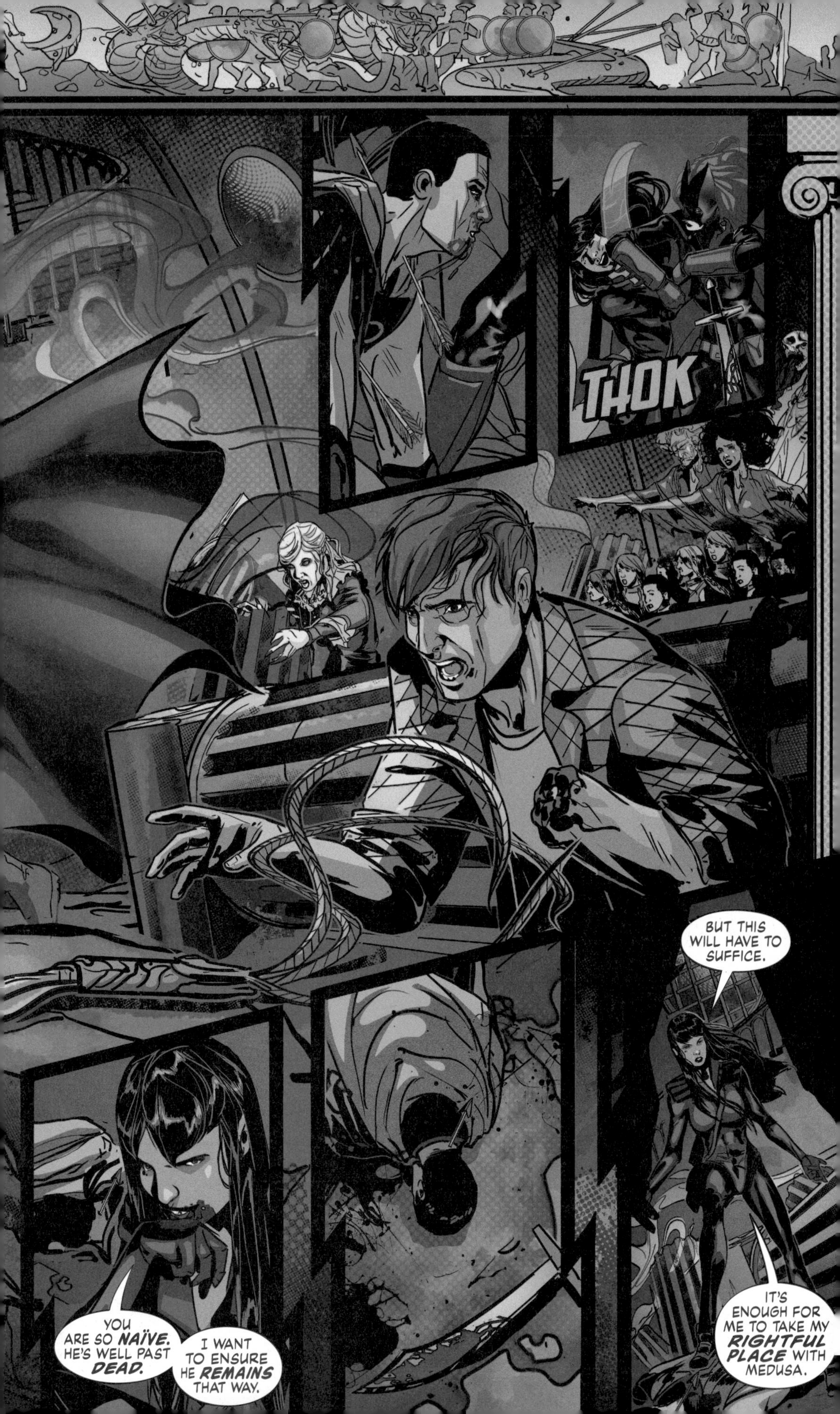
THOK
BUT THIS WILL HAVE TO SUFFICE.
YOU ARE SO **NAÏVE.** HE'S WELL PAST **DEAD.**
I WANT TO ENSURE HE **REMAINS** THAT WAY.
IT'S ENOUGH FOR ME TO TAKE MY **RIGHTFUL PLACE** WITH MEDUSA.

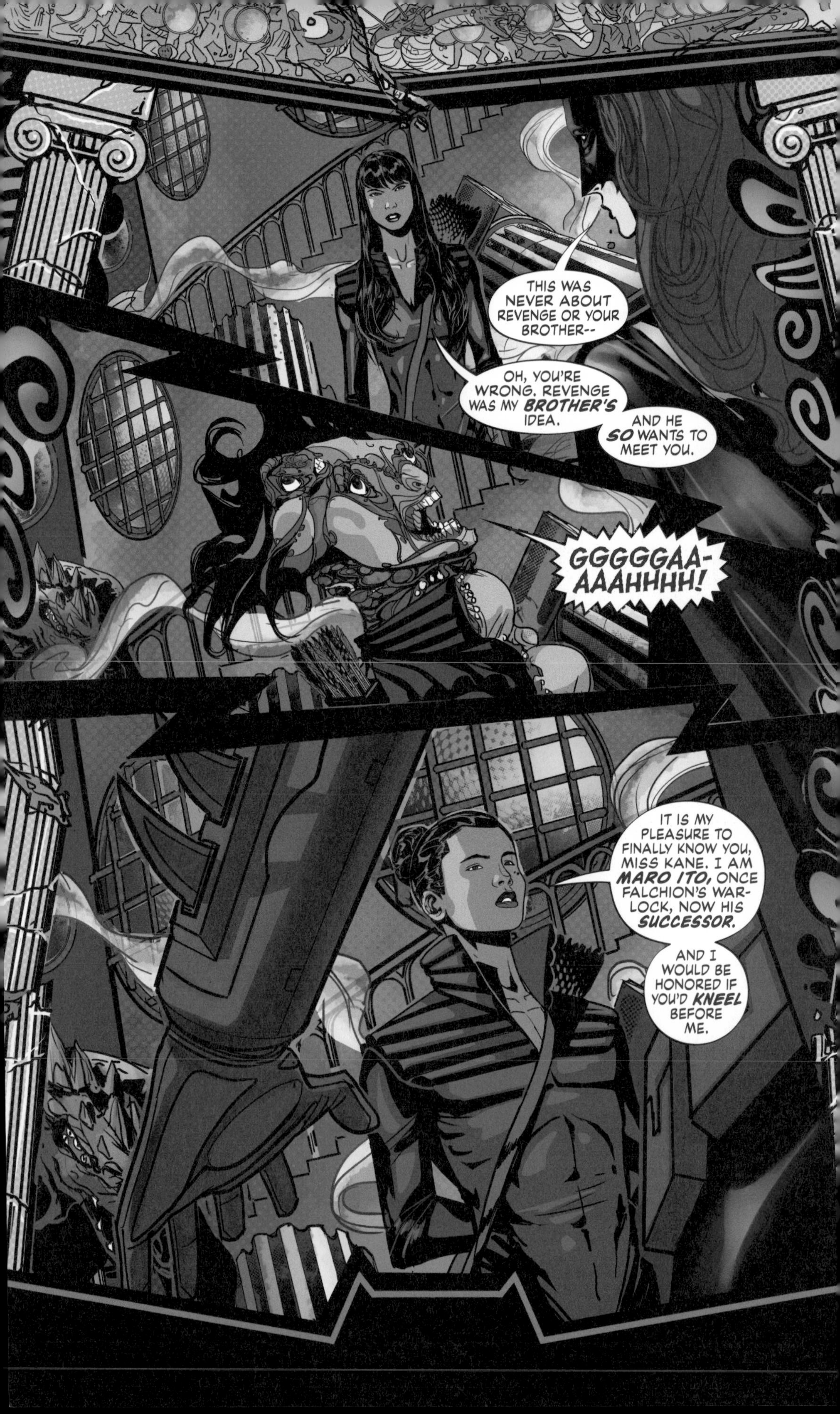
THIS WAS NEVER ABOUT REVENGE OR YOUR BROTHER--
OH, YOU'RE WRONG. REVENGE WAS MY BROTHER'S IDEA.
AND HE SO WANTS TO MEET YOU.
GGGGGAA-AAAHHHH!
IT IS MY PLEASURE TO FINALLY KNOW YOU, MISS KANE. I AM MARO ITO, ONCE FALCHION'S WAR-LOCK, NOW HIS SUCCESSOR.
AND I WOULD BE HONORED IF YOU'D KNEEL BEFORE ME.

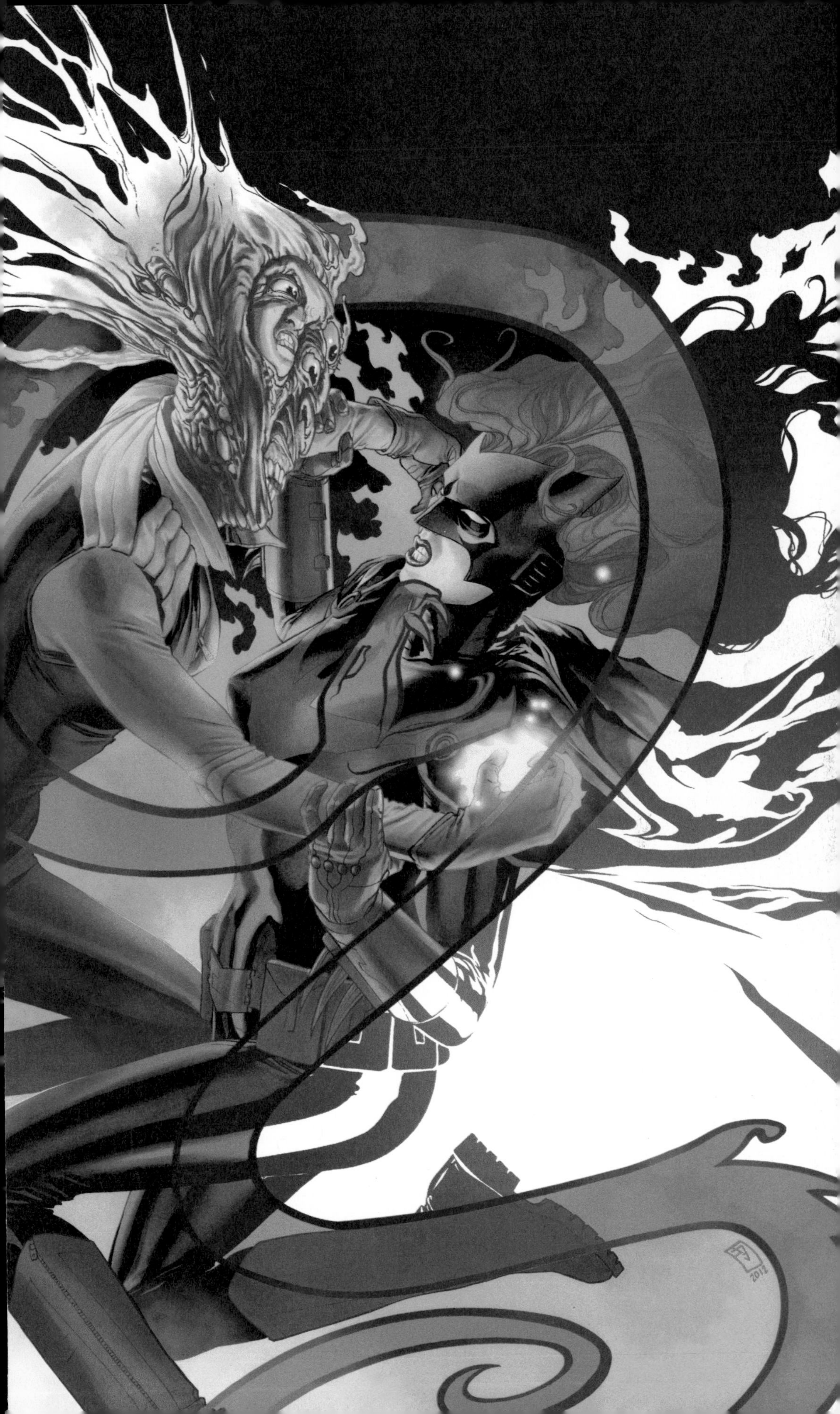
2012

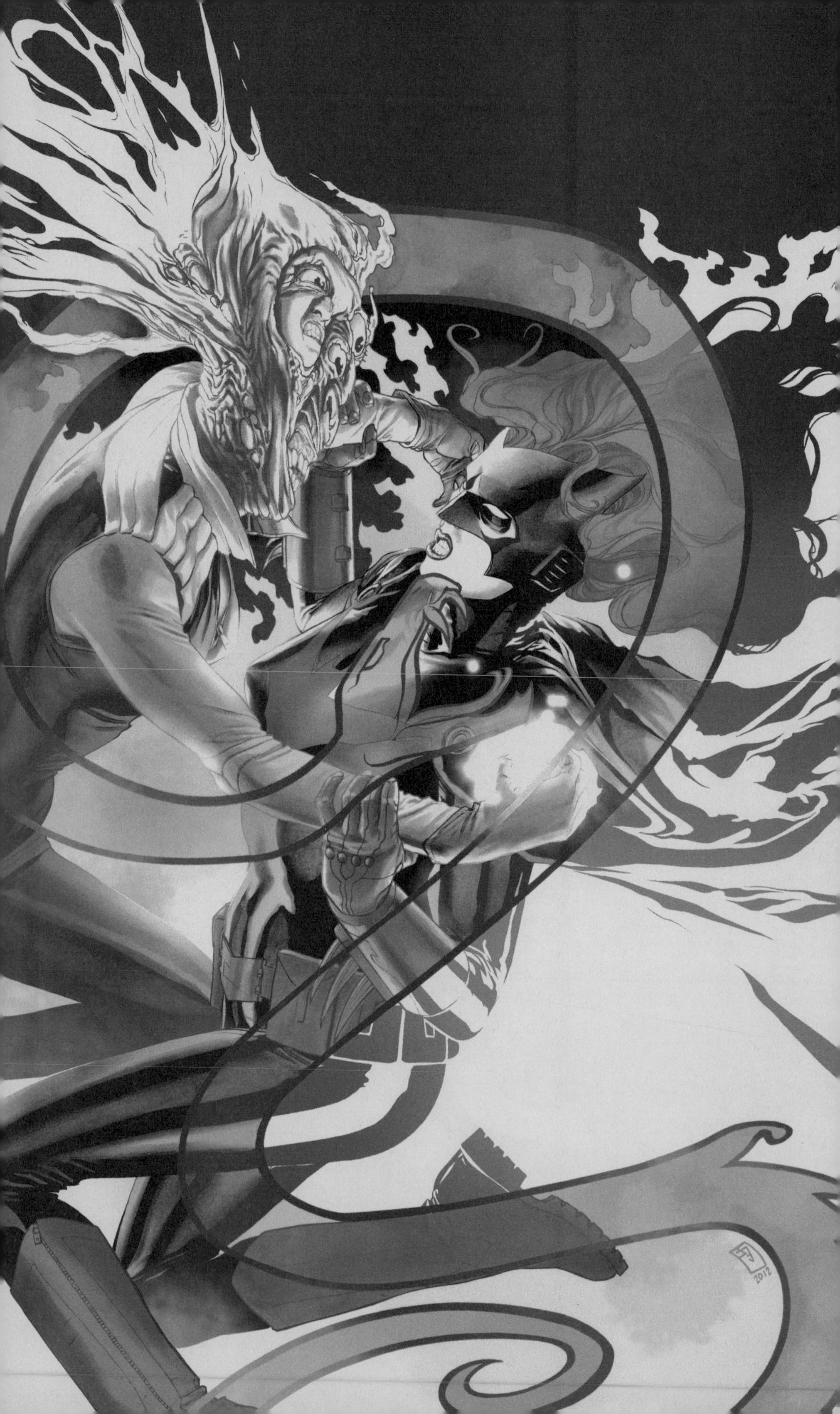

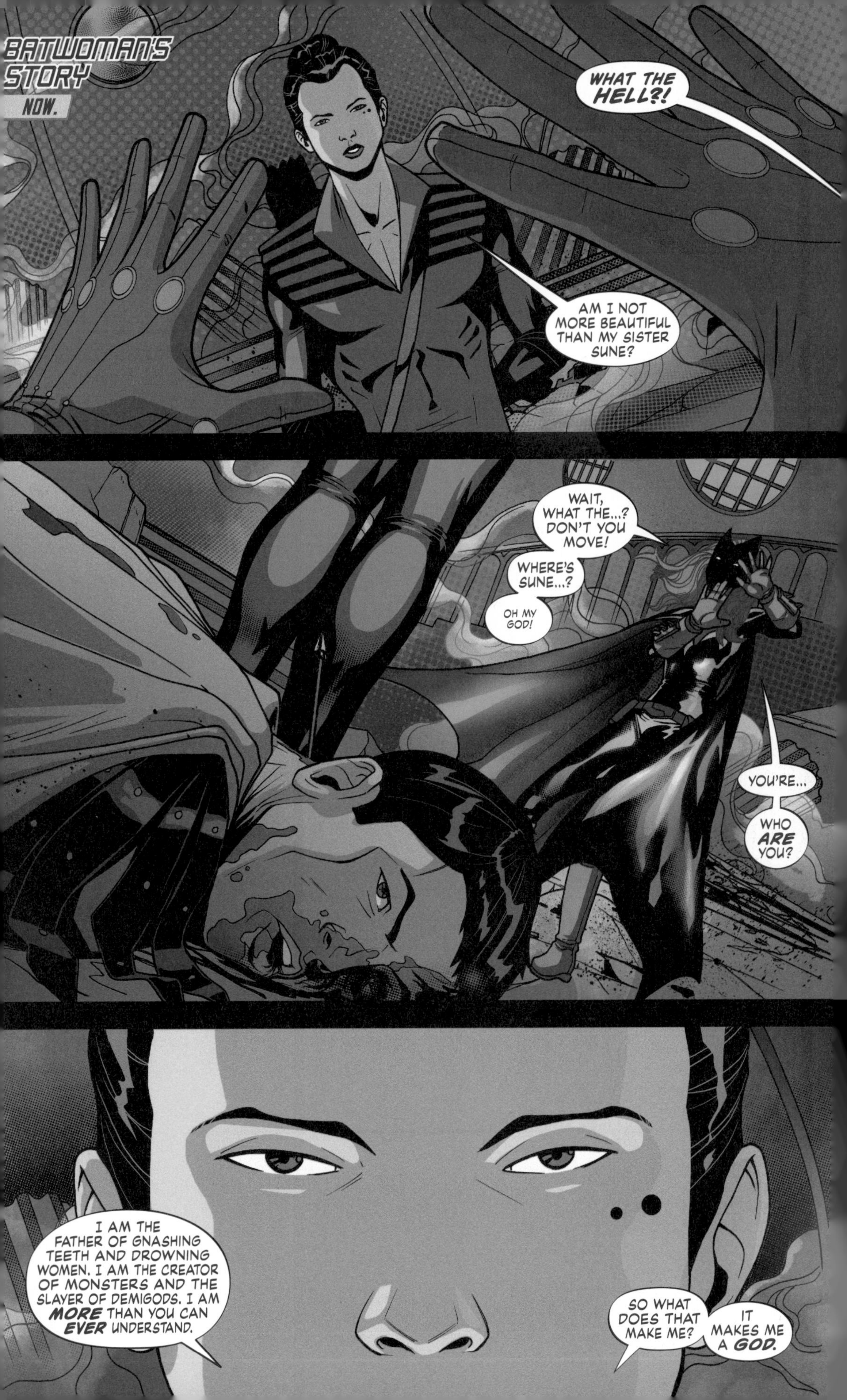
BATWOMAN'S STORY
NOW.
WHAT THE HELL?!
AM I NOT MORE BEAUTIFUL THAN MY SISTER SUNE?
WAIT, WHAT THE...? DON'T YOU MOVE!
WHERE'S SUNE...?
OH MY GOD!
YOU'RE...
WHO ARE YOU?
I AM THE FATHER OF GNASHING TEETH AND DROWNING WOMEN. I AM THE CREATOR OF MONSTERS AND THE SLAYER OF DEMIGODS. I AM MORE THAN YOU CAN EVER UNDERSTAND.
SO WHAT DOES THAT MAKE ME?
IT MAKES ME A GOD.

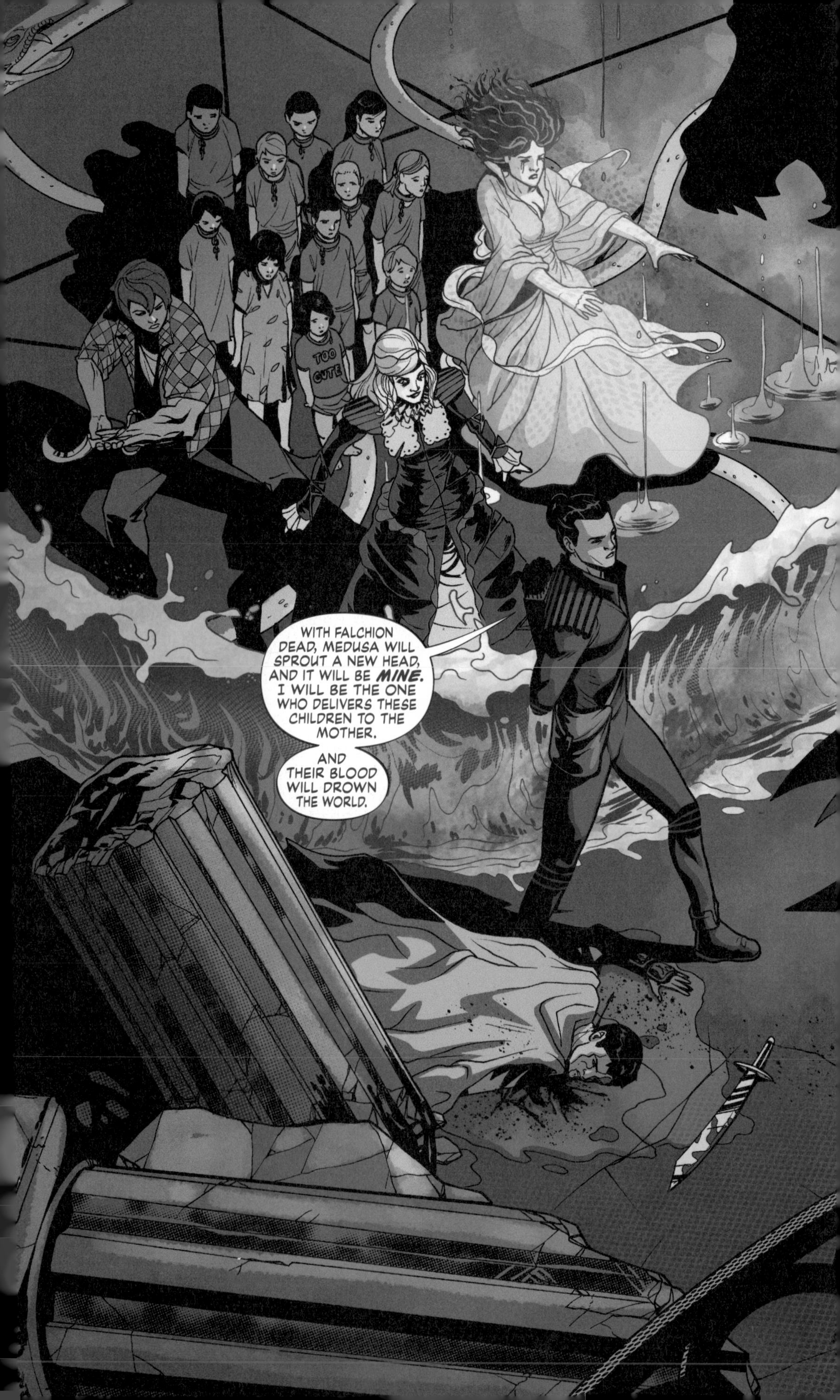
TOO CUTE
WITH FALCHION DEAD, MEDUSA WILL SPROUT A NEW HEAD, AND IT WILL BE *MINE.* I WILL BE THE ONE WHO DELIVERS THESE CHILDREN TO THE MOTHER.
AND THEIR BLOOD WILL DROWN THE WORLD.

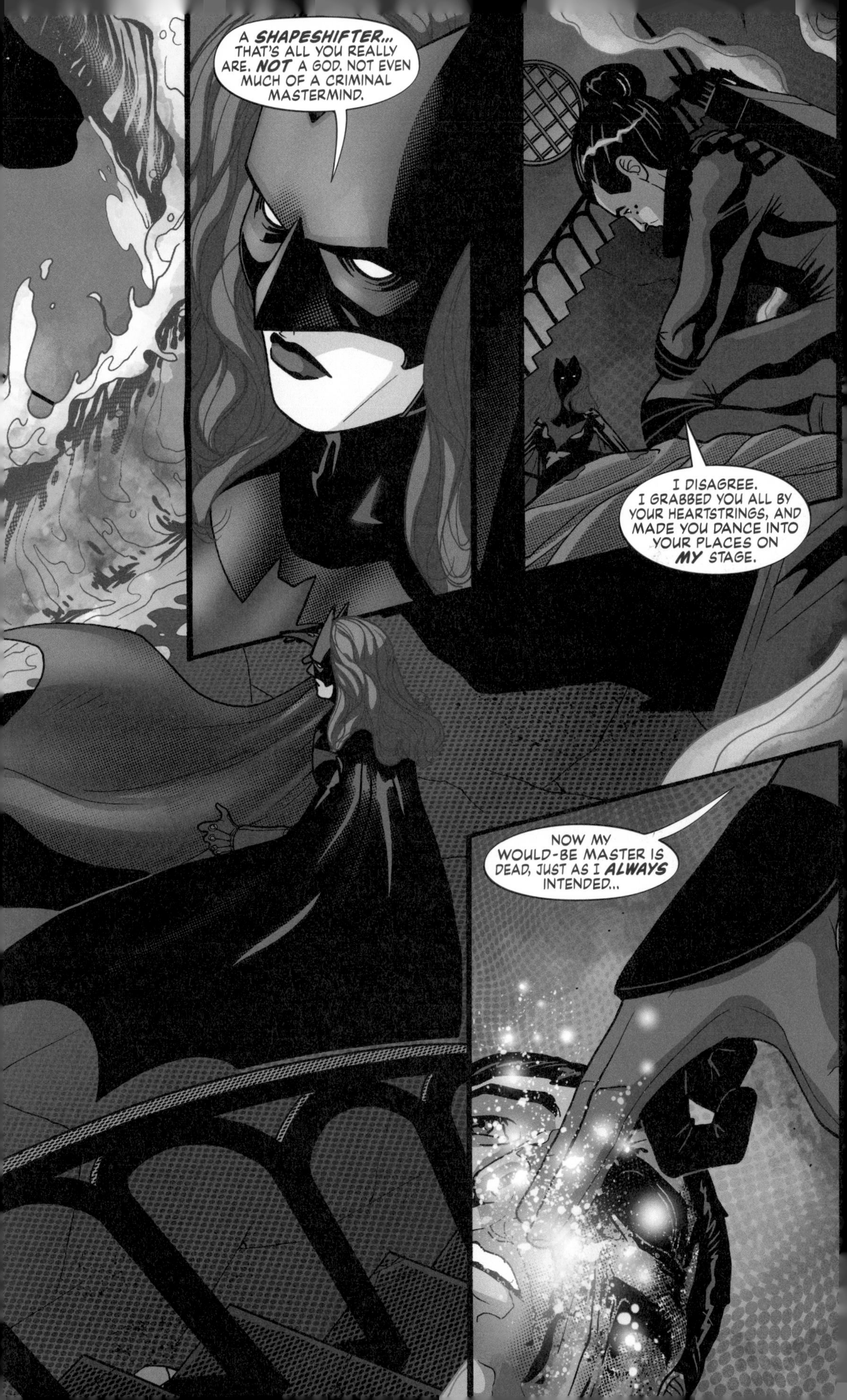
A SHAPESHIFTER... THAT'S ALL YOU REALLY ARE. NOT A GOD. NOT EVEN MUCH OF A CRIMINAL MASTERMIND.
I DISAGREE. I GRABBED YOU ALL BY YOUR HEARTSTRINGS, AND MADE YOU DANCE INTO YOUR PLACES ON MY STAGE.
NOW MY WOULD-BE MASTER IS DEAD, JUST AS I ALWAYS INTENDED...

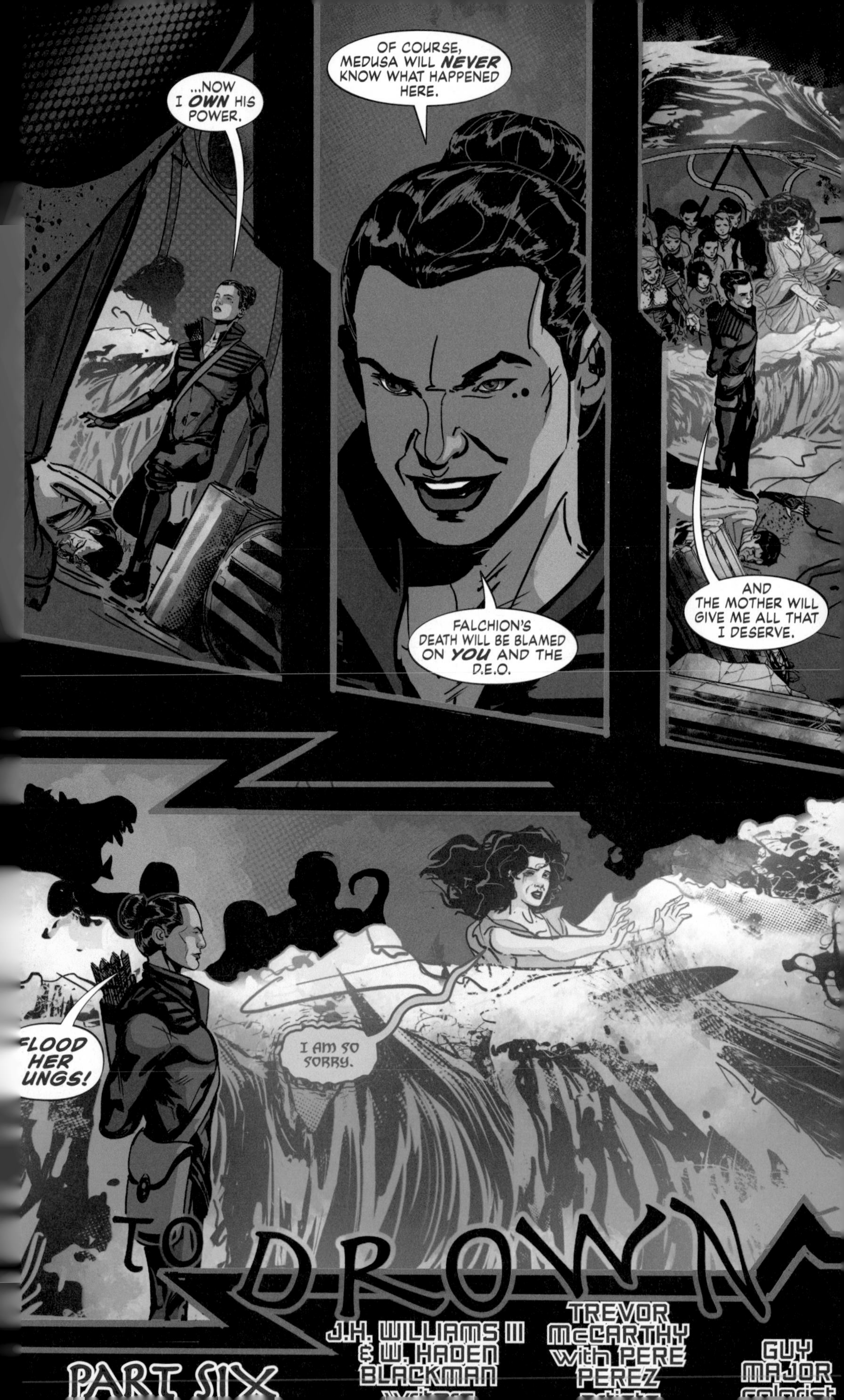
...NOW I OWN HIS POWER.
OF COURSE, MEDUSA WILL NEVER KNOW WHAT HAPPENED HERE.
FALCHION'S DEATH WILL BE BLAMED ON YOU AND THE D.E.O.
AND THE MOTHER WILL GIVE ME ALL THAT I DESERVE.
FLOOD HER UNGS!
I AM SO SORRY.
TO DROWN
PART SIX
J.H. WILLIAMS III & W. HADEN BLACKMAN
TREVOR McCARTHY with PERE PEREZ
GUY MAJOR

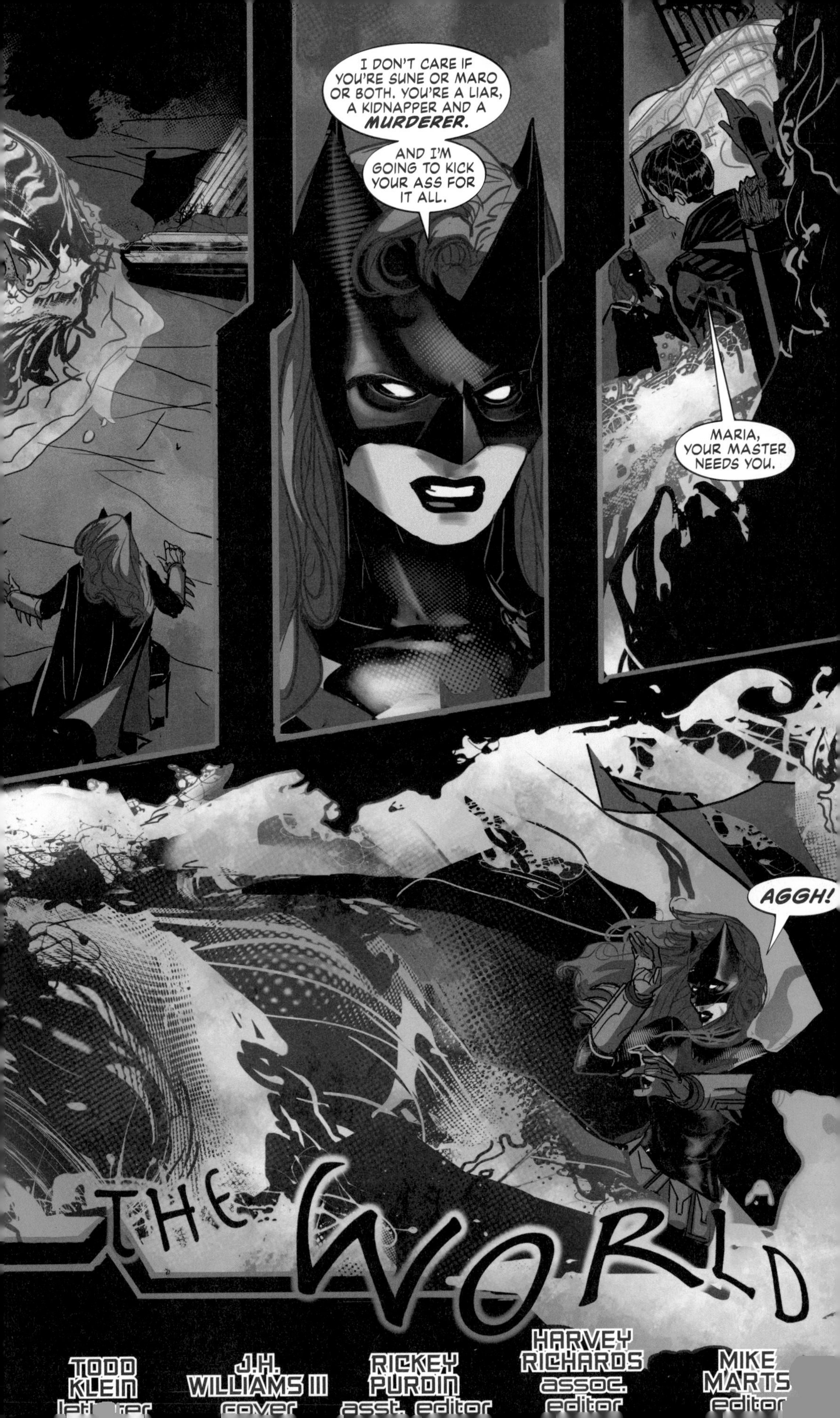
I DON'T CARE IF YOU'RE SUNE OR MARO OR BOTH. YOU'RE A LIAR, A KIDNAPPER AND A **MURDERER.**
AND I'M GOING TO KICK YOUR ASS FOR IT ALL.
MARIA, YOUR MASTER NEEDS YOU.
AGGH!
THE WORLD
TODD KLEIN
J.H. WILLIAMS III cover
RICKEY PURDIN asst. editor
HARVEY RICHARDS assoc. editor
MIKE MARTS editor

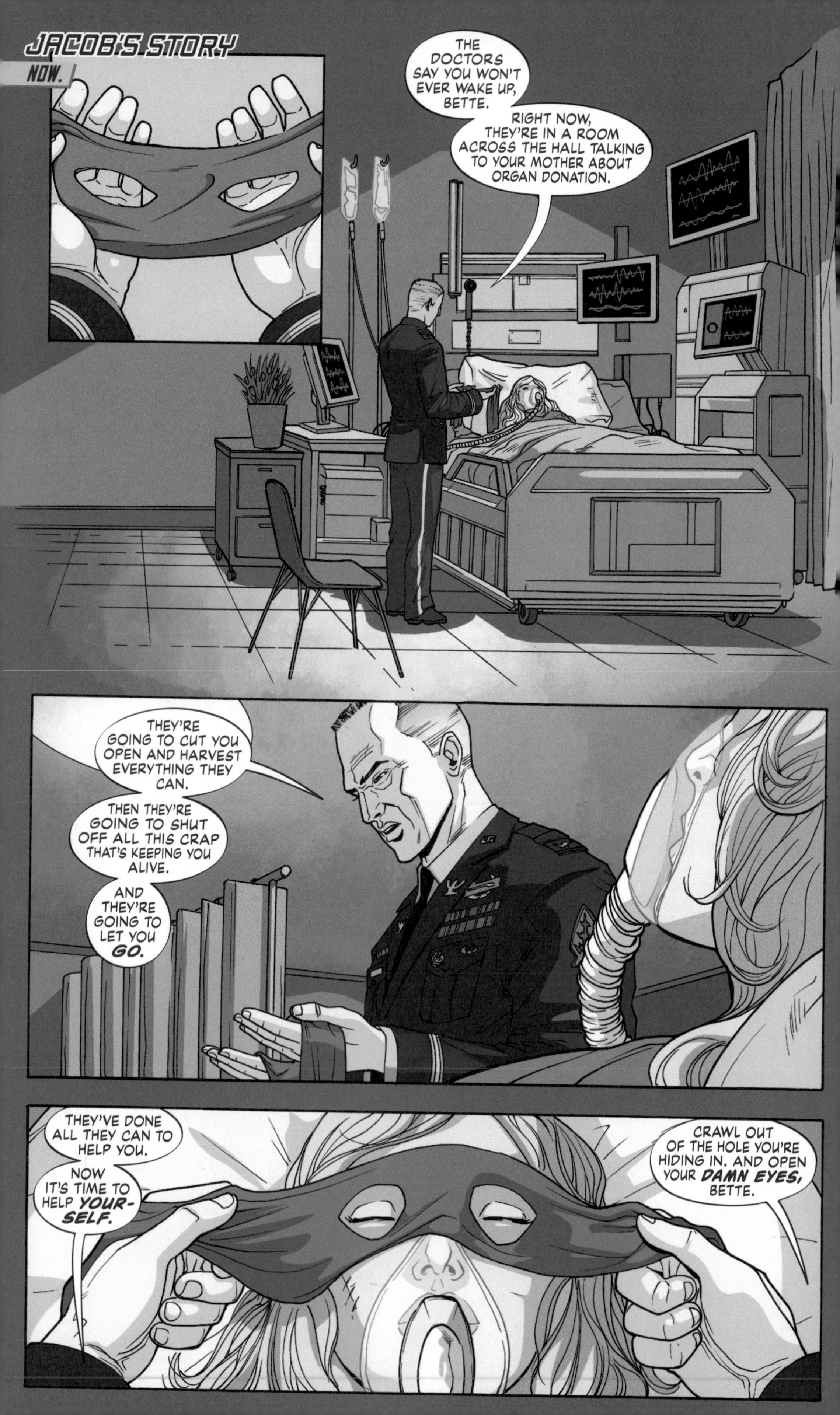

JACOB'S STORY
NOW.
THE DOCTORS SAY YOU WON'T EVER WAKE UP, BETTE.
RIGHT NOW, THEY'RE IN A ROOM ACROSS THE HALL TALKING TO YOUR MOTHER ABOUT ORGAN DONATION.
THEY'RE GOING TO CUT YOU OPEN AND HARVEST EVERYTHING THEY CAN.
THEN THEY'RE GOING TO SHUT OFF ALL THIS CRAP THAT'S KEEPING YOU ALIVE.
AND THEY'RE GOING TO LET YOU GO.
THEY'VE DONE ALL THEY CAN TO HELP YOU.
NOW IT'S TIME TO HELP YOURSELF.
CRAWL OUT OF THE HOLE YOU'RE HIDING IN. AND OPEN YOUR DAMN EYES, BETTE.

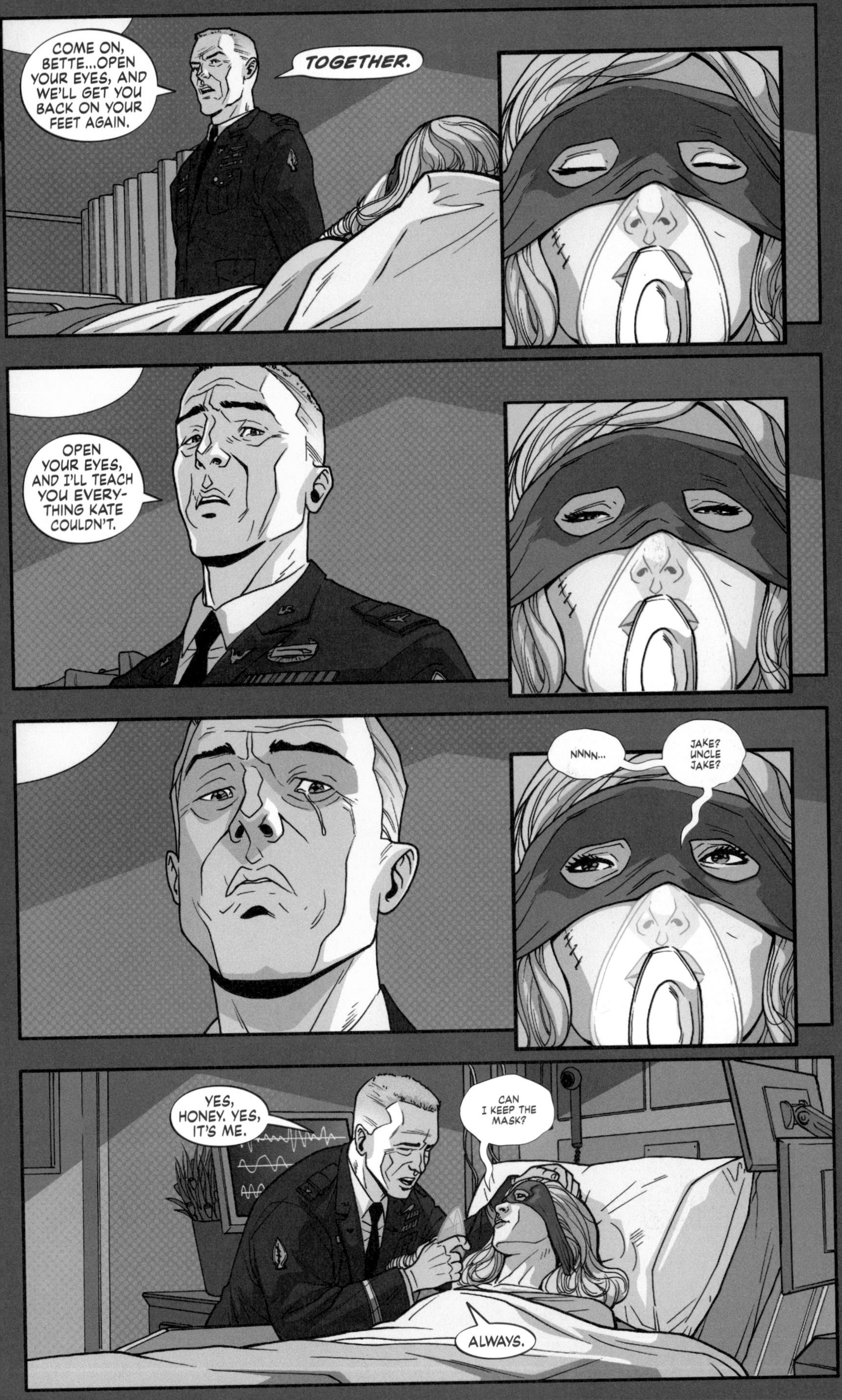
COME ON, BETTE...OPEN YOUR EYES, AND WE'LL GET YOU BACK ON YOUR FEET AGAIN.
TOGETHER.
OPEN YOUR EYES, AND I'LL TEACH YOU EVERY-THING KATE COULDN'T.
NNNN...
JAKE? UNCLE JAKE?
YES, HONEY. YES, IT'S ME.
CAN I KEEP THE MASK?
ALWAYS.

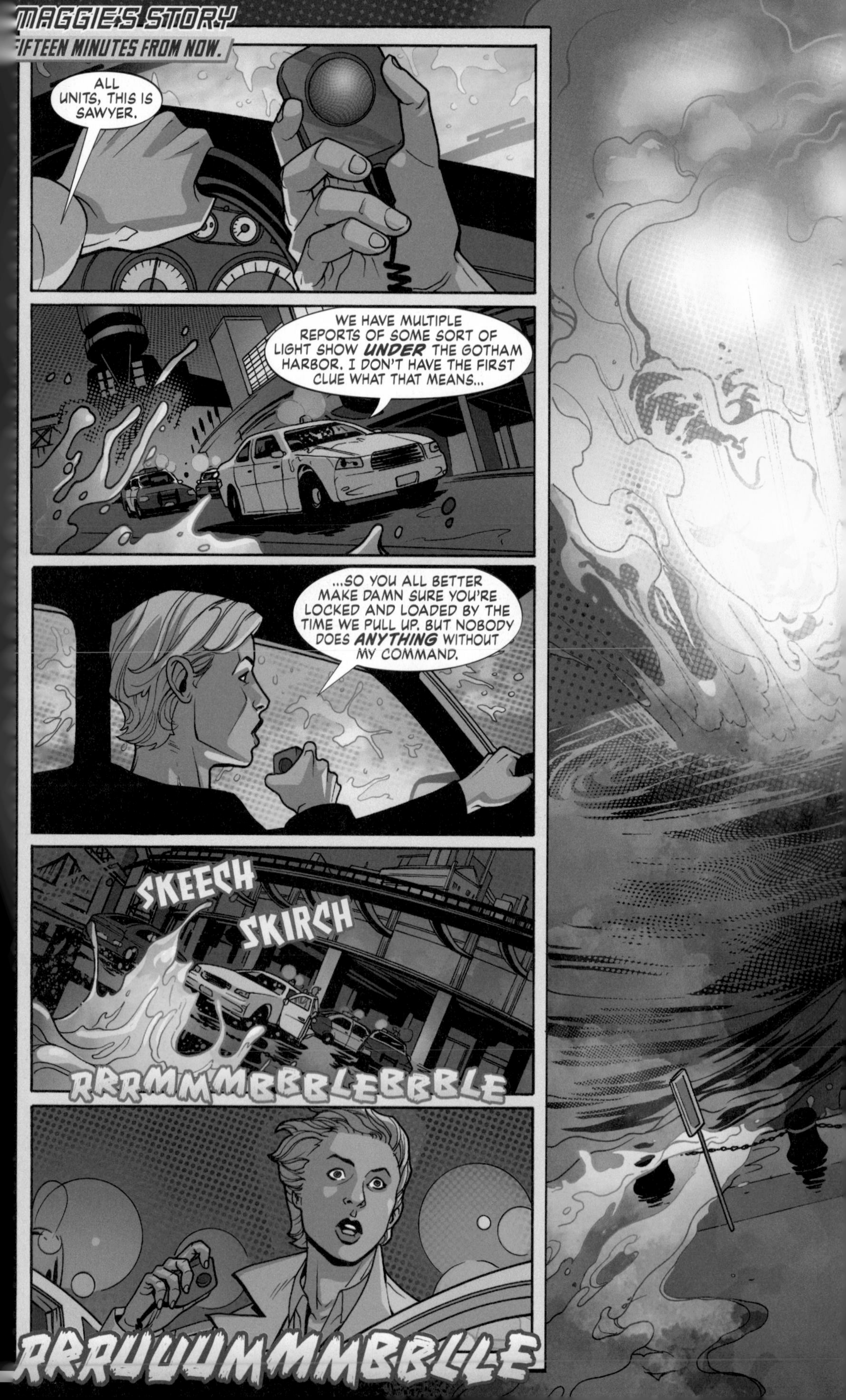

MAGGIE'S STORY
FIFTEEN MINUTES FROM NOW.
ALL UNITS, THIS IS SAWYER.
WE HAVE MULTIPLE REPORTS OF SOME SORT OF LIGHT SHOW UNDER THE GOTHAM HARBOR. I DON'T HAVE THE FIRST CLUE WHAT THAT MEANS...
...SO YOU ALL BETTER MAKE DAMN SURE YOU'RE LOCKED AND LOADED BY THE TIME WE PULL UP. BUT NOBODY DOES ANYTHING WITHOUT MY COMMAND.
SKEECH
SKIRCH
RRRMMMMBBBLEBBBLE
RRRUUUMMMBBLLE

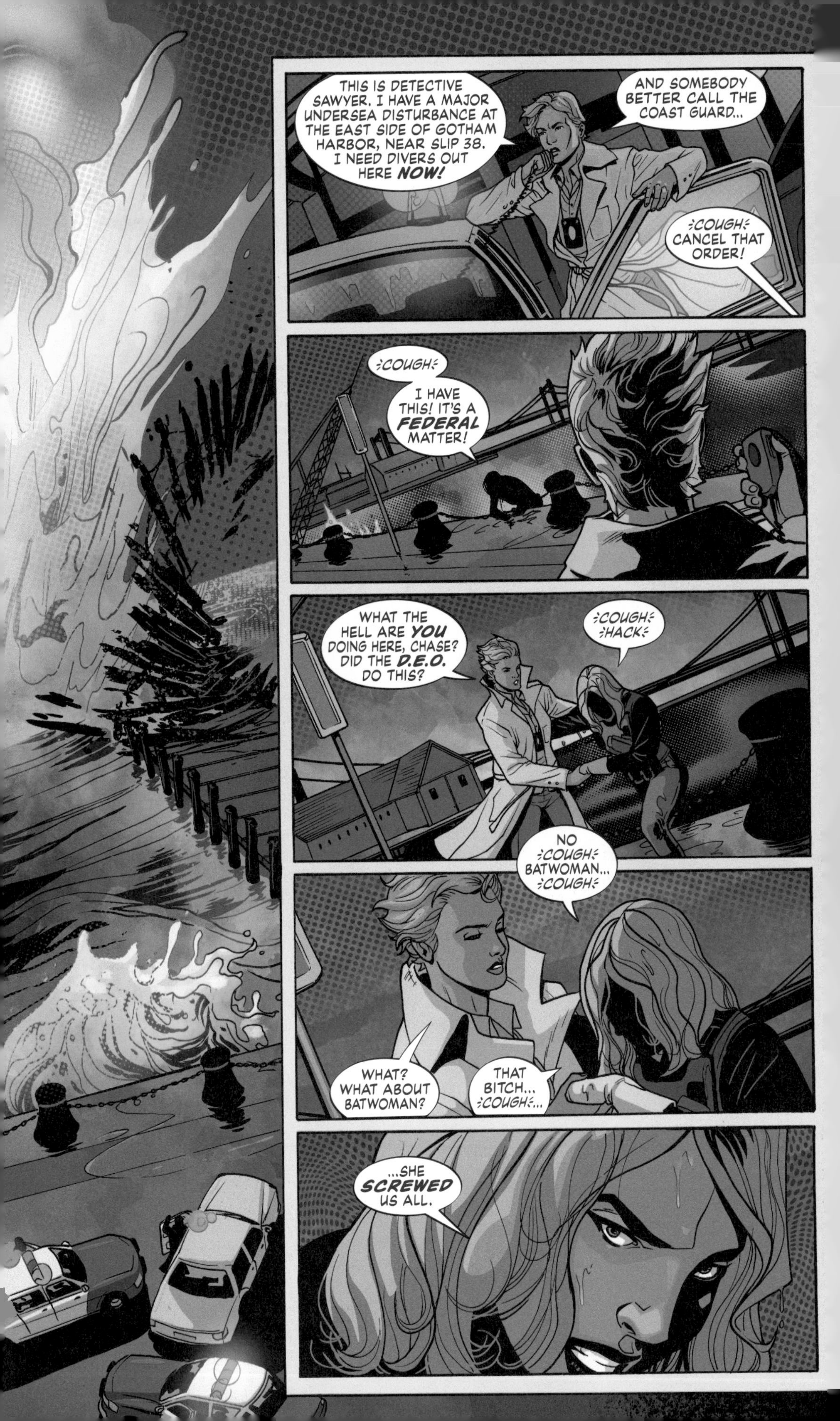
THIS IS DETECTIVE SAWYER. I HAVE A MAJOR UNDERSEA DISTURBANCE AT THE EAST SIDE OF GOTHAM HARBOR, NEAR SLIP 38. I NEED DIVERS OUT HERE NOW!
AND SOMEBODY BETTER CALL THE COAST GUARD...
COUGH CANCEL THAT ORDER!
COUGH
I HAVE THIS! IT'S A FEDERAL MATTER!
WHAT THE HELL ARE YOU DOING HERE, CHASE? DID THE D.E.O. DO THIS?
COUGH HACK
NO COUGH BATWOMAN... COUGH
WHAT? WHAT ABOUT BATWOMAN?
THAT BITCH... COUGH...
...SHE SCREWED US ALL.

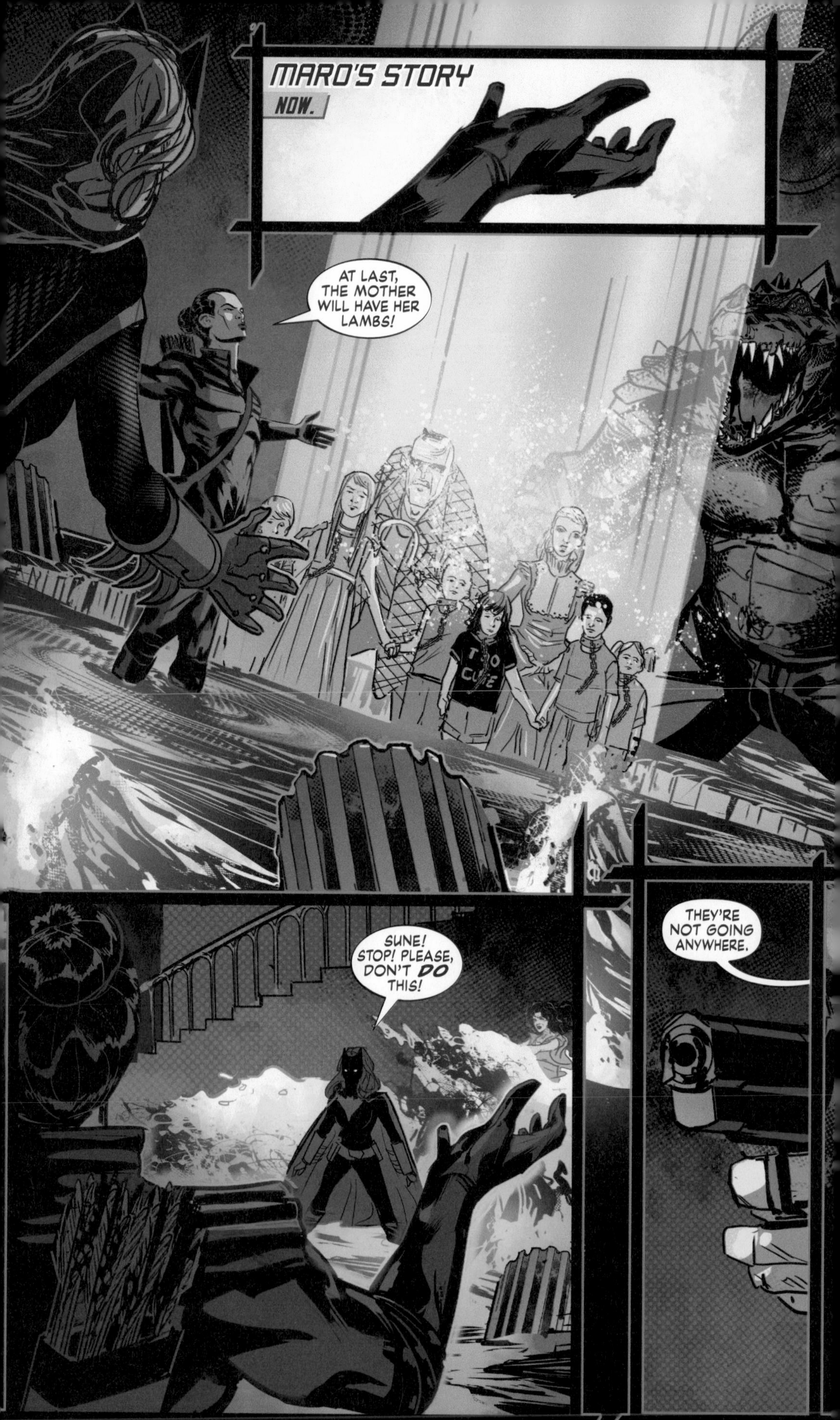
MARO'S STORY
NOW.
AT LAST, THE MOTHER WILL HAVE HER LAMBS!
SUNE! STOP! PLEASE, DON'T DO THIS!
THEY'RE NOT GOING ANYWHERE.

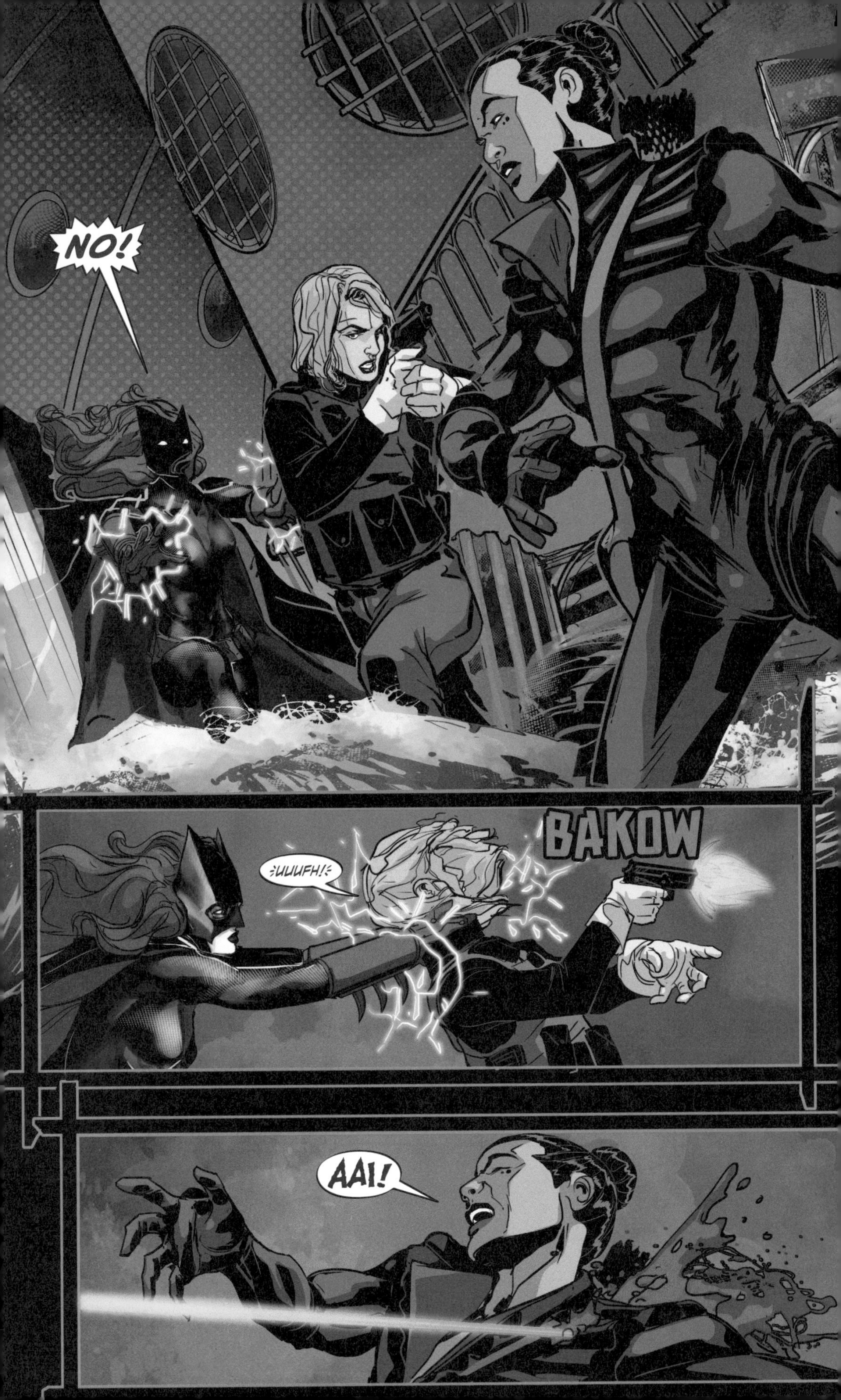
NO!
BAKOW
UUUFH!
AAI!

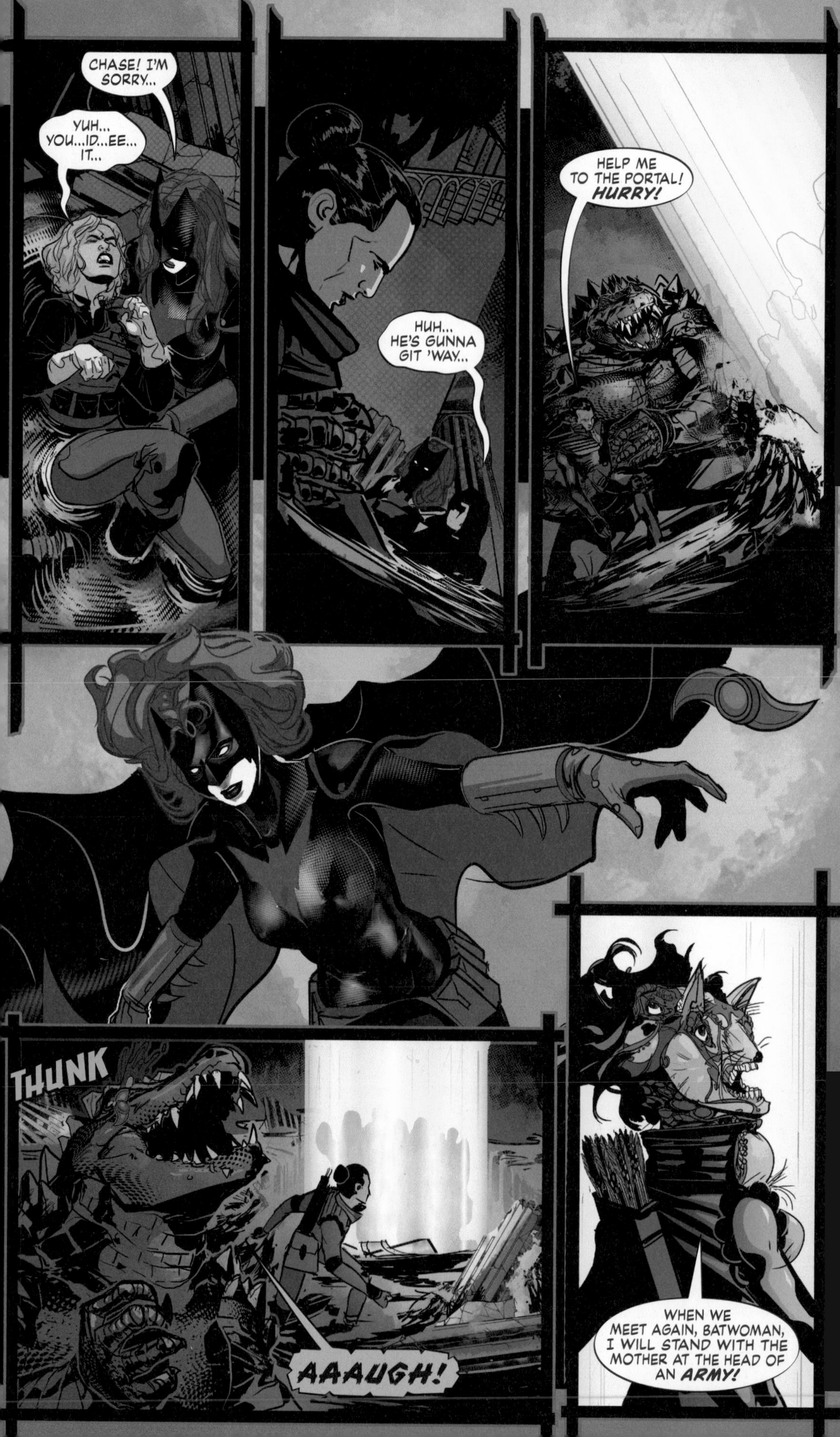

CHASE! I'M SORRY...
YUH... YOU...ID...EE... IT...
HUH... HE'S GUNNA GIT 'WAY...
HELP ME TO THE PORTAL! *HURRY!*
THUNK
AAAUGH!
WHEN WE MEET AGAIN, BATWOMAN, I WILL STAND WITH THE MOTHER AT THE HEAD OF AN *ARMY!*

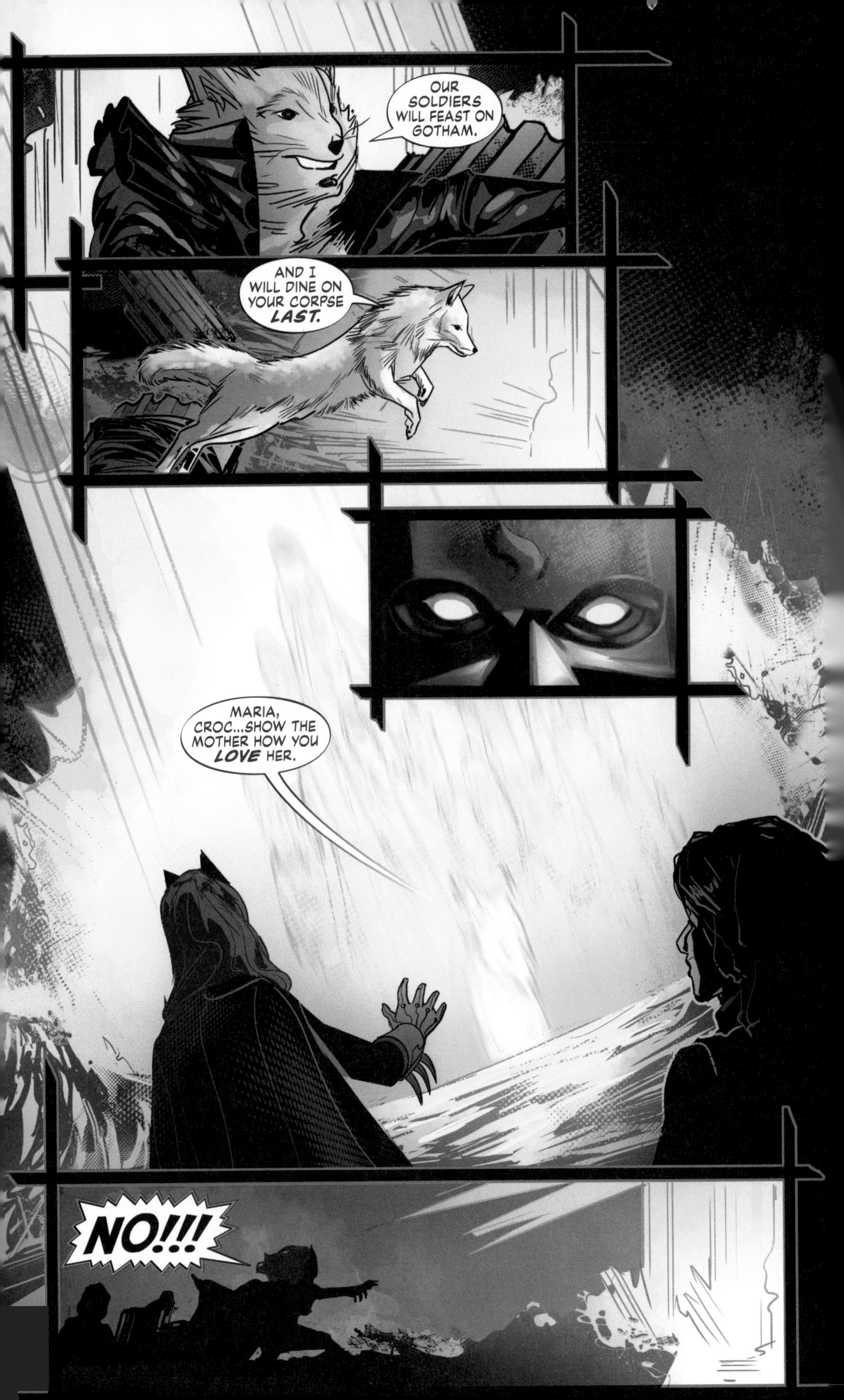
OUR SOLDIERS WILL FEAST ON GOTHAM.
AND I WILL DINE ON YOUR CORPSE *LAST.*
MARIA, CROC...SHOW THE MOTHER HOW YOU *LOVE* HER.
NO!!!

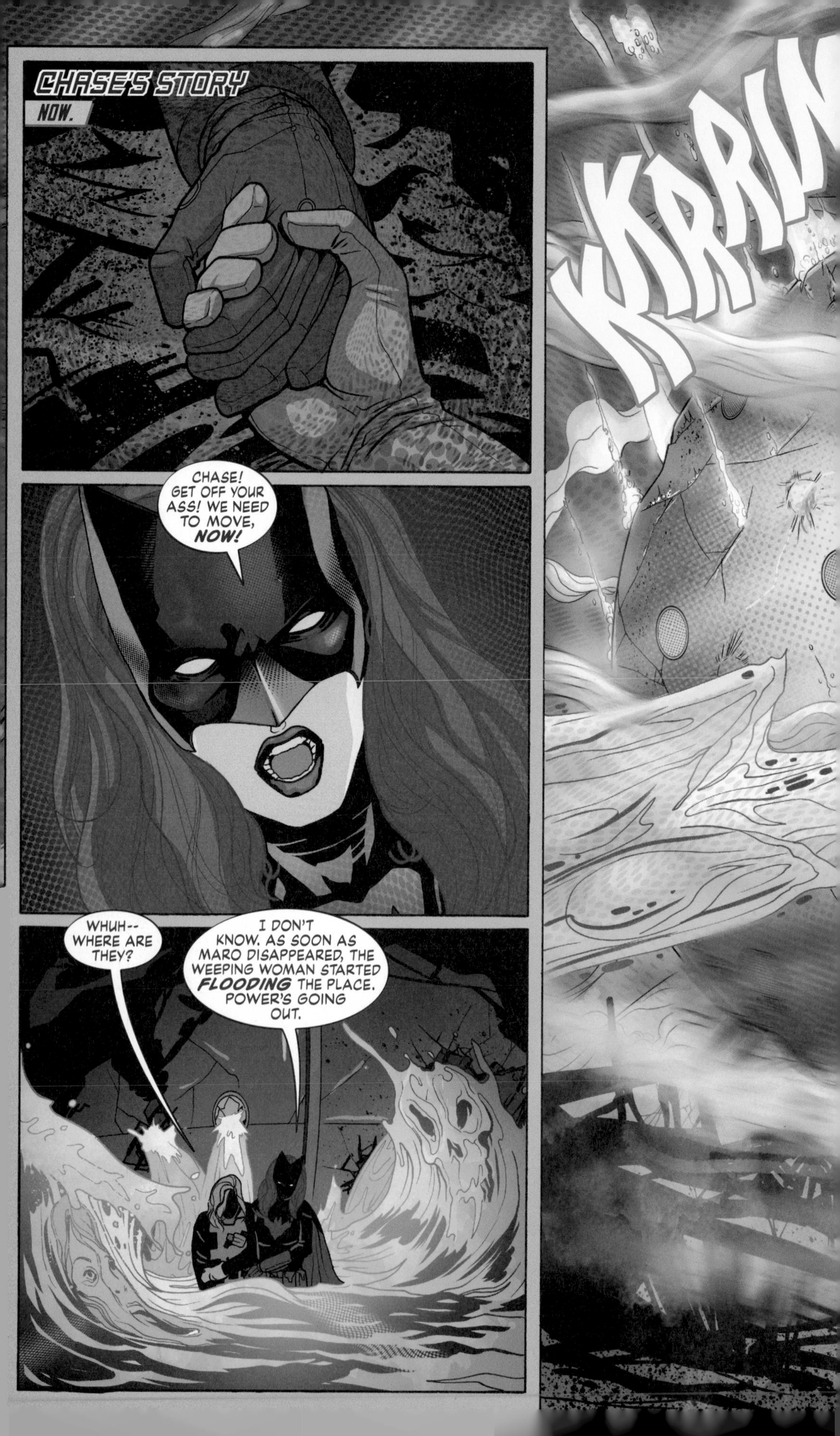
CHASE'S STORY
NOW.
CHASE! GET OFF YOUR ASS! WE NEED TO MOVE, NOW!
WHUH-- WHERE ARE THEY?
I DON'T KNOW. AS SOON AS MARO DISAPPEARED, THE WEEPING WOMAN STARTED FLOODING THE PLACE. POWER'S GOING OUT.
KRRIN

NGGK

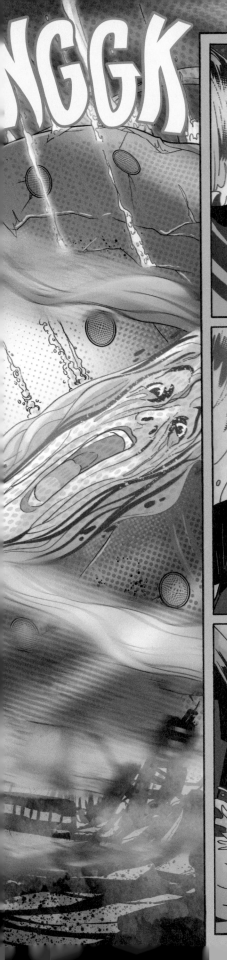

AND CROC?

HE'S STILL IN HERE WITH *US.*

AND MARIA IS TEARING THIS PLACE APART...

HERE. HOLD ONTO THIS. I THINK YOU'RE GOING TO *NEED* IT.

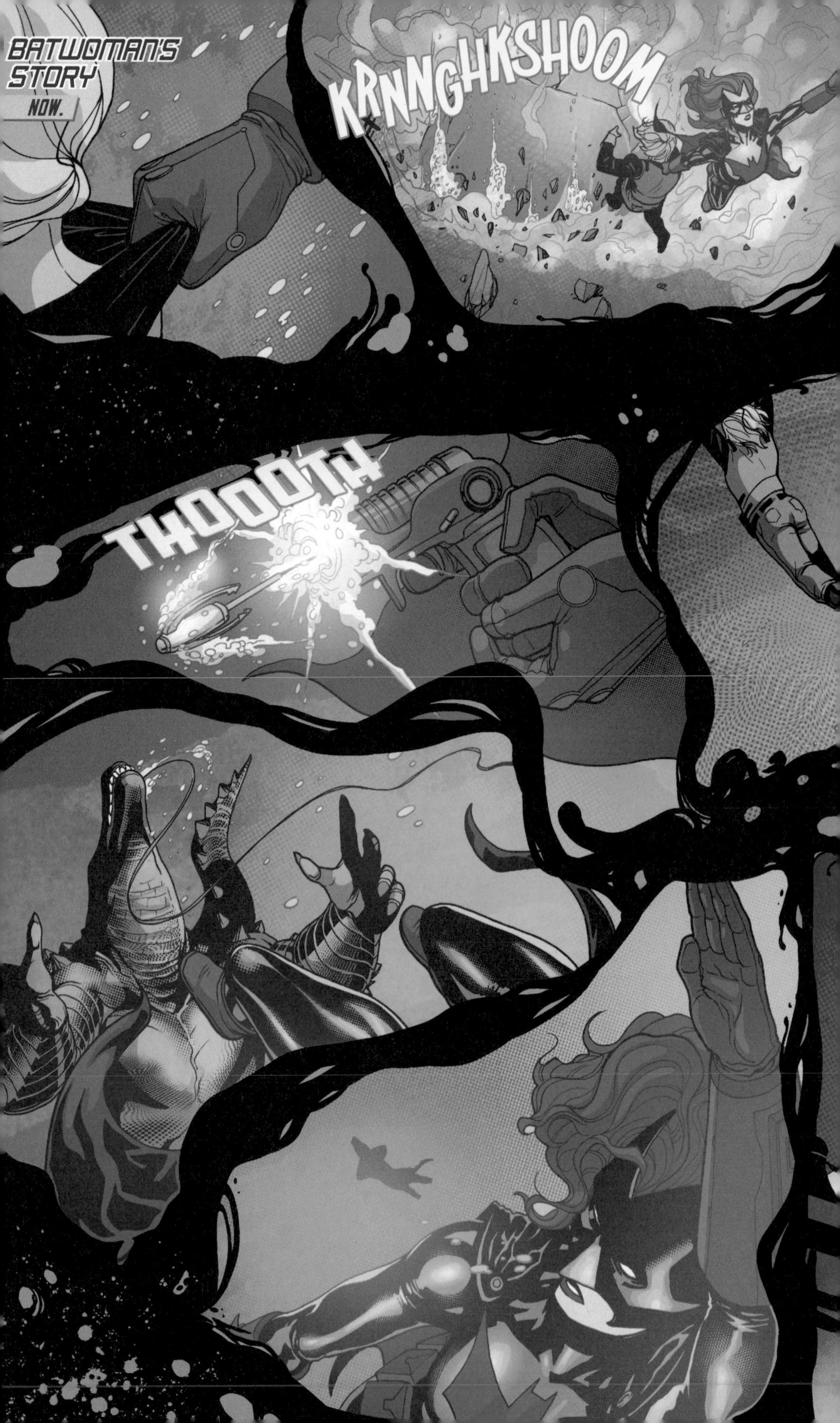
BATWOMAN'S STORY
NOW.
KRNNGHKSHOOM
THOOOTH

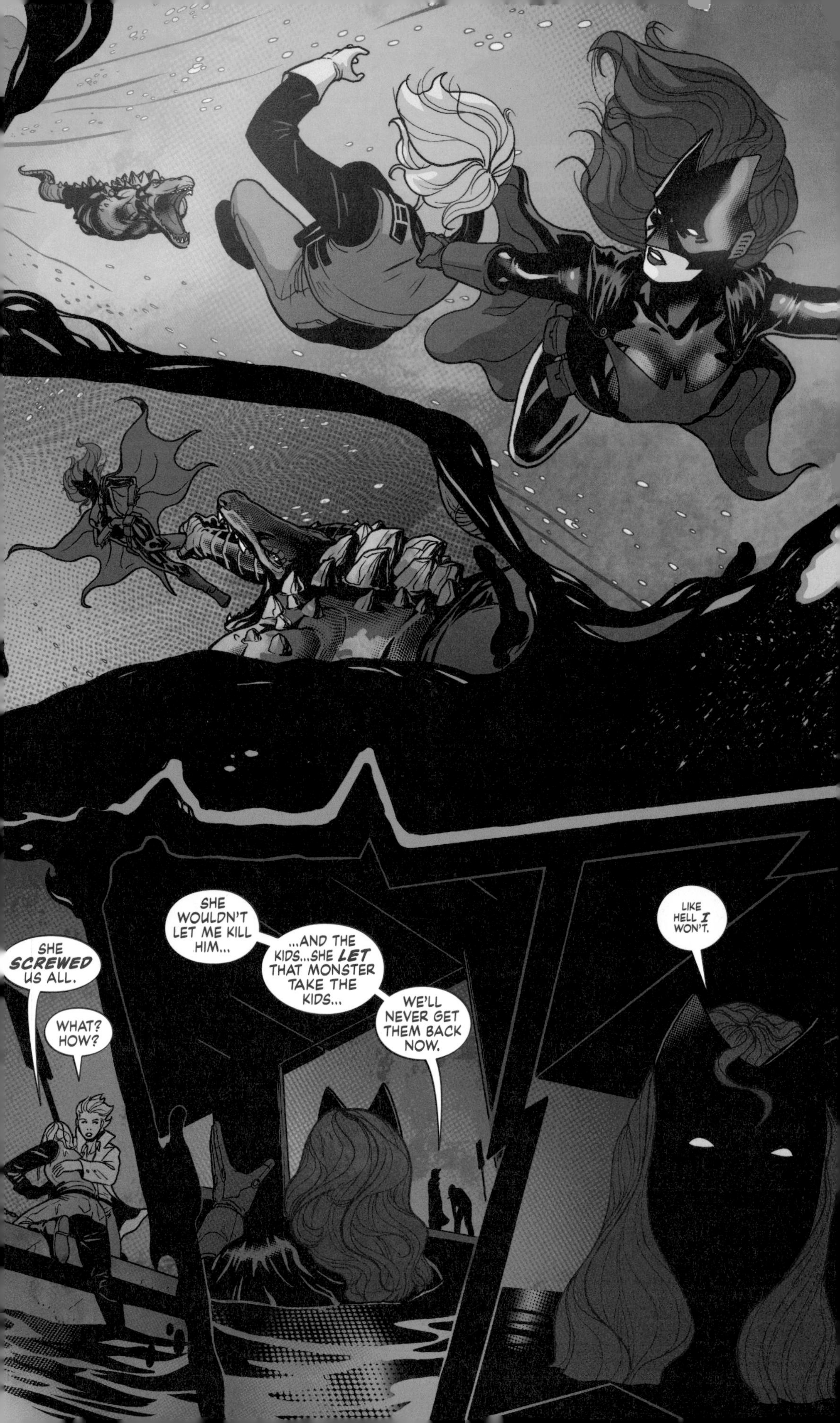
SHE SCREWED US ALL.
WHAT? HOW?
SHE WOULDN'T LET ME KILL HIM...
...AND THE KIDS...SHE LET THAT MONSTER TAKE THE KIDS...
WE'LL NEVER GET THEM BACK NOW.
LIKE HELL I WON'T.

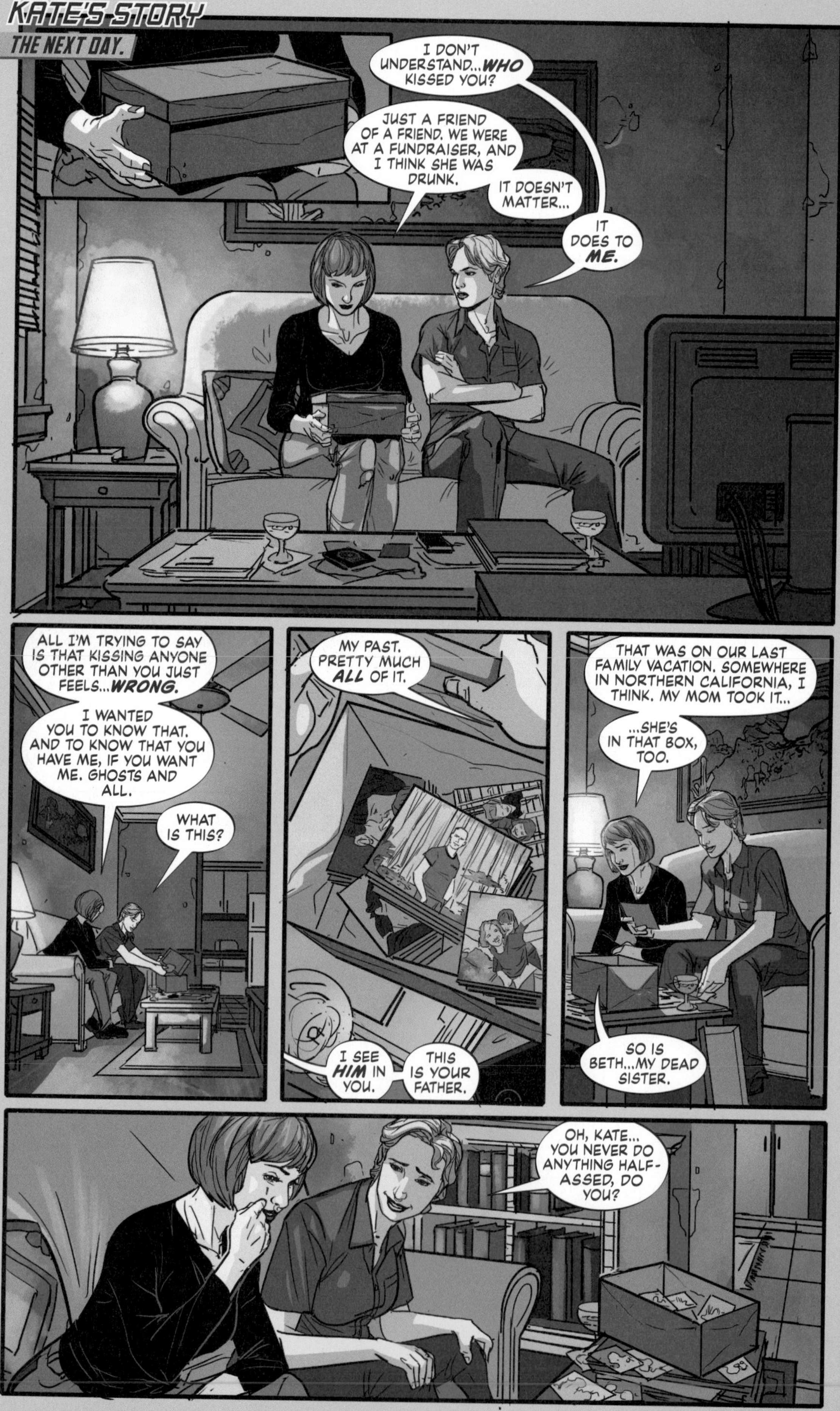
KATE'S STORY
THE NEXT DAY.
I DON'T UNDERSTAND... WHO KISSED YOU?
JUST A FRIEND OF A FRIEND. WE WERE AT A FUNDRAISER, AND I THINK SHE WAS DRUNK.
IT DOESN'T MATTER...
IT DOES TO ME.
ALL I'M TRYING TO SAY IS THAT KISSING ANYONE OTHER THAN YOU JUST FEELS... WRONG.
I WANTED YOU TO KNOW THAT. AND TO KNOW THAT YOU HAVE ME, IF YOU WANT ME. GHOSTS AND ALL.
WHAT IS THIS?
MY PAST. PRETTY MUCH ALL OF IT.
THIS IS YOUR FATHER.
I SEE HIM IN YOU.
THAT WAS ON OUR LAST FAMILY VACATION. SOMEWHERE IN NORTHERN CALIFORNIA, I THINK. MY MOM TOOK IT...
...SHE'S IN THAT BOX, TOO.
SO IS BETH... MY DEAD SISTER.
OH, KATE... YOU NEVER DO ANYTHING HALF-ASSED, DO YOU?

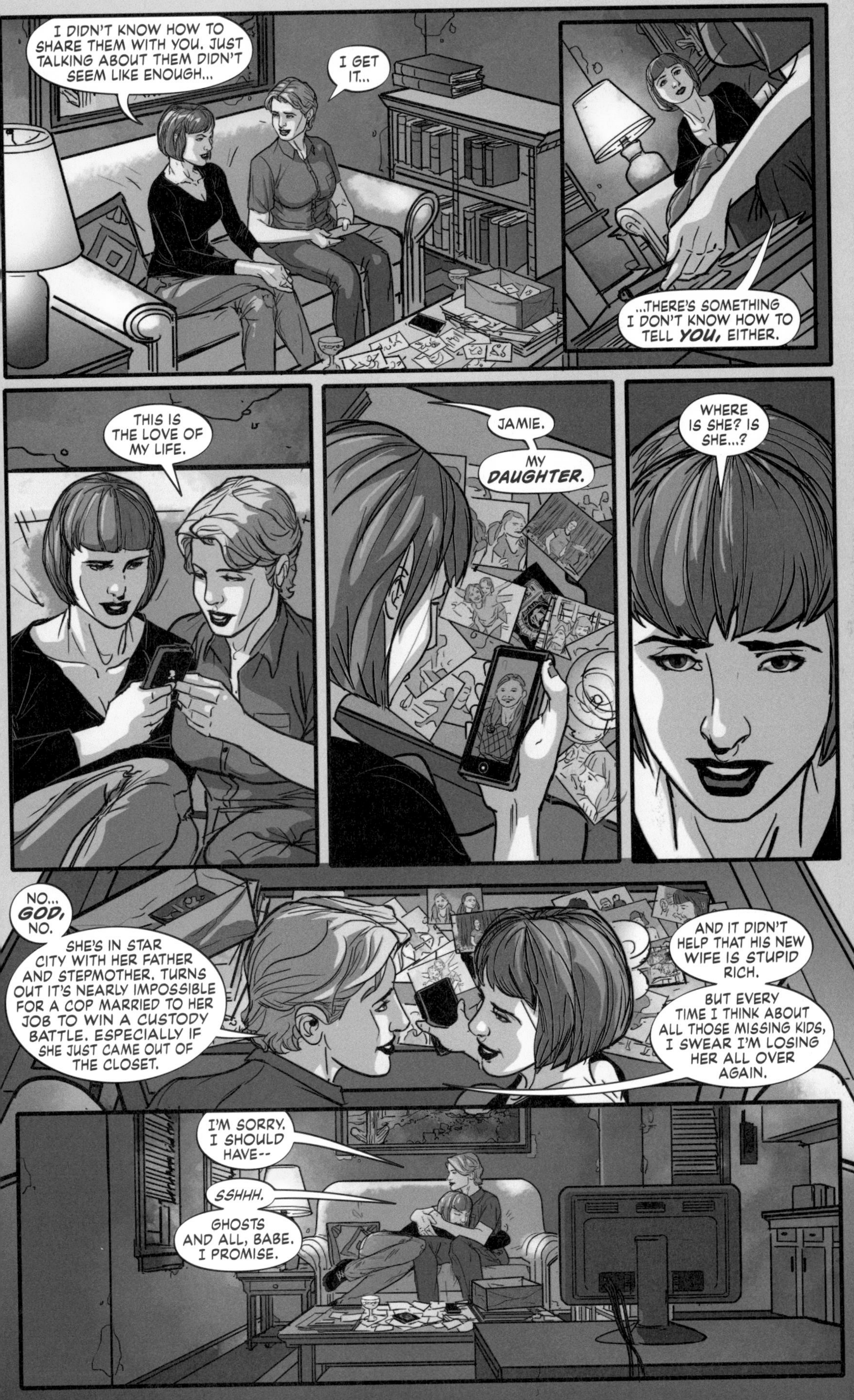
I DIDN'T KNOW HOW TO SHARE THEM WITH YOU. JUST TALKING ABOUT THEM DIDN'T SEEM LIKE ENOUGH...
I GET IT...
...THERE'S SOMETHING I DON'T KNOW HOW TO TELL *YOU,* EITHER.
THIS IS THE LOVE OF MY LIFE.
JAMIE.
MY *DAUGHTER.*
WHERE IS SHE? IS SHE...?
NO... *GOD,* NO.
SHE'S IN STAR CITY WITH HER FATHER AND STEPMOTHER. TURNS OUT IT'S NEARLY IMPOSSIBLE FOR A COP MARRIED TO HER JOB TO WIN A CUSTODY BATTLE. ESPECIALLY IF SHE JUST CAME OUT OF THE CLOSET.
AND IT DIDN'T HELP THAT HIS NEW WIFE IS STUPID RICH.
BUT EVERY TIME I THINK ABOUT ALL THOSE MISSING KIDS, I SWEAR I'M LOSING HER ALL OVER AGAIN.
I'M SORRY. I SHOULD HAVE--
SSHHH.
GHOSTS AND ALL, BABE. I PROMISE.

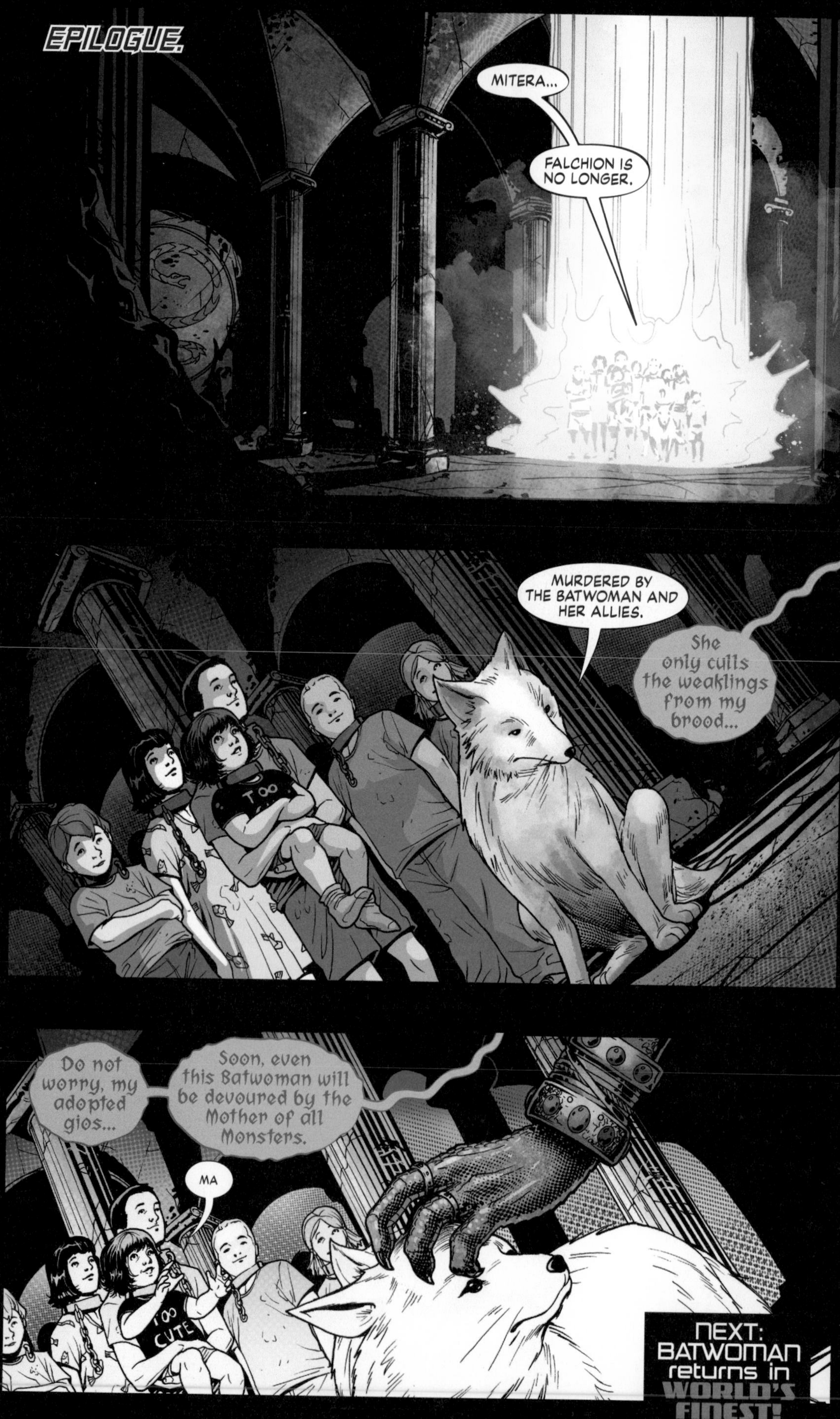
EPILOGUE.
MITERA...
FALCHION IS NO LONGER.
MURDERED BY THE BATWOMAN AND HER ALLIES.
She only culls the weaklings from my brood...
TOO
Do not worry, my adopted gios...
Soon, even this Batwoman will be devoured by the Mother of all Monsters.
MA
TOO CUTE
NEXT: BATWOMAN returns in WORLD'S FINEST!

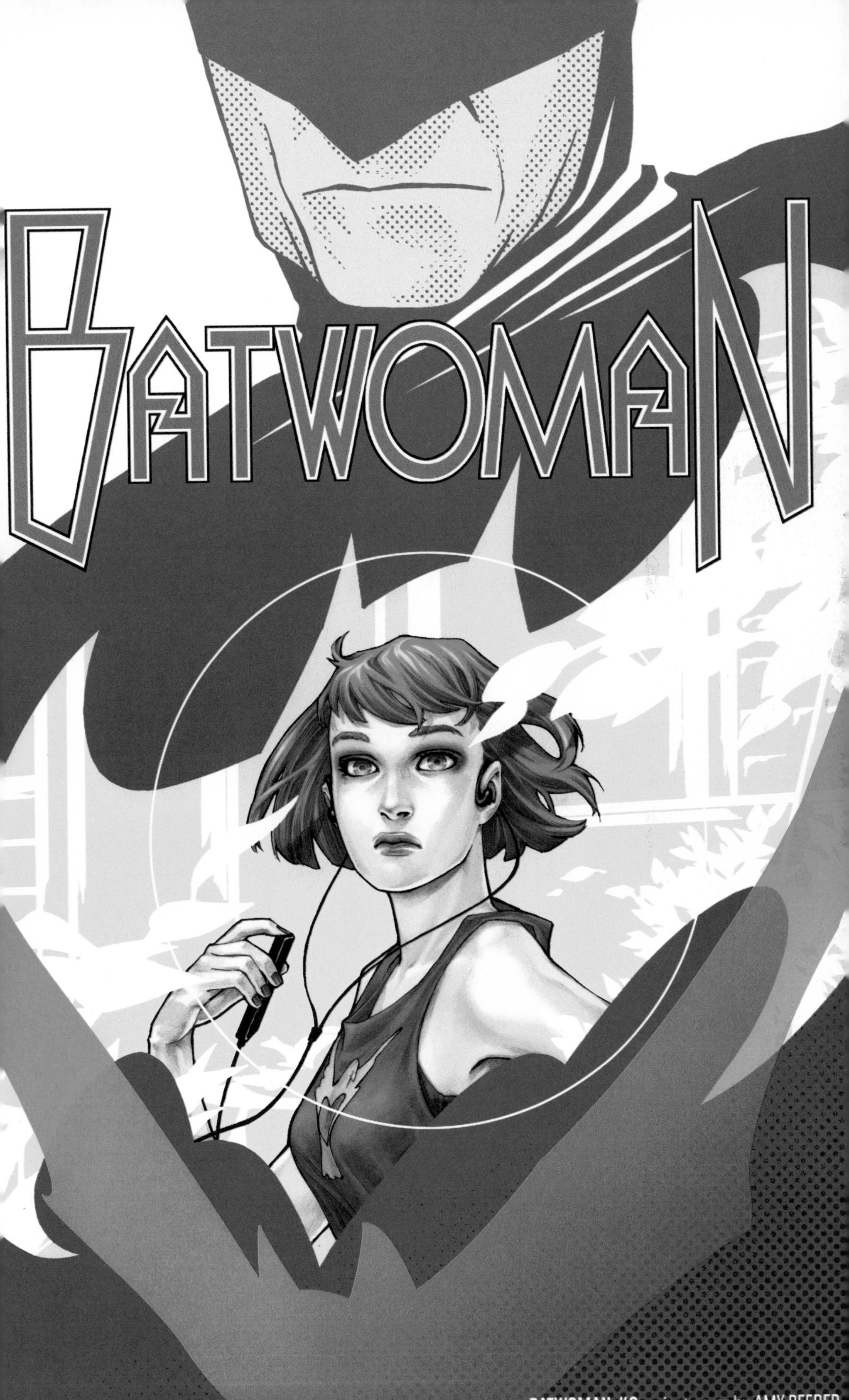
BATWOMAN

BATWOMAN #0 variant cover by AMY REEDER

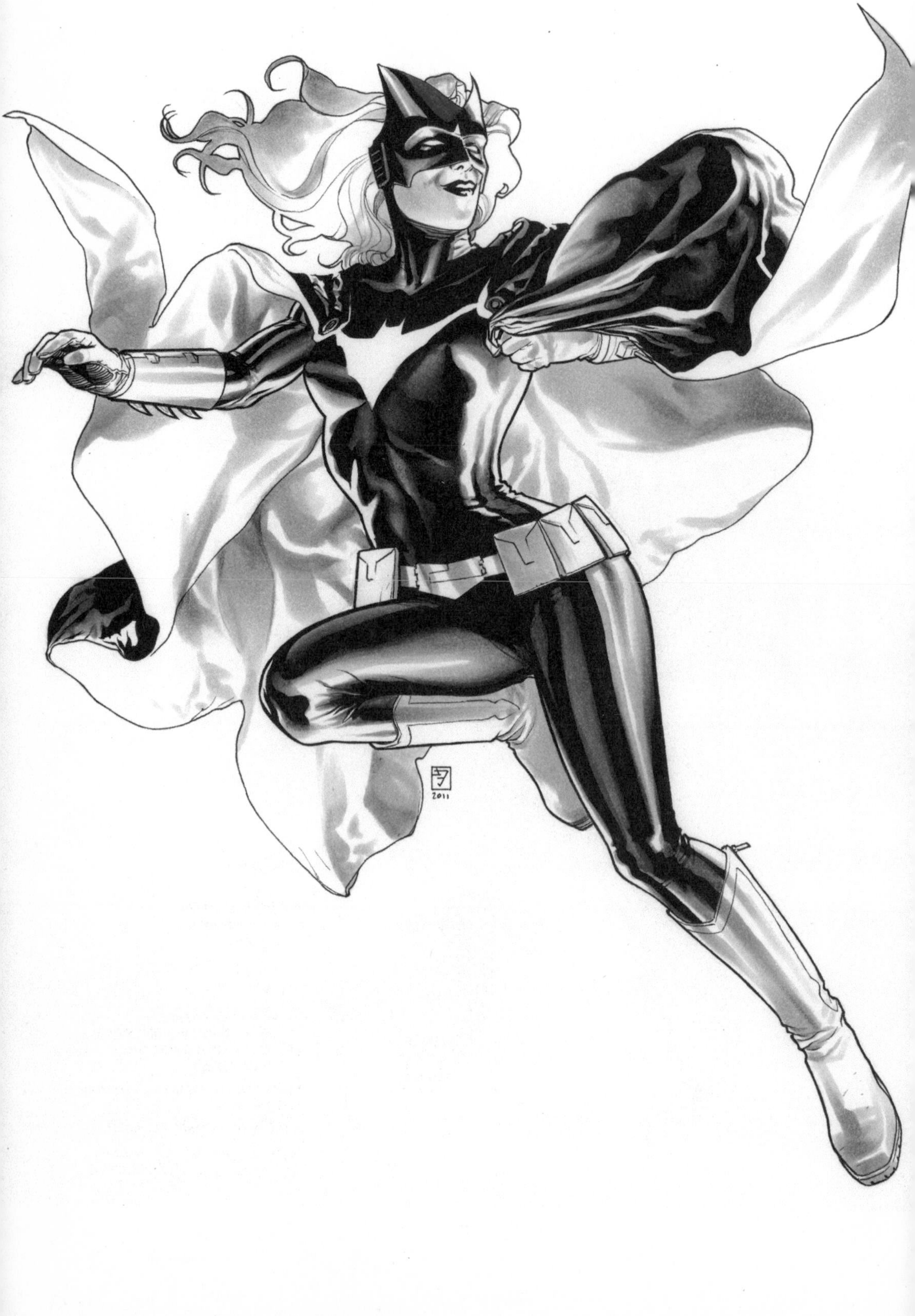

This image of Batwoman, illustrated by **J.H. Williams III**,
was used for a DC Universe mural, which is displayed in the DC offices.

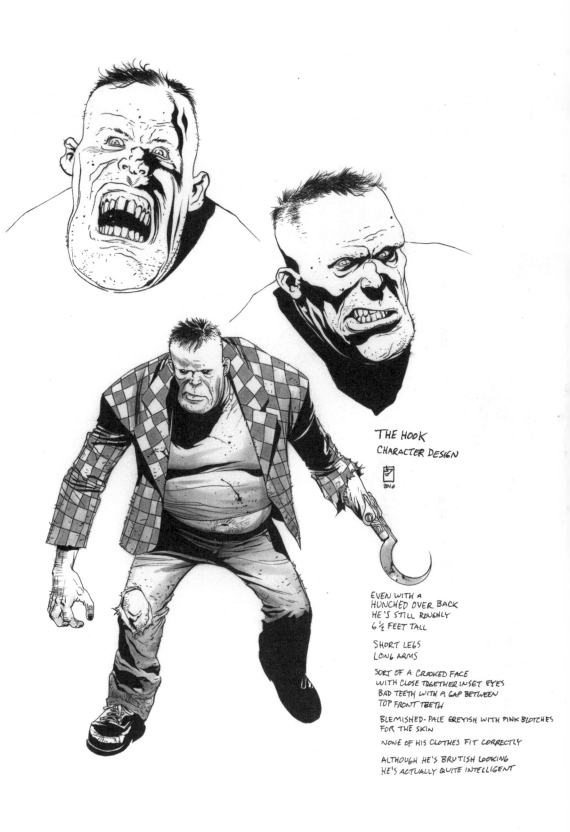

THE HOOK
CHARACTER DESIGN

EVEN WITH A
HUNCHED OVER BACK
HE'S STILL ROUGHLY
6 ½ FEET TALL

SHORT LEGS
LONG ARMS

SORT OF A CROOKED FACE
WITH CLOSE TOGETHER INSET EYES
BAD TEETH WITH A GAP BETWEEN
TOP FRONT TEETH

BLEMISHED - PALE GREYISH WITH PINK BLOTCHES
FOR THE SKIN

NONE OF HIS CLOTHES FIT CORRECTLY

ALTHOUGH HE'S BRUTISH LOOKING
HE'S ACTUALLY QUITE INTELLIGENT

THE HOOK character design by **J.H. WILLIAMS III**

BOATHOUSE design by **J.H. WILLIAMS III**

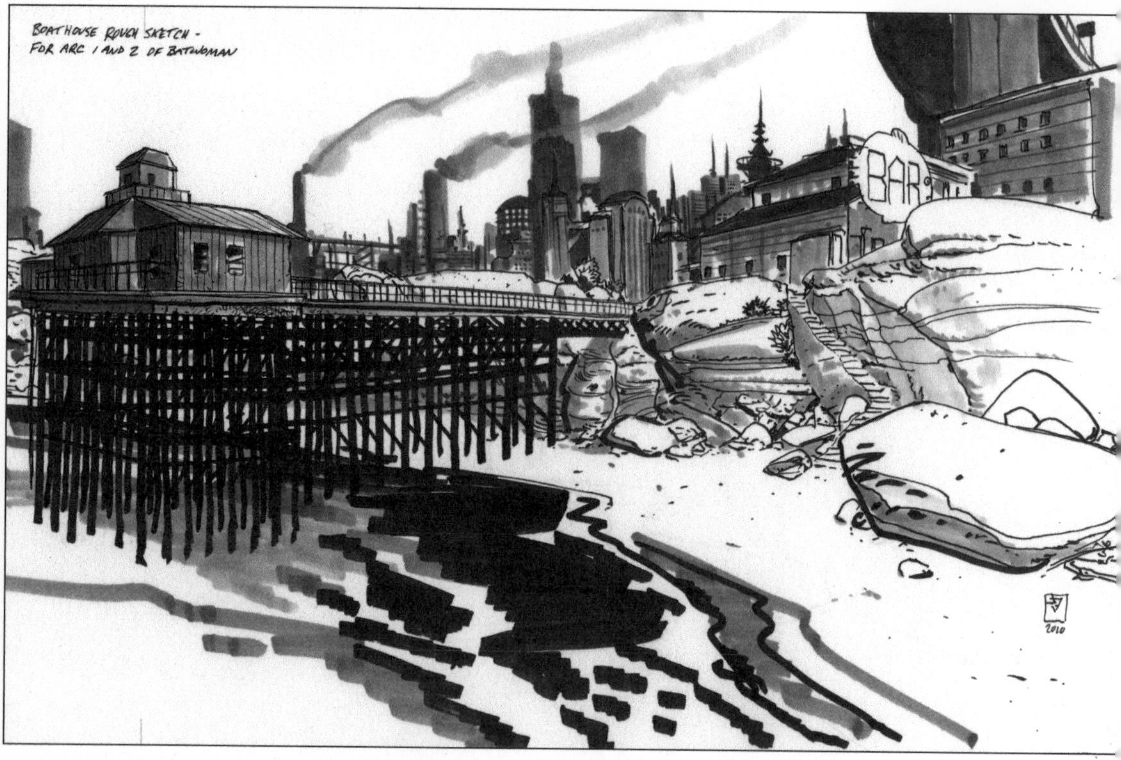
BOATHOUSE ROUGH SKETCH -
FOR ARC 1 AND 2 OF BATWOMAN
BAR
2010

Cover sketches by **J.H. WILLIAMS III** for BATWOMAN issues #0, #1, #4 and #5

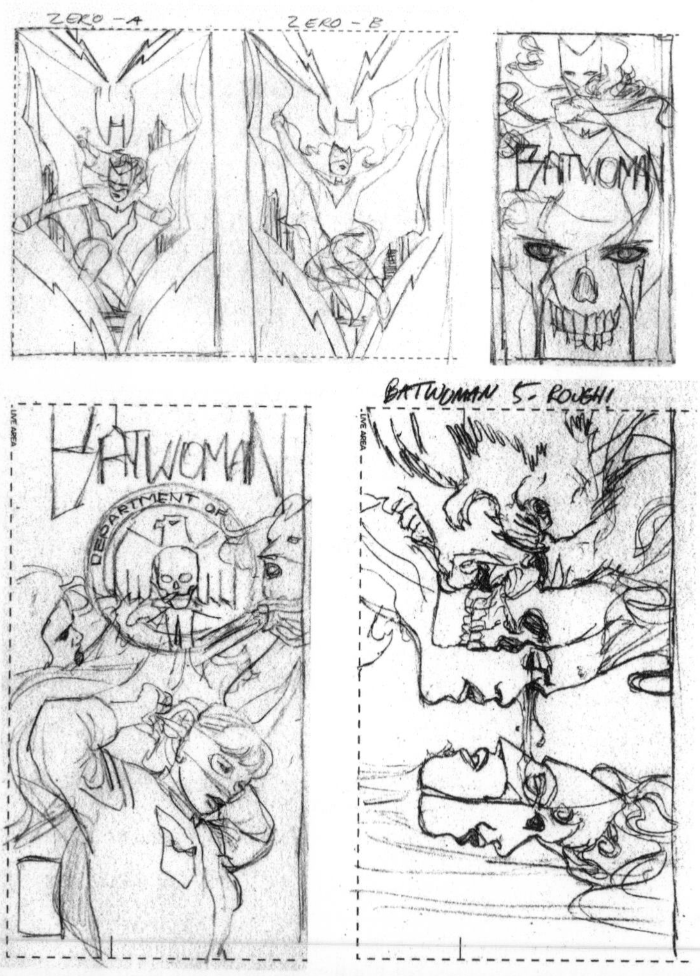
ZERO - A
ZERO - B
BATWOMAN
BATWOMAN
DEPARTMENT OF
BATWOMAN 5- ROUGH!

BATWOMAN
Art by TREVOR McCARTHY
Script by J.H. WILLIAMS III and W. HADEN BLACKMAN

Script excerpt from BATWOMAN #9

PAGE SIXTEEN (6 Panels)

Panel 1. Kate's hand holding a pair of high-heeled shoes that match her gown. We're now back at the gala that Falchion was holding, the same one from earlier in the issue. But now it's all from Kate's point of view, as we get to see where she was when Maggie was looking for her.

   1. CAP: Kate's story.

   2. CAP: Three nights ago.

   3. KATE (OP): It's not here.

Panel 2. Big panel. We're in Falchion's massive bedroom. There's a big four-poster bed against one wall, with serpents carved into the posts. Kate is standing near a desk with a laptop on it, looking at the screen intently. She looks gorgeous, but is definitely playing the part of the socialite, in the same evening gown with bare shoulders and jewelry as you drew in the ballroom scene earlier in this issue, at the gala on the yacht. She's holding her high heels, and her posture here is all business. Sune is reclining on the bed behind her, not necessarily seductive, but relaxed as she is removing the golden mask she was wearing in previous panels. She is also dressed as seen before, all in black. There's a big ornately carved chest at the foot of the bed.

   4. KATE: The D.E.O. *data worm* punched through every security protocol and there are no maps, no schematics, no blueprints.

Panel 3. Sune, sitting up, looking around the room, she's setting her mask on the bedding with one hand. And pulling a thin lockpick from her hair with the other. We can see how beautiful she actually is here, as her long black hair falls softly around her shoulders.

   5. SUNE: Perhaps we're searching through the wrong *chest*...

Panel 4. Sune has dropped to a knee in front of the chest and is already working on the lock. Kate has come up behind her.

   6. KATE: Do we have *time* to look through his *luggage*?

   7. SUNE: The guards are of no concern. They believe that five defensive *runes*, two fingerprint access doors and three laser tripwires will do the job.

   8. KATE: Right. I still want to know how you *deactivated* those runes.

Panel 5. Sune, both hands on the chest now, stopping for a moment. She is hanging her head, looking away from Kate—the most vulnerable we've seen her, a little like a victim here. If we can see any details of the chest here it of course has snake designs carved into it, and looks very old.

   9. SUNE: Falchion *forced* me to learn many counter spells. Among *other* things.

Panel 6. Kate is kneeling now too, right next to Sune. She has already taken over on the lock.

   10. KATE: Here, let *me* try.

   11. KATE: How did you fall in with Medusa?

PAGE SEVENTEEN (7 Panels)

Most of the panels on this page should be from basically the foot of the bed, looking over the front of the chest at Sune and Kate, kneeling side-by-side in front of the chest.

Panel 1. Sune. She hasn't moved much, but she's looking at Kate next to her, eyes shimmering. Again we can see how beautiful she is, and there seems to be a vulnerable warmth to her gaze here. Nothing outright seductive (yet), but still somehow inviting.

   1. SUNE: My *brother*. He promised me to Falchion, and became his *lieutenant* in exchange.

   2. SUNE: When Falchion realized that I had certain *skills* valuable beyond this room, he sent me into the field.

Panel 2. A small panel inset into the next, larger panel 3. Here, we just see Kate's hands as she fusses with the lock, using the pick here. We can see that the lock is ornate and built into the chest itself – it's not a padlock or anything like that. It has an old-fashioned keyhole.

   3. KATE: Is *that* why you're helping us? *Revenge*?

Panel 3. Kate is still looking at the lock, but Sune is looking at Kate, and has a hand on her shoulder. There is a subtle earnestness from her here, but not overplayed.

   4. SUNE: In part. But I also know that anyone caught in Medusa's *coils* will someday be crushed.

   5. KATE (small, sort of to herself): ...damn this lock is squirrely...

   6. KATE: Well, by joining the D.E.O., you're probably just trading in *one* snake for another.

   7. SUNE: I do not want to be allied with that Cameron Chase, *or* her D.E.O.

Panel 4. Sune has hands on both of Kate's shoulders now. It could either be a gesture signifying that they are comrades, or she could be moving in for a kiss... We will never know. Kate is a little taken aback, looking at her. But Sune does seem to have an unspoken ulterior motive beyond the words she is saying, it's intimate enough. Her beauty can't help but be noticed by Kate.

   8. SUNE: I want to be allied with *you*.

   9. SFX (OP, make sure this falls after the above dialogue): KLICK

Panel 5. Almost identical to Panel 4. The two are still looking at each other. Kate hasn't responded, her mouth is still open slightly. Sune is smiling, letting her words sink in.

10. KATE: I... think I got it.

11. SUNE: Yes.

Panel 6. The chest is now unlocked and its lid is already open. Make sure we can see the open chest here but not everything in it, so the storytelling is clear. Kate has pulled a large rolled parchment from the chest and has already mostly unrolled it with two hands. The "camera" should be positioned so that we can see her face—she's grinning.

12. KATE: Huh. How about that? An analog crime lord...

13. SUNE: That is it!

Panel 7. Looking over their shoulders as they study an intricately hand-drawn blueprint for Falchion's underwater lair, indicating the small travel tube that runs from the bottom of the yacht to the submerged lair/vessel deeper in the waters below. Refer to previous descriptions of this in the artist notes at the beginning of the script, to enhance what you do here for the "blueprint" schematic. The ink is rust red, like it's been drawn in blood, there is also a blood red pentagram sort of placed like a watermark off to one corner, and the parchment itself is yellowed and frayed along the edges. Sune has a hand on the small of Kate's back.

14. KATE: Good. I'll snap a few pictures.

15. KATE: Then I *need* to get back to the party before I'm missed.

16. SUNE: Of course.

PAGES EIGHTEEN & NINETEEN (12 Panels)

The design layout for this spread matches the layout concept for the spread on Pages 4 & 5: Blackness and very fine wavy panel borderlines, creating oddly shaped panels that seem organic, unstructured. But here, as the action will be removing the shadow-bomb stuff, the panel shapes slowly morph into standard-shaped panels as the spread moves along. The progression of this effect should be in line with the panel descriptions, timing the dissipation of the murky shadow fx so that by the end of the scene, we are completely back to normal square-shaped panels for the last few images of the spread.

Panel 1. Sune and Batwoman are holding hands. The darkness is complete around their hands, the Shadowland bombs still in effect from where we left off earlier.

1. CAP: Batwoman's Story.

2. CAP: Now.

3. BATWOMAN (OP) (whisper): This way.

Panel 2. Pan out to show Sune and Batwoman in darkness. Batwoman is leading Sune over some large rubble in the nearly-destroyed lair. Both are still wearing their funky goggles from the beginning, and the darkness is thick behind them. Batwoman is still holding Sune's hand, but now we can see it's because she's helping her clamber over the chunks of a fallen pillar or statue or machinery or whatever—it's not a romantic stroll. In her free hand, Sune still has her bow. (Based on this, it's key that we see large debris at the opening sequence to this issue.)

NO COPY

Panel 3. They have descended the other side of the rubble. Batwoman is kneeling next to a huge hulking form—the still unconscious Mutant Killer Croc, though only partially visible. He's so large and the darkness is so thick that we can only see his back and shoulders, as Batwoman and Sune are almost on top of him. She is touching him, checking his vital signs.

4: BATWOMAN (whisper): Killer Croc. Still down.

5: BATWOMAN (whisper): No sign of the other *freak*jobs. That would *suck* in this blackout...

6: SUNE: Falchion is *still* here. I can *feel* him.

Panel 4. Falchion bursts from the darkness. His blade is glowing golden light as it becomes a magical tool to fight the fx of the shadow-stuff. He's slashing downward—as he does so, the sword literally cuts through the darkness as if it were cloth. The Shadowland darkness dissipates when the glowing blade touches it, so we can start to see a bit of the backgrounds of the lair behind Falchion as he swings. He still has arrows sticking out of him everywhere, blue blood running from the punctures—he looks spattered with the stuff. As he lurches toward us, it's almost frightening, like a startle scene in a suspense thriller.

7. FALCHION (very large): *And I can always see you, slattern!*

Panel 5. Falchion is swinging at Sune. Again, the darkness is being rent apart, revealing more the room's details beyond. Batwoman is shoving or pulling Sune out of the way, but the blade still connects with Sune's side.

8. BATWOMAN (large): Sune!

9. SUNE (large): *Aaagh!*

Panel 6. Sune is on the ground, clutching her side. Batwoman is facing Falchion, pissed. She's pulling something out of her belt again. This has to be clear for storytelling here. More of the darkness has been dispelled or is being sliced open by Falchion's blade.

10. FALCHION: Do not *weep* for Sune. We have *both* misjudged her. I would have made her a *goddess*...

11. BATWOMAN: You think you're a *god* just because you look down on the rest of us?

Panel 7. Close-up of Batwoman's fingertips holding a small, pointed explosive device used for blasting open locks or door hinges. No bigger than half the length of a pen or pencil. One end is a metal spike, suitable for ramming into concrete or other dense material in order to mount the explosive. The other end is a small, round explosive laced with thin electrodes. There is a little tiny activation light that comes to life here.

12. BATWOMAN: Because you *use* us?

13. SFX (small): deet

Panel 8. Batwoman has leapt into the air, propelling herself higher than Falchion's head, and is ramming the spike-end of the explosive into Falchion's eye. She has both hands clutched as she drives the device home. Falchion is stumbling backwards, stunned, surprised. We should see remnants of the darkness swirling around his legs, but otherwise it's mostly gone. This shot needs to convey intense violent action on Batwoman's part.

14. BATWOMAN: *Enslave* us?

15. FALCHION: *Aaaaaagh!*

16. SFX (larger): DEET!

Panel 9. Batwoman is shoving Falchion's head to one side, away from her, as the device explodes. The explosion looks like it is blowing out a small portion of Falchion's face—his eye socket and part of his cheek. It's clearly doing disfiguring damage to his face, but it's still small enough that Batwoman isn't getting hurt by it, and it clearly won't kill Falchion, just serious painful damage.

17. BATWOMAN: *Murder* us?

18. FALCHION (large): Urk!

19. SFX (larger): DEE--

20. SFX (directly connecting to above sfx): POMF!

Panel 10. Falchion has dropped to one knee, clutching at his face. Smoke seeps through his fingers, and the area around his eye socket is blackened and scorched. His flesh around this portion of his face is mottled, burned, hamburger. All of his other wounds from the various arrow strikes are still present and seem even more profound here—pouring blue blood. Batwoman is standing over him, tough, committed, a boot on his shoulder.

21. FALCHION: Nnfff...

22. BATWOMAN: Try looking *down* on us *now*.

Panel 11. Batwoman kicks Falchion over, he clutches at his face.

23. FALCHION: Unnngh...

Panel 12. Pull back into an aerial shot, looking down at Falchion on his back. We can see about three-quarters of his body. He looks up at nothing with his one good eye swimming, clutching with his hands or hand at the other eye. Again, we can see all of his wounds here—he looks defeated, broken, arrows still embedded in his body, blood leaking from everywhere. Blue blood is splattered across the floor, on the walls and debris, and pools of blood are forming around his body. He is clearly in agony.

24. FALCHION (small): Have I failed you Mother?

PAGE TWENTY (3 Panels)

Panel 1. Sune, trying to roll over. She's bleeding badly, holding her side. We can see Batwoman's boots in the frame. Sune has ripped off the goggles, and they dangle in one hand.

1. BATWOMAN: Sune. Hang on.

Panel 2. Batwoman at her side now, helping her sit up. We can see that she too has removed her goggles. Sune is reaching up, putting a hand on Batwoman's cheek. It's bloody and leaves blood streaks on Batwoman's mask and skin.

2. BATWOMAN: D.E.O. should be here soon.

3. SUNE: You saved *me*.

Panel 3. Sune kisses Batwoman. She has one hand on the back of Batwoman's head, pulling her towards her as she lifts up a bit to deliver the kiss. Her eyes are closed, but Batwoman's are wide open.

4. NEXT: Hidden Faces Revealed

Black-and-white art from BATWOMAN #9 page 20

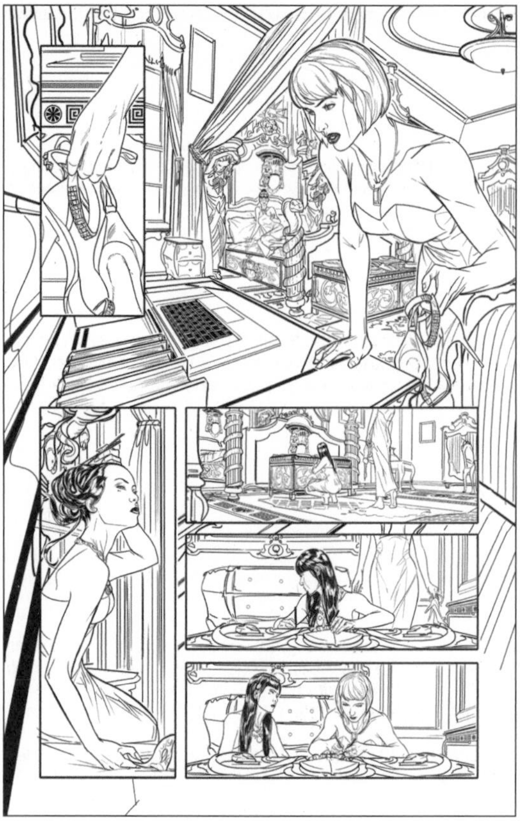

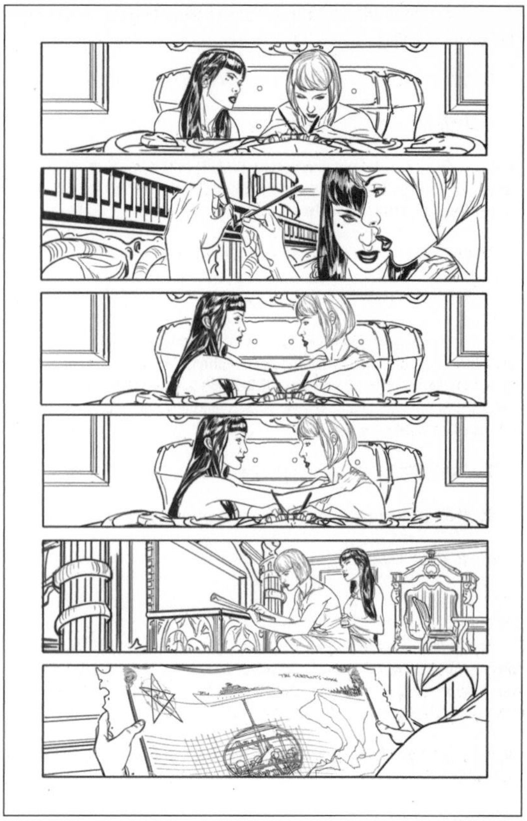

Black-and-white art from BATWOMAN #9 pages 16-17 (above) and 18-19 (below)

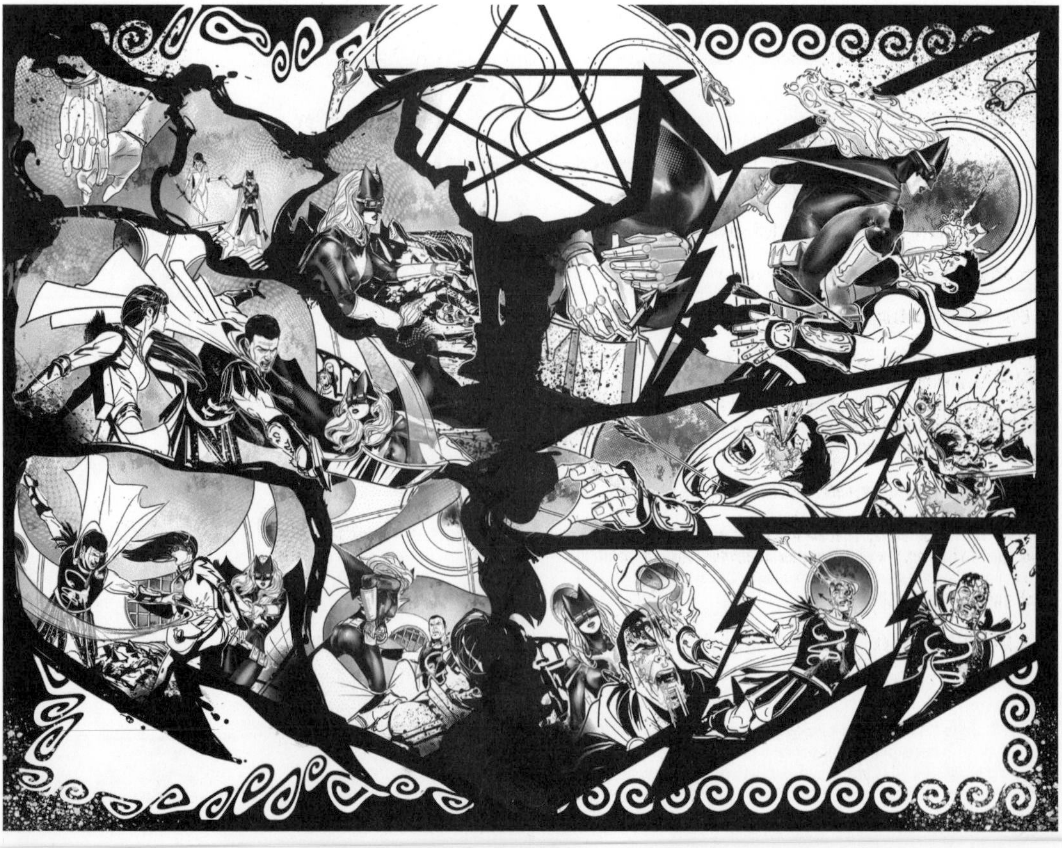